The People's Welfare

STUDIES IN LEGAL HISTORY

Published by the University of North Carolina Press

in association with the American Society for Legal History

Thomas A. Green and Hendrik Hartog, editors

WILLIAM J. NOVAK

The People's Welfare

Law and Regulation in Nineteenth-Century America

The University of North Carolina Press

Chapel Hill and London

The paper in this book meets the guidelines for permanence
and durability of the Committee on Production Guidelines
for Book Longevity of the Council on Library Resources.

Library of Congress Cataloging-in-Publication Data

Novak, William J., 1961–

The people's welfare : law and regulation in nineteenth-
century America / by William J. Novak.

p. cm.—(Studies in legal history)

Includes bibliographical references and index.

ISBN 0-8078-2292-2 (cloth : alk. paper)

ISBN 0-8078-4611-2 (pbk. : alk. paper)

1. Law—United States—History.   I. Title.   II. Series.

KF366.N68   1996

349.73′09′034—dc20   95-51850

[347.3009034]   CIP

07 06 05 04 03   7 6 5 4 3

For My Parents

CONTENTS

Preface ix

— INTRODUCTION —

Governance, Police, and American Liberal Mythology

1

— CHAPTER ONE —

The Common Law Vision of a Well-Regulated Society

19

— CHAPTER TWO —

Public Safety: Fire and the Relative Right of Property

51

— CHAPTER THREE —

Public Economy: The Well-Ordered Market

83

— CHAPTER FOUR —

Public Ways: The Legal Construction of Public Space

115

— CHAPTER FIVE —

Public Morality: Disorderly Houses and Demon Rum

149

— CHAPTER SIX —

Public Health: Quarantine, Noxious Trades, and Medical Police

191

— CONCLUSION —

The Invention of American Constitutional Law

235

Every history bears the impress of its times. This book is no exception. At the close of the twentieth century, one cannot help but be provoked by the changes and problems greeting the new millennium. Of particular concern for this book is a set of challenges bound up in what some scholars have called the three crises or malaises of modernity: (1) an epistemological crisis wrought by the continued ascendancy of a thin, instrumental rationality in public as well as private life; (2) a social crisis perpetuated by the impoverished ethics of atomistic individualism and hedonistic consumerism; and (3) a political crisis marked by the dangerous coupling of an enervated democracy and public sphere with a relentlessly aggrandizing state. In the economic sphere, the fall of communism has done nothing to diminish Karl Marx's initial apprehension about new forms of alienation and oppression emerging from within the liberation of capital.

One response to present crises is a rush to the past—a mythical American past. The failure of one version of socialist utopia has been accompanied by a blind return to its alter ego—neoclassical liberalism. As Marx and the twentieth-century Soviet Union have faltered, John Stuart Mill and the nineteenth-century United States have enjoyed something of a rebirth. Critiques of modern state power and public institutions attend a simple revival of faith in the naturalistic workings of the market and civil society. Contemporary politicians and commentators suggest that most of America's current problems stem from the excesses of twentieth-century statism, socialism, and welfarism. They proffer an uncomplicated solution—a return to the golden age of American liberalism, the nineteenth-century Jeffersonian world of minimal government, low taxes, absolute private property, individual rights, self-interested entrepreneurship, and laissez-faire economics. This book argues that such a world never existed, that nineteenth-century America was home to powerful traditions of governance, police, and regulation that refuse to conform to our twentieth-century ideological and psychological imperatives.

But though we cannot go back to a past that never existed to meet our current crises, nineteenth-century history remains a useful schoolhouse. The centrality of public spirit, self-government, and an active citizenry to the early American state reminds a struggling twentieth-century polity about the indispensable role of participation and the people's welfare in a democratic republic. Similarly, the local and social nature of nineteenth-century governance hold out alternatives to the twin tendencies of modern political change, centralization and individualization. It is also comforting to know that nineteenth-century Americans could find room for a political faith between the Scylla of socialism and the Charybdis of economic liberalism, skeptical of the claims that a good society could only come from a surrender to *either* the state *or* the civil society. Finally, much can be learned simply by encountering an early American legal-political tradition that departs so markedly from its advance billing, a tradition in which individual rights were inseparable from social duties, liberty was regulated, and the private and the public were inextricably intertwined in a vision of a well-regulated society. In the end, history provides no simple answers to fall back on, only better understandings with which to go forward.

This book also bears the impress of some extraordinary people who deserve mention and thanks. In my dissertation, I indulged the modern penchant for elaborate acknowledgments. Here I simply would like to list those most indispensable to my life and work. Good lists and their edifying power are at the heart of this book. This list is closest to my own: my mentor, Morton Keller; my teachers, Michael Grossberg, Hendrik Hartog, Morton Horwitz, Willard Hurst, James Kloppenberg, and Carl Ubbelohde; my advisers, Robert Gordon, Thomas Green, Arthur McEvoy, and Christopher Tomlins; my colleagues, George Chauncey, Kathleen Conzen, Julius Kirshner, Steven Pincus, and Richard Ross; my research assistants, David Tanenhaus and Scott Lien; my friends, Ben Brown, Elizabeth Clark, Sarah Gordon, Richard John, Thomas Pegram, Linda Przybyszewski, Nayan Shah, Stephen Smith, Manfred Ungemach, Victoria Woeste, Barbara Welke, Michael Willrich, and Charles Yanesh. And, most importantly, my parents, Louis and Elizabeth Novak; my love, Margaret Sikon Novak; and my joy, Max and Gabe. Anyone acquainted with them knows how fortunate I have been. Anyone acquainted with me knows how indebted I am. Anyone getting acquainted with this book should know that I alone am responsible for its shortcomings.

The People's Welfare

Governance, Police, and

American Liberal Mythology

She starts old, old, wrinkled and writhing

In an old skin. And there is a gradual sloughing

off of the old skin, towards a new youth.

It is the myth of America.

—D. H. Lawrence

A distinctive and powerful governmental tradition devoted in theory and practice to the vision of a well-regulated society dominated United States social and economic policymaking from 1787 to 1877. With deep and diverse roots in colonial, English, and continental European customs, laws, and public practices, that tradition matured into a full-fledged science of government by midcentury. At the heart of the well-regulated society was a plethora of bylaws, ordinances, statutes, and common law restrictions regulating nearly every aspect of early American economy and society, from Sunday observance to the carting of offal. These laws—the work of mayors, common councils, state legislators, town and county officers, and powerful state and local judges—comprise a remarkable and previously neglected record of governmental aspiration and practice. Taken together they explode tenacious myths about nineteenth-century government (or its absence) and demonstrate the pervasiveness of regulation in early American versions of the good society: regulations for *public safety* and security (protecting the very existence of the population from catastrophic enemies like fire and invasion); the construction of a *public economy* (determining the rules by which the people would acquire and exchange food and goods); the policing of *public space* (defining common rights in roads, rivers, and public squares); all-important restraints on *public morals* (establishing

—1—

the social and cultural conditions of public order); and the open-ended regulatory powers granted to public officials to guarantee *public health* (securing the population's well-being, longevity, and productivity). Public regulation—the power of the state to restrict individual liberty and property for the common welfare—colored all facets of early American development. It was the central component of a reigning theory and practice of governance committed to the pursuit of the people's welfare and happiness in a well-ordered society and polity.

These laws, this regulatory tradition, and this vision of governance—what I collectively refer to as "the well-regulated society"—are the subjects of this book. To the omnipresent and skeptical social-historical question, Were such laws enforced?, the thousand cases examined here testify simply and unequivocally, yes.[1] A second question is more interesting, more complicated, and more controversial: Why is this governmental regulatory practice so invisible in our traditional accounts of nineteenth-century American history? Why is it at all surprising to discover the pivotal role played by public law, regulation, order, discipline, and governance in early American society?

The question is especially perplexing given the rich traditions in American political, legal, and historical scholarship establishing the public underpinnings of nineteenth-century social and economic life. American political science, after all, was born amid a veritable obsession with the systematic investigation of nineteenth-century governmental facts and institutions cataloged in endless Johns Hopkins and Columbia University volumes on history and political economy.[2] Almost concurrently, serious sociolegal study began in the United States with the investigations of sociological jurists and legal realists into the distributive, coercive, and decidedly public nature of nineteenth-century common law doctrines like property and contract.[3] The commonwealth school of American history perfected the monograph while definitively demonstrating the role of the positive state in forging the infrastructural, commercial, and legal prerequisites for nineteenth-century capitalism.[4] The republican synthesis[5] is thus only the latest scholarly attempt to collar that elusive associational, corporative, governmental, and public-spirited strand in early American life that has captivated political commentators since Alexis de Tocqueville and James Bryce.[6]

Despite this abundance of learned opinion, America's nineteenth-century regulatory past remains something of a trade secret. No comprehensive history of antebellum regulation exists, and the mention of an American regulatory heritage prompts a familiar incredulity if not outright denial. Why? The culprit is a set of four interrelated and surprisingly resilient myths about

nineteenth-century America challenged by this book: the myth of stateless-ness, the myth of liberal individualism, the myth of the great transformation, and the myth of American exceptionalism.

The myth of American statelessness is about institutions and public power. Its adherents range from Hegel, who denied America status as a "Real State," to Walter Dean Burnham, who argued that "the chief distinguishing char-acteristic of the American political system before 1861 is that *there was no state*."[7] Cousin to the most notorious fallacy in American historiography, the laissez-faire thesis, the myth of statelessness holds that the essence of nineteenth-century government was its absence.[8] America was essentially born free, without elaborate bureaucratic, governmental, or political-philosophical traditions.

Encouraged by the "society" turn that has characterized much historical scholarship since the Second World War, the myth of American statelessness ironically has received support from contemporary state theory as well. There, Franco-Germanic models of development predominate; and doses of mod-ernization theory dictate an emphasis on rationalized and centralized govern-ment, national bureaucratic capacity, and the presence of a positive and ab-solute sovereignty. Since arguably the United States failed to achieve those things before the twentieth century, state theory yields an impoverished dis-course about lag, the negative state, and the Tudor polity, on the one hand, and teleological narratives about the road to the New Deal and general-welfare state, on the other.[9]

In its weak version, suggesting a lack of formal correspondence with the ideal-typical state of theory, there is a grain of tired truth in the stateless thesis. But in its more common, strong rendition, implying a substantive absence of power or activity on the part of public officials, the myth of American state-lessness is *groundless*. One simple illustration. In 1837 (a reputed heyday of laissez-faire) the Illinois legislature cataloged the governmental powers of the new city of Chicago:

First. To prevent all obstructions in the waters which are public highways in said city.

Second. To prevent and punish forestalling and regrating, and to prevent and restrain every kind of fraudulent device and practice.

Third. To restrain and prohibit all descriptions of gaming and fraudulent devices in said city, and all playing of dice, cards and other games of chance, with or without betting, in any grocery, shop or store.

Fourth. To regulate the selling or giving away of any ardent spirits, by any storekeeper, trader or grocer, to be drank in any shop, store or grocery, outhouse, yard, garden or other place within the city, except by inn-keepers, duly licensed.

Fifth. To forbid the selling or giving away of ardent spirits or other intoxi-cating liquors, to any child, apprentice or servant, without the consent of his or her parent, guardian, master or mistress, or to any Indian.

Sixth. To regulate, license or prohibit the exhibition of common show-men, and of shows of every kind, or the exhibition of any natural or artificial curiosities, caravans, circuses or theatrical performances.

Seventh. To prevent any riot or noise, disturbance, or disorderly assem-blage.

Eighth. To suppress and restrain disorderly houses and groceries, houses of ill-fame, billiard tables, nine or ten pin alleys or tables, and ball al-leys, and to authorize the destruction and demolition of all instru-ments and devices used for the purpose of gaming.

Ninth. To compel the owner or occupant of any grocery, cellar, tallow-chandler's shop, soap factory, tannery, stable, barn, privy, sewer, or other unwholesome, nauseous house or place, to cleanse, remove or abate the same, from time to time, as often as may be necessary for the health, comfort and convenience of the inhabitants of said city.

Tenth. To direct the location and management of all slaughterhouses, markets, and houses for storing powder.

Eleventh. To regulate the keeping and conveying of gunpowder, and other combustibles and dangerous materials, and the use of candles and lights in barns and stables.[10]

Twelfth. To prevent horse-racing, immoderate riding or driving in the streets, and to authorize persons immoderately riding or driving as aforesaid, to be stopped by any person.

Thirteenth. To prevent the incumbering of the streets, sidewalks, lanes, alleys, public wharves and docks, with carriages, carts, sleighs, sleds, wheel-barrows, boxes, lumber, timbers, firewood, or any other sub-stance or material whatsoever.

Fourteenth. To regulate and determine the times and places of bathing and swimming in the canals, rivers, harbors, and other waters in and adjoining the city.

Fifteenth. To restrain and punish vagrants, mendicants, street beggars, common prostitutes.

Sixteenth. To restrain and regulate the running at large of cattle, horses, swine, sheep, goats and geese, and to authorize the distraining, impounding, and sale of the same, for the penalty incurred and the costs of proceeding.

Seventeenth. To prevent the running at large of dogs, and to authorize the destruction of the same when at large, contrary to the ordinance.

Eighteenth. To prevent any person from bringing, depositing or having within the limits of said city, any dead carcass or any other unwholesome substance, and to require the removal or destruction by any person who shall have upon or near his premises any such substance, or any putrid or unsound beef, pork or fish, hides or skins of any kind, and on his default, to authorize the removal or destruction thereof by some officer of said city.

Nineteenth. To prevent the rolling of hoops, playing at ball, or flying of kites, or any other amusement or practice having a tendency to annoy persons passing in the streets or on the sidewalks of said city, or to frighten teams and horses within the same.

Twentieth. To compel all persons to keep the snow and ice and dirt from the sidewalks in front of the premises owned or occupied by them.

Twenty-first. To prevent the ringing of bells, blowing of horns and bugles, crying of goods and other things within the limits of said city.

Twenty-second. To abate and remove nuisances.

Twenty-third. To regulate and restrain runners for boats and stages.

Twenty-fourth. To survey the boundaries of said city.

Twenty-fifth. To regulate the burial of the dead.

Twenty-sixth. To direct the returning and keeping of bills of mortality, and to impose penalties on physicians, sextons and others, for any default in their premises.

Twenty-seventh. To regulate gauging, the place and manner of selling and weighing hay, of selling pickled and other fish, and of selling and measuring of wood, lime and coal, and to appoint suitable persons to superintend and conduct the same.

Twenty-eighth. To appoint watchmen, and prescribe their duties and powers.

Twenty-ninth. To regulate cartmen and cartage.

Thirtieth. To regulate the police of said city.

Thirty-first. To establish, make and regulate public pumps, wells, cisterns, and reservoirs, and to prevent the unnecessary waste of water.

Thirty-second. To establish and regulate public pounds.

Thirty-third. To erect lamps, and regulate the lighting thereof.

Thirty-fourth. To regulate and license ferries.[11]

This first of many regulatory lists in this book is intended physically to confront hypotheses about the absence of state with the overwhelming presence of regulatory governance.

The cultural and ideological complement to the myth of statelessness is the myth of liberal individualism. It owes its most lasting exposition to Louis Hartz. Since Hartz's *The Liberal Tradition in America* (1955), American liberalism has been defined narrowly with primary emphasis on its possessive, transactional, self-interested, and individualistic attributes.[12] Nineteenth-century political ideology, according to Hartzian mythology, was quintessentially Lockean, suffused with a passion for private right and predestined for market capitalism. Unassociative by nature, early Americans clung to an absolutist faith in the private legal mechanics of property and contract to carry out the necessary social negotiations among otherwise isolated, autonomous individuals. Over the past twenty years, historians working on classical republicanism, evangelical Protestantism, Scottish moral philosophy, and neo-Stoic ethics have unearthed rich countertraditions in the American past committed to civic virtue, moral rectitude, and the public good.[13] This book builds on these revisions. But the "well-regulated society" is not so much an attempt to offer another historical antidote to liberalism as an effort to recover the distinctiveness of a nineteenth-century political culture pervaded by regulation, police, law, and powerfully anti-individualistic sentiments about social duties, public obligations, and restraints on private rights and interests. Changes in the meaning of liberalism in American history are much more complicated and compelling than the one-dimensional tale of a shift from negative to positive definitions of liberty and freedom.[14]

Along with national myths about culture and institutions come fictions about time and sequence. One of the most powerful in Western history is the notion of a deep rupture separating modernity from its past. A product of nineteenth-century deterministic theories about social and economic evolution, the idea of a "great transformation" focuses attention on the inevitable transition from *Gemeinschaft* to *Gesellschaft*, status to contract, feudalism to capitalism, or traditional to modern social relations. In American history the pivotal date is 1776, the coaxing event the American Revolution. Legal and constitutional historians have been especially seduced by the power of transformative theory, positing a sharp divide between colonial folkways and "the

formative era of American law." Examining constitution, property, and contract, historians contend that 1776 marked the beginning of a new positivistic and instrumental legal order, where ancient notions like natural law, oracular styles of judging, and community justice were jettisoned to forge a fungible and useful legality suited to a modernizing, capitalist society. Reinforcing myths of individualism and statelessness, this legal transformation is said to have ushered in a modern liberal society and a nightwatchman state.[15] The regulatory legal order examined in this book contests this linear, evolutionary chronology. In place of the simple transition to liberal legalism, the well-regulated society intrudes as a wholly distinctive nineteenth-century legal-governmental regime that does not merely echo past nor anticipate future public practice.

Finally, all these myths about the opening of American society, the victory of individual rights, and the arrival of economic and market freedom are part of a general theory of Americanization that pervades histories of the early nineteenth century. By the time Alexis de Tocqueville arrived in the United States in the 1830s, it is argued, Americans had divested themselves of decrepit European attitudes and practices like deference, hierarchy, and statism and embraced the unique virtues bequeathed by American soil, democracy, and constitution. Those virtues now enjoy the status of cant: individualism, independence, industry, opportunity, enterprise, and self-sufficiency. Though it would be a mistake to overlook the distinctiveness of many aspects of early American society and government, the cult of American exceptionalism (with its tendency to remove American identity from the stream of history) has led us to underestimate the degree to which older European ideas and institutions remained vital parts of the American polity. The well-regulated society owed much of its institutional framework and underlying political philosophy to transatlantic customs and traditions.[16]

Together these four organizing myths constitute a master narrative of American political development in which liberty *against* government serves as the fulcrum of a constant and distinctively American liberal-constitutional tradition. The reigning paradigms of American politics (self-interested liberalism), law (constitutionalism), and economics (neoclassical market theory) conspire with this mythic historiography to produce a gross overemphasis on individual rights, constitutional limitations, and the invisible hand; and a terminal neglect of the positive activities and public responsibilities of American government over time.

This ideologically charged interpretive template was first fashioned almost fifty years ago as American liberal scholars cut themselves off from an earlier

progressive reform tradition and pieced together a more contented, compensatory liberalism.[17] But even after the critical inroads of class, gender, and race histories, descriptions of mainstream nineteenth-century political faith continue to echo Richard Hofstadter's version of the American creed: "the sanctity of private property, the right of the individual to dispose of and invest it, the value of opportunity, and the natural evolution of self-interest and self-assertion, within broad legal limits, into a beneficent social order."[18] This single nineteenth-century American mythology has proved assimilable to the whole spectrum of modern political positioning: conservative, liberal, critical, and feminist.[19]

Despite the cacophony of consensus, the governmental theory and practice described in this book defy the foregoing characterization at every point. Abandoning historical and ideological preoccupation with "the state" in the "American liberal tradition," this book instead emphasizes the actual day-to-day *conduct* of governance. For, at bottom, governance is not primarily a matter of philosophy, plutocracy, or bureaucracy. It is a constitutive public practice—a technology of public action with its own history, structures, and rationalities that produce as much as they are produced by economics, ideology, and culture. The power to make, the willingness to obey, and the decision to contest rules and commands is an ineradicable part of everyday social relations. Governance as conduct highlights the nexus of political and social history, marking that point where state and civil society enter into most deep and prolonged reciprocal contact. It is far more likely to be found in family law, state health reports, or local court decrees than the *Federalist Papers* or the *Congressional Record*.[20]

In the endless contest between state-centered and society-centered approaches to the public and its problems (a debate as old as Machiavelli's *Prince* versus Rousseau's *Social Contract*), the recent rise of the social has spawned a tendency to see politics, law, and the state as but alternative arenas or sites for the playing out of more fundamental social-historical forces, such as class, ethnicity, race, gender, sexuality. A corrective is warranted. But in place of a pendulous return to state-centeredness or attempts to identify a third, autonomous sphere ("public," "social," or "associative")[21] between state and society, governance as conduct turns our attention to points of reciprocal interaction and mutually constitutive contact. Over sixty years ago, progressive political economists and legal realists demonstrated the critical power of thinking about the state in terms of "what its officials *do*."[22] In "bringing the state back in,"[23] we should heed their example, building a public history around the intersection of polity and society and the actual everyday conduct

and consequences of government.[24] A history of politics without such a thick and realistic conception of governance is akin to a history of capitalism that avoids economics or a history of slavery that ignores race.

The notion of governance as a relatively autonomous field of public conduct ascribes new significance to the regulatory practices of nineteenth-century America. Almost erased from American history because of its lack of fit with liberal mythology, the well-regulated society is often misconstrued as a lagging mercantilist stage of development or as the lesser half of an ever present tension within liberalism between individualist and communitarian renderings of freedom. In contrast, this book posits well-regulated governance as a separate and independent set of governmental aspirations and practices. The well-regulated society is a regime of governmental conduct with its own distinctive structure, rationality, and social impact. It defies categorization within the traditional, transitional genealogies of liberal political evolution (e.g., feudalism, mercantilism, or Whiggism). The well-regulated society confronts the myths of statelessness, individualism, transformation, and exceptionalism with four distinguishing principles of positive governance: public spirit, local self-government, civil liberty, and law. While very much at odds with modern conceptions of the sovereign state and the rights-bearing individual, these principles were the heart of the nineteenth-century vision of a well-regulated society.

Public spirit. Salus populi (the people's welfare) is the title of this book, an abridgment of the influential common law maxim *salus populi suprema lex est* (the welfare of the people is the supreme law) and one of the fundamental ordering principles of the early American polity.[25] Nineteenth-century America was a *public* society in ways hard to imagine after the invention of twentieth-century privacy. Its governance was predicated on the elemental assumption that public interest was superior to private interest. Government and society were not created to protect preexisting private rights, but to further the welfare of the whole people and community. The public regulations examined in this book were consistently and routinely legitimated by the principle canonized by New York Chancellor James Kent: "Private interest must be made subservient to the general interest of the community."[26] Any reversal of that sentiment—any attempt to subsume public welfare in private interest—was a perversion of republicanism and a reversion to that dark age when governance was captured by private lords and manors.[27] Historians of civic republicanism have alerted us to the prominence in early American thought of an autonomous conception of the public good between the extremes of abstract idealism and crude utilitarianism. But the *salus populi* tradition was not so

much a product of formal political philosophizing (despite important codifi-
cations in Cicero, Grotius, and Montesquieu) as a product of governance. It
was embedded in the practices of local institutions and common laws. This
political moment owed much more to magistracy than to Machiavelli.

Local self-government. Despite the jilting of the Articles of Confederation
and the new supremacy clause in the federal Constitution, nineteenth-century
American governance remained decidedly local. Towns, local courts, common
councils, and state legislatures were the basic institutions of governance, and
they continued to function in ways not unlike their colonial and European
forebears. As Francis Hilliard remarked in 1835, the Constitution established
certain "general principles" and specific "national purposes," but it relied on
states and municipalities "to carry into operation a newly formed government, by . . . regulating those innumerable details, which the exigencies of society present."[28] The very label "municipal law," used throughout this period
to represent the whole of human (as opposed to divine) rules, customs, and
governmental contrivances, bespeaks the local origins and orientation of governance in the republic.[29] The reason to introduce this history of regulation
with a list of the powers of a municipality (Chicago) rather than the U.S.
Statutes at Large is because they were infinitely more important to regular
governance.

But self-government implied more than a particular level for the exertion
of public authority. It was part of a broader, more substantive understanding
of the freedoms and obligations accorded citizens as contributing members of
self-regulating communities.[30] Though its antidespotic thrust is often mistaken for liberal individualism, local self-government conceived of liberty and
autonomy as collective attributes—badges of participation, things achieved in
common through social and political interaction with others. The independent law-making authority of local communities (what Francis Lieber called
"the formative action of citizens") was to be defended from usurpation by
despots, courtly mandarins, or other central powers.[31] But within communities, individuals were expected to conform their behavior to local rules and expectations. No community was deemed free without the power and right of
members to govern themselves, *that is*, to determine the rules under which the
locality as a whole would be organized and regulated. Such open-ended local
regulatory power was simply a necessary attribute of any truly popular sovereignty. A paradigmatic example of local self-government was the constitution
created by the Wisconsin Pike Creek Claimants Union in 1836 (made famous
by Willard Hurst). This local government was established to foil the attempts

of "unprincipled and avaricious men" to "produce anarchy, confusion and the like among us, destroy our fair prospects, [and] subvert the good order of society."[32] Self-government had little to do with possessive individualism or laissez-faire, and it was just as likely to be found in frontier Wisconsin as in the New England town.

Civil liberty. Integral to local self-government was a unique conception of civil or regulated liberty. In an 1853 treatise *The Science of Government*, Charles B. Goodrich effectively captured its meaning: "Liberty is a relative term. Some persons regard it as a right in every individual to act in accordance with his own judgment. Such liberty is unknown to, and cannot be found in connection with or as a result of government, or of the law of society. Government and societies are established for the *regulation* of social intercourse, of social institutions."[33] Civil liberty consisted only in those freedoms consistent with the laws of the land. Such liberty was never absolute, it always had to conform to the superior power of self-governing communities to legislate and regulate in the public interest. From time immemorial, as the common law saying went, this liberty was subject to local bylaws for the promotion and maintenance of community order, comfort, safety, health, and well-being.[34] Local police ordinances and regulations were seen as the foundation for the simultaneous freedom and order enjoyed in communities and associations such as the legendary Greek city-state, the English hundred, and the German mark.[35] Freedom and regulation in this tradition were not viewed as antithetical but as complementary and mutually reinforcing. At the Constitutional Convention, James Wilson could argue without any sense of contradiction: "The state governments ought to be preserved—the *freedom of the people* and their *internal good police* depends on their existence in full vigor."[36]

Law. By definition, any history of early American government must also be a legal history. For this was a common law polity where the boundaries between law and government were indecipherable. As Thomas Paine noted, "In America the law is king." John Adams famously added (invoking James Harrington) that this was "a government of laws."[37] The terse, revolutionary document that established the constitutional framework for American government provided only a rough outline to be interpreted and filled in according to the established standards and practices of Anglo-American law.[38] What was a bill of attainder, an ex post facto law, the obligation of contracts, due process, or a privilege of citizenship? These were legal questions. Like most aspects of early American governance, their ultimate determination was left up to legislators, courts, and judges working in older, preconstitutional legal traditions.

No one captured this sense of American governance as part of a longer preestablished legal tradition better than Massachusetts Chief Justice Lemuel Shaw:

> The constitution was not first prepared and drawn up by and for a people who were then, for the first time, establishing political and civil institutions, for their security and government; it was rather a slight remodelling of a social system, by a people who had long enjoyed the protection of law, and the security of social order, under a government, nearly as free, and practically nearly as popular, as the lot of humanity would admit. *The constitution itself recognises this [pre]condition of law and social order.*[39]

Synthesizing the four principles of early American government, Shaw went on to suggest that the welfare of the community depended upon constant legislative and judicial reference "to established laws and institutions, and to the principles and maxims of civil liberty, secured and regulated by mild, equal and efficient laws."[40]

Law was certainly the American modality of governance. As Christopher Tomlins has noted, "Between the Revolution and the beginning of the nineteenth century, law became *the* paradigmatic discourse explaining life in America."[41] But the content of the common legal tradition undergirding the well-regulated society runs counter to some classic interpretations of American bench and bar that emphasize solely devotion to private (usually economic) interests and hostility to government. The legal doctrines and practices guaranteeing the rights of municipalities to regulate social and economic life were testaments to the importance of nonconstitutional public law to the American polity. The nineteenth century was not simply an age of private contract and public constitutional limitations. It was an epoch in which strong common law notions of public prerogatives and the duties and obligations of government persisted amid a torrent of private adjudication and constitution writing. The rule of law, a distinctly public and social ideal antedating both Lockean liberalism and Machiavellian civic humanism, dominated most thinking about governance in the nineteenth century. This book attempts to recover the neglected public side of the American rule of law.

Public spirit, local self-government, civil liberty, and common law were part of a worldview decidedly different from our own and from the one we have imposed on an unsuspecting past. Their reference point was the relationship of a citizen to a republic rather than an individual subject to a sovereign

nation-state. But *salus populi* and well-regulated governance entailed more than a particular legal-political worldview. It was a governmental practice embedded in some of the most important public policies and initiatives of the nineteenth century. In particular, the four principles outlined here found clearest expression in countless[42] nineteenth-century exertions of what is known in legal parlance as *state police power,* what Richard Ely dubbed "one of the most remarkable developments in the history of jurisprudence" and "the centre of socio-economic conflict in the United States."[43]

The state police power is one of the most enigmatic phenomena in American legal and political history. To begin with, the phrase "state police power" is triply misleading. First, police power has little to do with our modern notion of a municipal police force. Second, the triumph of this particular legal terminology was part of a late nineteenth-century effort to rein in, constitutionalize, and centralize the disparate powers of states and localities. Using the term to describe earlier developments thus risks importing some anachronistic assumptions. Finally, despite being a "state" power, the police power was usually exercised by local officials.

Generations of judges and scholars have suggested that, in fact, state police power is undefinable.[44] Ernst Freund, author of the most important treatises on regulatory and administrative law, made the bravest attempt, defining it in 1904 as "the power of promoting the public welfare by restraining and regulating the use of liberty and property." Lewis Hockheimer, Freund's contemporary, added that "The police power is the inherent plenary power of a State . . . to prescribe regulations to preserve and promote the public safety, health, and morals, and to prohibit all things hurtful to the comfort and welfare of society."[45] Together these definitions cover three essential components of police power: law, regulation, and people's welfare. Police power was the ability of a state or locality to enact and enforce public laws regulating or even destroying private right, interest, liberty, or property for the common good (i.e., for the public safety, comfort, welfare, morals, or health). Such broad compass has led some to conclude that state police power was the essence of governance, the hallmark of sovereignty and statecraft.

The American constitutional basis of state police power was the Tenth Amendment, reserving to the states all power not explicitly delegated or prohibited in the Constitution. But more significant than this formal constitutional sanction were the substantive roots of state regulatory power in early modern notions of police or *Polizei*. A product of the epochal transfer of civil power from church and lord to polity that dominated Europe after the Reformation,

police took on a multiplicity of forms by the eighteenth century. They ranged from the Scottish Enlightenment and English mercantilist context of Adam Smith's *Lectures on Justice, Police, Revenue and Arms* (1762–63), to the German cameralism of Johann Justi's *Polizeiwissenschaft* (1756), to the French *droit administratif* tradition represented by Nicolas Delamare's *Traité de la Police* (1722).[46] What all had in common was a focus on the polity's newfound responsibility for the happiness and welfare of its population. Police was a science and mode of governance where the polity assumed control over, and became implicated in, the basic conduct of social life. Thus William Blackstone defined "public police and oeconomy" as "the due regulation and domestic order of the kingdom; whereby the individuals of the state, like members of a well-governed family, are bound to conform their behavior to the rules of propriety, good neighbourhood, and good manners; and to be decent, industrious, and inoffensive in their respective stations."[47] But police goals and objectives did not end with the preservation of a neo-Stoical public order.[48] Police aspirations also included enriching population and state, increasing agricultural yields, minimizing threats to health and safety, promoting communication and commerce, and improving the overall quality of the people's existence.

Such sweeping objectives required the intense regulation and public monitoring of economy and society. Indeed the effect of police was a vast proliferation of regulatory intrusions into the remotest corners of public and private activity. As Michel Foucault suggested, "The *police* includes everything."[49] The detailed regulatory lists that dot this book are meant to capture this depth of inclusiveness. Delamare's initial treatise laid out eleven expansive categories of police regulation and administration: (1) religion, (2) manners (and morals), (3) health, (4) provisions, (5) travel (roads and highways), (6) public tranquillity and safety, (7) the sciences and liberal arts, (8) commerce and trade, (9) manufactures and mechanical arts, (10) labor, and (11) the poor.[50] No aspect of human intercourse remained outside the purview of police science.

Nineteenth-century America never experienced the centralized police state anticipated by the German cameralists and partially realized in Colbert's France and Catherine II's Russia (in part because the American police tradition remained so connected to local self-government). But the notion of a well-regulated society secured by a state police power was an essential part of the American governmental tradition. The influential description of police power offered up by Justice Samuel Miller in the *Slaughterhouse Cases* (1872) clearly resonated with the broad reach of *Polizei*: "The power is, and must be

from its very nature, incapable of any very exact definition or limitation. Upon it depends the security of the social order, the life and health of the citizen, the comfort of an existence in a thickly populated community, the enjoyment of private and social life, and the beneficial use of property."[51]

Similar police rationales undergirded the deluge of laws and ordinances passed by states and municipalities regulating American life between 1787 and 1877. Between 1781 and 1801, the New York legislature enacted special laws regulating lotteries; hawkers and peddlers; the firing of guns; usury; frauds; the buying and selling of offices; beggars and disorderly persons; rents and leases; firing woods; the destruction of deer; stray cattle and sheep; mines; ferries; apprentices and servants; bastards; idiots and lunatics; counselors, attorneys, and solicitors; travel, labor, or play on Sunday; cursing and swearing; drunkenness; the exportation of flaxseed; gaming; the inspection of lumber; dogs; the culling of staves and heading; debtors and creditors; the quarantining of ships; sales by public auction; stock jobbing; fisheries; the inspection of flour and meal; the practice of physic and surgery; the packing and inspection of beef and pork; soal leather; strong liquors; inns and taverns; pot and pearl ashes; poor relief; highways; and quit rents.[52] Most of these regulations were passed in 1801 while the legislature was busy reestablishing the basic institutions and infrastructure of state government: elections, legislative sessions, courts, towns, sheriffs, the militia, basic criminal laws, weights and measures, land laws, banks, turnpikes, and bridges.

This regulatory pattern continued well into the nineteenth century. Like many states, Michigan revised its statutes in the late 1830s.[53] Under familiar titles and headings, the state organized its regulations of highways, bridges, and ferries; trade (including the inspection and regulation of beef, pork, butter, fish, flour and meal, leather, pot and pearl ashes, beer and ale, and staves and heading; the licensing and regulation of auctions; and weights and measures); public health (including regulations for quarantines, the removal of nuisances, offensive trades, contaminated vessels, homes or buildings, the burial of the dead, travelers, boards of health, medical societies, physic and surgery); the internal police of the state (including regulations for paupers and the poor, disorderly persons,[54] taverns and other licensed houses, illegitimate children, Sunday observance, the law of the road and public carriages, the firing of woods and prairies, timber on water and land, lost goods and stray beasts, theatrical exhibitions and public shows, gunpowder, and unauthorized banking); and corporations. In addition, separate criminal provisions helped restrain such conduct as obstructing highways, dueling, defrauding or cheating at common

law, unlawfully assembling or rioting, the importing and selling of obscene books or prints, exciting disturbance at public meetings or elections, and selling corrupt or unwholesome provisions.[55]

Lists such as these could be multiplied a thousandfold across the various jurisdictions of nineteenth-century America. And each item listed is more than likely the focus of scores of more particular regulations and specifications. Under the police power, railroads were ordered to reconstruct bridges for the public welfare, disorderly houses were closed and their contents sold for offending public morals, and private dwellings were summarily destroyed when found inimical to the public health or safety. Unlike the power of eminent domain, deprivations of private property owing to police regulations were not compensated. Thomas Cooley, often too quickly dismissed as an opponent of the police power, suggested that it "pervades every department of business and reaches to every interest and every subject of enjoyment."[56]

This power of police and the larger governmental and regulatory tradition of which it was part are the subjects of the next six chapters. Chapter 1 explores the intellectual and jurisprudential foundation of the well-regulated society— the distinctive common law vision that inspired American police regulation. The following five chapters then form the empirical heart of this study—five detailed case studies into the central substantive areas of nineteenth-century police regulation: public safety and security, public economy, public property, public morality, and public health. These focused examinations of police regulations regarding fires, urban marketplaces, corporations, highways and riverways, prostitution, liquor, quarantine, and offensive trades demonstrate the well-regulated society's pervasive force in nineteenth-century America. But even these seemingly all-encompassing categories barely begin the process of recapturing the nineteenth-century regulatory state. Enormous areas of regulation and state policing remain outside the parameters of this study: public education, public lands, public defense, public charities, public dependents, public communications, public finance, public taxation, public utilities, public works, public carriers, crime, the family, religion, natural resources, labor, servitude, and slavery.

Over the past thirty years, historians have successfully deconstructed the American myth of equality. Countless histories (from Edmund Morgan's *American Slavery, American Freedom* to Nancy Cott's *Bonds of Womanhood* to Ronald Takaki's *Iron Cages*) have demonstrated how the idealistic pretension of the Declaration of Independence's claim that "all men are created equal" masked a deeper reality and ongoing paradox in American history wherein

unprecedented freedom for some was continually purchased with the enslavement of others.[57] The vast, largely unwritten history of American governance and police regulation suggests that it is time to refocus attention on that other founding paradox—the myth of American liberty. For this book argues that the storied history of liberty in the United States, with its vaunted rhetoric of unprecedented rights of property, contract, mobility, privacy, and bodily integrity, was built directly upon a strong and consistent willingness to employ the full, coercive, and regulatory powers of law and government. The public conditions of private freedom remains the great problem of American governmental and legal history.[58]

Two final introductory caveats on two staples of historical analysis: conflict and change. First, though this book posits a dominant, overarching tradition of common regulation in nineteenth-century governance, it by no means implies an absence of conflict vis-à-vis particular regulatory policies. As Chapters 5 and 6 make clear, early American morals and health policies were rife with group contest and ethnic, racial, and gender divisions. Indeed, the legal record that makes up the bulk of the evidence for this study is inherently adversarial. Every case mentioned is by definition contested on one issue or another. This book argues that one distinctive understanding of public powers and rights was consistently victorious in nineteenth-century courtrooms, assembly halls, and council chambers. But an ineradicable strain of dissent, discontent, and dispute (accompanied by important changes in society and economy) ultimately resulted in the transformation of American liberalism and the demise of the well-regulated society.

Which brings me to caveat number two. A good part of this book's analysis is somewhat synchronic in tone, outlining the major features of the tradition of well-regulated governance that existed more or less intact in the United States from 1787 to 1877. I make only general allusions to important continuities with a colonial American and early modern European past. But while continuity is a major theme in this book, after midcentury emphasis shifts to harbingers of change. A product of the crucible of the Civil War and longer-term alterations in the nature of state power, individual rights, and constitutionalism, a fundamentally new mode of governance and political discourse displaced the public, local, and legal regulatory tradition described in this book after 1877. At the end of each substantive chapter and in the conclusion, I venture some hypotheses on the erosion of the well-regulated society and the

rise of a new governmental regime in the late nineteenth century. But any adequate explanation of these important events must await a subsequent volume on "The Creation of the American Liberal State, 1877–1937."

On the whole, however, this book unapologetically emphasizes the contiguity of the past. Government and law are complex beasts. The way people order their lives and societies order their people are not revised overnight. Despite the revolutionary events of the late eighteenth and early nineteenth centuries, American communities continued to organize and regulate themselves according to long-held beliefs and practices. In our (typically modern and American) fascination with the new—the Constitution, fee simple property, self-interested liberalism, and market economics—we have underestimated the tenacity of the old—the common law, the social obligations of property, *salus populi*, and public institutions and customs. This is not to say that American government and law did not undergo deep changes in the nineteenth century. Only that change occurred under the heavy weight of past public traditions. Marx's notion of individuals making history on terrains not of their own choosing was presaged more eloquently by his early hero Hegel:

> The bud disappears when the blossom breaks through, and we might say that the former is refuted by the latter; in the same way when the fruit comes, the blossom may be explained to be a false form of the plant's existence, for the fruit appears as its true nature in place of the blossom. These stages are not merely differentiated; they supplant one another as being incompatible with one another. But the ceaseless activity of their own inherent nature makes them at the same time moments of an organic unity, where they not merely do not contradict one another, but where one is as necessary as the other; and this equal necessity of all moments constitutes alone and thereby the life of the whole.[59]

Hegel's notion of organic historical change—of past and present in constant dialectic tension—is very close to what some early American legal thinkers understood to be the essence of a common law tradition. That tradition, especially its vision of a well-regulated society, was the foundation for the blossoming of state police power in the nineteenth century.

The Common Law Vision of a Well-Regulated Society

The central parent-publick calls

Its utmost effort forth, awakes each sense,

The comely, grand, and tender. Without this,

This awful pant, shook from sublimer powers

Than those of self, this heaven-infused delight,

This moral gravitation, rushing prone

To press the publick good, *our* system soon,

Traverse, to several *selfish* centres drawn,

Will reel to ruin.

—James Thomson, quoted in James Wilson,

Lectures on Law (1791)

The usual starting point for the history of police power and the American regulatory state is Chief Justice Lemuel Shaw's decision in *Commonwealth v. Alger* (1851).[1] There, the Supreme Judicial Court of Massachusetts upheld the power of the legislature to regulate the use of private property in Boston harbor by establishing a wharf line beyond which no private structure could be built. The regulation aimed to keep the harbor free of obstructions. Cyrus Alger was prosecuted for maintaining a pier built squarely on his own property but beyond the legislative wharf limit.[2] Shaw justified this public restriction of private property rights with one of the most famous paragraphs in the jurisprudential history of police regulation:

We think it is a settled principle, growing out of the nature of well ordered civil society, that every holder of property, however absolute and

unqualified may be his title, holds it under the implied liability that his use of it may be so regulated, that it shall not be injurious to the equal enjoyment of others having an equal right to the enjoyment of their property, nor injurious to the rights of the community. All property in this commonwealth . . . is derived directly or indirectly from the government, and held subject to those general regulations, which are necessary to the common good and general welfare. Rights of property, like all other social and conventional rights, are subject to such reasonable limitations in their enjoyment, as shall prevent them from being injurious, and to such reasonable restraints and regulations established by law, as the legislature, under the governing and controlling power vested in them by the constitution, may think necessary and expedient. This is very different from the right of eminent domain, —the right of a government to take and appropriate private property whenever the public exigency requires it, which can be done only on condition of providing a reasonable compensation therefor. The power we allude to is rather the police power; the power vested in the legislature by the constitution to make, ordain, and establish all manner of wholesome and reasonable laws, statutes, and ordinances, either with penalties or without, not repugnant to the constitution, as they shall judge to be for the good and welfare of the Commonwealth. . . . It is much easier to perceive and realize the existence and sources of this power than to mark its boundaries, or prescribe limits to its exercise.[3]

In this comprehensive passage, Shaw offered several powerful ideas that endorse his reputation as "the greatest *magistrate* which this country has produced."[4] He articulated a substantive notion of "the rights of the community." He pointed out the limited, "conventional" nature of property rights—the idea that property came with an implied restriction that it should be used so as not to injure others. He defended the legislature's open-ended police power to make "general regulations" for the "common good and general welfare." And he made perfectly clear the sharp nineteenth-century distinction between such police regulations and state powers of eminent domain.[5]

The problem with *Commonwealth v. Alger* is that it is usually treated as a *hard* case—a case outside the regular ambit of early American jurisprudence. Shaw's ideas are perceived as new and exceptional in 1851. When not ignored by legal and constitutional historians,[6] *Alger* is discussed primarily as a novelty, a unique product of a judicial mind ahead of its time. Lemuel Shaw is

seen as pioneering a conception of state regulatory power that ultimately belonged in the Progressive Era.[7]

Such interpretations are anachronistic. *Commonwealth v. Alger* was a common and *easy* case, firmly entrenched in the intellectual, political, and legal traditions of nineteenth-century America. Far from being the springboard for the development of police power, it was more like the capstone of a distinct era in which courts routinely upheld the state and local regulation of dangerous buildings; railways and public conveyances; corporations; the use of streets, highways, wharves, docks, and navigable waters; objectionable trades; obscene publications; disorderly houses; lotteries; liquor; cemeteries; Sunday observance; the storage of gunpowder; the sale of food; traffic in poisonous or dangerous drugs; occupations; the hours of labor; the safety of employees; the removal of dead animals and offal; and a score of other social and economic activities.[8]

Shaw's arguments and language were eloquent and powerful. They were not unprecedented. In 1817 the New Hampshire Supreme Court validated a state statute prohibiting travel on Sunday with the observation that "All society is founded upon the principle, that each individual shall submit to the will of the whole. When we become members of society, then we surrender our natural right, to be governed by our own wills in every case."[9] Sustaining a New York harbor regulation, Justice Woodworth preempted Shaw by twenty-four years in *Vanderbilt v. Adams* (1827): "The sovereign power in a community, therefore, may and ought to prescribe the manner of exercising individual rights over property. . . . The powers rest on the implied right and duty of the supreme power to protect all by statutory regulations, so that, on the whole, the benefit of all is promoted. . . . Such a power is incident to every well regulated society."[10] *Commonwealth v. Alger* occupied a central place in nineteenth-century jurisprudence; but Lemuel Shaw's great achievement lay in accurately gauging the pulse of his present, not in seeing our future.

Much of the confusion surrounding *Alger* and the police power in the early American polity is owed to the hold of modern liberal mythology. In law, that mythology takes two distinct forms: the public law paradigm of *liberal constitutionalism* and the private law thesis of *legal instrumentalism*.

The hallmark of liberal constitutionalism is a vision of law and society emphasizing a harsh, overarching separation of the private and the public, the individual and the state. The dichotomy is total and the two are often seen as intrinsically hostile and antagonistic, as in Herbert Spencer's *The Man versus the State*.[11] Judges derive their distinctive political authority in the liberal

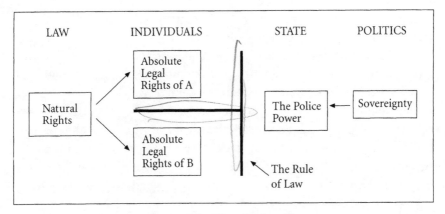

Figure 1. The liberal rule of law

constitutional order as the border guards of an all-important frontier between public powers and private rights. Duncan Kennedy illustrated the conceptual power of the liberal rule of law with a diagram (Figure 1). In the liberal schema, the rule of law is the only thing protecting us from the simultaneous threats of the private other and the public state.[12]

American constitutional history, from this perspective, is basically a one-dimensional tale of a continuous judicial maintenance of the line between public and private, power and right, political sovereignty and fundamental law, protecting the latter from the former. Edward S. Corwin best exemplified that tradition. In a set of authoritative articles, Corwin argued that the essence of American constitutionalism was a triumvirate of sacred limiting doctrines: judicial review, vested rights, and due process.[13] Those doctrines were rooted in a higher law tradition as old as Western civilization that happily realized its telos in the work of the Founders, the *Federalist Papers*, John Marshall, and the Supreme Court. Together those sources yielded American constitutionalism's "basic doctrine" of shielding private property and individual rights from legislative attack via an independent, naysaying judiciary. As Robert McCloskey summarized, "The essential business of the Supreme Court is to say 'No' to government."[14]

The new legal history of American private law originated in critique of some of the excesses of liberal constitutional history. Willard Hurst and Morton Horwitz, two of its most influential practitioners, attacked constitutional history's obsession with a few great cases and statesmen. In contrast to Corwin's emphasis on Founder's talk, vested rights, and the negative function of constitutionalism, the new legal history stressed private law's creative potential—its proactive role in the release of capitalist energy in the market revolution.[15]

The centerpiece of this historiographical reorientation was a more realistic, sociological interpretation of law's role in history—legal instrumentalism.[16]

In place of liberal constitutionalism's vision of law as protector of an ever increasing sphere of private liberty, legal instrumentalism substituted law as dependent variable. The instrumentalist perspective emphasized private law's reflexive qualities as a mirror and facilitator of basic social processes, most importantly capitalist development. Beginning in 1776, the story goes, American laws of property, contract, tort, and crime were revolutionized and transformed to meet the economic demands of a modernizing, industrializing society (e.g., demands for certainty, predictability, subsidy, fungibility, a reliable labor force, and the distribution of risk). Legal instrumentalism supported both conservative (a consensual freeing up of entrepreneurial initiative) and radical (a conspiracy of the bar and commercial interests) glosses.

While correcting the Whiggish tendencies of liberal constitutionalism, legal instrumentalism introduced new problems of its own. Its reductionist materialism has been ably criticized by critical legal scholars charting law's constructive and constitutive capabilities and attacking the overdetermined notion of law as the epiphenomenal product of economic imperative.[17] Indeed, the structural-functionalist sociology underlying instrumentalism has been undermined by recent developments in social and literary theory demonstrating the underdetermined nature of all human creations from language and consciousness to interests and institutions. The mechanistic separation of law from the rest of society at the heart of legal instrumentalism (law-in-the-books from law-in-action; legal concept from social fact) is no longer tenable.

The possibility of a third interpretive route beyond liberal constitutionalism and legal instrumentalism seems implicit in these critiques. Unfortunately, American legal history thus far has relied on a rough and unsatisfactory synthesis of public and private law paradigms. The two strands of legal interpretation are usually tied together in a caricature of early American legal change wherein jurists wield a conservative constitutionalism to protect property from unreasonable legislative intervention *and* a flexible, instrumental conception of private law to hammer away at antidevelopmental common law doctrines. A jurisprudential commitment to dynamic individual rights over the people's welfare is seen as meeting the needs of both liberal political philosophy and a market economy. As Kent Newmyer summed up the liberal consensus: "Like judge-made private law, judge-made constitutional law responded mainly to dynamic capitalists." The road from this understanding of the formative era of modern legalism to the Lochner Court runs straight and narrow.[18]

Within these two interpretive schemas, there is little room for the decision of Chief Justice Shaw in *Commonwealth v. Alger*. *Alger* was not a constitutional or a liberal opinion in the ordinary usage of those terms. Shaw's opinion was based primarily on the principles and doctrines of the common law. His decision trumped individual property rights with a larger notion of the "rights of the community." *Alger* was also not a particularly modern or forward-looking decision. Shaw grounded his entire opinion in the "views of the law of England, as it had existed long anterior to the emigration of our ancestors to America."[19] *Alger* can be seen as instrumentally rational or ends-oriented only by assuming Shaw to be artfully disingenuous through fifty pages of careful legal opinion (an argument one might not want to make about the Captain Vere of American legal history).[20] So, Shaw and *Alger* become anomalies.[21]

In this chapter, I take the supposed anomaly seriously, keeping at bay the two interpretive paradigms into which it does not fit. The approach employs what Thomas Kuhn and other intellectual historians have called a "hermeneutic method." Kuhn defined it simply enough as something like sensitive reading: "When reading the works of an important thinker, look first for the apparent absurdities in the text and ask yourself how a sensible person could have written them. When you find an answer, I continue, when those passages make sense, then you may find that the more central passages, ones you previously thought you understood, have changed their meaning."[22] Among the central passages of liberal constitutionalism and legal instrumentalism, *Commonwealth v. Alger* is an apparent absurdity. Kuhn holds out the promise that once we understand *Alger*, we might rethink some previously unchallenged assumptions about law, liberalism, and the early American state.

The first step in this methodology is to take seriously the language and ideas of Shaw's opinion and others like it. Whereas legal instrumentalism marginalizes the efficacy of legal ideas (or at least renders them secondary to interests),[23] this chapter treats the language of these regulatory decisions as crucial. A generation of intellectual historians has now convincingly demonstrated that language is not epiphenomenal; it is an important, inseparable part of culture and social life. By ascribing meaning and significance to social reality, ideas actually shape and constitute reality. Legal thought especially, far from being incidental to social and economic action, is a central "*activity* of communication," distributing authority, rewards, and penalties through "linguistic means." Legal ideas occupy one of those rare niches where abstract concepts necessarily run smack into more mundane considerations of polity, economy, and society.[24]

Getting at these ideas and beliefs is not easy, however. Early nineteenth-century police power decisions were often short, much of their rationale taken for granted. Even when one gets a rich opinion like Shaw's, the work of fleshing out layers of assumed meaning remains difficult. What does Shaw mean by the "nature" of society? What does he mean by a "well ordered civil society?" What is the significance of his referring to "well ordered" or "regulated" six times in one page in 1851? How can he call "rights of property" "social and conventional rights?" What is the significance of his references to limits on property and rights in an era when we are used to hearing about limits on legislatures? How unusual are his references to "the common good" and "the general welfare?" What is one to make of Shaw's use of the common law as a basis for decision?

To begin to understand *Commonwealth v. Alger* and early American regulation, therefore, we must reconstruct an older world of meaning—the common presuppositions and assumptions swirling around early nineteenth-century legal thought that make Shaw's statements and countless others like them intelligible. In recovering these underlying metaphysics of the police power, court records alone are insufficient. Though they are the soul of doctrinal development, the actual regulatory decisions only hint at the broader discursive backdrop to legal change. A proper contextualization requires a fresh look at the major legal and constitutional texts of the early nineteenth century—the general discussions of law and government that illuminate the political idiom of the time. When these treatises, law lectures, and speeches are confronted with the unanswered questions that jump from opinions like *Alger*, the outline of a previously elusive discourse about man, society, governance, and the people's welfare begins to emerge.

The central texts in this legal discourse were an eclectic lot, ranging from James Wilson's published law lectures at the College of Philadelphia (1804) to Chancellor James Kent's studied and comprehensive *Commentaries on American Law* (1826) to the basic political grammars of William Sullivan and Edward Mansfield.[25] Authors were no less diverse in temperament and politics, from the austere Federalism of Zephaniah Swift, a Connecticut jurist and sponsor of the Hartford Convention, to the Southern agrarian democracy advocated by Thomas Cooper, president of South Carolina College.[26] Mix in the German and French expatriate sensibilities of Francis Lieber and Peter (alias Pierre Etienne) Du Ponceau and one senses the variety within this legal conversation.[27] Isolating "key words" (e.g., "utility," "natural law," "individual rights," "common good," "the people," "government," "sovereignty") is difficult; most were present.[28] Citations to Bacon, Blackstone, Burke, Cicero,

Coke, Gibbon, Grotius, Hale, Harrington, Hobbes, Hooker, Hume, Locke, Milton, Montesquieu, Paley, Reid, Rousseau, and Vattel were bandied about as if their ideas were not often in tension.

Such diversities and ambiguities reflect the supple and pluralistic nature of this nascent public philosophy. These legal commentators were not in the business of producing a single, coherent intellectual system with which to coax the ready assent of all reasonable people. They were jurists and lawyers very much engaged in the messy, everyday practice of law and governance. Consequently, what one finds in the legal texts of the period is not so much a scientific political theory as a persuasion or vision, a fuzzy intellectual matrix not quite captured by the prevailing models of intellectual and legal history.[29] The legal ideas discussed here no doubt resonate with the moral and political-philosophical traditions unearthed by historians Henry May, Gordon Wood, J. G. A. Pocock, and Peter Miller.[30] But to anchor the intellectual origins of the well-regulated society in any one great textual tradition in political thought would be a mistake. The broad public vision that springs from these treatises and cases evades categorizations like "Ciceronian" or "Harringtonian" or "Burkean" as easily as it skirts the interpretive paradigms of constitutionalism and instrumentalism.

These texts yield instead a peculiar hybrid legal mentality—a self-proclaimed science skeptical of reason, a moral philosophy that shunned metaphysics, a theory of law that often ignored precedents and rules. Although difficult to define as a philosophy, it is possible to delineate four interrelated components of this legal persuasion: (1) a focus on man[31] as a social being in society; (2) a relative and relational theory of individual rights; (3) a pragmatic, historical methodology enshrined in a dynamic, pre-Enlightenment conception of the rule of common law; and (4) an overall concern with the people's welfare obtainable within a well-regulated society. Together, these four sets of assumptions composed the legal worldview that fostered and legitimated the pervasive role of police and regulation in early American economy and society: the common law vision of a well-regulated society.

Man of a Social Nature

In 1794, James Kent began his career as legal educator at Columbia with "An Introductory Lecture to a Course of Law Lectures."[32] There Kent succinctly captured the general approach to law that dominated legal thought up to the Civil War. His starting point was not rules, statutes, or procedure. He excoriated the "mere Mechanical Professor of our Laws" and stressed instead the

"doctrines of Moral Philosophy" as the "foundation of Human Laws" and an "essential part of Juridical Education." By moral philosophy Kent had in mind a particular sort of exercise or methodology. The science of jurisprudence and government had to begin with an examination of "the nature and moral character of Man," man not in some empty, individualized form, but in "the relations he stands to the Great Author of his being, and to his Fellow-Men." Only through such an examination could one decipher "the duties, the rights, and happiness resulting from those relations." On such duties, rights, and happiness stood the moral and obligatory force of law.[33]

This methodology, anchoring a science of law and government in the moral nature of man and society, permeated the work of James Wilson, Nathaniel Chipman, David Hoffman, Zephaniah Swift, and others.[34] It was even the fundamental starting point for practical political manuals like William Sullivan's *Political Class Book* (1831).[35] Moral philosophy, after all, was the common intellectual framework for all the human sciences in antebellum America, providing the necessary bridge between Protestant theology and more naturalistic forms of inquiry. As the culminating course in a pious college education, moral philosophy—the science of obligation and duty—provided a pedagogical foundation whereby all further learning and vocation were simple extensions of the fundamental requirements of virtue, order, and ambitious moral improvement.[36]

The sciences of law and governance were no exception. To early American jurists, law was no mere instrument or rule or profession. Their legal treatises were extended works of moral, ethical, and political theory. They strove to undergird their entire system of law with "first principles." As political and moral theory, these legal writings went beyond descriptions of existing legal knowledge and arrangements. They were part of an older moral-political tradition that sought actively to transfigure and perfect social and legal relationships through what Sheldon Wolin has called an "illuminating vision of the Good."[37] David Hoffman advised law students in 1817 that law was "a moral science of great sublimity." It was founded not on "an unconnected series of decrees or ordinances," but on "principle" that distinguished right from wrong, employed "the noblest faculties of the soul," and exerted "*in practice* the cardinal virtues of the heart."[38]

As Kent suggested, the starting point for these thinkers' reflections on law was the nature of man. But they offered a conception of nature different from some of the dominant philosophies of the time. Nathaniel Chipman began his extraordinary treatise *Principles of Government* (1833) with a critique of the "state of nature" theories of Hobbes, Locke, and Rousseau. All these theories,

he argued, whether they conceived the state of nature as noble savagery or a brute war of all against all, posited society and nature as fundamental opposites. Society and civil government were portrayed as contrived impositions on man's natural state, at best necessary evils. Chipman was particularly impatient with the views of Locke, Blackstone, and Beccaria, who defended civil government but insisted that man sacrificed something to get there, a portion of his "natural" liberty.[39] This "back-door" theory of state and society—the idea that human beings only grudgingly and furtively conceded to civil institutions—came under repeated attack in nineteenth-century legal literature. It was the beginning of a vibrant American hostility to state-of-nature thinking that stretched from James Wilson to Woodrow Wilson.[40] Uncomfortable with the implications of these ideas, Nathaniel Chipman and others advocated an alternative conception of the nature of man, a view in which society, government, association, and ultimately law were perceived not only as necessary but natural, keenly suited to human appetites. Implicit in this conception of the *social* nature of man was a spirited critique of the individualistic excesses of Hobbes and Locke.[41]

The notion of the social nature of man was rooted in a particular strand of moralistic thinking on the law of nature and nations that has received scant attention from historians of American political and constitutional thought. Since the progressive histories of Edward Corwin, Charles Grove Haines, and Benjamin Fletcher Wright, the higher and fundamental law of nature has been interpreted primarily as a conservative, antidemocratic cornerstone of the doctrines of judicial review, private rights, and supraconstitutional limitations.[42] Excessive natural law thinking, after all, was the abhorred weapon of choice in the "Lochner Court's" early twentieth-century campaign to frustrate benevolent reform in the name of absolute rights of property and contract. This progressive legacy has obscured the diversity within law-of-nature thinking and marginalized the central preoccupation of natural law writers with theories of the common good.[43]

One of the classic early American defenses of the law of nature and nations was James Duane's opinion in the case of *Rutgers v. Waddington* in the New York Mayor's Court (1784). Duane professed to "revere the rights of human nature; at every hazard we have vindicated, and successfully established them in our land! and we cannot but reverence a law which is their chief guardian."[44] But Duane's law of nature bore little resemblance to the negative, individualistic higher law of progressive demonology. When Samuel Loudon reported the case in 1784, he appended a note outlining the "Principles of the Law of Nature" of which Duane spoke:

That man was made for *society*—that society is absolutely necessary for *man*—that the *public good* ought always to be the supreme rule—that the spirit of *sociability* ought to be *universal*—that we ought to have the same disposition towards other men, as we desire they should have towards us—that we should behave in the same manner towards other men, as we would be willing they should behave towards us in the like circumstances—that we should preserve a benevolence even towards our *enemies*—that although the *exercise* of benevolence towards our enemies may be *suspended,* yet we are not allowed to *stifle* its principle; that revenge introducing, instead of benevolence, a sentiment of hatred and animosity is condemned; because such a sentiment is vicious in itself and contrary to the public good.[45]

This law of nature culminated not in theories of judicial review, absolute rights, and constitutional limitations but in recommendations for good governance and the pursuit of *salus populi* (the people's welfare).

American law writers cited most of the natural law canon: Grotius, Pufendorf, Wolff, Burlamaqui, Rutherford. But they were particularly fond of Emmerich de Vattel's *Law of Nations* (especially his chapter on "The Duties of a Nation towards Herself"), the most frequently acknowledged source of their notion of the social nature of man. Vattel, whom Kent deemed "the most popular, and most elegant writer on the law of nations," provided a theory of nature and man in tune with American moral-philosophical thinking.[46] Skeptical of an abstracted Enlightenment faith in pure reason—a faith that resulted in a rather empty, highly individuated concept of man's nature—Vattel (like Hume and Montesquieu) looked instead to human experience. Vattel's laws of nature were not a priori truths imposed from on high, but tentative conclusions drawn from the study of the "circumstances" of living human beings. One of the first principles deduced from such study, a principle reaffirmed over and over again in the legal texts of the period, was that man was a fundamentally social or relational being. Man's natural state was not to be found outside of community or in isolation from others but *in society.* For "in a state of lonely separation from the rest of his species, he cannot attain his great end—happiness."

This simple idea had rippling ramifications for the way one perceived the world, society, and law. Vattel gave an inkling of the revolutionary potential in this definition of natural law when he concluded, "Nature, herself, therefore, has established that society, whose great end is the common advantage of all its members; and the means of attaining that end constitute the rules that each

individual is bound to observe in his whole conduct."[47] Instead of positing a society and government beholden to and derived from the needs and interests of autonomous individuals, Vattel envisioned individuals as obligated to and inseparable from the greater good and welfare of the society as a whole.

In the hands of Chipman, Swift, Wilson, and Kent, such suggestions were molded into the foundation of an impressive jurisprudence. Nathaniel Chipman devoted his entire treatise to proving the fact that "man is, by the constitution and laws of his nature, fitted for society." Nature and society were not opposed. Rather, society was the "natural state to which the laws of his nature, general and particular, all tend."[48] Zephaniah Swift, building on Chipman's early writings, clearly sketched the break with conventional natural law thinking: "To contrast the social state, to the natural state, as tho the former was artificial, and the latter natural, is contrary to the truth. No principle of human conduct is more perfectly natural than that which prompts mankind to associate together for mutual benefit."[49] For these legal theorists, man was naturally and fundamentally a *social* being. Chipman put it most forcefully: "He was not made for independence, but for mutual connexion, mutual dependence, and to this everything in his nature is more or less relative."[50] Swift added, "Man will as soon put an end to his existence, as withdraw himself from society, or cease to maintain it. . . . The happiness of men depend upon their connexion and union with their fellow creatures. . . . We must eradicate from the human heart, the desire of happiness before man will cease to adhere to community."[51]

The language of "connexion," "union," and "society" was ubiquitous in these treatises.[52] In an appendix to William Sullivan's *Political Class Book,* George B. Emerson echoed the ideas of Swift published forty years before: "We find ourselves existing in such connexion with those about us, that we depend, in a thousand ways, upon them, and are able, in an equal degree, to contribute to their good. The dependence is mutual. The benefits we receive from others are such, that life would hardly be worth having, without them." Like Vattel, Emerson reached a conclusion quite contrary to the dogma of Adam Smith. Far from allowing public good to flow from individual interest, Emerson reasoned that it was the duty "of each individual in society to contribute his proportion towards that common good, from which the happiness of each one, and of the whole, is derived."[53]

But by far the most powerful spokesman for a social view of the nature of man was James Wilson. Wilson began his seventh law lecture, "Of Man, as a Member of Society," with Genesis: "'It is not fit that man should be alone,' said the all-wise and all-gracious Author of our frame, who knew it, because

he made it; and who looked with compassion on the first solitary state of the work in his hands. Society is the powerful magnet, which, by its unceasing though silent operation, attracts and influences our dispositions, our desires, our passions, and our enjoyments. . . . Does self-interest predominate here? No. Our social affection acts here unmixed and uncontrolled."[54] Wilson illustrated the force of the social affections with one of the most amazing (and, by today's standards, mawkish) tales to be found in an American legal treatise. He related the story of an imprisoned French nobleman cut off from all social contact, whose only solace came through the discovery of a spider sharing the same abode. Wilson noted, "He immediately formed a social intercourse with the joint inhabitant" and "enjoyed without molestation, this society" until discovered by a guard "long tutored and accustomed to all the ingenious inventions and refinements of barbarity." As a "consummate master of his art," the guard killed the spider and sent the nobleman reeling once again into complete solitude. According to Wilson, once freed, the nobleman often declared that he suffered most when he lost "his companion in confinement."[55]

Wilson used this extraordinary story to further a critique of what he called the "selfish philosophy" of Hobbes and Locke and to emphasize his own conception of man's social rather than individualistic nature. He found the "narrow and hideous" philosophies that posited universal self-love as the fulcrum of humanity "totally repugnant to all human sentiment and all human experience." Rather, the "passion for commonweal," the propensity to society, were natural as well as necessary "to support life, to satisfy our natural appetites, to obtain those agreeable enjoyments of which our nature is susceptible." Even Robinson Crusoe, that popular rugged individualist, needed society. Wilson pointed out, "All the comforts which he afterwards provided and collected, was laid in the useful instruments and machines, which he saved from his shipwreck. These were the productions of society."[56]

Nathaniel Chipman summed up this perspective as early as 1793. Quite simply, "the laws of nature" were "laws of social nature": "man is formed for a state of society and civil government. He is furnished with appetites, passions, and faculties, which in no other state have either gratification or use. In society, in civil society only, can man act agreeable to the laws of his nature. . . . It is, in truth, his ultimate state of nature."[57] John Bouvier began his influential *Institutes of American Law* (1854) with the widely accepted first principle of law and governance: "*Man is a social being.*"[58] For these jurists, the nature of man was not something to be deduced by contemplating the essence of an isolated, abstracted, presocial individual. Such a hypothetical individual was shorn of the very qualities they deemed most human—the desire to associate

with others, the feeling of pleasure at the approach of one's kind, moral perceptions, passions, sentiments, and emotions. All these traits were fundamentally relational in nature.[59] Instead of abstract reasoning, these thinkers embraced an experience-based induction, rooted in "observation on real life and manners," to get at the nature of man.[60] This perspective led them to conclude unequivocally that man's nature was social, realized within society and impossible without. It also led them to one of the most explicit and uncompromising repudiations of possessive individualism in early American legal and political literature.[61]

Rights (or Duties) of a Social (or Relative) Nature

If these legal theorists stopped here, with the mere recognition of man's social nature, their tales of spiders, French noblemen, and Robinson Crusoe could be dismissed as curiosities. But this focus on man *in society* rather than in nature was but the first step in an extended intellectual journey, the beginnings of jurisprudence. The first ramification of the rejection of the nature/society dichotomy was an original conception of the relative nature of individual rights or, more aptly, individual duties.

William Blackstone's omnipresence in early nineteenth-century legal literature is no secret. What is surprising is the degree to which some of his most important ideas came under vigorous assault. One such idea was his notion of the "absolute [or natural] rights of individuals."[62] Blackstone's conception of individual rights was a direct product of his juxtaposition of nature and society, natural liberty and civil liberty. Through this bifurcation, he derived certain "natural" or "absolute" rights that existed outside of and beyond the reach of society and its laws. Indeed, though man sacrificed a part of natural liberty to enter society, society's first duty was to protect individuals in the enjoyment of those preeminent, presocial rights.[63] The individual and his interests preceded and trumped society and social interests. Individuals backed into a society and government whose legitimacy hinged not so much on what it substantively accomplished but on how little it disturbed preordained private rights.

What would become of Blackstone's "*absolute* rights of individuals" when confronted with Wilson's or Swift's notion of the *social* nature of man? What were natural rights, if "natural" in fact meant "social?" Nathaniel Chipman answered dismissively that there "cannot, strictly speaking, be any such thing as absolute rights" as Blackstone described them. In excluding the "notion of social from his law of nature," Blackstone "confounded the natural liberty of

man, with the range of action permitted to all animals of the brute creation." Such "liberty" or "right" cut off from social relations was simply animalistic "locomotion." It did not warrant the label "natural right." When man's nature was defined by his social interaction with others, natural rights could only consist of those actions conducive and not antagonistic to that interaction. Wilson neatly captured the thrust of this argument when he challenged Blackstone's claim that man sacrificed a portion of his natural liberty, or his right to do "mischief to his fellow citizens," when he entered society. Wilson rejoined with a simple rhetorical question: "Is it a part of natural liberty to do mischief to any one?"[64]

As an alternative to the "savage" and "selfish" power of one to "do what he please with his own," the theorists of the well-regulated society offered a vision of liberty that Chipman labeled "the moral" or "social kind." Rights such as personal liberty, personal security, and private property universally resulted "from the social relations" and had their roots in the "social nature of man."[65] A natural or legal right was not something to be exerted against society, but was intimately connected to the duties and moral obligations incumbent on social beings. A "right," in other words, was not a "wrong." For Vattel, rights emerged out of moral obligation as that which enabled one to carry out duties, as "nothing more than the power of doing what is morally possible." The right of self-defense in this understanding came not from an individual right to fend off others, but from the moral and social imperative to take care of one's body. Man's social nature, in Charles Goodrich's "science of government," bequeathed not rights to act in accordance with "individual will or caprice," but obligations to perform public duties. As Mark Hopkins, a Williams College instructor in "moral science," simply put it, "A man has rights in order that he may do right."[66]

With this "most important elementary truth"—that "the idea of right cannot be philosophically stated without the idea of obligation"—Francis Lieber extracted political science from moral philosophy.[67] For the obligation or duty intrinsic to this conception of right and rights was not an abstract debt to God or some transcendent moral law, but a responsibility to others, to one's neighbors, in society. Rights were of the distinctly human realm of law, governance, legislation, and regulation. Jesse Root introduced the first volume of Connecticut's *Supreme Court Reports* observing, "The great end of civil government . . . is to induce us to respect the rights, interests, and feelings of others as our own." James Wilson similarly acknowledged the fundamental human right and duty to "give to others every assistance." In society, men were "brethren" mutually obliged to one another; rights and duties were

relational "from man to man." Both Root and George Emerson reduced this philosophy to the injunction of the golden rule "*to love our neighbor as ourselves*, and to do all as we would they should do to us; knowing that the rights and enjoyments of others are the same to them as ours are to others."[68]

Rights were thus not only social (as opposed to individual) and affirmative (as opposed to defensive), they were also distinctly relative (as opposed to absolute). In contrast to the Blackstonian notion of inviolable, individual guarantees against social or governmental intrusion, these nineteenth-century jurists emphasized the relational and qualified nature of rights. All rights were defined by and subject to the larger society from which they sprang, particularly the coincident rights of others and the superior rights of the whole. Nathaniel Chipman argued that "man, sociable by the laws of his nature, has no right to pursue his own interest or happiness, to the exclusion of that of his fellow man."[69] James Wilson elaborated that one had a right to exercise "intellectual" and "active powers" *provided* "he does no injury to others; and *provided* some publick interests do not demand his labours."[70] These two great social qualifications on individual rights—hallmarks of the well-regulated society[71]—were at the core of these theorists' definition of *civil* liberty. Opposed to the anarchic notion of freedom as "unrestrainedness of action," civil liberty was "relative and limited." Its essence was the "mutual grant and check" embedded in "the idea of granting to [one's] fellows the same liberty which he claims for himself, and of desiring to be limited in his own power of trenching on the same liberty of others."[72]

This nineteenth-century understanding of the social, positive, and relative nature of rights poses some problems for contemporary legal and historical scholars who insist on seeing rights, first, as absolute shields and trumps protecting individuals from society and government; and, second, as the definitive achievement of a unitary and continuous liberal constitutionalism.[73] The writings of Wilson, Chipman, Lieber, and others confront such interpretations with a dominant early American legal discourse that took duties, not rights, seriously. Rights and liberties were secondary to (indeed derived from) the larger social obligations of man. As the theorists of the well-regulated society were fond of pointing out, rights and liberties were "not of a negative character."[74] They did not consist of merely saying "no" to government. On the contrary, they served as the central source and rationale for legal and governmental power. As Nathaniel Chipman summarized, "The rights of man are relative to his social nature, and the rights of the individual exist, in a coincidence only with the rights of the whole, *in a well-ordered state of society and civil government*."[75] The social nature of man, James Wilson tantalizingly

observed, yielded "a very close and interesting connection . . . between the law of nature and municipal law."[76]

The Rule of Common Law

In state-of-nature, social contract, and invisible-hand thinking, law and governance are by definition second-order concerns. The common good is best obtained by keeping an undistracted eye on the autonomous self, its presocial rights, and its ability to decipher and pursue its own individual interests. Law and governance are essentially remedial mechanisms—policemen and night-watchmen intermittently summoned to mediate private disputes, correct market failures, or restrain the occasional rogue individualist. In their unyielding attacks on Hobbes, Locke, Rousseau, Blackstone, and Smith, the theorists of the well-regulated society developed a radically different conception of governance and law. If man was a social being, and if all individual rights and liberties were relative to the rights of others and the good of the whole, then governance and law were not peripheral, yet alone antithetical, to man's nature. Indeed, law and governance embodied man's social essence as the indispensable regulators of the whole panoply of relative rights and duties. Francis Lieber captured this interdependence of individual liberty *and* social order, private right *and* public power when he concluded, "[Civil] liberty requires the supremacy of the law."[77]

Law was the cornerstone of the well-regulated society. Effusive tributes to law pervaded early American intellectual life.[78] The *North American Review* greeted the publication of Kent's *Commentaries* by invoking Hooker: "Of law no less can be acknowledged than that her seat is in the bosom of God; her voice, the harmony of the world; all things in heaven and earth do her homage, the very least as feeling her care, and the greatest as not exempted from her power." Such legal reverence involved much more than a prevailing cultural idiom or the political power of a handful of pioneering judges or a burgeoning alliance between bar and commercial interests. The overweening power of law between 1787 and 1877 was based on its pivotal role in the vision of a well-ordered society. As the *North American Review* elaborated, "In the accustomed security of a well regulated community we meet with but few occurrences to remind us of the influence of the laws that are blended in all our transactions, safely conducting us in the crossings and windings of our diverse pursuits."[79]

In the well-regulated society, the rights of individuals were not protected absolutely, according to some simple transcendent, antesocietal code or a set

of unchanging, natural laws of economic or individual behavior. Rather, rights and duties were guaranteed actively and relatively in an ongoing calculation of the reciprocal rights and duties of others and the good of the whole in a constantly changing society. A "well administered system of laws" served as that all-important calculator and calibrator "conferring upon rulers all the necessary powers, and only those, with the requisite counterpoises, checks, and limitations; confining each to his own sphere; distinctly explaining to the citizens their rights and duties in their multiplied and almost numberless relations among themselves and to the government; offering large encouragement to arts, industry, intellectual efforts, and public spirit; and arraying all the moral and physical power of the community on the side of the general welfare, and in defence of the rights and possessions of each individual member."[80] "Legal obedience and conformity" rather than the "absolute and uncontrolled power of doing whatever [one] pleases" constituted the first rule of behavior in a well-regulated society. Legal constraints on "wild and savage liberty," simultaneously protecting other individuals and securing "the general advantage of the public," were precisely what distinguished natural right from wrong in elaborations of the social nature of man.[81] Civil liberty, in short, was liberty restrained by *law*.

But not just any law. By the nineteenth century, a host of jurisprudential theories vied for the attention of Western social and political thinkers. Theorists of the well-regulated society were very particular about the kind of law that could perform these complicated and delicate social tasks. Indeed, they began their theory of law (like their theory of man) with an extended critique of three different schools of legal thought: natural law, legal positivism, and constitutionalism.

Though these thinkers relied on writers like Grotius and Vattel and constantly used the language of "nature" and "natural law," they distinguished their ideas from the great mass of natural law theory. They reserved particular hostility for the a priori character of most versions of natural law—the idea that natural law was a system of rules and principles anterior to experience and accessible only through pure reason. Attacking the natural law theories of Hobbes, Locke, and Rousseau, James Wilson observed, "The defects and blemishes of the received philosophy, which have most exposed it to ridicule and contempt, have been chiefly owing to a prejudice of the votaries of this philosophy in favour of reason. They have endeavoured to extend her jurisdiction beyond its just limits." Building on Scottish and common sense critiques of the preeminence of enlightened reason, early American jurists advocated a legal approach to man and society much more historical and experiential.[82]

David Hoffman advised in 1817, "The law more than any other science, should be known in all the various stages of its progression: its history discloses its philosophy."[83] Collapsing the natural and the social (natural law and municipal law) through their concept of "social nature," the theorists of the well-regulated society tried to close the gap between norm and reality, reason and experience, autonomy and heteronomy. They tried to locate a source of value and morality within rather than without human lives, communities, and histories.[84]

With similar passion, these jurists assailed legal positivism, which came to them primarily through the "will" or "command" theory of law articulated by William Blackstone. Blackstone defined municipal law simply as "a rule of civil conduct prescribed by the supreme power in a state, commanding what is right and prohibiting what is wrong." He rested obedience and the obligation of law not on the "approbation" of an inferior but on the "will" of a superior.[85] Such ideas, James Wilson challenged, could not come from "a zealous friend of republicanism." Blackstone's rooting of law in power and interest was "dangerous and unsound," containing within it the "seeds of despotism" and the "germ of divine right." "Bare force," he insisted, "far from producing an obligation to obey, produces an obligation to resist."[86] Nathaniel Chipman concurred, "What a triumphant defence of all the villains, public and private, that have ever infested society—of all the tyrants civil and ecclesiastical, who have ever existed from the days of Nimrod down to the present period of the holy alliance!" Power or force could impose necessity but never "obligation."[87] In constructing an alternative to Blackstone's positivism and his "misconception of the nature of our civil and political institutions," the theorists of the well-regulated society looked again to history and experience. "The sole legitimate principle of obedience to human laws," they argued, was "human *consent*," especially consent after "long, approved, uninterrupted experience."[88]

Finally, given the flurry of postrevolutionary constitution-making and the historic decisions of John Marshall's Supreme Court, one might conclude that constitutionalism was the reigning approach to law and legislation in the nineteenth century.[89] But early American law writers even contested the novelty and exaggerated significance of constitutions. Constitutions were simple and practical political documents, they argued.[90] They were not the first or the last word on American law and governance. Francis Hilliard observed that constitutionalism concerned only "political" rights, not the more general "civil rights and obligations of the citizen"—"the relations between man and man." Justice Henry Baldwin devoted an entire treatise to an attack on the use of exclusively constitutional sources (i.e., the books, essays, and speeches of

the Framers) in legal interpretation. John Holmes contended simply and provocatively that, "The Government of Massachusetts did not spring out of the revolution. The people of that colony were not obliged to begin anew."[91] For these theorists, constitutionalism was derived from and always secondary to an older body of law that remained the "national law" of the Union and the individual states—"the general law of the land."[92] That law was the common law.

The common law was the law of the Revolution and the "birthright of American citizens."[93] Early American jurists were unwavering in their devotion. For Nathaniel Chipman the common law was the Founders' native language—"not merely the language of their lips, but of their thoughts upon law, government, and all institutions, civil and political."[94] Statutes and even constitutions were to be construed according to its dictates.[95] James Wilson declared it "one of the noblest births of time." Peter Du Ponceau mused in almost biblical cadence, "We live in the midst of the common law, we inhale it at every breath, imbibe it at every power; we meet it when we wake and when we lay down to sleep, when we travel and when we stay home; it is interwoven with the very idiom we speak, and we cannot learn another system of laws without learning at the same time another language. We cannot think of right or of wrong but through the medium of the ideas that we have derived from the common law."[96]

The common law rather than natural law, positivism, or constitutionalism was the legal foundation for the well-regulated society. But the common law that inspired these thinkers was not the private, static, or individualistic common law described by Roscoe Pound, Daniel Boorstin, and countless twentieth-century legal scholars.[97] It was dynamic, social, and visionary. Its essence was a historical, organic understanding of the world in which public and private, individual and community, rights and duties were inextricably intertwined in a conception of a well-ordered, constantly changing, society. It challenged natural law, legal positivism, and constitutionalism with a social vision of law embedded in a vast array of contingent human experiences rather than the timeless, external truths of God, Reason, Sovereign, or Text. In particular, early American jurists celebrated four aspects of the common law that fit their overall faith in man's social nature, their commitment to a natural, noncoercive public happiness, and their rejection of both metaphysical and positivistic conceptions of law: consent, history, accommodation, and public spirit.

One of the most talked-about common law qualities lacking in other visions of law was consent. James Sullivan insisted that the common law was not

"a coercive institution," but "certain rules, which have a legal and acknowledged force, from our own consent."[98] James Wilson contrasted the harsh, thunderous edicts of Blackstonian legal positivism to the "calm and placid accents" of common or customary law: "I never intruded upon you: I was invited upon trial: this trial has been had: you have long known me: you have long approved of me: shall I now obtain an establishment in your family?" In customary, common law, "every lovely feature beam[ed] consent," the only "true origin of the obligation of human laws":

> How was a custom introduced? By voluntary adoption. How did it become general? By the instances of voluntary adoption being increased. How did it become lasting? By voluntary and satisfactory experience, which ratified and confirmed what voluntary adoption had introduced. In the introduction, in the extension, in the continuance of customary law, we find the operations of consent universally predominant. Customs . . . are laws written in living tables.[99]

According to common law theory, law's obligatory force came not from theory or from power but from the "rightness" that flowed from a consonance with the "habits and thoughts" and the "genius and manners" of the people.[100] Such consent did not amount to mere majoritarianism or an aggregate of individual preferences. An instrumental tabulation of current opinions, interests, or utilities was not what these theorists had in mind.[101] In the common law they located a more organic, weighty notion of consent and a grounding for their standards of sense and value in the accumulated human experiences of time.

History, then, was the second important feature of the common law persuasion. Skeptical of the power of reason and fearful of the power of hubris, theorists of the well-regulated society honed instead a common law historical sensibility.[102] Nathaniel Chipman recommended "the study of the history of man in society"—"actual observation on real life and manners"—as the best method of deriving principles of law and government.[103] Others simply invoked Matthew Hale's historical insight that the common law "was not the product of the wisdom of one man or society of men, in any one age; but of the wisdom, counsel, experience, and observation of many ages of wise and observing men."[104] Experience, "the faithful guide of life and business," was imbedded in the principles and usages of the common law. As James Wilson put it, "In every period of its existence, we find imprinted on it the most distinct and legible characters of a customary law—a law produced, extended, translated, adopted, and moulded by practice and consent."[105] The common

law was not the product of edict, or philosophy, or mere present-day need. Its authority rested instead on "reception, approbation, custom, long and established."[106] It was based not on a theory of man outside society, but on a living record of man's practices and experiences within society.

This historical vision of the common law might have given way to mere conservatism or formalism if by history these thinkers had in mind Edward Coke's static notion of an ancient constitution—the idea of the common law as unchanging and immemorial. But they took their notion of law's historicism not from Coke but from Matthew Hale. Hale furnished a more dynamic conception of a revisable and changing common law—a historicism that understood law as an "ever-changing product of the historical process."[107] The common law was not fixed from "time out of mind," but accommodating. "While to vulgar eyes it appears fixed and stationary," Peter Du Ponceau argued, it was "from its very nature uncertain and fluctuating," experiencing "great changes at different periods."[108] James Wilson called it "experimental."[109] He labeled this malleability and flexibility "the accommodating spirit of the common law"—the common law's ability to "adjust itself to every grade and species of improvement by practice, commerce, observation, study, or refinement."[110] Consent, history, improvement, and flexibility, then, went hand in hand with common law understanding. The common law accommodated "the circumstances, the exigencies, and the conveniences of the people." It changed as "circumstances, and exigencies, and conveniences change[d]," allowing for "the accumulated wisdom of ages."[111]

In this idea of a changeable yet tenacious common law, the treatise writers propounded a naturalistic legalism that avoided the extremes of formalism and instrumentalism. The common law, though ultimately flexible to the demands of the present, retained a residual authority and "principled-ness" from the weight of the past. As historian James Stoner observed, the common law mind "view[ed] each controversy as a matter, not for free invention or for fresh deduction from first principles, but for judicious choice, with attention to precedent always in order but authoritative solution always elusive."[112] The dialectic of past and present produced an experienced-based vision of law as a ongoing dialogue between needs and rules, interests and ideas, man and society. It emphasized law as process, engaged with history, rather than as rule or instrument. J. G. A. Pocock captured this aspect of Matthew Hale's thought: "Each law is the product of many past moments and is being tested at the present moment by a wisdom which in turn relies on the past. Each law will change, but society and its wisdom will go on."[113] Zephaniah Swift also caught

this double vision of the common law: "It establishes one permanent uniform, universal directory for the conduct of the whole community, and opens the door for a constant progressive improvement in the laws."[114]

The common law persuasion offered legal thinkers a way around some troubling theoretical antinomies: nature versus society, individual versus community, continuity versus change. Just as significantly, it took them beyond the public/private distinction, paving the way for some of the central political insights of the well-regulated society. Although Roscoe Pound described nineteenth-century common law as "characterized by an extreme individualism," traces of an alternative perspective are evident in the very adjective "common."[115]

"Common" was a constant ingredient in nineteenth-century political and legal discourse. Though still a rich word today, it was especially layered with meanings then. It was a synonym for "public," identifying objects, goals, traits, of a general nature, belonging to the whole. It stressed those things shared rather than individually possessed, binding society and mankind together rather than pulling it apart. "Common" rippled with larger notions of "community," "ordinariness" (as in "commoners" or House of Commons), "intercourse" (as in "communication" or "communion"), and "public goods" (as in "the commons"). Even alone it resonated with hints of the ideas associated with some of its more famous couplings: "common good," "common rights," "common people," and "common weal." It was the central component of the English translation ("commonwealth") of the Latin *res publica*— the source of our own "republic."[116] Such rich etymological roots suggest there is much more to "common" law than individualism, private right, and limited government.

Justice Henry Baldwin, after deciding that the common law should be the measure of constitutional interpretation, declared that one of the first rules of common law construction was that "laws and acts which tend to public utility, should receive the most liberal and benign interpretation . . . so as to make the *private* yield to the *public* interest."[117] James Sullivan's common law constitutionalism went even further, equating the broad goals of the Constitution's preamble—perfect union, justice, domestic tranquillity, common defence, general welfare, and liberty—with the spirit of "the common law of the whole country." He argued that "whatever is necessary to those important ends is an innate principle of government, and is solemnly made the will of the nation."[118] For these thinkers, the common law was a source of distinctly public values. Francis Hilliard found the common law's "*strong common*

sense" not in individualism but in the extent to which it sacrificed "immediate advantage or superficial equity, to its far-reaching views of permanent and universal good."[119]

The public vision of the common law was best expressed in two of its most influential, commonly cited maxims: *salus populi suprema lex est* (the welfare of the people is the supreme law) and *sic utere tuo ut alienum non laedas* (use your own so as not to injure another). These two maxims were the common law foundation for American police regulation. But to treat them as narrow legal rules would be a mistake. *Salus populi* and *sic utere tuo*, in fact, embodied complete and powerful moral and political philosophies. They were the common law blueprints for governance in a well-regulated society.

Well-Regulated Governance

So far we have seen the way early American legal thinkers, beginning with a moral-philosophical conception of the social nature of man, were led to jurisprudence—to an investigation of the many relative rights and duties of man in society. The rule of law was the necessary mechanism that identified and enforced the constantly shifting powers and mutual obligations of citizens. But only a rule of truly *common* law met these theorists' demands for consent, history, experience, accommodation, and public spirit. The end of this rule of common law and the crowning achievement of this whole body of thought was good governance in a well-regulated society: laws were tools of regulation; regulation was the condition for social order and the pursuit of the people's welfare; social order and the people's welfare were the primary objects of governance.

Though man was a social being, theorists of the well-regulated society were too naturalistic and historicist to place their hopes for society and government in some self-realizing general will or invisible hand. As Nathaniel Chipman pointed out, "Although men have a relish for society; . . . yet no goodness of heart can enable them to enjoy its benefits without an establishment of laws." "The general happiness of the whole human race [was] an object too vast for the limited faculties of man"; therefore, regulations (rules, ordinances, by-laws) were necessary to guide and encourage communities and citizens to promote "jointly and effectually, the publick security and happiness."[120] As Vattel put it, "Every political society must necessarily establish a public authority to regulate their common affairs, —to prescribe each individual the conduct he ought to observe with a view to the public welfare, and to possess

the means of procuring obedience."[121] Only through the meticulous legal regulation of relative rights and duties could man's social nature, his tendency toward society and the public good, be realized. Even James Fenimore Cooper admitted that "man is known to exist in no part of the world, without certain rules for the regulation of his intercourse with those around him."[122] Such regulation was the essence of self-government and the guarantor of true civil liberty. A government without regulatory power, "a weak government," as Francis Lieber put it, was ultimately "a negation of liberty."[123]

Consequently, the conception of governance in the well-regulated society could not contrast more completely with negative liberal notions of a minimalist or night-watchman state. Across the political spectrum from Federalist to Jeffersonian to Jacksonian to Whig, jurists of the well-regulated society passionately defended the positive responsibilities and obligations of government. James Wilson decried the prevalence "even among enlightened writers" of the "mistaken opinion, that government is subversive of equality and nature!" Forty years later, Cooper railed against the same "untenable" opinion: "[I]t is a common error to suppose that the nation which possesses the mildest laws, or the laws that impose the least personal restrictions is the freest. . . . [N]o country can properly be deemed free, unless the body of the nation possesses, in the last resort, the legal power to frame its laws according to its wants."[124] Over and over again, these thinkers defended the "energy in government" necessary to society's preservation, security, improvement, and happiness.[125] Government was not extraneous to society, it was not a necessary evil, and it did not originate sheepishly in a coerced bargain struck to preserve presocial liberties. Government was integral to the interconnected goals of man and society. As William Sullivan argued, "government . . . springs out of society and society cannot exist without it." These theorists devoted themselves to a "vigorous maintenance of the legitimate and wholesome power of government."[126]

But the concept of well-regulated governance should not be confused with modern notions of a positivist state. These theorists' sense of government was not inconsistent with the same general outlook that led them to challenge William Blackstone's idea of law as the command of a sovereign. Although government needed to be "energetic," it could not be capricious or even merely expedient. The regulations and laws of government had to meet standards of consent, experience, and accommodation. Charles Goodrich demanded that laws and regulations had to "coincide with and follow the habits of the people."[127] In other words, the role of government in a well-regulated

society was firmly ensconced within the common law tradition. Indeed its two substantive objectives—social order and the people's welfare—closely followed the broad outlines of the ruling common law maxims *sic utere tuo* and *salus populi*.

Sic utere tuo represented the more negative, constraining facet of well-regulated governance. That is, it defined the limits of individual rights, liberties, and activities within a well-ordered, civil society. *Sic utere tuo* embraced those preliminary rules and regulations necessary to secure a basic social ordering—to protect individuals from each other. *Sic utere tuo* built directly on these theorists' notion of the relative nature of social rights and civil liberty.

The "first rule" and "fundamental principle" of well-regulated governance, Nathaniel Chipman and William Sullivan pointed out, was the *sic utere tuo* maxim: "so use your own right, that you injure not the rights of others." Since "men cannot live each one by himself, but must live together, in society," it was imperative "that the wants and rights of each member shall be regulated by the rights and wants of every other."[128] An individual certainly had a "right" to utilize "powers" or "faculties" to obtain happiness, but only to the degree that he did not "destroy or impair those which appertain to every other individual."[129] Rights and liberties did not consist of the absolute, "unlimited power of every person to act" upon their immediate wishes, Charles Goodrich and James Fenimore Cooper argued, but in the "controlling authority" of government to regulate liberty by law.[130] Inverting one of the canons of American constitutional dogma that rights and liberties entailed limits on government, these thinkers posited a well-regulated society wherein the object of government was "to sustain and enforce limitations upon the supposed . . . rights of individuals."[131] *Sic utere tuo* was the common law standard by which government established regulations and restrictions to prevent one individual's liberty and property from injuring another. It was the essence of civil liberty—liberty regulated by common law.

But though negative in form (i.e., forbidding one from treading on the rights of neighbors in society), *sic utere tuo* was hardly a timid doctrine. Indeed, it was the substantive reference point for the whole common law of nuisance (public as well as private). And as will be seen in the following chapters, nuisance law was one of the most important regulatory tools of the nineteenth-century American state. Ernst Freund dubbed nuisance law "the common law of the police power, striking at all gross violations of health, safety, order, and morals."[132] Horace Wood captured something of the power of *sic utere tuo* and the reach of the common law vision of a well-regulated society in his 1875 treatise on the *Law of Nuisances*:

No man is at liberty to use his own without any reference to the health, comfort or reasonable enjoyment of like public or private rights by others. Every man gives up something of this absolute right of dominion and use of his own, to be regulated or restrained by law, so that others may not be hurt or hindered in the use or enjoyment of their property. This is the fundamental principle of all regulated civil communities, and without it society could hardly exist, except by the law of the strongest.[133]

For these thinkers, *sic utere tuo* constrained individual behavior, but it did not limit or detract from individual liberty. By abating a nuisance or imprisoning a criminal, courts were not destroying liberties, they were defending the rights, actually expanding the liberty, of wronged citizens. The theorists of the well-regulated society, it is important to remember, saw themselves as champions, not critics, of liberty and rights. They merely pointed out that true freedom was always a product of reciprocal protection and respect. Liberty and the common good were not antagonistic in this formulation; they were mutually reinforcing.

But *sic utere tuo* was only part of the equation of well-regulated governance. Nathaniel Chipman called it a "mere rule of forbearance." Social order was important—a necessary, but not sufficient, condition for good government and society. "Society ought to be preserved in peace," James Wilson observed, "But [was] that all? Ought it not to be improved as well as protected?"[134] In addition to shielding individuals from one another according to the *sic utere tuo* maxim, the well-regulated society aspired to an even greater protection and pursuit of the people's welfare as a whole. *Sic utere tuo* was always secondary to "the more general rule, which require[d] that all the actions of individuals be so directed as to promote the good of the whole."[135] The well-regulated society demanded the higher obligations associated with the maxim *salus populi*: the welfare of the people is the supreme law.

With their positive and social rather than negative and individual conception of the rights and obligations of man, the theorists of the well-regulated society pushed beyond a critique and description of existing law toward a more prescriptive moral vision—a vision of the good, a vision of what society ought to be. They were perfectionists. They envisioned not a defensive society and government, summoned to action sporadically when individual rights were endangered, but a public society in motion, ever reaching to secure the general welfare, public happiness, and even love. Vattel counseled that one of the major duties a nation owed to itself was "to labour at its own perfection."[136] James Wilson again echoed, "A nation should aim at its perfection.

The advantage and improvement of the citizens are the ends proposed by the social union."[137] Perfection was defined as something more than securing minimal living standards, balancing interest groups, or preserving peace. Many theorists joined Nathaniel Chipman in finding the key to perfecting "the happiness of the species" in love—the biblical command "Love thy neighbor as thyself."[138] William Sullivan and Thomas Cooper rooted improvement in the supreme law to promote the "common welfare" of society and "the happiness of the community."[139]

Like civic republicanism, the perfectionist vision of the well-regulated society embodied in the *salus populi* maxim championed public good over private interest. The social nature of man, the consequent rejection of absolute individual rights, and the emphasis on man's moral obligations toward others led these thinkers overwhelmingly to favor the "rights of the whole"—the society in general—over the selfish interests of individuals. Since man's entire nature was inextricably linked with and defined by society and its well-being, it followed that the existence, welfare, and improvement of that public took precedence over the concerns of private individuals. Treatise writers were unambiguous. Hugh Henry Brackenridge labeled the community "superior" and the individual "inferior" in reaching the conclusions that "the whole is greater than the part," and "private convenience must give way to the general good."[140] Charles Goodrich's *Science of Government* rested upon the unquestioned premise that "the public interests are more important and essential than any mere individual rights."[141] Inverting the Smithian notion of an invisible hand, these jurists championed the primary, active pursuit of a common good, which in turn would accrue advantages to all individuals. James Wilson reasoned, "He who acts on such principles, and is governed by such affections as sever him from the common good and publick interest, works, in reality towards his own misery; while he, on the other hand, who operates for the good of the whole . . . pursues, in truth, and at the same time, his own felicity."[142]

The theorists of the well-regulated society replaced political philosophies rooted in selfishness and individualism with a theory of governance in which "passion for commonweal" would "preserve inviolate the connexion of interest between the whole and all its parts." *Salus populi* culminated in the open-ended obligation of government to pursue the people's welfare above all else. With that governmental obligation came governmental power. As Zephaniah Swift described the law-making power of government, "It is difficult to define or limit its extent. It can be bounded only by the wants, necessities, and the welfare of society."[143] Charles Goodrich captured the full governmental implications of *salus populi* when he deemed it "the bounden duty of a state to ad-

vance the safety, happiness, and prosperity of its people, and to provide for its general welfare, by any and every act of legislation which it may deem to be conducive to these ends."[144] Minimalist governmental theories were simply incompatible with the broad public aspirations with which James Wilson closed his discussion of "Man in Confederation": "Let us, then, cherish; let us encourage; let us admire; let us teach; let us practise this '*devotion to the publick*,' so meritorious, and so necessary to the peace, and greatness, and happiness of the United States."[145]

Together *salus populi* and *sic utere tuo*, interpreted through the consensual, historical, and accommodationist tendencies of the rule of common law, made up the general conceptions early American jurists had in mind when they invoked the well-regulated society. From these two seemingly unassuming common law principles flowed a multitude of governmental restrictions on property, contract, morality, and a host of other aspects of social life.[146] The right of property, these thinkers were fond of pointing out, was a social, relative, and hence regulatable right. Zephaniah Swift declared, "It is in virtue of his being a member of society that a man is a proprietor . . . and not in virtue of any natural right."[147] Consequently, even a defender of property like John Taylor had to admit that "like all other passions it ought to be regulated and restrained, to extract from it the benefits it can produce, and to counteract the evils it can inflict."[148] So too with the right of contract. "In every well regulated community," John Holmes suggested, "there should exist a power to control parties in making their contracts, in providing how they shall be executed and even in prohibitions such as are against public policy."[149] Even religious freedom was subject to the strictures of *salus populi* and *sic utere tuo*. "Religious profession and sentiments are free from restraint," Charles Goodrich noted, "*provided* they are not made so as to disturb the public peace, or interfere with the profession or sentiment of another."[150] More mundane rights and freedoms received even less consideration. Thomas Cooper summed things up rather bluntly: "The great object of all laws is the general welfare. . . . There can be no rights inconsistent with this. If a man cannot be safely trusted with liquor or with arms, he has no right to them."[151]

The common law vision of a well-regulated society not only greatly affected the way one thought about property, contract, and civil rights, it incorporated a wholly separate logic of American public law and constitutional interpretation. Treatise writer William Sullivan provided a perfect example concerning state bankruptcy laws and the contracts clause of the Constitution.[152] In the early nineteenth century, Sullivan asserted, there were two ways to interpret the contracts clause. One interpretation held "that the 'obligation of a contract'

was that duty which arises from the immutable laws of natural justice, the obligation of which men are presumed to carry with them into society; and that the laws of society do no more than enforce the performance of that duty." Those who accepted this first absolutist, Blackstonian version understood the right of contract as existing outside of society, and law as government's mechanism to protect and preserve that presocial right. Hence a bankruptcy statute, "which *substitutes* something, for the exact performance of the contract, was a law impairing the obligation of contract," and was "repugnant to the constitution."

The second interpretation—the view compatible with the well-regulated society—held "that all contracts are made by persons, who are already members of society, and are made with reference to the existing laws of the society of which they are members; and that the 'obligation' of the contract is that *only*, which laws make it to be." Under this more social vision of man and government, all contracts were made subject to the human laws in force at the time of the contract, whether or not such laws altered, discharged, or negated the particular contract altogether. Contracts were social, presumed to be made according to society's demands and regulations: *sic utere tuo* and *salus populi*. Bankruptcy laws did not impair the "obligation of contracts." They defined that very obligation.

Thus, jurisprudential thinking of the most abstract sort—on the nature of man, society, and government—formed an important intellectual template for general nineteenth-century policymaking. William Sullivan found such perspectives absolutely crucial to the conflicting opinions of U.S. Supreme Court justices in *Sturges v. Crowninshield* (1819) and *Ogden v. Saunders* (1827).[153] So too with Lemuel Shaw's decision in *Commonwealth v. Alger*. Only after reconstructing the jurisprudential context of the common law vision of a well-regulated society can one see the potency of Shaw's argument from "settled principles" on "the nature of well-ordered society," the meaning of his reference to property rights as "social and conventional," and the logic of his defense of "general regulations . . . necessary to the common good."[154] Shaw's decision was not anomalous or unusually difficult or prescient. It fit perfectly into a prevailing governmental and regulatory tradition keenly attuned to the "rights of the community" and a dominant vision of law "shook from sublimer powers than those of self."[155]

The ideas and rhetoric of the common law vision of a well-regulated society were certainly powerful, but even more impressive was the way in which *salus populi* and *sic utere tuo* were translated into a practice of governance, encompassing "all the ordinary transactions of the community; the obligations and

liabilities resulting from the relations of life."[156] From these principles flowed not only bankruptcy laws and wharf lines (which alone greatly affected the early American economy) but the criminal code, taxation, eminent domain, and the police power. In *salus populi* and *sic utere tuo*, Nathaniel Chipman located the general law-making powers of nineteenth-century state and local governments "to protect their respective citizens in the secure enjoyment of all their personal rights; to regulate the mode of acquiring, and to secure the acquisitions of property; to cherish and protect all the social relations; to provide for an equal administration of justice; to provide the means of education, and to facilitate the diffusion of useful knowledge; to animadvert upon morals, and to provide for the prevention and punishment of all those crimes, that attack private property, or in any way violate the rights, or disturb the peace of the community." The effect of this regulatory police power was "constant," and it operated upon "the most important interests of society."[157]

Demonstrating the reach of the well-regulated society in nineteenth-century American public policies regarding public safety, public economy, public property, public morals, and public health is the task of the next five chapters. But though the common law vision of a well-regulated society was particularly influential in the development of American public law, it would be a mistake to see it simply as the offsetting public corollary to a private law discourse of individual right and laissez-faire. The well-regulated society was not the lesser and lighter public half of a perennial balancing act in American history between society and government, individualism and communitarianism, private interests and people's welfare. Nor was it some fading vestige of feudalism, mercantilism, or civic republicanism. The vision of a well-regulated society was a coherent, distinctive, and dominant legal-political discourse that permeated even the most unlikely texts and practices in nineteenth-century American life, private as well as public. Its assumed and commonly accepted nature only makes it that much harder to recognize.

One could read, for example, James Kent's famed chapter "Of the History, Progress, and Absolute Rights of Property," and see only a traditional concern for the sanctity of private right. But even this sacred tract on American property rights was infused with the doctrines of the well-regulated society. Tossed here and there between the cracks of Kent's main argument were comments indicating the presence of a less explicit, subterranean conversation going on. In these interstitial passages one finds layers of assumed meaning and the large shadow of the well-regulated society. Kent argued, "Every individual has as much freedom in the acquisition, use, and disposition of his property, as is consistent with good order and the reciprocal rights of others." Rights of

property, while important, "must be made subservient to the public welfare. The maxim of law is, that a private mischief is to be endured rather than a public inconvenience." Kent ended his lecture with a caveat describing the ultimate regulating power of society and government: "Though property be thus protected, . . . the lawgiver has a right to prescribe the mode and manner of using it, so far as may be necessary to prevent the abuse of the right, to the injury or annoyance of others, or of the public." Nuisances, unwholesome trades, slaughterhouses, gunpowder, combustible materials, and burials could be regulated "on the general and rational principle, that every person ought so to use his property as not to injure his neighbours, and that private interest must be made subservient to the general interest of the community." Kent thus ended his great statement on private property rights by invoking nothing less than the two great principles of the well-regulated society, *sic utere tuo* and *salus populi*.

Two of the most comprehensive American legal minds met in the twelfth edition of Kent's *Commentaries* (1873), when Oliver Wendell Holmes Jr. superimposed his comments on Kent's masterpiece. Holmes added a footnote to Kent's final passage on property: "This power is now called the police power." The vision of the well-regulated society that lurks beneath Kent's discussion of private property was indeed the basis for modern notions of police power. But in the translation into a Holmes-era constitutional doctrine, many changes took place. One reason to recreate or piece back together the common law vision of a well-regulated society is that so much of it has been lost or misunderstood. American history is short. Oliver Wendell Holmes himself knew both John Quincy Adams and Alger Hiss.[158] The question is, How well did Holmes know the *world* of John Quincy Adams? More particularly, how well did his "police power" capture the meanings of James Kent's "general interest of the community?" Was Holmes's understanding of the police power broad enough to fathom a philosophy of property and rights that opened with the premise "Man was fitted and intended by the Author of his being for society and government?"[159]

Public Safety:

Fire and the Relative Right of Property

Among the many objects to which a wise and free people

find it necessary to direct their attention, that of providing

for their *safety* seems to be the first.

—John Jay, *Federalist*, No. 3

A s an abstract theory of man, society, and government, the common law vision of a well-regulated society was an important part of the intellectual environment of nineteenth-century America. But the ideas and perspectives captured by this body of thought were not simply the speculations of theorists, relevant only to those pursuing the minutia of the American mind. The jurisprudential ideas outlined in chapter 1 were especially significant in the way they were woven into the institutional and social fabric of American life. As Pierre Bourdieu pointed out, legal ideas and texts are peculiarly performative, having a special power to produce immediate social effects—to make things happen simply by saying so.[1] The linguistic turns and ideas of the jurists of the well-regulated society were ideas *in action*. They governed the way courts, legislatures, and local officials acted on countless public policy issues involving the state, the economy, property, social order, and the people's welfare. Marvin Meyers was right to caution us that a full picture of political culture means watching politicians' (and jurists') feet as well as their mouths.[2] Accordingly, it is time to turn to the actual practices of nineteenth-century governance—the particular policies by which officials pursued the main objectives of the well-regulated society: public safety, public economy, public mobility, public morality, and public health. Of these, none surpassed the importance of public safety.

Public safety involved the polity's duty to protect the life and limb of the citizenry. Without a people to rule, of course, there was little need for rulers; without subjects there was no state. Before addressing the concerns of order, prosperity, or morality, a government first had to secure and ensure (later insure) the population's existence and longevity. Public safety was the cornerstone of governmental obligation. It had been so for some time.

The long history of governmental preoccupation with public safety is evident in the very evolution of *salus populi* (sometimes translated as "the *safety* of the people*"). The ancient Roman version "*Salus Populi Romani,*" signifying the overarching public responsibility to the health and safety of the people of Rome, infused religious iconography in the Middle Ages. Blending the secular notion of public safety with pastoral, Christian concern for the people's salvation, icons were used in religious processions to ward off the dangers of invasion or epidemic.[3] But more significant for nineteenth-century governance was the pivotal role of public safety and security in early modern conceptions of police or *Polizei*. Having little to do with modern law enforcement, early modern police encompassed the loftiest ambitions and powers of government—the general pursuit of public good and the people's happiness. Police did so (as demonstrated best in Marc Raeff's detailed examination of German *Landes-* and *Polizeiordnungen*) through the proposed regulation and control of almost every aspect of daily life.[4] As the polity reclaimed jurisdiction over the people's well-being from the church, public safety—securing the population in number and health—returned as a primary reason of state. Even Adam Smith's police theory first acknowledged the dependence of the "peace of the state" on the "security of the people" (thus the necessity of town guards and fire regulations) before taking up the wealth of nations, that is, "the proper means of introducing plenty and abundance."[5]

Despite the historical tendency to contrast police and common-law regimes,[6] the nineteenth-century American vision of a well-regulated society emulated police concern for public safety. The extended life of the republic hinged on a healthy and secure population, on first guaranteeing the "life" of the people. Liberty, happiness, and property (yet alone comfort and wealth) were by definition secondary concerns. Early American jurists often used public safety as a synonym for the "domestic tranquillity" insured by the Constitution's preamble. In the Constitution itself, public safety appeared as the only justification for the suspension of habeas corpus.[7] "Mutual safety," Justice Henry Baldwin observed, was one of the prime motives of society and, consequently, an important obligation of constitutional governance.[8]

Public safety was a central component of early American conceptions of the

people's welfare, triggering the common law directives *sic utere tuo* (use your own so as not to injure another) and *salus populi* (the welfare of the people is the supreme law). All private rights and individual interests were subject and relative to the overriding public concern for the people's survival and security. One could exercise rights of property and liberty, *provided* they did not endanger the public safety. As Supreme Court Justice James Iredell held in 1795, the public safety was that "to which all private rights ought and must forever give way."[9] Public safety was also a source of a more proactive and open-ended legislative regulatory power. New York attorney David B. Ogden argued before the Supreme Court in 1837, "The object of all well-regulated governments is, to promote the public good, and to secure the public safety; and the power of that legislation necessarily extends to all those objects."[10] When the public safety was threatened, public officials could summon the full, creative powers of governance. The common law of nuisance and the law of overruling necessity, legal embodiments of *sic utere tuo* and *salus populi*, figured prominently in cases involving dangers to the people's safety.

Many hazards to public safety existed in nineteenth-century America, but three were particularly threatening to population, social order, and civil government. The first was invasion or insurrection (unfortunately, it would take three more volumes to trace the role of *salus populi* in American foreign policy, American Indian policy, and the coercive structure of American slave law).[11] The second was epidemic, which, as will be seen in chapter 6, galvanized an entire movement for medical police and public health reform. The third overarching public safety concern, and the one most revealing of the underlying assumptions of nineteenth-century American governance, was . . . "Fire!"

The "Giant Terror"[12]

One of the most important lawyer-judge exchanges in the constitutional history of the police power took place in 1827 in *Brown v. Maryland*, which Charles Warren dubbed "one of the great fundamental decisions of American constitutional law."[13] There, the two chief justices who would dominate the U.S. Supreme Court until the Civil War confronted each other over a Maryland statute imposing a license tax on importers and vendors of foreign commodities. Roger Taney, then representing the state of Maryland, defended the state's right to license and regulate all merchants and dealers within its borders. Without such a right, he argued, states would be defenseless against numerous offenses in the name of commerce. Taney offered a pointed example:

if the right to sell was a "vested right" unaffected by state legislation, then a merchant could wantonly "offer for sale large quantities of gunpowder in the heart of a city and thus endanger the lives of the citizens."[14]

John Marshall ruled against his successor to the chief justiceship, finding the Maryland statute in conflict with the commerce clause and the constitutional prohibition against state duties on imports or exports. But Marshall could not ignore Taney's concerns about unregulatable selling or gunpowder. He made it clear that his decision was about the boundaries of American federalism, not the absolute rights of sellers. "The power to direct the removal of gunpowder," Marshall reasoned, "is a branch of the police power, which unquestionably remains, and ought to remain with the States." This police power formed "an express exception" to the prohibitions of the commerce clause.[15] With this short, unelaborate response to Taney's argument, the phrase "police power" for the first time made its way into the constitutional lexicon.

It is neither unimportant nor unusual that "police power" was constitutionally coined amid a discussion of gunpowder. Taney's counterfactual caught Marshall's attention because its ramifications were too important to be dismissed or ignored. Marshall's affirmation was so short because what he said was a fact of everyday life taken for granted in early nineteenth-century society. The specter of a large deposit of gunpowder in the middle of early New York, Boston, or Philadelphia demanded recognition because it evoked one of the central policy concerns of an emerging nation of towns and cities—the threat of fire. Marshall felt no need to elaborate on the police power because it was never doubted in this well-regulated society that something as potentially injurious to the public as gunpowder, whether imported or exported, bought or sold, or considered "commerce," "property," "contract," or a "market transaction," was decidedly regulatable. Nothing in the nascent Constitution or John Marshall's jurisprudence would change that.

Fire emerged early as one of the crucial public safety concerns of the young republic. Fire did not merely endanger the people's health or economy or morality; it threatened their very being, their existence. And like most things in early America identified as inimical or hazardous to the people's welfare, fire became the focus of formidable common law and legislative regulations. The public fight against fires ignited a comprehensive and diverse regulatory effort employing most of the legal technologies and rationales of the well-regulated society. This legal fire fighting nicely illuminates the degree to which early American law and polity were solicitous of the paramount claims of

public safety and *salus populi*. It also demonstrates the nineteenth-century limits on individual rights, especially the relative right of private property.

Though fire remains an important public concern today, a shift in perspective is necessary to capture its significance for nineteenth-century Americans living in cities or towns. To these individuals, fire and epidemic disease made up two of the most constant, catastrophic threats to safety and well-being. In early Philadelphia or Boston, fire's menace was no longer symbolized by the ignition of an isolated barn, but by the general conflagration capable of devouring an entire city. Crowded conditions, wooden buildings and chimneys, narrow streets, the use of open fires and combustibles in daily living, primitive water supplies, and inadequate fire-fighting equipment and organization made the early nineteenth-century city a veritable tinderbox.[16] One person's carelessness or folly could put the public safety and common welfare at immediate and severe risk. But fire was more than a threat or idle anxiety in antebellum America. All too often, fear and concern were products of fatal experience.

From 1818 to 1856, David Dana reported 425 "large" fires in the thirty principal cities of the United States with estimated losses of over $190 million.[17] Boston suffered serious, general conflagrations in 1653, 1676, 1679, 1682, 1691, 1711, 1753, 1760, 1787, 1794, 1824, 1825, 1850, and 1852. Smaller fires were a way of town and city life, the ringing of fire bells constant, the burning of a home, warehouse, or row of businesses routine. A Cincinnati editor complained in 1807, "We seldom pass a week, without reading some melancholy account of the disasters occasioned by the most destructive of all elements—fire."[18] If the constancy of fires in early America brought with it the danger of numbing familiarity, it was soon snapped by the massive infernos the engulfed Savannah in 1820, New York in 1835 and 1845, Charleston in 1838, Pittsburgh in 1845, St. Louis in 1849, San Francisco in 1851, and Portland in 1866. The Charleston fire consumed 700 densely settled acres.[19] The 1835 New York fire leveled the whole first ward of the city, the central financial and business district.[20] Fires of this magnitude shook society to its core.

Large fires brought the citizenry face-to-face with the apotheosis of unregulated, disordered society. Descriptions of "chaos," "confusion," "uncontrollability," and "panic" dot early nineteenth-century accounts of urban fires. Jeremiads of general social collapse joined doomsday sermons as the two most common forms of social commentary accompanying "great fires."[21] Disorder and the fear of social disintegration manifested themselves in a pervasive paranoia of incendiarism and an obsession with security and police at fires. The

lone, crazed, criminal arsonist—the antithesis of civilized, ordered life—
became a focus of antebellum society's effort to explain the uncontrollable, ir-
rational, and antisocial force of fire. Arsonists were vilified in the popular
press. One Mississippi editor was particularly vituperative (and alliterative):
"Some sneaking, savage, sanguine, scorbutic, scraggy, scrofulous, scurrilous,
shameless, sinister, slouchy, slavish, slinking, slovenly, sordid, skulky, soulless,
slubberede guillion, set fire to a frame house on Washington Street on Satur-
day morning last, before day, which, but for its accidental and early discovery
would certainly have laid in ruins a large portion of the city."[22] As early as 1796,
the mayor of Philadelphia petitioned the Pennsylvania legislature for power to
take measures against a "gang of incendiaries" setting fire to the city with a
view to plunder.[23] Whether fears of rampant arson were warranted, they usually kindled calls for better security before, during, and after fires. Provisions
for the constable's watch and fire prevention emerged simultaneously in
South Carolina for the "preservation," "good order," and "peace and good
weal" of Charleston.[24] While actual fire-fighting troops were still grossly inadequate, up to 400 "watchmen" were ordered to report to all New York fires in
1826 to prevent looting, burglary, and general disorder.[25] A special guard of
1,300 watchmen, constables, marshals, militia, marines, sailors, and civilians
was assembled to restore and preserve the peace for several days after the New
York disaster of 1835.[26] Fire was more than an unfortunate occurrence in the
early nineteenth century; it was all too often an exercise in social dissolution.

Given common assumptions about statelessness, individualism, and private property, one might assume that the early American governmental
response to the peril of fire went no further than the organization of some
well-publicized volunteer fire companies. Given the common law vision of a
well-regulated society, however, that was unthinkable. Fire posed dire threats
to two of the fundamental concerns of the well-regulated society: social order
and the people's welfare. Consequently, it met with immediate state action
that was restrictive, forceful, and anything but voluntary. Statute and ordinance books offer the first inklings of an alternative "police" story in the case
of fire.

While New York City was still known as New Amsterdam, Peter Stuyvesant
introduced ordinances prohibiting wooden or plaster chimneys, straw or reed
roofs, hayricks or haystacks; requiring each household to have a ladder; appointing fire wardens and inspectors with powers to levy harsh fines (up to
100 guilders); and compelling householders to keep chimneys clean. Fines and
taxes went toward the purchase of community fire buckets, hooks, and lad-

ders.[27] After Dutch rule, the colonial legislature supplemented those regulations with a more comprehensive policy that included appointing "firemen"; establishing "fire limits" that required new buildings to be "made of Stone or Brick and Roofed with tile or slate"; restricting the storage of pitch, tar, and turpentine; prohibiting more than six pounds of gunpowder (twenty-eight pounds for retailers—"in four stone jugs or leather bags not more than seven pounds each") to be kept within two miles of City Hall; regulating the transportation of gunpowder on city streets; and limiting the height of buildings. Extensive fines were imposed for violations of these regulations, and buildings erected contrary to explicit provisions were indictable as "public nuisances."[28]

By 1813, when the legislature condensed and revised its municipal regulations, New York City had the beginnings of an ample fire code.[29] Provisions followed the general outlines laid down before the Revolution: fire limits, building regulations, bans and restrictions on dangerous materials, the appointment of administrative officers and fire personnel, inspection, and penalties. In addition to materials of brick or stone, the 1813 code required party or fire walls between structures. Offending buildings were deemed nuisances, which might be "abated and removed," in addition to having the proprietor or builder prosecuted. Gunpowder regulations grew to two pages, adding provisions for a public magazine, restrictions on ships and wharves,[30] public carriage,[31] and concealment. Sulphur, hemp, flax, rosin, and linseed oil joined gunpowder, pitch, tar, and turpentine as prohibited or heavily restricted materials. The firing or discharge of guns, pistols, rockets, crackers, squibs, or any other fireworks in populated areas of the city was prohibited. The statute also included detailed instructions for the behavior of the sheriff, common council, firemen, marshals, and constables during fires. It empowered these officials to *compel* the service of the citizenry (and their buckets) to extinguish fires. The mayor with the consent of two aldermen was given the special power to direct the destruction of buildings to prevent the spread of fire. If these specifics were not enough, the common council was finally granted an omnibus power to pass ordinances as it "may deem proper, for the more effectual prevention and extinguishment of fires," including the power to regulate lights and candles in livery and other stables, "to remove or prevent the construction of any fire-place, hearth, chimney, stove, oven, boiler, kettle or apparatus used in any manufactory or business which may be dangerous in causing or promoting fires," and to direct deposits for ashes.[32] Inspectors were authorized "to enter into and examine all dwelling-houses, lots, yards, inclosures and buildings of every description within the said city, to ex-

amine and discover whether any danger exists therein." Fines grew, as did a range of other penalties like imprisonment, forfeiture, abatement, and seizure.

Fire laws proliferated in almost every major settlement, from the sophisticated fire codes of coastal cities to frontier bans on the firing of woods.[33] As early as 1638, Boston forbade smoking outdoors, imposed curfews on household fires, and enacted penalties for incendiarism. In this fire-plagued city, Carl Bridenbaugh pointed out, "hardly a Town Meeting convened without prolonged discussions" of fire prevention. After devastating experiences with fire in 1679 and 1711, the Massachusetts General Court required brick or stone buildings with slate or tile roofs in the city and empowered fire wardens to order assistance and pull down houses during fires. Quantities of gunpowder over twenty pounds were to be stored at Robert Gibb's warehouse on the outskirts of town.[34] William Penn brought to Pennsylvania a heightened awareness of the dangers of fire inherited from his father's experience in the infamous London conflagration of 1666.[35] Ben Franklin had his volunteer fire department, but Penn deserves credit for making Philadelphia a well-regulated, remarkably fire-resistant city. Philadelphia's fire regulations included prohibitions on wooden buildings, the boiling of pitch or tar, and gunpowder.[36] Chimneys and the manufacture of gunpowder were regularly inspected, and households were required to keep leather buckets solely for extinguishing fires. In South Carolina, eighteen of the twenty-six legislative acts governing Charleston before 1751 dealt with public safety: the watch, fortifications, and the prevention of fires.[37] Rhode Island enacted similar fire regulations for Providence, Newport, Bristol, and Warren.[38]

Legislative penalties and remedies were as diverse and potentially severe as the regulations themselves. Fines could be substantial. In 1811, New Jersey imposed a staggering $2,000 fine for the manufacture of gunpowder within a quarter-mile of any town or house.[39] Imprisonment was also a distinct possibility, especially if the fine was not paid or the nuisance was left unabated. Legislatures also devised some ingenious schemes for enforcement and deterrence. Rhode Island imposed an annual $50 tax on wooden buildings within the fire limits of Providence, accumulating until wood was replaced with brick or stone.[40] Private prosecution accompanied by forfeiture provisions were also commonly used tools, turning every citizen into a potential police officer and prosecutor. In New York, a violation of gunpowder laws could result in a forfeiture of all gunpowder "to any person or persons who will sue and prosecute."[41]

Finally, buildings and goods held and used contrary to fire law were susceptible to one of the most remarkable remedies of the nineteenth-century legal order: summary *destruction* by public officers and private citizens. In a striking illustration of the powerful ramifications of *sic utere tuo* and *salus populi*, private property used so as to endanger the public welfare by increasing the hazards of fire was condemned by the common law of nuisance and subject to summary removal, abatement, or being simply "pulled down."[42] The demolition and confiscation of private property figured prominently in Charleston, South Carolina's fire-prevention techniques, which included legislative prohibitions on wooden chimneys; wooden buildings; gunpowder; the storage of straw and fodder in houses; the boiling of pitch, tar, rosin, or turpentine; and the keeping of stills and stillhouses. Except for the boiling of pitch and tar, summary destruction was a remedy for every statutory violation.[43] From the perspective of the well-regulated society (with its relative and conditional understanding of private right), such destruction of public safety nuisances was a "necessary" regulation for the people's welfare, not a "taking" of private property entitled to compensation under the Fifth Amendment to the Constitution.[44]

These statutory regulations and remedies supplemented a larger fire policy that included the more familiar tale of emerging fire companies, fire departments, fire insurance, and more effective fire-fighting equipment. Adequate fire protection, after all, was much more than a matter of quenching existing fires. It required a marshaling of social resources and a rigorous ordering of social life — central elements in the ideal of a well-regulated society. The legislative record reflects a society committed to that ideal. From an early date, state legislatures and local governments imposed stringent restrictions on property (building laws), liberty (mandatory assistance in firefighting), and the market (the sale of gunpowder). In the interest of the people's welfare, they enacted regulations governing how an individual built a home or business, how it was heated, how it was lighted, what it had to contain (leather buckets and hooks), the cleanliness of its chimneys, and the goods or activities or trades pursued therein. Additionally, legislatures granted municipalities ample power to regulate even more for "the purposes of a well-ordered police, and for the good government of the city."[45] The statutes and ordinances seemed to regard no behavior, personalty, realty, or set of rights as ultimately beyond the ambit of state and local regulations to prevent fires.

But there are limits to what the legislative record alone can tell us about the character and extent of early American safety regulation. First, the statutes

themselves reveal little about the actual implementation or enforcement of regulation. A small cottage industry has grown up in legal history exploring the gaps between law on the statute books and law in action. A convincing challenge to pervasive myths of lax law enforcement in nineteenth-century America (whether in safety, criminal, market, or morals law) requires a deeper investigation of prosecution, litigation, and local governance.[46] Second, the legislative record is also weak on underlying rationale. Fire regulations were often the product of imitation, at times passed hastily after a particular disaster. Issues of governmental power, constitutionality, precedent, the historical roots of authority, and the like were often assumed rather than made explicit. The New York Assembly, for example, established a fire company in Schenectady with the cursory observation that the need for this legislation was "too obvious to require particular detail."[47] As with the question of implementation, it is necessary to turn elsewhere for a closer examination of the underlying assumptions of early nineteenth-century fire regulation.

American courts were constant and crucial players in nineteenth-century governance and regulation. The cases they heard offer direct evidence of the actual operation and enforcement of fire laws. Moreover, the requirement that appellate courts justify and explicate the legal and constitutional context of their decisions in written opinions provides a more comprehensive picture of the legal-philosophical framework of nineteenth-century public safety regulation. Indeed, two of the central doctrines behind fire laws were the products of courts, not legislatures. The law of nuisance and the law of overruling necessity were two powerful legal technologies that governed public safety issues such as the prohibition of hazardous materials, the regulation of buildings and land use, and the conduct of public officials in actual fires.

Nuisance: Gunpowder and Wooden Buildings

The common law of nuisance was one of the most important public legal doctrines of nineteenth-century regulatory governance. Its object was securing social order according to the maxim of the well-regulated society: *sic utere tuo ut alienum non laedas* (use your own so as not to injure another). Nathan Dane suggested the potential within this "very important and extensive branch of the law," when he observed, "Strictly whatever annoys or damages another is a nuisance." Horace Wood elaborated that nuisances were "that class of wrongs that arise from the unreasonable, unwarrantable or unlawful use by a person of his own property . . . or personal conduct, working an obstruction of or injury to a right of another or of the public."[48]

Since Blackstone, it has been common to think of nuisance in two categories, private and public. A private nuisance consisted of a trespass- or tort-like invasion of one individual's rights by a neighbor. The classic cases involved either a physical intrusion like the construction of a house so as to overhang adjoining property, or the less corporeal maintenance of a hogsty or drainage system so as to flood a neighbor's hereditament with noxious smells or water. Public nuisances consisted of similarly troublesome behavior or uses of property, but so as to injure the whole community rather than a single individual. Livery stables, slaughterhouses, disorderly inns, bawdy houses, and malarial ponds were all considered public nuisances at common law.[49] Private nuisances were civil offenses; public nuisances made up a category of crimes and misdemeanors. Taken together, the law of private and public nuisance greeted damaging and asocial uses of private property and individual liberty with an impressive array of legal remedies: civil suit, damages, equitable injunction, private destruction, criminal indictment, fine, and summary abatement.

Two historical misconceptions, however, have hindered an accurate appraisal of the role of nuisance in nineteenth-century public policymaking. First is the tendency to see nuisance in modern terms as a "trifling inconvenience" and nuisance law as an archaic technology for addressing the somewhat irritating land-use habits of a not-so-good neighbor. This perspective deems nuisance law's individuated, ex post facto, court-centered mode of resolving petty conflicts as the very antithesis of the preventive legislative measures required of modern regulatory states.[50] Second, the provocative work of historians Joel Brenner and Morton Horwitz has overemphasized the instrumental transformation of *private* nuisance law on behalf of commerce at the expense of the continued regulatory significance of *public* nuisance law. Nuisance law was not simply a site for creative, capital-friendly judges to relax antidevelopmental standards of private liability.[51]

On the contrary, nineteenth-century jurists were quite explicit about both the overarching significance and the public power of the law of nuisance.[52] Horace Wood's formulation of private nuisance encompassed almost the whole of modern tort law. Joel Bishop attributed a significant chunk of nineteenth-century criminal law (from barratry to sepulture) to public nuisance precepts. And James Kent foreshadowed Ernst Freund's notion of nuisance as the common law of the police power, suggesting that the governmental power to "interdict such uses of property as would create nuisances" was the font of general law-making authority.[53] Nuisance law, far from being ineffective or emasculated by a market-minded judiciary, remained a powerful juris-

prudential reference point for nineteenth-century discussions of private and public power.

Nineteenth-century nuisance law was neither trivial nor timid. Along with every unneighborly hogsty or spite fence abated as a nuisance came dozens of ships, hospitals, steam engines, furnaces, dairies, sewers, slaughterhouses, stables, pumping stations, foundries, manufactories, and saloons. Almost every major innovation in transportation and industry at one time or other came within the purview of nuisance law: mills, dams, railroads, smokestacks, and public works. Declaring an activity or establishment a nuisance in the nineteenth century unleashed the full power and authority of the state. Perhaps under no other circumstances (short of martial law) could private property and liberty be so quickly and completely restrained or destroyed.

In sum, nuisance law was not primarily a matter of technical, private law at all. The *sic utere tuo* rationale of nuisance was a public ordering principle of "every civilized community." Sidney and Beatrice Webb pointed out that the heart of nuisance was an all-embracing notion of social obligation, wherein any breach of one's irreducibly public duties to society and to others was deemed an actionable nuisance. The redress of nuisance thus came to include nearly "every conceivable neglect or offence"—a good part of the "framework of law in which the ordinary citizen found himself."[54] *Sic utere tuo*, Horace Wood argued, was but "the legal application of the gospel rule of doing unto others as we would that they should do unto us." Indeed, nuisance law encapsulated the ultimate statement of the relative right of private property in a well-regulated society: "Every person yields a portion of his right of absolute dominion and use of property, in recognition of, and obedience to, the rights of others . . . for the mutual protection and benefit of every member of society." These public principles of nuisance law formed the jurisprudential framework for the regulation of such diverse subjects as noxious trades, adulterated food, obscenity, contagious diseases, theaters, and monopolies.[55] They also decidedly shaped the response of the nineteenth-century American polity to the public safety threat posed by two enormous fire hazards: gunpowder and wooden buildings.

The policing of the manufacture, storage, and sale of gunpowder marked an important episode in the development of the early American regulatory state. Though trade regulations had deep roots in the colonial era, gunpowder was one of several emerging industrial manufactures that met extensive governmental restraints after the Revolution. Powder mills, like the extensive textile manufactories of the Boston Associates, symbolized the dramatic take-off of the early American economy.[56] Gunpowder was grist for early American

capitalism. In addition to its obvious importance for public defense, frontier security, and hunting, gunpowder was increasingly in demand for a host of developmental projects in a labor-scarce economy, including mining, canal building, and road building.[57] Before the Revolution, American gunpowder supply was dependent on a handful of mills, scattered household production, and imports.[58] Five years after hostilities with Britain, Pennsylvania had 21 powder mills producing 625 tons of powder annually. The 1810 United States census listed 200 mills scattered among sixteen states, the most promising being the Du Pont works on the Brandywine River in Delaware.[59] Gunpowder production fast became a central component of early American commerce, industry, and trade. And it just as quickly encountered the force of early American governance in the guise of the law of public nuisance.

Gunpowder's tendency to explode, with dramatic consequences for nearby surroundings, made it particularly susceptible to nuisance law's admonition that one should use property so as not to injure another. As early as 1700, Lord Holt made it clear that "though gunpowder be a necessary thing, and for the defence of the kingdom, yet if it be kept in such a place as it is dangerous to the inhabitants or passengers, it will be a nuisance."[60] The manufacture and storage of gunpowder joined an array of economic activities including brewhouses, glasshouses, limekilns, dyehouses, smelting houses, tan pits, chandler's shops, and swine-sties subject to common law nuisance restrictions on behalf of the people's health and safety.[61]

Early American legislative and municipal enactments regulating gunpowder were extensive, but control over antisocial uses of private property in the early republic did not depend on codification. The regulation of gunpowder through the common law of public nuisance in lieu of statute remained an integral part of the American fight against fires throughout the nineteenth century—this, despite a somewhat inauspicious start. In *People v. Sands* (1806), C. & L. Sands were indicted for maintaining a public nuisance. They were accused of keeping fifty barrels of gunpowder in a Brooklyn house "near the dwellinghouses of divers good citizens of the state, and also, near a certain public street . . . to the great damage, danger, and common nuisance of all the good citizens."[62] Statute law explicitly regulated dangerous caches of powder in New York City, but Brooklyn had no similar written requirement.[63] Though the trial court declared the powderhouse to be a public nuisance, the New York Supreme Court reversed.

None of the justices in *Sands* denied that a gunpowder storehouse could be a common nuisance. Indeed, they all agreed with Lord Holt that if kept in such a place "as it is dangerous" to the public, it would certainly be indictable.

But they refused to accept the district attorney's contention that fifty barrels of gunpowder stored near a dwelling house was a public nuisance per se, as a matter of law. They wanted the circumstances of the nuisance—time, place, manner, and/or evidence of negligence or lack of due care—spelled out in the indictment for a jury's inspection and determination.[64] Indeed, in an outrageous example of judicial notice, Justice Livingston offered that he knew the house in question, identified it as a "powder-house," and personally deemed it "safe." From his own observation, Livingston described the structure as a "brick building, constructed for the storing of powder, and secured by conductors, and every other usual guard against accident." He concluded, "A safer mode of keeping this article than in a building thus constructed, cannot well be devised. . . . The danger of a magazine's exploding, when properly built and secured is remote indeed."[65] In other words, this was truly a decision about a particular powderhouse rather than a general policy insulating dealers of gunpowder from the regulatory impact of nuisance. In addition to agreeing with Lord Holt's general condemnation of dangerous powderhouses, Livingston advocated legislative interference if the common law should ultimately prove an insufficient safeguard.[66]

Still the justices' refusal in *Sands* to acknowledge a powderhouse in a populated area as ipso facto a common nuisance was significant. If it predominated in American case law, the regulation of gunpowder (in lieu of statute or ordinance) would necessitate a case-by-case judicial evaluation of the peculiar circumstances surrounding each alleged nuisance. Such solicitousness for idiosyncratic facts could severely inhibit public nuisance law's usefulness as a general regulatory instrument.[67] A negligence requirement could disable it altogether.

That was not to be the case, however. Perhaps because the Brooklyn powderhouse at issue in *Sands* exploded six months later (no doubt to Livingston's surprise), future courts were much more willing to find gunpowder stored in populous areas common nuisances as a matter of law.[68] In *Myers v. Malcolm* (1844), after 600 pounds of gunpowder exploded killing and wounding several people, the New York Supreme Court ruled that the keeping of a large quantity of gunpowder in a wooden building near other buildings was indeed a public nuisance.[69] Ending some confusion after *Sands*, Chief Justice Nelson made it clear that negligence was not a part of public nuisance determinations.[70] Tennessee's Supreme Court went even further in *Cheatham v. Shearon* (1851), holding that a powder magazine in a populous part of Nashville was a nuisance per se as a matter of law.[71] Directly challenging the decision in *Sands*, Justice Green ruled that no matter what the circumstances and no matter how

solidly constructed, a large storehouse of gunpowder in the heart of a populous city was in and of itself a public nuisance.[72] Green's argument closely followed the main outlines of the well-regulated society. Citing Blackstone, Green defined common nuisances as "offenses against the public order and economical regimen of the state." Invoking the *sic utere tuo* rationale of nuisance, he suggested that there were "few things one could do that would annoy the community more than the deposit of a large quantity of gunpowder in the midst of a populous city." Concluding with public safety and *salus populi*, Green asked, "Can it be possible that the law shall protect us from the annoyance of a pig-sty, or a slaughterhouse, and yet that it affords no protection from a danger that might be a constant annoyance, and which may, and sometimes does, result in a great destruction of life and property?"[73] He answered and decided, of course, "No."

Although few courts were as explicit as Justice Green in deeming powderhouses nuisances per se, they continued to abate and in some cases enjoin them with reference to little else than the presence of nearby dwellings.[74] In 1873, the Pennsylvania Supreme Court afforded the extraordinary relief of an equity injunction against a partially constructed powderhouse in a "suburban village" of Sharpsburg.[75] Here, the facts deemed so crucial in *Sands* were unavailable—the powderhouse had not yet been built.

The public calculation was not always easy. After all, powderhouses were a "great convenience to the public, and of advantage to the commerce of [a] city."[76] But ultimately, public safety trumped commerce as it trumped the relative property rights of powderhouse owners. Whereas Justice Livingston could argue in *Sands* that "the danger of a magazine's exploding . . . is remote indeed," later justices had to deal with the fact that they were exploding all the time.[77] Once the threat to public safety became apparent, *People v. Sands* was a dead letter.[78]

Early American nuisance restrictions on gunpowder aptly reflected the pull and power of the common law vision of a well-regulated society. Even without legislative action, uses of property and modes of production that endangered the people's welfare were subjected to restraints and penalties. As Lemuel Shaw pointed out, a gunpowder nuisance prosecution involved not only the punishment of the offender, but "the seizure and confiscation of the property, by the removal, sale, or destruction of the noxious articles."[79] Nuisance law was a powerful and punitive technology of public action. The well-regulated society was not insensitive to the claims of commerce and property; it was merely adamant about the superior rights of the public. Property rights were protected, but relatively, not absolutely. Under the common law of nuisance

one did not have a right to accumulate gunpowder in one's tenement. On the contrary, neighboring property owners (and the community as a whole) had a right to be protected from just such dangerous accumulations—*sic utere tuo ut alienum non laedas.*

State statutes and municipal ordinances regulating gunpowder essentially codified the underlying principles of the common law of nuisance.[80] These written laws themselves were rarely challenged in the early nineteenth century and were never struck down by an appellate court. In 1843 the New York Supreme Court upheld the constitutionality of New York City's gunpowder restrictions with the simple observation, "The statute is a mere police regulation—an act to prevent a nuisance to the city."[81] In the *License Cases* (1847), U.S. Supreme Court Justice McLean was unequivocal about written prohibitions on gunpowder: "Now this is an article of commerce, . . . yet, to guard against a contingent injury, a city may prohibit its introduction." McLean defended such regulatory power as "essential to [the] self-preservation" of "every organized community" upon that "acknowledged principle" of ordered society: "Individuals in the enjoyment of their own rights must be careful not to injure the rights of others."[82]

Gunpowder regulation, then, was an easy case. As Roger Taney anticipated in his argument in *Brown v. Maryland*, no one would defend a private right to sell or store gunpowder in the heart of early American cities. Restrictions on gunpowder were so well rooted in the common law of nuisance and the vision of a well-regulated society that they spawned little controversy and required little elaboration. Perhaps because the regulation of wooden buildings entailed a more distinct departure from common law norms, judges handled this kind of fire regulation with fuller discussions of the implications of nuisance, police, regulation, and the people's safety.

On the whole, legal prohibitions on wooden buildings in early American cities closely followed the evolution of gunpowder restrictions. Both were security and safety measures, passed to protect the public from the dangers of fire; and both relied heavily on the common law of nuisance for remedies as well as underlying rationale. But bans on wooden buildings involved a somewhat different species of public regulation. Unlike gunpowder, there was nothing inherently dangerous or hazardous about a wooden structure. In and of itself it was largely benign vis-à-vis adjoining property owners and the community at large. Unlike traditional public nuisances (slaughterhouses, pigsties, tanneries), no physical characteristics made a wooden building particularly noxious, offensive, or threatening to the surrounding public. It became a nuisance solely because the legislature or municipality drew an

arbitrary line (analogous to the wharf line in *Commonwealth v. Alger*) known as a "fire limit" around a community declaring otherwise innocent conduct within that boundary "offensive" as a matter of law.

Fire limits, then, were hardly a timid or primitive form of public regulation. They were prospective and preventative (rather than merely remedial), and they operated on behavior not inherently evil or pernicious. They represented a distinct effort to prevent urban development from becoming simply a function of a free market of private decision-makers to the detriment of public safety. Fire limits involved the kind of foresight, public planning, and mandated social ordering that many claim is an exclusive product of the twentieth century.[83] Indeed, in the fire-limit ordinances of the early nineteenth century we see a form of urban land-use regulation different only in degree from the comprehensive zoning ordinances of the Progressive Era.

One of the first American discussions of the legal and constitutional legitimacy of fire limits occurred in 1799. Philip Urbin Duquet was indicted for maintaining a "common and most dangerous nuisance"—a wooden house erected contrary to a 1796 Philadelphia ordinance prohibiting wooden structures (houses, shops, warehouses, stores, or stables) on pain of $500 fine.[84] Jared Ingersoll argued the case for the Commonwealth in *Republica v. Duquet*. Citing English Chief Justice Lord Holt, Ingersoll defended Philadelphia as a "great community that have a legislative power intrusted to them for their better government" to "make laws to *bind the property* of those that live within."[85] He rooted Philadelphia's overarching regulatory power in its incorporation statute authorizing it to make laws "as shall be necessary or convenient for the government and welfare" of the city. And he invoked a 1795 state act explicitly empowering Philadelphia to establish fire limits.[86] "We have no unfavorable precedents against us," Ingersoll declared, noting similar fire and safety regulations in New York City and Charleston.[87]

In a very short opinion, Chief Justice Shippen simply cited the two state statutes and matter-of-factly upheld the constitutionality of the fire-limit ordinance. The only question in this case was whether legislative authority was properly delegated to the municipal corporation. Neither the judge nor the defendant's attorneys thought to question the legislature's ultimate authority to restrict and restrain private property by banning the use of wood in buildings. As was suggested in the very statute creating the "Corporation of the City of Philadelphia," the intention of civil government was to "provide for the order, safety and happiness of the people."[88] The power of government to "bind" property in pursuit of these larger ends—to protect against fire—hardly was contestable.

Respublica v. Duquet quickly emerged as the leading American case on the constitutionality of municipal fire limits.[89] But the court's spartan opinion did not really offer a compelling explanation for the legal legitimacy of fire ordinances. We can only infer that public power to regulate private property to protect against fire was so apparent and assumed by the Pennsylvania court that close scrutiny was unnecessary. Thirty-six years after *Duquet* in *Wadleigh v. Gilman*, the Maine Supreme Court fleshed out some of the common assumptions left implicit by Chief Justice Shippen.[90]

Like Philadelphia, New York, Boston, and Charleston, Bangor, Maine, had a fire-limit ordinance in the early nineteenth century prohibiting new wooden buildings (existing buildings were exempt). The penalty for violation of the ordinance was $50. When Wadleigh moved a preexisting wooden building from one part of Bangor to another, it was deemed new construction and, in a twist reflective of the swiftness and power of nuisance law, was summarily demolished by the street commissioner and city marshal. Wadleigh brought an action of trespass against the municipal officers for breaking and entering his close. The defendants justified their action as merely the enforcement of Bangor's fire regulation. In a short but comprehensive opinion, Chief Justice Weston exonerated the municipal officials.[91]

Wadleigh is notable for several reasons. First, it illustrates the extent to which some communities were willing to go to enforce their police regulations. At issue in *Wadleigh* was a quite common, but striking, nineteenth-century remedy for antisocial uses of private property—the physical destruction and removal of offensive structures. As we shall see in later chapters, demolition was used throughout this period to deal with noxious milldams, disorderly houses, saloons, hospitals and infectious buildings, as well as the accoutrements of the illegal liquor trade.[92] In *Wadleigh*, the plaintiff's wooden building was torn down by public officials despite the fact that the municipal ordinance only authorized a $50 fine. Chief Justice Weston had no trouble amplifying the public remedy. "Is this all they can do?" he questioned, "After exacting the penalty, must [the city] submit to the continuance of a mass of combustible matter, erected in defiance of their ordinance, in the heart of the city?" He found otherwise: "If it was lawful for them to forbid the erection, we hold it lawful for them to cause it to be removed."[93] Such incidents of the actual *destruction* of private property without compensation (in the interests of public safety, morals, health, and welfare) indicate just how different nineteenth-century common law assumptions about public regulation could be from twentieth-century constitutional hairsplitting over what constitutes a

"taking" of private property. In the early nineteenth century, a taking was not contingent on how much private property rights were impaired (after all, property could be confiscated or destroyed). And a police regulation by definition was not a "taking."[94] Maine's chief justice found the complete leveling of Wadleigh's building simply the carrying out of "a salutary and lawful regulation."[95]

Just as notable as the particular remedy in this case was Chief Justice Weston's carefully reasoned defense of fire-limit regulations. Like Lemuel Shaw, Weston attempted to make clear what had been left implicit and assumed in *Duquet* and so many other regulatory cases before the Civil War—the exact nature and relationship of public police regulations and private property in a well-regulated community. Unlike Philadelphia, Bangor enacted its wooden building prohibition without explicit legislative authorization. Nevertheless, Weston found that the mere incorporation of Bangor with power to make laws "as shall be needful to the good order of said body politic" was sufficient to allow it to pass fire regulations.[96] This general grant of power (found in some form in almost all municipal charters) entitled Bangor to make "all necessary police regulations" essential to "the well ordering of the body politic." For Weston, fire limits were simply a legitimate form of police regulation. He noted, "It is an object, in the highest degree worthy of the attention of the city authorities, to take such measures, as may be practicable, to lessen the hazard and danger of fire. No city, compactly built, can be said to be *well ordered or well regulated*, which neglects precautions of this sort."[97]

With such language, Weston plugged into an established discourse on the role of law and regulation in a well-ordered society. The goal of police regulations was to "forbid such a use, and such modifications, of private property, as would prove injurious to the citizens generally." To be protected from such noxious private behavior was "one of the benefits which men derive from associating in communities." Though restrictions on private conduct "may sometimes occasion an inconvenience to an individual," compensation comes from "participating in the general advantage." Police regulations, so defined, were "unquestionably within the scope of the legislative power, without impairing any constitutional provision." A police regulation, like the fire limit at issue here, was not a "taking" or an appropriation of property requiring compensation—it merely regulated such property's enjoyment.[98]

In Weston's view, people associated in communities for general advantages and benefits, superior to the interests of any single individual. To protect and preserve the common good and welfare, the well-ordered community had the

power to enact regulations that restricted private rights and property. This was a power with deep roots in the common law (especially the law of nuisance)— a common law not abrogated by the specific strictures of constitutionalism.

But by 1835, Chief Justice Weston did not need to rely simply on the vision and persuasiveness of an abstract intellectual-jurisprudential tradition. By 1835, the powerful sentiments that James Wilson and his peers divined in the common law had begun to congeal into a coherent mass of American case law on police regulation. At the behest of the Bangor city solicitor, Weston placed the legitimacy of this fire regulation squarely in that emerging American legal tradition. He cited *Vanderbilt v. Adams* (1827), *Stuyvesant v. Mayor of New York* (1827), *Baker v. Boston* (1831), and *Village of Buffalo v. Webster* (1833) as unequivocally establishing the constitutionality of municipal and state police regulations restricting individual liberty and private property in the interest of public safety, morality, health, and welfare.[99] These precedents along with later decisions like *Commonwealth v. Alger* would eventually become staples of early American police power citation. For Weston, they embodied the legal legitimacy of police statutes and ordinances regulating harbors (*Vanderbilt*), cemeteries (*Stuyvesant*), the use of water by milldams (*Baker*), and public markets (*Webster*).

But these cases were more than examples of particular regulations. They were also explicit manifestations of the well-regulated society in American case law. *Salus populi* accented government's affirmative duties and the necessity of pursuing a distinctly *public* good. From *Baker v. Boston*: The municipality is "fully empowered to adopt measures of police, for the purpose of preserving the health, and promoting the comfort, convenience and general welfare of the inhabitants within the city." *Sic utere tuo* recognized the social, relative nature of rights. From *Stuyvesant v. Mayor of New York*: "Every right from an absolute ownership of property, down to a mere easement, is purchased and holden subject to the restriction, that it shall be so exercised as not to injure others." The well-regulated society held that the people's welfare was best realized in an ordered society that regulated the noxious, threatening behaviors and properties of private individuals. From *Vanderbilt v. Adams*: "The sovereign power in a community . . . ought to prescribe the manner of exercising individual rights over property. . . . The powers rest on the implied right and duty of the supreme power to protect all by statutory regulations, so that, on the whole, the benefit of all is promoted. . . . [S]uch a power is incident to every well regulated society; and without which it could not well exist."[100] In *Wadleigh v. Gilman*, the people's welfare and safety dictated that a municipality had the power to restrict wooden buildings. As Weston reasoned, "Where

the owner of a city lot intends to build of wood, he holds it to be clearly within the competency of the constituted authorities, to say to him, 'you must not exercise that right, it is dangerous to all. You may build of brick or stone; because the safety of all is, in this way, promoted.'"[101]

The decisions of the Michigan and Louisiana supreme courts in *Brady v. Northwestern Insurance Co.* (1863) and *Mayor of Monroe v. Hoffman* (1877) ratified the earlier decisions in *Duquet* and *Wadleigh*.[102] Justice Marr of Louisiana may well have been speaking about gunpowder restrictions as well when he upheld the power of municipal corporations "to restrict the right of property" as within their "police power." As Marr suggested, the common law maxim *sic utere tuo* forbade "the owner so to use his property as to imperil that of his neighbors, or to endanger their lives or their health." Consequently, states and cities could "prohibit the erection of works and factories, and the pursuit of industries within the corporate limits, which would be injurious to the public health and destructive of the comfort of the inhabitants."[103] Gunpowder and wooden building laws were particularly conspicuous examples of legislatures and municipalities doing just that, and state courts upholding their power to do so. They were illustrations of "a police power necessary to the safety" of the people.[104] They reflected the extent to which private behavior and property could be restricted in this well-regulated society when the public's safety and security were at stake. But even these strong fire-prevention statutes do not fully capture how prepared nineteenth-century legal culture was to sacrifice individual and private interest to the people's welfare. That is better reflected in the way public officials could and did behave in cases of necessity, cases of actual catastrophic fire.

Necessity: New York City's Great Fire of 1835

Prohibitions on gunpowder and wooden buildings demonstrate the regulatory power of public nuisance law and the *sic utere tuo* philosophy of the well-regulated society. Nuisance law clearly entailed much more than a set of civil constraints on private irritations and trespasses. It restrained a whole range of noninvasive uses of property that threatened public safety. Moreover, authorities did not have to wait for gunpowder to explode or wooden buildings to catch fire to respond. They were able to identify, abate, and sometimes destroy potentially dangerous nuisances as part of a comprehensive and preventative regulatory strategy.

But the well-regulated society and state were not confined to *sic utere tuo*, policing the relative rights of private property and individual liberty. *Salus*

populi embraced an even more affirmative and expansive vision of public power positively pursuing the common good—doing whatever was *necessary* to secure the people's happiness and safety. The legal doctrine of overruling necessity was a direct manifestation of this open-ended, perfectionist impulse. Indeed, two treatise writers rooted the entire nineteenth-century police power in "the law of overruling necessity."[105]

The doctrine of overruling necessity flowed directly from the assumptions of *salus populi*. If the people's welfare and safety were the highest law, it followed that when the preservation of society was at stake lesser rules and conventions gave way. In its most basic form, the law of overruling necessity was a social version of the law of self-defense.[106] American courts and commentators consistently referred to a long line of English cases making it "well settled at common law" that in cases of calamity, such as fire, pestilence, or war, individual interests and rights would not inhibit the preservation of the common weal. Thus private houses could be pulled down or bulwarks raised on private property *without compensation* when the safety and security of the many depended on it.[107] As Thomas Cooley later reasoned, "Here the individual is in no degree in fault, but his interest must yield to that 'necessity' which 'knows no law.'" The injury to the individual was *damnum absque injuria* (an injury without a remedy) under the reasoning that "a private mischief shall be endured, rather than a public inconvenience." The higher prerogatives of the common law often made it necessary for individual injuries to go unredressed in the common interest.[108]

But overruling necessity was more than a social self-defense mechanism. Early on, natural law writers suggested the wider potential of the law of necessity. Thomas Rutherford argued that "necessity sets property aside"—things necessary "continue in common." Like Grotius and Pufendorf, Rutherford contended that an extreme want of food or clothing justified theft. Property was relational, dependent on the common consent of all. No one could be assumed to have consented away the right to use another's property when self or social preservation were in jeopardy.[109] Necessity revived a "community of goods," where all things were available to common use for common benefit. Although, as Blackstone made clear, civil law ideas on theft never made their way into English common law, the broader conceptions of consent, conventional and relational property rights, the community of goods, and public necessity trumping private interest did.[110] These notions provided a more open-ended backdrop for defending municipal, legislative, and sovereign prerogatives in cases of pressing public need. Just such a case engulfed the city of New York in 1835.

A few minutes after nine o'clock on the evening of December 16, 1835, Comstock and Andrews's dry goods house on Merchant Street in New York City caught fire—hardly a rare occurrence in a city reporting 500 conflagrations that year.[111] This fire, however, was destined to be unique. A subzero temperature, a strong southerly wind, frozen rivers and hydrants, and a fire department and water supply exhausted from a large fire two nights earlier combined to produce a devastating conflagration. The fire's glow was soon noticed as far away as Poughkeepsie. By noon the next day, the entire first ward of the city—fifty-two acres—was in ruins. This was a very special fifty-two acres. It comprised the city's central commercial and mercantile district. From Wall Street and Broad Street to Coenties Slip and South Street, the city's grandest financial, business, and merchant houses—674 buildings in all—surrendered to the flames. The fabulous stores and buildings of Exchange Place and Merchant Street, including the Merchant's Exchange, the U.S. Post Office, and a newly dedicated statue of Alexander Hamilton, were destroyed. Estimated losses approached $20 million. As James Gordon Bennett of the New York Herald lamented, "[I]n one night we have lost the whole amount for which the nation is ready to go to war with France!"[112] New York had twenty-five prosperous insurance companies capitalized at $8 million before the fire. Afterward, fourteen were insolvent and the rest in trouble after paying out $7 million for insured losses. A fire this size and this destructive had never occurred in America, and was comparable only with the burning of Moscow in 1812 and the Great Fire of London in 1666.[113]

For our purposes, one of the most important aspects of the Great Fire of 1835 was the way it ended. At approximately three o'clock in the morning, with the Merchant's Exchange in ruins and water congealing soon after it left hose or hydrant, Mayor Cornelius W. Lawrence in consultation with Chief Engineer James Gulick decided to resort to gunpowder. The plan drew on an age-old method of fighting fire in congested areas—the creation of an artificial firebreak by pulling down or otherwise destroying buildings in the path of the fire.

As early as 1653, houses were pulled down in an unsuccessful effort to squelch the first of many Boston fires.[114] Early fire statutes almost always directly empowered local officials to "order assistance" and "pull down houses" to extinguish fires.[115] As essential to early fire fighting as leather buckets and ladders was a strong iron hook connected to a long rope or pole. The hook was attached to the roof or upper wall of a building and yanked until the structure fell apart.[116] Gunpowder was later found to be a quicker and more effective means of creating a firebreak. The destruction of buildings to stop

fire was so common in this period, it acquired a special place in "great fire" folklore. Equal to Nero's fabled fiddling was the folly of London's Mayor Bludworth, who in 1666 refused to order the pulling down of buildings for fear of lawsuits. In consequence, the story goes, "half that great city was burned."[117]

Cornelius Lawrence was determined to avoid such infamy. But despite his relatively quick decision to resort to gunpowder, delay was not avoidable. Ironically, well-enforced powder regulations had successfully banned large stores of gunpowder from the vicinity of New York and Brooklyn. Powder arrived from Governor's Island only at dawn. By eleven o'clock on December 17, the blowing-up of buildings in the path of the fire effectively contained the flames. Cornelius Lawrence saved New York. His triumph was short-lived, however. Within months, Mayor Lawrence ran smack into Mayor Bludworth's worst fears—lawsuits—with over thirty-three filed in New Jersey alone. For almost two decades, Lawrence fought off compensation demands for private losses suffered in his city-saving efforts. This litigation produced an unusually rich discussion of the lengths to which public authorities could go when public necessity and public safety demanded action.

At issue in the subsequent legal actions against the mayor of New York was the doctrine of overruling necessity. A sentiment expressed early in the Year Books of Henry VIII soon became embedded in American common law: "The commonwealth shall be preferred before private wealth; for on behalf of the commonwealth one shall suffer damage, as when a house is plucked down if the next house is burning, and suburbs of cities shall be plucked down in time of war, because that is for the common wealth."[118] The idea that in times of great necessity, like fire, private property could be destroyed to protect the public good and safety was consistently ratified by English courts. *Maleverer v. Spinke* (1538), *The Case of the King's Prerogative in Salt-peter* (1607), and *Mouse's Case* (1609), held that such "private damages" endured "*pro bono publico*" (for the public good) were not actionable.[119] Justice Buller summed up these early English statements of the law of necessity in 1792: "There are many cases in which individuals sustain an injury, for which the law gives no action; for instance, pulling down houses, or raising bulwarks, for the preservation and defence of the kingdom. . . . This is one of those cases to which the maxim applies, *salus populi suprema est lex*."[120]

Within a year of the Constitutional Convention, Chief Justice M'Kean of the Pennsylvania Supreme Court made it clear that "rights of necessity" formed a part of "our law." In *Respublica v. Sparhawk* (1788), he drew on a host of common law decisions establishing that "it is better to suffer a private

mischief, than a public inconvenience" and that "the safety of the people is a law above all others." In particular, M'Kean argued, "Houses may be razed to prevent the spreading of fire, because for the public good."[121] Chancellor Kent only solidified the standing of necessity in American law when, citing *Maleverer* and *Sparhawk*, he delivered his ultimate statement on public rights:

> [T]here are many cases in which the rights of property must be made subservient to the public welfare. The maxim of law is, that a private mischief is to be endured rather than a public inconvenience. On this ground rest the rights of public necessity. If a common highway be out of repair, a passenger may lawfully go through an adjoining private enclosure. So, it is lawful to raze houses to the ground to prevent the spreading of a conflagration.[122]

None of these common law precedents required compensation for "necessary" public destructions.

One would think that with such undisputed authority New York jurists would have little trouble laying to rest the numerous cases generated by Mayor Lawrence's order to "raze houses to the ground." Two things, however, muddied the jurisprudential waters. First, article 7 of New York's 1821 constitution, like the federal Constitution's Fifth Amendment, declared that "private property [shall not] be taken for public use without just compensation." Second, New York's legislature passed a statute governing the mayor's conduct in cases of fire. The 1813 law explicitly authorized the mayor and two aldermen "to direct and order . . . any other building which they may deem hazardous, and likely to take fire, or to convey the fire to other buildings, to be pulled down or destroyed."[123] But the statute also specified that owners of buildings so pulled down and "all persons having any estate or interest therein" were entitled to "damages" to be determined and assessed in proceedings like those to award compensation for property *taken* for public use.[124] The statute thus amended the common law rule of necessity in New York City, allowing damages for buildings destroyed in the path of fire. But though the statute was clear on the issue of damages to owners and tenants of buildings, it was silent on what was to be done for the owners of goods without an "interest or estate" in those buildings. The fire of 1835 struck the heart of the mercantile district chocked full of warehouses piled high with imported and traded goods. Though one would not want to be to cynical about the parochialism of the New York legislature, it might have been more than an oversight that the owners and tenants of buildings (likely to be New Yorkers) were compensated, while the mere

owners of goods (more likely to be out-of-staters) were not.[125] In any event, this statutory situation produced a host of civil cases in New York, and, not surprisingly, in New Jersey.

In 1837, the first cases against the mayor and corporation of New York reached the appellate courts.[126] In *Mayor v. Lord* (I), the city contested a jury award of $163,000 made to Rufus and David Lord in compensation for the destruction of their building and goods by municipal officials. As the structure's owner, Rufus Lord received $7,168.50. David Lord, as tenant and owner of the goods in the building, received $156,274.80.[127] Chief Justice Nelson dismissed the city's argument that damages should only be awarded for the building and liberally construed the 1813 statute to authorize "the assessment of damages for the loss of merchandize and other personal property" by owners, landlords, and tenants.[128] Citing *King's Prerogative* and *Mouse's Case*, Nelson had no doubt that it was "well-settled" at common law that buildings might be pulled down in cases of necessity without redress. "For the commonwealth, a man shall suffer damage," he quoted.[129] But given the statutory remedy specified, he treated this case as falling within the purview of the "great fundamental principle" codified in the New York constitution that "private property shall not be taken for public use, without just compensation."[130] Although even Nelson was unwilling to hold that article seven compelled the legislature to provide compensation, once it did so, he felt the statute should be broadly construed to include all damages actually sustained.

The city appealed Nelson's judgment to the New York Court of Errors, a unique judicial body composed of the president of the Senate, the chancellor, and select state senators. The outcome was the same. In a sixteen-to-six decision, the Court of Errors upheld the damage award made to the Lords. Once again the court had no trouble with the common law of necessity:

> The principle appears to be well settled, that in a case of actual necessity, to prevent the spreading of a fire, the ravages of pestilence, the advance of a hostile army, or any other great public calamity, the private property of an individual may be lawfully taken and used or destroyed, for the relief, protection or safety of the many, without subjecting those whose duty it is to protect the public interests, by whom, or under whose direction such private property was taken or destroyed, to personal liability for the damage which the owner has thereby sustained.[131]

But, Chancellor Walworth suggested, once the statute was passed, remedying the common law's lack of compensation, it should be construed equitably. Those who benefited from the sacrifice "ought in equity and justice to make

good the loss which the individual has sustained for the common benefit of all."[132]

In *Stone v. Mayor of New York* (1840) and *Russell v. Mayor of New York* (1845) the Court of Errors drew back from the far-reaching dicta of *Mayor v. Lord* (I & II) and began to cut off the city's responsibility for private damages.[133] *Stone* and *Russell* originated in claims that the city was liable for *all* property destroyed by the mayor's order (not merely the property of those with an "interest or estate" in the building as provided by statute) under the "just compensation" requirement of the New York constitution. Such arguments forced the court to clearly define the character of the mayor's action. Was the demolition of buildings, irrespective of statute, a "taking"—an act of eminent domain? If so, article 7 of the New York constitution required that *all* property "taken" for public use be compensated. The court in *Stone* and *Russell* refused to accept that constitutional argument. The mayor's action was not a "taking" of private property, but an act of public necessity covered alternatively by the common law and statute. The statute did not abrogate the common law, but merely specified a separate remedy pursuable by those explicitly designated—those with "interests" in the building. The statute made no reference to goods or personal property.[134]

Stone and *Russell* reaffirmed the principles of the law of necessity. As Senator Edwards put it, "There are many cases in which the maxim, *salus populi suprema lex*, applies; and I know not but this case may with propriety be considered one of them. . . . [P]rivate mischief is to be endured rather than public inconvenience."[135] In *Russell* Senator Sherman even more vigorously attacked the "fallacy" that Mayor Lawrence was exercising eminent domain powers: "The destruction of this property was authorized by the law of overruling necessity. . . . [I]n a case of actual necessity, to prevent the spreading of a fire, the ravages of a pestilence, or any other great public calamity, *the private property of any individual may be lawfully destroyed for the relief, protection, or safety of the many*, without subjecting the actors to personal responsibility for the damages which the owner has sustained."[136] The statute of 1813 was simply a police law designed to regulate the implementation of the law of overruling necessity in New York. It was not an exercise of the sovereign right of eminent domain.[137] Nor did article 7 of the state constitution suspend the common law rule of necessity. Justice Porter reasoned, "[Necessity] is founded upon principles which are above or beyond the reach of constitutional restriction."[138] In simple terms, the New York Court of Errors held that nothing in the federal or state constitutions kept governmental officials from blowing up valuable private property without compensation when the "public interest" necessitated it.

With avenues to satisfaction blocked in New York, litigators opted for the next best option—they went to New Jersey. Over thirty cases were filed there seeking damages from Mayor Lawrence for goods destroyed and not compensated under New York statute law.[139] After some initial success convincing judges that the mayor was exercising eminent domain powers, the New Jersey Supreme Court ultimately resisted the temptation to reinterpret New York law. In *American Print Works v. Lawrence* (1851), the court ruled that the "common law doctrine of necessity is one that is now too firmly established to be drawn in question." "The necessity which arises from the danger of conflagration in a great city . . . and which rests for its exercise upon the subservience of private rights to the public good" legitimated Mayor Lawrence's destruction of private goods for the safety of the common weal.[140]

The New York fire cases exemplify the power and persistence of the common law vision of a well-regulated society dedicated to the *salus populi*. The first thing to note about them is that no one challenged the statute itself. The power of the legislature to authorize the demolition of private buildings in conflagrations was not questioned. The 1813 statute was simply assumed to be a legitimate police regulation. Second, the mayor's behavior in these cases diverged somewhat from a typical act of regulation. Like the wooden building in *Wadleigh v. Gilman*, property was actually destroyed. But unlike *Wadleigh*, the property at issue did not violate any prescribed restrictions, written or unwritten. These goods were simply in the wrong place at the wrong time. The fire cases show that public power over private property in the early nineteenth century was not restricted to passing prospective rules or limitations. In cases of necessity, it could act swiftly and expediently, without notice, to protect the people's welfare.

The New York fire cases also reveal the tenacity of common law standards (especially those protecting public prerogatives) in nineteenth-century America. Here, two potent rivals had ample chance to stifle the common law of necessity. The 1813 statute provided judges sufficient room to compensate all sufferers. Furthermore, article 7 provided New York with a clear constitutional mandate to compensate takings of private property for public use. It would be hard to imagine a better scenario for a takings clause to trump police power than in cases of the summary destruction of perfectly harmless private properties. Nonetheless, the common law rule of necessity persevered through statute and constitution. The New York and New Jersey courts ultimately refused to interpret Mayor Lawrence's action as within the constitutionally protected realm of eminent domain. Though buildings were certainly compensable via statute, this was simply a legislative bonus or "bounty."[141] All other

property losses were *damnum absque injuria* (injuries without remedies) according to the principle that the people's welfare was the supreme law.

But could it be that the New York fire cases were simply flukes, an unusual and strange climax to a rare occurrence? Or were New York judges simply relying on ancient precedents to shrewdly cut off liability to New Jersey merchants? Such explanations would certainly curtail the usefulness of these cases for drawing general conclusions about early American law. But the New York fire cases did not stand alone. In addition to becoming precedential tinder for a host of general regulatory cases, the New York and New Jersey decisions were ratified in fire cases in California, Indiana, Massachusetts, and Minnesota.[142] In *Bowditch v. Boston* (1880), the United States Supreme Court gave its sanction to the common law of necessity.[143] By 1881, John Dillon could cite a slew of American decisions for the proposition:

> The rights of private property, sacred as the law regards them, are yet subordinate to the higher demands of the public welfare. *Salus populi suprema est lex.* Upon this principle, *in cases of imminent and urgent public necessity, an individual or municipal officer may raze or demolish houses and other combustible structures* in a city or compact town, to prevent the spreading of an existing conflagration. This he may do independently of statute, and without responsibility to the owner for damages he thereby sustains.[144]

The New York fire of 1835 vividly demonstrated just how interconnected people's lives were in early American cities. Individual uses of private property could have staggering effects on the well-being of the whole. The well-regulated society was designed to guard against such unfortunate consequences. The lesson of the fire of 1835 in court was that the common law could be aggressively responsive to the people's safety even at the expense of private interests. In these cases, property—supposedly that most sacrosanct of American institutions—was not merely restricted, taxed, or appropriated to public use with compensation. It was blown up by public officials to save New York City. Early American judges, often perceived as the conservative bulwark of such property interests, found nothing in early American common, statute, or constitutional law to stand in the way.

Conclusion

By the late nineteenth century most American cities vigorously regulated combustibles, buildings, and behavior to guard against the dire public safety

threat posed by fire. Elaborate building codes presaged comprehensive zoning laws in an effort to create fire-proof cities. In turn-of-the-century Philadelphia, for example, a theater owner had to comply with 87 special provisions governing everything from radiators to proscenium curtains in addition to the 158 restrictions applicable to buildings in general.[145] Invariably the constitutionality of these fire regulations was upheld by late nineteenth-century courts.[146]

Indeed, by the late nineteenth century, fire regulations became a paradigm for constitutional exertions of state police power. Treatise writers as diverse as Christopher Tiedeman and Ernst Freund accepted the patent constitutionality of police power prohibitions on gunpowder and wooden structures in urban areas.[147] Thomas Cooley and John Dillon both used fire regulations to epitomize police power limitations on private property. Cooley observed that fire limits might look like the "destruction of private property," but they were merely "a just restraint of an injurious use of property"[148] Dillon added that the power of public officials to raze private buildings to prevent the spread of fire was the classic example of private property deferring to "the higher demands of the public welfare"—"*salus populi suprema est lex.*"[149]

Such statements testify to the power and persistence of the well-regulated society. Fire regulations embodied the concerns for public welfare, local self-government, common law, and the relative nature of property at the heart of that vision of social governance. In a society dedicated to the people's welfare, no right was fixed or absolute unto itself, no matter how innocent its exercise might appear on the surface. Rights existed relative to surrounding others. The maintenance of a cache of gunpowder in Brooklyn or a wooden building on the outskirts of Philadelphia could be perfectly legitimate for decades. But once conditions and populations fluctuated so as to make such conduct harmful in relation to the surrounding community, the right to store gunpowder or build of wood evaporated. Rights did not sprout magically from the land, nor did they inhere in title. Rights were social creations, products of continual change and regulation. The well-regulated society recognized no individual right, written or unwritten, natural or absolute, that trumped the people's safety. Indeed, when that safety was threatened, public officials could summon a powerful array of legal technologies, from nuisance indictment to equity injunction to summary destruction, in response. A swarm of local officials (mayors, aldermen, constables, sheriffs, justices of the peace, fire commissioners, fire wardens, and night watchmen) as well as private citizens readily enforced the underlying principles of the police power, the common

law of nuisance, and the law of overruling necessity: *sic utere tuo* and *salus populi*.[150]

As clearly as fire regulation speaks to the presence of the well-regulated society in nineteenth-century law, it speaks to the absence of one of the staples of liberal constitutionalism—an absolutist protection of private right, especially the right of property. In case after case, judges comfortably defended a far-reaching state power to enact fire regulations and control private property rights for the public safety. Constitutional standards like the commerce clause, state takings requirements, and anything resembling substantive due process protections for individual rights were consistently trumped by the *sic utere tuo* and *salus populi* prerogatives of nonconstitutional public law. Houses, goods, occupations, trades, industries, manufactures, sales, exchanges, land uses, and the like were all subject to regular and harsh public limitations when the safety of the people was threatened by fire.

But though the well-regulated society persisted through Cooley, Dillon, and Tiedeman, change was imminent. At issue in *United States v. Dewitt* (1869) was a section of the *federal* Internal Revenue Act of 1867 that prohibited the dangerous mixing of naphtha and other illuminating oils. Such national police and safety legislation conflicted with the principles of localism, federalism, and self-government at the heart of the well-regulated society.[151] Indeed, a new legal and governmental regime had displaced the *salus populi* tradition by the time Oliver Wendell Holmes Jr. issued his famous opinion in *Pennsylvania Coal v. Mahon* (1922), holding that "though property may be regulated . . . if regulation goes too far it will be recognized as a taking." In imposing a new constitutional limitation on exercises of police power, Holmes felt obligated to respond to the seemingly unlimited power behind nineteenth-century fire regulations. But by 1922, the common law assumptions and principles that made sense of those regulations had all but evaporated. The turn-of-the-century paradigm shift to liberal constitutionalism left Holmes with only an indecipherable anomaly: "It may be doubted how far exceptional cases, like the blowing up of a house to stop a conflagration, go—and if they go beyond the general rule, whether they do not stand as much upon tradition as upon principle."[152]

But like *Commonwealth v. Alger*, of course, gunpowder prohibitions, *Wadleigh v. Gilman*, and the public safety measures of Cornelius Lawrence were *not* anomalies. The nineteenth-century fire cases almost instantly became precedents and reference points for the whole spectrum of nineteenth-century public policymaking, from public economy to public health. They

were at the center of a dominant early American regulatory tradition quite at odds with modern renderings of legal instrumentalism or liberal constitutionalism. Perhaps Louis Brandeis was simply more attuned to nineteenth-century verities when he dissented from Holmes's opinion in *Penn Coal*, arguing that in a "civilized community" if "the public safety is imperiled, surely neither grant, nor contract, can prevail against the exercise of the police power." Any other conclusion, Brandeis mused echoing Lemuel Shaw, threatened the "paramount rights of the public."[153]

Public Economy:
The Well-Ordered Market

So the markets are regulated.—Thomas M. Cooley

P ublic safety was a first-order concern of the well-regulated society to which all private rights and interests were subordinated. An examination of fire regulations thus goes far toward demystifying American private property. Property rights in the early nineteenth century were social, relative, and historical, not individual, absolute, and natural. A second aspect of American liberal mythology that stands in need of disenchantment concerns that mysterious and value-laden sociohistorical force known as "the market." Polity and economy have a very special relationship. But despite being at the center of American historical research for over a century, basic assumptions about the American state and the market have remained surprisingly static. First, state regulation and market economics are seen as diametrical opposites. Regulation is a contrived and public interference in a field of invisible economic relations otherwise natural and private.[1] Second, American economic regulation is understood as a relatively recent invention. As Thomas McCraw argued in 1975 (perhaps with the Massachusetts Board of Railroad Commissioners in mind), "regulation is barely a century old."[2]

This chapter takes aim at both of these assumptions. Through a historical reconstruction of nineteenth-century notions of *public* economy and the *well-ordered* market, it establishes the predominance in theory and practice of an approach to economic life in early America antithetical to the classical separation of market and state. The cases, statutes, and ordinances analyzed here

suggest that early Americans understood the economy as simply another part of their well-regulated society, intertwined with public safety, morals, health, and welfare and subject to the same kinds of legal controls. Far from viewing the state and the economy as adversarial, public economy was part of a world-view slow to separate public and private, government and society. It understood commerce, trade, and economics, like health and morals, as fundamentally public in nature, created, shaped, and regulated by the polity via public law.

This chapter also demonstrates the deep roots of economic regulation in America. In contrast to historical depictions of the period from 1776 to 1860 as an era of Americanization, transformation, and modernization heralding the ascendancy of liberal constitutionalism and free-market economics, it documents the pervasiveness of a commitment to a regulated economy in a well-ordered society. Indeed, the deluge of restrictions on economic life passed by state and local authorities in this period suggests that "regulation" might supplant "the market" as a better metaphor for the age. Regulations were not quaint residues of a feudal regime doomed to obsolescence. Rather public economy and the well-regulated society functioned as central, compelling philosophies in early American public law—philosophies busily put into practice through a host of particular rules and prosecutions solicitous of public goods over individual interests.

The market did not burst on the American stage circa 1776 of its own natural self-volition. It was a human, historical, and political creation. Postrevolutionary America was indeed the site of an economic transformation. But it owed more to the visible laws of police than the natural laws of economics. This was a revolution that had more to do with the conspicuous invention of political economy than the invisible hand of the free market.

Market Revolution or Legal-Political Economy?

The first hurdle blocking a reconstruction of the notion of public economy in nineteenth-century America is a twentieth-century perspective that separates public and private and understands economy as an autonomous and natural force in history. One of its most persistent historical themes is the notion of antebellum America as a site for the pivotal transition from colonial mercantilism to laissez-faire capitalism. The publication of Adam Smith's *Wealth of Nations* (1776), the story goes, "inaugurated an economic revolution by emphasizing laissez-faire and individualism in place of the mercantilist emphasis on government intervention and statism."[3] Building on accounts of the ascen-

dancy of a self-regulating market in England, histories of early American economic development continue to rely on a rather narrow and apolitical rendering of the great capitalist transformation. Capitalism is defined as a state of affairs where "most property is privately owned," "economic decisions are determined in a relatively unfettered market," and "profit is the goal." A free market, private property, and self-interested profit maximization set the conditions for an "age of boundlessness" and unprecedented economic growth.[4]

Recently social historians have taken to the phrase "market revolution" to characterize the impact of antebellum industrial and agricultural change on ordinary Americans. They too emphasize the invisible force of "new markets" in land, labor, and produce that eroded artisan handicrafts and subsistence farming, creating a sea change in human relations and American history. As in the case of capitalist transformation, these market changes transcended legal, governmental, or other forms of public action.[5] In both the theses of "market revolution" and "capitalist transformation," the public and political dimensions of change are subordinated (if not made invisible) to the more primary relationships of society and economy. Law and the state appear as separate, external spheres whose ramifications can be captured in a simple, binary assessment of whether they were "in" or "out" of the economy. There is no room in such interpretations for a common law tradition in which state, economy, and society were mutually interwoven in an overarching practice of well-regulated governance.

As one might expect, political and legal histories of the nineteenth century do stress the governmental and institutional contexts of market and capitalist change. Indeed, political history since Oscar and Mary Handlin's *Commonwealth*[6] and legal history since Willard Hurst's *Law and the Conditions of Freedom*[7] have exploded the "myth of laissez-faire" and demonstrated the myriad ways that law and active state governments furnished the necessary *conditions* for early American economic development, from the state promotion of canals and railroads to the transformation of the laws of property and contract. Without downplaying this extraordinarily important insight, however, the commonwealth studies and the new legal histories nonetheless remain predominantly instrumentalist in orientation. The state had an important *role* in early American capitalism, and the law was a crucial *tool* of economic development. But polity and economy, public and private remained separate spheres. The needs of capitalism was still the dominant engine of change in nineteenth-century America. At bottom, the state and the law in these legal-political studies were mere public mechanisms for the advancement of economic individualism and an ultimately private, self-regulating market. As

Arthur Miller observed in a commonly accepted depiction of nineteenth-century law and economy: "The basic emphasis of government . . . may be summed up in the hypothesis that the legal system was used to encourage and protect business enterprise."[8]

In contrast, I would like to rehabilitate a different conception of the relationship between polity and economy that predominated in nineteenth-century America. Law and state were not simply instrumentalities of a fundamentally economic transformation. Rather, they were the central creators of the notion of economy as a special sphere of social activity, a sphere distinctly cognizable as an object of governance. In the early nineteenth century as a product of state policy and legal change, the economy emerged from the shadows of colonial household management into the public sphere as an object of police and statecraft. The basic relations of the American economy were subsequently formed and transformed as a result of the overt policies of government and law *not* the invisible laws of supply and demand. Indeed, one of the most important attributes of this antebellum debut of economics as a distinctly public practice was its accompaniment by extensive police regulation.[9]

First and foremost, the economy was seen in antebellum America as a site for the exercise of public power, that is, for the execution of the ubiquitous rules and restrictions of the well-regulated society. The discourses of governance, police, and political economy grew up together. Vattel captured this confluence when he described as the principal object of government "the business of providing for all the wants of the people, and producing a *happy plenty* of all the necessaries of life, with its conveniences and innocent and laudable enjoyments." In a well-regulated society, the happiness of the nation and the welfare of the people depended upon the public management of economy and market. It was a duty (as well as reason) of state to encourage labor and industry, to provide sufficient working men, to prevent the emigration of useful laborers, to encourage cultivation (e.g., by the establishment of public granaries), to cultivate home trade, to promote public communication and transportation, and to enact and enforce regulations for preventing scarcity.[10] Charles Goodrich, who labeled political economy "only another term for jurisprudence," was quite explicit about this interconnection of police and economy: "The regulation of internal trade is a matter of public concernment, and is regulated by state authority."[11] Regulation was an inseparable and indispensable part of the early American notion of "public economy."

In unpacking this understanding of public economy, it is important to remember that the word "economy" meant something different in the eighteenth and nineteenth centuries. The Latin *oeconomia* had Greek roots and

meant "the management of a household." The notion of management or control was inherent in the word, as was its connection to family matters. By the eighteenth century, under the influence of police and cameralist thinking, the word was broadened to include any society ordered after the manner of a family or, similarly, the general administration of the concerns of a community with a view to orderly conduct and productiveness.[12] That was, of course, exactly William Blackstone's meaning when he referred to "Offenses against Public Police or Oeconomy" in his *Commentaries*.[13] Blackstone used the words "public police" and "oeconomy" interchangeably to represent "the due regulation and domestic order of the kingdom."[14]

The nineteenth-century American notion of public economy resonated with the eighteenth-century English "moral economy" implied by Blackstone but more critically described by E. P. Thompson (the historian along with Marx and Weber who best illuminated the legal and political construction of market capitalism). But there was a crucial difference. Thompson argued that English law and legislation quickly capitulated to the overwhelming "intellectual victories" of the "new political economy" of Adam Smith. Thus, enforcement of the precepts of the old moral economy fell to the ultimately futile "extralegal" activities of the English crowd.[15] In contrast, American public economy remained firmly rooted in law and legislation until after the Civil War.[16]

Indeed, despite historical depictions of free trade, "laggard" regulation, and the opening of American society,[17] the early nineteenth century was home to a deluge of formal economic regulations and vigorous defenses of the power of the state over trade and commerce. Regulations of public trade and the *jus publicum* of commerce, like those governing public justice and public peace, were crucial building blocks of the well-regulated society and antebellum public policy. The commerce clause of the United States Constitution, empowering Congress to "regulate commerce," was only the nation's most visible economic police law.[18] In 1823, Nathan Dane (who established the first law chair at Harvard University) outlined a series of economic offenses against "public polity and good order of the government."[19] He enumerated a variety of common law and statutory regulations of "public trade," violations of which "no well-governed state can suffer to exist unpunished." Among these were: cheating, deceits, and frauds; the operation of an inn, tavern, or licensed house without a license; offensive trades; the sale of unwholesome provisions; peddlers and hawkers; forestalling, engrossing monopolies, and regrating; luxury; usury; and illegal weights and measures.[20] Though Dane's list was short, the broad policy concerns represented by each offense stretched across

the spectrum of the antebellum economy and included thousands of particular state economic regulations.

The broad, political understanding of economy as the object of police and regulation dominated thinking about exchange, trade, and commerce well into the nineteenth century. Rather than moving to the whims of an invisible, self-regulating law of supply and demand, early Americans perceived the economy as inseparable from the basic institutions and public concerns of their daily lives. As such, it was held to the same rigorous controls and legal standards that governed all aspects of life. Indeed, ultimately the early American economy is only interpretable through the mass of economic rules, controls, customs, and regulations passed by state and local governments to protect and pursue *salus populi*, the people's welfare.

Product Laws

Under "cheating, deceit, and fraud in trade," Nathan Dane discussed a host of state and common law regulations meant to ensure fair trade and "fair dealing." Nearly all state legislatures in the early nineteenth century passed laws directing "trades to be conducted, and wares and goods to be fabricated, and put up for market in a certain manner."[21] Between 1780 and 1835, the Massachusetts legislature passed regulations that closely specified and controlled the way the following products were manufactured and sold: boards, shingles, clapboards, hoops, and staves (1783); flaxseed, barreled fish, and dried fish (1784); tobacco and onions (1785); pot and pearl ashes (1791); firewood, bark, and coal (1796); beef and pork (1799); boots, half-boots, shoes, pumps, sandals, slippers, and galoshes (1799); butter (1799); bread (1800); nails (1800); chocolate (1803); hops (1806); lime (1806); smoked alewives and herrings (1807); gunpowder (1809); pickled fish (1810); Indian and rye meal (1813); firearms (1814); salt and grain (1817); paper (1818); spruce and pine timber (1822); hay (1825); ale, beer, and cider (1829); sole leather (1831); oils (1833); and beef cattle (1833).[22] Surveys of the statute books of Maryland, South Carolina, Michigan, and Ohio reveal similar stories.[23]

But a mere list of restricted products (even if it contains the staples of the antebellum economy) does not capture how deeply embedded public regulation was in the American economy. That is more apparent in the far-reaching detail of the statutes. A Maryland law regulating the sale, inspection, and export of pickled or salted fish was typical.[24] It employed most of the antebellum strategies for regulating the sale of food products (short of outright price-fixing): strict controls on packaging, weights and measures, and quality and

merchantability; branding; inspection and certification; restrictions on exportation; oaths; and, of course, penalties (fines and seizure).

Maryland borrowed liberally from a Massachusetts statute which in turn was based on English Parliamentary Acts dating from the seventeenth century. The Maryland act demanded rigorous packaging standards:

> [A]ll barrels . . . shall be made of sound well seasoned oak, ash or chestnut staves, of rift timber, not less than half an inch thick, with heading of either of the said kinds of wood, not less than five-eighths of an inch thick, and sound and well seasoned, the said heading to be well planed or shaved, the barrels, half barrels and tierces, to be well hooped, with at least three hoops on each bilge, and three hoops on each chine, all of which shall be good hoops of sufficient substance; the barrel staves to be twenty-eight inches in length, and the heads to be seventeen inches between the chines, and to contain not less than twenty-nine or more than thirty-one gallons; and the barrels, half barrels and tierces, shall be made in a good workman-like manner, so as to hold pickle, the tierces to hold not less than forty-five gallons, and the half barrels not less than fifteen gallons.[25]

Owners or importers of any fish in Baltimore were required to arrange for an inspection within forty-eight hours. The state inspector was charged with ensuring that the fish were "well struck with salt or pickle . . . and preserved sweet and free from rust, taint or damage." Those "of a good and fat quality, with sweet pickle in the barrels, and sufficient salt to preserve them" were branded "No. 1." Others were branded "No. 2" or condemned. Fish of a very superior quality were further branded with the owner's name and the word "prime."[26] No fish could be exported from Maryland without certification of inspection and an oath by the ship's master that all fish on board had been properly inspected.[27] Further restrictions were placed on the landing of fish at the public wharf and the storage of more than forty-eight barrels in a warehouse. Penalties were imposed for violating any part of the act or for tampering with stamps or brands.

Similar regulations accompanied the sale and exportation of almost all important commodities. Before being sold, wood had to be measured (conforming to precise dimensions); inspected for sap, shakes, wormholes, rots, knots, splits, and seasonedness; certified; and cut, split, landed, stored, and carted according to the dictates of statute.[28] Legislatures empowered a small army of inspectors, measurers, surveyors, viewers, cullers, weighers, provers, and gaugers, as well as mayors, aldermen, justices of the peace, and private citizens,

to protect the public against the evils of unregulated commerce and trade.[29] The fear was fraud and deceit—the same motivation for laws regulating weights and measures and outlawing cheating.[30] But there was also a ubiquitous concern for quality, merchantability, and fair dealing.[31] In a public economy, the buying and selling of goods was intimately bound up with community identity and social order. Nothing so important could be left to the invisible laws of a marketplace or the private law stricture that a buyer should beware.

Demands for a moral and well-regulated economy did not die with the American Revolution or a subsequent economic one.[32] As late as 1841, the Supreme Court of Alabama unequivocally upheld the assize of bread, suggesting that "whatever doubts have been thrown over the question by the theories of political economists, it would seem that experience has shown that this great end [the urban bread supply] is better secured by licensing a sufficient number of bakers and by an assize of bread, than by leaving it to the voluntary acts of individuals." In *Turner v. Maryland* (1882), the U.S. Supreme Court reviewed state product and inspection laws dating from the late eighteenth century and found them decidedly constitutional.[33]

Licensing

Licensing, another item in Nathan Dane's analysis of public trade, was just as far-reaching and important to the public economy as inspection and product laws. Nineteenth-century legislators used licensing to regulate and control a host of economic activities, trades, callings, and professions. The goals of particular license laws were mixed and sometimes confused, including prohibition, regulation, administration, and revenue. But the overall justification for licensing was the same as the police power generally—the public good and the people's welfare.[34]

To get at the public significance of licensing in the nineteenth century, it is necessary to suspend our twentieth-century conception of licensing as little more than routine public registration. As Thomas Cooley pointed out in 1876, the license (like an early act of incorporation) was understood as a special "privilege granted by the state."[35] Licensing was an exertion of the public prerogative granting permission to do that which was otherwise illegal or against public policy.[36]

So what were some of the activities that were considered special privileges in the early nineteenth century—illegal without public sanction? In some states, one was the basic economic act of *selling for profit*. Beginning in 1827,

Maryland put together a series of statutes that established a "license to trade." An act of the legislature made it unlawful for anyone (other than the grower, maker, or manufacturer of goods) to set up any shop or stand "for the purpose of selling by wholesale or retail, or bartering any dry goods, groceries, spirituous or fermented liquor, imported dried fruit, glass, crockery, hardware, drugs or medicines, paints, printed books, stationery, saddlery, gold, silver or plated ware, jewelry, toys, wearing apparel, salted provisions, grain, meal, flour, timber, tobacco, cotton, leather, hides, lime, wrought or cast iron, copper or tin, or any other kind of goods, wares or merchandise, foreign or domestic, without first obtaining a license."[37] By 1832, it was illegal in Maryland to "expose for sale, or sell, any goods, wares or merchandise, with a view to profit in the way of trade" unless one first obtained a state "license to trade."[38] Tennessee, Missouri, Pennsylvania, and California all passed similar statutes around midcentury requiring the licensing of merchants, retailers, and wholesalers. In *French v. Baker* (1856), the Tennessee Supreme Court joined other state courts in holding that the occupation of merchant was a *privilege* sanctioned by government and not a natural right of individuals.[39] That most basic of economic activities—the selling of goods in a shop—was understood as flowing from the state, which retained the right and duty to control, regulate, and tax it for the common good.

But merchants and retailers were not the only economic actors subject to licensing restrictions. By 1868 Alabama required a license for over thirty occupations and businesses, including public race tracks, lottery ticket dealers, gift enterprises, liquor dealers, distillers, brewers, dealers in tobacco or cigars, livery stable keepers, keepers of stud horses, horse and mule dealers, brokers, pawnbrokers, real-estate agents, insurance agents, dentists, physicians and surgeons, lawyers, druggists, commission merchants, peddlers, bowling alleys, billiard tables, gaming tables, theaters, dealers in firearms, auctioneers, and newspapers. The Alabama Supreme Court upheld this statute (and the indictment of a lawyer for practicing without a license) with the observation, "The right to regulate the property and the avocations of its citizens by the State is sovereign."[40] By 1881, a Tennessee legislature declared more than fifty such occupations "privileges" requiring a license.[41]

General licensing statutes were significant in establishing the power of the state over nineteenth-century businesses and occupations. But even more important were statutes that used the license as the first step in a more comprehensive regulatory strategy. This was the case with many antebellum businesses, but especially in the licensing and regulation of three central economic operations: inns and taverns, auctioneers, and public carriers.

Inn and tavern owners were not only licensed but were treated as virtual public officials. Drawing on its own colonial laws and English precedents dating from William III, Massachusetts passed an act for the regulation of "licensed houses" in 1786.[42] It held that no person could be a common victualler, innholder, taverner, or seller of strong liquors by retail without a license. To obtain such a license, tavern owners had first to obtain a certificate from the selectmen of their town recommending them as "persons of sober life and conversation, suitably qualified and provided for the exercise of such an employment." They then had to take an oath bearing allegiance and faith to the commonwealth and post a recognizance of twenty pounds that they would "keep and maintain good order and rule, and shall suffer no disorders nor unlawful games to be used . . . and shall not break any of the laws for the regulation of such houses." Such regulations included requirements for suitable provisions and lodging for all strangers and travelers; pasturing and stable room, hay and provender for horses and cattle; a conspicuous sign; a duty to provide for all travelers; a prohibition on gaming implements, dancing or reveling, excessive drinking, and service to minors or servants. In addition, selectmen posted the names of common drunkards and idlers in all inns and taverns, prohibiting service to such individuals. Tithingmen were appointed to inspect all licensed houses and inform on all disorders or violations of the statute. Substantial fines and forfeiture of a license were the penalties for violating these regulations. Tavern owning was neither a right nor a private economic activity; it was understood as a public responsibility. American statutes echoed English Justice Coleridge's suggestion that "innkeepers are a sort of public servant."[43] Justices of the peace were charged with issuing no more licenses than "necessary for the public good."[44] In South Carolina and Maryland, county courts set prices and rates for food, drink, lodging, and horse care at licensed inns and taverns.[45]

Auctioneers were as much economic officers of the state as tavern keepers. The auction (or vendue) was an ancient institution still integral to nineteenth-century economic exchange. Auctions were strictly regulated public events. The auctioneer was usually appointed by the governor, and the number in any city limited by law.[46] He was required to post bond or recognizance to cover all duties, satisfy any claims against him, and guarantee good and honest public behavior (in Baltimore $30,000 in 1827). License fees could amount to more than $750. Accounts were to be rendered to public officials and duties paid on all items sold every three to six months. Auctioneers were required to take oaths attesting to the accuracy of the accounts. Auctions were restricted to certain times and places, and their commissions were fixed by state law.

If one's business was carting people or hay, firewood, lime, charcoal, or manure in an antebellum city, there was little room for free bargaining. All were licensed and regulated occupations. In early New York City, cartmen were appointed and licensed by the mayor.[47] Each sled or cart in New York at the turn of the century had to be "two feet, five inches wide between the foremost rungs, and two feet, nine inches wide between the hindmost rungs." The iron or tire around the wheels had to be "in breadth not less than three inches, and . . . nails shall not project beyond the surface thereof."[48] The number of the cart's license was to be painted on the side of the cart in red paint. Licensed cartmen had an obligation to serve all customers and had to observe precise limits on loads. Indeed, New York City demanded special carts with special dimensions and load limits for the carting of hay, firewood, lime, charcoal, manure, sand, and clay. Finally, the rates for the carting of people and products to various points in town were closely circumscribed by state and municipal government. As was the case with ferriage, carriage rates often went on for pages in the statute books. New York City rates began:

> For loading, carting, and unloading every common load of European goods, wheat, meal, or flour in bags (twelve bags to the load) and of firewood and other articles not herein after mentioned to any place within this city, not exceeding half a mile, one shilling and six-pence. And for every load of lime, bricks, staves, heading, hoops, hoop-poles, cocoa, bar-iron, pimento, slate, all kinds of dye-wood, every seven barrels of flour, every four tierces of bread, every two bales of cotton, every fifteen bushels of salt, every load of cheese or gammons, every load of sails, every load of white sand, building sand, paving sand or clay, containing twelve bushels, every load of beef, pork, pitch, tar, turpentine, beer, cyder, or other goods or things in tight barrels, allowing five barrels to each load (excepting oil and pot-ash which shall be four barrels to the load) not exceeding half a mile, one shilling and six-pence, and if housed, six-pence more for each load.[49]

Two more pages listed rates, quantities, and mileage for iron pots and kettles, household goods, hay, calves, sheep lambs, shingles, brick, earthen ware, pantiles, coal, fish, hemp or flax, oyster shells, rum, liquor, molasses, wine, strong liquor, sugar, coffee, cocoa, tobacco, rice, flaxseed, cable, and cordage. Baltimore broke up its 1837 rates (from twelve and one-half cents to one dollar) for carting people according to these classifications: "1. From steamboats and rail road depots to any part of the city; 2. To steamboats and rail road depots; 3. Within certain prescribed limits, east, west, north, and south from Calvert

street, the centre of the city; 4. By the hour; 5. Evening and night; 6. Between the Exchange and Fell's Point."[50] The carting of noxious products through city streets, such as offal (the hazardous waste of the nineteenth century), often was prohibited.[51]

The license was used in several other areas to restrict and regulate economic activity. Traveling salesmen, known as "hawkers and peddlers," continuously encountered legislation controlling or prohibiting their activities. In New York, the annual license fee for hawkers in 1813 was $50 if on foot, $80 on horse or boat, and $100 if one was prosperous enough to come by carriage. In 1831 South Carolina required a $1,000 fee and an additional recognizance of $1,000. Hawkers or peddlers without a license were susceptible to a $5,000 fine.[52] Other regulated licensed trades were butchers, bakers, grocers, lawyers, and doctors.[53] The multiplicity of motives behind license laws can be seen in a Maryland act requiring free blacks selling corn, wheat, or tobacco to be specially licensed and a gold-rush California statute demanding a license for "foreign" miners.[54]

Licensing left little in the early American economy untouched. Indeed, it turned several occupations and trades into veritable offshoots of the state or municipality. In all cases, licensing established the predominant public interest in policing the economy. Licensed activities were privileges, not rights, and were subject to police regulation when the public health, safety, and welfare demanded.

Extensive as licensing and inspection statutes were, they still made up only part of the array of regulatory technologies used to control the public economy. As Dane noted, laws against the sale of unwholesome provisions were widespread. In New York, unsound beef, pork, fish, or hides were to be destroyed by municipal officials by "casting them into the streams of the East or Hudson rivers."[55] Though public health (rather than water pollution) was a main concern in these statutes, one must also not overlook a general legislative aversion to what Dane called "luxury." An early Massachusetts provision law was directed at "evilly disposed persons, [who] *from motives of avarice and filthy lucre*, have been induced to sell diseased, corrupted, contagious or unwholesome provisions, to the great nuisance of public health and peace."[56]

The reining-in of avarice and lucre also was one of the goals of laws against regrating, forestalling, and engrossing. As Dane suggested, this trio of offenses against public trade "existed in all countries and ages, and will probably exist as long as men shall be influenced by avarice and a sordid love of gain; as long as many of them prefer living and gaining property by arts and contrivances, to honest and laborious industry."[57] Regrating, forestalling, and engrossing re-

mained a focus of economic regulations into the late nineteenth century. Their objective was to discountenance economic conduct that falsely raised the price of products. Thus buying goods already on the way to market with the intention of selling again at a higher price was prohibited. So too, licensing laws almost always exempted or favored sellers of their own goods over middlemen and retailers. Though profit is supposed to be the central attribute of market capitalism, its simple maximization was not a discernible purpose of the public statute books of the early nineteenth century. On the contrary, profit was continually subsumed by a larger public interest in fair dealing, fair price, honest labor, wholesome provisions, public health, and the orderly exchange of the necessities of life. These were the goals of a public economy. If there was one overarching symbol of the predominance of this well-ordered conception of economic relations in the nineteenth century, it was the urban market house.

The Urban Marketplace

In studying buying and selling, economists and economic historians have been drawn to a methodology that hinges on the workings of an abstract "boundless and timeless" process known as "the market."[58] I would like to focus instead on a more concrete and historical phenomenon. For most antebellum Americans, "the market" was not an invisible set of economic principles but that place near the center of town where farmers, butchers, and householders exchanged necessary provisions. This market bore little resemblance to the market of theory. For one thing, the economic activity that went on there could hardly be called "free." Indeed, the urban marketplace was probably the most visible, potent expression of public control over buying and selling in the antebellum public economy.

The public marketplace had deep roots in the Domesday Book and beyond.[59] Indeed, scholars place its origins in that strange mixture of commerce, magic, and religion that attended ancient religious observances and pilgrimages.[60] Throughout its early history, the market was closely identified with state and municipality (e.g., the notion of "market towns") and was controlled by rigorous public rules and regulations. In England, the establishment of marts and fairs was the exclusive prerogative of the king, to be exercised for the public benefit.[61] They came into being by a legal grant or franchise from the crown. In 1765, Lord Mansfield justified formal market grants on the need for the "preservation of order, and prevention of irregular behavior."[62] As public institutions, markets came with special restrictions: a prohibition of

buying and selling outside the market; prescribed places, times, days, and hours; the use of just weights and measures; the payment of tolls or duties; prohibitions of certain goods, hawking, and peddling; and laws against forestalling, regrating, and engrossing. English markets required a special public official, the clerk, to keep order and enforce rules. Special courts known as piepowders administered market justice.[63]

American colonies duplicated English market ways soon after settlement.[64] Many scholars have suggested that these "feudal" restrictions did not last much beyond the 1820s, as a new "free-trade attitude" and "ideal of open competition," fueled by the natural rights rhetoric of the Revolution, supplanted the notion of "regulated concord."[65] But a close look at state and local laws along with subsequent legal cases across the country tells a different story. Not only were public market restrictions still very much part of economic life at the time of the Civil War, but the state judiciary overwhelmingly upheld a variety of regulations passed in the 1840s, 1850s, and 1860s. By the time John Dillon wrote his definitive treatise on municipal corporation law in 1872, there were ample precedents supporting a municipality's power to build and regulate public markets, thereby restricting alternative methods of buying and selling provisions.[66]

Rationales for public market regulations also proved remarkably resilient. In 1719, Reverend Benjamin Colman supported the establishment of markets in Boston to discourage "hucksters, forestalling, engrossing and buying up the Provisions that come into Town," thus artificially raising prices for townspeople. In 1856, Boston's Committee on Public Buildings sought to reopen the market under Faneuil Hall to combat the increased "cost of the necessaries of life" caused by the proliferation of some 600 private provision and produce stores in the city.[67] American public markets, like their Roman and English predecessors, were created to ensure an adequate supply of wholesome, fairly priced food and provisions accessible to the general population. The health, comfort, convenience, and welfare of the people depended upon such provisions. It was a duty of sovereignty and an obligation of government to act affirmatively. To leave unregulated something as central to the general welfare as the supply of basic foodstuffs was an abdication of public responsibility. Consequently, nineteenth-century states and municipalities used their police powers to construct regulated marketplaces to protect their populations from high prices, unhealthy goods, unsanitary conditions, fraud and cheating, and the adverse effects of simple profiteering by hucksters, forestallers, middlemen, and other second hand sellers. Though across-the-board price controls were rare after the eighteenth century (except in the case of bread and flour),

nineteenth-century state judges left some clues to the answers to these questions. Their opinions suggest that the problem lies not with the presence of market restrictions, but with conventional interpretations of the era and American law into which they do not fit.

Philadelphia's High Street Market was demolished between 1859 and 1860 so that a $1 million public market could be built on new ground. When country farmers brought suit to prevent the destruction, claiming a "vested right" to sell in the market, Chief Justice Black of the Pennsylvania Supreme Court delivered a staunch defense of the market's publicness and the power of local government to control it: "The necessity of a public market, where the producers and consumers of fresh provisions can be brought together at stated times for the sale of those commodities, is very apparent. There is nothing which more imperatively requires the constant supervision of some authority which can regulate it and control it. Such authority is seldom, if ever vested in individuals."[79] Black championed the local community's right to regulate itself: "The daily supply of food to the people of a city is emphatically their own affair." The all-too-visible "laws of a market" were "always made by the persons who reside at the place." Black declared that according to the "common law of Pennsylvania," all cities with powers "to promote the general welfare and preserve the peace" could "fix the time or places of holding public markets for the sale of food, and make such other regulations concerning them as may conduce to the public interest." Black deemed this wide grant of authority over the sale of food the "true rule"—"necessary and proper, in harmony with the sentiments of the people, universally practised by the towns, and universally submitted to the residents of the country."[80]

Justice Black was unequivocal about local power to regulate the urban food market, because his 1859 opinion followed the reasoning of a long line of jurists. Often, more was at stake than the power of a city to replace its market house. Two of the earliest state decisions dealt with the most controversial and potent of municipal market powers: the ability to prohibit all trading and selling of food outside the established public marketplace. The villages of Poughkeepsie and Buffalo, New York, were incorporated with general police powers to make laws respecting markets and the "good government" and "good improvement" of the village.[81] Both villages subsequently established public markets and market regulations prohibiting the "hawking" or "selling by retail" of meat anywhere except the public marketplace. In *Bush v. Seabury* (1811) and *Village of Buffalo v. Webster* (1833), the New York Supreme Court validated local proceedings against two defendants for trading meat outside the market.[82] In *Bush*, the defendant was selling meat out of his wagon in the

streets of Poughkeepsie. In *Buffalo v. Webster*, a farmer was convicted for trading a quarter of lamb for tea in a Buffalo grocery. The *Bush* court was matter of fact: "The fixing the *place* and times at which markets shall be held and kept open, and the prohibition to sell at other places and times, is among the most ordinary regulations of a city or town police."[83] In *Webster*, Chief Justice Savage had to contend with Webster's assertion that the local bylaw was "bad, as unreasonable and improperly restraining trade." Unfortunately for Webster, English common law had sanctioned public market restrictions "from time out of mind." Savage distinguished illegal restraints of trade from legitimate public regulations, observing that "a by-law that no meat should be sold in the village would be bad, being a general restraint; but that meat shall not be sold except in a particular place is good, not being a restraint of the *right to sell* meat, but a *regulation* of that right. . . . Laws relating to public markets must necessarily embrace the power to require all meats to be sold there." Savage cited *Bush* and Lord Mansfield in *Pierce v. Bartrum* (1775) holding the prohibition of all slaughtering in Exeter a regulation and not a restraint of trade.[84]

Nineteenth-century judges also readily sanctioned the broad powers of the market clerk to enforce weights, regulate stalls, and rein in forestallers and hucksters. The clerk of Boston's Faneuil Hall Market was the focus of two important antiforestalling decisions. In 1830, Clerk Caleb Hayward filed a complaint in Boston's Police Court against Josiah Nightingale of Quincy.[85] Hayward accused Nightingale of occupying a stand in South Market Street at Faneuil Hall for the resale of sheep carcasses (bought months before in the cattle market at Brighton), lambs (bought a week before in Hingham), and other articles not the product of his own Quincy farm. Nightingale refused to obey Hayward's order to leave the market for violating Boston's 1826 market ordinance against the sale of secondhand produce.[86] Judge Thacher of Boston's Municipal Court upheld a Police Court conviction, condemning the evil of forestalling and championing market regulations as a remedy: "From a period coeval with the settlement of this city, there has been established in it a public market. The right to establish a market has not been questioned in this trial; and considering the city as having that right, it follows that they may establish such good and wholesome regulations as shall be found necessary for its good government."[87] On appeal, Justice Wilde of the Shaw Supreme Court agreed. The ordinance giving the market clerk power to eject traders not selling their own produce was simply a valid police law, not unlike the licensing, harbor, and cemetery regulations validated by earlier Massachusetts and New York courts.[88] It was neither a violation of private rights nor an improper restraint of trade. Boston's bylaw was a "wholesome regulation of [trade]."[89]

In 1845, Chief Justice Lemuel Shaw added his own voice to a chorus of judicial opinion supporting urban market regulations. In *Commonwealth v. Rice*, he backed Faneuil Hall Clerk Daniel Rhodes's action against Barnabus Rice for vending poultry he obtained from a farm in New Hampshire.[90] Shaw defended Boston's 1843 market ordinance. The bylaw, he argued, was "founded on the old policy of the law inhibiting forestalling." Its very purpose was "to secure a dealing between the producer and the consumer, without the intervention of any intermediate agent." Shaw denied that restrictions on resale and secondhand goods were "contrary to common right" or "in restraint of trade" as claimed by Rice. He held instead that "the city have, at great expense provided accommodations; and they have a right so to control them, as best to promote the welfare of all citizens." Here, the "public and general benefit" of city and country was secured by a regulated market providing "free and convenient stands for actual producers."[91]

Although particular opprobrium was reserved for forestallers and hucksters (perhaps the preeminent agricultural capitalists), courts also supported market clerks' powers to evict, penalize, and prosecute other market offenders. The authority to demand rents or fees, require public weighing before sale, and even the general discretion to remove sellers and dole out summary justice were ratified by state judges.[92] In *Charleston v. Goldsmith* (1844), some extreme circumstances produced a quite common defense of the powers delegated to market clerks and commissioners.[93] Moses Goldsmith was summarily expelled from the Charleston market in 1842 after he stabbed "one Kennedy" with a butcher's knife (so much for tradesman solidarity). Justice Wardlaw vigorously supported broad, discretionary power in the hands of local officials in rhetoric steeped in the vision of a well-regulated society:

> [W]hen it is considered that in cities, policy necessarily requires many restraints upon individual freedom and that especially in relation to markets — objects of universal interest — numerous minute regulations prevail in all large cities, advantageous to both buyer and seller. Although arbitrary and vexatious, there can remain no doubt that the summary exercise of severe powers here authorized, and committed to the commissioners of the markets, may be required by the public convenience, and is altogether consistent with the rights secured to the citizen.

To deny such powers, Wardlaw argued, would be to deprive a community "the power of preserving order" and "the peace and prosperity of the city."[94] In *Cincinnati v. Buckingham* (1840), Ohio Chief Justice Lane declared that "the prompt and strong enforcement of market regulations" was the rule "from

the days of the court of pie poudre to the present." A system of closely enforced police regulations, "fixing market hours, making provisions for lighting, watching, cleaning, detecting false weights and unwholesome food, and other arrangements calculated to facilitate the intercourse, and insure the honesty, of buyer and seller," was part of Lane's very definition of a municipal market.[95]

Dissent crept into judicial deference to local market regulations only in the years immediately preceding the Civil War. In the late 1850s and 1860s, courts in Georgia, Minnesota, and Illinois temporarily challenged the municipality's right to prohibit trade outside the marketplace.[96] Justice Lumpkin of the Georgia Supreme Court went furthest, challenging the fundamental rationales for a public market and positing a vision of law, state, citizen, and economy in tension with the well-regulated society. At issue in *Bethune v. Hughes* (1859) was a plaintiff's habeas corpus petition to be released from prison for violating an 1858 Columbus city ordinance against selling provisions outside the public marketplace. Lumpkin indulged in a tirade against this "coercive," "excessive," "anti-free-trade," and "class legislation": "Let anything and everything be done rather than restrict commerce, rather than force and imprison tradespeople, to coerce them to submit to all kinds of discomfort and inconvenience, not to say loss, to gratify the selfishness or avarice of a few municipal lords." He recommended that a popular convention be called to impose restraints on the powers of the legislature. He set Bethune free with a testament to the value of a free economy:

> A peaceable citizen, who discharges punctually all his public duties, and respects scrupulously the rights of others, should be left free and untrammeled as the air he breathes in the pursuit of his business and happiness. Fetters are equally galling, whether imposed by one man or by a community; and I am not ashamed to confess that the best sympathies of my heart are, and always will be, interested for one who is, or may be, incarcerated, because, in proud consciousness of a freeman, he claims the right to offer for sale, at any hour of the day, on the highway or in the streets, as interest or inclination may prompt him, any commodity he may possess, the traffic in which is not forbidden by the laws of the land.[97]

Despite his closing qualification (obviously in deference to government's power to prohibit the sale of goods like liquor), Lumpkin's rhetoric certainly contrasted with common law precedent and the ideal of a well-regulated society. His cynicism about local officials' true motives also was something not often seen in earlier market cases.[98]

Economic ideas like those expressed in Judge Lumpkin's opinions were clearly in the air well before the Civil War and became increasingly common in the courts of late nineteenth-century police power jurisprudence. But they failed to hold the day in 1859. Cities continued to build and regulate public markets in the 1850s and 1860s and close down private groceries, stands, and butcher shops in which food products were retailed contrary to law.[99] In 1869, Missouri Justice Bliss dismissed counsel's use of Georgia and Minnesota precedents, calling Judge Lumpkin's broad language "peculiar."[100] Such cases "would establish absolute free trade throughout the city in butcher's meats, and indeed in every other commodity, and would render it impossible to keep up the market system for family supplies in cities of the State—a system believed to be, in the larger towns, for the benefit of both seller and buyer, and conducive to the public order, cleanliness, and health." Instead, Bliss rested his legitimation of St. Louis's 1864 prohibition of meat shops outside market limits on the New York precedents of *Bush* and *Webster*.[101] In 1875, the Georgia Supreme Court itself overrode Lumpkin, claiming: "The right of the legislature to regulate trade . . . has been recognized by this court from the time of its organization." Justice Trippe cited Georgia police ordinances regulating carts and wagons in Augusta, prohibiting the cultivation of rice in Savannah, and the licensing of retail liquors in Covington.[102]

The public economy and the notion of regulated trade were thus still crucial parts of American legal discourse in 1875. This is apparent not only in the long lists of prohibited economic activities, but also, occasionally, in the kinds of things lawmakers found it necessary to positively sanction and allow. In 1866, the Louisiana legislature for the first time explicitly *legalized* "private markets, stores, or stands" in New Orleans "for the sale of meats, game, poultry, vegetables, fruit, and fresh fruit."[103] The idea that the private selling of vegetables in New Orleans had to be established by positive law is a good indicator of just how different nineteenth-century notions of polity and economy were from our own. This law aptly captured the prevalent early American view that selling, trade, and occupations were not natural rights or constitutionally protected "pursuits of happiness." They were privileges subject to the larger demands and concerns of well-regulated communities.

Even after the 1866 act legalizing private stores, New Orleans continued to control the sale of food through licensing and a legislative ban on sales within twelve miles of a market house.[104] In *New Orleans v. Stafford* (1875), the Louisiana Supreme Court upheld an injunction against a previously licensed *private* market on St. Peter and Decatur Streets.[105] In doing so, the court had to overcome a new challenge to market regulation—the defendant's claim

that it "creates an involuntary servitude; that it abridges the privileges and immunities of the citizens; that it deprives them of their property under due process of law." The grocer, of course, was invoking the newly minted language of the Thirteenth and Fourteenth Amendments to the United States Constitution. The court responded to this new attack with an old defense of legislative power to regulate:

> [T]he power arises from the nature of things, and is what is termed a police power. It springs from the great principle '*salus populi suprema est lex.*' There is in the defendant's case no room for any well-grounded complaint of the violation of a vested right, for the privilege, if he really possessed it, of keeping a private market, was acquired subordinately to the right existing in the sovereign to exercise the police power to regulate the peace and good order of the city, and to provide for and maintain its cleanliness, and salubrity.

And what of the defendant's right to earn a living? Justice Taliaferro's opinion suggested that "private benefit would have to yield to the public advantage. It would be a perversion of the principles of organized society and regulated liberty to permit an individual to continue a business or occupation endangering the public health in order that he might derive profit from such occupation."[106]

Public market regulations and the broader notions of public economy that lay behind them were alive and well in 1875. But the free trade rhetoric of Judge Lumpkin and the new constitutionalism evident in the defense's argument in *Stafford* expanded in the late nineteenth century. When free trade and constitutionalism were fused together in the rights-conscious years after Reconstruction, a full-fledged challenge to the well-regulated society was born. Ironically, by the time this challenge rose to prominence, a new positivist and federal definition of regulatory power emerged to greet it. Substantive due process and modern administrative regulatory strategies grew up together.[107]

Prior to the Civil War, public market regulations proliferated—infrequently challenged and almost never declared substantively unconstitutional. They were a strong testament to the power of the visions of a well-regulated society and a public economy. It was simply assumed that the state and community had the inherent power to restrict and even prohibit private individuals and shopkeepers from selling meat and produce. The welfare of the people demanded that this basic economic act be performed according to the public standards of the community rather than the private profit motive of the entrepreneur. In most large cities that meant that sales of food were restricted to certain places and times and subject to innumerable conditions. Hawkers,

peddlers, hucksters, forestallers, middlemen, agents, and even honest butchers and grocers (let alone cheats) were prosecuted, fined, and sometimes imprisoned for selling their wares according to the laws of "the market" rather than the regulations of the market house. They were following the dictates of economics but violating the rules of public economy.

A Note on Corporations, Charters, and Contract

The law of the urban marketplace epitomized the nineteenth-century economy's debt to the well-regulated society. But economic regulation was not limited to urban centers or the policing of foodstuffs and necessaries. The laws, ordinances, and regulations of the nineteenth-century polity—what Willard Hurst sometimes emphasized as the "conditions" of freedom—permeated the economy, structuring its basic relationships and controlling its varied activities. The public regulatory histories of commercial, corporation, and contract law are too massive to receive fair treatment in this survey (and are still in search of their historians). Nonetheless, at least a word is necessary to dispel the myth that these economic subjects were primarily matters of private law and interest, beyond the public purview of state police power.

As Patrick Atiyah noted the histories of corporation and contract law are closely linked.[108] Indeed, the legal history of the corporation in the United States begins with the controversial problem of the status of corporate charters. In contemporary "liberal" or "classical" theory, the corporation is simply the normal unit of business—an efficient device for assembling capital. Its legal status and personality is significant only as a convenient juristic mechanism for encouraging commercial and industrial activity.[109] One might expect that this has long been the case, especially in the era of "market revolution." But, as always, it is wise to heed L. P. Hartley's warning: "The past is a foreign country; they do things differently there."[110]

Before the predominance of general incorporation statutes around 1875,[111] most corporations came into being via a special charter from the state legislature. That special, public act signified the corporation's status as a creature of governance. It was as an artificial legal entity dependent upon sovereign authority for existence and power. The right of incorporation as practiced in early America was a special gift (accompanied by special privileges) bestowed by the polity upon select associations as quid pro quo for the performance of special duties and obligations. The essential publicness of this arrangement cannot be denied despite subsequent wranglings over the extent of those privileges and obligations. Indeed, most early American corporate charters were

granted to organizations with a distinct public-utility or community-interest cast. Of the 335 profit-seeking corporations formed before 1800 (317 of which were chartered after 1780), 219 were turnpike, bridge, and canal companies; 67 were banks and insurance companies; and 36 concerned water, fire protection, or harbor facilities.[112] Between 1790 and 1860, 88 percent of Pennsylvania's 2,333 special charters remained in the hands of transport, utility, and financial corporations (only 8 percent went to manufacturing or general business firms).[113] The early American business corporation shared a legal identity and ancestry with such public and quasi-public institutions as municipalities, schools, churches, charities, guilds, and the great trading companies of the sixteenth and seventeenth centuries.

The special charter system was inherently regulatory. Corporations were not citizens possessing natural and absolute rights. They were (in the words of both John Marshall and Roger Taney) "artificial beings" existing only "by force of [state] law" and subject to extensive legislative conditions and restrictions.[114] The early corporate charter was simultaneously a tool of promotion, regulation, and control. An association received important, special benefits of incorporation: (1) a unitary legal personality and concomitant rights to sue and be sued, acquire and liquidate property as a single corporate entity irrespective of changes in ownership; (2) limited liability; and (3) a host of more specific privileges and special-action franchises (e.g., powers of monopoly; eminent domain; rights of way for roads, canals, or railroads; tolltaking). In return, legislatures extracted what Ernst Freund dubbed "an enlarged police power."[115] First, the common law doctrine of *ultra vires* held that corporations (as finite creatures of legislative prerogative) were strictly limited to those powers, objects, and purposes explicitly designated in their charters. Second, legislatures reserved and imposed special statutory conditions regulating general and specific corporate behavior.[116] Finally, and most important, corporations were not immune from the general functioning of state police power— the legislature's ongoing ability to enact regulations for the public safety, morals, health, and welfare.

The basic outlines of this original position of the business corporation in American law are not in dispute.[117] But a string of great constitutional cases— *Dartmouth College* (1819), *Charles River Bridge* (1837), and *Santa Clara* (1886)— has led some legal historians to exaggerate its demise.[118] According to Herbert Hovenkamp, those constitutional developments marked the emergence of the "classical [as in classical economics] corporation."[119] By the 1830s, the corporate regime of special charters, privilege, and regulation is said to have given

way to general incorporation, democracy, and laissez faire. The crucial legal achievements of this process were corporate separation from the state and corporate insulation from government regulation—a status befitting the flagship of free-market capitalism.

The classical liberal story begins with the *Dartmouth College Case* which initiated the great transformation of the business corporation from public into private entity. John Marshall's interpretation of the corporate charter as a "contract" constitutionally protected from retrospective state revision (coupled with Joseph Story's clear delineation of private as opposed to public corporations) advanced the cause of privatization and protection by restricting state "discretion to deal with vested property rights."[120] Together with Jacksonian-era general incorporation laws, the *Charles River Bridge Case* then further normalized the business corporation by vitiating the residual privileged and monopolist characteristics favored by John Marshall in *Dartmouth College*. Whether characterized as a shift from static to dynamic property rights, from the protection of property to the release of creative energy, or from special privilege to general utility, the move from *Dartmouth College* to *Charles River Bridge* usually is interpreted in classic political-economic terms as releasing the corporate entrepreneur to compete and lure capital in a freer marketplace.[121] Finally, *Santa Clara v. Southern Pacific Railroad* sealed this legal revolution by declaring corporations "persons" entitled to the constitutional rights and protections guaranteed by the Fourteenth Amendment.[122] With the emergence of "substantive due process," corporations finally achieved their "natural," economic status as ordinary, private, constitutionally protected enterprises rather than as special, public creations of the state.

While there is no doubt that the corporation became a less exclusive legal institution after 1819, this classical portrait of insistent and inevitable liberalization and privatization is problematic. Indeed, hints of an alternative history appear within the key decisions themselves. Joseph Story's concurrence in *Dartmouth College* famously suggested that states could escape contract clause limitations simply by reserving the right to amend or repeal in every corporate charter.[123] *Charles River Bridge* contained some of Roger Taney's strongest defenses of an open-ended state police power: "The object and end of all government is to promote the happiness and prosperity of the community by which it is established; and it can never be assumed, that the government intended to diminish its power of accomplishing the end for which it was created."[124] Despite some important exceptions, special charters with special conditions remained the rule of American incorporation until the Civil War. Finally, prior

to *Santa Clara* (and for a good bit of time afterward), the generally accepted standard on corporate identity was *Bank of Augusta v. Earle* (1839), in which the Taney Court insisted that the corporation was an artificial state creation, not a "citizen" protected by the privileges and immunities clause of the U.S. Constitution.[125]

Such incongruities beg a substantive revision of the legal evolution of the business corporation that is ultimately beyond the scope of this chapter. Still, three public economy cases at least outline the degree to which nineteenth-century interpretations of contract and corporation remained rooted in the assumptions and practices of the well-regulated society.

Brick Presbyterian Church v. Mayor of New York (1826) and *Coates v. Mayor of New York* (1827) grew out of New York's attempt to regulate cemeteries as nuisances to public health.[126] In 1823, the municipal corporation passed an ordinance prohibiting all burials within city limits. The ordinance essentially divested several important private churches of long-held rights—rights secured by explicit covenants from the city and royal grants and corporate patents dating from the seventeenth century. The Corporation of the Brick Presbyterian Church challenged the ordinance, suggesting that it violated the city's original 1766 conveyance of property for church and cemetery, wherein the municipality covenanted for "quiet use" and enjoyment "without any let or hindrance." In *Coates*, the sexton of Trinity Church produced a similar deed from the city as well as a corporate grant from William III.[127]

Certainly after John Marshall's 1819 decision in *Dartmouth College*, such deeds, covenants, and patents would be constitutionally protected as "contracts," the obligations of which states and localities could not impair. But to the contrary, the New York Supreme Court unambiguously sustained the complete disinterment of the churches' vested property and corporate rights. In *Brick Presbyterian Church*, Justice Savage emphasized the public obligations of the municipality to take "care of the public morals and the public health." The city had no power to covenant or contract away legislative powers and duties of police. The church's covenant for quiet enjoyment was trumped by *salus populi*—the threat the cemetery posed to the "health" and "lives" of the "citizens."[128] The *per curiam* opinion in *Coates* was even more emphatic. This health regulation "repealed all covenants entered into by the corporation incompatible with the by-law." Nevertheless, it was legitimate and constitutional. All local police regulations rested on the city's acknowledged power "so to order the use of private property in the city, as to prevent its proving pernicious to the citizens generally. . . . Every right, from an absolute ownership

in property, down to a mere easement, is purchased and holden subject to the restriction, that it shall be so exercised as not to injure others."[129] The New York cemetery regulation summarily abolished vested rights, annulled previous covenants, and uprooted established customs and expectations; but it was a "salutary application of police powers," not an unconstitutional "taking" of property without compensation or an unconstitutional impairment of the obligation of contracts.[130]

The post–*Dartmouth College* treatment of conveyances, deeds, and grants in the New York cemetery cases was but a prelude to one of the most definitive statements on police power and corporate rights in nineteenth-century law. In *Thorpe v. Rutland and Burlington Railroad Company* (1855), Chief Justice Isaac Redfield sustained an 1849 Vermont statute requiring railroads to fence their lines and maintain cattle guards at farm crossings or be held strictly liable for all damages to animals.[131] Rutland and Burlington Railroad contested the regulation claiming that their 1843 corporate charter was a contract with the state, containing nothing about a costly obligation to erect cattle guards. Redfield responded by directly challenging the misconception that charters (after *Dartmouth College*) granted corporations "immunity and exemption from legislative control." Rather, citing John Marshall and Roger Taney, Redfield insisted the corporate grants be construed strictly—"in favor of the public"—so as not to abridge legislative power to regulate persons and property and "civil institutions adopted for internal government."[132] This was not a contract case or a property case but a police power case concerning the general "law-making power" of free states residing "perpetually and inalienably in the legislature." Isaac Redfield contributed one of the classic definitions: "This police power of the state extends to the protection of the lives, limbs, health, comfort, and quiet of all persons, and the protection of all property within the state [a]ccording to the maxim, *Sic utere tuo ut alienum non laedas*. . . . Persons and property are subjected to all kinds of restraints and burdens, in order to secure the general comfort, health, and prosperity of the state."[133] After listing examples of the "thousand things" legislatures could regulate regarding railroad corporations, Redfield concluded unambiguously that state legislatures had the power "as public exigencies may require, to regulate corporations in their franchises, so as to provide for the public safety."[134] According to Redfield, John Marshall on charters and Joseph Story on corporations did not displace the deeply rooted traditions of public economy and *salus populi*.

To the end of his opinion in *Thorpe*, Redfield appended a series of police power cases (a veritable field guide to the well-regulated society circa 1854),

suggesting that there was no end to such illustrations of "the police of the large cities."[135] He dismissed skeptics with a knowledge and confidence befitting his status as a great jurist:

> One in any degree familiar with this subject would never question the right [of police regulation]. . . . To such men any doubt of the right to subject persons and property to such regulations as the public security and health may require, regardless of merely private convenience, looks like mere badinage. They can scarcely regard the objector as altogether serious. And generally, these doubts in regard to the extent of governmental authority come from those who have had small experience.

In 1895, James Bradley Thayer reproduced Redfield's note in its entirety in his pioneering casebook on American constitutional law, perhaps vainly trying to stave off the badinage and ignorance of late nineteenth-century constitutional idealogues.[136]

What *Commonwealth v. Alger* did for property and police power, *Thorpe v. Rutland* did for corporations and contract. *Salus populi* was the supreme law. Corporations and contract were not above or outside of the general powers of states and localities to regulate for the public welfare. The reification of select constitutional language from a few great Supreme Court cases should not blind us to the continuous mass of nineteenth-century law and legislation regulating and controlling corporate behavior. Such regulations continued right through the supposed golden ages of "laissez-faire constitutionalism," "liberty of contract," and "corporate capitalism." Indeed, two reputed idealogues of postbellum constitutionalism had nothing but good things to say about *Thorpe v. Rutland*. Thomas Cooley made Redfield's opinion the linchpin of his discussion of corporations and police power: "All contracts and all rights, it is held, are subject to this power; and all regulations which affect them may not only be established by the State, but must also be subject to change from time to time, with reference to the general well-being of the community. . . . Rights insured to private corporations by their charters, and the manner of their exercise, are subject to such new regulations as from time to time may be made by the State with a view to the public protection, health, and safety."[137] Christopher Tiedeman added, "It would be an exceedingly liberal, and hence wrongful, construction of the constitutional protection against the impairment of the obligation of contracts, to place corporations above and beyond the ordinary police power of the state."[138]

By the late nineteenth century, the treatises of Cooley and Tiedeman helped solidify the notion advanced in *Thorpe* and the cemetery cases that police

powers could not be "contracted away."[139] That doctrine became known as the "inalienable police power" and it essentially mooted *Dartmouth College*–style arguments about charters limiting state regulatory power. In *Boston Beer Company v. Massachusetts* (1877), the U.S. Supreme Court held that a brewery charter did not preclude the state from subsequently prohibiting altogether the manufacture of intoxicating liquors. A prohibition on offal had the same, drastic ex post facto consequences for the Northwestern Fertilizing Company. Again the Supreme Court sustained the police regulation over vested charter provisions.[140] But ultimately it makes little sense to discuss these decisions now as purely matters of "corporation" or "economic" or "commercial" law. For they were firmly embedded in the long legal histories of public morals and public health to be taken up in the final two chapters of this book. Still, one late nineteenth-century corporation case does capture the tenuous persistence of earlier notions of public economy and corporate responsibility to the general welfare. In 1898 (four years after conviction of Eugene Debs for his role in the notorious Pullman strike), the Illinois Supreme Court declared that Pullman's Palace Car Company (one of the great ogres of American corporate capitalism) had no authority to own an entire "company" town. Such behavior was an *ultra vires* act of the corporation, contrary to the "good public policy" of the state and "incompatible with the theory and spirit of our institutions."[141] Nineteenth-century American corporations were neither self-generating nor self-regulating. They were creatures of law and governance, subject to the visible hand of regulation in a distinctly public economy.

Conclusion

Roger Taney suggested in his argument before Chief Justice Marshall in *Brown v. Maryland* that there was no such thing in American jurisprudence as a vested right to sell. If there had been, Taney argued, one could not only peddle gunpowder in the heart of New York City, but "he may offer hides, fish, and articles of that description, in places offensive and inconvenient to the public, and dangerous to the health of the citizens; he may hold an auction at his own warehouse, and refuse to pay any tax to the State; he may sell at retail; he may sell as a hawker and pedlar."[142] Taney well knew in this argument reductio ad absurdum that no antebellum jurist could accept such consequences. As surely as the Constitution granted the federal government power to regulate interstate commerce, selling, trading, and exchange within a state were subject to long-held state and local regulations of police.

The Blackstonian notion of "public oeconomy" so apparent in Nathan Dane's offenses against public trade was tenacious and inclusive. But even Dane's list of offenses illuminates only the most obvious controls on the early American economy. Additionally, one-seventh of all potential trading, manufacturing, and dealing was immediately restricted by laws limiting activity on Sundays.[143] Pilot, port, and wharfage laws significantly proscribed freedom of action in the nation's harbors.[144] Public safety, health, and morals laws restricted or prohibited the sale of hazardous, noxious, or immoral goods. In addition, large bodies of regulation circumscribed economic activity in areas that remain unexamined here, including taxation, bankruptcy, mills, railroads, banking, insurance, and labor laws.

These police regulations formed the basic outline of early American public economy. Taken together, they reflect a society devoted to a vision of economic relations subject to the larger dictates of community and social mores. An array of local and public officials supervised and cleared the exchange of primary economic goods. Those same goods had often already passed stringent public requirements regarding manufacturing, packaging, and transport. In some communities and cities, almost all modes of selling anything, and a wide variety of other occupations and trades were considered privileges, specially licensed and sanctioned by government. Many economic activities were prohibited because they conflicted with grander social objectives. No business, occupation, trade, or economic activity was immune from the state's police powers for the protection and promotion of public safety, morals, health, comfort, and welfare.

In theory, the nineteenth-century market was "free." In practice, it was "well-ordered" and "well-regulated." The legal and local regulation of economic life in early America was pervasive. The rules of public economy were extremely detailed and were governed by the overarching legal principle that private interest must be made subservient to the public welfare. As judge after judge put it when such regulations were contested in court, *salus populi suprema est lex*—the welfare of the people is the supreme law.

The relationship of public and private, and law and economy in American capitalism are complicated and crucial historical questions—too important to remain hidden beneath resilient national myths about a golden age of contract, possessive individualism, and free enterprise. The common legal notion of public economy uncovered in nineteenth-century statutes, cases, and legal commentaries bears no resemblance to such shibboleths. It reflects a legal culture resistant to the abstract theories of "the state," "the individual," and "the market" at the heart of such myths and committed to understandings of

"property," "rights," and "government" irreducible to the a priori assumptions of neoclassical economics or a negative liberal injunction to leave alone. The form and substance of the early American economy was a product of law and regulation. Capitalism and active governance were not incompatible; they were interdependent. There is nothing natural or private or particularly surprising about the forms of power operating under the aegis of contemporary notions of economics. For the primary relationships of the modern American economy were constructed in the early nineteenth century with the full public powers of police and governance.

Public Ways:
The Legal Construction of Public Space

Smooth the road and make easy the way.—George Washington

Regulations of public safety and public economy were central to the creation of the early American state in the guise of the well-regulated society. But powerful as was their reach into social and economic life, fire and market regulations alone convey a rather limited picture of *salus populi*. Indeed, the ancient origins of overruling necessity and the regulated market house risk leaving the false impression that early American safety and economic policy was but a continuation of age-old habits of local governance. That would be a mistake. The well-regulated society was not a residual colonial communalism but a new and positive extension of police power over society and economy as part and parcel of the establishment of early republican governance.

The best example of the new, creative, and perfectionist (as opposed to old, negative, and preservationist) dimensions of the well-regulated society was the degree to which the early American polity seized control over the nation's infrastructure—its primary mechanisms of transportation, communication, association, and trade. In the early nineteenth century, public officials working in the *salus populi* tradition radically extended governmental powers over roads, rivers, harbors, bridges, buildings, monuments, commons, parks, and marketplaces. They used the governmental rhetoric and legal tools of the well-regulated society to create and carve out distinctly public properties and public spaces. This positive construction of public rights and powers in common

resources bolstered the authority and expanded the jurisdiction of new state governments. It laid the groundwork for a wider assertion of state power throughout the society and economy. Indeed, the development of public thoroughfares and public squares was routinely followed by regulation—a broad-based policing of the streets.

The American story of the invention of public property and the development of a public infrastructure must be seen in the larger context of the emergence of modern states. Sociologist Michael Mann has identified "infrastructural power"—"the capacity of the state actually to penetrate civil society, and to implement logistically political decisions throughout the realm"—as a defining and indispensable element of modern governance. Central to such logistical permeation of society by state (which included such diverse things as literacy, coinage, and weights and measures) was the efficient and controlled transportation of people, goods, and messages via improved roads, waterways, and means of communication.[1] Pasquale Pasquino has rooted most forms of European police regulation in the first attempts of early modern states to take infrastructural control over lands and spaces outside traditional feudal jurisdictions, for example, squares, markets, roads, bridges, rivers.[2] The public recapturing and regulating of these crucial grids of connection, transport, and assembly was a first object of police and modern statecraft. Well into the twentieth century, roads, rivers, ports, and communication networks remained the "measure of civilization"—the measure of nation-states.

Although the context of state-formation was similar, the American version of this infrastructural transformation waited the postrevolutionary establishment of nationhood. In the early nineteenth century, American officials embarked on a concerted and extensive campaign to improve and expand state power over public ways and to imagine, map, and control new public geographies. Parts of this story are familiar to historians. This is the era of internal improvements and "Transportation Revolution." Commonwealth historians from George Rogers Taylor to Carter Goodrich to Harry Scheiber have explored in marvelous detail the explosion of public interest and investment in great infrastructural works like the Cumberland Road, the Ohio and Erie Canals, and ubiquitous local efforts to encourage turnpike and railroad development.[3] Such studies challenge theories of governmental "drift and default," and demonstrate the importance of a comprehensive system of public improvements to early American economic development.

While social historians have tended to downplay macrolevel changes in economy, transportation, and communications, they have remained quite attuned to the cultural significance of the policing of public space. Elizabeth

Blackmar, Mary Ryan, and David Scobey, for example, have depicted public spaces (e.g., squares, parks, main streets, promenades, riverfronts) as one of the key nineteenth-century terrains for the playing out of the cultural politics of race, class, and gender.[4] The American system of public infrastructural development, in other words, had powerful social-regulatory as well as economic-promotional dimensions. The creation, regulation, and policing of public space and property was central not only to early American state building, but to the general conduct of economic and social life. The relationship between the abridging of distance (whether by technological change or concerted governmental investment) and the formation of national, sectional, and cultural identities was fundamental.

The cultural and morals policing of streets, inns, and theaters will be addressed in the next chapter. For now, I would like to concentrate on the initial problem of the legal construction of publicity—the way public officials as part of a vast American transportation and improvements revolution first established the public's priority and stake in properties of connection, mobility, exchange, and communication.[5] In particular, this chapter will investigate the juridical creation and protection of public rights in some taken-for-granted settings: roads, rivers, ports, and squares. Today public powers and rights in such locales seem self-evident. But the outcome of nineteenth-century policy was more in dispute. There was, after all, nothing *inherently public* about a highway or riverway. "Publicness" had to be constructed and defended in a political and social milieu fraught with conflict and tension. Nineteenth-century towns and populations expanded and moved through spaces and properties that for long periods of time had been considered exclusively private. The process of building public thruways, bridges, wharfs, and even parks involved the public expropriation and extinguishment of preexisting rights, usages, and expectations.[6] The invention of public space was contested terrain in the early nineteenth century, requiring a full deployment of the rhetorics and techniques of the well-regulated society.

Roads, rivers, and ports were singled out early as territory for the extension and elaboration of state powers of police. As bearers of valuable social resources like mobility, communication, and commerce, public "highways"[7] aroused the attention and the passions of the new nation's leading politicians and jurists. In *Federalist* No. 14 James Madison endorsed immediate infrastructural improvement:

The intercourse throughout the Union will be daily facilitated by new improvements. Roads will everywhere be shortened, and kept in better

order; accommodations for travelers will be multiplied and meliorated; an interior navigation on our eastern side will be opened. . . . The communication between the western and Atlantic districts . . . will be rendered more and more easy, by those numerous canals, with which the beneficence of nature has intersected our country, and which art finds it so little difficult to connect and complete.[8]

Madison's enthusiasm for connection, intersection, communication, navigation, and intercourse as a foundation for union and good government echoed throughout the period. Joseph Angell's pioneering treatise on the *Law of Highways* invoked French police theorist Jean Domat: rivers and ports were gifts of God securing "communication with all the world."[9] They were "gates of the republic" and "facilities to husbandry, commerce, and manufactures" on which the growth and prosperity of a well-regulated society depended.[10] Francis Lieber devoted a full chapter of his founding political textbook to "Communion—Locomotion, Emigration," arguing that connection and communication were "indispensable elements of all advancing humanity."[11] Early American police and civil policy had among their principal objects not only the creation of well-regulated cities and towns, but the establishment of ordered connections between them "by thoroughfares."[12] As Albert Gallatin confessed in 1807, the public significance of roads and rivers was so "universally admitted, as hardly to require any additional proofs."[13]

Such police rhetoric reflected a deeper legal and governmental reality. Nineteenth-century statute books were swollen with legislation regarding highways, internal improvements, and infrastructure. Almost every state that revised its statutes in the 1830s and 1840s provided a separate title for "Highways, Bridges, and Ferries" where they dictated the procedure for laying out public roads, appointed officers for the superintendence of highways and bridges, specified persons liable to work on highways, provided for assessments, and enumerated the regulations and penalties attending the obstruction of public ways.[14] Cities and towns were separately incorporated with elaborate and open-ended powers to "regulate, keep in repair, and alter the streets, highways, bridges, wharves and slips."[15] Nineteenth-century ferry regulations were paradigms for the kind of minute and controlling detail that suffused the well-regulated society. An 1810 New York statute regulating rates on the New York City–Nassau Island ferry was typical:

For every fat ox, steer or bull, twenty-five cents, for all other neat cattle eighteen cents, the ferry-master to find the necessary head ropes to fasten

and secure the cattle in the boats; for every dead calf, hog or sheep, two cents; for every lamb, pig or shote, one cent; for every quarter of beef, three cents; for every firkin of butter, lard or tallow, two cents; for every other package of butter, lard or tallow, per cwt. three cents; for every ham, an half cent; for every bale of cotton or wool, ten cents; for every crate of earthen ware, twelve cents and an half; for every bear skin, dry hide or horse skin, an half cent; for every cask of flax seed, dry beans or peas of seven bushels, seven cents; for every hundred oysters or clams, one cent; for every sheaf of straw, an half cent; for every one horse chaise with standing top, thirty-one cents; for every hundred bricks, six cents; for every full trunk or chest four feet long, six cents; three feet long four cents; for every full trunk or chest two feet long, two cents, all under, one cent; for every empty trunk or chest of the above sizes, half the above rates; for every bookcase or cupboard, twenty-five cents; for every secretary, bookcase or chest of drawers, twenty cents; for every mahogany dining table, eights cents; for every tea or card table, four cents; of other kind of wood, half of the above rates; for every piano forte, twenty cents; for every mahogany bedstead, four cents; of other wood, two cents; for every clock and case, twenty-five cents; for every sideboard, thirty-seven cents and an half; for every mahogany settee, twenty cents; of other wood, six cents; for every feather bed, three cents; for every cat-tail or straw bed, one cent; for every matrass of hair or wool, two cents; for every looking glass the plate six feet long, fifty cents; five feet long or upwards, eight cents; three feet, six cents; two feet, two cents; all under, one cent; for every chaldron of coals, fifty cents; for every cord of nutwood, eighty cents; for every cord of oak or other wood, seventy cents; for every kettle of milk of eight gallons or upwards, two cents; for every empty milk kettle, one cent; for every musket or fowling piece, one cent; for every large or horse boat of household furniture where a single boat is required, one hundred and fifty cents; for every ton of hemp or flax, sixty-two cents and an half; for every ton of cordage, sixty-two cents and an half; for every ream of paper one cent; for every fruit or other tree more than six or less than ten feet long, an half cent; all under, one quarter cent; flowers or shrubs in pots or boxes, an half cent; for every corpse of an adult, twenty-five cents; of children, twelve cents and an half; for every cheese, one quarter cent; for every dog, four cents; for every hundred of pipe staves or heading, fifteen cents; for every hundred of hogshead staves or heading, twelve cents and an half; for every hundred

of barrel staves or heading, eight cents; for every hundred weight of hay, ten cents.[16]

In 1846, New York synthesized its general canal laws and regulations in a 129-page volume containing some 500 separate provisions.[17] Add the surfeit of charters granted to corporations for the construction of roads, turnpikes, bridges, ferries, and canals, and it should be clear that public property and public highways were major preoccupations of the early American state.

The public and police significance of roads and waterways was not lost on jurists and legal commentators. In William Blackstone's classic description of offenses against "the public order and oeconomical regimen of the state," he went first to "*highways, bridges,* and public *rivers.*"[18] Horace Wood, who perhaps better than anyone in the period understood the importance of public as opposed to private nuisances, devoted much of his treatise to the exploration of public nuisances in highways and navigable streams.[19] After the Civil War, Thomas Cooley and John Dillon continued the legal tradition of beginning discussions of state power in nineteenth-century America with an exploration of public authority over public ways.[20] Indeed, most of the formative legal cases of the nineteenth century involved transportation, infrastructure, or public properties and utilities. Excluding ubiquitous railroad cases, the list still includes *Palmer v. Mulligan* (1805), *Callender v. Marsh* (1823), *Gibbons v. Ogden* (1824), *Willson v. Black-Bird Creek Marsh Company* (1829), *New York v. Miln* (1837), *Charles River Bridge Case* (1837), *Commonwealth v. Tewksbury* (1846), *Passenger Cases* (1849), *Commonwealth v. Alger* (1851), *Cooley v. Board of Wardens* (1851), *Genesee Chief v. Fitzhugh* (1851), *Wheeling Bridge Case* (1852), *Munn v. Illinois* (1877), and *Pensacola Telegraph Co. v. Western Union Telegraph Co.* (1877).[21]

This chapter explores this extensive legal tradition of police regulation in roads, rivers, and other public properties. If the overarching lesson of fire and market regulations concerned the *relative* nature of private rights (especially when in conflict with public safety, economy, and welfare), regulations of public space reflected the *absolute* nature of public rights in the well-regulated society. Indeed, perhaps in no other area of nineteenth-century social and economic life was state power wielded so effectively and unambiguously to define and uphold the rights of the public. By midcentury, courts, legislatures, and common councils made it perfectly clear that private claims to public properties and spaces would always be trumped by the great public objectives of regulated and improved transportation, communication, and assembly. In the process, these legal actions and reasonings poured new content and

meaning into that tortuous and elusive adjective "public" that came to define the early American way.

Roadways

The simplest meaning of "public" is nonprivate. Consequently, the first hurdle confronting the publicization of early American roadways was their original status as private property. At the start of the nineteenth century, the ownership of the land constituting roads (and, by analogy, navigable rivers) remained in the hands of adjacent landowners. As James Kent stated the original common law rule, the "owners of the land on each side go to the centre of the road, and they have exclusive right to the soil."[22] Title to lands making up the highway belonged to bordering property owners as part of their private domain. The public acquired only an "easement" in the road—what Kent described aptly as "charges on one estate for the benefit of another."[23] In this case, the easement was "the right of passage" for the benefit of the public. Horace Wood summed up the system: "At the common law, the only right which the public acquired in highways was that of passage over it, and any interference with the soil, other than that necessary to the full enjoyment of this right, . . . [was] regarded as an interference with the rights of the owner of the fee."[24]

Thus, the establishment of public jurisdiction over streets and roads first necessitated an aggressive use of state power to extinguish private, common law claims and expand the public easement. Invoking the *salus populi* tradition, nineteenth-century jurists did just that. They dissolved vested interests and private property rights and reinvented the roadway as a distinctly public phenomenon, an object of governance and police. By 1857, Joseph Angell expanded the public easement to include "the more general purposes of sewerage, the distribution of light and water, and the furtherance of public morality, health, trade, and convenience."[25] Horace Wood similarly flipped public/private priorities by 1875, arguing that "the public easement is superior to all other rights, and no one has any right to impair it in the slightest degree—not even the owner of the soil."[26] The construction of this strong public tradition in the American rules of the road had three separate components: the initial assertion of publicity, the subsequent policing of newly established public rights, and the expansion of public remedies.

The initial assertion of a highway's publicity was a product of two rather arcane but enormously important jurisprudential developments: the revival of Matthew Hale's concept of public rights in public ways and the simultaneous

expansion of the doctrine of implied dedication. Historians Harry Scheiber and Molly Selvin have demonstrated the power and reach of Matthew Hale's manuscripts "*De Jure Maris*" and "*De Portibus Maris*" in nineteenth-century American law.[27] In those two works on public waterways and highways, Hale basically argued that beyond the private rights (*jus privatum*) of adjacent property owners, there existed public rights (*jus publicum*) in certain rivers, ports, and roads that could not be violated. Public highways had to be "free and open for subjects and foreigners." They were not subject to the private whim of titleholders. Hale entrusted the sovereign with the ultimate "patronage and protection" of such *juris publici* (common highways, common bridges, common rivers, and common ports). It was an obligation of governance to police such public properties, preventing all impediments and nuisances that might "damnify the public."[28]

Hale's ideas manifested themselves in American case law as strong statements of the sovereign's prerogative regarding public ways. Chief Justice Gibson of the Pennsylvania Supreme Court best captured this commonwealth theory of public property in 1851:

> To the Commonwealth here, as to the king in England, belongs the franchise of every highway as a trustee for the public; and streets . . . are as much highways as are rivers, railroads, canals, or public roads laid out by the authority of a municipal corporation. In England a public road is called the king's highway; and though it is not usually called the Commonwealth's highway here, it is so in contemplation of law, for it exists only by force of the Commonwealth's authority. . . . Every highway, toll or free, is licensed, constructed, and regulated by the immediate or delegated action of the sovereign power; and in every Commonwealth the people in the aggregate constitute the sovereign.[29]

Such a theory of sovereign control over highways gave the state "full power to provide all proper regulations of police to govern the actions of persons using them." It took away from all private persons (adjacent property owners as well as passersby) any private interest in the way. As Wood put it, "No person can acquire a private easement in a public highway." Private rights were "in abeyance and subject to the superior rights of the public."[30]

Hale's public rights and Gibson's sovereign prerogative greatly enhanced public powers over existing streets and roads. Indeed, by midcentury they essentially destroyed anything left of private claims to the road and deemed it a fundamentally public property. But such doctrines did not actually bring new properties into the public sphere. For that purpose, another legal technique

was much more effective.[31] The doctrine of implied dedication loosened the requirements for establishing a road's essential publicness in the first place.[32]

Public roads were not built on neutral space; they were carved out through previously private lands, necessitating a public expropriation of private right. The doctrine of implied dedication accomplished this (without the compensation demanded of eminent domain) by holding that when a property owner left his land open to public travel for a certain period of time, the courts could infer an intention to dedicate this land to public use.[33] Simple acquiescence, time, or the selling of lots could be used by judges to create this public priority. Historian Carol Rose has gone so far as to venture that the only thing a landowner could do to prevent an implication of public access and control was to make the way "physically impassable."[34]

Indeed, early nineteenth-century courts defended a presumption that roads had been dedicated to public use. They were extremely reluctant to support assertions of age-old private rights. In *State v. Wilkinson* (1829), for example, Curtis Wilkinson was indicted for erecting a building on a common highway through the public square of the village of St. Albans, Vermont.[35] Wilkinson argued that his ancestor Silas Hathaway had never formally dedicated the land to public use, and that consequently it was his to do with as he wished. The Vermont Supreme Court disagreed finding an implied dedication: "If the way is of public convenience and has been treated by the public without interruption, a presumption arises of their right, and a dedication of it to them by the owner may be inferred."[36] Public use of the property as a highway for thirty years grew into an irreversible and preeminent public right. Throughout the nineteenth-century, similar doubts as to title and dedication were resolved overwhelmingly in favor of public property. The consequences could be enormous. Private ferry-houses, stables, homes, walls, and other buildings constructed on what landowners thought was their own property could be pulled down for violating the public easement and interfering with common right.[37]

The pulling down of private structures signals the second component in the consolidation of public power over public ways—the policing of newly created rights of public access and thoroughfare. An effective infrastructure depended not only on the transformation of private property into public highway, but on the state's subsequent ability to guarantee and defend public transportation and communication from impediments. Public roads had to be kept free of private intrusions, usurpations, and obstructions. That became another important job for the common law of public nuisance.

The public power to remove and abate nuisances and encroachments on highways was a crucial instrument of sovereignty and an important develop-

ment in early American law. Indeed, the legal power to abate highway nuisances complemented (and, in some of its ramifications, surpassed) the state power of eminent domain. While the law of eminent domain held that the state could expropriate private property with adequate compensation, the encroachment doctrine held that the inverse case was not possible. A private individual could not expropriate the public (and, therefore, preeminent) domain. Public rights in roads and waterways were inviolable. Moreover, there was nothing particularly trivial or obscure about highway "encroachments" or "obstructions" in the early nineteenth century. Though fines for common nuisances were sometimes small, the abatement and destruction of costly buildings and wharves entailed public sanctions of the highest order.[38]

The leading early American case of an obstructive nuisance to a public road was *People v. Cunningham* (1845).[39] Cunningham was the owner of a Brooklyn distillery that since 1810 had been delivering excess slops to farmers via a peculiar but efficient technology. Iron pipes ran out of the distillery ("at a sufficient elevation to be above the heads of persons passing on the sidewalk") and into the street, where slops were discharged into casks in waiting carts and wagons.[40] The state asserted that the long lines of wagons obstructing Front Street from early morning to late evening amounted to a public nuisance. The expansive "obstruction to streets" rationale reached all kinds of noxious conduct. Evidence was admitted on the noisome effects of this whole process of delivering slops, the "great quantities of offensive filth in the street" and the "offensive smells and stenches." The whole disordered scene clashed with the vision of a well-regulated society: "From an early hour in the morning until late in the evening every day the street at this point was thronged with teams of 'swill-drivers,' waiting to be served by the defendants, the drivers of which indulged in coarse and obscene language and crowded and fought for priority, and travel upon the street was constantly and greatly impeded."[41] Obstructing the right of way was important, but Cunningham was also guilty of offending a range of community sensibilities from order and morality to health and aesthetics.

Despite the private rights involved, despite the efficiency and convenience of this mode of delivering slops, despite the fact that the distillery had been operating this way for thirty-five years, and despite the fact that it would greatly injure the defendant's business and dependent trades and commerce, the New York court ordered the public nuisance abated. Justice Jewett reasoned, "The citizens in general have a right of passage in the street or highway . . . to its utmost extent unobstructed by any impediments."[42] The court admitted that this "mode of delivery was decidedly preferable, as well for pri-

vate as public convenience," and that "this business [could] not be carried on in any other manner at that place so advantageously either to individuals or the public." Still, in legally absolutist rather than economically instrumental fashion, it held the defendant "could not legally carry on any part of his business in the public street."[43] One could not "eke out the inconvenience of his own premises by taking the public highway."[44] Jewett concluded with Kent's open-ended endorsement of the well-regulated society: "Private interest must be made subservient to the general interest of the community."[45]

Cunningham was a clear victory for state police power over public highways, defending several important principles of publicity. First, public rights of passage and convenience were absolute. Time, habit, or even formal municipal acquiescence did not legitimate private intrusions on public rights. The fact that Cunningham had been doing business like this for thirty-five years with the explicit sanction of the Brooklyn city council did not weaken the public's claim to the highway.[46] Cunningham's customary right was expropriated, for there could be no such thing as a vested right to obstruct public roads. The displacement of Cunningham's customary private rights by an absolute rendering of public rights was followed up with a broad-based defense of public power to police the streets. Was Cunningham prosecuted simply for blocking a public way? More likely it was the general character of this public inconvenience—the filth, the stench, the general disorderliness. The prosecution of public property nuisances and the power to remove highway encroachments were effective mechanisms of broader social and cultural regulation. The policing of the streets was but prelude to a general extension of police powers throughout American economy and society.

People v. Cunningham did not stand alone. In *State v. Morris and Essex Railroad Company* (1852) and *Morton v. Moore* (1860), a railroad and a sawmill bore the brunt of the courts' hostility to private obstructions on public ways.[47] In *Morris and Essex Railroad*, the court ordered a building torn down and several railroad cars removed, warning that a railroad's corporate identity brought no special privileges to intrude on the public domain. It required no great ingenuity, the court declared, to show that "a company, as such," was guilty of a public nuisance when it annoyed or impaired "the common rights of the community."[48] In *Morton*, the court denounced the sawmill's sixty-year practice of abusing the *jus publicum*, arguing that "the right of the public in a common highway is paramount and controlling."[49] Even milldams, by all accounts a most favored form of property in statute law and private adjudication, did not fare well when public rights were at stake.[50] In *Dygert v. Schenk* (1840), the defendant allowed a bridge covering his millrace that crossed the

public road to fall into disrepair.[51] The court ruled that he "came short of his obligation to the public. . . . Any act of an individual done to a highway, though performed on his own soil, if it detract from the safety of travelers, is a nuisance." The court excoriated the defendant's selfishness: "Things began and ended in himself; the land, the mill, the water, the raceway, the profit, and therefore the bridge. The public [derived] nothing but mischief."[52] In *Dimmett v. Eskridge* (1819), the Virginia court upheld the right of a private citizen to cut down a milldam obstructing both the Great Cacepehon River and a public road "to the great damage and *common nuisance* of the Citizens of [the] Commonwealth."[53]

In a host of similar cases, early American state courts defended the principles of public rights in public property. The Michigan Supreme Court refused to interpret an 1807 act of the state legislature giving property owners ten feet for the erection of steps, porches, and awnings as vesting rights in proprietors. The court cited forty years of English and American jurisprudence against making public rights "subservient to the convenience or cupidity of individuals."[54] In Massachusetts and Maine, judges resisted attempts to limit public rights solely to the traveled part of the road: "obligation to the public . . . required the full and entire use of the whole located highway."[55] Chief Justice Shaw extended these doctrines to turnpikes.[56] Similar judicial reasonings accompanied defenses of public rights against lesser obstructions like stones, logs, steps, ditches, and fences.[57]

This body of case law vigorously defended the well-regulated society's interests in a publicly controlled infrastructure. Throughout the period, courts refused to allow private businesses, be they millowners, distillery owners, railroads, or auctioneers, to encroach on the commonwealth's highways. The arguments were unequivocal. Private individuals would not be allowed to benefit by appropriating what belonged to the public. In *Commonwealth v. Passmore*, the Pennsylvania court urged that one's private "emoluments or inconvenience can have no weight, when they come in competition with the established rights of the community at large." It endorsed instead the higher social obligations of *sic utere tuo*: "He is bound to exercise the duties of his station without injuring the rights of others."[58] A New York court opted for the even stronger public admonition of Lord Denman to rebut a railroad's arguments from utility: "In the infinite variety of active operations always going forward in this industrious community, no greater evil can be conceived than the encouragement of capitalists and adventurers to interfere with known public rights from motives of personal interest."[59] Such pervasive regard for public rights and hostility to private intrusions cannot be reconciled with

purely instrumentalist or vested rights theories of early American law. Rather, they were part of a police and regulatory tradition fundamental to economic development, social regulation, and the emergence of an early American state.

The third and final component anchoring this potent public property regime was a willingness to expand available procedures and legal remedies to defend public rights and powers in public highways. Traditional indictments and abatements were powerful weapons against private intrusions on public ways. But early nineteenth-century courts also developed two alternative technologies to promote and protect community prerogative: the use of the equity injunction and the doctrine *damnum absque injuria* (an injury without a remedy). Though matters of somewhat complicated and technical doctrinal development, these two legal inventions had a huge impact on the early American creation of public properties. They also illustrated just how far early nineteenth century courts were prepared to go to protect new public rights and powers in the new nation's transportation and communications network.

The equity injunction was one of the most powerful legal remedies available in the early republic. Indeed equity's summary, juryless mode of justice placed so much remedial discretion in the hands of chancellors that it supposedly relinquished its criminal jurisdiction with the abolition of the infamous English Court of Star Chamber in 1641. Nonetheless, early American jurists enlisted criminal equity and its potent injunctive remedies in their fight against private encroachments on public ways.[60] Judges cleared the way for this public equity revival by building on the somewhat improbable legal notion of purpresture, lending credence to Mr. Dooley's observation that in the hands of a lawyer, the brick wall can indeed become a triumphal arch.

In English common law, purpresture denoted a very special kind of public nuisance—an encroachment upon the king and his demesne lands. Since the king was considered the owner of public lands, an encroacher upon public property in England essentially violated two different kinds of rights—the private rights of the Crown (as property owner) as well as public rights of travel and passage (a public obligation of sovereignty). Loath to deny the king a legal remedy available to all other property owners, English courts began to carve out purpresture as a special exception to the usual prohibition on the equity injunction in criminal cases. From 1795 English courts began to uphold the power of the attorney general acting on behalf of the Crown to enjoin encroachments and obstructions on public ways.[61]

In importing and expanding this doctrine, American jurists had to overcome the fact that private encroachments on highways, rivers, and harbors in the United States entailed no similar violation of a regent's personal right.

Jurists resolved this problem by ignoring it, decidedly shifting the basis for equity jurisdiction away from property (albeit royal property) concerns and toward a more general protection of the people's welfare. Public power over public property became matters of policy and sovereignty, not title, charter rights, or the state's capacity as landowner.[62]

Following Joseph Story's endorsement of equity's "more complete and perfect" remedies, American judges invoked the injunctive remedy to restrain all kinds of encroachments on public lands and ways.[63] In *Commonwealth v. Rush* a perpetual injunction was granted to prevent the erection of a house on the public's square.[64] Justice Hepburn of the Pennsylvania Supreme Court based equity jurisdiction on the irreparable mischief threatened by the appropriation of "the property of the public to private use."[65] Alabama and Georgia used the injunction to prohibit the building of elaborate market houses and other structures across old rights of way in Mobile and Columbus.[66] And the injunction was applied with equal vigor against encroachments on public rivers, where even much needed milldams were enjoined when they interfered with public navigation and welfare.[67] Once again, utility was not the measure of public rights. Mills, market houses, aqueducts, railroads, and other important commercial enterprises met "the strong arm of the Court" when they encroached on public ways. Though some legal historians have argued that public nuisance doctrine was primarily a vehicle for protecting private capital,[68] the forceful use of the equity injunction against highway obstructions suggests an alternative objective: the creation and protection of public rights and state interests in an emerging national infrastructure. Though private rights were clearly placed at greater risk through the adoption of equity's summary processes, courts invoked *salus populi*—the "political maxim . . . that individual interests must yield to that of the many."[69] Potent remedies were needed "to compel persons so to use their own property as not to injure others."[70]

Another legal weapon employed in the fight to protect public rights from private interference was the common law doctrine *damnum absque injuria* (an injury without a remedy). In an important and intriguing turn in the public law of the road, courts made it exceedingly difficult to collect private damages as a consequence of the ubiquitous public works projects of the early nineteenth century. When public officials interfered with private rights in repairing or altering highways, courts increasingly refused to grant private property owners damages or compensation, arguing that such private injuries warranted no public remedies. *Damnum absque injuria* and the complementary notion of "consequential injury" insulated the public sector from a slew of

private damage claims and helped establish the jurisprudential distinctiveness and priority of public powers—an important ingredient in early American state building.

The proximate common law origin of *damnum absque injuria* was the English case *Governor v. Meredith* (1792).[71] There English pavers changed the grade of a street, forcing the plaintiffs to heighten an arch admitting wagons to their warehouses. Chief Justice Kenyon denied an action for damages, warning that it would jeopardize every turnpike act, paving act, and navigation act in the kingdom. Justice Buller issued a famous concurrence: "There are many cases in which individuals sustain an injury, for which the law gives no action; for instance, pulling down houses or raising bulwarks for the preservation and defence of the kingdom against the king's enemies. . . . This is one of those cases to which the maxim applies, *salus populi suprema est lex.*"[72] *Meredith* held that the common law would tolerate without remedy extensive interferences with private rights when the public welfare demanded.

The early American transportation revolution involved some radical interferences with just such private rights. In the influential case *Callender v. Marsh* (1823), the regrading of a Boston street laid bare the foundation of a private dwelling house forcing a costly rebuilding.[73] Nonetheless, Chief Justice Parker found the surveyor's actions authorized by statute and well within the "right use of property already belonging to the public."[74] The damage sustained by the homeowner was not a "taking" of private property deserving compensation under Article 10 of the Massachusetts Constitution, for that article had "ever been confined . . . to the case of property actually taken and appropriated by government." Rather, the government was merely making "right use" of property already belonging to the public, which included the power to "repair and amend the street . . . to make the passage safe and convenient." The injury sustained by the plaintiff in the process was "indirect," "consequential," and *damnum absque injuria.*[75] As in the New York fire cases, sometimes the forceful promotion of the public welfare entailed private, uncompensated costs. The road to a national public infrastructure would not be held hostage to private damage claims.

Although much has been made of some famous dissents to the rule in *Callender v. Marsh* (most importantly Chancellor Kent's opinion in *Gardner v. Newburgh*), it remained the dominant doctrine into the late nineteenth century.[76] Courts continued to evaluate cases of private damage from public works not from the perspective of property rights and eminent domain, but in terms of the police powers and sovereign prerogatives belonging to the state to

promote the people's welfare through well-regulated public thruways. In *Radcliff's Executors v. Mayor of Brooklyn*, Chief Justice Bronson summed up the rule of *damnum absque injuria* in public works cases:

> If any one will take the trouble to reflect, he will find it a very common case, that the property of individuals suffers an indirect injury from the constructing of public works; and yet I find but a single instance of providing for the payment of damages in such a case. . . . The construction of the Erie Canal destroyed the business of hundreds of tavern-keepers and common carriers between Albany and Buffalo, and greatly depreciated the value of their property, and yet they got no compensation. . . . Railroads destroy the business of stage proprietors, and yet no one has ever thought a railroad charter unconstitutional, because it gave no damages to stage owners. The Hudson river railroad will soon drive many fine steamboats from the river; but no one will think the charter void because it does not provide for the payment of damages to the boat owners. A fort, jail, workshop, fever hospital, or lunatic asylum, erected by the government, may have the effect of reducing the value of a dwelling house in the immediate neighborhood; and yet no provision for compensating the owner of the house has ever been made in such a case.[77]

Other grand statements in this *damnum absque injuria* tradition included *Charles River Bridge* (1837) and *Barron v. Baltimore* (1833). In the former, Chief Justice Taney refused to compensate the proprietors of the Charles River Bridge when they were disfranchised by the new, improved, and free Warren Bridge arguing that if all private injuries suffered on account of new public works were compensated, "we shall be thrown back to the improvements of the last century, and obliged to stand still, . . . [unable] to partake of the benefit of those improvements which are now adding to the wealth and prosperity, and the convenience and comfort, of every other part of the civilized world." In the latter, Chief Justice Marshall refused compensation to a wharf owner left high and dry by a Baltimore harbor project lowering water levels. Marshall argued famously that the Fifth Amendment's takings provision applied only to the general government and not to the states.[78]

Like *Callendar* and *Radcliff*, these classic cases were not simply about takings or limited liability or the creative and instrumental destruction of vested property rights. Rather, these cases were argued and decided squarely within a vibrant and expansive tradition of state power and police. A key part of that tradition was the refusal of courts to restrict themselves to a private jurispru-

dence of Right—Injury—Compensation. Instead of reasoning upward from private rights and particular injuries, these decisions reasoned downward from autonomous conceptions of state powers, public rights, and the general welfare of the society. If some private individuals were injured as a consequence of public-spirited improvements, early American judges were comfortable leaving them without a remedy. *Damnum absque injuria* was not a hole in their jurisprudence, it was a solution.[79] In the creation of a powerful tradition of regulated public space and public property, this solution meshed perfectly with concomitant changes in the laws of dedication, purpresture, and public nuisance. Private rights were relative; public rights were absolute. Such doctrines were crucial to the emergence of an early American state tradition that went well beyond the common law negotiation of private conflicts and economic transactions.

Riverways

Given the condition of most early American roads (one Ohio maintenance statute required that stumps be cut to within one foot of the road surface),[80] rivers assumed even greater importance in early American economy and society. Indeed, it is almost impossible to overestimate the significance of rivers in the settlement of towns and cities, the marketing of crops, and the migration of populations. In 1818, two thirds of the market crops in South Carolina were harvested within five miles of a river.[81] Before 1820, most of the population of Ohio huddled around the Ohio River and its tributaries.[82] As Joseph Angell awkwardly rhapsodized, to rivers "has the public at large been extensively indebted for the easy and convenient communication by them afforded, between the maritime cities and the rapidly growing productive regions of the interior. They have imparted energy to the enterprising genius of the people, and been the means of transforming deserts and forests into cultivated and fruitful fields, flourishing settlements, and opulent cities."[83]

Consequently, rivers, like roads, became a key site for the exertion of state power over grids of transportation and communication. Once again, the first step to asserting state regulatory power over rights in rivers hinged on the legal declaration of a river as public highway. This was a trickier enterprise with waterways than with roadways. Without denying the variety encountered on American roads, it was relatively easy to categorize them legally as either public or private. In contrast, waterways ran the gamut from majestic seaports hosting the largest international vessels to trickling streams and brooks

navigated only by crayfish and salamanders. Drawing lines and allocating public and private rights was a more difficult and variegated business.

For most American jurists, the starting point for sorting out the tangled relationship of public and private in rivers was the English common law. Though English experience was diverse, most acknowledged that the test of a river's publicness in England was "navigability," which the common law equated with the ebb and flow of the tide.[84] Waters that moved with the tide were regarded as "navigable"—distinctly public and under the control and regulations of the Crown. Waters resisting the fluctuations of the tide were "nonnavigable" and under local or private control. Given England's island status, this legal equation of navigability, tidewater, and publicness had a reasonable basis in reality and policy. Most rivers capable of useful, public navigation by boats were more than likely affected by the tide. But from an American perspective the common law rule equating navigability with tidewater made little sense (especially as settlement moved westward). If strictly construed, the tidewater rule immunized America's great inland rivers—the Mississippi, Ohio, Susquehanna, and Hudson—from public regulation. Almost immediately, American courts, legislatures, and commentators began searching for a way around the stringent requirements of the common law rule.

Once again, Matthew Hale came to their assistance. In *"De Jure Maris,"* Hale portrayed an English common law experience in ports and rivers much more diverse, flexible, and public than implied by the natural rule of tidewaters.[85] Hale admitted that riparian owners had property interests in nontidewater streams, but he refused to see such rivers as insulated from public use and regulation: "There be other rivers, as well fresh as salt, that are of common or publick use for the carriage of boats and lighters. And these, whether they are fresh or salt, whether they flow and reflow or not, are *prima facie publici juris,* common highways for man or goods or both from one inland town to another."[86] Hale made it clear that the common law equation of navigability and tidewater did not mean that other rivers and streams were unburdened by a public easement of passage and special restrictions for the public safety and convenience.

Early American jurists and public officials took their cue from Hale's expansive conception of public waterways, applying to riverways the same range of public remedies, powers, and rights applied to early American roadways.[87] Hale offered a way around "the absurdity of applying the supposed Common Law to our great rivers, measuring their navigability [and publicness] by the ebb and flow of the tide."[88] Invoking Hale, American courts and legislators

moved steadily toward making most American rivers, navigable *in fact*, susceptible to public jurisdiction and state power.[89] In some jurisdictions, mere "floatability"—the ability of a stream to carry logs or other products—became the measure for public easements and regulatory claims.[90] The result was a complete repudiation of the limited common law definition of navigability. Like roads, most American rivers came to be seen as public rather than private property, serving common rather than individual interests. This fundamental, redistributive shift in the definition of early American public waterways was accomplished without paying compensation to riparian owners. In the well-regulated society, important lines of communication, prosperity, mobility, and intercourse were to be controlled by the state, not private decision makers.

When looking at early nineteenth-century riparian law, legal historians have made much of courts' instrumentalist tendency to favor large and efficient, private developmental interests in the release of capitalist energies.[91] According to this interpretation, when private interests clashed, as they did in the paradigmatic water rights case *Palmer v. Mulligan* (1805), courts usually sided with the newer and larger developmental enterprise. The problem with such a private and economic determinist interpretation of riparian law, however, is that it ignores the larger public law context of the well-regulated society. In the early nineteenth century, private riparian disputes took place on a terrain increasingly being redefined as the exclusive province of public prerogative and police power.

Palmer v. Mulligan involved a private law dispute between millowners on New York's Hudson River.[92] The plaintiff charged that the defendant's newer and larger upstream dam obstructed his flow of water and damaged his forty-year-old sluiceway and mill. The New York Supreme Court's denial of relief to the old downstream millowner usually has been interpreted as a key episode in the liberalization of the common law rules of priority and natural use in the interest of private, economic development—"one of the best instances of the emerging [instrumentalist] legal mentality."[93] Things look a bit different, however, in the context of New York's burgeoning state powers over the all-important Hudson River.

After delineating the Hudson River's definitive status as a "public highway," Justice Spencer declared: "The erection of both dams are nuisances, and it is questionable whether the plaintiffs can . . . complain that the defendant's nuisance is injurious to their nuisance."[94] Spencer wrestled with the problem of weighing private rights on an increasingly public river. But in the end, he

refused to grant private damages to a mill equally intrusive on a public waterway. Justice Livingston concurred with this public perspective: "Whatever [the plaintiffs'] pretensions to build a dam and mills adjoining their own land may have been, it must be conceded that, *as far as the public are concerned*, the defendants had the same right opposite their ground, provided it could be done without injury to the navigation of the river."[95] Assertions of exclusive private rights on free and public ways were inherently suspect. Spencer and Livingston refused to treat *Palmer v. Mulligan* simply as another private dispute entailing a judicial calculation of damages. Rather, consulting the "public advantage," they ruled that one private enterprise could not benefit from the use of public waters to the exclusion of all others. And, of course, if any one private interest made use of the public river so as to obstruct navigation, it became a public nuisance subject to the sternest penalties of early American law.

In remarkably similar language, later courts continued to rebuff private claims made on public rivers and to order the abatement of obstructions and encroachments. New York City's East River was the site of a private dispute over a popular nineteenth-century river obstruction, a floating dock.[96] In *Hecker v. New York Balance Dock Company*, the New York court found such a floating obstruction a straightforward public nuisance: "To place a floating dock in the river, . . . although beneficial in repairing ships, is a common nuisance."[97] In a strikingly antimonopolistic opinion, the court challenged the exclusive, private appropriation of public waterways: "The business of the defendants, although highly beneficial to the commerce of the port, is, in fact and in its very nature, a monopoly. It is an exclusive appropriation to the few of the rights belonging equally to the many."[98] The river was a "common highway" not subject to such private claims and obstructions. Even the local dockmaster had no power to dole out public rights-of-way to private interests.[99]

In *Veazie v. Dwinel* (1862) the Maine Supreme Court ended a prolonged dispute between private milldam owners by again appealing to the superior rights of the public.[100] Citing Hale's "De Jure Maris" as well as *People v. Cunningham*, Justice Rice established the publicity of the entire Penobscot River and defended the public's right to unobstructed navigation and floatage.[101] He summarized a range of similar cases:

The authorities, ancient and modern, are all consistent, and point in one direction. Highways whether on land or water, are designed for the accommodation of the public, for travel and transportation, and any unauthorized or unreasonable obstruction thereof is a public nuisance in

judgment of the law. They cannot be made the receptacles of waste materials, filth or trash, nor the depositaries of valuable property even, so as to obstruct their use as public highways.[102]

Massachusetts and Maine had long-standing policies to encourage the construction and maintenance of mills; still, the court put greater emphasis on the competing demands of public property. The distinct privileges of the mill-owner had to be "so exercised as not to interfere with the substantial rights of the public in the stream, as a highway."[103]

Private disputes on public rivers, then, were more than mere private disputes. Early nineteenth century courts consistently recognized the common interests and rights in the highway when deciding such cases. Mills, docks, and dams, no matter how central to economic development, were checked when they interfered with or obstructed public rights. As the Illinois Supreme Court put it in 1848, "A private citizen may not take the public welfare into his own hands, and justify himself for such a violation of its rights, under a plea of general benefit."[104] The courts refused to acknowledge arguments from either absolute property rights or general utility. Instead, they clung to a notion of the public interest inherent in the common law doctrines that protected against obstructions and encroachments on public ways.

When dam owners attempted to claim immunity from such common law restrictions under state mill acts, they met responses like that of Chief Justice Gibson of Pennsylvania: "The legislature never consented to part with a particle of the public franchise for purposes of merely private convenience."[105] Corporate charters also failed to provide an exemption from public nuisance law. Most state legislatures included a provision in their bridge and dock company charters requiring them to conduct their businesses without obstructing or injuring public navigation. Any ambiguity in such charters operated "against the adventurers and in favor of the public."[106] Even winter did not inhibit public responsibility. In *French v. Camp* (1841), the Penobscot was held to be a public highway whether fluid or "congealed."[107] To cut a hole in the ice near a well-known passageway was "a direct violation of that great principle of social duty, by which each one of us is required to use his own rights, as not to injure the rights of others."[108]

With few exceptions, state appellate courts in this period expanded the definition of a public river, widening the applicability of public nuisance restrictions on the private use of riparian property.[109] At the same time, they ignored a range of justifications for infringements of public rights from private property to charter privileges to ice. These legal changes limited public

liability, immunized public works projects from private compensation demands, and creatively destroyed previously enjoyed private rights and usages of property. But their ultimate objective went beyond the legal subsidization of particular industries or an inherent preference for dynamic (as opposed to static) uses of property and economy. These cases reflected the overwhelming force of an emergent state power over public space, public ways, and natural resources. Building on a powerful common law tradition that viewed private rights as subservient to a larger common good,[110] judges in these cases disenfranchised private riparian owners of previous rights and expectations in order to assert the preeminence of public powers in newly established public spaces. In a well-ordered society, public rights and public powers of police were the main legal reference points regulating and redistributing rights-of-way on American rivers.

Ports: New Orleans, Albany, New York, and Boston

The vigorous public property tradition hammered out in early American road and river cases played a substantial role in the histories of some diverse and distinguished riparian real estate. It would be hard to identify bodies of water more important to nineteenth-century development than the port of New Orleans, Albany's Hudson River–Erie Canal Basin, and the harbors of New York City and Boston. It also would be difficult to find bodies of water with more diverse legal and social histories. Yet despite rather drastic cultural, legal, political, and geographical differences, Louisiana, New York, and Massachusetts courts and legislatures came to remarkably similar conclusions about the limits of private rights and the priority of public powers on these all-important waterways.

Louisiana's French civil law heritage guaranteed New Orleans a distinctive approach to the negotiation of public and private claims on the Mississippi waterfront at New Orleans.[111] The extensive regard for public rights in the civil law tradition was reflected in Louisiana's Civil Code of 1808. The code formally defined "public things" as "the property of which belongs to a whole nation, and the use of which is allowed to all the members of the nation." It included under that designation navigable rivers, seaports, roads, harbors, and highways.[112] Private individuals exercised no rights of property in such "public things." The Louisiana code also made special provision for riverbanks. Banks and shores remained in the hands of private owners, but *use* of them was open to the public: "Every one has a right freely to bring his ships to land

there, to make fast the same to the trees which are there planted, to unload his vessels, to deposit his goods, to dry his nets, and the like."[113] In 1825, the code specified levees as part of the "banks" of the Mississippi.[114] And in Louisiana, there was never any question that the Mississippi itself was a decidedly public river.[115]

But civil law and codification did not preclude legal conflict on the Mississippi at New Orleans. One of the most famous disputes was the New Orleans Batture controversy.[116] That legal-political struggle centered on Edward Livingston's claim under a Spanish land grant to a major part of the New Orleans alluvion known as the Batture St. Mary. French civil law deemed alluvion (the accretion of land due to river deposits) to be public property.[117] Livingston, a former New Yorker and well-known law reformer, began to make "improvements" to the land in 1807, outraging a citizenry that had come to see the Batture as a distinctly public space. The federal government at the behest of Thomas Jefferson evicted Livingston from the property in 1808. The subsequent maze of litigation ended in 1836 when a Louisiana court upheld Livingston's Spanish claim to title but, consistent with Louisiana Code, subjected the property to inalienable public rights of usage. This was a repeated pattern in Louisiana water law. Courts regularly defended public rights in the alluvion—rights of use, passage, and mooring—and upheld the power of state and city to regulate and police such property in the public interest.

The classic case was *Hanson v. City Council of Lafayette* (1841). Like many early nineteenth-century regulatory cases, *Hanson* was a hybrid phenomenon—part police power, part public nuisance law, part *damnum absque injuria*, and part public works.[118] It emerged from the decision of the neighboring cities of Lafayette and New Orleans to construct a new levee on the Mississippi. The old levee was worn out by travel, neglect, and various destructive acts.[119] With the demise of the old levee, an assortment of houses, stores, and buildings immediately sprung up on the adjoining batture.[120] To remedy the situation, the Lafayette City Council passed an ordinance ordering the banks of the river cleared and the removal and destruction of all buildings obstructing new levee construction. After a number of houses were demolished, a group of thirteen riparian owners sued for an injunction to prevent the council from obliterating $300,000 worth of their property without compensation. The Louisiana Supreme Court refused the injunction and ratified the City Council's strong public prerogative.

"The subject of roads and levees," the court began, "has repeatedly occupied the attention of the Legislature. . . . No subject is more important." No highway was more important to the state of Louisiana than the Mississippi

River. Public rights in that river and its banks were "well established" by code and statute. On the Mississippi, levees were banks. This was "a servitude" or easement, "established for the public or common utility, and all that relates to it, is regulated by particular laws."[121] In antimonopoly, antiprivilege rhetoric similar to the New York court in *Hecker v. New York Balance Dock Company*, Justice Garland argued that in constructing their buildings on the old levee the plaintiffs exceeded their individual private property rights and violated the rights of the public. No provision of law was clearer, Garland contended, than that "no man has a right to take exclusive possession of the banks of a navigable river, and appropriate them to his own use, and particularly the banks of the Mississippi." The proprietors of adjacent lands, though the right of property be in them, had no right to obstruct the free use of the banks by the public.[122] Though these thirteen plaintiffs built directly on their own land, though their buildings had been there for two to fifteen years, and though these personal and commercial properties were valued at $300,000, Justice Garland held that the property owners were unlawfully obstructing and impeding superior rights of the public expressly delimited in code and statute. Such unlawful private acts and interests would not be allowed to trump "the safety of the whole community."[123]

As unequivocally as the Louisiana court rejected the plaintiffs' private property claims, it ratified the city council's powers of regulation and self-government. The safety of the cities of Lafayette and New Orleans demanded a new and more substantial levee. The power to make all "necessary and needful regulations respecting streets, levees, roads, ditches, bridges, etc.; and to repair old levees, and lay out and construct new ones" was inherited by the city council from the "police jury" of the parish of Jefferson. The city charter and subsequent legislative acts expressly gave the council "the power of pulling down and removing all buildings and other incumbrances, that may obstruct the levee or the space between the levee and the river . . . at the expense of those who have erected them."[124] The Louisiana Code itself authorized "the destruction of any works built on the banks of rivers at the expense of those who claim them, and the owner of those works cannot prevent their being destroyed under any pretext of prescription or possession, even if immemorial."[125] The court held that this series of unambiguous state acts clearly endowed the council with ample regulatory and police authority to construct the new levee and remove anything on the old levee obstructing the public way.

The *Hanson* case was a testament to Louisiana's strong tradition of public rights in rivers and other public properties. In that tradition, the banks of the

Mississippi (though title remained in private hands) were subject to a broad and inalienable public easement. The state legislature and delegated localities were armed with strong powers to police and maintain that easement. Private property violating the public easement, jeopardizing public safety or interests, was subject to the most summary and severe of public remedies.[126] Louisiana law consistently deferred to the public importance and public status of its chief means of transportation, communication, and commerce.

The city of Albany had no state code defining "public things," and it had no levees (though a history of devastating floods indicated they might have been useful). Nor was New York law particularly solicitous of the rights of the public in the banks or batture of the Hudson River. Albany had a common law rather than a civil law heritage. But despite the conservative and individualistic glosses frequently imposed on New York State's jurisprudence, the common law vision of a well-regulated society could be just as intolerant as the French civil law of the private appropriation of public ways and just as aggressive in the assertion of public rights to ports and harbors.

Albany also had the Albany Basin, constructed in 1825 and billed as "one of the greatest works connected with the [Erie] canal."[127] The basin was essentially an artificial harbor built at the point where the Hudson met the completed Erie Canal. The state constructed a 4,000-foot pier, accommodating a road, plenty of warehouses, and dry dock facilities, to separate the river from the harbor. The pier was 250 feet from the shore, thereby enclosing a basin of thirty-two acres. The basin offered moorings for 1,000 canal boats and 50 steamboats. The space was needed: in the canal's first year an estimated 12,000 boats passed through the basin. By 1852 well over a million tons of property moved up and down the canal annually, and Albany's population quadrupled.[128]

Albany was also the beneficiary of extensive regulatory powers granted by the New York state legislature. As in Louisiana, New York legislated extensively on the use of its public roads and rivers. The Erie Canal alone was the focus of eighty special acts from 1810 to 1857.[129] The Albany Basin was constructed according to a special act of the legislature with extensive provisions for building specifications, financing, improvements, wharfage, and tolls.[130] New York State was careful to expressly grant its major municipal corporations general police power "to regulate, keep in repair, and alter the streets, highways, bridges, wharves and slips, and . . . to prevent all obstructions in the river near or opposite to such wharves, docks, or slips."[131] These were not idle regulatory statutes. They were enforced by the New York courts with a vigor befitting their public-oriented, civil law counterparts in Louisiana.

Hart v. Mayor of Albany (1832) was the premier public nuisance case in the Albany Basin.[132] It was to the Hudson River what *Hanson* was to the Mississippi, and it was to navigable rivers generally what *People v. Cunningham* was to public roads. The facts of *Hart* were remarkably similar to *Hecker v. New York Balance Dock Company*. The plaintiffs, merchants engaged in trade on the Hudson from New York to Albany, rented two lots with stores on the 4,000-foot pier that created the Albany Basin. To expedite the loading and unloading of merchandise, they constructed and moored in the basin opposite their lots a $3,000 floating dock (120 foot by 42 foot). In response to this monstrosity, the mayor and alderman of Albany passed a special ordinance directing the dockmaster to fix a notice to any nonnavigating vessel in the Hudson requiring removal within ten days. If not so removed, the ordinance authorized the dockmaster to remove and sell the obstruction at auction. In this case, removal entailed destruction of the float. As in *Hecker*, the plaintiffs appealed to the chancellor for an injunction restraining the city from destroying their property.

When Chancellor Walworth denied the plaintiffs an injunction, they took their case to the New York Court of Errors prompting an extensive discussion of police, nuisance, and public and private rights in public ways.[133] Voting twenty-one to two against an injunction, the Court of Errors attacked the plaintiff's selfish appropriation of a way designed for the convenience of all, and upheld the city's suppression of the public nuisance as a legitimate police regulation.[134]

The court denounced the plaintiff's claim in the strongest terms as "not merely doubtful, but . . . clearly and obviously unfounded."[135] The Albany Basin was a great public highway. As such, it was for the "common, free, and uninterrupted use" of all vessels that might enter it. "No individual," Justice Sutherland argued, "can appropriate a portion of it to his own exclusive use and shield himself from responsibility to the public by saying that enough is still left for the accommodation of others."[136] Senator Edmunds concurred, "It is sufficient to know that [the plaintiffs] have without right appropriated to their own use a portion of that which was designed for the benefit of all; that they have obstructed the free navigation of this public basin, which was the primary object of its construction, and have adopted a practice which, if sanctioned, would result in the entire destruction of public and common benefits."[137] The plaintiffs' actions were anchored solely in private, material considerations—a floating dock saved them the cost of storing their goods on shore. Such selfish motivations betrayed the great public purposes underlying the construction of the basin and the public rights inherent in navigable waters.

As strongly as the New York court derided the plaintiffs' private assault on common rights, it supported the municipality's right to take action against it. First, this floating dock was a common nuisance—an unauthorized obstruction of a public highway. As such, it was abatable by any person.[138] This was an unlawful act injurious to the whole community; all had a right to abate it. To the plaintiffs' objection that this amounted to a destruction of property without the benefit of a trial by jury, Senator Edmunds contended, "Nothing is clearer or better settled than the right to exercise this power in a summary manner," especially where the whole community was affected. The right to abate a common nuisance, obstructing or annoying things of daily convenience and use, was "a right necessary to the good order of society."[139] The entire common law of public nuisances from Blackstone onward stood behind the summary destruction of public "inconveniences" of this sort.

But the court did not rest its decision on the common law alone. In opinions that aptly reveal the links between the common law of nuisance and the police power, Justice Sutherland and Senators Allen and Edmunds validated Albany's actions as part of its statutory authority "to regulate the police of the city; to be commissioners of highways in and for the city, and generally to make all such rules, by-laws, and regulations for the order and good government of the city."[140] The court broadly construed these statutory powers as expressly authorizing the removal of "the evil complained of" as an obstruction to navigation or a common nuisance. The object of this statute was "to produce the greatest amount of public good."[141] No judicial construction could allow such a law to "advance a private interest to the destruction of that of the public."[142]

Albany had no code declaring the Hudson a "public thing" and requiring the demolition of private intrusions, but the common law of public nuisances and police regulations passed by the state legislature were ample sources of strong public rights and broad public powers. Common law rules of statutory construction only provided further protections for the public good. The result was a defense of public rights in the Albany Basin as clearcut as anything coming out of the Mississippi Delta. Once again, a northeastern court staunchly guarded public claims against potent arguments from vested rights, private property, *and* general utility. Despite the fact that this floating warehouse might have greatly facilitated the transhipment of goods up and down the Hudson, the order and good government of the city and the right of the public to freely navigate an unobstructed basin required the uncompensated public destruction of another piece of valuable antebellum private property.[143]

If the moral of the *Hart* case was that private rights could not intrude on public rights, *Lansing v. Smith* (1829) made it clear that public rights in the Albany Basin were so crucial they could impair the private rights of individuals without compensation.[144] *Lansing* was a classic public *damnum absque injuria* case. The plaintiff claimed that, in building the basin, the state of New York cut off his wharf's direct access to the Hudson and diverted his natural flow of water. He claimed that the 1823 statute authorizing the construction of the basin was unconstitutional, violating the implicit contract and property rights guaranteed by his waterlot grant.

Chancellor Walworth, who first dissolved the injunction in *Hart*, upheld the constitutionality of the statute in the strongest public rights terms. He likened the state's power over navigable waters to the king's sovereign prerogative. The right to navigate the public waters of the state were public rights belonging to the people at large not "the private inalienable rights of each individual." The legislature, as the representative of the public, had the right to "restrict and regulate the exercise of those rights in such a manner as may be deemed most beneficial to the public at large."[145] Charter, contract, and property rights were not inalienable in a well-regulated society; they were subject to general regulations on behalf of the public. In Walworth's words, "[I]t would be directly in opposition to the spirit of the law to give a construction to this grant which would deprive the state of the power to regulate the wharves, ports, harbors, and navigable waters within its boundaries."[146] Though the plaintiff may have suffered a real injury or a loss of business or convenience due to the construction of the basin, the state was pursuing a distinctly constitutional public improvement. The private injury was without remedy—*damnum absque injuria*. Waterlot grants did not endow proprietors with immunity from legislative regulation, legislative change, or legislative improvements.[147]

The Albany experience, then like New Orleans's regulation of life on the Mississippi, reflected deeply rooted notions about public rights on public ways, be they on land or water. Those rights were not abstract phenomena. They were encased in particular rules of statutory construction, the common law of nuisance, notions of the sovereign prerogative, and state police power. Private rights that conflicted with common rights of navigation in the Albany Basin were summarily denied or destroyed. In short, the Albany Basin was held to the standards of the well-regulated society. Neither the static vested rights of previous owners, nor the dynamic hand of the market was allowed to dictate the course of development in these waters. The state, as guarantor and

promoter of the public interest, was given the *duty* of constructing the basin and keeping it clear, free, and in the service of the people's welfare.

Of course, for anyone living in New York City or Boston in the early nineteenth century, there were really only two bodies of water worth their salt—the great harbors on which those two cities were built. And, indeed, those harbors yielded some of the most influential statements of the common law vision of a well-regulated society. But the sweeping rhetoric of Lemuel Shaw in *Commonwealth v. Alger* and Justice Woodworth in *Vanderbilt v. Adams* that led off chapter 1 did not spring from the individual genius of two exceptional jurists or from a peculiar commonwealth or New York view of the world. Rather, they were part of a broad, well-understood tradition of public rights and public powers in American roads, rivers, and ports that cut across diverse legal jurisdictions and cultures. In many ways, the New York and Boston harbor cases were merely the most powerful articulations of legal and political ideas that governed public properties and spaces from the streets of Brooklyn to the waterfront of New Orleans.

Justice Woodworth's opinion in *Vanderbilt v. Adams* (1827) was one of the most complete discussions of police regulation before Shaw.[148] The case turned on an 1819 New York statute bestowing on the harbor master of the port of New York the power to make room on private wharves for incoming vessels.[149] The harbor master ordered the defendant to move his steamboat, the *Thistle*, stationed at a private wharf in the North River, to make room for the newly arriving *Legislator*. The defendant refused and was fined. In the ensuing action to collect, the defendant challenged the constitutionality of the statute regulating his ship while on private property.[150] Such a power, he argued, impaired the obligation of contracts.

Woodworth had little trouble defending this police power over private property and contract, asserting that government and society brought distinct limits on individual rights. Property did not exempt one from regulatory power. As Woodworth explained, when city officials "convey a lot of land, or waterlot, their sovereignty, as to the subject matter, is not gone. They possess the same power, for the common benefit, as they possessed prior to the grant." This particular statute was passed "for the preservation of good order in the harbor." It was a necessary police regulation, and not void, even though it interfered with individual rights.[151] Such legislative power was "incident to every well regulated society; and without which it could not well exist." The sovereign power in a community to prescribe the manner of exercising individual rights over property rested upon "the implied right and duty of the

supreme power to protect all by statutory regulations, so that, on the whole, the benefit of all is promoted."[152] The restriction of individual rights that always accompanied police regulations did not amount to an injury that required either remedy or compensation.

Lemuel Shaw amplified Justice Woodworth's police claims in *Commonwealth v. Tewksbury* (1846) and *Commonwealth v. Alger* (1851)—the culmination of a half century of American jurisprudence creating and defending public rights and public powers in American public spaces. In *Commonwealth v. Tewksbury*, William Tewksbury was indicted for removing sand and gravel from his own beach contrary to a Massachusetts statute preserving the natural embankments of Boston harbor.[153] Tewksbury argued that any statute prohibiting a private property owner from removing soil from his own property amounted to an unconstitutional public taking of private property without compensation. For Chief Justice Shaw, however, this was merely another example of a government's power to issue police regulations restricting uses of property hostile to the people's welfare. The Massachusetts statute was a "just and legitimate exercise of the power of the legislature to regulate and restrain such particular use of property as would be inconsistent with, or injurious to, the rights of the public." "All property," Shaw elaborated, was "held under the tacit condition that it shall not be so used as to injure the equal rights of others, or to destroy or greatly impair the public rights and interests of the community; under the maxim of the common law, *sic utere tuo ut alienum non laedas*."[154] When public rights were violated, the common law of public nuisance provided for punishment by indictment and abatement. But Shaw was unwilling to rely solely on the common law to protect the safety, health, and comfort of the community. In situations like this, with the natural boundaries of a great harbor at stake, the legislature could also intervene to *prevent* nuisances through "positive enactment" prohibiting uses of property injurious to the public.[155] In strong civil law fashion, Shaw held that the beaches and embankments of public ports and harbors were "of great public importance," subject to extensive public regulation.[156]

But Shaw's opinion in *Commonwealth v. Alger* remained his ultimate statement on police regulation and private property.[157] In *Alger*, Shaw defended the wharf lines of Boston harbor established by the legislature to prevent the kinds of obstructions and encroachments described throughout this chapter. Shaw upheld the statute as a legitimate exertion of the commonwealth's police power: "the power vested in the legislature by the constitution, to make, ordain and establish all manner of wholesome and reasonable laws, statutes and ordinances . . . not repugnant to the constitution, as they shall judge to be for

the good and welfare of the commonwealth."[158] But far from pioneering a new brand of state power, Shaw's opinion in *Alger* ratified, consolidated, and applied to Boston harbor a growing body of legal rules and political practices governing public highways throughout the antebellum era.

Indeed, many of the grander claims Shaw made in *Alger* were already well-established when he appeared as counsel for the commonwealth before the Municipal Court of Boston in 1829 in another wharf case, *Commonwealth v. Wright and Dame*. There Shaw argued for the indictment and abatement of the defendant's 100-foot wharf protruding beyond the low-water mark in Boston harbor to the detriment of public navigation.[159] Though it is unclear exactly how many of the jury instructions in this case were owed to Shaw (Judge Thacher admitted "noticing" Shaw's points in his opinion), much of *Tewksbury* and *Alger* was presaged here. The public significance of harbor and highway did not escape Judge Thacher, nor did the obligations of government therein. He told the jury, "It is the right and duty of the government, to preserve the highways from obstruction both by land and water; since both are of the highest moment, the one for the navigation of boats and vessels, the other for land carriage." Destroy the free and public harbor with private impediments and nuisances, "and you will soon make the city desolate."[160] Thacher left little question as to the relative weight of public and private rights in the harbor: "If a citizen . . . shall infringe upon the right of all the other citizens, by extending his wharf beyond the line of low water, and into the channel, to the common detriment . . . he has offended against a principle of law, which is as ancient as it is reasonable, and as well known as any other principle in our code."[161] In such cases, it was not only a constitutional power, but a moral duty for the sovereign, as trustee for the public rights, to "keep the sea shore free from encroachment, and not to suffer any individual . . . to intrude on it."[162] On these instructions, the jury found William Wright and Abraham A. Dame guilty of a public nuisance. They were fined $20 each. Their wharf "with all the piers and timbers under, and the materials belonging to the same," was ordered to "be dug up, demolished and abated" at their own expense.[163] Shaw won his case. But more significantly, he became well acquainted with the limits of private rights in public spaces and the legal-political ramifications of the well-regulated society.

Conclusion: Whose "Public" Square?

The cases documented in this chapter reflected the overwhelming assertion of state power over public spaces and properties in the early nineteenth-century

United States. The extensive public works projects of the early republic, accompanied by the redefinition of public rights in roads, rivers, and harbors, marked the emergence of a nascent American state and the power of the well-regulated society. By the Civil War, legislators and courts successfully secured formal public authority and control over the nation's most important communication and transportation thoroughfares. This development was as significant as any transformation in American private law.

But was that all American courts meant by their defenses of public rights in these cases—the simple vindication of the formal powers of law-making bodies? Some cases already examined suggest otherwise. In *Hecker v. New York Balance Dock Company*, the official permission of a public dockmaster did not legitimate the maintenance of a public nuisance. State mill acts and corporate charters—the products of state legislatures—also brought no exemption from a more general duty to regard the people's welfare. When the Albany Basin itself became polluted, "the people" brought suit against the mayor and aldermen for maintaining a public nuisance "injurious to the health of persons living in the vicinity."[164]

But the best example of the judicial notice of a disjunction between public authority and public welfare came in a series of odd cases involving the sale of public squares by financially strapped municipalities. In 1849, for example, the mayor and council of Allegheny decided to sell the public square to private citizens to pay off public debts from the construction of new city waterworks. Edmund Wesley Grier purchased one of the lots and built a house. The state attorney general brought suit defending public rights in public space against such new, private obstructions.[165] In ruling in favor of the "public," Justice Hepburn of Pennsylvania argued that the public square could be appropriated "to no private use." The square was not the council's or the mayor's to sell or dispose of as they saw fit. Rather, it was the public's square, "and any private erection upon it, even by authority of the city council, [was] an offense against the public, and indictable as a common nuisance."[166] Public interest and public rights did not necessarily follow the positive enactments of municipal governments.

In *State v. Woodward* (1850), the Vermont Supreme Court similarly refused to authorize the sale of public property to private individuals. A dedication to "public purpose" was "irrevocable."[167] The public rights could not be traded, bought, sold, or bargained away to private interests, no matter what the alleged benefits. In language mirroring eminent domain law, the Vermont court held that the "taking of property dedicated to the use of the public, and appropriating it to private use, thereby wholly excluding the public from the en-

joyment of it" was not to be tolerated.[168] The public good was not to be made subservient to private convenience.

"Public rights" in the early nineteenth century did not simply mean the actions of formally constituted public authorities. Indeed, the legal renderings of "public" in the public square cases seem equally removed from legal positivism, majoritarianism, and instrumental calculations of utility. In *Commonwealth v. Bowman and Duncan* (1846), Pennsylvania Chief Justice Gibson condemned county commissioners for constructing an office building on the public's square, declaring that they had "no inherent right to property . . . dedicated not to its use, but to the use of all the citizens of the Commonwealth."[169] No matter how necessary a multiplicity of county buildings, no matter how many people voted for their construction, and no matter how many municipal ordinances were passed, the public square was a common highway belonging to the whole public. Public officials had no more right to obstruct public ways and invade public rights than private individuals. The legal construction of public space in early America was so successful that public officials were sometimes caught in their own creations.[170]

This powerful, relatively autonomous legal conception of public rights in public spaces had immense ramifications for the American state and its powers of regulation and police. The law of public highways was a concern of the highest order in the early nineteenth century, prompting discourses on public and private that reached to the very roots of the social and economic order. Cases such as *People v. Cunningham, Callender v. Marsh, Vanderbilt v. Adams,* and *Commonwealth v. Alger* were the jurisprudential foundation for more general nineteenth-century American elaborations of *salus populi* and state police power. The swiftness and completeness with which early American courts and legislators successfully secured a public tradition of policing public space had implications for the well-regulated society well beyond the confines of public ways.

Barker v. Commonwealth (1852) involved an indictment for the obstruction of a Pittsburgh street.[171] Barker's offense was "causing to assemble and remain therein for a long space of time, great numbers of men and boys . . . and idle, dissolute, and disorderly people." He was accused of "openly and publicly speaking with a loud voice, in the hearing of the citizens, &c., wicked, scandalous, and infamous words, representing men and women in obscene and indecent positions and attitudes."[172] Asserting that "common highways were designed for no such purpose," the court upheld the defendant's conviction. The manifest tendency of this obstruction "to debauch and corrupt the public morals" made the offense complete.[173] As streets and highways became

increasingly *public*, the regulatory powers of the state were enhanced. State control of streets, rivers, ports, and other public places involved not only the power to keep them free and open to public access but a more general duty to police them. Expanding public powers over public ways involved the regulation of an increased range of social and economic activities deemed hostile to the people's welfare, including public morality and public health. Policing these things first on public properties paved the way for the public regulation of some of the most private of American spaces.

Public Morality:
Disorderly Houses and Demon Rum

Morals are regulated by religion or by laws.—John Taylor

B y the standards of late twentieth-century law, the public regulation of morality is increasingly suspect. The burgeoning public/private distinction, the jurisprudential separation of law and morality, and the expansion of constitutionally protected rights of expression and privacy have yielded a polity whose legitimacy theoretically rests on its ability to keep out of the private moral affairs of its citizens. As the American Law Institute declared in the 1955 Model Penal Code, "We deem it inappropriate for the government to attempt to control behavior that has no substantial significance except as to the morality of the actor." "Public morality" may soon become an oxymoron.[1]

The relationship between law and morals in the nineteenth century could not have been more different. Of all of the contests over public power in that period, morals regulation was the easy case. That is not surprising. For the regulation of morality and a more general concern for order, ethics, good manners, respectable habits, and standards of decency were principal objects of police. Emmerich de Vattel's influential discussion of "Justice and Police" suggested that police was all about preserving order: "By a wise police, the sovereign accustoms the people to order and obedience, and preserves peace, tranquility, and concord among the citizens."[2] A well-ordered state of society depended upon a due regard for public morals. Historian Gerhard Oestreich has argued that neo-Stoicism—a methodology of moral order and ethical constancy—was an important attribute of the early modern state and its quest

to adjust "the spiritual, moral, and psychological make-up" of citizens, educating them "to a discipline of work and frugality."[3] Regulations in this ordering, disciplining spirit were hardly antagonistic to nineteenth-century economic and social development. Indeed, a new generation of social histories has begun to illuminate the absolute centrality to nineteenth-century culture and economy of legal and regulatory techniques for *policing* the city, the family, labor, and assorted "dangerous classes."[4]

A key technology in morals and cultural policing was the criminal law. The nexus of crime, morality, and police in this period was a close one. Indeed, the substance of nineteenth-century "criminal law" barely resembles the closely bounded legal technicality of modern criminal jurisprudence. Cesare Beccaria, the most influential of criminal law reformers, was also a leading Italian exponent of cameralism and police science.[5] Early criminal law treatises and reporters supplemented conduct guides and ethics tracts as manuals of proper moral instruction. Jacob Wheeler addressed his 1854 New York *Criminal Law Cases* to "every person," suggesting that the rules of criminal jurisprudence "have a direct and positive operation on the sentiments and manners of mankind, in a moral point of view . . . [and] may be considered as the continuation of an extended system of morality." Comparing criminal laws to Gospel strictures, Wheeler extolled the social philosophy of the well-regulated society:

> Man is not only a social, but a reasonable being, not only rational, but moral, and, therefore, accountable. It is in this state we find him, and it is in this state that he is subject to those regulations mankind has adopted for their government. . . . It is here where those salutary principles of criminal law operate with effect, admonishing, restraining, and punishing the foolish, the rash, and the wicked: binding the parts of society together in one bond of equal justice.[6]

The overlapping nature of criminal law, moral reform, and police regulation was also captured in the main categories of Joel Bishop's *Commentaries on the Criminal Law* (1865) where "Protection to Individuals" *followed* (1) "Protection to the Government"; (2) "Protection to the Public Health"; (3) "Protection to the Public Morals, Religion, and Education"; (4) "Protection to the Public Wealth and to Population"; (5) "Protection to the Public Convenience and Safety"; and (6) "Protection to the Public Order and Tranquility." Bishop, the preeminent nineteenth-century commentator on criminal law, defended the confluence of criminal law and morality matter-of-factly, "Morality, religion and education are the three main pillars of the state . . . they should be objects of primary regard by the laws."[7]

In addition to police and criminal law, morals regulation was also deeply rooted in American colonial experience. The biblical injunctions of Massachusetts's *Laws and Liberties* were but the most famous of a surfeit of morals restrictions passed by the "civil and Christian states" and "well-ordered plantations" of colonial America.[8] Statute books were bolstered by sermons like Increase Mather's *An Arrow against Profane and Promiscuous Dancing* and John Barnard's *The Throne Established by Righteousness*. The latter aptly captured the moralistic thrust of Puritan governance: "[S]ince Sin has broke in upon the World . . . there is but so much the more Reason and Necessity for Government among Creatures that are become so very weak, and depraved; to restrain their unruly Lusts, and keep, within due Bounds, the rampant Passions of Men, which else would soon throw humane Society into the last Disorder and Confusion."[9] For Cotton Mather, laws were "important machines, to keep very much evil out of the world."[10] Colonial officials from Boston to Charleston devoted an obsessive amount of attention to such evil, outlawing "carnal wickedness," prostitution, drunkenness, gambling, profanity, blasphemy, profanation of the Lord's day, and countless other debaucheries and improprieties.[11]

But as with other aspects of early modern law, historians have dismissed colonial morals and police regulation as an aberration—as another quirky, unfortunate prelude to "the formative era of American law."[12] William Nelson's thesis of Americanization and modernization goes furthest, suggesting that 1776 ushered in a collapse of morals prosecutions and a "shift in law's basic function . . . from the preservation of morality to the protection of property."[13] Lawrence Friedman argues more persuasively for the constancy of morals concerns in law, but posits a nineteenth-century "Victorian Compromise" whereby only the most "truly evil," open, and notorious morals violations were prosecuted while the "not quite so bad" were tolerated.[14] Certainly Nelson and Friedman are correct to detect an increased attention to violence and theft in early republican criminal law.[15] And the focus of morals police certainly did permutate from pastoral, otherworldly sin to social, thisworldly discipline—authority shifting from minister to magistrate. But as this chapter will make clear, legal support for morals restrictions barely wavered in the nineteenth century. Public morality remained a primary objective of criminal, municipal, and police regulation and a crucial obligation of local and state governments. This close relationship between law and morality was not a holdover from an atypical and austere Puritan heritage or the last vestige of decaying peaceable kingdoms. Rather, a regard for public morals had deep roots in Anglo-American common law and a persistent conception of well-

ordered governance. If there was a transformation in attitudes toward morality around 1776, it lay in the direction of *increased* rather than decreased public attention. The postrevolutionary era witnessed the origins of one of the most concerted and energetic moral reform movements in American history. The movement for the reformation of morals and manners stretched law's responsibility for public morality to unprecedented levels with profound constitutional consequences.

Movement for the Reformation of Morals and Manners

The antebellum benevolence and reform movement was an exceedingly disparate effort.[16] Despite intriguing precedents like Cotton Mather's 1710 call for "reforming societies," the movement was founded in the dramatic increase in religious revivalism known as the Second Great Awakening (1795–1837).[17] Evangelical missionary societies, tract and Bible societies, and Sunday schools spawned a host of voluntaristic moral organizations devoted to cleansing towns and cities of sin and evil. In Connecticut, the Missionary Society set up in the 1790s to spread the gospel westward gave way to Lyman Beecher's Society for the Suppression of Vice and the Promotion of Good Morals, organized in 1812. Beecher's inaugural sermon cataloged the ills to be remedied: "traveling, and worldly labor, and amusement on the Sabbath," "the enormous consumption of ardent spirit," "the neglect of family government and family prayer," "the increase of slander, falsehood, and perjury," and "profane swearing." Viewing "Sabbath-breakers, rum-selling tippling folk, infidels, and ruff-scruff" as portents of a more general breakdown in society, Beecher called for "the guardians of the public morals" to "be vigilant and efficient in the execution of the laws" and "stop the contamination of vice."[18] As if to underscore the interdependence of religion, morality, and law, Beecher was joined in the Good Morals Society by Litchfield parishioner Tapping Reeve and Zephaniah Swift. Reeve founded America's first law school at Litchfield in 1784; Swift was chief justice of the Connecticut Supreme Court from 1806 to 1819.[19]

Beecher's Morals Society was but the most conspicuous of reform organizations that spread rapidly throughout antebellum America.[20] Historian Charles Foster has conservatively listed 158 such organizations formed before 1850.[21] Some like the Andover South Parish Society for the Reformation of Morals remained committed to general moral uplift: "to discountenance immorality, particularly Sabbath-breaking, intemperance and profanity; and to promote industry, order, piety, and good morals."[22] Other societies focused on specific moral evils: the Anti-Duelling Society (1809), the Massachusetts Society for

the Suppression of Intemperance (1813), the Massachusetts Peace Society (1815), the Society for the Prevention of Pauperism in the City of New York (1817), the Boston Prison Discipline Society (1825), and the New York Female Moral Reform Society (1834). Arguably, one of the most radical aspects of antebellum reform was its culmination in abolitionism and women's suffrage. But just as consequential was its revolutionary implications for governance.

Despite an early commitment to moral suasion, reform organizations from the beginning proposed new laws and advocated rigorous enforcement of existing legislation. Constant agitation for the suppression of intemperance, the elimination of bawdy houses and gambling dens, and an end to other forms of urban disorder (especially the urban riots that convulsed Jacksonian America) precipitated a reworking of traditional notions of police. On top of the broad, organic conception of "police" as governance for the public welfare, urban reformers pioneered a narrower, instrumental version—police as crime prevention, moral control, and prelude to incarceration. Following the lead of late eighteenth-century British police theorists like Patrick Colquhoun, reformers advanced a vision of police more concerned with security and protection (of property, of person, of middle-class sensibilities) than some overarching pursuit of civic well-being.[23] These were the roots of our modern notion of the function of police and criminal law as the straightforward suppression of crimes and misdemeanors.

Charles Christian's *Treatise on the Police of New York City* (1812) was an extraordinary early statement in this reorientation. Christian argued, "When the population of a city becomes so numerous that the citizens are not all known to each other, then may depredators merge in the mass, and spoliate in secret and safety, and then is the precise time for the organization of a vigilant Police to develope."[24] Christian's treatise was essentially a tract on morals regulation championing increased police authority over dangerous classes: prostitutes, brothel keepers, gamblers, vagabonds, drunkards, and rum sellers. His vision of urban police as "the Cerberus of society, guarding from danger every man's door" made consistent gains through the antebellum years, reaching its apotheosis in the professional police and prison reforms of midcentury.[25]

Historians have attributed this explosion of moral and police reform to a variety of causes. Growing class antagonisms and disparities have headed the list since Daniel DeFoe's *Poor Man's Plea*.[26] The impact of religious zeal has been continuously documented.[27] The status frustrations and anxieties of old leadership groups in uncertain times certainly illuminate temperance and other reform alignments.[28] And there can be little doubt that nascent capitalists had a lot to gain from an effort to instill habits of restraint, self-control,

temperance, industry, and order in laboring classes.[29] More recently, historians have examined race and ethnicity in the categorization of new urban "others" as "dangerous classes" to be reformed or policed. The central role of women as reformers and reformed has also focused attention on the "ideology of domesticity" and the gender/sexual politics of benevolence.[30]

All of these factors are crucial to a comprehensive historical explanation of antebellum reform. But in the pages that follow, I would like to take a different tack and stress the public framework for reform, that is, the institutions and inherited assumptions about state power, local government, and the nature of a well-ordered community that shaped this extraordinary response to social and economic change. For, at bottom, the movement for the reformation of morals and manners was still a legal and political movement. It was an attempt to reorder communities by deploying established public languages and the diverse public technologies of the nineteenth-century state. It can only be fully understood by taking these languages and technologies seriously and on their own terms. Moreover, the ability of particular groups to master these languages and control these technologies had real and important *consequences.* Despite impressive tales of personal agency and everyday resistance, morals police was not simply a malleable arena for social-cultural struggle and definition. The legal structure of reform distinctly empowered certain definitions of public morality and silenced others. As Robert Cover eloquently argued, for all of law's supple normative capacity to embrace shifting social and personal narratives of justice and right, its hallmark remains an irreducible element of force and violence.[31]

One of the more important aspects of this public backdrop to reform was the deeply held legal-political assumption that community life should be well ordered and well regulated. Morality in this tradition was not a private, individual, or discretionary matter. Rather, it was a responsibility of government and a quid pro quo of community membership. When Lyman Beecher, Ward Stafford, and others extolled the virtues of "the well-regulated village" and "domestic discipline," they were drawing on well-established beliefs about the organization of community life—beliefs embedded in the institutional fabric of early American governance.[32] The Massachusetts Declaration of Rights (1780) codified Blackstonian notions of "public police" and "good neighbourhood": "A frequent recurrence to the fundamental principles of the constitution, and a constant adherence to those of piety, justice, moderation, temperance, industry, and frugality, are absolutely necessary to preserve the advantages of liberty, and to maintain a free government."[33] By invoking the "well-regulated society," moral reformers were calling public officials to arms.

They were mustering a public tradition ensconced in a score of local and legal institutions, practices, and doctrines.

Nineteenth-century criminal law was replete with morals restrictions. Joel Bishop's commentaries surveyed a host of common law[34] and statutory offenses respecting sexuality and chastity (adultery, fornication, solicitation, incest, bigamy, polygamy, bestiality, and sodomy—"the horrible crime not to be named among Christians"), obscenity and lewdness (keeping bawdy houses, publishing obscene prints and writings, obscene speech, indecent exposure, and all acts of "gross and open lewdness"), Christianity (Sabbath-breaking, profane swearing, blasphemy, and corpse stealing and dissection), and public houses and shows (common gaming houses, disorderly alehouses or inns, mountebank stages, cockfighting, and "every public show and exhibition which outrages decency, shocks humanity, or is contrary to good morals").[35] State criminal codes mirrored Bishop's categories. Connecticut's codification of 1830 contained the usual crimes against "chastity," "decency," and "public policy," while adding special provisions for "lascivious carriage and behavior," drunkenness, unauthorized and foreign lotteries, horse racing and wagering, billiard tables, playing cards (or selling them) for money, circuses, horse and animal shows, theatrical exhibitions, and other indecent public displays: "games, tricks, plays, shows, tumbling, rope dancing, puppet shows, or feats of uncommon dexterity or agility of body."[36]

But the public regulation of morality did not begin and end with penal codes in the nineteenth century. As Joel Bishop suggested, "The criminal and civil departments of the law somewhat blend in each other." A decentralized, loosely structured state coupled with strong traditions of private prosecution and local police regulation allowed for a stunning degree of diversity, experimentation, and discretion in dealing with threats to a community's moral standards.[37] States enacted separate police regulations ranging from the licensing of inns and taverns to the outright prohibition (and confiscation) of gambling implements. State legislatures delegated open-ended authority to municipalities to deal with moral hazards.[38] Local justices of the peace and town and county officers continued to exercise common law jurisdiction over morals nuisances like illegal saloons and brothels.[39] Even the poor law came into play as commissioners and overseers arbitrarily seized vagrants, idlers, prostitutes, and other "morals offenders" for the workhouse without any legal process whatsoever.[40] The typical technologies of the criminal law—fine and imprisonment—were only the most visible aspects of a morals regulatory apparatus, which included licensing, inspection, prohibition, search and seizure, summary abatement of morals nuisances, private abatement, private

prosecution, a pioneering use of the equity injunction, informal community sanctions,[41] and even extralegal crowd actions and riots. Like threats to public safety, property, and economy, morals dangers roused the full spectrum of nineteenth-century public powers. In 1868, Thomas Cooley devoted little attention to limitations on governmental powers over morality, suggesting instead, "The preservation of public morals is *peculiarly* subject to legislative supervision."[42]

Early American judges upheld such morals regulations as part and parcel of the well-regulated society. In 1817 New Hampshire Chief Justice Richardson defended a prosecution for traveling on Sunday with common *salus populi* rhetoric: "All society is founded upon the principle, that each individual shall submit to the will of the whole. . . . We agree to conform our actions to the rules prescribed by the whole, and we agree to pay the forfeiture which the general will may impose upon the violation of those rules, whether it be the loss of property, of liberty, or of life."[43] Like peace, order, and safety, morality belonged to that group of public concerns that defined the essence of nineteenth-century governmental obligation. As an Illinois jurist mused in 1852, "A government that did not possess the power to protect itself" from moral evils like liquor, lotteries, and gambling "would scarcely be worth preserving."[44] Such a perspective justified aggressive public action against perceived morals nuisances. Maine Chief Justice Shepley closed down a bowling alley, asserting that "bad habits are in such places often introduced or confirmed. The moral sense, the correct principles, the temperate, regular and industrious habits, which are the basis of a prosperous and happy community, are frequently impaired or destroyed."[45] Similar legal-moral reasonings accompanied prohibitions on a wide range of "immoral" conduct from indecent exposure to singing a ribald song, from exhibiting a stud horse to a magician's sleight of hand.[46]

The rest of this chapter is devoted to unpacking and analyzing this public tradition of morals regulation, especially in the areas of morals nuisances (disorderly houses) and antiliquor legislation. After examining safety, economic, and public property regulations, these restrictions should hardly be startling. Indeed only after twentieth-century constitutional innovations like privacy and civil liberties could one expect anything remotely approaching laissez-faire or caveat emptor in morals. As Lawrence Friedman suggested, "Free enterprise in liquor, lottery tickets, gambling and sex never appealed much to nineteenth century judges."[47] What is surprising and revealing, however, is how far reformers, legislators, and judges were willing to go to secure a public morality commensurate with the well-regulated society. In an unprecedented

campaign to secure traditional social values, these groups and individuals succeeded ultimately in transforming American government and revolutionizing
American constitutionalism.

"A House Is Not a Home"

One of the most sacred and enduring myths in Anglo-American constitutionalism is Edward Coke's adage "a man's house is his castle." The notion of a
house as fortress, refuge, and "little commonwealth" where private patriarchs
ruled absolutely without fear of interference was best captured by William Pitt:
"The poorest man may in his cottage bid defiance to all the forces of the
Crown. It may be frail—its roof may shake—the wind may blow through
it—the storm may enter—the rain may enter—but the King of England cannot enter; all his force dares not cross the threshold of that ruined tenement!"[48]

Despite such sentimental attachment to houses as quintessentially private
spheres, public realities intruded all the time. As the New York fire cases made
clear, all the king's men could not only cross a tenement's threshold, they
could tear it down. Still, this line between rhetoric and reality warrants closer
scrutiny. What were the specific conditions under which a house as a supposedly impregnable private domain gave way to the public powers of state?
Answers to that question help illuminate the slippery and overlapping nature
of nineteenth-century conceptions of public and private.

One of the most important keys unlocking early American houses to public
access was the legal designation "*disorderly.*" As an integral part of antebellum
moral reform, mayors, aldermen, constables, and private citizens joined judges
and lawyers in an almost constant construction and application of that designation. Once a home or business became a "disorderly house," little stood in
the way of the full force of early American public power. Why?

Once again the main legal rationalizations followed the outlines of *salus
populi* (the welfare of the people is the supreme law), *sic utere tuo* (use your
own so as not to injure another), and the common law of nuisance. First, disorder was the antithesis of the well-regulated society; it marked a temporary
disintegration of civil society, threatening the very existence of fragile antebellum communities. The *salus populi* tradition acknowledged the right of communities to defend themselves aggressively by imposing stringent requirements of orderliness on all spaces and activities. As Chief Justice Booth of
Delaware insisted, "Every man is responsible for the good government of his
house or store, so far as the public is concerned."[49] In addition to this broad
argument from "overruling public necessity," judges and commentators also

utilized the more consequentialist *sic utere tuo* rationale to attack immoral and disorderly houses. Alleged deleterious effects on neighbors and the community brought these houses into the regulated public sphere. Justice Yeates of Pennsylvania made the case explicitly, "Although a man has the exclusive right of governing his own house as he thinks proper, which I hope never to see invaded, yet he must do so in subservience to the laws and rights of others. *Sic utere tuo, ut alienum non laedas.*" Disorderly houses, according to Yeates, violated that principle as "great temptations to idleness, . . . apt to draw together a great number of disorderly persons, which cannot but be very inconvenient to the neighborhood."[50]

Such characterizations triggered the common law of public nuisance. As shown in chapter 2, public nuisance law was one of the most potent regulatory weapons in the common law arsenal, subjecting an offender to bold public remedies. According to Coke, Hawkins, Blackstone, Dane, and Kent, the disorderly house was a paradigmatic case of nuisance.[51] Horace Wood in the definitive American treatise deemed disorderly houses of an "immoral" or "indecent" nature nuisances per se, that is, nuisances irrespective of results, injury, or location. Although judges sometimes differed in their characterizations of "immorality" and their standards of proof, they overwhelmingly agreed with Wood's conclusion: "The experience of all mankind condemns any occupation that tampers with the public morals, tends to idleness and the promotion of evil manners, and anything that produces that result . . . is universally regarded and condemned by it as a public nuisance."[52]

The common law rationales of *salus populi, sic utere tuo*, and nuisance help explain why disorderly houses were susceptible to legal regulation and prohibition, but the question remains, What was a disorderly house? Beyond the tantalizing hints of Horace Wood and Justice Yeates, what tangible conditions systematically branded structures or activities as immoral, indecent, and disorderly?

One key ingredient (though by no means a requirement) of disorder was publicity. The more public the behavior, the more likely courts were to impose constraints. The common law nuisance offense of indecent exposure, for example, obviously hinged on performance in public.[53] Owners of *public* houses (licensed inns and taverns) were held to higher standards of orderliness. In *Alfred S. Pell's Case* (1818), the keeper of a public garden was obliged to establish rules and regulations "calculated to prevent acts of disorder and licentiousness," including requiring a light for each couple present in the garden after dark.[54] In *Barker v. Commonwealth* (1852), proximity to public highways helped to convict a defendant "speaking and uttering wicked, scan-

dalous, and infamous words, representing men and women in obscene and indecent positions, with design to debase and corrupt the morals of the youth."[55] Ill-governed houses in sparsely populated rural areas, at a distance from neighbors and roads, were far more likely to be tolerated than their more visible, more public, urban counterparts.[56]

Another common characteristic of disorderly house prosecutions was a sense of dissimilitude. Disorderly houses were different. They subverted established social practices and violated expectations about the way houses and businesses were governed. In an almost carnivalesque way, disorderly houses mixed, flipped, and ignored the customary hierarchies and social rules that defined antebellum orderliness. This oppositional quality has led Timothy Gilfoyle to describe New York City brothels as part of an extended, erotic "sub-culture."[57] An awareness of this "otherness" and the dangers posed by such inversions pervaded indictments, which routinely described disorderly houses as frequented by persons "old and young, male and female, black and white, by night and day."[58] The inclusion of "night and day" suggested such places disregarded even the natural regularities of time itself.

But though publicity and alterity did characterize a good number of disorderly house prosecutions, they were not determinative. "Disorderly house" was stamped on buildings and businesses of great diversity. No structure was immune from the prescriptions of nuisance law. Even a facade of respectability, privacy, and orderliness did not immunize an "immoral" establishment. As the New Jersey Supreme Court explained, "Although they may be quiet and orderly places, . . . although the most scrupulous cleanliness may be observed, and they may be magnificent in ornament, and luxurious in their provisions for mere sensual gratifications, they are notable nuisances at common law, . . . [when] injurious to the public health, public quiet, or public morals."[59] As a catchall offense against "ill-governed" gatherings of "evil-disposed" persons, the "disorderly house" charge was wielded against everything from private dwellings to swank hotels. Sailors' boardinghouses with their "drunken, bawdy songs," "frolicsome gambols," and "jovial hilarity" seemed particularly vulnerable to the charge.[60] But authorities were also willing to close down Amos Broad's riot-prone Baptist Church in New York City as an "ill-governed house."[61]

As a general rule, however, disorderly houses did tend to fall into one of the following categories: (1) gambling or gaming houses (i.e., houses harboring cards, faro banks, roulette wheels, illegal lottery tickets, shuffle board, billiard tables, bowling alleys, and/or cockfights);[62] (2) theaters, dancehalls, and shows; (3) bawdy houses (i.e., brothels, houses of prostitution, houses of ill fame,

houses of assignation); and (4) inns and taverns. Each of these social evils brought its own set of moral concerns and justifications for public action.

The regulation of gaming and gambling houses drew on a long legal and moralistic tradition. Blackstone incorporated Tacitus's indictment of gambling "addicts" into his own attack on gaming, "an offence of the most alarming nature; tending by necessary consequence to promote public idleness, theft, and debauchery." In 1812 Charles Christian infused this old complaint with new urgency demanding forcible police removal of New York gambling dens: "No pains should be spared to uproot them; in them are to be found sharpers, leading to ruin unsuspecting players, and the habitual idlers, that have dissipated in low excesses, the property left them by industrious parents."[63] The association of gaming and gambling with idleness, cheating, intemperance, vagabondage, gangs, penury, and volatile social descent was constant in nineteenth-century cases and commentary. Judges articulated a widespread social fear about the power of such places to lure the hardworking and upright into indolence and immorality. Gambling houses were dangerous to the neighborhood and disorderly nuisances, according to Justice Harrington of Delaware, because of their power to draw "the sober and industrious into habits of idleness and vice, corrupting the young and unwary."[64] Accordingly, gaming and gambling houses were routinely prosecuted as public nuisances at common law; and most states added special statutory regulations.[65] South Carolina made void all notes and securities won by gaming, allowed losers and third parties to sue winners, outlawed cheating, prohibited gaming at taverns, inns, retail stores, or other public places, and specially protected a ten-mile zone around South Carolina College.[66] Billiard tables like bowling alleys were routinely suppressed despite traditionally low stakes, such as playing for drinks or "for the rub."[67] Gambling implements and tables were subject to summary searches, seizures, and destructions.[68] Particular outrage was reserved for that most odious of games, the cockfight, where "dissolute persons of ill name, fame and dishonest conversation" bet on which bird would kill the other. Testimony of mysterious temptations, outrageous losses, and familial ruin prodded Lemuel Shaw to invoke a common law and constitutional duty to "inculcate principles of humanity." He reckoned cockfighting (like prizefighting and bearbaiting) a public nuisance and an unlawful sport, "being barbarous and cruel, leading to disorder and danger, and tending to deaden the feeling of humanity."[69]

Gaming and gambling were manifest evils in nineteenth-century society; but in a well-regulated community, all public displays and common exhibi-

tions (e.g., pageants, performances, parades, circuses, minstrel shows, magic acts) were subjected to moral strictures, official supervision, and Shaw's "principles of humanity." As arenas of public discourse and producers of public culture, such events exacted constant monitoring and moral policing. The nineteenth-century American "public sphere" (popular as well as bourgeois) was not autonomous from state powers of police and morals regulation.[70] Matthew Hale set the tone and English precedent in 1671 enjoining the erection of a stage at Charing-Cross for ropedancing.[71] American judges and treatise writers generalized Hale's fear of rogues and broils suggesting, "A public exhibition of any kind that tends to the corruption of morals, to a disturbance of the peace, or the general good order and welfare of society, is a public nuisance."[72] Magicians, minstrels, monster displays, and ethnic effigies were easy prey for antebellum authorities, but the low culture/high culture distinction was muted somewhat when theaters and opera houses fell victim to the law of disorderly nuisance.[73] In 1822, allegations of boisterous noise, profane language, mixed dressing rooms, prostitution, and nakedness brought a disorderly house prosecution down on the City Theatre in New York's Warren Street. The court observed, "The good of the community was a paramount object; . . . when [the theater] became a scene of disorder and riot—when the original design of those institutions was so far lost sight of as to allow indecent and immoral conduct, to the disturbance of the neighborhood, it then became a nuisance, and punishable as such." In 1878, the Society for the Prevention of Crime successfully prosecuted the Columbia Opera House for exhibiting "Mock Modesty" and "Silken Meshes," productions showing men and women "in various impudent, lascivious, lewd, wicked, scandalous and obscene groupings, dancings, movements, attitudes, positions, postures and songs, to the manifest corruption of morals."[74] The policing of public performance drew on a rich Anglo-American legal tradition. Through the nineteenth century, the public surveillance and regulation of "disorderly" meetings, halls, and theaters was constant.[75]

If liquor, gaming, and lewd theatrics prefigured a judicial finding of "disorderliness," the addition of race often helped assure conviction. Race often found its way into the primary legal statement of disorder—an indictment describing a house of men and women, young and old, white and black. Just as the "firewater myth" legitimated extensive governmental control over the sale of liquor to Indians, allegations of "drunken negroes" triggered disorderly house prosecutions, especially in lower courts, especially in the South.[76] The case *Smith v. Commonwealth* (Kentucky, 1845) made the color line explicit.

There the indictment of a grocery owner who sold and served liquor to slaves and free persons of color was quashed for not specifying the race of the customers. Chief Justice Ewing elaborated, "The keeping of a grocery, at which *that class* of the community are habitually allowed to assemble and buy whiskey and tipple and drink at pleasure, is calculated to corrupt their morals, to tempt them to petty larcenies, . . . to lead them to dissipation, insubordination and vice, and obstruct the good government, well-being and harmony of society."[77] Race determined whether such a grocery was an illegal, disorderly nuisance. Ewing went on, "The peaceable and habitual assembling of white persons, in the same or any other number, at the grocery for the same purposes, and who even indulged in the same practices as those proven against the slaves, it is believed would not constitute the house a public nuisance, as such assemblies and indulgences would not be of the same evil consequences to the public." Had there been cursing, swearing, noise, or the disturbance of neighbors, whites would have been as guilty of "disorder" as blacks. But when the behavior consisted solely of drinking and congregating, race alone turned the peaceable into the dangerous, the legal into the illegal, and the grocery into a "disorderly house."[78]

When race and slavery were involved, the line between public and private, civility and disorder grew exceedingly thin. On Christmas night 1846, a North Carolina slave patrol invaded a "common, ill governed and disorderly house" brimming with "evil practices." The house was the private plantation of Jacob Boyce where his family, his slaves and some of their relations from neighboring plantations had gathered to celebrate the holiday with conversation, music, and dance.[79] Despite neighbors' testimony that they heard nothing and that Boyce's household was "orderly, peaceable, and quiet," a jury convicted on judicial instructions that if Boyce had "suffered white persons and negroes, of both sexes, to meet together at his house and fiddle and dance together, and get drunk and make noise," they should find Boyce guilty. As Chief Justice Ruffin noted on appeal, the criminality seemed to inhere in "the mingling of the two colors together in the same house and dance."[80]

Race and class hierarchies powerfully shaped, and in some cases determined, antebellum conceptions of immorality and disorder. But nineteenth-century morals regulation was also shot through with gender. The notion of well-governed households at the heart of the moral, well-ordered society was one that clearly demarcated and regulated the roles of men and women, particularly in their sexuality. Nowhere did such assumptions operate more baldly than in the attempted suppression of that most notorious of disorderly houses, the bawdy house.

The Bawdy House

Of all the alleged disorderly houses in nineteenth-century America, the one that powerfully captured the attention and imagination of judges, commentators, and reformers was the bawdy house. Dubbed "The House of Death" by the pulp fiction of the time, the house of prostitution was the most vilified of antebellum morals nuisances.[81] In an attack on brothel keepers, Charles Christian captured the vitriol reserved for this offense:

> This corrupt, and contagious class of persons, whose tartarean depravity spares not even their own children, seize on the earliest opportunity to expose them to sale and prostitution, are fit subjects of the unremitting vengeance of the law, a neighbourhood of them may be truly termed, "hell upon earth." . . . The amount of mischief they do in this way, in what is termed the lower orders of society, is great and calamitous. The breaking up of families—dispersion of children—the ruin of husbands—and the public prostitution of wives, are often the consequences of their vile industry.[82]

Christian's prescription for such rampant moral corruption, police reform and a female penitentiary, also reflected the intimate relationship between changing notions of morality, sexuality, womanhood, and the role of the state.

As a prodigious historical literature has made clear, Christian was joined in his antiprostitution crusade by a bevy of moral reformers ranging from Reverend John R. McDowall, who inspired the New York Magdalen Society, to Dr. William Sanger, author of the most influential sociomedical study of New York prostitution in 1858.[83] But law and its exposition by law writers and courts remained at the center of the moral reform campaign. The New York *City-Hall Recorder* was compiled and published by Daniel Rogers as a complete register of the principal business of the local court of sessions between 1816 and 1820. This record was not meant for esoteric study by professional practitioners. Rather, according to Rogers, the goal of the trial reports was "To illustrate and enforce . . . the genuine principles of morality; and to convey to the public, in language clear and perspicuous, legal principles, important to be understood and known by every citizen."[84] Like the execution sermons of an earlier generation, the local legal record was printed to provide moral lessons—to instruct the public in the expectations and obligations of well-ordered citizenship.[85]

One of first cases in the *City-Hall Recorder* was *Mary Rothbone's Case*, a bawdy house prosecution of paradigmatic proportions.[86] Rogers began with

an epigram: "Ye generous fair, attend while I disclose; The mournful story of a mother's woes." Like many disorderly house cases, Mary Rothbone was *privately* prosecuted (before the mayor and two aldermen) by a mother on behalf of her fallen daughter of nineteen years. Rogers's description of parent and child encapsulated the whole morality tale:

> This mother, a respectable matron, who had once seen happier days, had a settled melancholy gloom of sorrow on her countenance, and her eyes were red with weeping. The daughter, once the hope and expectation of the fond parent, was no longer what she had once been under the fostering influence of a tender mother. The roses of modesty had fled from her cheeks; no longer her eyes beamed with the expressive mildness of virtue, and the sweet enchanting graces of innocence, which inspire even the libertine with a holy reverence. She had been led astray—seduced—debauched—and that guardian genius which was once her attendant, and protected her innocence had fled forever. But with the wild and impudent glance, the vacant, inexpressive stare, which, in the female countenance, so strongly indicates familiarity with vice, you might nevertheless discover some faint traces, not wholly effaced, which might induce the indulgent beholder, in the language of poetry, to pronounce her not "Less than Archangel ruined."[87]

Such maudlin invocations of feminine virtue defiled worked not to console a mother or exculpate a daughter but to convince a jury—a male jury—to let the state act. The prosecution acknowledged the gendered character of public power when issues of sexual morality were at stake by appealing almost literally to *parens patriae*, the notion of the state as parent/father: "Gentlemen. I speak to you on this occasion as fathers, as brothers, nay, as the guardians of the public morals of this community. Will you, by your verdict, sanction vice and corruption? . . . Will you permit women of this description to seduce and lead astray your daughters, your sisters, your female servants, with impunity?"[88]

The argument drew on a deeply rooted ideology about young women's proper place in early American society, beside their mothers or helping their husbands. This particular tragedy was resolved when the daughter was, as counsel put it, "reclaimed, and returned to the domestic fireside." But, though redomesticated, the daughter remained "polluted indeed," the natural progression from daughter to wife fatally interrupted. Those responsible for such meddling with the order of things—those "authors of public infamy" and "destroyers of female innocence"—were accountable to the state.[89]

By the end of this melodrama, Mary Rothbone, the bawdy house operator, did not stand a chance. The jury "immediately" found her guilty. She was sentenced to one year in the city prison. The evidence turned almost exclusively on her "general reputation" for keeping a disorderly house for the purposes of prostitution.[90]

This tale was repeated endlessly in the nineteenth century as authorities battled prostitution. Madams and landlords routinely appeared before magistrates and police juries. Findings of guilty "without leaving the box" fill the criminal reports. Brothels were nuisances at common law and violated a host of supplementary criminal statutes and municipal ordinances. State and local judges had no trouble upholding the broad use of public power against the house of prostitution.[91]

When the landlord of a bawdy house challenged Nashville's power to regulate and suppress it, the city responded with a typical defense of its powers of police, "One of the highest duties of a municipal corporation is to promote the morals, health, and comfort of its inhabitants. It may prevent or regulate any thing that tends to conflict with . . . these great interests." A house of prostitution was an obvious morals nuisance. The Tennessee Supreme Court agreed: "It not only tends to corrupt the public morals by an open profession of prostitution, but it likewise endangers public peace and good order, by drawing together profligate and disorderly persons."[92] Prostitution remained a clear-cut morals offense throughout the century. Its social intractability (in the words of a Kentucky jurist, "The bawd we have always had with us,") did not imply a lenient, individualistic political culture or an ineffectual American state.[93]

Nineteenth-century jurists boasted about the enforcement and deterrent effect of existing morals laws. Jacob Wheeler noted in his *Criminal Cases*, "Prosecutions for disorderly houses are very common, there is scarcely a term but one or more cases are tried; and . . . in almost every case, a conviction is had."[94] New York Chief Justice Nelson took pride in antibrothel remedies ranging from common law and statutory indictment to the voidability of leases and contracts aiding and abetting prostitution, concluding, "The public are pretty well guarded against the offence of keeping houses of ill fame."[95] Nelson balked at adding to New York's regulatory arsenal criminal proceedings against brothel landlords. But other judges and jurisdictions eagerly adopted this and other radical legal measures to weed out immoral establishments.[96] In *Hamilton v. Whitridge* (1857), a Maryland court pioneered the use of the equity injunction against Margaret Hamilton's brothel—a potent legal

innovation that ultimately sealed the fate of many urban red-light districts in the Progressive Era.[97] Historical depictions of the early nineteenth-century as an era of lax enforcement, toleration, or officially sanctioned sexual revolution are misleading. They ignore formidable innovations in equity and nuisance law and marginalize one of the most extensive moral reform and police movements in American history. They also obscure the very real costs (and victims) of nineteenth-century morals prosecutions.[98] After being sentenced to one year in the penitentiary for keeping a disorderly house, Mary Ann Clark relinquished a young child to local officials, and was then accompanied to her house for the quick disposal of her goods.[99]

The fate of Mary Ann Clark and Margaret Hamilton hints at the special vulnerability of certain kinds of people to antiprostitution measures. Without question, women rather than men were the focus of these morals regulations. Prostitution was by legal definition "a sexual vice peculiar to women."[100] Though the "frequenting" of houses of ill-fame was also a public nuisance (and was responsible for the same litany of social evils), it was not regularly prosecuted in the nineteenth century.[101] But even more suggestive of the female centeredness of this regulation was the treatment of married brothel keepers. Though the law of coverture supposedly immunized wives from criminal prosecution, bawdy houses were an express exception. As judges and commentators were fond of pointing out, a wife might not have a property interest in a brothel, but she surely shared in the "government" of the household, especially in matters "usually managed by the intrigues of her sex." In *People v. John Brougham and Bridget His Wife* (1822), the court reached the common conclusion that "the husband was not so much to blame as his wife."[102]

Given the expectations and status hierarchies of antebellum America, unattached, single women were even more susceptible to morals policing. Indeed, in many bawdy house and prostitution prosecutions, it is difficult to determine if the defendant is a prostitute or just a single woman with too many male companions. In many nineteenth-century communities, the distinction was perhaps irrelevant. In *State v. Evans* (1845), Augusta Ann Evans, a "spinster" abandoned by her husband for over a year, was found guilty of keeping an "ill-governed" and disorderly bawdy house.[103] The evidence consisted solely of neighbors' testimony of the early evening visits of a few different men. The Superior Court judge charged the jury that "while one or two acts of adulterous intercourse" do not a bawdy house make, "yet if this had become habitual and common . . . she would be guilty of the offense."[104]

The vulnerability of single women to such morals prosecutions was only

heightened by extraordinarily loose standards of evidence and proof. Evidence like that in *Evans*—the opinion and observation of neighbors—was usually dispositive. Bawdy house prosecutions were one of the few areas of the criminal law where hearsay evidence of one's "general reputation" was enough to convict. In 1838, for example, Margaret M'Dowell and five others were convicted as "notorious" prostitutes and bawdy house keepers without the aid of any facts except public opinion. Justice O'Neall of South Carolina defended the practice: "When it shown that their houses were notorious—that is, known to the whole community—as common bawdy houses, it is the same thing as if it was proved that over the door of each house was written . . . 'bawdy within.'"[105] Though an untolerated anachronism in the commercial law of 1838, O'Neall sought support in the maxim, "What every body says must be true." Only in morals regulation were due process concerns this lax and local voices this determinative. O'Neall assuaged fears of abuse: "To say that there is any danger of a virtuous woman being convicted on such testimony, is utterly absurd. She cannot even be suspected until she has lost her character. . . . [I]f such a charge should ever be made against a virtuous woman, her character will be her shield."[106] This emphasis on character and reputation reflects a morals law still devoted as much to reinforcing local status relationships as to punishing criminal actions. Antebellum judges did not obsess about the line separating "unvirtuous" womanhood from the crime of prostitution.[107]

A reliance on ill-defined offenses such as vagrancy, criminal idleness, "known thief," and "suspicious person" further illustrates the extraordinary degree of informality and discretion at the heart of early American morals regulation. Soon after independence, most states passed laws for the punishment of "rogues, vagabonds, common beggars, and other idle, disorderly and lewd persons."[108] Modeled on English precedent, these statutes began with open-ended enumerations of classes of people deemed vagrants. Massachusetts included

all rogues, vagabonds and idle persons, going about in any town or place in the county, begging; or persons using any subtle craft, juggling or unlawful games or plays, or feigning themselves to have knowledge in physiognomy, palmistry, or pretending that they can tell destinies or fortunes, or discover where lost or stolen goods may be found; common pipers, fiddlers, runaways, stubborn servants or children, common drunkards, common night-walkers, pilferers, wanton and lascivious persons in

speech, conduct or behavior; common railers or brawlers, such as neglect their callings or employment, mispend what they earn, and do not provide for themselves or the support of their families.[109]

The adjective "common" before "drunkards," "night-walkers," and "railers" implied that one need not commit specific illegal acts to be guilty of vagrancy. A bad reputation and a tainted character were enough. As the Ohio Supreme Court remarked, "The offense does not consist in particular acts but in the mode of life, the habits and practices of the accused in respect to the character or traits" deemed "prejudicial to public welfare."[110] In addition to open-ended definitions and proofs of criminality, vagrancy statutes also advocated summary judicial procedures patterned after the latitude granted English justices of the peace over the poor and "not of good fame."[111] In Massachusetts any justice of the peace could summarily commit "idlers" and "lewd persons" to the house of correction.[112]

Such local power and discretion did not bode well for unattached women accused of moral failing. Portland, Maine, made a habit out of bypassing criminal and judicial processes altogether in dealing with its alleged morals offenders. In 1853 Betsey Brown and her daughter Almedia (again abandoned by husband and father) were indefinitely committed to the Portland workhouse by edict of town overseers George Pearson and Benjamin Larrabee. The charge? They were deemed paupers "living a dissolute, vagrant life" whose house was "reputed to be a house of ill-fame."[113] There was no trial, no jury, no lawyer, no rights of the accused, no evidence beyond the "notoriety" of their Green Street home. The Browns were arrested by a constable and placed in the workhouse solely on the word and at the discretion of overseers of the poor. A legal record exists only because Portland later sued Bangor (the Browns's legal settlement) for the costs of commitment and support. Those costs were halved when Almedia Brown died a year later at age twenty-two.[114]

The Brown case was not anomalous or an exceptional incident of local abuse. Nineteen years earlier, Adeline G. Nott tried unsuccessfully to challenge Portland's practice after being similarly committed to the workhouse as a prostitute.[115] Nott's lawyer argued before the Maine Supreme Court that such process (or the lack thereof) was "unconstitutional and void," violating the "absolute and natural right" of a citizen to a trial or hearing before a judge. The court responded with an unwavering defense of a community's superior, paternal power to police immorality and to protect itself from indigence:

[Nott's] health and strength constitutes a fund, of which [the town] have a right reasonably to avail themselves, to contribute to her maintenance.

She is prostrating both by dissolute habits. . . . What has been done [in this case], is to preserve her health and strength, and to render it productive. For whose benefit? For her own. That she may thence draw an honest livelihood. That she may be removed from temptation, and compelled to cultivate habits of industry, to be again restored to society, as a useful member, as soon as may be. It is, under the circumstances a measure calculated for her own good. . . . [S]he will regard the interposition as parental; as calculated to save instead of punishing.[116]

In *Shafer v. Mumma* (1861), Maryland Chief Justice LeGrand similarly defended the discretionary, ministerial authority of mayors to imprison "lewd women." He described such morals policing as separate from the criminal law and the judicial power and immune from traditional constitutional protections. "It has always been understood," LeGrand argued, "that under the police power, persons disturbing the public peace, persons guilty of a nuisance, or obstructing the public highways, and the like offenses, may be summarily arrested and fined, without any infraction of that part of the Constitution which apportions the administration of the judicial power."[117]

The power of summary procedures, local discretion, and "character" evidence in nineteenth-century morals regulation reflects the tenacity of traditional conceptions of public power and community order. This regulatory regime embraced notions of criminality, constitutional right, and the relationship of public and private radically different from those of twentieth-century liberal constitutionalism. Status and the concomitant moralistic judgments of a local populace continued to matter more than hard evidence of specific criminal acts in punishing morals offenders. Individual due process was routinely subordinated to the local police powers necessary to secure the moral fiber and general welfare of a community. The kinds of conduct and types of people permitted in "private" houses were everybody's business. The well-ordered society depended on well-ordered families and households. The ultimate guardian of "order" was community sentiment and public opinion. Courts reinforced the role of public scrutiny in morals policing with legal conclusions like, "A man careful of the *reputation* of his house and regulating it upon correct principles, is not accustomed to have found there women *notoriously* charged with the offence of prostitution."[118] So much for a man's castle.

From a twentieth-century perspective, these ideas and practices seem arbitrary and even scary. The fate of women like Almedia Brown should certainly give one pause. But these notions were the essence of nineteenth-century

conceptions of local self-government.[119] They were part of the same vision of society that held market imperatives subject to the larger dictates of community well-being and that staunchly defended the publicness of roads and rivers. The "well-regulated society" presumed a correspondence between legal rules and community standards. In morals cases, law was primarily expected to enforce local codes of proper moral behavior, not to protect a private sphere of individual right from overzealous majoritarianism.

But as demonstrated here, antebellum notions of "proper moral behavior" were not neutral or consensual; they were shot through with tilted assumptions about race, gender, and ethnicity. Although disorderly house prosecutions did befall "respectable" citizens and establishments,[120] the status of single women and people of color made them inherently suspect and especially vulnerable. The tags "immoral" and "disorderly" were key terms unlocking the extensive, summary powers of the early American state. Once linked in the public imagination with particular segments of the population, they allowed for a powerful nexus between social bias and state police power.

The local and discretionary nature of early American morals regulation was directly challenged only in the late nineteenth century. The attack came from the same two forces that ultimately dislodged the common law vision of a well-regulated society: the centralization and constitutionalization of state power, and the rights revolution precipitated by the Civil War and Reconstruction. The Browns and Adeline Nott were finally vindicated in 1876 when the Maine Supreme Court struck down the Portland pauper law for violating the new Fourteenth Amendment. Justice Walton argued, "That article declares that no state shall deprive any person of life, *liberty*, or property, without due process of law; and while it may not be easy to determine in advance what will in every case constitute due process of law, it needs no argument to prove that an *ex parte* determination of two overseers of the poor is not such a process."[121] Assessing the constitutional implications of a world without slavery or servitudes, Walton elaborated, "If white men and women may be thus summarily disposed of at the north, of course black ones may be disposed of in the same way at the south; and thus the very evil which it was particularly the object of the fourteenth amendment to eradicate will still exist." He thus also vindicated Justice Rice who argued in dissent in the Browns' case that Portland's treatment of paupers was "but little removed from that of chattel slavery."[122] The end of slavery marked the beginning of a broad-based constitutional revolution in private rights.[123]

The most definitive statement of the new constitutional limits on moral reform came in the famous Illinois decision *People v. Turner* (1870).[124] There the

laws.[153] In nine separate opinions on three cases, the justices echoed Shaw that liquor licensing was a case of police power and not a violation of the commerce clause of the Constitution. Chief Justice Roger Taney reached for a broader and novel equation of police power and positive state sovereignty, but ultimately liquor licensing required no constitutional innovation.[154] State police power was potent and extensive enough, leading often to "the destruction of property." Justice McLean introduced the familiar regulatory defense:

> A nuisance may be abated. Every thing prejudicial to the health or morals of a city may be removed. Merchandise from a port where a contagious disease prevails, being liable to communicate the disease, may be excluded; and in extreme cases, it may be thrown into the sea. This comes into direct conflict with the regulation of commerce, and yet no one doubts the local power. It is a power essential to self-preservation, and exists, necessarily, in every organized community.[155]

On the last page of the sprawling, 128-page disquisition, Justice Grier summated that the police power included "every law for the restraint and punishment of crime, for the preservation of public peace, health, and morals." Such laws were "of primary importance," lying at "the foundation of social existence . . . *salus populi suprema lex*."[156]

Thus the first attempts of temperance reformers to tighten local liquor regulations met little in the way of sustained constitutional opposition.[157] Robert Rantoul reified the Massachusetts Declaration of Rights and Daniel Webster[158] waxed eloquently about the commerce clause of the Constitution, but local liquor regulation (even if it resulted in de facto prohibition) was too well ensconced in traditions of self-government and the common law vision of a well-regulated society. Even a Supreme Court torn by the impending crises of slavery and sectionalism (in which constitutional interpretations of "natural rights," "property," and "commerce" figured prominently) concluded unanimously that liquor licensing was an appropriate exercise of state police power. State licensing and nonlicensing conflicted with neither property rights, guarantees of contract,[159] or the commerce clause of the Constitution. No-license and local-option reforms certainly triggered social conflict, local resistance, and litigation. But they ultimately posed no fundamental problems for and forced no lasting reassessment of early American government. Indeed, those contests provided a forum for some of the most forceful defenses of well-regulated governance.[160]

All that changed suddenly when temperance reformers ratcheted up the polity for a new wave of legislative experimentation—state prohibition.

Prohibition marked a stunning departure in the legal and legislative history of morals and liquor regulation. Power and discretion were summarily taken out of the hands of communities and local officials and replaced with blanket state-wide legislative bans on a remarkably profitable activity (De Bow's reported 1,217 distilleries and breweries capitalized at over $8 million in 1850)[161] that previously enjoyed the sanction of law. Thomas Cooley reflected on the momentous consequences: "The trade in alcoholic drinks being lawful, and the capital employed in it fully protected by law, the legislature then steps in, and, by enactment based on general reasons of public utility, annihilates the traffic, destroyes altogether the employment, and reduces to a nominal value the property on hand." He added, "The merchant of yesterday becomes the criminal of to-day, and the very building in which he lives becomes perhaps a nuisance."[162] The radical implications of American state prohibition even elicited the attention of John Stuart Mill in *On Liberty* (1859).[163] For good reason. Together with other legislative revolutions in this era (e.g., police reform, Married Women's Property Acts, general incorporation laws, and Field codes), prohibition and its legal/political repercussions transformed traditional understandings of the scope of legislation, the nature of rights, and the locus of public power.[164]

A product of a gradual shift in the temperance movement toward total abstinence and public coercion, prohibition repudiated the local, piecemeal, regulatory regime of the license system. Despite the success of no-license organizing (including no-license in 728 of 856 New York towns in 1846, an Ohio no-license constitutional amendment in 1851, and success in every county of Massachusetts by 1851),[165] reformers still bristled at the formal legality of the liquor trade and the capriciousness and inconsistencies attending "half-way" police measures. The "License System" became increasingly viewed as part of the problem, "barter[ing] away the peace and morals of society," offering legal comfort to the enemy, and branding good temperance men and women as fanatical zealots opposed to the "law of the land."[166] Reformers demanded more vigorous and complete legal solutions. As a Massachusetts district attorney put it, "Legal and moral agencies should be combined. They are like the soul and body, and in the present state of existence can not well act separately."[167]

After a brief experiment in Massachusetts in 1838, prohibition burst on the national scene with the Maine Law crusade of Neal Dow, mayor of Portland and the "Napoleon of Temperance," in 1850. A committed prohibitionist frustrated by the spotty enforcement and low penalties of Portland's no-license system, Dow and the Maine Temperance Union pressured the state legislature into a far-reaching revision of its liquor laws. The resultant "Act for the Sup-

pression of Drinking Houses and Tippling Shops" (1851) included a series of revolutionary provisions:[168]

1. A complete statewide ban on the manufacture and sale of spirituous or intoxicating liquors (except by special municipal agents for medicinal and mechanical purposes).
2. Broad powers of search, seizure, and forfeiture that placed a burden of positive proof on the owner of confiscated liquors.[169]
3. Substantial penalties (including a loss of certain jury privileges), heavy fines, and stiff jail sentences for repeat offenders.
4. Additional provisions to deter appeals (by requiring additional bonds, guarantees, and double fines), to expedite prosecution (including a duty to prosecute when informed), and to restrict the discretion of judges.

The Maine Law triggered an unprecedented chain reaction of prohibitionist activity and imitative state legislation. Between 1851 and 1855, twelve more states enacted prohibition statutes modeled on Maine's initiative: Connecticut, Delaware, Illinois, Indiana, Iowa, Massachusetts, Michigan, Nebraska, New Hampshire, New York, Rhode Island, and Vermont.[170]

State prohibition was initially received with testimonials and great expectations. Some of them were engraved on a pitcher presented to Neal Dow by the citizens of Portland. The background depicted a tenantless jail and the prosperous commerce of ships under full sail. In the foreground, police officials administered the Maine law by emptying numerous casks of confiscated liquor onto the ground.[171] The former squared nicely with the aspirations of a well-regulated society. Courts and jurists were left to work out the legal and constitutional implications of the latter.

In *State v. Gurney* (1853), the Maine Supreme Court proclaimed the constitutionality of Dow's legislation: "The Legislature [has] a right to regulate by law the sale of any article, the use of which would be detrimental to the morals of the people."[172] Overall, that was the response of most of the country's state judiciary.[173] The U.S. Supreme Court's favorable review of restrictive licensing (especially Roger Taney's capacious rendering of state sovereignty), together with the high political and economic stakes of prohibition, emboldened juridical defenses of state police power. Justice Bennett upheld Vermont's version in *Lincoln v. Smith* (1855) declaring, "The law in question falls within that large class of powers, which are essential to the regulation, promotion, and preservation of morals, health and the general well being and prosperity of the people of this state; and it may in an eminent degree be regarded as a police regulation."[174] Such regulations, added Justice Storrs of Connecticut in *State*

v. Wheeler (1856), "[had] been passed in almost all civilized communities, and in ours from the earliest settlement of our state, . . . based on the power possessed by every sovereign state, to provide . . . for the health, morals, peace and general welfare of the state."[175] Liquor and intemperance, these jurists agreed, harmed public health, produced "pauperism and crime," and inflicted a great "moral injury upon society." "If a public evil of this character, and of this magnitude cannot be suppressed," Michigan Justice Johnson concluded emphatically in *People v. Gallagher* (1856), then "it may well be said that there is an end to all legislative power."[176]

These jurists supplemented staunch defenses of state legislative power with equally strong repudiations of the property and rights claims of defendants. In doing so, they drew explicitly on the social and relational philosophy of rights so much a part of the well-regulated society. In *State v. Allmond* (1856), Delaware Chief Justice Harrington made the classic case: "The Legislature may by general laws regulate and restrict the use of property which it deems dangerous to the existence, peace or welfare of society, and may prevent the acquisition of such kinds of property as it considers as to require such prohibition. The Legislature of this State has done so from the beginning, . . . regulating not only property itself but the personal industry and enterprise through which property is acquired." Examples? Harrington listed a litany of long-standing property and trade regulations: the statute of wills, intestate laws, license laws, weights and measures, and laws regarding physicians, surgeons, attorneys, millers, ferries, fisheries, and innkeepers.[177] But what of the speedy seizure, forfeiture, and destruction of liquor that accompanied Maine-style prohibition? Harrington's colleague in Vermont rejoined with the deep roots of summary abatement at common law:

> Nuisances may be abated in the most summary manner; dogs found chasing sheep may be shot down; bucks running at large . . . may become the property of the captor; and race horses may be declared forfeited; gambling implements may be destroyed; lottery tickets and obscene prints may be prohibited, and under the quarantine laws, the health officer of a city, to prevent the spread of infection or contagion, may destroy bedding or clothing, or any part of the cargo of a vessel, subject to quarantine, and which "he may deem infected." Gunpowder kept in improper places, may be seized and confiscated; and the exercise of these powers, is a power of prevention, highly conservative in its character, and essential to the well being of the body politic, and ought not to be characterized as arbitrary or despotic.[178]

As Mill and Cooley recognized, prohibition obliterated established property and economic rights in the liquor trade. But according to these state jurists, such destruction was simply an extension of the principles and practices of well-regulated governance serving public morality. As Justice Storrs concluded, "The subjection of private property in the mode of its enjoyment to the public good . . . is a principle lying at the foundation of government. It is a condition of the social state; the price of its enjoyment."[179]

But despite the heroic efforts of state judges to reconcile Maine laws with the well-regulated society, there was no escaping the fact that something about prohibition was new and different. In *Fisher v. McGirr* (1854), Lemuel Shaw began to elucidate that distinctiveness. The facts of *Fisher* also provide an opportunity to see a prohibition law in action (in this case the 1852 Massachusetts version).[180]

The critical events of the case all took place within a single day, August 4, 1852. Isaac Keith, Francis Kern, and William Chipman, all citizens and voters of the town of Sandwich, brought a complaint before the Barnstable County justice of the peace charging Theodore Fisher with keeping intoxicating liquors in his dwelling house contrary to the state's new prohibition law. Justice of the Peace Lothrop Davis promptly ordered the constable of Sandwich Patrick McGirr to forcibly enter Fisher's dwelling house during the day, make a careful search, and seize and keep all liquors he found. As Neal Dow once declared, all that was needed to make prohibition work was three good temperance men, a loyal constable, and an efficient magistrate.[181] The constable was further instructed to summon Fisher to appear before Davis and show cause why such liquors should not be forfeited and destroyed (the burden of proof was statutorily placed on the defendant). Constable McGirr found liquor: one-half barrel of cherry brandy, one demijohn and one bottle of brandy, one jug and one bottle of New England rum, and one bottle of gin. When Fisher failed to prove that such liquors were "legally kept" (i.e., of foreign origin in original packaging), Davis ordered the intoxicants destroyed and fined Fisher an additional twenty dollars and costs. Fisher challenged the constitutionality of these prohibition proceedings and sued to recover the value of his lost property.[182]

In a spate of liquor cases over the next twenty years, the Massachusetts Supreme Judicial Court never seriously questioned the overall constitutionality of the legislature's power to prohibit the manufacturing, selling, and keeping of intoxicating liquors.[183] In *Fisher v. McGirr*, however, Lemuel Shaw began subjecting particular components of the prohibition regime to close constitutional scrutiny, especially its formidable search, seizure, and forfeiture

provisions. Shaw was too well schooled in the well-ordered society to deny the *substantive* police power to ban, search, and destroy private properties deemed hostile to the general welfare.[184] So instead, he zeroed in on the *process* of prohibition. First, Shaw challenged the sweeping search and seizure powers enforcing the liquor law. The search of Fisher's dwelling, Shaw concluded, was "unreasonable" and "unconstitutional" because of the overly broad mandate given Constable McGirr. This search was not limited to specifically described properties or particular owners, nor did it safeguard imported/exported liquors. This was an express violation of the Declaration of Rights (article 14) protection against "general warrants and unreasonable searches."[185] Second, and even more significant, Shaw decried the utter lack of any proceedings remotely resembling a trial or "due process of law." The ex parte complaint of "three good temperance men" provided no opportunity to confront accusers, no examinations, no day in court, and no personal notice. The seizure of liquor amounted to a prima facie case against the defendant. Shaw railed that "No provision is made by the statute for a trial, for a determination by judicial proofs of the facts, upon the truth of which alone the property can be justly confiscated and destroyed." Such a trial was the requirement of article 12 of the Declaration of Rights, declaring "that no subject shall be arrested, or deprived of his property, immunities or privileges, or his life, liberty or estate, but by the judgement of his peers, or the law of the land."[186] This judgment of Theodore Fisher passed without trial, without proof, and consequently, according to Shaw, without constitutional muster.

Shaw's constitutional objections in *Fisher* forced the Massachusetts legislature to pass a revised 1855 prohibition statute *sans* the problematic enforcement procedures of section 14.[187] But the implications of Shaw's decision went beyond mere statutory revision. In *Fisher*, Shaw explicitly and powerfully elevated "procedural due process of law" into a regular and formal check on legislative exertions of state police power. Shaw defended the general legislative power to prohibit liquor as a nuisance. But he also served notice that such sweeping, unprecedented legislative endeavors would be accompanied by increased judicial solicitude for those "precautions and safeguards for the security of persons and property, and the most valuable rights of the subject, so sedulously required and insisted on . . . in our Declaration of Rights"—the right to a trial by jury, the right to be free of unreasonable searches and seizures, the right to common processes of law.[188] Though a regard for procedural due process had common law origins through Magna Charta, it now became an automatic and axiomatic part of the judicial review of police regu-

lation.[189] Consequently, the Supreme Judicial Court for the first time declared a substantial portion of a general Massachusetts statute unconstitutional.[190]

This was a new development in the story of the well-regulated society. And the crucial question is, why? After all, Shaw was only too aware of the prominent and historic role played by summary destructions, confiscations, ex parte proceedings, and local discretion in the administration of justice in well-ordered communities. He knew all about the pulling down of houses during fires, the summary removal of obstructions to public ways, the seizure of unwholesome meats by market clerks, the quick penalties inflicted on prostitutes and common drunkards. Why were identical processes deemed nefarious when appended to a prohibition statute in the 1850s? Shaw left one clue near the end of his opinion in *Fisher*:

> In a law directing a series of measures, which in their operation are in danger of encroaching upon private rights; vesting in sub officers large powers, which when most carefully guarded, are liable to be mistaken or abused, and which are to direct, limit and regulate the judicial conduct of a large class of magistrates; it is highly important that the powers conferred, and the practical directions given, be so clear and well defined, that they may serve as safe guides to all such officers and magistrates, in their respective duties; and in these respects, the statute itself must, on its face, be conformable to the constitution.[191]

Prohibition was not analogous to local fire or market regulations. It was a comprehensive statutory revocation of preexisting liberties, properties, and rights. It replaced local, discretionary liquor licensing with a formal, centralized, and uniform system of rules guiding the administrative and judicial conduct of law enforcement officials throughout the state. Such newly delineated "public" powers were met by careful defenses of more closely designated "private" rights.[192]

Shaw was not the only jurist to notice the transformative nature of prohibition laws. Indeed, Shaw's reaction was tame compared with the vitriolic rhetoric and constitutional creativity it inspired in other jurists. In Michigan and Vermont, prohibition was sustained only over vigorous dissents. In *People v. Gallagher*, dissenting Justice Pratt marshaled wide-ranging defenses of wine and property (from the Decalogue and Hume to Kent, Story, and Webster) to battle "the despotic and highly penal act"—"a bold and daring invasion of private property."[193] When Chief Justice Redfield failed to convince his colleagues to follow Shaw's example and insist upon ordinary modes of trial and

proof in the enforcement of Vermont prohibition, he left them with a dire warning:

> In regard to the mode of trial, if it can be applied to one offence it may be applied to all, and in times of tyranny and oppression, no mode of resort has been more common, than to treat an accusation, by public officers, as evidence of guilt and to demand of the accused proof of innocence. . . . In all abuses of authority there is no return, *nulla vestigia retrorsum*, and it always begins in a good cause, in defence of religion, or morality, or public decorum, or order, or decency.[194]

Such sentiments did not always remain in the minority. In a rare burst of aggressive judicial review, justices in Indiana and New York threw down the gauntlet and declared prohibition an unconstitutional exercise of legislative power.[195] In the process they developed an uncompromising critique of the *salus populi* tradition and pioneered a conception of "due process of law" well beyond Lemuel Shaw's concerns about procedure.

Central to the invention of a new legal-constitutional tradition was the dismantling of the old. In *Beebe v. State* and *Herman v. State* (1855), Justice Perkins of Indiana put together the most thoroughgoing assault on the principles of the well-regulated society found in antebellum law.[196] The question at hand: Could the state legislature enact a prohibitory liquor law? The state of Indiana, of course, argued affirmatively, defending a broad, legislative power under the mandate "the safety of the people is the supreme law." In *Beebe* Justice Perkins launched a devastating attack with a classic delegitimating argument: that might be "*European*" jurisprudence, but it was not "*American*" law.[197] Perkins argued that the roots of *salus populi* lay in "*European* writers on natural, public, and civil law" who were "dangerous, indeed utterly blind guides to follow in our free and limited government." The whole European tradition was corrupt. Perkins noted, it was the product of governments that were "paternal" in character:

> All power was in them by divine right, and, hence, absolute; the people of a country had no rights except what the government of that country graciously saw fit to confer upon them; and it was its duty, like as a father towards his children to command whatever it deemed expedient for the public good. . . . [Such governments] could prescribe what the people should eat and drink, what political, moral and religious creeds they should believe in, and punish heresy by burning at the stake, all for the public good.[198]

Justice Perkins asserted unambiguously in 1855 that the maxim *salus populi suprema lex est*, as applied to American legislative power, was foreign and "without meaning."[199]

In *Herman v. State*, Perkins did the same to the other key maxim of the well-regulated society, *sic utere tuo ut alienum non laedas*. The state of Indiana argued that the regulation of liquor was justified by the legislature's duty to make sure that all used their own so as not to injure others. Perkins retorted that prohibition implied "that a man shall not use at all for enjoyment what his neighbor may abuse." Such a doctrine, if given the sanction of law, would "annihilate society, make eunuchs of all men, or drive them into the cells of the monks, and bring the human race to an end, or continue it under the direction of licensed county agents."[200] Perkins invoked Genesis and John Milton's *Areopagitica* (1644). Prohibition based upon *sic utere tuo* was not the way the Almighty governed his world:

> [God] made man a free agent, to give him an opportunity to exercise his will, to be virtuous or vicious as he should choose, he placed evil as well as good before him, he put the apple into the garden of Eden, and left upon man the responsibility of his choice, made it a moral question, and left it so. He enacted as to that, a moral, not a physical prohibition. *He could have easily enacted a physical prohibitory law by declaring the fatal apple a nuisance and removing it.* He did not. His purpose was otherwise, and he has since declared that the tares and wheat shall grow together to the end of the world.[201]

Prohibition laws, Perkins dramatically concluded, robbed man of "free agency."

Two principles replaced *salus populi* and *sic utere tuo* in the "*American*" governmental tradition being created by Justice Perkins and colleagues: "the great doctrine of rights in the people as *against* the government"; and the notion of fundamental constitutional limitations on legislative power—limitations enforced by a vigilant judiciary. As Perkins summarized, "Over the people of this state hangs the shield of written constitutions, which are the supreme law, . . . which grant a restricted legislative power, within which the legislators must limit their action for the public welfare, and whose barriers they can not overleap under any pretext of supposed safety of the people." The rights of citizens to liberty, property, and pursuits of happiness were among the most important of those constitutional limitations against government. And since *Marbury v. Madison*, according to Perkins, the principal mechanism for "securing to the people safety from legislative aggression" was judicial review.[202] The "safety of

the people" ostensibly remained the law of the land. But suddenly it became the responsibility of an active judiciary policing state legislatures with potent new renderings of constitutional limitations and the substantive rights of individual citizens.

Wynehamer v. People (1856) was the first complete, positive statement of this new constitutionalism. It was a watershed in the history of American public law.[203] There the New York Court of Appeals transformed the due process clause of the state constitution into a *substantive* and determinative restraint on legislative prerogative. Substantive due process superseded *salus populi* as the American rule of law. It befell a new justice George F. Comstock to explicate this transformation. The only question before the court was whether New York's 1855 prohibition statute "for the prevention of intemperance, pauperism, and crime" was valid and constitutional. Comstock began by presenting New York's two chief constitutional limitations on legislative power:

> Article 1, section 1. No member of this state shall be disfranchised or deprived of any of the rights or privileges secured to any citizen thereof, unless by the law of the land or the judgment of his peers.

> Article 1, section 6. No persons shall be deprived of life, liberty or property without due process of law; nor shall private property be taken for public use without just compensation.

Next Comstock established that rights in liquor and its accoutrements were indeed forms of private property worthy of constitutional protection. Property was "an institution of law, and not a result of speculations in science, in morals, or economy." In New York law, alcoholic beverages "were bought and sold like other property" since settlement. The chief legal characteristic of all property for Comstock was "inviolability": "All property is equally sacred in the constitution, and therefore speculations as to its chemical or scientific qualities, or the mischief engendered by its abuse, have very little do with the inquiry."[204] So much for *sic utere tuo*. Liquor was protected *qua* property. And the remarkable novelty of *Wynehamer* was that this protection was fundamental, absolute, and sacrosanct. Legislative theories of the public welfare or general good did not legitimate interference. Comstock was unequivocal: "In a government like ours, theories of public good or public necessity may be so plausible, or even so truthful, as to command popular majorities. But whether truthful or plausible merely, and by whatever numbers they are assented to, there are some *absolute private rights beyond their reach, and among these the constitution places the right of property.*"[205] That was the *substantive* guarantee

attending the storied constitutional phrases "the law of the land" and "due process of law." These were not merely the procedural protections outlined by Lemuel Shaw in *Fisher v. McGirr*, requiring proper legal form and process before the legislative or administrative extinguishment of rights in property (e.g., trial by jury, notice, hearing, limited search and seizure). Rather, the "true interpretation" of these constitutional phrases, according to Comstock, was that "where rights are acquired by the citizen under the existing law, there is no power in any branch of government to take them away. . . . Where rights of property are admitted to exist, the legislature cannot say they shall exist no longer."[206] This was a powerful and revolutionary inauguration of a new constitutional creed. Comstock was saying that *any* law judicially interpreted to "annihilate the value of property" or "strip it of its attributes" was on its face a denial of due process and, consequently, an unconstitutional abuse of legislative authority.

Wynehamer v. People was a complete repudiation of the organizing principles of the well-regulated society. As in the Indiana decisions, it derided legal theories of public good and *salus populi*. It similarly left *sic utere tuo* in tatters. Property rights, according to *Wynehamer*, were absolute and inviolable. They were not subject to novel legislative schemes and regulations to keep one from using property so as not to injure another or the community at large. The social and relational understanding of rights and property that pervaded American public jurisprudence from James Wilson to Lemuel Shaw was not a part of the reasoning of the New York Court of Appeals in striking down prohibition. Public spirit, local self-government, and regulated liberty were replaced in Comstock's rule of law by a new (and, by twentieth-century standards, familiar) formula composed of absolute individual rights, strict judicial review of police regulation, and explicit[207] constitutional limitations upon legislative power. *Wynehamer* was the origin of a narrow, but remarkably popular and resilient, strand of American liberal constitutionalism that would later count among its jurisprudential triumphs such politically disparate cases as *Lochner v. New York* (1905) and *Roe v. Wade* (1973).

For the time being, however, *Wynehamer* and *Beebe* remained anomalous. Most state courts sustained the constitutionality of prohibition with vigorous defenses of state police power. And despite continued haggling over revenue laws and foreign and interstate commerce, the U.S. Supreme Court unambiguously declared in 1877 that, "as a measure of police regulation looking to the preservation of public morals, a State law prohibiting the manufacture and sale of intoxicating liquors is not repugnant to the Constitution of the United States"—"*salus populi suprema lex.*"[208]

But the die of a new constitutional regime was cast. The terms of debate had decisively shifted. On one side, a new constitutional language of private rights, limited government, and substantive (as well as procedural) due process of law began to displace the moral and common law philosophy of well-regulated governance in the public interest. This new private rights orientation was not self-generating. It was a direct response to an equally dramatic change in the exercise of public powers. State prohibition involved a distinctively upward shift in the locus of public decision-making power in the American polity. Morals police, including controls on intoxicating liquors, had been the pre-rogative of local self-regulating communities for centuries. With a simple fiat, state legislatures dissolved this tradition and a whole set of time-honored ex-pectations. It replaced a local, customary, and discretionary regime with a centralized, rule-based, and stream-lined enforcement apparatus. Even as state jurists attempted to reconcile these powers with the language of *salus populi* and *sic utere tuo*, defenses of prohibition redefined the nature and ex-tent of state power. "Sovereignty" increasingly replaced "police" as the key word[209] in regulatory apologetics. And the local-historical sensibility of the common law tradition was supplanted by straightforward renderings of inter-est and power. In *Beer Company v. Massachusetts* (1877), the U.S. Supreme Court upheld Massachusetts prohibition with a defense of an inalienable po-lice power allowing the discontinuance of any manufacture or traffic "the public safety or the public morals require."[210] Even in *Wynehamer*, Justice Hubbard managed this description of state power:

> The sovereign power of the state in all matters pertaining to the public good, the health, good order and morals of the people, is omnipotent. . . . The police power is, of necessity, despotic in its character commensurate with the sovereignty of the state; and individual rights of property, be-yond the express constitutional limits, must yield to its exercise. And in emergencies, it may be exercised to the destruction of property, without compensation to the owner, and even without the formality of a legal in-vestigation. . . . I know of no limits of self-preservation to the body politic.[211]

Increasingly differentiated conceptions of public powers and private rights ex-panded concurrently at midcentury—a prelude to the creation of a liberal state *simultaneously* individualizing and totalizing in its manifestations.

Postbellum American constitutionalism traditionally has been interpreted as the strange harvest of America's slave past and industrial future. Without downplaying the crucial significance of race and economy in late nineteenth-

century law, the question remains, why liquor? Why do we find the earliest, definitive statements of both substantive due process and the inalienable police power in cases involving intoxicants?[212] This chapter has suggested an answer in the powerful, persistent, and contested role of morals policing in the nineteenth-century American polity. Morals regulation did not recede in the nineteenth century. It exploded. Public morals were the focus of an unprecedented burst of reform activity and radical legal and legislative initiatives with important ramifications for American statecraft and political thought. Despite historical talk of tolerance, cities of eros, Victorian compromises, or a wholesale paradigm shift from morals to property, the regulation of public morality continued to play an absolutely central role in nineteenth-century American life. Morals police remained one of the matter-of-fact obligations of government in a well-regulated society. Our linear, liberal histories of constitutional rights and liberties obscure the degree to which new ideas about privacy and personal freedom grew up in cooperation with rather than in isolation from competing ideals of social order and public power.

Public Health:

Quarantine, Noxious Trades,

and Medical Police

Public Health is Public Wealth.—Benjamin Franklin

T he abilities of the polity to maintain social and moral order, to regulate trade and secure an urban food supply, to promote internal improvements and manage public properties, and to guarantee the safety and security of the populace were all central attributes of nineteenth-century conceptions of good governance and well-ordered society. But often overlooked and undervalued in histories and theories of modern state-formation is the crucial role of public health. Public health and public hygiene emerged simultaneously with new ideas about the affirmative responsibilities of "the state" in the seventeenth and eighteenth centuries, including English mercantilism, Scottish and French policing, and German cameralism and *Polizeiwissenschaft*.[1] From the medico-mercantilism of William Petty to Johann Peter Frank's enlightened vision of "medical police," a succession of political and medical thinkers asserted that as the principal aim of government was the welfare of land and population, the health of the people must be a primary object of public attention and official action.[2] Revolutions in science, medicine, and governance were interrelated and were perceived as mutually reinforcing. As William Petty remarked on the wider implications of Francis Bacon's work, "[T]he *Advancement of Learning*, hath made a judicious *Parallel* in many particulars, between the *Body Natural*, and *Body Politick*, and between the Arts of preserving both in Health and Strength."[3]

Michel Foucault described this new governmental focus on "thisworldly" salvation (i.e., wealth, well-being, security, protection against accidents) as a

revised "pastoral power"—a prelude to the creation of modern states and subjects. As governmental legitimacy and reason of state came to rest on a polity's ability to guarantee and improve the population's welfare (the *salus populi*), the public policing of health, hygiene, and urban supplies and environment assumed central importance. Disease came to be seen as an economic and political problem for societies to remedy and manage as a regular part of public policymaking.[4] Public health became a duty and a privilege of sovereignty.

Johann Peter Frank's definition of medical police captured this confluence of developments: "The internal security of the state is the subject of general police science. A very considerable part of this science is to apply certain principles for the health care of people living in society."[5] Frank outlined a "womb-to-tomb" public health program that included the regulation of midwives; pregnancy assistance; child education and welfare; orphan care; sewage and garbage disposal; water supply; the hygiene of food, clothing, recreation, and housing; accident prevention; vital statistics; hospitals; and the policing of epidemics and communicable diseases. Similar health regulations and rules of hygiene figured prominently in Nicolas Delamare's authoritative treatise on French police. By the end of the eighteenth century, the politics of health joined safety, order, economy, and morals as key concerns of the state and ongoing foci of political discourse and legal, administrative, and regulatory practice.[6]

The United States was not immune from these social, scientific, and governmental influences (though simple transatlantic germ theories elide the complexities of American public health history). Many early American political and medical theorists echoed their European counterparts on the alliance of health and polity. Dr. John Bell's *Report on the Importance and Economy of Sanitary Measures to Cities* noted the role of health in generating the "community of interests" necessary to well-ordered government: "The power of a state depends on the population, wealth, and productive industry, and on the cultivated intelligence of its people; trammels on all of which are created by whatever deteriorates the physical strength and the health of any portion of them."[7] Dr. John Griscom of New York, was even more specific and forensic, rooting American public health in the very documents of the Founding:

> I regard government as instituted for the protection of the lives of the people. Life is one of the first subjects mentioned in the Declaration of Independence as belonging particularly to the care of the government—

"Life, liberty, and the pursuit of happiness." I do not know what that means, if it is not the protection of the lives of the people against any approaches whatever, whether from internal or external causes of disease, or any other source that can be named. And as I believe that the strength of an individual depends upon his own health, so I believe that the strength of a State depends upon the health of the people who collectively compose it.[8]

American legal thinkers were just as insistent about public health priorities. Nathan Dane paraphrased Blackstone, "Injuries affecting a man's health are those, where by any *unwholesome* practices of another, a man sustains any apparent damage in his vigour or constitution, as by selling him bad provision or wine, by the exercise of noisome trade, which infects the air in his neighbourhood, or by the neglect or unskilful management of his physician, surgeon, or apothecary. . . . These injuries to health cannot be too carefully guarded against."[9] The Supreme Court history of the police power began with Chief Justice John Marshall's dictum in *Gibbons v. Ogden* (1824) that inspection laws, quarantine laws, and "health laws of every description" remained part of "the acknowledged power of a State to provide for the health of its citizens."[10]

Public health was so vital to nineteenth-century American governance that it sometimes served as a raison d'être for political organization. One of the key motivations behind the incorporation of Chicago in August 1833 was the desire of residents to organize against a recurrence of the cholera epidemic of 1832. By November, the city had its first sanitary regulation prohibiting the disposal of animal carcasses in the Chicago River. By June a stringent health code (including provisions for the removal of nuisances, the disposal of waste, street cleaning, house inspection, mandatory public works, a cholera hospital, and Committees of Vigilance) greeted the onset of a new cholera season.[11]

Public health and hygiene were not narrow, innocuous subspecialties of early American medicine. They were public police philosophies closely intertwined with the growth of the early American polity. As George Wilson defined it, the "science of public hygiene" was part of a comprehensive effort to improve the lives and happiness of the people: "It enlists the services of the people themselves in continuous efforts at self-improvement; of the teachers of the people, to inculcate the best rules of life and action; of physicians, in preventing as well as curing disease; and of law-givers, to legalize and enforce measures of health preservation."[12] Developments in American government,

law, and health went hand in hand in the nineteenth century. Indeed, public health was at the center of a legal and political revolution that culminated in the creation of modern constitutional law and a positive administrative state.

Medical Police

The role of public health and hygiene in the evolution of American public law has been obscured by the modern liberal tendency to separate medicine (like the market and civil society) from the state. Indeed, histories of public health before the Civil War resonate with a typology devised by George Rosen in 1958: individual action versus social regulation. Rosen argued that whereas continental Europe responded to the ills of industrialization and urbanization with extensive governmental regulatory strategies and police mechanisms, Americans continued to cling to a Jeffersonian faith in private initiative, voluntarism, and laissez-faire.[13] Effective health regulation in the United States awaited the creation of public health equivalents of the Interstate Commerce Commission. That process began only in 1866 with the pioneering New York Metropolitan Board of Health, and did not achieve critical mass until the health, medical, and social-welfare reforms of the Progressive Era.[14] Prior to that, urban and environmental historians have agreed that regulatory efforts in the name of public health were feeble, episodic (usually rising and falling with the tide of epidemic disease), and administratively immature. This diagnosis of regulatory neurasthenia in public health matters meshes well with the impression of nineteenth-century statecraft (or its absence) bequeathed to us by legal instrumentalism and liberal constitutionalism. Hygiene (like public safety, comfort, morals, and welfare) should be expected to take a back seat to property and commerce.[15]

Although it has become common to think about medicine and health in the United States in exclusively private and liberal terms (as straightforward products of the demands of the market and individual decisionmakers), public hygiene and health police were constant concerns in nineteenth-century American law and legislation. They were governmental duties of a primary nature.[16] Evidence of their observance is strewn across the landscape of early American intellectual, social, and political history.

In contrast to George Rosen's depiction of Jeffersonian nonchalance in health matters, historian James Mohr has established the force of medical jurisprudence and police in the early republic.[17] Benjamin Rush of Philadelphia was an early protagonist, exhorting his medical students in the early 1810s to tend to the inescapable social and legal dimensions of their profession:

I beg you will recollect the extent of the services you will thereby be enabled to render to individuals and the public. Fraud and violence may be detected and published; unmerited infamy and death may be prevented; the widow and the orphan may be saved from ruin; virgin purity and innocence may be vindicated; conjugal harmony and happiness may be restored; unjust and oppressive demands upon the services of your fellow citizens may be obviated; and the sources of public misery in epidemic diseases may be removed.[18]

Rush's student Charles Caldwell continued the hygienic crusade arguing that medicine "embraces the preservation not only of the health of individuals and families, but also that of the health of cities and communities." The "welfare of society" demanded not only individual cures and preventive habits, but the "medical police of cities," including street cleaning and paving, improved water supply, temperance, prohibitions on noxious slaughterhouses and manufactures, the regulation of burials and building, and the efficient administration of hygienic regulations.[19] Reflecting on public health progress at the nation's centennial, Henry I. Bowditch concluded, "Public Hygiene is the most important matter any community can discuss, for upon it, in its perfection, depend all the powers, moral, intellectual, and physical, of a State." Around midcentury such ideas began to jell into a full "sanitary jurisprudence" or "state preventive medicine."[20]

At the center of this public health jurisprudence was a vigorous conception of the regulatory powers of the state and a commitment to the vision of a well-ordered society dedicated to the *salus populi*. U.S. Army Surgeon John Billings began his inquiry into the relations of sociology, hygiene, and law with a familiar critique of individualism—"a mode of life . . . impossible except in a case like that of Robinson Crusoe." Billings constructed his "jurisprudence of hygiene" instead on "principles of State polity which concern the jural and moral relations of human life." The cardinal rule of sanitary legislation was that "every member of the community is entitled to protection in regard to his health, just as he is in regard to his liberty and property, and that on the other hand his liberty and his control of his property are only guaranteed to him on the condition that they shall be so exercised as not to interfere with the similar rights of others, nor be injurious to the health of the community at large." This, of course, was the language of the police power and the common law of nuisance (especially its maxim *sic utere tuo ut alienum non laedas*—use your own so as not to injure another). For Billings these were the essential justifications when "the State" approached the citizen and commanded: "'You shall

not, as heretofore, allow the waste from your factory to contaminate the stream upon which it is placed; you shall not slaughter cattle in the buildings which you have erected for that purpose; you shall not build a house on a certain lot of yours, unless you make the walls of a certain thickness and arrange the timbers in a certain way.'"[21]

One of the key judicial building blocks for Billings's jurisprudence of hygiene was Massachusetts Chief Justice Lemuel Shaw's definition of the police power in *Commonwealth v. Alger*: the power of the legislature to make all laws "for the good and welfare of the commonwealth." For Shaw health regulations were among those "many cases in which such a power is exercised by all well ordered governments, and where its fitness is so obvious that all well regulated minds will regard it as reasonable."[22] In 1850, the Massachusetts Sanitary Commission used similar Shaw-court arguments to defend the creation of a powerful State Board of Health. To the objection that public health interfered with private matters (e.g., "If a child is born, if a marriage takes place, or if a person dies [of a disease], in my house, it is my own affair"), the commission replied in classic Shaw-like fashion on the social nature and obligations of human beings: "Men who object and reason in this manner have very inadequate conceptions of the obligations they owe to themselves or to others. No family,—no person liveth to himself alone. Every person has a direct or indirect interest in every other person. We are social beings—bound together by indissoluble ties."[23] On the issue of interference with private rights (e.g., "If I own an estate haven't I a right to do with it as I please . . . to create or continue a nuisance—to allow disease of any kind on my premises, without accountability to others?"), the sanitary survey, citing *Shaw v. Cummiskey* (1828) and *Baker v. Boston* (1831), retorted:

> Every man who chooses to hold property in a town must learn that there are certain duties connected with that property, by the very nature of it, which must be fulfilled. He cannot use it as he would. He must, on the contrary, submit to those wise legislative measures which in all ages have been found necessary to protect the common weal. . . . We must revert to the ancient laws, and permit nothing to be done, come what may, which shall injure the health or comfort of the inhabitants.

The commission ultimately rested public health interventions on that fundamental principle of early American jurisprudence: "*salus populi suprema lex*, to protect one set of human beings from being the victims of disease and death through the selfish cupidity of others."[24]

In using *Baker v. Boston* to buttress its case, the Massachusetts Sanitary

Commission made a classic choice. The case originated when Edmund Baker sued the city of Boston for filling in Mill Creek, thereby obstructing navigation and violating his private riparian and usage rights. The city responded that this stagnant, artificial mill run had become a noxious sewer endangering the health of the citizens of Boston. Summing up early American sanitary jurisprudence, Justice Wilde of the Shaw court defended the overriding duty of municipal authorities to suppress nuisances to public health. "It [cannot] be denied," he argued, "that the mayor and aldermen are . . . fully empowered to adopt measures of police, for the purpose of preserving the health, and promoting the comfort, convenience, and general welfare of the inhabitants within the city. Among these powers no one is more important than that for the preservation of public health."[25] It was not only the right, but "the duty" of municipalities to "watch over the health of the citizens" and to remove every endangering nuisance. The damage suffered by private individuals in such cases was "*damnum absque injuria*" (an injury without a remedy), where the law presumes compensation via the general societal advantages secured by "beneficial regulations." Wilde made it clear that this governmental action could not be construed as a taking of private property subject to the compensation provisions of the law of eminent domain. Rather, this was a police regulation—a health law to which "every citizen holds his property subject."[26] Building on the veritable treatise of early American police regulation offered up by the city solicitor (including the New York cemetery cases, *Vanderbilt v. Adams, Lansing v. Smith, Callender v. Marsh*, and the commentaries of James Kent and Nathan Dane), Wilde firmly established the legal priority of public health (encoded in fire regulations, quarantine laws, and procedures governing nuisance removal) over and above the competing claims of navigability, riparian rights, and private property. This was the "well-regulated society" and the *salus populi* tradition in exemplary form.[27]

Police defenses of public health regulation were forceful and unequivocal as early as 1831. Public health was placed squarely within a public law tradition defending the right of states and localities to take aggressive measures to protect their populations from disease and death. Leroy Parker and Robert Worthington introduced their pioneering treatise on *The Law of Public Health and Safety* (1892) with this summation of decades of judicial rhetoric on the primacy of public health:

It needs no argument to prove that the highest welfare of the State is subserved by protecting the life and health of its citizens by laws which will compel the ignorant, the selfish, the careless and the vicious, to so regu-

late their lives and use their property, as not to be a source of danger to others. If this be so, then the State has the right to enact such laws as shall best accomplish this purpose, even if their effect is to interfere with individual freedom and the untrammelled enjoyment of property. Such right in the State has been universally recognized by the courts. . . . The principle which forms the basis of this right is, that every man owes a duty to do or maintain nothing that shall imperil the life or health of his fellow man.[28]

But powerful and provocative as was this legal discourse on health police (especially in its inversion of some classic liberal priorities), even more significant was the nature of its implementation. Public health did not exist solely in the mind and rhetoric of an isolated judge or sanitary reformer. It was an ongoing practice and technique of governance. It was institutionalized in the myriad actions of the central constituents of the nineteenth-century American polity: mayors and legislators, local administrative agencies, and state courts. And once again, written laws on the statute and ordinance books provide a good first indication of the extent of such public health regulations.

In 1860, New York City health regulations filled an entire volume. Provisions included the establishment of a board of health and Marine Hospital, the quarantining of vessels in port, vaccination, the regulation of "infected places," inspection, the "cleansing and purifying" of buildings and lots, the removal and destruction of putrid or dangerous cargo, the duties of physicians, the packing of salted provisions, street cleaning, dumping, the cleansing of tenement houses, the filling up and draining of land, the regulation of markets and the sale of foodstuffs, garbage, the removal of putrid and unsound meat, privies, sinks, and cesspools, slaughterhouses, the removal of dead animals, the keeping of swine and cattle, the regulation of swill carts, waste water, the washing and drying of clothes, the prohibition of stagnant water, burials and cemeteries, the removal of night soil, sewers and drains, the prohibition of the business of bone boiling, bone burning, bone grinding, horse skinning, cow skinning, or skinning of dead animals, or the boiling of offal, and the abatement and removal of nuisances generally.[29] By 1872, the Sanitary Code swelled to 181 provisions, covering New York persons, places, and things from A to Y:[30]

alcoholic spirits	ashes	bells
animals	ash-boxes	birds
animal matter	ash-carts	births
animal food	asses	blasting
apartments	bedding	blacksmiths

boarding-houses

bone-boiling

bone-burning

bone-grinding

brick

brine

Brooklyn

buildings

burial

burning-fluid

butchers

butter

calves

cargo

carpets

carts

cats

cattle

cattle-yards

cellars

cemeteries

cesspools

cheese

churches

church bells

cinders

cisterns

clam-shells

clergymen

coal

coal dust

coalyards

colts

concert saloons

contractors

coroners

corpses

cotton

cows

curbstones

decoctions

dead bodies

deadly weapons

dentists

dirt and filth

distilleries

docks

dogs

drainage

drink and food

drinks, poisonous

drinking-hydrants

driving fast

drovers

drugs

dust

eggs

emigrant vessels

entrails

excavations

farcy

fat

fat-boiling

feathers

feet of animals

fevers

fighting

filth and dirt

filling grounds

firearms

firecrackers

fish

flagstones

food and drink

forges

foundries

fowls

furnaces

garbage

garbage carts

gas

gas-tar

gas-works

geese

glanders

gluemaking

goatsgraves

grease

ground

guns

gut-fat

gut-cleaning

gutters

gymnasiums

hair

halls

heads of animals

hide-tanning

hides

hogs

horns of animals

horses

horse-racing

hotel-keepers

hotels

houses

hydrants

hydrophobia

ice

infected places

infected vessels

innkeepers

inns

inspection

interments

jails

kerosene

kite-flying
lambs
lampblack
lard-boiling
leather-dressing
lessee
life
light
lime
lobster-shells
liquids
lodging-houses
mad animals
manufactories
manure
markets
marriages
matter, offensive
meat
medicines
midwives
milk
milk-dealers
mules
night-soil
nurses
occupations
odors
offal
oil-boiling
oil
overcrowding
oyster-shells
oyster-saloons
pavement

petroleum
physicians
piers
pig-pens
poisons
police
pound-keepers
pounds
prisons
privies
public places
quarantine
racing
railroad cars
rags
receptacles
refrigerators
rendering
reservoirs
rooms
rubbish
saloons
sand
scavengers
schools
scouring
scrap
sewers
sextons
sheep
shell-burning
shells
ship fever
shops
sick persons

sidewalks
sinks
skinning animals
skins
slaughtering
slaughter-houses
smoke
snow
spirits
stone-throwing
stables
stalls
straw
streets
swill
swine
tallow
tanning
tar manufactory
tenement house
theatres
tombs
tubs
turpentine
urine
undertakers
vaccination
varnish factories
vats
vaults
vegetables
vessels
water
weapons
yarding cattle

Though state and municipal legislation varied widely, most political sub-divisions in the United States officially responded to the major concerns reflected in the New York code.[31] Still, vast codified inventories marked only the

beginning of nineteenth-century public efforts to police health and hygiene. Joel Bishop included "protection to the public health" among the main objectives of both criminal and common law, suggesting, "Without health, the members of the community cannot discharge duties either to the government or to one another." He cataloged a range of behaviors inimical to public health that were indictable *at common law* without the aid of any legislation: for example, bringing an infected animal into a public space, distributing unwholesome provisions, or carrying on an offensive trade.[32] The fact that the state of Arkansas had no comprehensive state health statute in 1876, or that Massachusetts's $7,500 appropriation for a board of health equaled only 1/28,858 of estimated state property values, did not translate into a lethargic medical police.[33] It means only that one must dig deeper into the legal and local substratum of the early American polity.

A good place to start is with one of the most important institutional innovations in early American health regulation—boards of health. The invention of boards of health was to public health what the prison was to public order and what the corporation (at least in its regulatory guise) was to public economy. Nineteenth-century boards of health fell into two primary categories—local and state. Local boards of health grew out of colonial antecedents, from the appointment of health officers and port physicians in New York to Massachusetts's practice of allowing selectmen and two justices of the peace assign places for offensive trades in market towns.[34] The yellow fever epidemic of 1793 galvanized more extensive administrative reforms. Philadelphia responded immediately by granting open-ended powers over public health to a junta composed of twenty-six citizens and the mayor. In 1794 and 1799, Pennsylvania formally institutionalized this regulatory arrangement by incorporating a board of health for the Philadelphia district with extensive administrative and law-making authority over quarantine, health nuisances, inspection, immigrant vessels, and the health office (a hospital, offices, and warehouses on State Island).[35] The same events compelled Massachusetts to grant all towns the authority to set up powerful health committees. By 1816 Boston had an independent board of health with staggering discretionary powers, including

> the power to make rules, regulations and orders for preventing, removing, or destroying nuisances, sources of filth, and causes of sickness, but such rules must be published before going into effect; to examine suspected places in Boston, the islands, or vessels in the harbor, by force, under a search warrant from a justice of the peace, if necessary, and to abate when found; to isolate cases of contagious disease or remove them

to Rainsford Island or elsewhere; to seize and destroy or remove unfit provisions; to make rules and regulations as to clothing or other articles capable of conveying contagious disease; to establish and regulate quarantine, the rules of the board to extend to all persons on board ship, to visitors from shore, and to the cargo; to appoint a principal physician, an assistant physician, and such other officers and servants as were necessary, and fix their salaries; to have the care of Rainsford Island, the hospital, and other property; to appoint scavengers, superintendents of burying grounds, undertakers and fix their fees; to make rules for the burial of the dead and appoint places of burial.[36]

New York invested similar powers of public health police in its Health Committee, Health Office, and Board of Health between 1793 and 1805.[37]

Thus the first real administrative agencies in the United States were born. Though always accountable to higher state and municipal authorities, local boards of health were one of the first political entities (outside basic civil subdivisions, i.e., villages, towns, cities, counties) to be delegated independent, discretionary powers to make rules, regulations, and laws regarding primary objects of governance. Although their responsibilities were constantly amended by legislators and reviewed by judges, they succeeded in defending a generally increasing jurisdiction to make regulations regarding quarantine; to appoint inspectors, physicians, and port officers; to abate public nuisances; to remove infected articles, vessels, and people; and to punish violators of their ordinances as criminals. These were vast governmental powers, concerning basic rights of property, economy, and personhood. Yet from an early date, delegation of quasi-legislative, -judicial, and -executive powers to this "fourth branch of government" was upheld as within state and municipal powers of police to "promote the health and protect the lives" of the citizenry. In 1868, the New York Court of Appeals reviewed local health policy and legislation from 1796 and concluded, "From the earliest organization of the government, the absolute control over persons and property, so far as the public health was concerned, was vested in boards or officers, who exercised a summary jurisdiction over the subject."[38]

State boards of health appeared only at midcentury and have received the bulk of the attention of public health historians. The product of a full-fledged sanitary reform movement akin to the movement for the reformation of morals and manners, state boards proliferated only after the Civil War, though Louisiana established an early version in 1855 (a key year as well for state prohibition experiments).[39] State and metropolitan boards were a much delayed

institutionalization of the recommendations of the legendary sanitary reformers John H. Griscom and Stephen Smith (New York), Lemuel Shattuck (Massachusetts), Wilson Jewell (Philadelphia), and Edward H. Barton and James Jones (New Orleans) and their blue-ribbon surveys, conferences, and commissions.[40] State boards were usually charged with the following responsibilities: (1) the organization of local boards; (2) the collection of medical and vital statistics; (3) the investigation of the causes of disease and mortality; (4) the removal of causes of disease (especially nuisances) with the cooperation of local sanitary officers; (5) the supervision of state hygiene institutions like prisons and asylums; and (6) the supervision of quarantine.[41] The overall thrust of this second wave of administrative reform was in the direction of centralization, professionalization, and uniformity. After attacking "the present health laws of the State" for being difficult, impracticable, and imprecise, Lemuel Shattuck's *General Plan for the Promotion of Public and Personal Health* (1850) recommended the establishment of a "central agency," analogous to the Massachusetts Board of Education, to give the sanitary movement "a uniform, wise, efficient, economical and useful direction." Nineteen years later, Massachusetts responded with one of the first significant state health departments.[42]

One should not underestimate the importance of sanitary reformers or the legal-governmental implications of this later "upward shift" in public health "decision-making power"—a shift that culminated in the establishment of a National Board of Health in 1879.[43] But an obsession with high-profile reformers like Shattuck and Smith and a willingness to take their critiques of local ineptitude, corruption, and inefficiency at face value[44] may have caused historians to overlook the real legal power of local and municipal health authorities in the antebellum era. The delegation of police powers to local boards and committees of health as early as the 1790s was legally and administratively momentous. Well before 1866, armies of mayors, aldermen, justices of the peace, appellate judges, and private citizens mobilized a powerful array of legal techniques to protect the public health of their communities. Their actions, decisions, and philosophies had important repercussions for American governance and constitutionalism, as well as for sanitary and medical police. They unequivocally contradict the notion of an anemic or neurasthenic state.

Illuminating this more obscure sociolegal story requires a narrowing of focus. Early American health policy is full of fascinating public issues that warrant closer scrutiny—vital statistics, inoculation and vaccination, the regulation of impure foods, milk control, disease and sexuality, mental hygiene, school hygiene, the construction of hospitals, and even such prosaic problems as the regulation of damp and night soil. Several sanitarian concerns have

already been treated elsewhere in this book—New York cemetery cases under "public economy," street-paving under "public ways," and the health hazards of liquor under "public morality."[45] In drawing out the local struggles and particular legal stakes involved in health regulation, I want to add but two more case studies. The two concerns that dominated boards of health and crowded legislative and judicial health records were quarantine and noxious trades.

Quarantine

Property and contract are usually thought of as cornerstones of American liberal theory. Yet throughout this book we have seen property and contract held subject to extensive safety, economy, and morality regulations according to the dictates of *sic utere tuo* and *salus populi*. So too with regulations concerning public health. In *Baker v. Boston*, introduced earlier, the Shaw court deemed Edmund Baker's property and riparian rights secondary (and relative) to the larger obligation of government to "watch over the health of the citizens."[46] In *Brick Presbyterian Church v. Mayor* and *Coates v. Mayor*, discussed in chapter 3, New York's charters, covenants, leases, and deeds were all trumped by the city's inalienable police powers to regulate burials for the "preservation" of the populace.[47]

If one were asked for the two other fundamental building blocks of the American liberal foursquare, commerce and personal liberty might come quickly to mind. But again the well-regulated society intruded. Public health officials advocated two kinds of quarantine in the nineteenth century: maritime and landed quarantine. At the heart of maritime quarantine was the imposition of onerous burdens and restrictions on commerce. Landed (or local) quarantine directly curtailed personal liberty.

Maritime Quarantine

Quarantine has long been defined as a limitation upon the freedom of movement of persons, animals, or especially vessels exposed to a communicable disease. It originally referred to the period of forty days during which a vessel could be detained away from shore when arriving from an infected port. Before the emergence of the germ theory of disease, evidence of contagion, transmissibility, and the "exotic origins" of smallpox, ship fever (typhus), yellow fever, and cholera encouraged the proliferation of this basically defensive, prophylactic technique.[48] Though forty days quickly eroded as a standard in-

cubation period, extended isolation and surveillance remained the core of the basic maritime quarantine process.

As one might surmise, the prospect of long stays at quarantine stations was a significant encumbrance on early American shipping and trade. By definition, quarantine laws interfered with commerce and intercourse. As Justice Miller admitted in the most direct Supreme Court ruling on maritime quarantine: "Undoubtedly it is in some sense a regulation of commerce. It arrests a vessel on a voyage which may have been a long one. . . . This interruption of the voyage may be for days or for weeks. It extends to the vessel, the cargo, the officers and seamen, and the passengers."[49] That was but the beginning. Maritime quarantine, as practiced in the early nineteenth century, imposed a bewildering variety of regulations and restrictions on the goods, vessels, passengers, and personnel of continually outraged shippers and merchants. Nevertheless, despite the all-important commerce clause of the United States Constitution—long interpreted as a principal bulwark of free enterprise and a check on intrusive state regulations—maritime quarantine regulations roused nary a complaint from the American judiciary.

Quarantine laws were early and regular features of American governmental and public health history. John Winthrop recorded that a "great mortality" plagued Barbadoes in 1647 prompting the General Court to issue a classic colonial quarantine order.[50] By 1717 Massachusetts had a hospital on Spectacle Island and an ongoing policy of directing infected vessels there for the removal of sick persons and infected articles. Ships remained at anchor until granted permission to put ashore by the governor and council, two justices of the peace, or Boston selectmen.[51] After battling yellow fever in 1798, Massachusetts took to cleansing ships with lime and empowered boards of health in Boston and Salem "to perform quarantine under such restrictions, regulations, and qualifications *as they may judge expedient.*"[52]

Such wide delegation of discretionary authority to administrative boards and officers signaled a new era in maritime quarantine regulation. By 1858 the Health Commissioners of the city of New York found it necessary to publish a separate volume to organize and synthesize the growing multiplicity of quarantine laws, ordinances, regulations, and rules.[53] These included provisions for the operation of the Quarantine Station and Marine Hospital at Staten Island[54] supervised by a health officer, deputy health officer, physician, assistant physician, apothecary and chemist, and special port warden. These officers were invested with extraordinary powers to direct and remove vessels, persons, and cargo to the quarantine grounds;[55] to inspect, examine, and observe

vessels for signs of infection; to determine appropriate lengths of stay (up to thirty days); to cleanse, fumigate, ventilate, and otherwise purify vessels, cargo, bedding, and clothing; to *destroy* any portion of such bedding, clothing, and cargo[56] incapable of purification; to *vaccinate* persons under quarantine as deemed necessary; to administer oaths and take affidavits during examination; to direct the arrest of those obstructing, "eloping," or violating quarantine;[57] to affix colors to quarantined vessels; to place indigent immigrants with the commissioners of emigration; to impose liens on vessels and cargo to cover the expense of removal; and to make all necessary rules and regulations for quarantined vessels (even on an individual or ad hoc basis).[58] In 1858, Health Officer Dr. R. H. Thompson posted his own additional rules governing colors, lighting, communication between vessels, contact between vessels and shore, spirituous liquors, universal cleanliness, bilge water, clothing and bedding, and the washing and liming of vessels. Thompson warned of fines up to $2,000 and imprisonment up to twelve months for infractions.[59]

The quarantine regimen was onerous and unpleasant. Vessels with personnel and cargo intact remained anchored for up to thirty days with severe limitations on movements and conduct.[60] Masters and crew were subject to the arbitrary directives, questions, and inspections of quarantine officers, and were forced to watch or participate in a thorough cleansing and "purification" of the vessel. The latter included such things as scrubbing, scraping, and washing forecastle and steerage with chloride of lime, whitewashing, fumigation (usually consisting of the burning of sulphur or treatment with carbolic acid), and often the outright destruction and burning of suspicious matter: cargo, clothing and bedding, and particularly offensive parts of the vessel itself.

The consequences of disinfection could be severe. In *Mitchell v. City of Rockland* a fumigating health officer set fire to an entire vessel; in *Beers v. Board of Health* the use of carbolic acid left a New Orleans shipper with $4,375 worth of black bananas.[61] In 1857 New York's commissioners of health procured an iron scow to keep up with the constant burning of infected articles and refuse.[62] While at quarantine, passengers and crew suspected of disease were forcibly removed to lazarettos and hospitals where they were subjected to another series of intrusive procedures from physical examination to vaccination. In 1837 Boston additionally required owners of vessels to post $1,000 bond for potential paupers on board.[63] An extreme example of how exacting antebellum quarantine could become accompanied the return of yellow fever to Boston in 1819. When the ship *Ten Brothers* arrived in condition so foul that it killed the customhouse officer, the ship was taken into the middle of Boston harbor and, on order of the Board of Health, scuttled.[64] No record of com-

pensation for this public sinking exists. On the contrary, perhaps adding insult to injury, vessel owners were required to pay for the whole range of quarantine procedures and services, upon which they were entitled to the official "clean bill of health."

Although the complete scuttling of a vessel by public health officials commands attention as an indicator of the public powers wielded at quarantine, one must not overlook more subtle and "gentle" forms of public intrusiveness.[65] Of all of the duties of health officers and quarantine physicians, one of the most consequential was the ongoing compilation of a vital statistical record of the health and movements of populations. New immigrants in particular were assiduously examined and documented. At issue in the pivotal Supreme Court case *New York v. Miln* (1837) was a New York statute requiring the master of every vessel to make a written report containing the name, age, place of birth, last legal settlement, and occupation of every person on board coming from a foreign country.[66] By 1880 New Orleans required all vessels to undergo inspection and submit to the following interrogation:[67]

1. Name of Vessel?
2. Name of Captain or Master?
3. Tonnage or Class of Vessel?
4. From whence is the Vessel you Command?
5. How many days have you been on the passage?
6. At what port or ports have you touched?
7. Were any Contagious or Infectious Diseases prevailing at the port from whence your vessel sailed?
8. If so, name the Diseases.
9. Were any Contagious or Infectious Diseases prevailing at the port or ports at which you touched?
10. If so, name the Diseases.
11. Was any freight or passengers received at the ports at which your vessel touched?
12. If so, give particulars.
13. Have you any Bills of Health?
14. If so, produce them.
15. During the course of your Cruise or Passage what cases of disease have occurred on board?
16. At what dates?
17. Have any deaths taken place on board your vessel since you last left the port?

18. If so, at what dates, and from what causes?

19. Are there any sick on your vessel at this time?

20. Has Yellow Fever, Small-Pox, Cholera or Plague ever existed on this ship?

21. If so, when?

22. What is the number of Officers?

23. What is the number of the Crew?

24. What is the number of Passengers?

25. What is your cargo?

26. To whom is the cargo consigned?

27. What is the present sanitary condition of the vessel, cargo, crew and passengers?

28. Have you a medical officer?

29. Give the name of the Medical Officer.

30. Produce the Reports of the Medical Officer.

Such detailed questionings, recordings, and reportings were part of a larger public health and social policy increasingly committed to counting, mapping, and officially recognizing "vital" occurrences and characteristics in the life of a population: for example, births, deaths, marriages, accidents, diseases, relocations, and racial and ethnic composition. Along with the maps and daily meteorological data that bloated sanitary and quarantine reports came relentless efforts to chart and quantify the health and condition of the people. Accompanying the quarantine questionnaire, the Louisiana Board of Health developed a "Weekly Statement of Mortality" for New Orleans plotting population ("white" and "colored" tabulated separately), ages (by race and sex), color, nativities (29 possibilities),[68] causes of death (including 201 general and local diseases and 73 other conditions), deaths in public institutions, still births, death rate (per 1,000 per annum per week, whites, colored), meteorological observations (barometer, temperature, relative humidity, rain).[69] The resultant proliferation of health statistics, inquiries, reports, and official circulars and forms (part of a larger nineteenth-century "history of detail"),[70] while stopping far short of social welfare bureaucracy, marked a decided change in the nature, focus, and extent of governmental preoccupation with the health and well-being of the citizenry. Statistical and actuarial constructions of "the public," its problems, and possible administrative and scientific solutions were important overtures to modern conceptions of governmentality and the nation-state's health and welfare authority.

But were quarantine laws enforced? Did public health actions match up

with public health words, reports, ordinances, and conferences? One clear indicator that quarantine practice and rhetoric often coincided was the constant and vociferous protest of shippers, merchants, and traders. In 1846 a New York House Committee on Quarantine compiled a register of mercantile complaint. Moses Taylor, a twenty-four-year veteran of the West India trade, denounced the great delay and heavy charges of quarantine, which he estimated at $250 to $1,000. Christopher Robert of the trading house Robert & Williams attacked the notion of thirty-day quarantine upon rumors of yellow fever in New Orleans: "On such slender evidence . . . the commerce between two of the most important places in the Union are shackled with regulations nearly equivalent to non-intercourse, burthened with onerous charges, and the parties engaged therein subjected to great inconvenience and loss, by the detention of property." J. H. Brower, consignee, further decried the increased costs, "loss of employ," and discretionary authority of health officers as "hurtful upon the trade and commerce of the city of New-York."[71] Such testimony was echoed by chambers of commerce, producer exchanges, and merchant associations throughout the nineteenth century.[72] The unequivocal opinion of those with direct economic interests at stake was that quarantine laws were implemented, indeed so well implemented as to become intolerably "burdensome" and "prejudicial" to commerce.

Despite such important and constant commercial opposition, American courts staunchly defended maritime quarantine regulations. Indeed the constitutional legitimacy of these exacting restraints was so taken for granted that early American quarantine provoked little sustained appellate litigation before the 1870s. In the small number of cases where maritime quarantine did raise substantive objections, they were expeditiously quashed. In *DuBois v. Augusta* (1831), a steamboat captain made the mistake of challenging a fine for evading quarantine. The Georgia Supreme Court defended the careful quarantine regulations "necessary for the security, welfare and convenience" of Augusta, and rebuked Captain DuBois: "The safety of the whole community is not to be hazarded upon the speculations of any captain of a boat."[73] When the ship *Ellen Brooks* arrived in Baltimore with cases of smallpox and typhus, the health officer insisted upon complete isolation, sent twenty-four passengers to the smallpox hospital, secured fresh provisions, ordered the vessel whitewashed, fumigated, and purified, and demanded $1,000 for expenses. The Maryland Supreme Court fully backed Baltimore's quarantine regime and the large discretion of the local health officer "to prevent the introduction of contagious diseases within the city."[74] A series of Missouri cases similarly sustained St. Louis's quarantine policies, noting simply that "this is a matter of

expediency, not of constitutional right."[75] State court opinions on quarantine were short and certain. Maritime quarantine was a long-standing, widely accepted health police measure deemed essential to the well-being of communities from the Atlantic to the Mississippi.[76]

The legal status of quarantine regulations was so unquestioned that they became a paradigm for the police power in the Supreme Court of the United States (where the politics of federalism and slavery invariably overshadowed substantive discussions of the well-regulated society). Federal deference to state quarantine regulations became the law of the land in the 1796 and 1799 quarantine acts of Congress. Both laws reserved a role for the federal government (especially revenue and military officers) in quarantine, but with the ultimate aim of executing "the quarantine and other restraints . . . established by the health laws of any state."[77] As Albert Gallatin argued before Congress in 1796, quarantine was the legitimate prerogative of states—a "regulation of police."[78] The Supreme Court followed suit, acknowledging some federal governmental role in quarantine (by virtue of its commerce powers) while unambiguously sustaining state health regulations. Building on John Marshall's *Gibbons v. Ogden* dicta, Roger Taney played the quarantine card in the *License Cases*:

> They subject the ship, and cargo, and crew to the inspection of a health-officer appointed by the State; they prevent the crew and cargo from landing until inspection is made, and destroy the cargo if deemed dangerous to health. And during all this time the vessel is detained at the place selected for the quarantine ground by State authority. The expenses of these precautionary measures are also usually, and I believe universally, charged upon the master, the owner, or the ship, and the amount regulated by the State law.[79]

Despite tremendous interferences with shipping, navigation, and commerce, Taney concluded, health and quarantine powers were "continually exercised by the States" and "continually recognized by Congress ever since the adoption of the constitution." Justice Grier adamantly concurred, "Quarantine laws, which protect the public health, compel mere commercial regulations to submit to their control."[80]

Justice Grier also defended state power to deny "paupers and convicts . . . admission into the country" as legitimate "police laws for the preservation of health, prevention of crime, and the protection of public welfare."[81] Issues of health, commerce, welfare, and social control were closely entwined in the

state passenger laws (essentially local immigration controls) reviewed by the Supreme Court in *Miln v. New York* (1837) and the *Passenger Cases* (1849). In *Miln* a New York statute requiring the registration (name, place of birth, legal settlement, age, and occupation) of every passenger brought into the port was sustained with a powerful defense of the state's police power "to advance the safety, happiness and prosperity of its people, and provide for its general welfare."[82] New York argued, and Justice Barbour agreed, that this was not a "commercial" but a "police" regulation with a long history and tradition: "The object of all well-regulated governments is to promote the public good and to secure the public safety. . . . It is under these principles that the acts relative to police, which may operate on persons brought into the state in the course of commercial operations, and the laws relative to quarantine and gunpowder are within the power of the states."[83] In the *Passenger Cases*, the Supreme Court refused to accept a state head tax on immigrants and passengers, but still endorsed state authority over "safety, health and morals" as part of the "supreme police power."[84] Supreme Court Justice Davis summed up the constitutional consensus on quarantine in *Peete v. Morgan* (1873): "That the power to establish quarantine laws rests with the States, and has not been surrendered to the General government is settled in *Gibbons v. Ogden*. The source of this power is in the acknowledged power of a State to provide for the health of its people."[85]

Throughout the contentious debate over federalism and the commerce clause that defined early Supreme Court history, quarantine, port, and pilot[86] regulations were consistently upheld as unassailable examples of state police power over health and welfare—as matter-of-fact as the regulation of gunpowder in crowded cities. Local officials were reined in when they exceeded delegated powers, and federal courts refused to allow states to impose direct head or tonnage taxes on passengers or goods. But the substantive power of states and localities to establish stringent quarantine rules to protect the public health, safety, and welfare was never judicially challenged, despite intense commercial opposition, despite the commerce clause of the Constitution, and despite the discretionary and draconian nature of the quarantine regime. In 1865 the New York Shipowner's Association charged that the local health officer was "clothed with more power than the President of the United States." One late nineteenth-century commentator offered an even better analogy, "In its effect upon the status of persons or property coming from the district quarantined against, a declaration of quarantine has been well compared to a declaration of war."[87]

Wartime is precisely the image conjured up by the early American practice of landed (or local) quarantine, especially under threat of epidemic. Antebellum localities viewed epidemic disease as catastrophic—as destructive, disabling, and disordering as the general conflagration. Accordingly, this enemy was met with a full mobilization of the public powers of the well-regulated society. The first line of defense consisted of local health boards and officers outfitted with summary powers and wide discretionary authority. The public rationale for such measures was the law of overruling necessity or community self-defense. The welfare of the community was the supreme law; the public life-and-death battle with epidemic disease trumped legal niceties like procedural due process and rights of private property.

During the cholera epidemic of 1832, Albany, New York, undertook just such a local public health mobilization complete with "shotgun" quarantine.[88] The *Albany Argus*, the local paper, tracked the disease through Paris, London, and Glasgow in May. With the first signs of the disease on the American continent—in Montreal in June—city officials sprang to action with intensive "precaution and police" measures that lasted throughout the summer. Special meetings of the Common Council directed the Board of Health and city marshal to prevent immigration from the north and to stop, inspect, and quarantine all carriages, wagons, and boats approaching the city. When guards reported a group of emigrants proceeding from Waterford on foot, the sheriff and an impromptu *posse comitatus* were sent to intercept them. In addition to this *cordon sanitaire*, the Board of Health deputized citizen "street committees" with plenary authority to "effect a prompt removal of all nuisances and to see that every house and building in the city is properly cleaned and ventilated."[89] Cadres of volunteers, local recruits, and citizen committees took it upon themselves to clean streets, improve drainage, fill and enclose vacant lots, burn tar and rosin, and examine private yards, cellars, and outhouses. The physicians of Albany met every evening in City Hall to record reports of disease and death. By September, 1,147 cases of cholera had killed 422 people.[90]

Under such extreme circumstances, landed quarantine and its concomitant police actions resembled nothing less than martial law. Yet American courts defended such local emergency health measures as necessary to public health and welfare. In *Van Wormer v. Mayor of Albany* (1836), the plaintiff objected to the summary destruction of his $3,000 barn and shed as a public health nuisance during the 1832 epidemic. Van Wormer claimed that the Albany Board of Health's action amounted to a trespass—an illegal infringement of his pri-

vate property rights. Chief Justice Savage of the New York Supreme Court disagreed, defending the extensive power entrusted to local officials for cleansing and purifying a city in a public health crisis. Savage argued that the state legislature had delegated to boards of health large discretionary police powers to make "such regulations as they shall think necessary and proper for the preservation of public health."[91] Among those was the power to summarily suppress and remove nuisances. "It is right," Savage concluded, "that such power should exist somewhere, to be exercised upon a proper emergency. If the civil authorities were obliged to await the slow progress of a public prosecution, the evil arising from nuisances would seldom be avoided."

Like New York's Great Fire of 1835, Albany's battle with cholera in 1832 was unusual. Landed quarantine, however, was not. It was a common and accepted feature of nineteenth-century public life. The inspection and isolation of particular houses and districts in cities and towns was a well-established practice.[92] Broad powers were exercised by local selectmen, boards of health, and health commissioners to discover, isolate, and sometimes destroy homes, buildings, and property deemed capable of spreading disease. By 1877 New Orleans had a formidable set of standard procedures for inspecting, quarantining, and abating public health nuisances. In the First Sanitary District, the annual house-to-house inspection included 10,693 premises. Inspector M. Edwin Schlatre, M.D., reported 2,357 nuisance abatements, 688 fumigations, 297 disinfections, as well as a bevy of formal notices, warnings, and orders. Only four individuals were cited for noncompliance.[93]

Like maritime quarantine, landed health police measures prompted relatively little appellate litigation before the 1880s. When they did, local regulatory authority was generally sustained. In *Commissioners of Salisbury v. Powe* (1858), North Carolina Justice Ruffin defended a community's power to enforce quarantine against travelers from diseased towns even as he denounced the loose construction of the Salisbury ordinance.[94] The Missouri Supreme Court similarly defended an extensive local police authority over the health of cities: "The power is intended to be an active, efficient power, to be exercised for the public good, and in its scope it reaches to whatever may be necessary for the preservation of the public health."[95] And in *Ferguson v. City of Selma*, Justice Peters upheld the most extreme use of power—the summary ability to remove and destroy buildings and property as public health nuisances. The Alabama Supreme Court cleared the way for Selma to remove a series of "filthy and crowded" tenements overflowing with smallpox patients. The court reasoned that Selma had a duty to "guard the health and comfort of its people"—"*Salus populi suprema lex.*"[96]

What were the legal limits of this local, landed health authority? In a few cases, judges offered warnings and reprimands. When Castleton officials quarantined a whole section of the town, prohibiting intercourse with the rest, the New York court insisted on the right of "healthy" persons to pass. While admitting that "public health is doubtless an interest of great delicacy and importance," the court argued that it did not "suspend the operation of the constitution" or "the natural rights of the citizen." The court ordered the release of Peter Roff from common jail.[97] Courts also balked at some extreme examples of seizure and impressment. The forcible removal of patients to makeshift hospitals and pesthouses was common practice in landed quarantine. But when Maine localities arbitrarily seized a private stagecoach and the commodious Lynde hotel (at an estimated $30,000 damages) for those purposes, the state's highest court held that health officers were acting beyond their delegated powers.[98] But ultimately such cases reveal less about substantive constitutional limits on health police power than they do about the seemingly boundless practices of local officials. Health officers thought it perfectly appropriate to forcibly remove the sick to county fair grounds; to impress horses, carriages, and assistants; and to seize private houses, buildings, and hotels for conversion into temporary municipal hospitals. Even those jurists who challenged such actions did so on the narrow ground of "undelegated authority." If the state legislature saw fit to confer upon local officials the explicit power to impress stagecoaches, the Chief Justice of Maine, for example, had no constitutional argument.[99] Moreover, the denial of delegated authority in these cases had the intriguing result of insulating the city as a public entity from liability for the actions of its officials.[100]

Public health was not an afterthought or a rationalization in American law and politics. It was a fundamental part of the nineteenth-century polity. Public health figured prominently in pivotal discussions of the state and its powers. This overarching legal solicitude for public health police illuminates some hitherto neglected aspects of early American governance and constitutionalism. For example, a knowledge of local quarantine processes makes it much easier to understand how just five years after defending federal power over interstate commerce on navigable waterways in *Gibbons v. Ogden*, John Marshall could defer to Delaware's decision to dam a navigable creek as a public health measure in *Willson v. Black Bird Creek Marsh Company* (1829).[101] Early American public law was not univalent, holding true to single externalist trajectories like "nationalism," "commerce," the "release of creative energy," or the "subsidization of economic growth." Instead, it encompassed a diverse set of legal and social priorities, one of the more significant being a keen appreci-

ation for the roles of health, medicine, and police in the well-regulated society. But even this concern for "public health" was multilayered, replete with alternative interpretations and contested meanings. One subtext that deserves special, if all too brief, mention is the role of class, ethnicity, and race in local constructions of what was necessary to the health of the public. Whose health? Whose public?[102]

One of the earliest recorded practices of landed quarantine can be found in the East Hampton Town Records in 1662. It was directed against Indians and servants.[103] Over two hundred years later, the earliest report of the California State Board of Health highlighted a special concern, "The Chinese from a Sanitary Standpoint," prelude to the quarantining of the whole of San Francisco's "Chinatown" as a public health nuisance.[104] As was the case with public morality, sanitary reforms and public health regulations were contaminated by particular local prejudices. All too often public health hazards were directly associated with the neighborhoods, housing, property, living conditions, habits, and manners of the poor, the different, and the new.

One of the buildings summarily pulled down during Albany's 1832 battle with cholera was a cramped tenement with five apartments—home to some forty to eighty Irish emigrants. Such "haunts of poverty, intemperance, and filth" were singled out continuously by the Board of Health for special attention. In *Meeker v. Van Rensselaer* (1836), Chief Justice Savage sustained the public destruction matter-of-factly: "A more offensive nuisance cannot be imagined than the buildings described."[105] But it did not take cholera or a board of health order to destroy the housing of the socially "undesirable." Well before the onset of cholera hysteria in Albany, the newspapers reported that a neighborhood mob pulled down a "noisy" house "tenanted by several families, black and white."[106] In 1877 New Orleans Sanitary Inspector Joseph Holt reported confidently that "all former observations establishing the rule that small-pox is peculiarly a disease of the vulgar and ignorant, and especially of negroes, have been confirmed." He recommended compulsory vaccination to protect the entire community from "the willfullness of prowling negroes and shabby whites."[107]

Such sentiments were not isolated excesses in landed or maritime quarantine. They were part and parcel of the general nineteenth-century practice and discourse of public health and hygiene. The first Sanitary Survey of Massachusetts took particular aim at "the sanitary evils arising from foreign emigration." Dr. Charles Caldwell's *Thoughts on Hygiene* carefully distinguished the health threats posed by New Orleans's "extraordinary assemblage of *ignorant* and *intemperate, unacclimated* and *reckless inhabitants*" from "the native,

acclimated, and orderly citizens" who enjoyed "sound and uninterrupted health [like] citizens of the same class in Baltimore or Philadelphia, New York, or Boston."[108] John Billings introduced the first comprehensive American treatise on public hygiene with concerns of the same order: "In the cities are found the extremes of poverty, ignorance, and vice; the dangers of contagion and the infective diseases are there at their maximum; there will always be certain localities in which the children cannot be healthy, intelligent, and virtuous, and those who survive in spite of the filth which they eat, drink, breathe, and live in, form the dangerous classes, an ever-present menace to society." Citing a report from the American Public Health Association, Billings even raised the possibility of a eugenics-style response from the "body politic" to "prevent the suffering, disease, and vice, with which hereditary influences from the insane, the syphilitic, or the drunkard, will afflict our children's children."[109]

Like the regulation of public morals, public health was closely entwined with the politics of social order and the policing of dangerous classes. The rhetorics and technologies of *salus populi* did not mean that everyone's welfare and safety was being pursued equally. At the center of public health discourse was a series of dichotomies separating the healthy from the unhealthy, the clean from the unclean, the safe from the dangerous, and the normal from the abnormal. Such distinctions were not simply the objective products of science or medicine. All too often, the line between wellness and sickness closely followed established hierarchies of social difference: class, ethnicity, and race. And as with the distinction between the orderly and the disorderly, a determination of healthy or unhealthy had great implications for private right and public power. While the healthy, the clean, and the normal remained relatively insulated from the interventions of medical police, the "sick" and "abnormal" triggered the full potential of the nineteenth-century state, including powers of segregation, destruction, and removal.[110] Although an exploration of the complex cultural politics underlying social policing in nineteenth-century America is ultimately beyond the scope of this work,[111] it is important to keep in mind the way cultural constructions of difference burrowed their way into the very legal-institutional structure of the American state.

But early American health policy and medical police was more than just another arena for social contest. Nineteenth-century jurisprudence conforms to simple models of social control no more than it does to one-dimensional notions of the release of entrepreneurial energy or the needs of capital. Quarantine was simultaneously the bane the nation's poorest immigrants *and* most prosperous merchants. The languages of dirt, disease, insalubrity, and un-

healthfulness (and the exercise of police powers they precipitated) were turned not only on the oppressed but on profitable manufactories and trades deemed noxious to the people's welfare.

Offensive Trades

The law of offensive trades drew directly on the principles of health police, especially the common law of nuisance and its *sic utere tuo* prescription that all should use property so as not to injure others. When certain trades or businesses (lawful in themselves) violated this precept by subjecting their neighbors to unhealthy smoke or offensive smells, they were subject to a range of public and private, common law, equitable, and statutory remedies. A private individual or a group of neighbors could bring a private nuisance suit against a noxious factory seeking money damages or an equitable injunction protecting them from future injury. Public officials could indict the proprietor for maintaining a public nuisance culminating in a fine, imprisonment, an injunction, or the final abatement of the nuisance. Legislators could grant municipal officials and boards of health summary police powers to shut down and remove the offending nuisance. Finally, in a few extreme cases, individuals tore down noxious establishments without legal process, much the way mayors tore down buildings in the path of fire. All of these remedies were employed against businesses deemed harmful to public health in the first three-quarters of the nineteenth century. They were varied strategies in a powerful public health policy built upon the common law of public nuisance.[112] Far from being eviscerated to accommodate the industrial revolution, public nuisance law remained a potent source of public regulatory and sanitary power.

The first developmental nuisance cases to appear in state appellate court records were not really against "noxious" trades at all. They were usually private nuisance actions against mills, canals, and early railroad companies for diverting water and obstructing ways. In New Jersey, the power of courts to grant both damages and injunctions against useful enterprises for such offenses was not questioned, and they did so about half of the time.[113] Public health and nuisance law merged only when burgeoning municipalities began to address such potential health hazards as stagnant water, cemeteries, the keeping of pigs, infectious hospitals, and even the growing of rice in city limits.[114] Such health offenses usually were challenged as public nuisances, and judges typically upheld their restriction with strong defenses of police regulation. In *Coates v. Mayor of New York*, the classic cemetery case, the New York court defended the city's power "so to order the use of private property in the

city, as to prevent its proving pernicious to the citizens generally. A contrary doctrine would strike at the root of all police regulations."[115]

Following such early health precedents, American courts in the 1840s, 1850s, and 1860s enforced restrictions on a growing array of common businesses and trades held to be noxious and unhealthy. In *Rhodes v. Dunbar* (1868), Justice Read of the Pennsylvania Supreme Court gave a partial listing of offensive trades deemed nuisances in Anglo-American law: a glasshouse, a chandler shop, a swine yard, a pigsty, a pig boardinghouse, a soap factory, a tallow furnace, a slaughterhouse, a bone-boiling establishment, a horse-boiling establishment, a milldam, a melting house of animal fat and tallow, a cotton press, steam boilers, the use of a public place for immigrants, brick burning, laying up wet jute, storing wood naphtha, gunpowder, petroleum or nitroglycerine, a limekiln, a dyehouse, a furnace, a smelting house, a smith forge, a livery stable, a tannery, and gasworks.[116] But two types of economic enterprises were singled out for especially harsh attack for their noxious effects on public health and comfort—those involving smoke and animals.

The former represented age-old phenomena—smoke, soot, and dirt—grown exponentially problematic in increasingly urban and industrial settings.[117] The polity responded by expanding existing regulatory techniques. By the 1860s, a variety of time-honored trades and manufactories—blacksmiths, tinsmiths, brick burning, pottery kilns, and limekilns—bore the regulatory brunt of the law of nuisance. The Maine Supreme Court decreed in suppressing a blacksmith's shop, "All the acts put forth by man, which tend directly to create evil consequence to the community at large, may be deemed nuisances. . . . However ancient, useful, or necessary the business be, if it is so managed as to occasion serious annoyance, injury, or inconvenience, the injury has a remedy."[118] Citing the common law maxim *sic utere tuo* and an array of English cases, American courts repeatedly issued injunctions and granted damages against "the prosecution of a legal trade, where it is carried on in such a manner as to injure an adjoining tenant, or to affect the air with noisome smells, gases, or smokes injurious to health, or rendering the enjoyment of life . . . uncomfortable." Were this not settled law, a Pennsylvania court argued, "unwholesome establishments, filthy styes, and distracting machinery might and would be erected at the very doors of private dwellings, to the destruction of all peace, health, and comfort of the inmates."[119]

But traditional smoky trades were only partly responsible for the noxious and offensive conditions in many nineteenth-century cities. The use of steam and coal to power new and extensive factories severely compounded the

problems of urban congestion, waste, noise, and air and water pollution. In 1812, the Boiling Spring Bleaching Co. was a small New Jersey fulling and dyeing operation pouring saw dust and small amounts of refuse into the Passaic River. By 1860, the company was a full-scale mill and works for bleaching and finishing cotton and woolen goods. In consequence, the Passaic took on an additional 450 pounds of lime, 250 pounds of vitriol, 650 pounds of soda ash, 300 pounds of chlorine, and 1,800 pounds of vegetable oil and fiber weekly.[120] The American legal response to such rampant and rapid transformation was hardly monolithic. But in a slew of midcentury cases, courts and public officials relied on the standards of nuisance law, public economy, and the well-regulated society to check some of the excesses of private industrial initiatives.

In *Whitney v. Bartholomew* (1851), a plaintiff was awarded damages for the cinders, ashes, and smoke thrown from the chimneys of a nearby carriage factory.[121] Chief Justice Church of the Connecticut Supreme Court rooted his opinion in the principle "that every man must so use his own property as not to injure another"—a maxim "known to every lawyer, and approved by every moralist." This was not a hard case. Despite the fact that carriage making was a lawful and useful trade, this factory was in an "improper place." Justice Church elaborated on the role of callings and trades in a well-regulated society:

> The first object of society and of the laws, should be, to protect life, health and property, and the comfortable enjoyment of them; and whatever essentially, injuriously, and unnecessarily affects these, must be wrong. They are paramount to the mere convenience of pursuing a lawful calling, in a particular place; and so the common law has considered it from the earliest times. The defendant assumes, that, as he erected his shop and pursued his business on his own land, there could be no wrong on his part, if the business was conducted with due care and caution. Herein, we think, is his mistake; and he will find no authority to sustain that position. He had a right to erect his shop on his own land; but he must so use it, even there, as not to injure his neighbor.

Church noted that it was uniformly held that a "swine-sty, slaughterhouse, tannery, tallow-furnace, steam-engine, smith's forge, or other erection" infecting nearby dwellings or producing "unhealthy vapours or offensive smells or noises" was a nuisance.[122]

With equal legal and rhetorical vigor, several midcentury courts supported the use of nuisance law against that harbinger of industrial revolution, the

steam engine. In 1845 Massachusetts passed a statute requiring a license for the operation of certain steam engines, boilers, and furnaces.[123] Chancellor Williamson of New Jersey held that the noise of a steam engine alone could be sufficient to deem it a nuisance: "The authorities are abundant to sustain the position that an individual cannot erect, in a densely settled portion of a city or town, occupied by private dwellings, any kind of manufacturing establishment, and so use the machinery and carry on the business as to render living in the neighborhood uncomfortable, either on account of the noise it occasions, or of its smoke and offensive smells."[124] Iron companies, gasworks, and railroads also fell victim to private and public nuisance regulation.[125]

But as one might guess, American courts were not uniform in their willingness to suppress new industrial enterprises. When a Lowell resident living in the vicinity of Norcross's Mills, Brook's Mills, Mechanic's Mills, and Sargent's Mills decided to bring a nuisance action against another nearby operation, the Massachusetts court balked.[126] So too, the New Jersey Court of Equity continually hesitated to employ what it termed the "heavy hand" of the chancellor's injunction against industrial nuisances.[127] Some cities were simply written off. A New Jersey chancellor suggested, "[I]f in Sheffield, Birmingham, or Pittsburgh, or any other city . . . clouded with the soot and smoke issuing from hundreds of engines, one more was added, such almost imperceptible addition the evil would not be restrained."[128] Many courts wrestled with the dilemma of where exactly *common* interest and *general* welfare actually lay in a rapidly industrializing, urbanizing society. Michigan Supreme Court Justice Thomas Cooley, quite familiar with Blackstone's condemnation of offensive trades and Lemuel Shaw's defense of public rights, could not bring himself to enjoin an important Detroit flour mill: "We cannot shut our eyes to the obvious truth that if the running of this mill can be enjoined, almost any manufactory in any of our cities can be enjoined upon similar reasons. Some resident must be incommoded or annoyed by almost any of them."[129] Where was one to draw the nuisance line in an increasingly interconnected economy where Supreme Court Justice Brewer could state by 1892: "There is scarcely any property in whose use the public has no interest. No man liveth unto himself alone, and no man's property is beyond the touch of another's welfare"?[130] Complicating matters further, knowledge of the health hazards of industrial pollution emerged only slowly. Citing a new article on smoke and coal in the *English Quarterly*, a Pennsylvania judge surprisingly announced in 1868, "Not only do our hands and faces contract dirt, but soot finds its way into the air-tubes of our lungs."[131]

Despite this jurisprudential uncertainty and unevenness, nuisance law remained a potent weapon for regulating noxious industrial manufactories into the early twentieth century. Though cases were not always brought and remedies not guaranteed, nuisance law certainly was not remade to accommodate American industrialism. On the contrary, courts at midcentury remained quite willing to issue injunctions, grant damages, and throw people in prison for fouling community health and environment. As Justice Read of Pennsylvania suggested, nuisance law was influential in pushing the most noxious industries (as was the case with gunpowder magazines) to the outskirts of town and beyond residential neighborhoods:

> Brick-kiln ponds are now covered with noble dwellings. . . . The old engine-house on Chestnut street [in Philadelphia], afterwards used as a china factory disappeared years ago. . . . On the south side of Chestnut street is the depot of the Philadelphia City Passenger Railway Company, which is to be removed over Schuylkill, and may therefore be considered as gone. . . . The first planing-machine or mill was, I believe, erected on Arch and Broad streets, and opposite the Arch street prison. They have disappeared, and Arch street, from Broad to the Schuylkill, is a magnificent street, covered with beautiful dwellings and churches.[132]

Early nuisance cases provided precedents and rationales for the more extensive legislative and municipal efforts to regulate industrial trades in the late nineteenth century. The potency of these precedents and rationales was most evident in the generally successful battle communities waged against the most patently offensive trades of the mid-nineteenth century: those involving animals.

Despite their usefulness and necessity, the building and operation of livery stables was not left to the whim of a landowning entrepreneur or market supply and demand. In *Coker v. Birge* (1851), James Coker successfully obtained an injunction against William Birge to prevent him from erecting a stable near Coker's tavern in Griffen, Georgia.[133] Judge Warner cited the stable's "unhealthy effluvia," flies, *sic utere tuo*, and Sir William Blackstone in denying Birge the right to build: "It is a nuisance . . . to do any act that, in its consequences, must necessarily tend to the prejudice of one's neighbor. So closely does the law of England enforce that excellent rule of gospel morality, of doing to others as we would they should do unto ourselves." Courts in Texas, North Carolina, New York, and Rhode Island followed suit.[134] Not all stables met with such swift and severe proscription,[135] but the fact that nineteenth-

century courts circumscribed so ordinary and universal a trade as stable keeping is indicative of the public bounds placed on threatening economic activities involving animals and the public health.

If the keeping of animals was a continuous problem for nineteenth-century nuisance law, their slaughtering in cluttered urban neighborhoods quickly became a public health nightmare. An 1865 report of the Citizens Association of New York declared its 173 slaughterhouses "gross impositions" and "sources of evil," "too offensive to health and decency to be longer permitted." They did not need to dwell on the specifics of midcentury butchering and slaughtering to make their point. The large collections of wild animals and decomposing offal, the continuous flow of blood, urine and fecal matter into gutters and streets, the fetid odor in the summer, and the effects of the daily spectacle on children and residential neighborhoods were enough.[136] Consequently, the entire arsenal of nineteenth-century regulatory strategies took aim at the problem of urban slaughterhouses. Public authorities were not timid about restricting private rights or stifling creative economic energies when faced with such egregious nuisances to public health and comfort. In *Catlin v. Valentine* (1842), New York's Chancellor Walworth enjoined the erection of a slaughterhouse, suggesting that such a use of private property was prima facie a nuisance to neighboring inhabitants. Later New York courts held that even if slaughterhouses were long-established and residential populations "came to the nuisance," they would be restrained from disturbing the comfort and senses of newcomers.[137] Courts upheld convictions and abatements with arguments steeped in the common law vision of a well-regulated society:

> No person can lawfully exercise an absolute dominion over the land of which he is the owner. His use and enjoyment of it must have reference to the rights of others, and be subordinate to general laws, which are established for the benefit of all. . . . *The public health, the welfare and safety of the community, are matters of paramount importance, to which all the pursuits, occupations and employments of individuals, inconsistent with their preservation, must yield.*[138]

Milwaukee restricted slaughtering to a municipally established site. San Francisco simply banned slaughtering, herding, curing, and "any other business or occupation offensive to the senses or prejudicial to public health."[139]

But contrary to popular belief, slaughterhouses were not the end of the line for most hogs and cattle. Animal "by-products" were a huge industry in the nineteenth century, spawning a school of horrendous "dependent" health nuisances. The unofficial motto of the nineteenth-century "porkopolis" Cin-

cinnati—"use everything but the hog's squeal"—was applicable to the industry as a whole. Leather, brushes, lard, tallow, soap, sausage casings, strings, ligatures, glue, gelatin, feed, fertilizer, chemicals, and, later, oleo margarine were all produced from slaughterhouse remains. A variety of melting, bone-boiling, soap-boiling, fat-boiling, curing, drying, and chemical establishments grew up in nineteenth-century cities pursuing this profitable trade.

Though Upton Sinclair has bequeathed twentieth-century Americans some idea of the horror of the slaughtering business, we must rely on our imaginations and the antiseptic language of trade manuals to recreate these abominations. Alexander Winter's handbook for butchers and abattoirs, containing "recipes" for the manufacture of lard, tallow, greases, oils, fertilizer, and the care of bone, blood, and offal, described the basic process employed in most of these trades—the boiling and steaming of residual animal matter. At one point, Winter cautioned against discarding "smothered" or diseased hogs, suggesting instead, "It is a very simple matter to render them in a tank, the whole carcass being thrown in and thoroughly boiled." A 300-pound dead hog could thus yield 130 pounds of "beautifully clear, white and odorless lard" at six cents per pound. The residue could be sold for fertilizer. However, Winter urged the use of gloves with such animals to avoid blood poisoning, "I have seen them lying on the platforms at the Union Stock Yards, Chicago, swollen to twice their natural size and burst open."[140]

If slaughterhouses were public nuisances, a fortiori boiling, rendering, and melting houses were regulatable offensive trades. Once again, injunctions, indictments, fines, and summary abatement by municipal officials were used to stifle such establishments. When the butchers of New York formed the Butchers' Melting Association to melt fat and tallow from the city's slaughterhouses on a large scale, they were indicted, fined, and perpetually enjoined from operating such a business.[141] Two hundred sixty citizens had earlier presented a written remonstrance to the butchers complaining of the noxious and offensive stenches, smells, vapor, and smoke from this "intolerable nuisance." A similar injunction was issued against a long-established soap-boiling factory on Broadway. Chief Justice Oakley declared, "The court can prohibit trades of this character from being carried on in a great city, or in a dense population, on the broad principle, that all trades which render the enjoyment of life and property uncomfortable, must recede with the advance of population, and be conducted in the outskirts of the city or in the country. This is on the principle of the law, that every man must so use his own property as not to injure the rights of his neighbors."[142] Massachusetts, which had a strong statutory tradition in dealing with noxious trades and common nuisances, applied the

same standards to a chemical works on the outskirts of Providence unlawfully using "large quantities of acid, guano, tar, oil, bone and dead bodies, and other noxious and offensive substances, in the manufacture of acids, colors, chemicals and chemical products."[143] The Louisiana Supreme Court upheld the power of the New Orleans street commissioner to summarily close up a hide-curing establishment noxious to the health of the city.[144]

But the regulation of offensive trades in the nineteenth century was not merely a matter of an isolated case here and a municipal ordinance there. Often, private nuisance actions, public prosecutions, state statutes, and municipal ordinances were mixed in a concerted and comprehensive effort to restrain a series of problematic enterprises. To get some idea of what such a regulatory strategy looked like in practice, it is necessary to magnify (and consequently restrict) our analytical lens.

Manhattan waged repeated wars on noxious trades throughout the century.[145] But its neighboring New Jersey peninsula, consisting of Hudson County between the Hudson and Hackensack Rivers and Newark and Jersey City, put up an even braver fight, perhaps because New York was the source of offensiveness. In 1865, the New Jersey legislature literally caught wind of the "offensive and noisome" manufactures growing up on the Jersey shore of the Hudson. It passed a special law making it unlawful in this area to "make, erect or set up any building or apparatus . . . or use the same when so made, for the purpose of boiling any part of the dead bodies of any animals, or of manufacturing the same into tallow, glue, ivory black, bone dust, manure or other substance, whereby any noisome, or offensive, or unwholesome, or annoying smokes, smells, or stenches may be emitted therefrom." Every person violating this act would not only be liable to indictment for nuisance but would be subject to an additional $75 fine for each offense.[146]

Relying on the statute, the New Jersey attorney general brought suit on behalf of several individuals against the New Jersey Stock Yard Company.[147] The company was a slaughterhouse chartered by the state, which was also engaged in boiling the viscera and intestines and extracting fat. Chancellor Zabriskie issued injunctions in this case prohibiting the company from keeping live hogs on the premises for more than three hours, from "permitting the blood of slaughtered animals, the contents of their stomachs and intestines, and other offal or parts of the animal to run, or to be deposited upon the shores or in the waters of the bay, or to remain on the premises," and from boiling the fat from slaughtered animals. The chancellor also generally condemned the condition of the buildings and pens and the disposal of waste products. Con-

vinced, however, of the scientific and practical improvements being made in keeping unoffensive abattoirs, he appointed a special commissioner to suggest permanent remedies for abating this nuisance.[148] The stockyard solved the problem of disposing of blood and offal by entering into an agreement with the Manhattan Manufacturing and Fertilizing Company.[149] The solution seemed ingenious. One could solve a nasty health and waste problem, turn a profit, and achieve a satisfying, organic wholeness by returning these remains to the fertile earth. As we shall see, however, fertilizing companies were not panaceas.

As if New Jersey's own slaughterhouses were not problem enough, the Garden State also had to contend with the animal waste of New York City. New Jersey fertilizing companies were magnets for nineteenth-century garbage barges and collateral industries. Residents of Bayonne on Newark Bay thought they won a reprieve when a drying and rendering business across the Hackensack burned down in 1870.[150] Hundreds of residents petitioned that it not be rebuilt. When it was, five brought suit. This establishment was particularly noxious. Refuse animal matter from the markets, abattoirs, and streets of New York was first sent to a New York City rendering operation in the Hudson. There, the material was boiled, and useful fat extracted. The residue of this process was pumped into the defendant's barges and sent south of Newark. The defendant dried this slop by heating it or by spreading it up to 6 feet deep on a 250-square-foot platform and letting the sun and wind do the rest. This dried mixture was then transported to the defendant's bone dust and poudrette (manure) factory on the Passaic. The five plaintiffs, "well-known citizens of the highest respectability," complained of "a noisome, unpleasant and sickening odor" which "enters their dwellings," "renders it impossible to be upon their piazzas or grounds with comfort," and "nauseates and actually sickens them and their families." They demanded an injunction.[151]

Chancellor Zabriskie obliged them. He argued, "The business of the defendants, conducting a bone factory and preparing the refuse of the streets, slaughterhouses, and markets of a great city for manufacture, is of a like kind with many other trades and business, perfectly lawful, that are universally recognized as nuisances; and where carried on, it requires clear and positive evidence to show that they do not affect those residing in the vicinity." Defense counsel probably chose the wrong argument when he urged that New York City needed "some place where it can deposit and utilize its filth." For Zabriskie responded, "That city, without the consent of New Jersey, has no right to make any part of this state its sewer or its pest-house." The owners of

the villas "in this most beautiful and desirable part of New Jersey" did not "hold their houses by the base tenure of being obliged to provide a cess-pool, or sewer, for the impurities of the city of New York."[152]

Injunctions, even when issued on behalf of private citizens, could be powerful public regulatory tools. But New Jersey was willing to go even further to restrain noxious and offensive trades. In 1872 the Manhattan Fertilizing Company itself fell victim to such a strong public remedy.[153] Located about 100 feet from the New Jersey Stock Yard in Jersey City, the company boiled residual blood and offal from the yard and mixed the cooked and solid result with sulphate of soda or salt. This was then dried in an oven, mixed with other chemicals, ground in a mill, and sold as usable fertilizer. That process went on for no more than two years when, upon local complaint, the street commissioner of Jersey City, Benjamin Van Keuren, gave notice that the company was a nuisance in violation of a Jersey City ordinance. He demanded that the nuisance, "consisting of putrid and decaying animal matter and offensive substances, emitting noxious and unwholesome smells," be abated within twenty-four hours. Seventeen days later, as fertilizing production went on as usual, Van Keuren took action. Together with twenty-five policemen and several others, the street commissioner entered the factory by force at one o'clock in the morning. They proceeded to "abate" the nuisance. In this case that meant the "taking of the eccentric rods of the machinery for grinding the baked blood, removing the belting or gearing, damaging and carrying off parts of machinery and property, and committing other acts to put a stop to complainants' works." Nineteenth-century public officials were willing to act decisively and powerfully against industries deemed harmful to the public.[154]

Like Mayor Cornelius Lawrence of New York,[155] Street Commissioner Van Keuren was taken to court for his strong-armed regulatory tactics. But also like Mayor Lawrence, the New Jersey courts ultimately vindicated Van Keuren's actions on behalf of the public. The Fertilizing Company marshaled some potent constitutional objections to this swift abatement, including unreasonable search and seizure, the taking of property without due process, deprivation of trial by jury, and the taking of property without compensation. Vice-Chancellor Dodd nevertheless validated the summary procedures used under state statute, municipal ordinance, and the police powers of a well-regulated society.

The Jersey City charter distinctly granted the board of alderman power to declare and remove nuisances.[156] The aldermen subsequently empowered the street commissioner, upon complaint, "to enter any building or premises to

ascertain if a nuisance exists," and, after twenty-four hours notice, "to abate it by the removal of such portions of the machinery, or other matter or thing, as may be necessary for the creating of the nuisance." Such seized property could then be sold at the public yard of the city. But Dodd did not rely solely on positive legislative power in disposing of the company's constitutional arguments. He placed Van Keuren's action within the scope of common law powers protecting public welfare. Dodd's defense of Van Keuren and the well-regulated society is second in eloquence and breadth only to Lemuel Shaw's argument in *Commonwealth v. Alger*:

> At common law, it was always the right of a citizen, without official authority, to abate a public nuisance, and without waiting to have it judged such by a legal tribunal. . . . This common law right still exists in full force. Any citizen, acting either as an individual or as a public official under the orders of local or municipal authorities, whether such orders be or be not in pursuance of special legislation or chartered provisions, may abate what the common law deemed a public nuisance. In abating it, property may be destroyed and the owner deprived of it without trial, without notice, and without compensation. Such destruction for the public safety or health, is not a taking of private property for public use, without compensation or due process of law in the sense of the Constitution. It is simply the prevention of its noxious and unlawful use, and depends upon the principles that every man must so use his property so as not to injure his neighbor [*sic utere tuo*], and that the safety of the public is the paramount law [*salus populi*]. These principles are legal maxims or axioms essential to the existence of regulated society. *Written constitutions pre-suppose them, are subordinate to them, and cannot set them aside.* They underlie and justify what is termed the police power of the state.[157]

Historians have suggested that at the time *Manhattan Manufacturing and Fertilizing Co. v. Van Keuren* (1872) was decided American legal and constitutional discourse were being reshaped by notions of "natural" and "higher law"—a higher law defined in terms of individual rights, due process, and the sanctity of private property.[158] But Vice-Chancellor Dodd's opinion suggests another kind of supraconstitutional law still at work. That law was the common law and its commitment to a well-regulated society devoted to the people's welfare. In *Van Keuren* the common law powerfully trumped explicit constitutional provisions and legitimated a major public health initiative against three of the most noxious polluters in Hudson County.

As late as 1872 then, the common law vision of a well-regulated society still dominated public health police. Trades, businesses, and industrial occupations deemed hazardous to the health and welfare of the community were held subject to the dictates of *salus populi*[159] and *sic utere tuo*. But public health law in the 1860s and 1870s also augured some important changes—changes in governance and law, changes in public power and private right. In the Manhattan Fertilizing Company's objections to summary abatement, we see the emergence of new ideas about constitutional rights as substantive limits on health police. Simultaneously, states and municipalities pioneered ever more powerful and centralized public controls in their attempts to guarantee public health. Liberty and authority, once fused in the notion of organic, self-regulating communities in which all were bound by customary rules of their own choosing, were slowly disentangling themselves. Eventually and reluctantly, they would reconverge in the liberal notion of a positivist state limited by absolute constitutional rights.

On the public powers side of the equation, the 1860s and 1870s witnessed a shift in the locus of prosecution of offensive trades from private individuals and diverse local officials to centralized boards of health with plenary power over public nuisances. In 1866, New York created the Metropolitan Sanitary District to consolidate the public health concerns of New York City and Brooklyn and place them under the direction of a single *state* agency. The Metropolitan Board of Health was given complete authority to control health hazards in the two cities. Almost immediately upon passage, the board began an unprecedented, coordinated attack on public nuisances in New York. Within two years, twelve cases involving the board's actions reached the New York appellate courts.[160]

The New York courts overwhelmingly upheld the board's legislatively granted powers. In *Coe v. Schultz* (1866), the owners of a poudrette manufactory at Hunter's Point challenged the board's order to discontinue their operations until altered so that odors and fumes could not escape into the air.[161] The plaintiff claimed that the execution of such an order without a trial and without a jury deprived him of his property "without due process of law." Justice Sutherland held such a contention "utterly without any colorable support," basing his decision on the long-held power of citizens to abate public nuisances at common law.[162] In *Metropolitan Board of Health v. Heister* (1868), the court approved the board's power to pass ordinances outlawing slaughterhouses and to close down violating establishments.[163] Chief Justice Hunt ar-

gued that such powers had long histories: "[F]rom the earliest organization of the government, the absolute control over persons and property, so far as the public health was concerned, was vested in boards or officers, who exercised a summary jurisdiction over the subject, and who were not bound to wait the slow course of the law." Almost every year, the legislature chartered some city or village with local powers to summarily remove noxious trades.[164]

But try as they might, New York judges had to be aware that something was new in these cases besides the due process arguments of plaintiffs. The Metropolitan Health District and Board of Health were distinctive phenomena in public health regulation. As in the Metropolitan Police Act of 1857, the New York legislature was creating new civil divisions of state.[165] It was granting *state* agencies extensive, independent power over regulatory matters traditionally left to local officials, citizens, and the common law. The Metropolitan Board of Health was given complete authority to investigate, give notice, grant hearings, pass ordinances, and close noxious establishments. Their orders were immediately enforceable by the Metropolitan police. The board was a fact-finding, law-making, and law-enforcing body—a legislature, court, and administrative agency rolled into one. The revolutionary implications of such a body became apparent in *Village of Jamaica v. Long Island Railroad Co.* (1869).[166] There the Queens County Court struck down a Jamaica ordinance against the loading and unloading of offensive substances in the village. The Municipal Health Act of 1866 vested public health authority *exclusively* in the Board of Health.[167] Local governments in the health district—the traditional repositories of such power—were disfranchised. Such ramifications made boards of health the site of continuous legal-political controversy.[168] It also made them progenitors of a new administrative state.[169]

The centralization and rationalization of American public health policy continued unabated through the late nineteenth century. The national quarantine conventions of the 1850s, the pioneering role of the United States Sanitary Commission during the Civil War, the revival of the national Marine Hospital Service, and the founding of the American Public Health Association conjoined to produce the first national quarantine act and the National Board of Health in 1879.[170] In 1878 in *Northwestern Fertilizing Company v. Hyde Park*, the U.S. Supreme Court defended an "inalienable" state police power to eliminate public health nuisances despite a fifty-year charter grant to manufacture the animal waste of Chicago.[171] Such unmistakable shifts in the locus and incidence of public health police powers eventually displaced the common law practices of self-regulating communities.[172] The consequences were legion.

As was the case with state prohibition experiments, novel exertions of public power were greeted with new delineations of private right. For example, after the Civil War, Louisiana experimented with a new mode of regulating and controlling the New Orleans slaughtering industry. Drawing on Paris's well-known, healthy experience with great centralized public abattoirs, the state in 1869 ordered a complete prohibition on slaughtering and stock landing in New Orleans except at the centralized, regulated facilities of the Crescent City Live Stock Landing and Slaughterhouse Company. Louisiana's ambitious public health measure precipitated the classic constitutional struggle known as the *Slaughterhouse Cases* (1872).[173]

As the site of the first Supreme Court interpretation of the Fourteenth Amendment, the *Slaughterhouse Cases* have been the subject of interminable interpretive debate. For decades progressive historians treated *Slaughterhouse* as the locus classicus of laissez-faire constitutionalism, focusing almost exclusively on Stephen Field's dissenting paean to an "inalienable right" to "the pursuit of the ordinary avocations of life."[174] *Slaughterhouse* has also been seen alternatively as a ridiculously belated "Jacksonian" response to corrupt monopoly or as a harbinger of the end of Reconstruction—the latter interpretation suggesting that the majority opinion's narrow rendering of Fourteenth Amendment freedoms was primarily a product of the politics of race and states' rights. Recently Herbert Hovenkamp spurned this court-centered approach in order to emphasize the economics of *Slaughterhouse*, especially the roles of market failure and new technology in the creation of an "ingenious," price-regulated public utility.[175]

Without minimizing the roles of the racial and sectional politics of Reconstruction or the economics of the meat industry, *Slaughterhouse* takes on a different significance when examined within the context of public health police and the history of the well-regulated society. Despite charges of a corrupt, partisan deal by the Louisiana legislature (charges not uncommon in the Reconstruction era), the public health concerns raised by established methods of slaughtering animals in New Orleans cannot be dismissed. As early as 1866, 1,100 citizens petitioned the legislature through the president of the Board of Health testifying:

> The immense quantity of filth and offal which is accumulated at and in the vicinity of the stock landing . . . goes into the Mississippi river, which if not prejudicial to health, is certainly very revolting. The immense suction pipe of the New Orleans water works is immediately below, and sucks in objects floating on the water, at a distance of fifty or sixty feet.

When the river is low, it is not uncommon to see intestines and portions of putrefied animal matter lodged immediately around the pipes. The liquid portion of this putrefied matter is sucked into the reservoir. Vessels arriving here with cattle, especially those that have been in a storm, invariable throw the dead cattle—of which they often have many—into the river at the stock landing.[176]

With such clear public health implications and so much antebellum precedent for the regulation and prohibition of slaughterhouses in urban areas, one would think the Crescent City solution would meet little legal opposition (even if it affected nearly a thousand butchers). And indeed the Louisiana court first sustained the measure with a familiar defense of the ideals of the well-regulated society: "Liberty is the right to do what the law permits. Freedom does not preclude the idea of subjection." Justice Taliaferro elaborated, "The sacrifice of the individual right in this case is of no consequence, in view of the general benefit and commerce of a great commercial community. The doctrine, then is elementary and well established, that in the public interest and for the public good, legislation which postpones the interests of a few to that of a whole community, is legitimate and proper."[177]

But after the Civil War the legitimacy of such propositions was no longer readily apparent. Amid the rhetoric of radical Republicanism and emancipation, the argument that "freedom does not preclude the idea of subjection" simply did not carry the same moral force. In the U.S. Supreme Court, John A. Campbell advanced the New Orleans butchers' claim that the Louisiana regulation violated Fourteenth Amendment guarantees of liberty and property. His argument resonated more deeply with the changing times:

Life, liberty and property, if not affected by [the Fourteenth Amendment, would be] entirely under the cognizance and control of the State Governments. The State Governments might divest vested rights. . . . The State Governments might fix the status of every person on its soil. [They] did so in the laws tolerating slavery. They admitted slaves, they created slaves by the laws, and they emancipated slaves.

But, Campbell asked pointedly, "How is the case now?" He went on to elaborate a new constitutionalism wherein "the Constitution, by declaring that every member in the empire is its citizen," prohibits states from disturbing "this citizen" in "his privileges or immunities or in his life, liberty or property."[178] Campbell promoted this new vision of constitutional rights in direct response to what he perceived as an unprecedented use of public force: "Can

there be any centralization more complete, or any despotism less responsible, than that of a State Legislature concerning itself with dominating the avocations, pursuits and modes of labor of populations, conferring monopolies on some, voting subsidies to others, restraining the freedom and independence of others and making merchandise of the whole?"[179]

John Campbell's question *"How is the case now?"* was the great constitutional issue of the late nineteenth century. It implied that public things had definitively changed—that all bets were off. The constitutional and federal ideas that supported and protected slavery were discredited. It was up to the Supreme Court to redefine a constitutionalism with which to "begin the nation anew"—to strike a new balance of power between the national government and the states and between new public powers and new individual rights.[180] The broad, substantive definitions of economic liberty, "equality of right," and "due process of law" in the *Slaughterhouse* dissents of Justices Field and Bradley played major roles in that process of redefinition.[181] The fate of the well-regulated society was ultimately sealed when the contrary constitutional rhetorics of substantive due process and inalienable police power replaced common law discussions of regulated liberty and *salus populi.*

But for the moment, Campbell, Field, and Bradley did not capture the majority of the Supreme Court which upheld the Louisiana slaughterhouse regulation. Citing Chancellor Kent, Justices Shaw and Redfield, and Chief Justice Marshall in *Gibbons v. Ogden,* Justice Miller argued, "The power here exercised by the legislature of Louisiana is, in its essential nature, one which has been, up to the present period in the constitutional history of this country always been conceded to belong to the States."[182] Miller was influenced by the weight of the past. If he needed reminding about the roots of regulation in America, Louisiana's counsel called up a panoply of antebellum regulatory legislation that had been sustained by state and federal courts (a catalog of the well-regulated society): laws respecting markets and fairs, ferries, bridges, railroads and turnpikes, fishing, navigation, gas companies, health and quarantine, offensive trades of all descriptions, slaughterhouses, the keeping of animals, statutes limiting the hours of labor and the employment of children, and the licensing of attorneys, auctioneers, brokers, innholders, peddlers, pilots, theaters, and retailers of liquors.[183]

If John Campbell were right—if the Fourteenth Amendment were construed broadly to include *all* privileges and immunities and *all* state interferences with property and liberty—Louisiana protested that the constitutionality of all state regulation would be called into question. And certainly that could not be the case. Justice Miller agreed, posing the rhetorical question,

"Was it the purpose of the fourteenth amendment, by the simple declaration that no State should make or enforce any law which shall abridge the privileges and immunities of the *citizens of the United States*, to transfer the security and protection of all civil rights which we have mentioned from the States to the Federal government?"[184] Certainly that could not be the case.

But, in fact, it was. The story of police power jurisprudence and social and economic regulation after 1877 primarily involved the reconsideration of age-old regulatory issues in the new context of nationalization and consolidation. This total postwar reconsideration of public power and private right entailed revolutionary changes in the conduct of American governance, including the "invention" of constitutional law, the constitutionalization of police regulation, and ultimately the creation of a new American liberal state.

The Invention of
American Constitutional Law

> The domestic problems of our country after the Recon-
> struction period may be said to have revolved in the main
> around the responsibilities of wealth to commonwealth.
> —Felix Frankfurter

The common law vision of a well-regulated society was a powerful public philosophy. But following Stendhal's observation that "all the truth lies in the details," the real significance of the *salus populi* tradition lay in the minute and ubiquitous regulations shaping the most important public policy concerns of the nineteenth century: public safety, public economy, public property, public morals, and public health. Close investigations of such pervasive and everyday governmental practices are essential to a complete picture of the American legal-political tradition and the elusive meanings of American democracy, liberalism, and republicanism. Indeed, even the partial surveys contained in this volume illuminate an alternative understanding of nineteenth-century conceptions of public practice, state power, and legal right.

The first historical lesson to be drawn from the well-regulated society concerns the overwhelming presence of the state and regulation in nineteenth-century American life. The countless regulations examined in this book reflect the power of a deeply rooted American tradition of police and regulatory governance vital to social and economic development. Armed with a far-reaching conception of law and state serving the people's welfare, public officials defined the safety, health, morals, and commercial concerns of citizens as objects of state policy and governmental regulation. All private interests and rights

were subordinated to these primary public objectives. The consequence was a new and intense regard in the science of government for the policing of society and economy. The nineteenth century was not an era of laissez-faire or statelessness where public inertia and political naiveté just happened to provide the perfect conditions for a burgeoning private market economy and a self-generating civil democracy. On the contrary, the fundamental social and economic relations of the nineteenth century—the market, the city and the countryside, the family, the laborer, the proprietor, the good neighbor, the good citizen—were formed and transformed in this period as the constant objects of governance and regulation. Law and the state were not simply reflectors or instruments or facilitators of natural evolutions in the market or civil society. They were creative and generative forces.

Seeing this public construction of early American society and economy is difficult given a modern liberal mythology that has naturalized and privatized such irreducibly historical and public matters as commerce, property, and contract. Consequently, the arguments of this book perhaps too frequently have had to be phrased in the negative—countering absolutist renderings of private property with the relative rights of social beings, confronting the free market with the regulated marketplace, challenging the neurasthenic state with a vigorous medical police. But this deconstructive strategy of contesting the excessive rhetoric of statelessness, possessive individualism, constitutional limitations, and American exceptionalism with the conspicuous state practices of well-regulated governance also provides a framework for some positive historical reconstructions.

The presence of a powerful legal regulatory apparatus, for example, simply makes more understandable the kinds of social power and economic control that social historians have been documenting in nineteenth-century America for the past twenty-five years. American slavery was not the product of a society hesitant to draw on the coercive powers of the state. The inequitable relationship established between railroad corporation and switchman was not the inadvertent excess of laissez-faire. Patriarchy was not the natural outcome of the unencumbered private choices of men and women. The trail of law, state, and police was over all. Similarly, the explosive changes of the late nineteenth and early twentieth centuries—industrialism, imperialism, progressivism (to name a few)—make more sense in the context of a much longer tradition of political economy, statecraft, and social welfare regulation.

But one must be cautious about substituting one set of anachronisms for another. It would be a serious mistake to read *salus populi* as demonstrating

the existence of a uniform and consistent American police-state tradition, a direct nineteenth-century precursor to the New Deal. For the second historical lesson to be drawn from the well-regulated society has everything to do with its distinctiveness—its deviation from modern understandings of law, the state, regulation, and private rights. Much of that difference is captured in a full appreciation of the well-regulated society as primarily a *common* legal tradition.

Common first implied localism. In contrast to the modern ideal of the state as centralized bureaucracy, the well-regulated society emphasized local control and autonomy. Indeed, the state and federal centralization of public economic, morals, and health authority signaled the decline of well-ordered governance. Second, common embraced a social conception of rights and duties in a well-regulated society. Whereas the modern American state has been quick to recognize new, absolute, and private civil rights and civil liberties, the well-regulated society endorsed a regime of local self-government where all such rights were subordinated to the community's ability to regulate for the good of the whole. Common also denied the clear separation of the private from the public—a hallmark of the modern liberal state. Finally, the superior rule of law in the well-regulated society was common, not constitutional, law. The common law's standards of consent, history, and accommodation embodied a humanistic and hermeneutic approach to the problem of authority and rule inconsistent with modern legal positivism.

The history of governance in America then is neither simple nor linear. Indeed, it is often fraught with paradox and contradiction, especially in the disjunction of rhetoric and reality. As early as 1888, Albert Shaw introduced James Bryce to the conundrum of the American rhetoric of laissez-faire amid a "profusion" of state regulatory legislation. Shaw chalked up this contradiction to an unequaled capacity in the American "for the entertainment of legal fictions and kindred delusions. He lives in one world of theory and in another world of practice." Bryce attempted an atypically feeble explanation, emphasizing American state experimentalism and a "strong moral sentiment, such as that which condemns intemperance."[1] Such explanations are inadequate if provocative. But Shaw and Bryce at least recognized the fundamental tension in the coexistence of a heightened American rhetoric of individual liberty with a constant and historic readiness to employ the coercive state powers of regulation and police. Paradoxical on its face, this crucial relationship of personal freedom and regulatory governance, of liberty and restraint, only makes sense in historical context. American notions of private right and public power do

	COLONIAL RULE	WELL-REGULATED GOVERNANCE	THE LIBERAL STATE
Time Period	17th–18th Century (to 1787)	19th Century (1787–1877)	20th Century (1877 to present)
Locus of Authority	Locality	State and Local Government	Central Government
Preferred Social Unit of Governance	Household	Self-Governed Community	Individual
Preferred Method of Governance	Mediation	Regulation	Administration
Rule of Law	Custom	Common Law	Constitutional Law

Figure 2. American governmental regimes

not hold true to a single and consistent idea or trajectory. They were the product of changing and conflicting everyday practices of governance—practices with distinct and particular histories.

One of the advantages of approaching the problem of government as constitutive public conduct (as opposed to political philosophy or bureaucracy) is that it allows one to chronologize important governmental changes that transcend the short-term give-and-take of electoral politics or presidential syntheses without falling prey to catchall, timeless teleologies like the rise of the modern state or the emergence of liberal politics. The practices of governance have a weightiness and stickiness that allows them to persist through some of the most seismic historical and sociological events. And transformations in governmental practice and logic often entail repercussions just as consequential as wars, elections, ethnocultural conflicts, business cycles, changes in the birthrate, or intellectual paradigm shifts. The well-regulated society embodied a particular set of governmental practices with important ramifications for nineteenth-century social and economic life. Those practices were not a postscript to feudalism or a prelude to the modern state. They also were not merely the residual public and communitarian safeguards of a dominant liberal and individualistic political culture. Rather they occupied their own niche in a larger history of American governmental practice.

In place of singular, linear histories of the evolution of liberalism or the

state, American public life on the whole is better understood in terms of three very distinctive, successive regimes of governmental practice: colonial rule; nineteenth-century well-regulated governance; and the twentieth-century liberal state. Though continuities between the three regimes certainly exist (with rather long and murky transitions), governmental conduct and rationality in 1730, 1830, and 1930 formally and substantively diverged. As ideal types (subject to the usual warnings about oversimplification), colonial rule, well-regulated governance, and the liberal state represent three categorically different, nonfungible ways of practicing and thinking about government. The schema of American governmental conduct presented in Figure 2 suggests the kinds of conceptual, structural, and practical factors that distinguish governmental regimes.

Figure 2 is suggestive and experimental rather than comprehensive and certain. Other markers could certainly be added (Theodore Lowi's tripartite division of economic policymaking into distributive, regulatory, and redistributive paradigms comes to mind);[2] and the categorization suggested is subject to endless qualification and contest (colonial rule, for example, raises the unique problem of a monarchical-imperial perspective at odds with the domestic regime represented here). The research in this book only supports the characterization of well-regulated governance. But the point is to identify a coherent matrix of public factors neglected by traditional approaches to politics that have an indubitable significance in history. Where is public power exercised (locally, regionally, centrally)? What form of law predominates? What types of governmental action and policymaking are legitimate (taxation, regulation, redistribution)? What are the appropriate objectives of governance? What mechanisms (judicial, legislative, administrative, actuarial) are available to meet those objectives? These are crucial questions. And when one detects across-the-board changes in the answers to such questions over time, a first-order historical variable if not a governmental paradigm shift has been identified. In the late nineteenth century, American governance underwent just such a shift.

Well into the 1870s, American social and political life continued to be governed by the principles and traditions of the well-regulated society. The American laws of public safety, public economy, public property, public morality, and public health, meticulously carved out by legislatures and courts since the earliest days of the republic, etched their influence deep into the institutional and ideological foundation of American public policy. Consequently, as late as

1877 one can still discern the powerful influence of the ideals and practices of *salus populi*, local self-government, and the common law. As they had since 1787, courts continued to uphold a slew of public regulations of individual liberties, properties, and activities with the general observation that private interests were subservient to the general welfare of society. An overarching public concern with police and well-orderedness trumped legal-political arguments about individual liberties and inalienable rights. Localism and notions of citizenship tied to membership in self-governing communities continued to control much thinking about the underpinnings of democracy and republican governance. In the first decades after the Civil War, Americans remained a remarkably associative people, constructing and defending political and personal identities through participation with others in particular localities, churches, organizations, charities, clubs, political parties, corporations, and unions. Finally, the public and historical sensibilities of a dynamic common law tradition still guided jurists, politicians, and lawyers as they hammered out the rules and maxims regulating American public and private life.

But by the end of Reconstruction, new social and economic forces were eroding the moral and political authority of *salus populi* and the well-regulated society. As early as the 1850s, new political voices and new legal languages challenged public controls on economy, morality, and health. The character of those controls themselves had already moved substantially away from traditional, local, and participatory origins. As Felix Frankfurter noted, the challenges of industrialism (wealth) placed increasing strains on the assumptions of the well-regulated society (commonwealth). By the 1870s trickles of change and discontent became a tidal flood. By century's end a new governmental regime was in place, and traces of the well-regulated society (past as well as contemporaneous) were being aggressively redrawn if not erased.

It will ultimately take another volume to address these transformations adequately, and quick generalizations on postbellum America are a risky enterprise. Nevertheless, a full appreciation of the power, problems, and peculiarity of the well-regulated society requires some concluding account of the reasons for its demise and an introductory sketch of the rough features of its conqueror.

What replaced the well-regulated society as a mode of law and governance was the American liberal state (a regime very much with us today). Its central attribute was the simultaneous pursuit of two seemingly antagonistic tendencies—the *centralization of power* and the *individualization of subjects*. The two would be ultimately mediated (and, again simultaneously, promoted) by the *constitutionalization of law*. By the early decades of the twentieth century,

a society legally and politically oriented around the relationship of individual subjects to a central nation-state had substantially replaced the well-regulated society's preference for articulating the roles of associative citizens in a confederated republic. Power and liberty, formerly interwoven in the notion of self-regulating, common law communities, were now necessary antipodes kept in balance only through the magnetic genius of an ascendant American constitutionalism.

The causes of this transformation were as complex as "modernity" itself and all the elusive accoutrements that historians embarrassedly try to capture under headings like industrialism and urbanization. But one that cannot be minimized was the mid-nineteenth-century crisis of slavery and Civil War. The Civil War played midwife to the American liberal state. It delivered new definitions of individual freedom, state power, nationalism, and constitutionalism.[3] Indeed, the paramount legal-political statement of that conflict—the Emancipation Proclamation—was an archetype of the new regime. Never before had the United States witnessed such a sweeping example of central power and authority: the federal, summary, and uncompensated abolition of vested property rights in other human beings. Never before had the United States witnessed such a sweeping testament to freedom and individual liberty. New powers and new liberties would become the twin pillars of liberal state building.

The well-regulated society was a belated casualty of the Civil War. But that conflict only brought to a boil some broader legal, political, social, and economic pressures simmering since the 1850s—pressures not released by the compromises of 1877. Those pressures ultimately undercut antebellum traditions of local self-government, *salus populi*, and common law and precipitated substantially revised understandings of state power, individual rights, and constitutional law.

State Power

Max Weber defined the modern state as the monopoly of the use of force—as the "system of order" claiming binding authority "not only over the members of the state, the citizens, . . . but also to a very large extent over all action taking place in the area of its jurisdiction."[4] Strictly construed, historians are perhaps justified for failing to find this kind of "state" in early nineteenth-century America. After the Civil War, however, Max Weber's creeping leviathan made its presence felt. A decidedly upward shift in decision-making power[5] characterized late nineteenth-century American police and regulatory policies. The legal and political autonomy of local, regional, and sectional entities

repeatedly lost out as federal and state governments centralized and consolidated their authority. Authorities unable to trace their legitimacy to explicit central delegations of power became inherently suspect.[6] Although the peculiarities of American federalism continued to confound any unitary sovereignty, power consistently flowed upward and outward. The roots of a positivist administrative and bureaucratic state insistently totalizing its reach into American social and economic life were clearly discernible in this period.[7] That state increasingly replaced well-ordered communities as the primary locus of legal-political power and public moral-ethical legitimacy.

The Civil War and its aftermath were fine proving grounds for experiments in state power. In addition to inspiring a wave of insurgent nationalism, the wartime presidency of Abraham Lincoln was awash in novel exertions of centralized governmental power, the suspension of habeas corpus and the first national income tax. The Reconstruction Amendments, securing the individual rights of newly freed men and women, also wrote into the Constitution new definitions of national citizenship and the supremacy of the federal government. This dramatic intrusion of centralized power into the local and "domestic" affairs of states would have been unimaginable to James Wilson or Zephaniah Swift, despite their aversion to slavery. Indeed, after the Civil War the common law philosophy of Wilson and Swift quickly succumbed to a founding political science interest in "The State."

In 1835, Alexis de Tocqueville began his classic inquiry into the political culture of the United States with a cautionary chapter five on the "Necessity of Examining the Condition of the States before That of the Union at Large." James Bryce, Tocqueville's late nineteenth-century counterpart, unapologetically began his investigation of the *American Commonwealth* with "The National Government."[8] Bryce was typical of a wave of postbellum reflections on government that moved quickly away from debates on the "nature of Union" to prescriptive analyses of the nature of the modern state.[9] Building on European theories of public law and state formation, particularly the work and lectures of German scholars like Johann Bluntschli and Rudolf von Gneist, American political theorists built a new discipline and a new political philosophy on the backs of state theories like Woodrow Wilson's *The State* (1889) and W. W. Willoughby's, *An Examination of the Nature of the State* (1896).[10] The emphasis was no longer on common law, localism, and confederation, but on the positive constitutional powers of a central state. The authoritative sphere of this new sovereignty, Theodore Woolsey revealed, "may reach as far as the nature and needs of man and of men may reach."[11]

But the consolidation of power and sovereignty was not simply a product of

political theorizing. Rather, the centralization of order-maintenance and accompanying prohibitions on private, local, and sectional uses of force were the consequence of hard-fought changes in legal and public policy. State prohibition statutes and the nationalization of public health initiatives were perfect examples of the kinds of policies that spearheaded transformations in conceptions of legitimate state power. State health and police measures essentially disfranchised localities (as well as private citizens) of common law powers to define and abate public nuisances. Morals regulations of liquor and lotteries prompted judicial invocations of an "inalienable police power" defined increasingly in terms of sovereignty and command rather than consent and common law precedent. State police regulation did not die after the Civil War. In fact, it proliferated as never before. But as the newly positivized and constitutionalized police power it ceased to encompass the same aspirations and consequences for governance. It traded in a local, historical, and popular orientation for a new status as a category of constitutional law demarcating the "bidding and forbidding power of the State."[12]

One of the culminating legal decisions of the well-regulated society was *United States v. DeWitt* (1870), where the U.S. Supreme Court ruled that there was no such thing as a "federal" police power—that is, a general, open-ended power in the *national* government to regulate liberty and property to protect the public safety, morals, health, comfort, and welfare.[13] Legal and political developments between 1877 and 1937 made that federal police power—an essential attribute of modern, centralized states—a practical if not a technical reality.

But centralization was not a linear or inevitable or inherently progressive process. Henry Adams warned as early as 1876: "From the moment the small state became merged in a great nation, the personal activity of the mass of free men in politics became impossible."[14] Adams's pessimistic and decidedly anti-Whiggish perspective allowed him to identify disintegration as a necessary and indispensable part of consolidation. One of the key accompaniments of the aggrandizement of state power was the dissolution of intermediate citizen loyalties and local authorities en route to a one-to-one relationship between the state and the individual.

Individual Rights

Otto von Gierke argued that one of the "universal tendencies" of modern history was the pursuit of an "absolute individuality" as a complement to the "absolute state." Such a constructive project was simultaneously destructive, requiring the "dissipation of all local communities and fellowships" so as to

leave "no intermediate links of any kind between the supreme universality of the all-caring state and the sum total of single individuals, comprising the people."[15]

The well-regulated society was all about the legal and political cultivation of just such intermediate links between the state and the individual. Power was diffused and flowed from the bottom up. General powers of social and economic police were situated and exercised primarily in towns, counties, and municipalities. The power of self-governing communities and associations to police themselves through the enactment of bylaws and ordinances regulating safety, economy, property, morals, and health were reviewed only irregularly by higher authorities and seldom were overturned. The ability of individuals to contest local controls on hawkers or peddlers, vagrants or prostitutes, noisome trades or disorderly houses, wooden buildings or unhealthy premises was severely circumscribed. Indeed, the whole idea of an individual *qua* citizen of a nation-state exercising rights through legal challenges to such police regulations was incongruent with the very concepts of self-government and *salus populi*. Soon after the Civil War, such challenges became the norm— both catalyst and product of the invention of a more liberal, constitutional law. In sum, the well-regulated society was built precisely on those local institutions and associational sympathies increasingly vulnerable in the late nineteenth century to the double-edged sword of statism and individualism.

One of the oddest things about the legal centralization of state power in late nineteenth-century America was that it was accompanied not by the expected enhancement of *salus populi*, common good rhetoric, but by its repudiation, and an offering in its stead of a heightened regard for *individual* right and liberty. The Civil War wrought the first changes in constitutional language since 1804 (just as its constitutional prologue brought the first judicial nullification of an act of Congress since *Marbury v. Madison*).[16] But the Thirteenth, Fourteenth, and Fifteenth Amendments were no simple textual revisions. Much like the *sic utere tuo* and *salus populi* maxims they ultimately replaced, the constitutional clauses "involuntary servitude," "privileges or immunities," "due process," "equal protection," and "right of citizens of the United States" embodied a wholly new political philosophy. The heart of that philosophy was a radical reconstruction of individual rights. Abolitionism, emancipation, and radical Republicanism renewed interest in the inherent, natural, and absolute rights of individuals, dethroning a public-spirited common law as the source of American fundamental law.[17] In contrast to the law of *salus populi*, this new "higher" constitutionalism emphasized individual freedoms and personal autonomy rather than the duties incumbent upon members of organized and

regulated communities. These were the roots of distinctly modern notions of individual civil rights and civil liberties.

Some forms of the new individualistic credo were distinctly oppositional vis-à-vis the expansion and centralization of state power—for example, the social Darwinism of William Graham Sumner and the constitutional libertarianism of Christopher Tiedeman. But, on the whole, the law and language of individual rights were not antagonistic to state building. For every postbellum equivalent of Justice Comstock in *Wynehamer v. People* articulating a libertarian, antistatist version of substantive due process, there was a Justice Shaw in *Fisher v. McGirr*, demarcating the procedural rights and individual protections the state should observe while expanding the scale and scope of its reach into American social, cultural, and economic life. After all, though the well-regulated society receded after 1877, the police power exploded. The sovereign power of the late nineteenth-century American state was ultimately enhanced by an individualism increasingly defined by national citizenship and directed against the intermediary pulls of locality, section, and association.

But this uneasy alliance of state and individual, power and liberty was not without fundamental tensions. Indeed, the central question of the late nineteenth-century polity was what would hold it all together. The answer came in the guise of a new American constitutionalism. The muddy jurisprudential waters of Anglo-American common law were not conducive to the bright political lines demanded of law by a new liberal ideology. The common law's emphasis on historic communities, local customs, and self-government clashed with both the needs of a centralized state and the resurgence of individualism. Like the reception of Roman law in early modern Europe, the invention of American constitutional law clinched the establishment of a modern nation-state.

Constitutional Law

Oliver Wendell Holmes's *The Common Law* (1881) was the perfect epitaph for a customary, historical, and experiential approach to law quickly being surpassed by new modes of private legal science and public constitutionalism. Prominent postwar battles between power and liberty exposed weaknesses in the common law and shifted the mantle of American fundamental law and governing tradition to a new liberal constitutionalism. Liberal constitutionalism thrived on (and reinforced) the separation of public from private, state power from individual right. Indeed, its identity and strength hinged on its role as the principal guardian of the sacrosanct boundaries between power

and liberty. The invention of this constitutional law entailed fundamentally new rationalities of regulation, social governance, and public order.

As early as the 1830s fights over codification exposed a rift in American conceptions of the rule of law.[18] Codifiers challenged the common law's consensual and apolitical claims, arguing that a less arbitrary, more democratic legalism required the clear, written commands of the sovereign. The grand legislative experiments of the 1840s and 1850s—prohibition, police reform, married women's property acts, Field codes, and general incorporation laws—also undermined a vision of law and legislation as the incremental adjustment of past principle to present need. Such statutes were not minor common law revisions but wholesale shake-ups in established legal relations via the written precepts of sovereign legislatures. As the gaps between law and legislation and law and politics widened, midcentury jurists reworked traditional notions of legislative and judicial roles. Theodore Sedgwick's 1857 treatise on statutory interpretation was an opening salvo in a redefinition of law's primary role as a check on positivist state legislative power.[19] Sedgwick opened the door for both modern judicial review and a thoroughgoing postbellum constitutionalization of American law and regulation.

A cult of constitutionalism greeted the end of the Civil War.[20] Unlike the Eleventh and Twelfth Amendments, the Reconstruction Amendments became the focus of an entirely new constitutional and political philosophy. Treatises by Thomas Cooley and Christopher Tiedeman moved constitutionalism from the periphery to the center of American jurisprudence as the definitive oracle on governmental power and individual liberty, public aspirations and private freedoms.[21] The substance of that constitutionalism was increasingly defined in terms of substantive due process and constitutional limitations on the one hand, and inalienable (eventually federal) police power on the other. Despite the *Dred Scott* debacle, the American judiciary quickly regained power as the ultimate mediator of modern liberal demands for more state power *and* more individual rights.

The consequence for the police power and social and economic regulation was a decisive constitutionalization. After the Civil War, the police power became a constitutional doctrine. Its roots in amorphous English common law and continental police traditions regarding well-regulated communities were obscured by its new status as a formal subheading of American constitutional law. Age-old regulatory issues were reexamined and redecided in a distinctly constitutional framework in the great police power cases of the late nineteenth-century: *Munn v. Illinois* (1877), *Mugler v. Kansas* (1887), *Powell v. Pennsylva-*

nia (1888), *Budd v. New York* (1892), and *Lawton v. Steele* (1894).[22] Lemuel Shaw–like arguments about well-ordered society and civil liberty in self-governing communities became increasingly rare. Indeed, they were ultimately written out of the American constitutional tradition in exchange for the more usable, victorious past of John Marshall's commercialism, Daniel Webster's individualism, Joseph Story's constitutionalism, and Abraham Lincoln's nationalism.

But liberal constitutionalism was not the only jurisprudential consequence attending the decline of the common law vision of the well-regulated society. Although historians have spent much time debating the shift from legal instrumentalism to legal formalism, it is clear that the rationality of late nineteenth-century private and public law was both more formalist and more instrumental than the customary and historical jurisprudence of the common law tradition. Late nineteenth-century law was simultaneously more committed to the logic and precision of legal form, category, and rule and more attuned to law's effectiveness as a tool for advancing external societal goals like economic efficiency. Less present in American law after 1877 was toleration for the unwieldy, ambiguous mess of substantive human and historical values (ethical, religious, political, communitarian, aesthetic) present in the experiential accretions of common law. Modern jurisprudence tended toward positive formulations of power and interest, constitutional delineations of individual right, scientific applications of legal rules, and economic calculations of general welfare and utility. None of these things were conducive to the old common law tradition. It was discarded, and a new law was invented. By the twentieth century, American constitutional law assumed its necessary place next to American individualism and the American state.

Between 1877 and 1937, then, American conceptions of state power, individual rights, and the rule of law were fundamentally transformed. The invention of American constitutional law was the final linchpin in a new governmental regime that radically separated private right and public power in simultaneous pursuit of a centralized state and an individualized subject. The result was modern American liberalism—the way we currently tend to break up and analyze the legal-political world. The conventions and mythologies of this twentieth-century American liberalism have made it only that much harder to reconstruct and interpret the nineteenth-century well-regulated society. Modern notions of public power and private right displaced social theories of rights and traditions of local self-government, and they continue to obscure historical understandings of the people's welfare.

All of these changes in state power, individual right, and constitutional law were evolutionary historical tendencies rather than final and complete transformations. No doubt one can still detect traces of the well-regulated society in contemporary law and society. But overall, a new legal-governmental regime displaced the one described in this book by the beginning of the twentieth century. Its repercussions bombard us today in the form of an increasingly centralized, bureaucratized sovereign state; a sociocultural politics centered around an ever more thinly defined conception of the self; and a formal and instrumental approach to law and governance that privileges realistic and radically presentist formulations of interest and power over idealistic and historical visions of *salus populi*.

A modern liberal perspective on these changes emphasizes progress. And, indeed, the demise of the well-regulated society gave rise to two of the most compelling achievements of twentieth-century politics and society: the creation of an American welfare state and the emancipatory movements for civil liberties and civil rights. Clearly we cannot go back. Despite nostalgia for community values and social order, one would not want to revive a legal-governmental system that coexisted so comfortably with slavery and patriarchy. Nonetheless, heeding the warnings of critical theorists about the dangers of instrumental rationality, atomized individualism, and authoritarian governance, one cannot help but feel uneasy about some of these tendencies. One cannot help but wonder about the prospects for new despotisms within the ostensibly liberating agenda of constitutional law, individual rights, and central state power. One worries for a late twentieth-century polity that continues to reject fundamental aspects of the American democratic-republican experiment—an autonomous conception of the public good, a commitment to self-government and participatory citizenship, and a vision of law and governance "shook from sublimer powers than those of self." *Salus populi suprema lex est* consisted of an unbreakable bond between its constituent parts. There was no people's welfare without a rule of law, and there was no rule of law without a due regard for the common good. When *res publica* (the public things) and *salus populi* (the people's welfare) become mere functions of individual interests, economic formulas, and political expediency, we have only laws of men, not government.

Introduction

1. Different aspects of this question will be addressed in almost every chapter. But, in general, the thousand or so cases that make up the raw material for this study all emanate from laws being explicitly enforced. But, more important, the overall approach of this book to the problem of governance and social policing attempts to move beyond the harsh separation of law from society, law-in-the-books from law-in-action, and social history from political history implied in the positivist "enforcement" question. For further discussion, see chapter 2, n. 46.

2. For a useful introduction see Charles Edward Merriam, "Systematic Studies of Politics," in *American Political Ideas: Studies in the Development of American Political Thought, 1865–1917* (New York, 1920), 370–431. But a true appreciation of the dimensions of this scholarly movement requires some substantive browsing in the Johns Hopkins University Series on Historical and Political Science starting in 1876 and Columbia University's Studies in History, Economics and Public Law starting in 1880. This first wave of political/institutional studies culminated in Andrew C. McLaughlin and Albert Bushnell Hart's *Cyclopaedia of American Government*, 3 vols. (New York, 1914).

3. No better statements in this tradition exist than Roscoe Pound, "Liberty of Contract," *Yale Law Journal* 18 (1909): 454–87; Morris R. Cohen, "Property and Sovereignty," *Cornell Law Quarterly* 13 (1927): 8–30; and Robert L. Hale, "Coercion and Distribution in a Supposedly Non-Coercive State," *Political Science Quarterly* 38 (1923): 470–94.

4. The best of the commonwealth studies are Oscar Handlin and Mary Flug Handlin, *Commonwealth: A Study of the Role of Government in the American Economy: Massachusetts, 1774–1861* (New York, 1947); Louis Hartz, *Economic Policy and Democratic Thought: Pennsylvania, 1776–1860* (Cambridge, Mass., 1948); Carter Goodrich, *Government Promotion of American Canals and Railroads, 1800–1890* (New York, 1960); Gerald D. Nash, *State Government and Economic Development: A History of Administrative Policies in California, 1849–1933* (Berkeley, Calif., 1964). But it is hard to get an idea of the full import of this school without also including the work of Harry Scheiber on the Ohio canal era, Milton Heath, Bray Hammond, James Neal Primm, George Miller, Paul Gates, and Edwin M. Dodd. For a more complete bibliography and analysis, see Robert A. Lively, "The American System: A Review Article," *Business History Review* 29 (1955): 81–96; and Harry N. Scheiber, "Government and the Economy: Studies of the 'Commonwealth' Policy in Nineteenth-Century America," *Journal of Interdisciplinary History* 3 (1972): 135–51.

5. The classics on civic humanism and republicanism are Bernard Bailyn, *The Ideological Origins of the American Revolution* (Cambridge, Mass., 1967); Gordon S. Wood, *The Creation of the American Republic, 1776–1787* (Chapel Hill, N.C., 1969); and J. G. A. Pocock, *The Machiavellian Moment: Florentine Political Thought and the Atlantic Republican Tradition* (Princeton, N.J., 1975). Also see the bibliographies in Robert E. Shalhope, "Toward a Republican Synthesis: The Emergence of an Understanding of Republicanism in American Historiography," *William and Mary Quarterly* 29 (1972): 49–80; Shalhope, "Republicanism in Early American Historiography," *William and Mary Quarterly* 39 (1982): 334–56; and Daniel T. Rodgers, "Republicanism: The Career of a Concept," *Journal of American History* 79 (1992): 11–38.

6. Alexis de Tocqueville, *Democracy in America*, ed. Phillips Bradley, 2 vols. (New York, 1945); James Bryce, *The American Commonwealth*, 2d ed., 2 vols. (New York, 1891).

7. Georg Friedrich Hegel, *The Philosophy of History* (New York, 1956), 84–87; Burnham quoted in John G. Ruggie, ed., *The Antinomies of Interdependence* (New York, 1983), 84. Even more recently, Allen Steinberg has argued, "The United States moved from a society that was scarcely governed to one in which, by century's end, government regularly touched the daily lives of the people." Steinberg, *The Transformation of Criminal Justice: Philadelphia, 1800–1880* (Chapel Hill, N.C., 1989). For excellent discussions of the problem of American statelessness, see Morton Keller, "Social Policy in Nineteenth-Century America," in *Federal Social Policy: The Historical Dimension*, ed. Donald T. Critchlow and Ellis W. Hawley (University Park, Pa., 1988), 99–115; Stephen Skowronek, *Building a New American State: The Expansion of National Administrative Capacities, 1877–1920* (Cambridge, 1982), 3–5; and Richard R. John, "State and Society in the Early American Republic, 1787–1835: Toward a New Synthesis," unpublished manuscript.

8. For classic attacks on the laissez-faire thesis see Frank P. Bourgin, *The Great Challenge: The Myth of Laissez Faire in the Early Republic* (New York, 1989); Handlin and Handlin, *Commonwealth*; Hartz, *Economic Policy and Democratic Thought*. The first attack on the myth of laissez-faire was coincident with its very ascendancy. See Albert Shaw, "The American State and the American Man," *Contemporary Review* 51 (1887): 695–711.

9. For examples of these perspectives, see Samuel P. Huntington, "Political Modernization: America vs. Europe," in his *Political Order in Changing Societies* (New Haven, Conn., 1968), 93–139; Skowronek, *Building a New American State*; Sidney Fine, *Laissez Faire and the General-Welfare State: A Study of Conflict in American Thought, 1865–1901* (Ann Arbor, Mich., 1956); Calvin Woodard, "Reality and Social Reform: The Transition from Laissez-Faire to the Welfare State," *Yale Law Journal* 72 (1962): 286.

10. Perhaps foreseeing the dangers of combining flame with Mrs. O'Leary's cow.

11. "An Act to Incorporate the City of Chicago, 1837," in *Laws and Ordinances Governing the City of Chicago, 1837*, ed. Joseph E. Gary (Chicago, 1866), 537–38. On the implementation of these powers by the city, see the ordinances collected in the rest of this volume. Provisions 22 and 30 on nuisances and police alone entail thousands of other rules, regulations, and legal proceedings.

12. Louis Hartz, *The Liberal Tradition in America: An Interpretation of American Political Thought since the Revolution* (New York, 1955). For updated versions of the liberal position, see Joyce Appleby, *Capitalism and a New Social Order: The Republican Vision of the 1790's* (New York, 1984); John P. Diggins, *The Lost Soul of American Politics: Virtue, Self-Interest, and the Foundations of Liberalism* (New York, 1984).

13. In addition to the republicanism literature, see Henry F. May, *The Enlightenment in America* (New York, 1976); Morton White, *The Philosophy of the American Revolution* (New York, 1978); William G. McLoughlin, "The Role of Religion in the Revolution: Liberty of Conscience and Cultural Cohesion in the New Nation," in *Essays on the American Revolution*, ed. Stephen G. Kurtz and James H. Hutson (Chapel Hill, N.C., 1973), 197–255; Peter N. Miller, *Defining the Common Good: Empire, Religion, and Philosophy in Eighteenth-Century Britain* (Cambridge, 1994).

14. For the best discussion of the way in which this diversity of early American political and social thought can be encompassed within a thicker, changing definition of liberalism, see James T. Kloppenberg, "The Virtues of Liberalism: Christianity, Republicanism, and Ethics in Early American Political Discourse," *Journal of American History* 74 (1987): 9–33.

15. Roscoe Pound, *The Formative Era in American Law* (Boston, 1938); James Willard Hurst, *Law and the Conditions of Freedom in the Nineteenth-Century United States* (Madi-

son, Wis., 1956); Grant Gilmore, *The Ages of American Law* (New Haven, Conn., 1977); William E. Nelson, *The Americanization of the Common Law: The Impact of Legal Change on Massachusetts, 1760–1830* (Cambridge, Mass., 1975); Morton J. Horwitz, *The Transformation of American Law, 1780–1860* (Cambridge, Mass., 1977); Hendrik Hartog, "Distancing Oneself from the Eighteenth Century: A Commentary on Changing Pictures of American Legal History," in *Law in the American Revolution and the Revolution in Law*, ed. Hendrik Hartog (New York, 1981), 229–57. For the most sophisticated, multifaceted presentation of this theme (complete with a critique of the preceding works), see Christopher L. Tomlins, *Law, Labor, and Ideology in the Early American Republic* (New York, 1993). Seventeenth- and eighteenth-century legal historians recently have attempted to shift the date of this crucial transformation deeper into the colonial period without really challenging the linear nature of legal evolution. See David Thomas Konig, *Law and Society in Puritan Massachusetts: Essex County, 1629–1692* (Chapel Hill, N.C., 1979); Bruce Mann, *Neighbors and Strangers: Law and Community in Early Connecticut* (Chapel Hill, N.C., 1987).

16. Terrence McDonald has argued that though labor, urban, and working-class historians have vigorously attacked the myth of American exceptionalism in the social sphere—demonstrating, for example, more working-class consciousness and less social mobility than was once thought—their findings have only reinforced an exceptional American political history (e.g., the ameliorating influence of an expansive suffrage and ethnic patronage democracy). See Terrence J. McDonald, "The Burdens of Urban History: The Theory of the State in Recent American Social History," *Studies in American Political Development* 3 (1989): 3–29.

17. The most provocative, overarching statement of this theme is Alan Brinkley, *The End of Reform: New Deal Liberalism in Recession and War* (New York, 1995). On the impact of the "end of reform" on historiography, see Richard Hofstadter, *The Progressive Historians* (New York, 1968).

18. Richard Hofstadter, *The American Political Tradition* (New York, 1948), viii. For some recent restatements of this liberal interpretation (despite important generational and methodological differences), see Wood, *The Creation of the American Republic* 609: "The liberty that was now emphasized was personal or private, the protection of individual rights against all governmental encroachments." Linda Kerber, "The Revolutionary Generation: Ideology, Politics, and Culture in the Early Republic," in *The New American History*, ed. Eric Foner (Philadelphia, 1990), 33: "Corporatist concepts were now challenged by a more individualistic liberalism, which offered a vision of social and economic relations as both free and self-regulating. This new vision was embedded both in the 'invisible hand' of Adam Smith's *Wealth of Nations* (1776) and the conceptualization of the federal Constitution of 1787 as 'a machine that would go of itself.'" Paula Baker, "The Domestication of Politics: Women and American Political Society, 1786–1920," in *Women, the State, and Welfare*, ed. Linda Gordon (Madison, Wis., 1990), 61: "State and local governments gradually relinquished to the marketplace the tasks of regulating economic activity. . . . For our purposes, the important point is that governments largely gave up the tasks of regulating the economic and social behavior of the citizenry."

19. For conservatives, nineteenth-century laissez-faire marks a golden age to be restored. For liberals (building on the legacy of Progressive historiography), negative liberalism provides a foundation on which to build a different, positive liberalism to meet the challenges of industrialization. For Marxists and critical scholars, exceptional American political traditions explain the absence of socialism in America. For feminists and civil rights advocates, the nineteenth-century liberal rights tradition provides a precedent for making twentieth-century private autonomy and personal liberty claims against the state. For an

example of this versatility, see the symmetry in interpretations of nineteenth-century law and economy in Horwitz, *Transformation, 1780–1860*; and Stuart Bruchey, *The Wealth of a Nation: An Economic History of the United States* (New York, 1988). An exception to this tendency is recent Foucauldian scholarship, which, recognizing the police and regulatory roots of the liberal constitutional state, views political liberalism as but a transitional prelude to the modern disciplinary society. See, for example, the essays in Graham Burchell, Colin Gordon, and Peter Miller, eds., *The Foucault Effect: Studies in Governmentality* (Chicago, 1991). For a superb critique of this perspective, see Laura Engelstein, "Combined Underdevelopment: Discipline and the Law in Imperial and Soviet Russia," *American Historical Review* 98 (April 1993): 338–53.

20. The notion of governance as constitutive public conduct draws on a host of diverse sources. Among the most significant are Morton Keller's histories of polity and policy; Hendrik Hartog's concept of "technologies of public action"; Michel Foucault's theory of governmentality; and legal realist and critical legal studies work on the relative autonomy and constitutive power of law. See Morton Keller, *Affairs of State: Public Life in Late Nineteenth Century America* (Cambridge, Mass., 1977); Keller, *Regulating a New Economy: Public Policy and Economic Change in America, 1900–1933* (Cambridge, Mass., 1990); Keller, *Regulating a New Society: Public Policy and Social Change in America, 1900–1933* (Cambridge, Mass., 1994); Hendrik Hartog, *Public Property and Private Power: The Corporation of the City of New York in American Law, 1730–1870* (Chapel Hill, N.C., 1983), 66; Michel Foucault, "*Omnes et Singulatim*: Towards a Critique of 'Political Reason,'" in *The Tanner Lectures of Human Values II*, ed. Sterling M. McMurrin (Stanford, Calif., 1979), 225–54; Burchell, Gordon, and Miller, *The Foucault Effect*; Robert W. Gordon, "Critical Legal Histories," *Stanford Law Review*, 36 (1984): 57–124. Also see Pierre Bourdieu, *Outline of a Theory of Practice* (New York, 1977); and Bourdieu, "The Force of Law: Toward a Sociology of the Juridical Field," *Hastings Law Journal* 38 (1987): 805–53.

21. This third way between state and society can be quite compelling, especially given the normative import of its classic formulations: Tocqueville on associations, Gierke on fellowship, Arendt on the rise of the social, and Habermas on the public sphere. Tocqueville, *Democracy in America*, I:198–205; Otto von Gierke, *The German Law of Fellowship*, volume 1: *The Legal and Moral History of the German Fellowship*, trans. Antony Black, in *Community in Historical Perspective* (Cambridge, 1990); Hannah Arendt, *The Human Condition* (Chicago, 1958); Jürgen Habermas, *The Structural Transformation of the Public Sphere: An Inquiry into a Category of Bourgeois Society*, trans. Thomas Berger (Cambridge, Mass., 1989). But ultimately I have found John Dewey's simple, pragmatic, and consequentialist demarcation of public and private to be more useful analytically: "If it is found that the consequences of a conversation [or transaction] extend beyond the two directly concerned, that they affect the welfare of many others, the act acquires a public capacity." Dewey further reasoned that when such public consequences of individual behavior were recognized, "there is an effort to regulate them, something having the traits of a state comes into existence." John Dewey, *The Public and Its Problems* (1927), reprinted in *The Later Works, 1925–1953*, ed. Jo Ann Boydston (Carbondale, Ill., 1984), 2:244. Dewey's definition emphasizes the direct intersection of politics and society rather than some autonomous mediating role for second-level associations or policies or publications between the state and individual.

22. The two classic statements of this perspective are John Commons on the policeman: "Within that field his will is the will of the state. He is the state-in-action. He *is* the state. The state is what its officials do." And Karl Llewellyn on law: "This doing of something about disputes, this doing of it reasonably, is the business of law. And the people who have

the doing in charge, whether they be judges or sheriffs or clerks or jailers or lawyers, are officials of the law. *What these officials do about disputes is, to my mind, the law itself.*" John R. Commons, *Legal Foundations of Capitalism* (New York, 1924; reprint, Madison, Wis., 1957), 122. Karl N. Llewellyn, *The Bramble Bush: On Our Law and Its Study* (1930; reprint, New York, 1960), 12.

23. The best recent calls for a revivified history of politics include Theda Skocpol, "Bringing the State Back In: Strategies in Current Research," in *Bringing the State Back In*, ed. Peter Evans, Dietrich Rueschemeyer, and Theda Skocpol (Cambridge, 1985), 3–37; William E. Leuchtenberg, "The Pertinence of Political History: Reflections on the Significance of the State in America," *Journal of American History* 73 (1986): 585–99; Ronald P. Formisano, "The Invention of the Ethnocultural Interpretation," *American Historical Review* 99 (1994): 453–77; Mark H. Leff, "Revisioning U.S. Political History," *American Historical Review* 100 (1995): 829–53; McDonald, "The Burdens of Urban History"; Richard John, "State and Society."

24. American labor law historians, for example, have radically expanded and revitalized their field by examining the power of legal concepts and practices like servitude, conspiracy, and incorporation to construct and officially maintain asymmetrical labor and class relations while simultaneously remaining attuned to the enormous creative agency of individuals, groups, and economic processes. See the work of Eileen Boris, Andrew Cohen, Daniel Ernst, William Forbath, Victoria Hattam, Gary Herrigel, Karen Orren, Christopher Tomlins, Amy Dru Stanley, and Robert Steinfeld excellently surveyed in Christopher L. Tomlins and Andrew J. King, eds., *Labor Law in America: Historical and Critical Essays* (Baltimore, 1992). David Montgomery has suggested the synthetic possibilities for this approach in American history in *Citizen Worker: The Experience of Workers in the United States with Democracy and the Free Market during the Nineteenth Century* (Cambridge, 1993).

25. "*Salus populi suprema lex*" was the very first maxim in the influential Herbert Broom, *A Selection of Legal Maxims, Classified and Illustrated* (London, 1845), 1.

26. James Kent, *Commentaries on American Law*, 4 vols. (New York, 1826), 2:265.

27. One of the best restatements of this theme came in the late nineteenth century by none other than Henry Adams in "The Anglo-Saxon Courts of Law": "The theory of the constitution was irretrievably lost. Justice was no longer a public trust, but a private property. The recognition of the legality of private tribunals for the church was a recognition of the legality of private tribunals in general. . . . The entire judicial system of England was torn in pieces; and a new theory of society, known as feudalism, took its place." Henry Adams, "The Anglo-Saxon Courts of Law," in *Essays in Anglo-Saxon Law* (Boston, 1876), 1–54.

28. Francis Hilliard, *The Elements of Law: Being a Comprehensive Summary of American Civil Jurisprudence* (Boston, 1835), 5.

29. Divine law, of course, was the domain of natural law. Blackstone defended the label "municipal law": "I call it *municipal* law, in compliance with common speech; for, tho' strictly that expression denotes the particular customs of one single *municipium* or free town, yet it may, with sufficient propriety, be applied to any one state or nation, which is governed by the same laws and customs." William Blackstone, *Commentaries on the Laws of England: A Facsimile of the First Edition of 1765–1769*, 4 vols. (Chicago, 1979), 1:44.

30. William Blackstone also captured this positive side of "municipal" governance: "Municipal or civil law regards him also as a citizen, and bound to other duties towards his neighbour, than those of mere nature and religion: duties, which he has engaged in by enjoying the benefits of the common union; and which amount to no more, than that he do contribute, on his part, to the subsistence and peace of the society." Blackstone, *Commentaries*, 1:45.

31. Francis Lieber, *On Civil Liberty and Self-Government*, 3d ed. (Philadelphia, 1891), 249. Daniel Webster's encomium to self-government came in a May 22, 1852, speech at Faneuil Hall: "I say to you and to our whole country, and to all the crowned heads and aristocratic powers and feudal systems that exist, that it is to self-government, the great principle of our popular representation and administration—the system that lets in all to participate in the counsels that are to assign the good or evil to all—that we may owe what we are and what we hope to be." Cited in Lieber, 247. On Lieber generally, see Frank Freidel, *Francis Lieber, Nineteenth-Century Liberal* (Baton Rouge, La., 1947).

32. Hurst, *Law and the Conditions of Freedom*, 3–6. Margaret R. Somers examines the deep roots of this long tradition of local self-government in "Rights, Relationality, and Membership: Rethinking the Making and Meaning of Citizenship," *Law and Social Inquiry* 19 (Winter 1994): 63–112.

33. Charles B. Goodrich, *The Science of Government* (Boston, 1853), 219. Again, Blackstone provides an early reference point for definition of what he called "civil or political liberty": "This liberty, rightly understood, consists in the power of doing whatever the laws permit; which is only to be effected by a general conformity of all orders and degrees to the equitable rules of action, by which the meanest individual is protected from the insults and oppression of the greatest." Blackstone, *Commentaries*, 1:6.

34. Francis Lieber held that such laws "of the by" (i.e., of the place, of the community, of the collection of dwellers) were the essence of Anglican self-government: "Every institution of local self-government shall have the right to pass such by-laws as it finds necessary for its own government. . . . I believe that it is in the Anglican system of liberty alone that by-laws are enacted and have full force without consent of superior power." Lieber, *On Civil Liberty*, 322–23. Ernst Freund concurred on the centrality and full legitimacy of restrictive bylaws arguing, "The common-law concept of civil liberty was by no means repugnant to regulation in the public interest, but recognized such regulation as a proper and ordinary incident and qualification." Ernst Freund, *Standards of American Legislation* (Chicago, 1965), 188.

35. My own idiosyncratic favorites on this theme are Alfred Zimmern, *The Greek Commonwealth*, 5th ed. (New York, 1931); Mack Walker, *German Home Towns: Community, State, and General Estate, 1648–1871* (Ithaca, N.Y., 1971); Frederic William Maitland, *Domesday Book and Beyond: Three Essays in the Early History of England* (1897; reprint, Cambridge, 1987).

36. Max Farrand, ed., *The Records of the Federal Convention of 1787*, rev. ed., 4 vols. (New Haven, Conn., 1966), 1:157 (emphasis added).

37. Thomas Paine, *Common Sense* (1776), in *The Complete Writings of Thomas Paine*, ed. Philip S. Foner, 2 vols. (New York, 1945), 1:29; Massachusetts Constitution, art. 30, 1780.

38. On the legal nature of the Revolution and Constitution generally, see John Philip Reid, *Constitutional History of the American Revolution: The Authority of Rights* (Madison, Wis., 1986); Reid, *Constitutional History of the American Revolution: The Authority to Tax* (Madison, Wis., 1986); Charles Howard McIlwain, *The American Revolution: A Constitutional Interpretation* (New York, 1923); Forrest McDonald, *Novus Ordo Seclorum: The Intellectual Origins of the Constitution* (Lawrence, Kan., 1985), 9–55.

39. *Commonwealth v. Blackington*, 24 Pick. 352 (Ma., 1837), 356 (emphasis added).

40. *Commonwealth v. Blackington*, 356–57.

41. Christopher Tomlins uses the phrase "modality of rule" to represent law's reflexive *and* constitutive properties as a set of practices that "have determinable consequences for human action, not least those actions which constitute the practice of rule itself." Tomlins, *Law, Labor, and Ideology*, 21, 29–30.

42. I began researching this book with the naive goal of reading every appellate police power case in the nineteenth century. That task is impossible. While one might be able to survey all of the cases mentioned in nineteenth-century digests or in the pioneering treatises of Thomas Cooley, Christopher Tiedeman, and Ernst Freund, each state jurisdiction is home to thousands of other unindexed and unnoticed appellate police power cases, not to mention an even greater litany of unrecorded local and summary proceedings. On top of this quantitative problem, there are also definitional quandaries (to be explored later). Thomas M. Cooley, *A Treatise on the Constitutional Limitations* (Boston, 1868); Christopher G. Tiedeman, *A Treatise on the Limitations of Police Power in the United States* (St. Louis, 1886); Ernst Freund, *The Police Power: Public Policy and Constitutional Rights* (Chicago, 1904).

43. Richard T. Ely, *Property and Contract in Their Relations to the Distribution of Wealth*, 2 vols. (New York, 1914), 1:200, 205–6.

44. Some examples of this ubiquitous complaint: "The police power is the dark continent of our jurisprudence. It is the convenient repository of everything for which our juristic classifications can find no other place." John W. Burgess, *Political Science and Comparative Constitutional Law*, 2 vols. (Boston, 1896), 1:216. "We deal in other words, with what traditionally has been known as the police power. An attempt to define its reach or trace its outer limits is fruitless." Justice Black in *Berman v. Parker*, 348 U.S. 26, 32 (1954). The "origins" of the police power have been traced to such diverse sources as Plato's *Republic*, Justinian's *Institutes*, Coke, Blackstone, Montesquieu, Madison, Kent, *Federalist Papers's* conception of "residual sovereignty," and the "domestic tranquility" clause of the federal constitution.

45. Freund, *Police Power*, iii; Lewis Hockheimer, "Police Power," *Central Law Journal* 44 (1897): 158.

46. Smith defined police as "originally derived from the Greek *politeia* signifying policy, politics, or the regulation of a government in general. . . . It comprehends in general three things: the attention paid by the public to the cleanliness of the roads, streets, etc.; 2d, security; and thirdly, cheapness or plenty, which is the constant source of it." This last police component, of course, became the focus of Smith's *Wealth of Nations* (1776). Adam Smith, *Lectures on Jurisprudence* (1762–63; Liberty Classics edition, Indianapolis, Ind., 1982), 331. Johann H. G. von Justi defined police science as "concerned with nothing but the preservation and increase of the total 'means' of the state through good internal institutions and with creating all sorts of internal power and strength for the republic: e.g., through (1) cultivating the land; (2) improving the laboring class; (3) maintaining good discipline and order in the community." Albion Small, *The Cameralists: The Pioneers of German Social Polity* (Chicago, 1909), 437. The French rendering is best captured in Maurice Block's *Dictionnaire de l'administration française*: "Police is that part of the public power which is charged with protecting persons and things against all attacks, against all the evils that human prudence can prevent, or at least diminish in their effects. To maintain public order, to protect individual liberty and property, to watch over morals, to secure public health,—such are the principal objects confided to the care of the police." Cited in T. D. Woolsey, "The Nature and Sphere of Police Power," *Journal of Social Science* 3 (1871): 99. Also see the fine discussion of police in Tomlins, *Law, Labor, and Ideology*, ch. 2.

47. Blackstone, *Commentaries*, 4:162.

48. This emphasis on order is also a part of Vattel's highly influential treatment of "Justice and Police": "Police consists in the attention of the prince and magistrates to preserve everything in order. Wise regulations ought to prescribe whatever will best contribute to the public safety, utility and convenience; and those who have authority in their hands,

cannot be too attentive to their being observed. By a wise police, the sovereign accustoms the people to order and obedience, and preserves peace, tranquility, and concord among the citizens." Emmerich de Vattel, *The Law of Nations*, ed. Edward D. Ingraham (1759; Philadelphia, 1852), bk. I, ch. xiii, sec. 174. For an excellent discussion of Blackstone and Vattel on police, see William W. Crosskey, *Politics and the Constitution in the History of the United States*, 2 vols. (Chicago, 1953), 1:146–55. Beware, however, Crosskey's presentist and incomplete survey of American permutations. On neo-Stoicism, see Gerhard Oestreich, *Neo-Stoicism and the Early Modern State*, trans. D. McLintock (Cambridge, 1983).

49. Michel Foucault, "*Omnes et Singulatim*: Towards a Criticism of 'Political Reason,'" 248.

50. Ibid., 249. Also see Woolsey, "Nature and Sphere of Police Power," 100–101.

51. *Slaughterhouse Cases*, 83 U.S. 36 (1872), 62.

52. *Laws of New York, 1781–1801*, 2 vols. (Albany, N.Y., 1802).

53. *The Revised Statutes of the State of Michigan* (Detroit, 1838). Similar provisions can be found in *The Revised Statutes of the Commonwealth of Massachusetts* (Boston, 1836).

54. The detail of these regulations is crucial. Regulated under the heading of "disorderly persons" are: "All persons who threaten to run away and leave their wives and children a burden on the public; all persons pretending to tell fortunes, or where lost or stolen goods may be found; all common prostitutes, all keepers of bawdy houses, or houses for the resort of prostitutes; all drunkards, tipplers, gamesters or other disorderly persons; all persons who have no visible profession or calling to maintain themselves by, but who do for the most part support themselves by gaming; all jugglers, common showmen and mountebanks, who exhibit or perform for profit and puppet-show, wire or rope dancing, or other idle shows, arts or feats; all persons who keep in any public highway, or in any place where spirituous liquors are sold, any keno table, wheel of fortune, thimblers, or other table, box, machine or device for the purpose of gaming; all persons who go about with such table, wheel, or other machine or device, exhibiting tricks or gaming therewith; all persons who play in the public streets or highways, with cards, dice, or any instrument or device for gaming; shall be deemed disorderly persons." *Revised Statutes of Michigan*, 199.

55. Ibid., 619–51. In addition to these state regulations, municipalities were usually incorporated with ample powers to pass regulations of their own. A perfect example involves the extensive "police" powers granted to the city of Albany by the New York legislature. An 1826 statute haphazardly lumps together some of the regulatory powers of the common council for the "more effectual suppression of vice and immorality" and "for preserving peace and good order." Included are hundreds of regulatable offenses, actions, professions, and economic interests: forestalling; regrating; disorderly and gaming houses; billiard tables; combustible and dangerous materials; the use of lights and candles in livery or other stables; the construction of fireplaces, hearths, chimneys, stoves, and any other apparatus capable of causing fires; the gauging of all casks of liquids and liquors; the place and manner of selling hay, pickled and other fish; the forestalling of poultry, butter, and eggs; the purchase of wheat, corn, and every kind of grain and other articles of country produce, by "runners"; the running of dogs; weights and measures; buildings; chimneys and chimney sweeps; roads; wharves and docks; the weighing and measuring of hay, fish, iron, cord wood, coal, grain, lime, and salt; markets; cartmen and porters; fires; highways and bridges; roof guards and railings; the selling of cakes and fruit; the paving or flagging of sidewalks; the assize and quality of bread; the running at large of horses, cows, or cattle; and vagrants, common mendicants, or street beggars. In addition, the legislature authorized Albany's common council "to make all rules, by-laws and regulations for the good order and government of the said city." *Laws of the State of New York* (Albany, N.Y., 1826), c. 185, 191–93.

56. Cooley, *Constitutional Limitations*, 572.

57. Edmund S. Morgan, *American Slavery, American Freedom: The Ordeal of Colonial Virginia* (New York, 1975); Nancy F. Cott, *The Bonds of Womanhood: "Woman's Sphere" in New England, 1780–1835* (New Haven, Conn., 1977); Ronald T. Takaki, *Iron Cages: Race and Culture in 19th-Century America* (New York, 1979).

58. Willard Hurst, of course, revolutionized American legal history with an emphasis on just such *conditions*. Unfortunately, most commentators have focused too exclusively on Hurst's definition of *freedom* and the release of energy. Hurst, *Law and the Conditions of Freedom*.

59. Georg Wilhelm Friedrich Hegel, *The Phenomenology of Mind*, trans. J. B. Baille, 2d ed. (New York, 1931), 68.

Chapter One

1. *Commonwealth v. Alger*, 7 Cush. 53 (Mass., 1851). James Bradley Thayer firmly established the tradition (begun with Thomas Cooley) of beginning discussions of the police power with *Alger* in his influential *Cases on Constitutional Law*, 2 vols. (Cambridge, 1895), 1:693–705. The phrase "police power" was used by John Marshall as early as 1827 in *Brown v. Maryland*, 12 Wheat. 419 (U.S., 1827). For a discussion of *Brown*, see chapter 2.

2. In Massachusetts tidewater riparian owners were granted property rights extending to low-water mark. The Boston wharf line at issue in *Alger* was set legislatively *inside* this standard.

3. *Commonwealth v. Alger*, 84–85. Thomas Cooley first canonized *Alger* in 1868 by quoting this section in its entirety to begin his discussion of "The Police Power of the States." Thomas M. Cooley, *A Treatise on the Constitutional Limitations* (Boston, 1868), 572–73. Harry Scheiber is most responsible for keeping discussion of *Alger* alive among legal historians. Harry N. Scheiber, "Public Rights and the Rule of Law in American Legal History," *California Law Review* 72 (1984), 217–51.

4. Oliver Wendell Holmes Jr., *The Common Law*, ed. Mark De Wolfe Howe (1881; Boston, 1963), 85. Holmes's reason for such praise was Shaw's sense of the requirements of the community. In Holmes's words, "few have lived who were his equals in their understanding of the grounds of public policy to which all laws must ultimately be referred." Of course, for anyone who has seen a portrait of Shaw, the best description is still that of Rufus Choate, who looked upon Shaw as the pagan did his wooden idol, "knowing that he was ugly, but feeling that he was great." Quoted in Leonard W. Levy, *The Law of the Commonwealth and Chief Justice Shaw* (Cambridge, Mass., 1957), 26.

5. This jurisprudential distinction would be made less clear in twentieth-century constitutionalism, beginning most obviously with Oliver Wendell Holmes's declaration in *Pennsylvania Coal Co. v. Mahon*, 260 U.S. 393 (1922), 415, that "if regulation goes too far it will be recognized as a taking." But the recent assertion of some constitutional scholars that the "just compensation" provision of the Fifth Amendment long functioned as a constitutional limitation on the police power is ahistorical and inaccurate. See Richard A. Epstein, *Takings: Private Property and the Power of Eminent Domain* (Cambridge, Mass., 1985).

6. *Alger* is not discussed in the three leading histories of American law and constitutionalism. Lawrence M. Friedman, *A History of American Law*, 2d ed. (New York, 1985); Kermit L. Hall, *The Magic Mirror: Law in American History* (New York, 1989); Alfred H. Kelly, Winfred A. Harbison, and Herman Belz, *The American Constitution: Its Origins and Development*, 6th ed. (New York, 1983).

7. See, for example, W. G. Hastings, "The Development of Law as Illustrated by the Deci-

sions Relating to the Police Power of the State," *Proceedings of the American Philosophical Society* 39 (1900): 418; Scott M. Reznick, "Empiricism and the Principle of Conditions in the Evolution of the Police Power: A Model for Definitional Scrutiny," *Washington University Law Quarterly* (1978): 12. Even Leonard Levy, whose brilliant biography of Shaw sets the standard for legal-historical biography, concludes, "Only Shaw at this early date recognized that the objective of the police power is the promotion of the public welfare, that it was to be accomplished by regulation, and that the regulation must trench upon private rights." Relying on the work of Oscar and Mary Handlin, he comes close to explaining Shaw's decision as the peculiar product of a distinctive Massachusetts Commonwealth tradition — "To call the police power a Massachusetts doctrine would be an exaggeration, though not a great one." Finally, he claims that Shaw's definition of the police power is essentially the same as that of Ernst Freund over fifty years later. Levy, *Law of the Commonwealth*, 244, 308, 253; Ernst Freund, *The Police Power: Public Policy and Constitutional Rights* (Chicago, 1904); Oscar Handlin and Mary Flug Handlin, *Commonwealth: A Study of the Role of Government in the American Economy: Massachusetts, 1774–1861* (New York, 1947).

8. Of course, this is but the tip of the very large iceberg that will be chipped at for the rest of this book. For a preliminary smattering, see *Stoughton v. Baker*, 4 Mass. 522 (1808); *Commonwealth v. Ruggles*, 10 Mass. 391 (1813); *Corning v. Lowerre*, 6 Johns. Ch. 439 (N.Y., 1822); *Attorney General v. Hunter*, 16 N.C. 12 (1826); *Stuyvesant v. Mayor of New York*, 7 Cow. 588 (N.Y., 1827); *Baker v. Boston*, 12 Pick. 184 (Mass., 1831); *Mills v. Hall and Richards*, 9 Wend. 315 (N.Y., 1832); *State v. Bertheol*, 6 Blackf. 474 (Ind., 1843); *Fisher v. McGirr*, 67 Gray 1 (Mass., 1854); *Republica v. Duquet*, 2 Yeates 493 (Pa., 1799); *State v. Mayor of Mobile*, 5 Port. 279 (Ala., 1837).

9. *Mayo v. Wilson*, 1 N.H. 53 (1817), 57.

10. *Vanderbilt v. Adams*, 7 Cow. 349 (N.Y., 1827), 351–52. The 1819 statute at issue in *Vanderbilt* required the harbormaster to make room on private wharves (like the one built by Alger) for incoming vessels.

11. Herbert Spencer, *The Man versus the State*, ed. Truxton Beale (New York, 1916).

12. Duncan Kennedy, "The Structure of Blackstone's Commentaries," *Buffalo Law Review* 28 (1979): 382. From this perspective, even a critic of liberalism like E. P. Thompson could admit that "the notion of the rule of law is itself an unqualified human good." E. P. Thompson, *Whigs and Hunters: The Origin of the Black Act* (New York, 1975), 267. The central problem with Kennedy's analysis is his assertion that Blackstone's *Commentaries* marks the ascendancy of a liberal legalism that by the nineteenth century structured all of Anglo-American law. This book's periodization suggests that Kennedy's diagram and liberal legalism failed to capture American jurisprudence until the turn of the twentieth century (Kennedy's date for liberalism's "final disintegration").

13. Edward S. Corwin, "The 'Higher Law' Background of American Constitutional Law," *Harvard Law Review* 42 (1929): 365–409; Edward S. Corwin, "The Doctrine of Due Process of Law before the Civil War," *Harvard Law Review* 24 (1911): 366–85, 460–79; Edward S. Corwin, "The Basic Doctrine of American Constitutional Law," *Michigan Law Review* 12 (1914): 247–76, 538–72; Edward S. Corwin, "Marbury v. Madison and the Doctrine of Judicial Review," *Michigan Law Review* 12 (1914): 538. An overview of Corwin's basic position can be found in his *Liberty against Government: The Rise, Flowering and Decline of a Famous Juridical Concept* (Baton Rouge, La., 1948). Of course, Corwin acknowledged that definitions of private right and legislative power changed significantly from the nineteenth to the twentieth century. Private right grew from a narrow, propertied conception to modern notions of personal liberty and civil rights; the locus of public power shifted from the states to the federal government.

14. Robert G. McCloskey, ed., *Essays in Constitutional Law* (New York, 1957), 6. Although they highlight different aspects of the "basic doctrine" (private property, classical political economy, and an antiredistributive judiciary), three of the most important new books in American constitutional history return to the progressive, Corwinian paradigm. Jennifer Nedelsky, *Private Property and the Limits of American Constitutionalism: The Madisonian Framework and Its Legacy* (Chicago, 1990); Herbert Hovenkamp, *Enterprise and American Law, 1836–1937* (Cambridge, Mass., 1991); Morton J. Horwitz, *The Transformation of American Law, 1870–1960: The Crisis of Legal Orthodoxy* (New York, 1992). On the continued predominance of this vision in modern constitutional scholarship, see "Symposium: When Is a Line As Long As a Rock Is Heavy?: Reconciling Public Values and Individual Rights in Constitutional Adjudication," *Hasting Law Journal* 45 (April 1994): 707–1120.

15. James Willard Hurst, *Law and the Conditions of Freedom in the Nineteenth-Century United States* (Madison, Wis., 1956); Morton J. Horwitz, *The Transformation of American Law, 1780–1860* (Cambridge, Mass., 1977). Also see Friedman, *A History of American Law*; William E. Nelson, *Americanization of the Common Law: The Impact of Legal Change on Massachusetts Society, 1760–1830* (Cambridge, Mass., 1975); Stanley I. Kutler, *Privilege and Creative Destruction: The Charles River Bridge Case* (New York, 1971).

16. It is important to distinguish "legal instrumentalism" as used here to define a general historiographical tendency from Morton Horwitz's more particular, time-bound description of antebellum judges *making* rather than *declaring* law. Horwitz's thesis about a dramatic early nineteenth-century shift in judicial style from oracle to policymaker has been challenged by a colonial legal historiography in which judges seem just as dynamic and policy-oriented as their antebellum counterparts. Indeed, as Donald Kelley has shown, the tension between immanence and instrumentality is as old as the Western legal tradition itself. Horwitz, "The Emergence of an Instrumental Conception of Law," in *Transformation, 1780–1860*, 1–30; Donald R. Kelley, *The Human Measure: Social Thought in the Western Legal Tradition* (Cambridge, 1990). Also see William E. Nelson, "The Impact of the Antislavery Movement upon Styles of Judicial Reasoning in Nineteenth Century America," *Harvard Law Review* 87 (1974): 513–66; and Harry N. Scheiber, "Instrumentalism and Property Rights: A Reconsideration of American 'Styles of Judicial Reasoning' in the Nineteenth Century," *Wisconsin Law Review* (1985): 1–18.

17. Robert W. Gordon, "Critical Legal Histories," *Stanford Law Review* 36 (1984): 57–125; Hendrik Hartog, "The Constitution of Aspiration and 'The Rights That Belong to Us All,'" *Journal of American History* 74 (1987): 1013–34; Christopher L. Tomlins, *Law, Labor, and Ideology in the Early American Republic* (New York, 1993), especially 19–34; James T. Kloppenberg, "The Theory and Practice of American Legal History," *Harvard Law Review* 106 (1993): 1332–51.

18. This is the explicit theme of most recent attempts to synthesize public and private, nineteenth- and twentieth-century legal histories. R. Kent Newmyer, "Harvard Law School, New England Legal Culture, and the Antebellum Origins of American Jurisprudence," *Journal of American History* 74 (1987): 820. Also see Morton Horwitz on the transition from instrumentalism to classical legal thought in *Transformation, 1870–1960*; and Herbert Hovenkamp on *Lochner* and classical political economy in *Enterprise and American Law*.

19. *Commonwealth v. Alger*, 94.

20. Shaw is often thought to be the model for Herman Melville's troubled but dutiful ship captain in *Billy Budd*. Shaw, Melville's father-in-law, went through much the same tortured, decision-making process as Vere in sending fugitive slaves back to their masters. Although there are many interpretations of Vere (including a positivist one), his personal in-

tegrity is never challenged. See Robert M. Cover, *Justice Accused: Antislavery and the Judicial Process* (New Haven, Conn., 1975), 2–7.

21. There is another possibility—reconcile *Alger* and similar cases to the paradigm through some intellectual or legal gymnastics. Edward S. Corwin and Ernst Freund do this when they interpret Shaw's references to the common law and the *sic utere tuo* maxim as limiting legislative power much the way later legal theorists would use the due process clause. Such an understanding denies the very outcome (as well as the reasoning) of this case. See Corwin, *The Twilight of the Supreme Court* (New Haven, Conn., 1934), 68; Freund, *Standards of American Legislation*, 2d ed. (1917; Chicago, 1965), 65–71; and Freund, *Police Power*, 425. Corwin's analysis is a perfect example of the way he consistently uses cases that *uphold* the validity of state power to show judicial concern for vested rights. Compare Corwin's discussions of *Coates v. Mayor of New York*, 7 Cow. 585 (N.Y., 1827), and *Vanderbilt v. Adams* with those of Hendrik Hartog. Corwin, "The Doctrine of Due Process of Law before the Civil War"; Hendrik Hartog, *Public Property and Private Power: The Corporation of the City of New York in American Law, 1730–1870* (Chapel Hill, N.C., 1983), 74–77, 202–3.

22. Thomas S. Kuhn, *The Essential Tension: Selected Studies in Scientific Tradition and Change* (Chicago, 1977), xii. Hermeneutics has a long and dense genealogy from Hans-Georg Gadamer back through early biblical exegesis. I have been most influenced by James Kloppenberg's reconstruction of a "pragmatic hermeneutics." See James T. Kloppenberg, *Uncertain Victory: Social Democracy and Progressivism in European and American Thought, 1870–1920* (New York, 1986); Kloppenberg, "Deconstruction and Hermeneutics As Strategies for Intellectual History," *Intellectual History Newsletter* 9 (1987): 4–20; Kloppenberg, "Democracy and Disenchantment: From Weber and Dewey to Habermas and Rorty," in *Modernist Impulses in the Human Sciences, 1870–1930*, ed. Dorothy Ross (Baltimore, 1994), 69–90.

23. From the classic instrumentalist viewpoint, legal and political ideas are "mirrors" or "masks" reflecting or hiding the felt needs of particular interest groups. Legal language is seen as separable from and less important than "who gets what" in particular cases. The "who gets what" (and, in this period, "who gets what" is intimately connected to the needs of capitalism) is deemed the real story of antebellum legal development. Lawrence M. Friedman has been one of the most consistent proponents of this view evidenced in his early critiques of intellectual approaches to legal history: "Formal jurisprudential literature made a slim contribution at best to American culture, and it had little impact even on the work and thought of the profession. . . . What it [the legal profession] did was more significant than what some of its more pretentious leaders said it was doing." Friedman, "Some Problems and Possibilities of American Legal History," *The State of American History*, ed. Herbert J. Bass (Chicago, 1970), 2–21, 13–14; Friedman, "Heart against Head: Perry Miller and the Legal Mind," *Yale Law Journal*, 77 (1968): 1244.

24. See James Tully, ed., *Meaning and Context: Quentin Skinner and His Critics* (Princeton, 1988); John Dunn, "The Identity of the History of Ideas," *Philosophy* 43 (1968): 85–104; J. G. A. Pocock, *Politics, Language and Time: Essays on Political Thought and History* (New York, 1973), 3–41; Pocock, *Virtue, Commerce, and History: Essays on Political Thought and History, Chiefly in the Eighteenth Century* (Cambridge, Mass., 1985), 1–34; Gordon S. Wood, "Intellectual History and the Social Sciences," in *New Directions in American Intellectual History*, ed. John Higham and Paul K. Conkin (Baltimore, 1979), 27–41. Legal historians in particular should heed the advice of this literature. Appellate court judges rely on ideas in their opinions, while at the same time they embed them in the institutional structure of the American polity. Ideas in law, of all places, are truly ideas *in action*. The conclusion to E. P. Thompson's *Whigs and Hunters* remains one of the best presentations on the

multifaceted relationship between legal ideas and social, political, and economic power. Thompson, *Whigs and Hunters*, 258–69.

25. James Wilson (1742–98), one of the most important and neglected jurists in American legal history, was a Federalist, a Founder (whom James Bryce called "one of the deepest thinkers and most exact reasoners among the members of the Convention of 1787"), a Supreme Court Justice, and one of the nation's first law professors at the College of Philadelphia (1790). See *The Works of James Wilson*, ed. Robert Green McCloskey, 2 vols. (Cambridge, Mass., 1967). James Kent of Columbia (1763–1847) and David Hoffman of Maryland (1784–1854) published highly influential and comprehensive commentaries and law lectures. See James Kent, *Commentaries on American Law*, 4 vols. (New York, 1826); David Hoffman, *A Course of Legal Study: Respectfully Addressed to the Students of Law in the United States* (Baltimore, 1817). William Sullivan (1774–1839) and Edward Mansfield (1801–80) were less well known but put together influential manuals on law and government called political "grammars" or "class books." See William Sullivan, *The Political Class Book* (Boston, 1831); Edward D. Mansfield, *The Political Grammar of the United States* (New York, 1834). Despite the congruence of some of their ideas, these authors lived diverse lives. Sullivan shared with Kent a keen interest in Federalist politics, Sullivan in Massachusetts, Kent in New York. Mansfield, an Ohio Whig, like Hoffman was more drawn to writing than to either politics or practice.

26. Zephaniah Swift (1759–1823) was chief justice of the Connecticut Supreme Court from 1806 to 1819. He published one of the first American law texts, *A System of the Laws of the State of Connecticut*, 2 vols. (Windham, Conn., 1795), and *Digest of the Laws of Connecticut* (New Haven, Conn., 1822). Swift shared a Federalist and antislavery temperament with Wilson and Nathaniel Chipman (1752–1843), author of *Sketches of the Principles of Government* (Burlington, Vt., 1793). See Swift, *An Oration on Domestic Slavery, Delivered at the North Meeting-House in Hartford* (1791). Thomas Cooper (1759–1839), along with John Taylor of Caroline (1753–1824), has often been portrayed as the southern, agrarian, statesrights, Jeffersonian/Democratic opposition to everything Hamiltonian or Federalist. Yet together with James Fenimore Cooper (1789–1851), a rather atypical and aristocratic Jacksonian Democrat, they shared much of the basic legal philosophy sketched by Wilson, Swift, and Chipman. See Thomas Cooper, *Two Essays: 1. On the Foundation of Civil Government; 2. On the Constitution of the United States* (Columbia, S.C., 1826); John Taylor, *Construction Construed and Constitutions Vindicated* (Richmond, 1820); James Fenimore Cooper, *The American Democrat: Or Hints on the Social and Civil Relations of the United States of America* (Cooperstown, N.Y., 1838).

27. If Wilson and Kent were the republic's most comprehensive legal minds, Francis Lieber (1800–1872) was its most far-reaching political thinker. Lieber edited the *Encyclopedia Americana* and wrote two definitive political texts, *Manual of Political Ethics Designed Chiefly for the Use of Colleges and Students of Law*, 2 vols. (Boston, 1838–39), and *On Civil Liberty and Self-Government* (1853; Philadelphia, 1891). Peter Du Ponceau (1760–1844), an apolitical French emigrant with a distinct expertise in civil and foreign law contributed *A Dissertation on the Nature and Extent of the Jurisdiction of the Courts of the United States* (Philadelphia, 1824). John Holmes (1773–1843), a Maine lawyer, politician, and author of *The Statesman, or Principles of Legislation and Law* (Augusta, Ga., 1840), nicely represents the fluid party affiliations of some of these thinkers. Over the course of his life he was a Federalist, a Democrat, and a Whig.

28. On the "key word" approach to American political thought, see Daniel T. Rodgers, *Contested Truths: Keywords in American Politics since Independence* (New York, 1987).

29. Marvin Meyers, *The Jacksonian Persuasion: Politics and Belief* (Stanford, Calif., 1957);

Sheldon S. Wolin, *Politics and Vision: Continuity and Innovation in Western Political Thought* (Boston, 1960). Meyers and Wolin use the terms "persuasion" and "vision" not only to convey the half-formed and unclear nature of some ideas, but also the moral and emotional force of belief.

30. Henry F. May, *The Enlightenment in America* (New York, 1976); Gordon S. Wood, *The Creation of the American Republic, 1776–1787* (Chapel Hill, N.C., 1969); J. G. A. Pocock, *The Machiavellian Moment: Florentine Political Thought and the Atlantic Republican Tradition* (Princeton, N.J., 1975); Peter N. Miller, *Defining the Common Good: Empire, Religion, and Philosophy in Eighteenth-Century Britain* (Cambridge, 1994).

31. Throughout this book, I rely on the language and usages of the time in fleshing out the vision of the well-regulated society. This seems particularly appropriate when approaching a topic distorted by the intrusion of twentieth-century categories and definitions (e.g., of police, rights, the state). Consequently, I have also chosen not to replace or degender these theorists' use of "man" in the elaboration of their ideas on government and society. It is not at all clear to me when their usage encompassed universal humanity and when they were talking more exclusively about men and not women.

32. James Kent, "An Introductory Lecture to a Course of Law Lectures" (1794), in *American Political Writing during the Founding Era, 1760–1805*, ed. Charles S. Hyneman and Donald S. Lutz, 2 vols. (Indianapolis, Ind., 1983). Kent did not include this lecture in his magnum opus *Commentaries on American Law.*

33. Kent, "Introductory," 945, 947.

34. Compare, for example, Nathaniel Chipman's statement that no philosophers "have attempted, or at least succeeded in an investigation of first principles; in analyzing the social nature of man, and deducing from the relations thence resulting, the principles that ought to be pursued in the formation of civil institutions." Chipman, *Principles of Government: A Treatise on Free Institutions* (Burlington, Vt., 1833), iii.

35. Sullivan, *Political Class Book.*

36. Dorothy Ross, *The Origins of American Social Science* (New York, 1991), 36–42; Rodgers, *Contested Truths*, 118–22; Donald H. Meyer, *The Instructed Conscience* (Philadelphia, 1972); Daniel Walker Howe, *The Unitarian Conscience: Harvard Moral Philosophy, 1805–1861* (Cambridge, Mass., 1970). The key text used in moral philosophy courses was William Paley's *The Principles of Moral and Political Philosophy*, 7th ed. (Philadelphia, 1788). Paley's work remained the primary discussion of things social and political until it was replaced by Francis Lieber's *Manual of Political Ethics* in 1839.

37. As Wolin wrote, "At the center of the enterprise of political theory was an imaginative element, an ordering vision of what the political system ought to be and what it might become." By Wolin's use of the word "vision," he attempts to get at the "projective" quality of political philosophy, for example, its effort to "project a more perfect order into future time." Wolin, *Politics and Vision*, 35.

38. Hoffman, *A Course of Legal Study*, viii, xi, xii. Hoffman best articulated this higher, moral nature of law when he characterized the duties of a lawyer as "the protection of the injured and the innocent, the defence of the weak and the poor, the conservation of the rights and prosperity of the citizen, and the vigorous maintenance of the legitimate and wholesome power of government." In his introduction Hoffman quoted Sophocles: "The noblest employment of Man, is to assist Man."

39. Chipman, *Principles*, 1–2.

40. In addition to Chipman's critique see, Henry Baldwin (1780–1844), *A General View of the Origin and Nature of the Constitution and Government of the United States* (Philadel-

phia, 1837), 25; Swift, *System*, 12–17; Wilson, *Works*, 1:228–35. Woodrow Wilson, *The State* (Boston, 1889).

41. For the standard "possessive individualist" reading of Hobbes and Locke, see C. B. Macpherson, *The Political Theory of Possessive Individualism* (Oxford, 1962). Of course, this standard has undergone some revision. See, for example, John Dunn, *Locke* (Oxford, 1984); and James Tully, *A Discourse on Property: John Locke and His Adversaries* (Cambridge, 1980).

42. Corwin, "'Higher Law' Background"; Charles Grove Haines, *The Revival of Natural Law Concepts* (Cambridge, Mass., 1930); Benjamin Fletcher Wright, *American Interpretations of Natural Law: A Study in the History of Political Thought* (Cambridge, Mass., 1931).

43. The definitive study on the persistence of Ciceronian ethics and a *salus populi* tradition in natural-law thinking is Miller, *Defining the Common Good*.

44. *Rutgers v. Waddington* (1784), in *Select Cases of the Mayor's Court of New York City, 1674–1784*, ed. Richard B. Morris (Washington, D.C., 1935), 312.

45. Ibid., 312, n. 1.

46. Emmerich de Vattel, *The Law of Nations*, ed. Edward D. Ingraham (Philadelphia, 1852), 54. Kent, *Commentaries*, 1:18. James Duane echoed Kent's praises, referring to "the great Vattel, whose work is entitled to the highest admiration!" *Rutgers v. Waddington*, 313. Vattel was first published in the United States in 1805. The edition used here is an American revision of Joseph Chitty's 1833 English edition. Vattel was repeatedly cited in the regulatory cases of the early nineteenth century. A computer search of federal appellate cases before 1870 turned up 158 cases, nearly half the number of citations to Blackstone. Vattel was also included on the standard law reading lists of the period. See *The Papers of Daniel Webster: Legal Papers*, Volume 1, *The New Hampshire Practice*, ed. Alfred S. Konefsky and Andrew J. King (Hanover, N.H., 1982), 3–8; John Theodore Horton, *James Kent: A Study in Conservatism, 1763–1847* (New York, 1939), 122.

47. Vattel suggested, "Man is so formed by nature, that he cannot supply all his own wants, but necessarily stands in need of the intercourse and assistance of his fellow-creatures, whether for his immediate preservation, or for the sake of perfecting his nature and enjoying such a life as is suitable to a rational being." Vattel, *Law of Nations*, lviii–lvix, 4–8, 54.

48. Chipman, *Principles*, 2, 16.

49. Swift, *System*, 14.

50. Chipman, *Principles*, 46.

51. Swift, *System*, 13.

52. See also Kent, *Commentaries on American Law*, 2:256; Charles B. Goodrich, *The Science of Government* (Boston, 1853), 219; Sullivan, *Political Class Book*, 11–12.

53. George B. Emerson, "Upon Studies for Practical Men," in Sullivan, *Political Class Book*, 18. For another repudiation of the "invisible hand," see Wilson, *Works*, 1:238. Like John Locke, the work of Adam Smith has also been discovered to be more complex than once thought. Particularly interesting is work linking the antimercantilist ideas of the *Wealth of Nations* (1776) to the moral philosophy of the *Theory of Moral Sentiments* (1759). See Richard Teichgraeber III, *"Free Trade" and Moral Philosophy: Rethinking the Sources of Adam Smith's Wealth of Nations* (Durham, N.C., 1986); and Donald Winch, *Adam Smith's Politics: An Essay in Historiographic Revision* (Cambridge, 1978).

54. Wilson, *Works*, 1:227. Wilson quoted Pope's *An Essay on Man*:

There's not a blessing individuals find,
But some way leans and hearkens to the kind.
No bandit fierce, no tyrant mad with pride,

No caverned hermit rests self-satisfied.
Who most to shun or hate mankind pretend
Seek an admirer, or would fix a friend.
Abstract what others feel, what others think,
All pleasures sicken, and all glories sink.

55. Ibid., 228.

56. Ibid., 229, 235–36.

57. Nathaniel Chipman, "Sketches of the Principles of Government," in *The Legal Mind in America: From Independence to the Civil War*, ed. Perry Miller (Ithaca, N.Y., 1962), 26.

58. John Bouvier, *Institutes of American Law* (Philadelphia, 1854), 1.

59. For a similar perspective in modern political theory, see Michael J. Sandel, *Liberalism and the Limits of Justice* (New York, 1982).

60. Chipman, *Principles*, 15.

61. The concept of civic virtue in the Atlantic republican tradition, that is, the notion of the constant sacrifice of individual interests to the greater needs of the whole, also rejected any kind of crude, selfish individualism. But most historians of republicanism seem to agree that some notion of an autonomous, independent, and empowered citizen remained at the center of this ideology. The idea of the social nature of man to some degree challenges the very notion of complete independence and autonomy through its organic vision of an interconnected and mutually dependent citizenry within a well-ordered society. Pocock, *The Machiavellian Moment*; James T. Kloppenberg, "Virtues of Liberalism: Christianity, Republicanism, and Ethics in Early American Political Discourse," *Journal of American History* 74 (1987): 9–33; Hendrik Hartog, "Imposing Constitutional Traditions," *William and Mary Law Review* 29 (1987): 75–82.

62. William Blackstone, *Commentaries on the Laws of England: A Facsimile of the First Edition of 1765–1769*, 4 vols. (Chicago, 1979), 1: chap. 1. As Forrest McDonald pointed out in discussing property rights, Blackstone often substantially qualified his bold generalizations on rights by the time he finished his more substantive, doctrinal discussions. Forrest McDonald, *Novus Ordo Seclorum: The Intellectual Origins of the Constitution* (Lawrence, Kans., 1985), 13. For an excellent example of this, compare Blackstone's discussion of absolute individual rights to his analysis of offenses against "public police and oeconomy" (4:162).

63. Blackstone, *Commentaries*, 1:119–22.

64. Chipman's ideas on natural right and liberty are found primarily in book 4, "Of Rights and Liberty," in *Principles*, 56–58. Wilson waited until lecture 12 of part 2 in his law lectures to discuss "Of the Natural Rights of Individuals." In that lecture, he launched not into a discussion of individual liberties but an explanation of the social relations of man: husband/wife, parent/child, and master/servant. Wilson, *Works*, 2:587.

65. Chipman, *Principles*, 55–59. For a remarkably similar conception by a Jacksonian Democrat, see James Fenimore Cooper, *The American Democrat*, 137.

66. Vattel, *Law of Nations*, lv; Goodrich, *Science*, 170. Hopkins quoted in Rodgers, *Contested Truths*, 120. On Francis Lieber's fetishization of the slogan "No Right without Its Duty; No Duty without Its Right," see Frank Freidel, *Francis Lieber: Nineteenth-Century Liberal* (Baton Rouge, La., 1947), 154, n. 24.

67. Francis Lieber, "Inaugural Address of Francis Lieber," in *Addresses of the Newly-Appointed Professors of Columbia College, February 1858* (New York, 1858), 97.

68. Wilson, *Works*, 1:160; Jesse Root, "Introduction," in 1 Root i (Connecticut, 1793), xvi; Emerson, "Studies," 19. Again, this notion of positive social duties resonates with Vattel:

"Each individual should do for others every thing which their necessities require, and which he can perform without neglecting the duty that he owes to himself: a law which all men must observe in order to live in a manner consonant to their nature, and conformable to the views of their common Creator,—a law which our own safety, our own happiness, our dearest interest, ought to render sacred to every one of us." Vattel, *Law of Nations*, lvix.

69. Chipman, *Principles*, 62.

70. Wilson, *Works*, 2:587 (emphasis added).

71. See the discussion of the common law maxims *sic utere tuo* and *salus populi*.

72. Lieber, *Civil Liberty*, 26, 37.

73. For some leading contemporary examples, see Ronald Dworkin, *Taking Rights Seriously* (Cambridge, Mass., 1978); Bruce Ackerman, *Private Property and the Constitution* (New Haven, Conn., 1977); Robert Nozick, *Anarchy, State, and Utopia* (New York, 1974); and Richard Epstein, *Simple Rules for a Complex World* (Cambridge, 1995). The Critical Legal Studies "critique of rights" and Critical Race Theory's "critique of the critique of rights" both reify the mainstream position that there has been only one hegemonic constitutional/rights discourse in American history. For the best examples of this work, see Mark Tushnet, "An Essay on Rights," *Texas Law Review* 62 (1984): 1363–1403; and Patricia J. Williams, "Alchemical Notes: Reconstructed Ideals from Deconstructed Rights," *Harvard Civil Rights/Civil Liberties Law Review* 22 (1987): 401–33. These divergent arguments all ignore the possibility that there might have been radically different ways of talking about rights and constitutionalism in American history. For some hints on the historical reconstruction of alternative constitutional rights traditions, see Hartog, "The Constitution of Aspiration."

74. Lieber, *Civil Liberty*, 144.

75. Chipman, *Principles*, 66 (emphasis added).

76. Wilson, *Works*, 2:587. As suggested in the introduction, Wilson's use of "municipal" here, refers to the entire statute and common law applicable to citizens of a state.

77. Lieber, *Civil Liberty*, 273.

78. The three best statements of this theme are Perry Miller, *The Life of the Mind in America: From the Revolution to the Civil War* (New York, 1965); Robert A. Ferguson, *Law and Letters in American Culture* (Cambridge, Mass., 1984); and Tomlins, *Law, Labor, and Ideology*.

79. "Review of James Kent's *Commentaries on American Law*," *North American Review* 24 (1827): 345–65.

80. Ibid., 346.

81. W. Hickey, *The Constitution of the United States of America* (Philadelphia, 1854), xxvi.

82. Wilson, *Works*, 1:212, 222–23. The influence of Scottish commonsense philosophy on theorists like James Wilson is quite apparent. Wilson was born in Scotland and was educated at Glasgow and Edinburgh. Wilson provided an example of the virtues of common sense and a historical sensibility over abstract theorizing in a bumptious American critique of Locke's theory of religious toleration. "Let it be known," Wilson declared championing George Calvert, "that before the doctrine of toleration was published in Europe, the *practice* of it was established in America." Ibid., 1:71. Similar critiques of reason and theory in favor of experience and history pervaded the legal thought of the period. Theoretical discussions of government bothered John Taylor: "To contend for forms only, is to fight for shadows." Thomas Cooper added, "Government is not merely a thing of theory and of abstract right. It is founded on public experience, guided by past experience." Even the constitution was spared abstract rhapsodizing or theorizing. Mordecai M'Kinney wrote in 1845, "Constitutions are instruments of a practical nature, founded on the common business of hu-

man life, adopted to common wants, designed for common use, and fitted for common understandings." Taylor, *Construction Construed and Constitutions Vindicated*, 13; Cooper, *Two Essays*, 15; Mordecai M'Kinney, *The United States Constitutional Manual* (Harrisburg, Pa., 1845), iv, 193. On the Scottish Enlightenment and its influence in the United States, see Istvan Hunt and Michael Ignatieff, eds., *Wealth and Virtue: The Shaping of Political Economy in the Scottish Enlightenment* (Cambridge, 1983); N. T. Phillipson, "The Scottish Enlightenment," in *The Enlightenment in National Context*, ed. R. Porter and M. Teich (Cambridge, 1981); Morton White, *The Philosophy of the American Revolution* (New York, 1978); Garry Wills, *Inventing America: Jefferson's Declaration of Independence* (Garden City, N.Y., 1978); Douglass Adair, *Fame and the Founding Fathers* (Williamsburg, Va., 1974), esp. 93–123; and Kloppenberg, "The Virtues of Liberalism," 17–18.

83. Hoffman, *A Course of Legal Study*, 98.

84. For the best contemporary analogue, see the work of Michael Walzer. Walzer, *Spheres of Justice* (New York, 1983); Walzer, *Exodus and Revolution* (New York, 1985); Walzer, *Interpretation and Social Criticism* (Cambridge, Mass., 1987).

85. Blackstone, *Commentaries*, 1:44.

86. Wilson, *Works*, 1:79, 103, 106, 168, 175.

87. Chipman, *Principles*, 93–96, 182, 188. Chipman offered a similar critique of the legal positivism lurking in Thomas Cooper's translation of the *Institutes of Justinian* (arguments he saw as too conducive to slaveholding). Also see Francis Hilliard, *The Elements of Law: Being a Comprehensive Summary of American Civil Jurisprudence* (Boston, 1835), iii.

88. Wilson, *Works*, 1:180–82; Chipman, *Principles*, 182.

89. Indeed, constitutional historians for over a century have assessed early American legal and political ideology primarily in terms of the evolution of constitutional ideas: from Coke to Otis to the *Federalist Papers* to the Bill of Rights to *Marbury v. Madison*, 1 Cranch 137 (U.S., 1803), and beyond. See the works examined and criticized in Paul L. Murphy, "Time to Reclaim: The Current Challenge of American Constitutional History," *American Historical Review* 69 (1963): 64–79; and Harry N. Scheiber, "American Constitutional History and the New Legal History," *Journal of American History* 68 (1981): 337–50. The "republican synthesis" is the most recent historiography to overemphasize explicitly constitutional language and problems.

90. M'Kinney, *Constitutional Manual*, iv, 193.

91. Hilliard, *Elements*, 5; Baldwin, *Constitution*, 24. Baldwin's treatise was essentially an alternative method of publishing his opinions in *Briscoe v. Bank of Kentucky*, 11 Pet. 257 (U.S., 1837), *Charles River Bridge*, 11 Pet. 420 (U.S., 1837), and *Mayor of New York v. Miln*, 11 Pet. 102 (U.S., 1837). Baldwin's jurisprudence has been treated rather shabbily by historians. Harold Hyman and William Wiecek concluded, "Baldwin adopted an extremely proslavery position but was otherwise not known for any significant opinion." G. Edward White questioned Baldwin's sanity. Harold M. Hyman and William M. Wiecek, *Equal Justice under Law: Constitutional Development, 1835–1875* (New York, 1982), 62; G. Edward White, *The Marshall Court and Cultural Change, 1815–1835*, abr. ed. (New York, 1991), 298–99.

92. Du Ponceau, *Dissertation*, ix, xv, 93.

93. Peter Du Ponceau argued, "The grievances which induced [the colonies] to separate from the mother country were considered as violations of the *common law*." Du Ponceau, *Dissertation*, ix. Justice Henry Baldwin's treatise made this same point by reproducing the seal of the First Continental Congress. It showed Magna Charta as "the pedestal on which the column and cap of liberty was raised, supported by the twelve colonies . . . declaring that 'on this we rely,' 'this we will defend.'" Baldwin, *A General View*, 6. For a more complete analysis of common law basis of the Revolution, see James Wilson, "Speech Delivered in

the Convention for the Province of Pennsylvania" (1775), in *Works*, 2:747–58. Also John Phillip Reid, *Constitutional History of the American Revolution: The Authority of Rights* (Madison, Wis., 1986).

94. Chipman, *Principles*, 254.

95. On statutory construction, Francis Hilliard wrote, "With regard to the *statutes of the State legislatures*, it may be remarked, that the object and effect of them is not in general to alter or abrogate the principles of the common law." Hilliard, *Elements*, 5. This powerful statement of the common law's continuing hold on American law and legislation was repeated in various forms throughout the antebellum period. In the words of James Kent, "Statutes are likewise to be construed in reference to the principles of the common law, for it is not to be presumed the legislature intended to make any innovation upon the common law, further than the case absolutely required." Kent, *Commentaries*, 1:433. Or again, James Sullivan: "If we examine the laws now existing, as acts of Legislature in the State, we shall find the use of them principally designed for the directing, and rendering efficacious, the system of the Common Law, adopted and established by the common consent of the people." James Sullivan, *The History of Land Titles in Massachusetts* (Boston, 1801; Arno reprint, New York, 1972), 17. See also, Swift, *System*, 47.

96. Wilson, *Works*, 1:334; Du Ponceau, *Dissertation*, 91. Daniel Klerman brought to my attention the similarities between Du Ponceau's paean to the common law and Deuteronomy 6:4–9 (RSV).

97. Roscoe Pound, *The Spirit of the Common Law* (Boston, 1921), especially 35–37; Daniel J. Boorstin, *The Americans: The National Experience* (New York, 1965), 35–42.

98. Sullivan, *History of Land Titles*, 16.

99. Wilson, *Works*, 1:121–22, 180–84. Also see Chipman, *Principles*, 182.

100. Goodrich, *Science*, 240, 187; Swift, *System*, 42.

101. See the degree to which these thinkers opposed constituent control over representatives. Swift wrote, "If the people at large are vested with the rights of reconsidering and deciding upon the acts of the legislature, all the advantages of representation are lost. The general will of the community could never be collected, different districts would form contradictory decrees, instead of law and order, there would be perpetual controversies and confusion." Swift, *System*, 36.

102. For the best modern presentation of a historical sensibility, see the work of James T. Kloppenberg on Wilhelm Dilthey and the philosophers of the *via media*. Kloppenberg, *Uncertain Victory*.

103. Chipman, *Principles*, 15. James Wilson concurred, "In free countries, especially [those] that boast the blessing of a common law, springing warm and spontaneous from the manners of the people—Law should be studied and taught as a historical science." Wilson, *Works*, 1:70.

104. Hugh Henry Brackenridge, *Law Miscellanies* (Philadelphia, 1814), 34; Wilson, *Works*, 1:183.

105. Wilson, *Works*, 1:183, 348.

106. Ibid., 353.

107. One of the best discussions of historicism, ancient constitutionalism, and the differences between Coke and Hale is J. G. A Pocock, *The Ancient Constitution and the Feudal Law* (Cambridge, Mass., 1957), especially chs. 2 and 7.

108. Du Ponceau, *Dissertation*, viii. After all, as theorist after theorist pointed out, the common law in the United States was English common law as "received and modified in reference to the genius of [American] institutions." Kent, *Commentaries*, 1:455; Du Ponceau, *Dissertation*, 96; Chipman, *Principles*, 254.

109. Wilson, *Works*, 1:183.

110. Du Ponceau, *Dissertation*, xviii.

111. Wilson, *Works*, 1:353–54.

112. James R. Stoner Jr., *Common Law and Liberal Theory: Coke, Hobbes, and the Origins of American Constitutionalism* (Lawrence, Kans., 1992), 177.

113. Pocock, *Ancient Constitution*, 178.

114. Swift, *System*, 40.

115. Pound, *Spirit of the Common Law*, 13. Pound admits that this is a "narrow" characterization, and his overall argument is more complex. But the rest of this passage testifies to the common law's underlying individualism: "A foreign observer has said that its distinguishing marks are 'unlimited valuation of individual liberty and respect for individual property.' It is concerned not with social righteousness but with individual rights. It tries questions of the highest social import as mere private controversies between John Doe and Richard Roe."

116. The *Oxford English Dictionary* is an excellent source for the many uses and versions of "common" available in the late eighteenth and early nineteenth centuries. Also see Carol Rose, "The Comedy of the Commons: Custom, Commerce, and Inherently Public Property," *University of Chicago Law Review* 53 (1986): 711–81; and Arthur F. McEvoy, *The Fisherman's Problem: Ecology and Law in the California Fisheries, 1850–1980* (New York, 1986), 10–15.

117. Baldwin, *Constitution*, 8.

118. Sullivan, *History of Land Titles*, 344–45. These thinkers approached constitutionalism generally with the same distinctive public vision that informed their discussions of common law. Like Sullivan, James Wilson analyzed the constitution by starting with the broad goals and outlines of the preamble. He reasoned from larger goals to specific powers and rules. He argued, for example, that one "great end of national government is 'to ensure domestick tranquillity.' That it may be enabled to accomplish this end, congress may call forth the militia to suppress insurrections." Or again, "It is an object of the national government to 'form a more perfect union.' On this principle, congress is empowered to regulate commerce among the several states, to establish post offices." This approach to the constitution contrasts with modern attempts to construct a general politics or philosophy from particular, enumerated powers or the Bill of Rights. Wilson, *Works*, 1:434–35.

119. Hilliard, *Elements*, vi.

120. Chipman, *Principles*, 52, 163–64; Wilson, *Works*, 1:172.

121. Vattel, *Law of Nations*, 8.

122. Cooper, *American Democrat*, 9.

123. Lieber, *Civil Liberty*, 298.

124. Wilson, *Works*, 2:595; Cooper, *American Democrat*, 50–51.

125. Swift, *System*, 4; Wilson, *Works*, 1:239.

126. Sullivan, *Political Class Book*, 15; Hoffman, *Course of Legal Study*, xii.

127. Goodrich, *Science*, 187. See also Chipman, *Principles*, 205.

128. Chipman, *Principles*, 164; Sullivan, *Political Class Book*, 12–13.

129. Goodrich, *Science*, 1; also see Wilson, *Works*, 1:242; Sullivan, *Political Class Book*, 26.

130. Goodrich, *Science*, 170; Cooper, *American Democrat*, 57. James Fenimore Cooper agreed wholeheartedly with Goodrich's definition of liberty as liberty regulated by law. He wrote, "The doctrine that any one 'may do what he please with his own,' however, is false. One may do with his own, whatever the laws and institutions of his country allow and no more." Cooper, 137. Thomas Cooper concurred, "The great object of all laws is the general

welfare—public utility. There can be no rights inconsistent with this." Cooper, *Two Essays*, 15.

131. Goodrich, *Science*, 2. The degree to which these thinkers completely flipped the categories usually used to describe early nineteenth-century American thought is a good indication of the limits of our historiography. Compare Goodrich's conception of government limiting rights (rather than rights limiting government) with the numerous inversions of Adam Smith's invisible hand, wherein these jurists derive the good of individuals from the good of the whole and not vice versa.

132. Ernst Freund, *Standards of American Legislation*, 66.

133. Horace G. Wood, *A Practical Treatise on the Law of Nuisances*, 2d ed. (Albany, N.Y., 1883), 21.

134. Chipman, *Principles*, 164–65; Wilson, *Works*, 1:84.

135. Chipman, *Principles*, 164–65.

136. Vattel, *Law of Nations*, 4.

137. Wilson, *Works*, 1:159. It is important to note that this perfectionism was not static; that is, it did not posit some final version of a social utopia. Rather, this common-law vision emphasized an ongoing *process* of social and political change, whereby society constantly worked to improve itself. Wilson wrote, "It is the glorious destiny of man to be always progressive." Ibid., 146.

138. Chipman, *Principles*, 93. James Wilson held nations to the same standard: "It may, perhaps, be uncommon, but it is certainly just, to say that nations ought to love one another. The offices of humanity ought to flow from this pure source." Zephaniah Swift tersely added: "live honestly, hurt nobody," and "render every one his due." Wilson, *Works*, 1:161; Swift, *System*, 37. The frequent references to "love" in these legal treatises is astonishing and is one indication of the depth of these theorists's antipositivism. For those who would put an individualistic or selfish spin on the golden rule, George Emerson cautioned that the "New Testament" command "teaches us to love our neighbor for his sake, and not for our own, and this excludes selfishness, and other unworthy motives." Emerson, "Studies," 19. Wilson's whole philosophy was built on a passionate and exacting repudiation of such selfish glosses on man's nature. He attacked those philosophers alleging that "by nature, men are wolves to men": "By a strange perversion of things, they would so explain all the social passions and natural affections, as to denominate them of the selfish species. Humanity and hospitality towards strangers or those in distress are represented as selfishness, only of a more deliberate kind. An honest heart is only a cunning one; and good nature is a well regulated self-love." Wilson judged such conclusions "narrow and hideous"—"repugnant to all human sentiment, and all human experience." Wilson, *Works*, 1:228–29.

139. Sullivan, *Political Class Book*, 18–20; Cooper, *Two Essays*, 9, 15, 17.

140. Brackenridge, *Law Miscellanies*, 77, 220. This led Brackenridge to caution legislators about adhering too strictly to the "temporary impulses" and the individual interests of their constituents. He held that a representative "must be activated by what he considers as the salus populi or good of the whole. Where such a sacrifice of popularity is made, the prima facie evidence always is that of *virtue*, if not *wisdom*." *Law Miscellanies*, 99. Zephaniah Swift agreed, "[W]hen elected, a person becomes the representative of the *community* at large; he cannot therefore regard the instructions of his immediate constituents, but must consult the *general good of the community* and not the particular advantage of a district." For Swift, this was the essence of a "government of laws and not of men." Swift, *System*, 35–36.

141. Goodrich, *Science*, 201.

142. Wilson, *Works*, 1:238.

143. Swift, *System*, 72.

144. Goodrich, *Science*, 2, 189.

145. Wilson, *Works*, 1:238, 268.

146. Goodrich, *Science*, 169–70.

147. Swift, *System*, 17. See also Chipman, *Principles*, 70; and Wilson, *Works*, 1:84.

148. Taylor, *Construction Construed*, 28.

149. Holmes, *The Statesman*, 239. See also Sullivan, *History of Land Titles*, 337.

150. Goodrich, *Science*, 168 (emphasis added).

151. Cooper, *Two Essays*, 15–16.

152. Sullivan, *Political Class Book*, 152.

153. *Sturges v. Crowninshield*, 4 Wheaton 122 (U.S., 1819); *Ogden v. Saunders*, 12 Wheaton 213 (U.S., 1827).

154. *Commonwealth v. Alger*, 84–85.

155. Wilson, *Works*, 1:268.

156. Goodrich, *Science*, 206.

157. Chipman, *Principles*, 274; Goodrich, *Science*, 188.

158. Morton Keller is my source for this wonderful insight into the brevity and connectedness of American history. But Holmes himself provided a similar perspective in a cherished reminiscence from Sidney Bartlett, who wrote him: "Deacon Spooner died in 1818 aged ninety-four. I saw him and talked with him. *He* talked with Elder Faunce, who talked with the Pilgrims and is said to have pointed out *the* rock." Oliver Wendell Holmes Jr., *Speeches* (Boston, 1918), 41.

159. Kent, *Commentaries*, 2:265, 274–76; Kent, *Commentaries*, 12th ed., ed. Oliver Wendell Holmes Jr., 4 vols. (Boston, 1873), 2:441, n. 2.

Chapter Two

1. Pierre Bourdieu, "The Force of Law: Toward a Sociology of the Juridical Field," *Hastings Law Journal* 38 (1987): 805–13.

2. Marvin Meyers, *The Jacksonian Persuasion: Politics and Belief* (Stanford, Calif., 1957), v.

3. I owe this observation to conversations with Rachel Fulton. See Fulton, "The Virgin Mary and the Song of Songs in the High Middle Ages" (Ph.D. diss., Columbia University, 1994).

4. Marc Raeff, *The Well-Ordered Police State: Social and Institutional Change through Law in the Germanies and Russia, 1600–1800* (New Haven, Conn., 1983).

5. Adam Smith, *Lectures on Jurisprudence* (1762–63; Liberty Classics edition, Indianapolis, Ind., 1982), 331–33. Also see Johann Justi's prioritization of security and safety in Albion W. Small, *The Cameralists: The Pioneers of German Social Policy* (Chicago, 1909), 332–93.

6. This is a crucial distinction in Christopher Tomlins's informative treatment of police. See Tomlins, *Law, Labor, and Ideology in the Early American Republic* (New York, 1993), 19–97.

7. *The Constitution of the United States*, art. 1, sec. 9: "The privilege of the writ of *habeas corpus* shall not be suspended, unless when in cases of rebellion or invasion the public safety may require it." On the linkages between tranquillity and safety, see John Taylor, *Construction Construed and Constitutions Vindicated* (Richmond, Va., 1820), 13; and Emmerich de Vattel, *The Law of Nations*, ed. Edward D. Ingraham (Philadelphia, 1852), 10.

8. Henry Baldwin, *A General View of the Origin and Nature of the Constitution of the United States* (Philadelphia, 1837), 25; William Sullivan, *The Political Class Book: Intended to*

Instruct the Higher Classes in Schools in the Origin, Nature, and Use of Political Power (Boston, 1831), 19.

9. Iredell elaborated, "If in any government, principles of patriotism and public good ought to predominate over mere private inclination, surely they ought to do so in a Republic." *Talbot v. Janson*, 3 Dallas 133 (U.S., 1795), 136.

10. *Mayor of New York v. Miln*, 11 Pet. 102 (U.S., 1837), 128. Ogden argued more important cases before the early American Supreme Court than any lawyer except Daniel Webster and William Wirt. See Charles Warren, *A History of the American Bar* (1911; Howard Fertig edition, New York, 1966), 303.

11. For some hints, see the role of "public safety" in the discussions of slavery and native Americans in the antebellum Supreme Court decisions *Cherokee Nation v. Georgia*, 5 Pet. 1 (U.S., 1831), 55; and *Prigg v. Pennsylvania*, 16 Pet. 539 (U.S., 1842), 563.

12. While with vast strides and bristling hair aloof,
Pale Danger glides along the falling roof,
And Giant Terror, howling in amaze,
Moves his dark limbs across the lurid blaze.

Quoted in Henry L. Champlin, *The American Firemen* (Chelsea, Mass., 1880), 240.

13. *Brown v. Maryland*, 12 Wheat. 419 (U.S., 1827); Charles Warren, *The Supreme Court in United States History*, 2 vols. (Boston, 1926), 1:693.

14. Philip B. Kurland and Gerhard Casper, eds., *Landmark Briefs and Arguments of the Supreme Court of the United States: Constitutional* (Washington, D.C., 1978), 2:427–28.

15. *Brown v. Maryland*, 443–44.

16. Carl Bridenbaugh, *Cities in the Wilderness: The First Century of Urban Life in America, 1625–1742* (New York, 1938), 55–58; Carl Bridenbaugh, *Cities in Revolt: Urban Life in America, 1743–1776* (New York, 1955), 98–100; Richard C. Wade, *The Urban Frontier: Pioneer Life in Early Pittsburgh, Cincinnati, Lexington, Louisville, and St. Louis* (Chicago, 1959), 91–94, 291–94; Jane H. Pease and William H. Pease, "The Blood-Thirsty Tiger: Charleston and the Psychology of Fire," *South Carolina Historical Magazine* 79 (1978): 281–95; Carey Hearn, "Fire Control in Antebellum Mississippi," *Journal of Mississippi History* 40 (1978): 319–27. On the persistence of such problems into the early twentieth century, see Christine Meisner Rosen, *The Limits of Power: Great Fires and the Process of City Growth in America* (Cambridge, 1986).

17. David D. Dana, *The Fireman: The Fire Departments of the United States* (Boston, 1858), 358–65.

18. Quoted in Wade, *Urban Frontier*, 91.

19. Pease and Pease, "Blood-Thirsty Tiger," 281.

20. Alexander J. Wall Jr., "The Great Fire of 1835," *New York Historical Society Quarterly Bulletin* 20 (1936): 3.

21. See, for example, James R. Wilson, "Tokens of the Divine Displeasure in the Late Conflagrations in New York and Other Judgments," cited in Wall, "Great Fire," 19.

22. Quoted in Hearn, "Fire Control," 322. Also see Pease and Pease, "Blood-Thirsty Tiger," 294–95; Stephen F. Ginsberg, "The Police and Fire Protection in New York City: 1800–1850," *New York History* 52 (1971): 138–40; Joseph Bird, *Protection against Fire* (New York, 1873), 137–46; William Worthington Fowler, *Fighting Fire: The Great Fires of History* (Hartford, Conn., 1873), 532–42.

23. *Pennsylvania Senate Journal* (Philadelphia, 1797): 46; *Pennsylvania House Journal* (Philadelphia, 1797): 51–52.

24. *Statutes at Large of South Carolina, 1682–1841*, ed. Thomas Cooper, 10 vols. (Charleston, S.C., 1836), 7 (1685), 2; 7(1698), 7–12; 7 (1701), 17–22.

25. Ginsberg, "Police and Fire Protection"; Stephen F. Ginsberg, "Above the Law: Volunteer Firemen in New York City, 1836–1837," *New York History* 50 (1969): 165.

26. Ginsberg, "Police and Fire Protection," 141, 145.

27. *Laws of New Netherland, 1638–1674*, ed. E. B. O'Callaghan (Albany, N.Y., 1868), (1648), 82; (1648), 102; (1657), 322; (1658), 363; (1673), 500; Bridenbaugh, *Cities in the Wilderness*, 56–61. As would be typical of fire legislation for the next 200 years, the first New Amsterdam chimney ordinance of 1648 was passed immediately after "two Houses were burned" because of neglected chimneys.

28. *Colonial Laws of New York, 1664–1775*, 5 vols. (Albany, N.Y., 1894), 2 (1737), 1064; 4 (1761), 571–73; 5 (1772), 363; 5 (1775), 743–46; Joseph D. McGoldrick et al., *Building Regulations in New York City: A Study in Administrative Law and Procedure* (New York, 1944), 27–35. The New York public nuisance provision did not go nearly as far as a similar provision in a 1713 South Carolina statute. Wooden buildings deemed common nuisances in Charleston were to be *demolished* by judgment of "three commissioners." Cooper, *Statutes at Large of South Carolina, 1682–1841*, 7 (1713), 58–59. See also *Acts and Resolves of the Province of Massachusetts Bay, 1692–1780*, 21 vols. (Boston, 1869), 1 (1692), 42, c. 13, 42; and "An Act for Preventing Common Nuisances," *The General Laws of Massachusetts, 1780–1822*, ed. Theron Metcalf (Boston 1823), 1 (1785), 193–94. New York only provided for indictment, fine, imprisonment and double taxation. *Colonial Laws of New York*, 5 (1775), 745–46.

29. *Laws of the State of New York*, 2 vols. (Albany, N.Y., 1813), 2 (1813), c. 86 (R.L.), 363–70.

30. "The commander or owner . . . of every ship or other vessel, arriving from sea, and having gun-powder on board shall, within twenty-four hours after her arrival in the harbor, and before such ship or other vessel be hauled alongside of any wharf, pier or key, within the said city, land the said gun-powder, by means of a boat or boats or other small craft, at any place on the East river, east of Walnut street, or any place on the North river, to the northward of the outlet of Lispenard's meadow, which may be most contiguous to any of the magazines, and shall cause the same to be stored in one of the magazines . . . on pain of forfeiting all such gun-powder, to any person or persons who will sue and prosecute for the same to effect." Ibid., 365.

31. "[A]ll gun-powder which shall be carried through the streets of the city by carts, carriages or by hand or otherwise, shall be in tight casks well headed and hooped, and shall be put into bags or leather cases and entirely covered therewith, so that no powder may be spilled or scattered in the passage thereof. . . . And it shall and may be lawful for any person or persons to seize the same to his or their own use and benefit, and to convey the same to one of the magazines aforesaid, and thereupon to prosecute the person or persons offending against this act." Ibid.

32. Ibid., 369. This omnibus provision made explicit what was only assumed earlier—that the municipal corporation had power to regulate for the prevention of fires under a legislative grant to "make by-laws for the Public good." See Hendrik Hartog, *Public Property and Private Power: The Corporation of the City of New York in American Law, 1730–1870* (Chapel Hill, N.C., 1983), especially 127–28.

33. O'Callaghan, *Laws of New Netherland, 1638–1674* (1673), 501; *Laws of Connecticut* (1673), 25; *Laws of Ohio* (1805), 501; *Laws of Michigan*, 1 (1817), 500; *Laws of Indiana* (1818), 361.

34. Bridenbaugh, *Cities in the Wilderness*, 58; *Acts and Resolves of Massachusetts Bay, 1692–1780*, 1 (1692), c. 13, 42–43; 1 (1711), 677–78; *Massachusetts Laws, 1780–1822*, 1 (1796), 532–34. This three-pronged regulatory attack, featuring restrictions on building and hazardous materials along with extensive fireward powers, remained Massachusetts's ap-

proach to the fire problem into the nineteenth century. *The Revised Statutes of the Commonwealth of Massachusetts* (Boston, 1836), 192–93, 269, 401–2.

35. John V. Morris, *Fire and Firefighters* (Boston, 1953), 18.

36. *The Statutes at Large of Pennsylvania from 1682–1809*, 18 vols. (Harrisburg, 1911) 12 (1787), 416; 15 (1795) 346, 354–55; 18 (1809), 983; *House Journal* (1792): 165; *Senate Journal* (1795): 188–89; Bridenbaugh, *Cities in the Wilderness*, 208–9.

37. Cooper, *Statutes at Large of South Carolina, 1682–1841*, 7:1–79. In 1783 Charleston was incorporated and endowed by the legislature with its own powers "to make and establish by-laws, rules and ordinances, respecting the harbour, streets, lanes, public buildings, work houses, markets, wharves, public houses, carriages, wagons, carts, drays, pumps, buckets, fire engines, the care of the poor, the regulation of seamen or disorderly people, negroes, and in general, every other bye-law or regulation that shall appear to them requisite and necessary for the security, welfare and convenience of the said city, or for preserving peace, order and good government within." Ibid., 7:97, 98.

38. *Public Laws of the State of Rhode Island* (Providence, 1822), 449–77.

39. *A Digest of the Laws of New Jersey, 1709–1861*, ed. John T. Nixon, 3d ed. (Trenton, 1861), (1811), 300. Fines also tended to increase rapidly when concern about fire grew. When a three-guilder fine for wooden or plaster chimneys failed to deter the practice in New Amsterdam, the fine was quickly raised to fifty guilders. O'Callaghan, *Laws of New Netherland, 1638–1674* (1648), 82–83; (1657) 322. The record, however, is diverse. Massachusetts, as late as 1836, tended to impose fines of no more than $20 for violating its gunpowder and fire regulations. *Revised Statutes of the Commonwealth of Massachusetts* (1836), 269, 401–2, 192–93. New York tended to favor fines in the $150–$500 range in 1813. *Laws of New York* (1813), c. 86 (R.L.), 361–70.

40. *Public Laws of Rhode Island* (1822), 471.

41. *Laws of New York* (1813), c. 86 (R.L.), 365. The best discussion of private prosecution in nineteenth-century America is Allen Steinberg, *The Transformation of Criminal Justice: Philadelphia, 1800–1880* (Chapel Hill, N.C., 1989).

42. *Laws of New York* (1813), c. 86 (R.L.), 364; Cooper, *Statutes at Large of South Carolina, 1682–1841*, 7 (1713), 58; *Acts and Resolves of Massachusetts Bay*, 1 (1693), c. 13, 42.

43. Cooper, *Statutes at Large of South Carolina, 1682–1841*, 7:10, 19, 20, 27, 41, 58, 69, 126, 150.

44. The only semblance of a concern for particular property rights in these statutes is a sometime requirement for compensation and reimbursement from the town or city (1) when one's (nonnuisance) house was destroyed by public officials to prevent the spread of fire (except when the house was already on fire), and (2) when one's personal buckets were lost or destroyed when fighting fire. The whole issue of necessity and taking, *salus populi* and compensation, will be discussed more fully in conjunction with the Great Fire of 1835.

45. Hartog, *Public Property and Private Power*, 127.

46. Willard Hurst is one of the most dedicated investigators of this phenomenon. His work on the Wisconsin lumber industry illustrates the ultimate ineffectiveness of attempts to regulate the harvesting of the Wisconsin forest. The failure of public authorities to control forest fires is one of his innumerable themes. James Willard Hurst, *Law and Economic Growth: The Legal History of the Lumber Industry in Wisconsin, 1836–1915* (Cambridge, Mass., 1964), 456–59. Also see Charles E. Rosenberg, *The Cholera Years: The United States in 1832, 1849, and 1866* (Chicago, 1962), on the ineffectiveness of health regulations; Arthur F. McEvoy, *The Fisherman's Problem: Ecology and Law in the California Fisheries, 1850–1980* (Cambridge, 1986), on the ineffectiveness of California fishery regulations; Hendrik Har-

tog, "Pigs and Positivism," *Wisconsin Law Review* (1985): 899–935, on the ineffectiveness of New York City's pig regulations; and Timothy J. Gilfoyle, *City of Eros: New York City, Prostitution, and the Commercialization of Sex, 1790–1920* (New York, 1992), on the official tolerance of prostitution despite antiprostitution rhetoric and legislation. This book challenges this overwhelming emphasis on legal, regulatory failure and concomitant descriptions of lax enforcement with four separate arguments. First, legal ideas and social action are intimately linked in ways obscured by an overly harsh, instrumental separation of law and society, ideas and action. For example, modern sodomy laws are by all accounts not actively enforced. Yet I would contend that one interested in law, sexuality, and the policing of morality in late twentieth-century American life ignores the statistically anomalous but ideologically powerful case of *Bowers v. Hardwick*, 478 U.S. 186 (1986), at his or her peril. Second, 100 percent effectiveness is rarely anticipated in human laws. One must resist the temptation to translate the *presence* of illegality (or the incidence of fire or the extinction of alewives) into the *absence* of law, regulation, or enforcement. Again, a telling contemporary example: Would anyone argue that the high incidence of illegal drug use in late twentieth-century America signals tolerance, lax enforcement, or a lethargic state, police, or prison system? Third, the local, informal, and discretionary nature of the early American legal and criminal justice system, with its vast array of summary proceedings, private prosecutions, and unrecorded neighborhood coercions, makes the enforcement issue a very difficult social history question. Examinations of formal police or public prosecution records are inadequate for making a case for or against enforcement. Finally, this book presents its cases—each case represents a statute, ordinance, or regulatory common law action that was distinctly *enforced*. The cases are selective in area and predominantly appellate in level. They are part of case studies that necessarily only hint at the full dimensions of safety, property, economy, morals, and health regulation in nineteenth-century America. In other words, they are but the tip of the iceberg in an extensive (and sometimes hidden) legal history of enforcement.

47. *New York Assembly Journal* (Albany, N.Y., 1800): 216. After the fire of 1835, New York passed radical measures for public relief with calls for "promptitude and liberality." The governor, mayor, and legislature consciously strove to avoid extended debate or close discussion of proposed provisions. *New York Assembly Documents* (Albany, N.Y., 1836), 1: docs. 1, 3, 7, 8.

48. Nathan Dane, *A General Abridgment and Digest of American Law*, 8 vols. (Boston, 1823), 3:39; Horace G. Wood, *A Practical Treatise on the Law of Nuisances* (1875; 2d ed., Albany, N.Y., 1883), 1.

49. William Blackstone, *Commentaries on the Laws of England: A Facsimile of the First Edition of 1765–1769*, 4 vols. (Chicago, 1979), 3:216; 4:167.

50. In this vein, Martin Melosi dismisses antebellum efforts at pollution control because they treated a major public policy problem as a mere matter of "nuisance." Martin V. Melosi, ed., *Pollution and Reform in American Cities, 1870–1930* (Austin, Tex., 1980), 18. Edward Corwin and Leonard Levy portray nuisance as something like a second-rate forerunner of state police and administrative power, more an obstacle to be overcome than a source of public power. Edward S. Corwin, *The Twilight of the Supreme Court* (New Haven, Conn., 1934), 68; Leonard W. Levy, *The Law of the Commonwealth and Chief Justice Shaw* (New York, 1957), 252–54.

51. Joel Franklin Brenner, "Nuisance Law and the Industrial Revolution," *Journal of Legal Studies* 3 (1974): 403–33; Morton J. Horwitz, *The Transformation of American Law, 1780–1860* (Cambridge, Mass., 1977), especially 74–78. On public nuisance, see the adaptation of Paul M. Kurtz, "Nineteenth Century Anti-Entrepreneurial Nuisance Injunctions—

Avoiding the Chancellor," *William and Mary Law Review* 17 (1976): 621–70. The Brenner-Horwitz thesis turns on first presenting a misleadingly static and absolutist conception of preindustrial property and nuisance law. It then asks the admittedly fascinating but already skewed historical question: if no use of property could ever affect another (under a "strict liability" rather than a "relative rights" interpretation of *sic utere tuo*), how could the industrial revolution and its accompanying bevy of adverse effects on neighboring property have happened? The answer: nuisance was a site of modern legal transformation, wherein instrumental judges eased "the substantive law of nuisance in favor of the entrepreneur," and "effectively emasculated [it] as a useful curb" on industrialism. According to Horwitz and Kurtz, one of the most clever mechanisms for this legal capitalist subsidization was a resurrection of the "*narrow and technical* public nuisance doctrine" to bar private suits. Kurtz, "Anti-Entrepreneurial Nuisance," 645; Horwitz, *Transformation, 1780–1860*, 77. Note that historical misconceptions 1 and 2 directly conflict—nuisance law cannot be both trivial (primitive, ineffective) *and* a nearly "insurmountable obstacle" to "all entrepreneurial activity." Kurtz, 623.

52. My own revision builds on some excellent recent attempts to move beyond the Brenner-Horwitz interpretation. See John P. S. McLaren, "Nuisance Law and the Industrial Revolution—Some Lessons from Social History," *Oxford Journal of Legal Studies* 3 (1983): 155–221; Robert G. Bone, "Normative Theory and Legal Doctrine in American Nuisance Law: 1850 to 1920," *Southern California Law Review* 59 (1986): 1101–1226; Peter Karsten, "Explaining the Fight over the Attractive Nuisance Doctrine: A Kinder, Gentler Instrumentalism in the 'Age of Formalism,'" *Law and History Review* 10 (1992): 45; Christine Rosen, "Differing Perceptions of the Value of Pollution Abatement across Time and Place: Balancing Doctrine in Pollution Nuisance Law, 1840–1906," *Law and History Review* 11 (1993), 303–81.

53. Wood, *Nuisances*, 1; Joel Prentiss Bishop, *Commentaries on the Criminal Law*, 4th ed., 2 vols. (1865; Boston, 1868), 1:598; James Kent, *Commentaries on American Law*, 4 vols. (New York, 1826), 2:340; Ernst Freund, *Standards of American Legislation*, 2d ed. (1917; Chicago, 1965), 66; William Packer Prentice, *Police Powers Arising under the Law of Overruling Necessity* (New York, 1894), 167.

54. Sidney Webb and Beatrice Webb, *The Development of English Local Government, 1689–1835* (London, 1963), 13.

55. Wood, *Nuisances*, 2, 20, 26–82. For some idea of the deep historical roots of nuisance law as a regulatory instrument (including its use to prevent fires), see Helena M. Chew and William Kellaway, *London Assize of Nuisance, 1301–1431* (London, 1973), ix–xxxiv.

56. Douglass C. North, *The Economic Growth of the United States, 1790–1860* (Englewood Cliffs, N.J., 1961); Stuart Bruchey, *The Roots of American Economic Growth, 1607–1860* (New York, 1965); Thomas C. Cochran, *Frontiers of Change: Early Industrialism in America* (New York, 1981).

57. Victor S. Clark, *History of Manufactures in the United States*, 2 vols. (1929; New York, 1949), 1:222.

58. Orlando W. Stephenson, "The Supply of Gunpowder in 1776," *American Historical Review* 30 (1925): 271–81; Arthur Pine VanGelder and Hugo Schlatter, *History of the Explosives Industry in America* (New York, 1927), 30–37.

59. VanGelder and Schlatter, *Explosives Industry*, 66–71; Max Dorian, *Du Ponts: From Gunpowder to Nylon* (Boston, 1962).

60. *Anonymous*, 12 Mod. 342 (1700). This particular indictment was for gunpowder kept in Brentford Town. Also see *Rex v. Taylor*, 2 Str. 1167 (Eng., 1742). London's Common Council had explicitly banned gunpowder from the city after the Great Fire of 1666. "An

Act for preventing and suppressing fires within the City of London" (1676), in Donald Goddard Wing, *Short-Title Catalogue of Books Printed in England, Scotland, Ireland, Wales, and British America, and of the English Books Printed in Other Countries, 1641–1700* (New York, 1972–88), reel 1637, 35. By 1770, gunpowder was regulated throughout Great Britain by statute. 5 Geo. I, c. 26 (1720); 2 Geo. III, c. 35 (1770).

61. *Wolcott v. Melick*, 11 NJE 204, 66 Am. Dec. 790 (1856), 793. In *Rhodes v. Dunbar*, 57 Pa. St. 274 (1868), Justice Read's list of useful economic establishments declared nuisances included: "A glass-house, a chandler-shop, a swine-yard, a pig-sty, a pig boarding-house, a soap factory, a tallow-furnace, a slaughterhouse, a bone-boiling establishment, a horse-boiling establishment, a mill-dam, a melting-house of animal fat and tallow, a cotton-press, finishing steam boilers, the use of a public place for immigrants, brick-burning, laying up wet jute, storing wood-naphtha, gunpowder, petroleum or nitro-glycerine, a lime-kiln, a dye-house, a furnace, a smelting-house, a smith-forge, a livery-stable, a tannery, gasworks." *Rhodes*, 275. Also see Thomas W. Waterman, *Waterman's Eden on the Law and Practice of Injunctions*, 3d ed., 2 vols. (New York, 1852), 2:264–65; Francis Wharton, *A Treatise on the Criminal Law of the United States* (Philadelphia, 1846), 504–6; Wood, *Nuisances*.

62. *People v. Sands*, 1 Johns. 78 (N.Y., 1806), 78.

63. *Laws of New York* (1804), c. 126.

64. *People v. Sands*, 88.

65. Ibid., 83–84.

66. Ibid., 86.

67. Here are some examples of the potentially extreme particularity in nuisance law prosecutions from the late nineteenth-century: "The leaving of a hand car on a public road at a railroad crossing, and hanging buckets and clothing thereon, whereby horses are frightened." *Cincinnati R.R. Co. v. Commonwealth*, 80 Ky. 137 (1882). "The singing of a ribald song containing the stanza charged in the indictment, in a loud and boisterous manner, on the public streets, in the presence of divers persons, continued for the space of ten minutes." *State v. Toole*, 106 N.C. 736 (1890).

68. This information is supplied by William Johnson in the second edition of his reports. At this time, the house was stocked with 400 quarter casks of powder. The explosion damaged a church and several dwelling houses nearby. *People v. Sands*, 84, n. a.

69. *Myers v. Malcolm*, 6 Hill 292, 41 Am. Dec. 744 (New York, 1844).

70. It should be noted that the private plaintiff in this suit sought a public nuisance ruling specifically to get around the tort law requirement of negligence. Ibid., 745. Thus, contrary to the Horwitz-Kurtz thesis discussed earlier, public nuisance law and its accompanying special damage provision made it distinctly *easier* for this private party to seek damages.

71. *Cheatham v. Shearon*, 1 Swan. 213, 55 Am. Dec. 734 (Tenn., 1851).

72. Ibid., 736.

73. Ibid., 737.

74. *Bradley v. People*, 56 Barb. 72 (N.Y., 1866); *Rhodes v. Dunbar*, 290 (planing mill at issue, but dictum on powderhouses); *Wier's Appeal*, 74 Pa. St. 230 (1873); *Heeg v. Licht*, 80 N.Y. 579 (1880); *McAndrews v. Collerd*, 42 N.J. 189 (1880); Wood, *Nuisances*, 70–71, n. 3.

75. *Wier's Appeal*, 243. The extraordinariness of this equitable remedy against public nuisances will be discussed in more detail in chapter 4. One of many reasons for granting an injunction here (in a neighborhood "not thickly settled") was the fact that "a public turnpike-road" ran very near the powderhouse. Ibid., 244.

76. *Dumesnil v. Dupont*, 18 B. Monroe 800, 68 Am. Dec. 750 (Ky., 1858) is the exception to the general trend away from *Sands*.

77. *People v. Sands*, 84. Although obtaining an accurate count of powderhouse explosions is difficult, it is significant that the actions in *Myers, Cheatham, Heeg,* and *McAndrews* were prompted by actual explosions. Also see the testimony of witnesses in *Wier's Appeal*, 243–44. Unplanned explosions were a very real part of the history of the explosives industry. The Bellona Mills in Baltimore, for example, exploded three times in its short early nineteenth-century existence. See VanGelder and Schlatter, *Explosives Industry*, 77.

78. See, for example, the shoddy treatment of *Sands* ("that case was disposed of upon the form of the indictment") by the time of *Heeg v. Licht* (1880), 657.

79. *Fisher v. McGirr*, 67 Gray 1 (Mass., 1854), 27.

80. Gunpowder in Brooklyn (the issue in *People v. Sands*) was ultimately regulated by statute in 1852. *Laws of New York* (1852), c.355, 552, 559.

81. *Foote v. Fire Department of the City of New-York*, 5 Hill 99 (N.Y., 1843). Also see *Williams v. The City Council of Augusta*, 4 Ga. 509 (1848). In *Davenport v. Richmond City*, 81 Va. 636 (1886), a municipal ordinance directing the removal of a powderhouse was upheld even though the property had been conveyed for that very purpose.

82. *License Cases*, 5 How. 504 (U.S., 1847), 589–90.

83. As a typical property law text puts it, "Zoning is a twentieth-century development. . . . What came before was piecemeal and limited." Jesse Dukeminier and James E. Krier, eds., *Property*, 3d ed. (Boston, 1993), 1115. Andrew J. King's pioneering history of late nineteenth-century precursors of modern zoning also invokes the standard generalization: "In the United States decisions regarding the use of urban land rested almost exclusively in private hands until the twentieth century. While state and local governmental agencies provided the legal framework for private action, nineteenth century Americans trusted the market to ordain and facilitate the appropriate decisions." Andrew J. King, "Law and Land Use in Chicago: A Prehistory of Modern Zoning" (Ph.D. diss., University of Wisconsin–Madison, 1976). See also Lawrence M. Friedman, *A History of American Law*, 2d ed. (New York, 1985), 678.

84. *Respublica v. Duquet*, 2 Yeates 493 (Penn., 1799), 499.

85. Ibid., 497 (emphasis added); *City of London v. Wood*, 12 Mod. 669 (Eng., 1702), 686. As Holt pointed out, municipal power was necessary as the "supreme jurisdiction [the legislature] cannot have leisure to inspect into the small matters that concern the whole order and regulation of matters within that society or community, as they that are members of it shall." The complex historical relationship between municipal and state power is most authoritatively explored in Hartog, *Public Property and Private Power*.

86. *Respublica v. Duquet*, 497–98. *The Statutes at Large of Pennsylvania from 1682 to 1809*, 18 vols. (Harrisburg, Pa., 1911), 12 (1789) 200; "An Act to Authorize the Corporation of the City of Philadelphia to Prevent the Erection of Wooden Buildings in Certain Parts of the City of Philadelphia," *Statutes at Large of Pennsylvania*, 15 (1795) 354–55. Philadelphia was incorporated with this prologue: "Whereas the intention of civil government is to provide for the order, safety and happiness of the people and where the general systems and regulations thereof are found to be ineffectual it is the duty of the legislature to remedy the defects: And whereas the administration of government within the city of Philadelphia is in its present form inadequate to the suppression of vice and immorality, to the advancement of the public health and order and to the promotion of trade, industry and happiness and in order to provide against the (evils) occasioned thereby it is necessary to invest the inhabitants thereof with more speedy, vigorous and effective powers of government than are at present established." *Statutes at Large of Pennsylvania*, 13:193.

87. *Respublica v. Duquet*, 498–99. To bring his argument close to home, Ingersoll re-

minded the court of the "dreadful fire" which had just consumed Ricket's Circus, "distant only one square from where the court now sits." Ibid., 499.

88. *Statutes at Large of Pennsylvania*, 13 (1789) 193.

89. Irving Browne, "Fire Limits," *Albany Law Journal* 21 (1880): 225–26. In *Douglass v. Commonwealth*, 2 Rawle 262 (Pa., 1830), the Pennsylvania Supreme Court again had a chance to rule on the 1796 Philadelphia fire limit. Once again, the statute itself was not even challenged as the court decided that alterations and additions made in converting an existing wooden blacksmith's shop into a cabinetmaker's warehouse entailed an "erection" of a wooden building indictable under the statute.

90. *Wadleigh v. Gilman*, 12 Me. 403 (1835).

91. At trial, a jury found for Wadleigh in the amount $154.07 after the judge ruled as a matter of law that the removal of this building to another lot was not an "erection" within the meaning of the ordinance. Ibid., 403.

92. Often this destruction was by a public official in accordance with a local ordinance or state statute. But the common law also allowed for the private "abatement" of public nuisances. Vigilante destruction was, of course, also a very real threat for violators of antebellum law or community standards and expectations.

93. Ibid., 404–5. Weston also had no trouble liberally extending the "erection" requirement of the ordinance to include buildings moved from one quarter of Bangor to another. Ibid., 406. In a series of cases, Connecticut opted for a stricter construction of statutory "erections." See *Daggett v. State*, 4 Conn. 60 (1821); *Booth v. State*, 4 Conn. 65 (1821); *Tuttle v. State*, 4 Conn. 68 (1821).

94. The two categories—"taking" and "regulation," "eminent domain" and "police power"—were mutually exclusive in the nineteenth century. Under a police regulation, it did not matter what happened to the property because of the regulation. Any injury, no matter how severe, was *damnum absque injuria* (an injury without remedy) and noncompensable. A "taking," on the other hand, involved a completely different type of public action—the direct appropriation of private property for public use. For the best historical discussions of eminent domain, see Harry N. Scheiber, "The Jurisprudence—and Mythology—of Eminent Domain in American Legal History," in *Liberty, Property and Government: Constitutional Interpretation before the New Deal*, ed. Ellen Frankel Paul and Howard Dickman (Albany, N.Y., 1989), 217–38; and Scheiber, "Property Law, Expropriation, and Resource Allocation by Government: The United States, 1789–1910," *Journal of Economic History* 33 (1973): 232–51, 242–43.

95. *Wadleigh*, 405.

96. Ibid., 404.

97. Ibid. (emphasis added).

98. Ibid., 405.

99. *Vanderbilt v. Adams*, 7 Cow. 349 (New York, 1827); *Stuyvesant v. Mayor of New York*, 7 Cow. 588 (New York, 1827); *Baker v. Boston*, 12 Pick. 184 (Mass., 1831); *Village of Buffalo v. Webster*, 10 Wendell 99 (N.Y., 1833). *Stuyvesant* is one of the four New York City cemetery cases argued simultaneously in 1827. The same opinion is also often cited as *Coates v. Mayor of New York*, 7 Cow. 585 (N.Y., 1827).

100. *Baker*, 193; *Stuyvesant*, 605; *Vanderbilt*, 351–52. In 1881, John Dillon used these very cases along with *Wadleigh* for his comprehensive definition of "Police Powers and Regulations": "Many of the powers most generally exercised by municipalities are derived from what is known as the *police power* of the state, and are delegated to them to be exercised for the public good. . . . [I]t may here be observed that every citizen holds his property subject to the proper exercise of this power. . . . And it is well settled that laws and regulations of

this character, though they may disturb the enjoyment of individual rights, are not unconstitutional, though no provision is made for compensation for such disturbances. They do not appropriate private property for public use, but simply regulate its use and enjoyment by the owner. . . . These regulations rest upon the maxim, *Salus populi suprema est lex.* . . . It is not a taking of private property for public use, but a salutary restraint on a noxious use by the owner, contrary to the maxim, *Sic utere tuo ut alienum non laedas.*" John F. Dillon, *The Law of Municipal Corporations*, 2d ed., 2 vols. (New York, 1873), 1:167, n. 2.

101. *Wadleigh*, 405–6.

102. *Brady v. Northwestern Insurance Co.*; *Mayor and Council of Monroe v. Hoffman*, 29 La. Ann. 651, 29 Am. Rep. 345 (1877). The only limit to judicial acceptance of municipal fire limits in the late nineteenth century was a tendency among some state courts to demand explicit statutory delegation of power before municipalities passed such ordinances. For an early precedent these cases relied on *Mayor of Hudson v. Thorne*, 7 Paige ch. 261 (N.Y., 1838). See *City of Olympia v. Mann*, 1 Wash. St. 389 (1890); *Keokuk v. Scroggs*, 39 Ia. 447 (1874); *Pye v. Peterson*, 45 Tx. 312 (1876); *Kneedler v. Norristown*, 100 Pa. St. 368 (1882).

103. *Monroe*, 345–46.

104. *Brady*, 447.

105. Prentice, *Overruling Necessity*; Platt Potter, *Dwarris on Statutes* (Albany, N.Y., 1871), 444–67.

106. Prentice, *Overruling Necessity*, 4. Also see James Kent, *Commentaries on American Law*, 4 vols. (New York, 1826), 2:274–75; Thomas M. Cooley, *A Treatise on the Constitutional Limitations* (Boston, 1868), 594–95; Potter, *Dwarris on Statutes*, 444–45; Scott M. Reznick, "Empiricism and the Principle of Conditions in the Evolution of the Police Power: A Model for Definitional Scrutiny," *Washington University Law Quarterly* (1978): 19–20; Harrison H. Brace, "To What Extent May Government in the Exercise of Its Police Power, Take, Destroy or Damage Private Property without Giving Compensation Therefor?" *Chicago Legal News* 18 (1886): 339–41; Thomas J. Pitts, "The Nature and Implications of the Police Power," *Kansas City Law Review* 6 (1937): 128–49.

107. *Maleverer v. Spinke*, 1 Dyer 32 (Eng., 1538); *Case of the King's Prerogative in Salt-peter*, 12 Coke 13 (Eng., 1607); *Mouse's Case*, 12 Coke 63 (Eng., 1609); *Governor and Company of the British Cast Plate Manufacturers v. Meredith*, 4 T.R. 794 (Eng., 1792). The doctrine first appeared in American case law in 1788 in *Respublica v. Sparhawk*, 1 Dallas 357 (Pa., 1788).

108. Cooley, *Limitations*, 594–95; Kent, *Commentaries*, 2:274. On *damnum absque injuria*, see Joseph William Singer, "The Legal Rights Debate in Analytical Jurisprudence from Bentham to Hohfeld," *Wisconsin Law Review* (1982): 975–1059.

109. Thomas Rutherford, *Institutes of Natural Law*, 2 vols. (Philadelphia, 1799), 1:93–96.

110. Blackstone, *Commentaries*, 4:31–32.

111. Wall, "Great Fire," 17, n. 11.

112. As quoted in ibid., 11.

113. I relied on the following in putting together this composite sketch: Speeches by the governor and mayor to the New York Assembly in *New York Assembly Documents* (1836), 1: docs. 3, 7, 8; Wall, "Great Fire"; Nathan Miller, *The Enterprise of a Free People: Aspects of Economic Development in New York State during the Canal Period, 1792–1838* (Ithaca, N.Y., 1962), 172–93; William Worthington Fowler, *Fighting Fire: The Great Fires of History* (Hartford, Conn., 1873), 405–17; John V. Morris, *Fires and Firefighters* (Boston, 1953), 117–30; E. J. Goodspeed, *History of the Great Fires in Chicago and the West* (New York, 1871), 654–55.

114. Morris, *Fires and Firefighters*, 13–15.

115. See, for example, "An Act for Building with Stone or Brick in the Town of Boston, and Preventing Fire" and "An Act Providing, in Case of Fire, For the More Speedy Extin-

guishment Thereof," *Acts and Resolves of Massachusetts Bay, 1692–1780*, 1 (1692), c. 13, 42–43; 1 (1711), c. 5, 677–78. See also *Laws of New York*, 2 (1813), c. 86 (R.L.), 363–70.

116. Such "hooks" were on Peter Stuyvesant's list of necessary fire-fighting equipment for "New Amsterdam." O'Callaghan, *Laws of New Netherland, 1638–1674*, (1648), 82; (1657), 322. See also, Bridenbaugh, *Cities in the Wilderness*, 58–59, 211–13.

117. The Bludworth legend achieved legal status in *Respublica v. Sparhawk*, 362. The source of the legend is perhaps Samuel Pepys, who followed the Great Fire in his *Diary* (1659–69). Pepys went to the king and the duke of York for an order to pull down houses when met with the mayor's hesitancy. Gunpowder was finally used two days too late to squelch remaining flames. Alternative renditions have the mayor hesitating because the first houses to be destroyed belonged to lawyers of the temple, city magnates, or aldermen. Harold Priestley, *London: The Years of Change* (London, 1966), 151–78; Fowler, *Fighting Fire*, 465–96.

118. *Year Books*, 13 Henry VIII, 16, pl. 1 (1522).

119. *Maleverer v. Spinke; Case of the King's Prerogative in Salt-peter; Mouse's Case.*

120. *Governor and Company of the British Cast Plate Manufacturers v. Meredith*, 797.

121. *Respublica v. Sparhawk.*

122. Kent, *Commentaries*, 1:275–75.

123. *Laws of New York*, 2 (1813), 368.

124. *Laws of New York*, 2 (1813), c. 86, 368–69. Such statutory provision was not rare. After Boston's bout with fire in 1653, it passed a town ordinance allowing public officials to order the demolition of houses. The ordinance explicitly stated that "noe person whoos house shall be so pulled down . . . shall . . . recover any satisfaktion by law." In 1659, the town reversed itself and ordered that buildings so destroyed should "againe be repayred and made good by the towne." Bridenbaugh, *Cities in the Wilderness*, 58.

125. An alternative explanation for the statutory distinction between buildings and goods is that goods could be removed and saved whereas the building was purely at the mercy of the fire or authorities.

126. *Mayor of New York v. Lord* (I), 17 Wend. 285 (N.Y., 1837); *Mayor of New York v. Lord* (II), 18 Wend. 126 (N.Y., 1837).

127. The jury awarded these amounts (the Lords had asked for $9,558 and $250,259.30 respectively) despite a judge's charge that damages should be confined "to such property as could have been saved with ordinary care and diligence, if the building had not been destroyed." Here, witnesses testified that the building would have been inevitably destroyed by fire if it had not been blown up. *Mayor v. Lord* (I), 288.

128. Ibid., 289.

129. Ibid., 290.

130. Ibid., 291–92.

131. *Mayor v. Lord* (II), 129–30.

132. Ibid., 130. Dissents in both *Lord* appeals objected to broad and equitable constructions of a statute that clearly provided damages for buildings only. *Mayor v. Lord* (I), 296–305; *Mayor v. Lord* (II), 136–40.

133. *Stone v. Mayor of New York* (which includes *Berthoud v. Mayor of New York*), 25 Wend. 157 (N.Y., 1840); *Russell v. Mayor of New York*, 2 Denio 461 (N.Y., 1845).

134. *Stone*, 160–64.

135. Ibid., 162.

136. *Russell*, 473–74 (emphasis added).

137. Ibid., 475–76. Sherman analogized the statute to public health and quarantine laws. Mariners and vessels were subject to such laws "without providing any compensation for

the loss and delay, and for the confinement of the crew and passengers to the prescribed limits." So too, during the cholera epidemic, boards of health were created with powers "arbitrarily to destroy an unlimited amount of the property of its citizens, for the purpose of preventing the spread of disease, without imposing any obligation or subjecting them to any responsibility whatever."

138. Ibid., 484.

139. *Hale v. Lawrence* (decided together with *Howe v. Lawrence*), 21 N.J. 714, 47 Am. Dec. 190 (N.J., 1848), 192.

140. *American Print Works v. Lawrence* (decided with *Hale v. Lawrence*), 3 Zabr. 590, 57 Am. Dec. 420 (N.J., 1851), 430–32.

141. *Bowditch v. Boston*, 101 U.S. 16 (1879), 19. As defined by *Bowditch*, a bounty entailed "that which could not have been claimed before."

142. *Surocco v. Geary*, 3 Cal. 69 (1853); *Conwell v. Emrie*, 2 Ind. 35 (1850); *Taylor v. Inhabitants of Plymouth*, 49 Mass. 462 (1844); *Coffin v. Nantucket*, 5 Cush. 269 (Mass., 1850); *Ruggles v. Nantucket*, 11 Cush. 433 (Mass., 1853); *Parsons v. Pettingell*, 11 Allen 507 (Mass., 1866); *McDonald v. City of Red Wing*, 13 Minn. 38 (1868). See also *White v. City Council of Charleston*, 2 Hill 571 (S.C., 1835); *Keller v. Corpus Christi*, 1 Tx. 614 (1879). In *Surocco v. Geary*, the California Supreme Court explicitly connected the law of necessity and the law of public nuisance: "A house on fire, or those in its immediate vicinity which serves to communicate the flames, becomes a nuisance, which it is lawful to abate, and the private rights of the individual yield to the considerations of general convenience and the interests of society. Were it otherwise, one stubborn person might involve the whole city in ruin, by refusing to allow the destruction of a building which would cut off the flames and check the progress of the fire." *Surocco*, 73.

143. *Bowditch v. Boston*.

144. Dillon, *Municipal Corporations*, 2:953. In addition to Dillon's commentary, see "Destruction of Private Property to Prevent the Spread of Fires," *Law Journal* 9 (1874): 484; Henry C. Hall and John H. Wigmore, "Compensation for Property Destroyed to Stop the Spread of a Conflagration," *Illinois Law Review* 1 (1907): 501–36; and the note following the report of *Hale v. Lawrence* in 47 Am. Dec. 190, 207–10.

145. *Stewart Purdon's Digest: A Digest of the Statute Law of the State of Pennsylvania from the Year 1700 to 1903*, 13th ed., 5 vols. (Philadelphia, 1905), 3:2780–83.

146. See, for example, *City Council of Montgomery v. Louisville & N.R. Co.*, 84 Ala. 127 (1887); *Canepa v. City of Birmingham*, 92 Ala. 358 (1890); *McCloskey v. Kreling*, 76 Cal. 511 (1888); *Ford v. Thralkill*, 84 Ga. 169 (1889); *King v. Davenport*, 98 Ill. 305 (1881); *Baumgartner v. Hasty*, 100 Ind. 575 (1884); *City of Des Moines v. Gilchrist*, 67 Ia. 210 (1885); *Alexander v. Town Council of Greenville*, 54 Miss. 659 (1877); *State v. Johnson*, 114 N.C. 846 (1894); *Hubbard v. Town of Medford*, 20 Or. 315 (1891); *Corporation of Knoxville v. Bird*, 80 Tenn. 121 (1883); *City of Olympia v. Mann*; *City of Charleston v. Reed*, 27 W. Va. 681 (1886); *City of Richmond v. Dudley*, 129 Ind. 112 (1891); *Commonwealth v. Parks*, 155 Mass. 531 (1892); *Clark v. City of South Bend*, 85 Ind. 276 (1882); *Anderson v. City of Savannah*, 69 Ga. 472 (1882).

147. Christopher G. Tiedeman, *A Treatise on the Limitations of Police Power in the United States* (St. Louis, 1886), 438–40; Ernst Freund, *The Police Power: Public Policy and Constitutional Rights* (Chicago, 1904), 131. Tiedeman went so far as to support the decision in *Corporation of Knoxville v. Bird*, where the Tennessee Supreme Court applied the ban to cases where wooden construction was contracted for before passage of an ordinance, even though such an interpretation made all contracts for wooden construction illegal, and negated contractual obligations. Tiedeman, *Limitations*, 439, n. 1. This is hardly the construction of the contracts clause one would expect from one of the "villainous" proponents

of laissez-faire constitutionalism. See Arnold Paul, *Conservative Crisis and the Rule of Law: Attitudes of Bar and Bench, 1887–1895* (Ithaca, N.Y., 1960); Clyde E. Jacobs, *Law Writers and the Courts: The Influence of Thomas M. Cooley, Christopher G. Tiedeman, and John F. Dillon upon American Constitutional Law* (Los Angeles, 1954); Benjamin Twiss, *Lawyers and the Constitution: How Laissez Faire Came to the Supreme Court* (New York, 1962). For the best general revisions of this Progressive school of late nineteenth-century constitutional historiography, see Michael Les Benedict, "Laissez-Faire and Liberty: A Re-evaluation of the Meaning and Origins of Laissez-Faire Constitutionalism," *Law and History Review* 3 (1985): 293–331; and Aviam Soifer, "The Paradox of Paternalism and Laissez-Faire Constitutionalism: United States Supreme Court, 1888–1921," *Law and History Review* 5 (1987): 249–79.

148. Cooley, *Limitations*, 595–96.

149. John F. Dillon, *Commentaries on the Law of Municipal Corporations*, 3d ed., 2 vols. (Boston, 1881), 953. On the same point, see Cooley, *Limitations*, 595; Freund, *Police Power*, 563–64; Kent, *Commentaries*, 2:275.

150. Examples of rigorous enforcement abound. In 1840 New York City's fire wardens seized twenty-five kegs of gunpowder kept by a liquor merchant. The powder evidently had been in the accused's store for only *fifteen minutes* in the process of being packed for shipment to Mobile. *Foote v. Fire Department of the City of New York*, 99–100. A series of cases in Connecticut also revealed a relatively aggressive enforcement of New Haven's wooden building regulation. In 1821, state actions against three separate owners of wooden structures simultaneously made their way to the Supreme Court. *Daggett v. State*; *Booth v. State*; *Tuttle v. State*.

151. The Supreme Court agreed and declared section 29 unconstitutional, as the exercise of a police power belonging exclusively to the state governments. *United States v. Dewitt*, 9 Wall. 41 (U.S., 1869); *United States Statutes at Large*, 14 (1867), c. 169, 484. Federal laws, however, were successful in regulating explosives in interstate commerce and on steam vessels. *United States Statutes at Large*, 14 (1866), c. 162, 81; 16 (1871), c. 100, 440–59.

152. *Pennsylvania Coal Co. v. Mahon*, 260 U.S. 393 (1922), 415. At issue was the constitutionality of the Pennsylvania Kohler Act of 1921 prohibiting the mining of anthracite coal in such a way as to cause the subsidence (and thus threaten the existence) of any structure used as a human habitation. Carol M. Rose, "*Mahon* Reconstructed: Why the Takings Issue Is Still a Muddle," *Southern California Law Review* 57 (1984): 561–99; Lawrence M. Friedman, "A Search for Seizure: *Pennsylvania Coal Co. v. Mahon* in Context," *Law and History Review* 4 (1986): 1–22.

153. *Pennsylvania Coal*, 420, 422. Brandeis's dissenting opinion indeed resonated with Shaw-like overtones: "Every restriction upon the use of property imposed in the exercise of the police power deprives the owner of some right theretofore enjoyed, and is, in that sense, an abridgment by the state of rights in property without making compensation. But restriction imposed to protect public health, safety or morals from dangers threatened is not a taking. The restriction here in question is merely the prohibition of a noxious use. The property so restricted remains in the possession of its owner. The state does not appropriate it or make any use of it. The state merely prevents the owner from making a use which interferes with paramount rights of the public." Ibid., 417.

Chapter Three

1. Barry M. Mitnick, *The Political Economy of Regulation* (New York, 1980); James W. McKie, "Regulation and the Free Market: The Problem of Boundaries," *Bell Journal of Economics and Management Science* 1 (1970): 6–26. This notion flows as much from the pub-

lic/private distinction in modern political thought as from classical economics. See Joyce Oldham Appleby, *Economic Thought and Ideology in Seventeenth-Century England* (Princeton, N.J., 1978); Appleby, *Capitalism and a New Social Order: The Republican Vision of the 1790's* (New York, 1984); P. S. Atiyah, *The Rise and Fall of Freedom of Contract* (Oxford, 1979); Morton J. Horwitz, "The History of the Public/Private Distinction," *Pennsylvania Law Review* 130 (1982): 1423–28. For an early challenge to this perspective, see Morris R. Cohen, "Property and Sovereignty," *Cornell Law Quarterly* 13 (1827): 8; Robert L. Hale, "Force and the State: A Comparison of 'Political' and 'Economic' Compulsion," *Columbia Law Review* 35 (1935): 149.

2. Thomas K. McCraw, "Regulation in America: A Review Article," *Business History Review* 49 (1975): 175.

3. Gerald D. Nash, "State and Local Governments," in *Encyclopedia of American Economic History*, ed. Glenn Porter, 3 vols. (New York, 1980), 2:509. Also see Sidney Fine, *Laissez Faire and the General-Welfare State* (Ann Arbor, Mich., 1956); Wallace D. Farnham, "'The Weakened Spring of Government': A Study in Nineteenth Century American History," *American Historical Review* 68 (1963): 662–80. This traditional interpretation of Adam Smith has been revised. See Donald Winch, *Adam Smith's Politics: An Essay in Historiographical Revision* (Cambridge, 1978); Michael Ignatieff and Istvan Hont, eds., *Wealth and Virtue: The Shaping of Political Economy in the Scottish Enlightenment* (Cambridge, 1983).

4. Karl Polanyi, *The Great Transformation* (New York, 1944); Harold D. Woodman, "Economy from 1815 to 1865," in Porter, *Encyclopedia of American Economic History*, 1:66; Stuart Bruchey, *The Wealth of a Nation: An Economic History of the United States* (New York, 1988), x. Also see Simon Kuznets, *Modern Economic Growth: Rate, Structure, and Spread* (New Haven, Conn., 1966); Stuart Bruchey, *The Roots of American Economic Growth, 1607–1861* (New York, 1965); Douglass C. North, *The Economic Growth of the United States, 1790–1860* (Englewood Cliffs, N.J., 1961); Douglass C. North, *Growth and Welfare in the American Past: A New Economic History* (Englewood Cliffs, N.J., 1966); Robert W. Fogel and Stanley L. Engerman, eds., *The Reinterpretation of American Economic History* (New York, 1971); Thomas C. Cochran, *Frontiers of Change: Early Industrialism in America* (New York, 1981). Most American economic historians have dispensed with Polanyi's biting critical stance toward this transformation: "Our thesis is that the idea of a self adjusting market implied a stark utopia. Such an institution could not exist for any length of time without annihilating the human and natural substance of society." Polanyi, *Transformation*, 3.

5. Sean Wilentz, "Society, Politics, and the Market Revolution, 1815–1848," in *The New American History*, ed. Eric Foner (Philadelphia, 1990), 51–71; Harry L. Watson, *Liberty and Power: The Politics of Jacksonian America* (New York, 1990); Charles G. Sellers, *The Market Revolution: Jacksonian America, 1815–1846* (New York, 1991). The social history literatures synthesized in these three works are immense. For capitalism and the countryside, see the bibliography and discussions contained in Alan Kulikoff, "The Transition to Capitalism in Rural America," *William and Mary Quarterly* 46 (1989): 120–44; Christopher Clark, *The Roots of Rural Capitalism: Western Massachusetts, 1780–1860* (Ithaca, N.Y., 1990), 3–17; Steven Hahn and Jonathan Prude, eds., *The Countryside in the Age of Capitalist Transformation: Essays in the Social History of Rural America* (Chapel Hill, N.C., 1985). On industrial capitalism, see Anthony F. C. Wallace, *Rockdale: The Growth of an American Village in the Early Industrial Revolution* (New York, 1978); Alan Dawley, *Class and Community: The Industrial Revolution in Lynn* (Cambridge, Mass., 1976); Paul G. Faler, *Mechanics and Manufacturers in the Early Industrial Revolution: Lynn, Massachusetts, 1780–1860* (Albany, N.Y., 1981). Alan Kulikoff has recently called for social historians looking at antebellum agricul-

tural transformation to pay more attention to the political, institutional, and legal contexts of change. Kulikoff, "Transition to Capitalism." I know of no such move in the industrial capitalism literature. For a cautionary note on the extent of the market's encroachment on antebellum agriculture, see Allen W. Dodge, *A Prize Essay on Fairs* (Boston, 1858). Written shortly before the Civil War, Dodge's essay decries the fact that in all of Massachusetts there were still only two established markets (in Cambridge and Brookline) for the buying and selling of livestock. Dodge's testimony suggests that one response to market agricultural historians might come from Longfellow's "Tales of a Wayside Inn":

> What's the use
> Of this bragging up and down,
> When three women and one goose
> Make a market in your town!

6. Oscar Handlin and Mary Flug Handlin, *Commonwealth: A Study of the Role of Government in the American Economy: Massachusetts, 1774–1861* (New York, 1947); Louis Hartz, *Economic Policy and Democratic Thought: Pennsylvania, 1776–1860* (Cambridge, Mass., 1948). Although the Handlins and Hartz portray a state constantly involved in the antebellum economy, that state is primarily promotional, encouraging entrepreneurial projects (like canals, banks, and railroads) and creating a hospitable institutional environment for capitalist economic development. As Robert Lively put it, in the commonwealth studies "the elected official" simply replaced "the individual enterpriser as the key figure in the release of capitalist energy." In the end, except for the myth of statelessness, the commonwealth studies did little to challenge the fundamentally liberal-capitalist portrait of nineteenth-century America outlined in the introduction. For an illustration of this, see the works Hartz produced directly before and after his commonwealth monograph. Louis Hartz, "The Individualist Philosophy of John Harlan, 1833–1911" (Honors Thesis, Harvard University, 1940); Hartz, *The Liberal Tradition in America: An Interpretation of American Political Thought since the Revolution* (New York, 1955). I am using the Handlins and Hartz here to stand for the entire corpus of commonwealth work. See the works cited in Robert A. Lively, "The American System: A Review Article," *Business History Review* 29 (1955): 81–96; and Harry N. Scheiber, "Government and the Economy: Studies of the 'Commonwealth' Policy in Nineteenth-Century America," *Journal of Interdisciplinary History* 3 (1972): 135–51. Harry Scheiber's studies of public rights and eminent domain are the only commonwealth-inspired work to directly challenge the liberal thesis. See Scheiber, "Public Rights and the Rule of Law in American History," *California Law Review* 72 (1984): 217–51; and "Law and the Imperatives of Progress: Private Rights and Public Values in American Legal History," in *Ethics, Economics and the Law*, ed. J. Roland Pennock and John W. Chapman (London, 1982), 303–20.

7. James Willard Hurst, *Law and the Conditions of Freedom in the Nineteenth-Century United States* (Madison, Wis., 1956); Morton J. Horwitz, *The Transformation of American Law, 1780–1860* (Cambridge, Mass., 1977). Hurst and Horwitz demonstrate the very different spins possible within a basically instrumentalist interpretation of law and economy. In Horwitz's view, law is sinisterly manipulated by the largest capitalists in alliance with an elite bar. For Hurst, law responds naturally to more consensual demands for a freeing up of creative economic energies and individual, entrepreneurial initiative. The other classic statements in this tradition are Lawrence M. Friedman, *A History of American Law*, 2d ed. (New York, 1985); Stanley I. Kutler, *Privilege and Creative Destruction: The Charles River Bridge Case* (New York, 1971); William E. Nelson, *Americanization of the Common Law: The Impact of Legal Change on Massachusetts Society, 1760–1830* (Cambridge, Mass., 1975); and

Hendrik Hartog, "Distancing Oneself from the Eighteenth Century: A Commentary on Changing Pictures of American Legal History," in *Law in the American Revolution and the Revolution in the Law*, ed. Hendrik Hartog (New York, 1981), 229–57. Hurst's *Law and Economic Growth: The Legal History of the Lumber Industry in Wisconsin, 1836–1915* (Cambridge, Mass., 1964) is perhaps the most subtle and extended demonstration of the formative influence of law in economy. The Wisconsin timber industry was almost completely dependent on state-created "conditions": land grants of the 35 million acres owned by the government, internal improvements like improved streams and the building of railroads, and the granting of such public privileges as corporate status, special licenses and franchises, and the power of eminent domain. In this work particularly, Hurst comes close to a theme later elaborated by critical legal historians that *all* markets are legally and socially constructed. See, for example, Robert W. Gordon, "Critical Legal Histories," *Stanford Law Review* 36 (1984): 57–125; Duncan Kennedy, "The Role of Law in Economic Thought: Essays on the Fetishism of Commodities," *American University Law Review* 34 (1985): 939–1001; Robert J. Steinfeld, "*The Philadelphia Cordwainers' Case* of 1806: The Struggle over Alternative Legal Constructions of a Free Market in Labor," in *Labor Law in America: Historical and Critical Essays*, ed. Christopher L. Tomlins and Andrew J. King (Baltimore, 1992), 20–43.

8. Arthur Selwyn Miller, *The Supreme Court and American Capitalism* (New York, 1968), 26. Here are some similar conclusions after reflecting on either commonwealth or legal/constitutional history. Cochran, *Frontiers of Change*, 21: "The most pervasive favorable factor in law, as in other institutions, was the culture itself, with its traditional bias toward the entrepreneur, or the person engaged in buying and selling." Bruchey, *Wealth of a Nation*, 65: "The Taney Court provided the legal foundation for a democratized capitalism." Robert Higgs, *The Transformation of Economy, 1865–1914: An Essay in Interpretation* (New York, 1971), 53: "[T]he Constitution laid the foundation of private property rights so as to curb the arbitrary powers of government and to promote the security required for the pursuit of productivity-raising activities of all kinds." Sellers, *The Market Revolution*, 47: "Lawyers were the shock troops of capitalism." More ominously, two of the most important new works in legal history have resurrected previously vanquished myths about nineteenth-century law and economics. Herbert Hovenkamp has suggested, "American constitutional law came to be built on the political economy of an unreconstructed Adam Smith." Morton Horwitz has returned to the one-dimensional notion of nineteenth-century law as a "buffer" between state and society, protecting private property and blocking public schemes to redistribute wealth. Herbert Hovenkamp, *Enterprise and American Law, 1836–1937* (Cambridge, Mass., 1991), 69; Morton J. Horwitz, *The Transformation of American Law, 1870–1960: The Crisis of Legal Orthodoxy* (New York, 1992), 9.

9. Helpful in reconstructing this interrelationship of police and economy are Marc Raeff, *The Well-Ordered Police State: Social and Institutional Change through Law in the Germanies and Russia, 1600–1800* (New Haven, Conn., 1983), 92–119; Albion W. Small, *The Cameralists: The Pioneers of German Social Polity* (Chicago, 1909); Michel Foucault, "Governmentality," in *The Foucault Effect: Studies in Governmentality*, ed. Graham Burchell, Colin Gordon, and Peter Miller (Chicago, 1991), 87–104, especially 92–93; Pasquale Pasquino, "*Theatrum Politicum*: The Genealogy of Capital—Police and the State of Prosperity," *Ideology and Consciousness* 4 (1978): 45; Steven C. A. Pincus, "From Holy Cause to Economic Interest: The Study of Population and the Invention of the State" (unpublished manuscript).

10. Emmerich de Vattel, *The Law of Nations*, ed. Edward D. Ingraham (Philadelphia, 1852), 33–47.

11. Charles B. Goodrich, *The Science of Government* (Boston, 1853), vi, 181.

12. *Oxford English Dictionary*, 2d ed. (Oxford, 1989), 5:60.

13. William Blackstone, *Commentaries on the Laws of England: A Facsimile of the First Edition of 1765–1769*, 4 vols. (Chicago, 1979), 4:161. William Crosskey cites a similar usage in a tract by Jeremy Dummer in 1745: "A great Minister once said to me, That the Regulation of [colonial] Charters must be look'd on as Part of *the publick Oeconomy*, and not as the Affair of any particular Person or Province." William W. Crosskey, *Politics and the Constitution in the History of the United States*, 2 vols. (Chicago, 1953), 2:1286, n. 82. See Crosskey generally in the text accompanying this note for a provocative discussion of the distinctions between early American usages of "public economy," "political economy," and "commercial economy."

14. Blackstone, *Commentaries*, 4:162. Under "offenses against public police or economy" Blackstone treated a wide variety of crimes and activities: clandestine marriage, bigamy and polygamy, idle and wandering soldiers and mariners (or those pretending to be such), "Egyptians" or "gypsies," *common nuisances* (which he defines as including offenses against "the public order *and oeconomical* regimen of the state"), annoyances in highways, bridges, and public rivers, the keeping of hogs in a city, disorderly inns or alehouses, bawdy houses, gaming houses, and unlicensed stage plays, lotteries, cottages harboring thieves or idle and dissolute persons, the making and selling of fireworks, eavesdroppers, common scolds, idleness, rogues and vagabonds, luxury and extravagant expenses in dress and diet, gambling, and the selling and hunting of game. Ibid., 163–75.

15. E. P. Thompson, "The Moral Economy of the English Crowd in the Eighteenth Century," in *Customs in Common: Studies in Traditional Popular Culture* (New York, 1991), 185–258. Karl Marx's best statement of the legal-political construction of the market is, of course, "The So-Called Primitive Accumulation," in *Capital: A Critique of Political Economy* (1867; International Publishers Edition, 3 vols., New York, 1967), 1:713–74. In the Thompson tradition, Douglas Hay dates the legal-political transformation with John Locke, who "distorted the oldest arguments of natural law to justify the liberation of wealth from all political or moral controls; he concluded that the unfettered accumulation of money, goods, and land was sanctioned by Nature and, implicitly, by God." Douglas Hay, "Property, Authority and the Criminal Law," in *Albion's Fatal Tree: Crime and Society in Eighteenth-Century England*, ed. Douglas Hay et al. (London, 1975), 17–63, 18.

16. As a mountain of social history has demonstrated, this does not mean that the United States was any more immune from class conflict and crowd actions in this period. See especially Paul Gilje, *The Road to Mobocracy: Popular Disorder in New York City, 1763–1834* (Chapel Hill, N.C., 1987).

17. Jon C. Teaford, *The Municipal Revolution in America: Origins of Modern Urban Government, 1650–1825* (Chicago, 1975), 39–43, 97–100; Robert H. Wiebe, *The Opening of American Society: From the Adoption of the Constitution to the Eve of Disunion* (New York, 1984). Richard L. McCormick, in summing up the contribution of the commonwealth studies to an understanding of antebellum economic policy, argued, "Forever giving things away, governments were laggard in regulating the economic activities they subsidized. . . . 'Policy' was little more than the accumulation of isolated, individual choices, usually of a distributive nature." McCormick, "The Party Period and Public Policy: An Exploratory Hypothesis," *Journal of American History* 66 (1979): 279, 284–85.

18. *Constitution of the United States*, art. 1, sec. 8: "The Congress shall have power . . . to regulate commerce with foreign nations, and among the several states, and with the Indian tribes."

19. Nathan Dane, *A General Abridgment and Digest of American Law*, 8 vols. (Boston, 1823), 4:728. Dane's organization of crimes against public policy closely mirrors Blackstones. For Blackstone's list of crimes against public trade, see *Commentaries*, 4:154–60. Also see Matthew Hale, *The Prerogatives of the King*, ed. D. E. C. Yale (London, 1976), 286–321.

20. Dane, *Abridgment*, 6:728–55; 7:33–111.

21. Ibid., 6:744. Throughout this section, my generalizations will be based on a close reading of statute books in Massachusetts, Maryland, South Carolina, Michigan, and Ohio.

22. *The General Laws of Massachusetts, 1780–1835*, ed. Asaheal Stearns and Theron Metcalf, 4 vols. (Boston, 1823–36), 1:88, 170, 200, 391, 519; 2:20, 15, 28, 46, 16, 85, 156, 212, 174, 198, 253, 339, 357, 437, 445, 566; 3:84, 268, 348; 4:109, 106.

23. *The General Public Statutory Law and Public Local Law of the State of Maryland, 1692–1839*, ed. Clement Dorsey, 3 vols. (Baltimore, 1840); *The Statutes at Large of South Carolina, 1682–1838*, ed. David J. McCord, 10 vols. (Columbia, S.C., 1841); *The Revised Statutes of the State of Michigan* (Detroit, 1838); *Statutes of Ohio and of the Northwestern Territory Adopted or Enacted from 1788 to 1833*, ed. Salmon P. Chase (Cincinnati, 1835).

24. "An Act to regulate the Inspection of Salted Fish," in Dorsey, *Law of Maryland*, 2 (1817), c. 114, 1483–94. See also, "An Act to prevent Fraud and Deception in the Packing of Pickled Fish, and to regulate the Size and Quality of Casks, and the Sale and Exportation thereof within and from this Commonwealth," Stearns and Metcalf, *Laws of Massachusetts*, 2 (1810), c. 120, 253–57.

25. Dorsey, *Law of Maryland*, 2:1483–84. Barrels, casks, hoops, and staves were a constant focus of antebellum legislation. Prior to 1841, South Carolina had enacted some eighty-seven provisions respecting barrels. McCord, *Statutes at Large of South Carolina, 1632–1835*, 10:41–42.

26. Dorsey, *Law of Maryland*, 2:1484–85. Inspectors received a fee for each barrel inspected and were given broad powers to condemn or to order barrels repacked and repickled. In 1818, the inspector was given further power to discharge any coopers producing barrels for fish that did not meet statutory requirements. Ibid., 1489.

27. In Maryland the oath was: "I, A.B. do swear, or affirm, according to the best of my knowledge and belief, the certificate hereunto annexed contains the whole quantity of pickled and barrelled fish on board the _____, _____ master, and that no fish is shipped on board said vessel for the ship's company, or on freight or cargo, but what is inspected and branded according to the law of this state; so help me God." Ibid., 1486.

28. See Stearns and Metcalf, *Laws of Massachusetts*, 1 (1783), 88; 1 (1796), 519; 2 (1799), 4.

29. From 1789 to 1818, Boston's town officers included: 9 selectmen, 12 overseers of the poor, 12 members of the school committee, 3 auditors, 24 firewards, 20 surveyors of lumber, 4 cullers of hoops and staves, 10 cullers of dry fish, 4 fence viewers, 4 hogreeves and haywards, 2 surveyors of hemp, 2 surveyors of wheat, 2 assay masters, and 2 inspectors of lime. *By-Laws and Orders of the Town of Boston* (Boston, 1818), 3–4. Also see Stearns and Metcalf, *Laws of Massachusetts*, 1 (1786), 250. Municipalities backed up their appointments with dollars. In early Philadelphia, salaries for clerks of the market and corders of wood exceeded the budget for watering the city. *Ordinances of the Corporation of the City of Philadelphia*, ed. John C. Lowber (Philadelphia, 1812), 208–9.

30. Stearns and Metcalf, *Laws of Massachusetts* 2 (1799), 11. An 1815 Massachusetts law recommended seven years hard labor for all persons "who knowingly and designedly, by false pretense or pretences, shall obtain from any person or persons, money goods, wares, merchandize or other things, with intent to cheat or defraud any person or persons of the

same." Ibid., 2 (1815), 403. *Laws of New York*, 1 (1813), c. 30, 376; Dorsey, *Law of Maryland*, 1 (1825), c. 206, 864; *Laws of New York*, 1 (1813), c. 44, 75.

31. An example of this overall concern for fairness and assurance of quality is the procedure prescribed for the economic transfer of hides and skins from butchers or slaughterers to leather manufacturers in Baltimore. Such a transaction could not take place without the intervention of an inspector who would stamp each hide for damage (holes, cuts, slashes, or wounds) and deduct total damages from the purchase price of a prime hide. Furthermore, the inspectors were charged with keeping a regular record of the damages to every hide slaughtered by Baltimore butchers, and butchers were subsequently fined for such damage. Dorsey, *Law of Maryland*, 2 (1831), c. 245, 1503; 2 (1835), c. 270, 1506; 2 (1831), c. 103, 1507. Also see the restrictions on usury: Stearns and Metcalf, *Laws of Massachusetts*, 1 (1784), 138; 3 (1826), 150; Dorsey, *Law of Maryland*, 1 (1704), c. 69, 5; *Laws of New York*, 1 (1813), c. 13, 64; McCord, *Statutes at Large of South Carolina, 1632–1838*, 10:307.

32. Historians have prematurely proclaimed the death of "mercantilist" restraints and economic controls like those just described at various points in the late eighteenth and early nineteenth century (part and parcel of the "market revolution" and the "Americanization" of law). But despite some legislative lapses and occasional temporary acts of repeal, the bulk of these kinds of regulations were intact at the Civil War. See, for example, *The General Statutes of the Commonwealth of Massachusetts* (Boston, 1860), especially title 13, "Of the Regulation of Trade in Certain Cases," 256–98; and title 15, "Of the Internal Police of the Commonwealth," 390–464. Perhaps one of the most significant lapses in the antebellum era was New York's repeal of its inspection laws in the constitutional convention of 1846. Article 5, section 8, of its new constitution stated: "All offices for the weighing, measuring, culling or inspecting of any merchandise, produce, manufacture or commodity whatever, are hereby abolished." The law excepted such offices created for public health, property, revenue, tolls, and weights and measures. It was not long, however, before such regulatory offices began creeping back into New York's public economy. See *Tinkham v. Tapscott*, 17 N.Y. 141 (1858).

33. *Mayor of Mobile v. Yuille*, 3 Ala. 137, 36 Am. Dec. 441 (1841), 445. Also see Stearns and Metcalf, *Laws of Massachusetts*, 2 (1800), c. 76, 46. *Turner v. Maryland*, 107 U.S. 38 (1882).

34. Antebellum licensing is an enormous and messy topic that I can only touch on here. The distinctions between and consequences of licensing for the purposes of prohibition, regulation, revenue, and administration are the subjects of great debate. It is clear, however, that licensing was used for all four purposes in the antebellum era. Though by the late nineteenth-century they were often classified with revenue laws, licensing statutes in their strongest form, as prohibitory legislation, remained a vital part of the state's public policymaking arsenal. For the best discussions of licensing, see Thomas M. Cooley, *A Treatise on the Law of Taxation* (Chicago, 1876), 403–15; John F. Dillon, *Commentaries on the Law of Municipal Corporations*, 3d ed., 2 vols. (Boston, 1881), 1:356–51; Ernst Freund, *Administrative Powers over Persons and Property: A Comparative Survey* (Chicago, 1928), 59–128; Ernst Freund, "Licensing," in *Encyclopedia of the Social Sciences* (New York, 1933), 9:447–51; "Power of State to Exact Licenses, and Charge Therefore," *American Decisions* 52 (1886): 331–35; and Malcolm B. Parsons, *The Use of Licensing Power by the City of Chicago* (Urbana, Ill., 1952).

35. Cooley, *Taxation*, 406.

36. Even today, licensing is formally understood as conferring a right or power that would not exist otherwise. *Corpus Juris Secundum*, ed. Arnold O. Ginnow and Milorad Nikolic (St. Paul, Minn., 1987), vol. 53, 323. Parsons, *The Use of Licensing Power*, 1; *Inter-City Coach Lines v. Harrison*, 172 Ga. 390 (1930).

37. Dorsey, *Law of Maryland*, 2 (1827), c. 117, 928.

38. Ibid., 2:1085. Also see Maryland acts of 1828, c. 85; 1829, c. 217; 1830, c. 184; 1831, c. 262; 1834, c. 232; 1837, c. 124.

39. *French v. Baker*, 36 Tenn. 193 (1856). Also see *Adams v. Mayor of Somerville*, 39 Tenn. 363 (1859), which upheld a Tennessee act granting a municipal corporation the power to "license, tax, and regulate auctioneers, grocers, merchants, retailers, brokers, coffee-houses, confectioneries, retailers of liquors, hawkers, pedlers, livery stable keepers, negro traders, and tavern keepers." *Laws of Tennessee* (1854), c. 17; *Laws of Missouri* (1859), 53; *Missouri v. Whittaker*, 33 Mo. 457 (1863); *Berks County v. Bertolet*, 13 Pa. St. 522 (1850); *Laws of Pennsylvania* (1846), 486–91; *City and County of Sacramento v. Crocker*, 16 Cal. 119 (1860). Revenue was certainly one of the main motivations of these later statutes. Like the original Maryland statute, these acts consistently exempted farmers or mechanics selling their own produce. This attempt to favor the sellers of their own products versus middlemen or profiteers can also be seen in market laws and restrictions against forestalling, regrating, and engrossing.

40. *Alabama Acts of the General Assembly* (1868), 329–35. *Cousins v. State*, 50 Ala. 113 (1874).

41. *Laws of Tennessee* (1881), c. 69.

42. Stearns and Metcalf, *Laws of Massachusetts*, 1 (1786), 297–304.

43. *Rex v. Ivens*, 7 Car. & P. 213 (Eng., 1835), 219.

44. Ibid., 302; Daniel Davis, *A Practical Treatise upon the Authority and Duty of Justices of the Peace* (Boston, 1824), 255. These provisions remained relatively unchanged throughout the period in Massachusetts. See Stearns and Metcalf, *Laws of Massachusetts*, 3 (1830), 375; *The General Statutes of the Commonwealth of Massachusetts* (1860), 455–57.

45. McCord, *Statutes at Large of South Carolina, 1632–1838*, 10 (1785), 236–37; Dorsey, *Law of Maryland*, 1 (1780), c. 24, 158.

46. Dorsey, *Law of Maryland*, 3 (1827), c. 111, 1433–43; *Laws of New York*, 2 (1813), c. 70, 181–87; Stearns and Metcalf, *Laws of Massachusetts*, 1 (1795), 473; 3 (1823), 20. The number of auctioneers in Baltimore was limited to twenty, in New York City to thirty-six. See generally Joseph Bateman, *A Practical Treatise on the Law of Auctions* (Boston, 1883). See also *Commonwealth v. Passmore*, 1 Serg. & R. 217 (Pa., 1814).

47. *Laws and Ordinances Ordained and Established by the Mayor, Aldermen, and Commonalty of the City of New-York* (New York, 1799), 42–60; *Laws of New York* (1813), 2:446.

48. *Ordinances of New York*, 42–43. At least temporarily, Massachusetts regulated wheels on all common highways. See Stearns and Metcalf, *Laws of Massachusetts*, 3 (1827), 211; 4 (1832), 32.

49. *Ordinances of New York*, 45.

50. Dorsey, *Law of Maryland*, 2 (1836), c. 285, 1472. These statutes were but surface expressions of rich and contested social and urban histories. See Isaac S. Lyon, *Recollections of an Old Cartman* (Newark, N.J., 1872); and Graham Russell Hodges, *New York City Cartmen, 1667–1850* (New York, 1986).

51. *Vandine's Case*, 23 Mass. 187 (1828).

52. "An Act concerning Hawkers, Pedlars, and Petty Chapmen," in Stearns and Metcalf, *Laws of Massachusetts*, 2 (1821), c. 45, 540–41; *Laws of New York*, 2 (1813), c. 9, 228; Dorsey, *Law of Maryland*, 1 (1784), c. 7, 182; McCord, *Statutes at Large of South Carolina, 1632–1838*, 6 (1831), 529. Also see Richardson Wright, *Hawkers and Walkers in Early America* (Philadelphia, 1927); J. R. Dolan, *The Yankee Peddlers of Early America* (New York, 1964).

53. Butchers: *Laws of New York*, 2 (1813), c. 272, 446. Bakers: *Mayor of Mobile v. Yuille*. Grocers: McCord, *Statutes at Large of South Carolina, 1632–1838*, 7 (1821), 142, *Thomas v. Town of Vernon*, 9 Oh. 290 (1839). Lawyers: Dorsey, *Law of Maryland*, 1 (1810), c. 126, 601

(setting fees); Stearns and Metcalf, *Laws of Massachusetts*, 1 (1785), 199; McCord, *Statutes at Large of South Carolina, 1632–1838*, 5 (1786), 289. In 1811, South Carolina passed a statute prohibiting ordinaries of the state from practicing law. See *Administrators of Byrne v. Administrators of Stewart*, 3 Des. Eq. 466 (S.C., 1812). Doctors: McCord, *Statutes at Large of South Carolina, 1632–1838*, 6:497 (1833); *Laws of New York*, 2 (1813), c. 94, 219; Stearns and Metcalf, *Laws of Massachusetts*, 2 (1818), 438; 2 (1819), 490. For a more comprehensive listing of cases and statutes, see the indexes to the *Century Digest* and the *American Law Reports*.

54. Dorsey, *Law of Maryland*, 1 (1805), c. 80, 510; *People v. Naglee*, 1 Calif. 232 (1850).

55. *Laws of New York*, 2 (1813), c. 261, 443. As urban historians have suggested, this technique was widespread in the nineteenth century. In New Orleans, the Mississippi was the cure for mangy and measly meat. *Ordinances Ordained and Established by the Mayor and City Council of the City of New-Orleans* (New Orleans, 1817), 124.

56. Stearns and Metcalf, *Laws of Massachusetts*, 1 (1785), 182 (emphasis added). Dane, *Abridgment*, 7:33, 48.

57. Dane, *Abridgment*, 205. Also see Dorsey, *Law of Maryland*, 2 (1788), c. 17, 1547. Blackstone defined the distinctions between forestalling, regrating, and engrossing as follows: Forestalling was "the buying or contracting for any merchandise or victual coming in the way to market; or dissuading persons from bringing their goods or provisions there; or persuading them to enhance the price when there. Regrating was . . . the buying of corn, or other dead victual, in any market, and selling it again in the same market, or within four miles of the place. . . . Engrossing was . . . the getting into one's possession, or buying up, large quantities of corn or other dead victuals, with intent to sell them again. This must of course be injurious to the public, by putting it in the power of one or two rich men to raise the price of provisions at their own discretion." Blackstone, *Commentaries*, 4:158. Though Dane equivocated on the *enforcement* of laws against forestalling, the market cases that follow indicate that they were taken very seriously.

58. Jean-Christophe Agnew, "The Threshold of Exchange: Speculations on the Market," *Radical History Review* 21 (1979): 109; Agnew, *Worlds Apart: The Market and Theater in Anglo-American Thought, 1550–1750* (Cambridge, 1986).

59. Frederic William Maitland, *Domesday Book and Beyond: Three Essays in the Early History of England* (1897; Cambridge, 1987), 192–95.

60. Agnew, "The Threshold of Exchange," 99–118; Cornelius Walford, *Fairs, Past and Present: A Chapter in the History of Commerce* (London, 1883), 1–11; Vernon A. Mund, *Open Markets: An Essential of Free Enterprise* (New York, 1948), 3–31.

61. Maitland, *Domesday*, 193–94; Mund, *Open Markets*, 32–51; Hale, *The Prerogatives of the King*, 313–17; Joseph Chitty, *A Treatise on the Law of the Prerogatives of the Crown* (London, 1820), 193–96; Susan Henderson, "Out of the Ashes: The Great Fire and the Transformation of London's Public Markets," *Radical History Review* 21 (1979): 119–30.

62. *Rex v. Marsden*, 3 Burr. 1812 (Eng., 1765), 1818.

63. These regulations were the product of a variety of English grants and statutes. For a quick sense of these see Matthew Bacon, *A New Abridgment of the Law*, ed. John Bouvier, 10 vols. (Philadelphia, 1876), 4:154–64; Earl of Halsbury, *The Laws of England* (London, 1911), 20:4–59; Blackstone, *Commentaries*, 4:158–59, 272. The ancient etymology of the market also hints at the public objectives. As Vernon Mund points out in his nicely researched but curiously argued book, sometimes a market was known as a "cheaping" from the Old English "ceap" (cheap), which meant "to bargain." One of the initial London markets was Cheapside. Early market laws, especially those aimed at forestalling, were certainly meant to ensure reasonable prices on country produce. The linkages between "market," "fair,"

and "fairness" are also fairly obvious. Mund, *Open Markets*, 57, n. 20; Agnew, "Threshold of Exchange," n. 33.

64. For the most comprehensive discussion of colonial and revolutionary era markets, see Carl Bridenbaugh, *Cities in the Wilderness: The First Century of Urban Life in America, 1625–1742* (London, 1938), 27–29, 192–95, 349–53; and Bridenbaugh, *Cities in Revolt: Urban Life in America, 1743–1776* (Oxford, 1955), 24, 80–82, 278. David Hackett Fisher, *Albion's Seed: Four British Folkways in America* (New York, 1989).

65. Teaford, *Municipal Revolution*, 39–43, 97–100; Nelson, *Americanization of the Common Law*, 145–64; Sidney Irving Pomerantz, *New York: An American City, 1783–1803* (New York, 1938), 170–78. Pomerantz argued that by 1801, "Paternalism was giving way to laissez-faire and more reliance was being placed on 'free competition' than on municipal by-laws" (172). Most adherents to this view have limited their primary research to Boston and New York City where market regulations did undergo several roller-coaster rides in the eighteenth and nineteenth centuries. At different points in time, market restrictions were repealed in these cities only to be reactivated at a later date. For a more subtle look at the complex forces and motivations behind New York City's market and trade regulations, see Howard B. Rock, *Artisans of the New Republic: The Tradesmen of New York City in the Age of Jefferson* (New York, 1979), 205–34; Sean Wilentz, *Chants Democratic: New York City and The Rise of the American Working Class, 1788–1850* (New York, 1984), 137–40; Hendrik Hartog, *Public Property and Private Power: The Corporation of the City of New York in American Law, 1730–1870* (Chapel Hill, N.C., 1983), 38–40, 151–54. Also see Thomas F. DeVoe, *The Market Book: A History of the Public Markets of the City of New York* (1862; reprint, New York, 1970). Richard Wade has suggested that in the exact period of time Jon Teaford proclaims the victory of free trade in New York, Boston, and Philadelphia, Pittsburgh, Cincinnati, and St. Louis were constructing elaborate new market buildings and tightening public regulations. Richard C. Wade, *The Urban Frontier: Pioneer Life in Early Pittsburgh, Cincinnati, Lexington, Louisville, and St. Louis* (Chicago, 1959), 280–82.

66. John F. Dillon, *Commentaries on the Law of Municipal Corporations*, 2d ed. (New York, 1873), secs. 313–25.

67. Benjamin Colman, *Some Reasons and Arguments Offered to the Good People of Boston and Adjacent Places for the Setting Up Markets in Boston* (Boston, 1719), 6; *Faneuil Hall Leases*, city doc. 23 (Boston, 1856), State Historical Society of Wisconsin Pamphlet Collection, 4–5. For a further discussion of Colman's argument, see Teaford, *Municipal Revolution*, 39–41.

68. On price controls, see DeVoe, *The Market Book*, 141–44; Dane, *Abridgment*, 39–40.

69. James Mease, *The Picture of Philadelphia* (Philadelphia, 1811), 116; Joseph Jackson, *Encyclopedia of Philadelphia* (Harrisburg, Pa., 1932), 3:874; Bridenbaugh, *Cities in Wilderness*, 28.

70. "Regulations for the Markets of Philadelphia, 1693," *Pennsylvania Magazine of History and Biography* 23 (1900): 408–9.

71. This provision for donating penalties to the poor was not uncommon in antebellum economic regulations. See, for example, "An Act to prevent Fraud in Firewood, Bark or Coal Exposed to Sale," in Stearns and Metcalf, *Laws of Massachusetts*, 1 (1796), 519; 1 (1785), 193. There is a nice symmetry in the idea that proceeds from economic crimes should go to those economically deprived.

72. An exception was made for the reselling of goods that had been in the market for two hours after the opening bell. The constant presence of forestalling as a legislative rationale for the establishment and regulation of urban markets should caution us against dismissing the importance of laws against forestalling (and its cousins regrating and engrossing) be-

cause of scant evidence of indictments. The informal and summary powers given the clerk or commissioner of the market may have kept the number of formal, recorded indictments low. In any event, much more quantitative research needs to be done on nineteenth-century mayor's courts, police courts, and justices of the peace before concluding that these crimes were not prosecuted. Dane, *Abridgment*, 7:33. For other state controls, see McCord, *Statutes at Large of South Carolina, 1632–1838*, 4 (1785), 652 (Winnsborough); 5 (1787), 21 (Georgetown); 9 (1739), 692 (Charlestown market). For further discussion of the enforcement question, see chapter 2, n. 46.

73. Agnes Addison Gilchrist, "Market Houses in High Street," in *Historic Philadelphia: From the Founding until the Early Nineteenth Century*, ed. American Philosophical Society (Philadelphia, 1953), 304–12; Mease, *Picture of Philadelphia*, 117; Jackson, *Encyclopedia of Philadelphia*, 3:874; Bridenbaugh, *Cities in Wilderness*, 193, 349–50.

74. *Ordinances of the Corporation of the City of Philadelphia*, ed. John C. Lowber (Philadelphia, 1812), 149–60. These regulations were from "An ordinance for the regulation of the Market held in High-Street" originally passed in 1798, but still in effect in 1812. Enforcement of these regulations is a tricky historical issue. James Mease, writing in 1811, hinted that cellars of houses near the market were often used for selling and huckstering, on the other hand he also suggested that butter, lard, and sausages were often seized by the clerks of the market for being deficient in weight. Mease, *Picture of Philadelphia*, 120, 122. See also Margaret B. Tinkcom, "The New Market in Second Street," *Pennsylvania Magazine of History and Biography* 82 (1958): 379–97.

75. Quoted in Tinkcom, "New Market in Second Street," 392.

76. Ibid., 395; Jackson, *Encyclopedia*, 3:876. On the general evolution of markets in New Orleans, see Robert A. Sauder, "The Origin and Spread of the Public Market System in New Orleans," *Louisiana History* 22 (1981): 281–97.

77. *Digest of the Ordinances of the City Council of Charleston, 1783–1818*, ed. John Geddes (Charleston, S.C., 1818), 147; *By-Laws and Orders of the Town of Boston*, 36–38, 48; *Ordinances Ordained and Established by the Mayor and City Council of the City of New-Orleans*, 124; *A Law to Regulate the Public Markets* (New York, 1814).

78. *Ash v. People*, 11 Mich. 347 (1863); *Shelton v. Mayor of Mobile*, 30 Ala. 540 (1857); *City of St. Paul v. Laidler*, 2 Minn. 159 (1858); *City of Cincinnati v. Buckingham*, 10 Oh. 257 (1840); *Iowa and Dubuque v. Leiber*, 11 Ia. 407 (1861); *City of St. Louis v. Jackson*, 25 Mo. 37 (1857); *Ketchum v. City of Buffalo and Austin*, 14 N.Y. 356 (1856); *Peck v. City of Austin*, 22 Tx. 261 (1858).

79. *Wartman v. City of Philadelphia*, 33 Pa. St. 202 (1859), 209.

80. *Wartman*, 209; also see *Woelpper v. City of Philadelphia*, 38 Pa. St. 203 (1861).

81. *Laws of New York* (1801), c. 130; *Laws of New York* (1822), c. 258, 293. Poughkeepsie was also given power to regulate the assize of bread, though it was expressly prohibited from fixing any other prices of provisions.

82. *Bush v. Seabury*, 8 Johns. R. 418 (N.Y., 1811); *Village of Buffalo v. Webster*, 10 Wend. 99 (N.Y., 1833).

83. *Bush*, 420.

84. *Webster*, 100, 101; *Pierce v. Bartrum*, 1 Cowp. 269 (Eng., 1775). These cases and the ones to follow show a seriousness about *enforcing* market regulations. At issue in each of these cases is a fine or other penalty enforced by a local court that is then reviewed usually by a state's highest tribunal. The number of cases that make it to state supreme courts are indicative of a good deal more lower court and informal, summary enforcement.

85. *Commonwealth v. Nightingale*, Thach. Crim. Cas. 251 (Mass., 1830); *Nightingale's Case*, 11 Pick. 168 (Mass., 1831).

86. Hayward also testified that Nightingale had been thrown out of the market once before for forestalling. *Commonwealth v. Nightingale*, 253.

87. Ibid., 257.

88. Pickering, the city solicitor, cited *Pierce v. Bartrum*, as well as *Vandine's Case*, 23 Mass. 187 (1828), upholding the licensing of cartmen; *Vanderbilt v. Adams*, 7 Cow. 349 (N.Y., 1827), upholding the regulation of harbors; and *Coates v. Mayor of New York*, 7 Cow. 585 (N.Y., 1827), upholding the regulation of cemeteries, to place market regulations squarely in a legitimated tradition of police regulation.

89. *Nightingale's Case*, 171.

90. *Commonwealth v. Rice*, 9 Metc. 253 (Mass., 1845).

91. Ibid., 256, 258–59. For Shaw's opinion on the legitimacy of taxation for the purposes of erecting market houses, see *Spaulding v. City of Lowell*, 23 Pick. 71 (Mass., 1839).

92. *Cincinnati v. Buckingham*, 10 Oh. 257 (1840) (fees); *City of Raleigh v. Sorrell*, 1 Jones Law 49 (N.C., 1853) (weights); *Hatch v. Pendergast*, 15 Md. 251 (1859) (eviction).

93. *City Council of Charleston v. Goldsmith*, 2 Spear's Law 428 (S.C., 1844).

94. Ibid., 429, 435.

95. *Cincinnati v. Buckingham*, 261–62.

96. *Bethune v. Hughes*, 28 Ga. 560; 73 Am. Dec. 789 (1859); *City of St. Paul v. Laidler*, 2 Minn. 159, 72 Am. Dec. 89 (1858); *Caldwell v. City of Alton*, 33 Ill. 416, 85 Am. Dec. 282 (1864). The Georgia Supreme Court later upheld an identical prohibition in Atlanta because that municipality had explicit legislative authorization to regulate the market. In 1866, the Minnesota Supreme Court allowed the strict licensing of the sale of meats outside the public market. *Badkins v. Robinson*, 53 Ga. 613 (1875); *City of St. Paul v. Colter*, 12 Minn. 41 (1866).

97. *Bethune v. Hughes*, 791–93. Also see Lumpkin's opinion in *Mayor and Council of Atlanta v. White & Kreis*, 33 Ga. 229 (1862). Like *Laidler* and *Caldwell v. Alton*, the issue in *Bethune* was whether the legislature actually delegated the power to prohibit trade outside the market to the municipality. Judge Lumpkin explicitly refused to rule on whether the state legislature itself had such a power. *Bethune*, 791.

98. Also see *St. Paul v. Laidler*, 93, on the Minnesota court's fears of a city monopoly and special grants to political partisans and friends.

99. *City of St. Louis v. Jackson*; *City of St. Louis v. Weber*, 44 Mo. 547 (1869); *Ash v. People*; *Shelton v. Mayor of Mobile*; *Davenport v. Kelly*, 7 Ia. 102 (1858); *Town Council of Winnsboro v. Smart*, 11 Rich. 551 (S.C. Law, 1858); *City of Bowling Green v. Carson*, 73 Ky. 64 (1873). Also see the earlier decisions of New York Chief Justice Nelson in *City of Brooklyn v. Cleves*, Hill & Denio 231 (N.Y., suppl., 1843); *Mayor of Rochester v. Rood*, Hill & Denio 146 (N.Y., suppl., 1843); *Trustees of Rochester v. Pettinger*, 17 Wend. 265 (N.Y., 1837).

100. *City of St. Louis v. Weber*, 551. Bliss was upholding a fine against a private butcher shop. His opinion followed the earlier Missouri precedent *City of St. Louis v. Jackson*.

101. *City of St. Louis v. Weber*, 551.

102. *Badkins v. Robinson*, 615. *Nagle v. City Council of Augusta*, 5 Ga. 546 (1848); *Green v. Mayor and Aldermen of Savannah*, 6 Ga. 1 (1849); *Whitten v. Mayor and Council of Covington*, 43 Ga. 421 (1871); *Perdue v. Ellis*, 18 Ga. 586 (1855).

103. *City of New Orleans v. Stafford*, 27 La. Ann. 417; 21 Am. Rep. 563 (1875), 564; Sauder, "Public Market System in New Orleans," 286. Also see the earlier New Orleans market decisions *Morano v. Mayor*, 2 La. 217 (1831); *First Municipality v. Cutting*, 4 La. Ann. 335 (1849). Also see *Cougot v. City of New Orleans*, 16 La. Ann. 21 (1861); *City of New Orleans v. Heirs of Guillotte*, 12 La. Ann. 818 (1857) (especially the dissent of Chief Justice Merrick).

104. The original 1866 act contained the provision that all private markets were still "subject to the general sanitary ordinances of the city council." New Orleans passed a

licensing statute in 1873 charging $300 for the privilege of keeping a private market. In 1874, the Louisiana legislature enacted the twelve-mile prohibition. *City of New Orleans v. Stafford*, 564.

105. Ibid.

106. *City of New Orleans v. Stafford*, 563, 565. As in the *Slaughterhouse Cases*, 83 U.S. 36 (1872), the defendant alleged that fraud, bribery, and corruption by state and local officials suffused the administration of New Orleans market laws. And indeed, there is no question that the *public revenues* of public markets were an important motivation for regulation by the 1870s. Part of the city's case against this private grocery was that it was subjecting New Orleans to a pecuniary loss of $1,000. See Sauder, "Public Market System in New Orleans," 287–89.

107. In this sense, Thomas McCraw is exactly right in finding a shift in regulatory strategy and procedure (though not regulation's birth) in the late nineteenth century. Thomas K. McCraw, *Prophets of Regulation* (Cambridge, Mass., 1984).

108. Atiyah, *The Rise and Fall of Freedom of Contract*, 562.

109. For an early statement of this position, see Gerard Carl Henderson, *The Position of Foreign Corporations in American Constitutional Law* (Cambridge, Mass., 1918). More recent expressions can be found in Hovenkamp, *Enterprise*, 11–41; and James Willard Hurst, *The Legitimacy of the Business Corporation in the Law of the United States, 1780–1970* (Charlottesville, Va., 1970). This work contains one of the clearest statements of Hurst's instrumentalism: "Corporation law has always been an instrument of wants and energies derived from sources outside the law; it has not been a prime mover. . . . We must not exaggerate the influence of men of law compared with the inventions and energies of promoters, financiers, managers, marketing men, trade union leaders, and a host of others. In the whole course of affairs lawyers produced only marginal effect." Hurst, *Business Corporation*, 10–11.

110. Quoted in Morton Keller, *Regulating a New Economy: Public Policy and Economic Change in America, 1900–1933* (Cambridge, Mass., 1990), 6.

111. Some states pioneered general incorporation very early (New York in 1811, Connecticut in 1837, New Jersey in 1846, Ohio in 1856), but it was not until 1875 that constitutional amendments made special charters obsolete for most enterprises in most states. See George Heberton Evans Jr., *Business Incorporations in the United States, 1800–1943* (New York, 1948), 10–12.

112. Adolf A. Berle and Gardiner C. Means, *The Modern Corporation and Private Property*, rev. ed. (New York, 1968), 11; Joseph S. Davis, *Essays in the Earlier History of American Corporations*, 2 vols. (Cambridge, Mass., 1917), 2:24–27.

113. Hurst, *Business Corporation*, 14–15; Hartz, *Economic Policy and Democratic Thought*, 38.

114. The language quoted is from Roger Taney in *Bank of Augusta v. Earle*, 13 Peters 519 (U.S., 1839), 588. John Marshall's classic statement appeared in *Dartmouth College v. Woodward*, 4 Wheat. 518 (1819), 636: "A corporation is an artificial being, invisible, intangible, and existing only in contemplation of law. Being the mere creature of law, it possesses only those properties which the charter of its creation confers upon it, either expressly, or as incidental to its very existence."

115. Ernst Freund, *The Police Power: Public Policy and Constitutional Rights* (Chicago, 1904), 358.

116. Ernst Freund lists the following as typical, general statutory restrictions: "The objects for which corporations may be organized: conditions as to minimum number of organizers, and sometimes as to their residence; conditions as to denomination of shares and their transferability; manner of organization, name, subscription and payment of capital, and

preliminary contracts; regarding officers and members rights, including general meetings, right to vote, qualification and number of directors, their election, term of office, and removal, the power to make and alter bye-laws; the management of corporate business, including payment of dividends, acquisition and disposition of real estate, and the contracting of loans; liability and power to assess; increase and reduction of capital; change of name and purposes; duration, extension, liquidation, consolidation; registration of officers and shareholders; and requirement of accounts and reports." Freund, *Police Power*, 359.

Willard Hurst provides examples of more particular reservations: "Distinctive to transportation company charters were statutory stipulations for provision of promised facilities (that, on pain of forfeiture, minimum capital be subscribed and paid in, operations begin within some specified time, and works be kept in good order and not abandoned), for tolls to be within set minimum and maximum levels, to be fair and reasonable, and to be conditioned on substantial service, and for certain operations reports to be regularly filed. Distinctive to bank charters were particular requirements as to minimum capital paid in, specie reserves, personal liability of bank directors for various kinds of misconduct, special liability of stockholders for debts of the bank, and the rendering of reports and the opening of books to legislative inquiry. Distinctive to insurance company charters was a slow elaboration of special financial regulations, directed at creating an adequate insurance fund and protecting its integrity against careless or fraudulent diversion." Hurst, *Business Corporation*, 39.

117. In addition to the sources cited, see E. Merrick Dodd Jr., *American Business Corporations until 1860* (Cambridge, Mass., 1954); John W. Cadman Jr., *The Corporation in New Jersey: Business and Politics, 1791–1875* (Cambridge, Mass., 1949); Oscar Handlin and Mary F. Handlin, "Origins of the American Business Corporation," in *Enterprise and Secular Change*, ed. Frederic C. Lane and Jelle C. Riemersma (Homewood, Ill., 1953), 102–24.

118. *Dartmouth College v. Woodward*; *Charles River Bridge v. Warren Bridge*, 11 Pet. 420 (U.S., 1837); *Santa Clara v. Southern Pacific Railroad*, 118 U.S. 394 (1886).

119. As Hovenkamp defined it, "Classical political economy was dedicated to the principle that the state could encourage economic development best by leaving entrepreneurs alone, free of both regulation and subsidy." Hovenkamp, *Enterprise*, 11–13.

120. Horwitz, *Transformation, 1780–1880*, 112–13. By the time of *Dartmouth College*, Horwitz suggests, "the conception of the corporation as a public body had been on the decline for almost a generation."

121. Hovenkamp, *Enterprise*, 25; Hurst, *Law and the Conditions of Freedom*, 27–29; Kutler, *Privilege and Creative Destruction: The Charles River Bridge Case*; Kermit L. Hall, *The Magic Mirror: Law in American History* (New York, 1989), 117–18; Oscar Handlin and Mary Handlin, *The Dimensions of Liberty* (New York, 1966), 98. Willard Hurst is one of the few historians to remain always keenly aware of the ongoing role of the state in the legal history of the American business corporation. But even Hurst displays a strong affinity for the role of classical political economy and constitutional limitations in nineteenth-century public policy: "The idea of constitutionally limited government—with its insistence that the state should use its power only for purposes of public interest and should not intervene in affairs merely of private concern—assumed that most business was 'private' precisely because the nonofficial discipline of the market existed to keep oppressive or wasteful practices from reaching such proportions as to make them properly subjects of 'public' attention. This proposition was present, though mostly implied, in the earlier years when the simple conditions of society offered little occasion to bring the matter to explicit statement. Locke grounded the moral legitimacy of private property on the assumption that men apply their labor to resources in situations 'where there is enough and as good left in common for others.' Jefferson urged that the guiding principle of legal order should be to achieve 'a wise

and frugal government, which shall restrain men from injuring one another, which shall leave them otherwise free to regulate their own pursuits of industry and improvement, and shall not take from the mouth of labor the bread it has earned.'" Hurst, *Business Corporation*, 41.

122. See Morton J. Horwitz, "*Santa Clara* Revisited: The Development of Corporate Theory," *West Virginia Law Review* 88 (1985): 173–224; Herbert Hovenkamp, "The Classical Corporation in American Legal Thought," *Georgetown Law Journal* 76 (1988): 1593–1689.

123. Some states had already experimented with such reservation clauses. See, for example, *Laws of Massachusetts*, sec. 7 (1809). The clause read: "*Provided always*, That the Legislature may from time to time, upon due notice to any corporation, make further provisions, and regulations for the management of the business of the corporation, and for the government thereof, or wholly to repeal any act, or part thereof, establishing any corporation as shall be deemed expedient." After Story's warning, such reservations were common practice, becoming part of general incorporation statutes as well as state constitutions. Freund, *Police Power*, 361.

124. *Charles River Bridge*, 547.

125. *Bank of Augusta v. Earle*. Consequently, a corporation did not have a constitutional right to do business outside of the state in which it was incorporated. The issue of the constitutional status of "foreign corporations" loomed large in nineteenth-century law and economy. The best discussion remains Henderson, *Foreign Corporations in American Constitutional Law*. But see also Horwitz, *Transformation, 1870–1960*, 65–107.

126. *Brick Presbyterian Church v. Mayor of New York*, 5 Cow. 538 (N.Y., 1826); *Coates v. Mayor of New York*, 7 Cow. 585 (N.Y., 1827). The *Coates* decision is reported jointly with *Slack v. Mayor of New York* and *Stuyvesant v. Mayor of New York*. For the best discussion of these cases see Hartog, *Public Property and Private Power*, 71–81.

127. *Brick Presbyterian Church*, 539; *Coates*, 586.

128. *Brick Presbyterian Church*, 540–42.

129. *Coates*, 604–5.

130. Ibid., 605–6. For a conflicting judicial interpretation see *Austin v. Murray*, 16 Pick. 121 (Mass., 1834), where the Massachusetts court invalidated an almost identical Charlestown ordinance. There are two explanations for this glaring anomaly during Lemuel Shaw's watch. First, expediency—allowing the towns ringing Boston to prohibit burials completely would leave Boston with no safe place to bury its dead. Second, as Leonard Levy pointed out, Charlestown regulatory practice discriminated against Catholic burials. Thus the Massachusetts court might have been justified in holding that this police regulation was not "made in *good faith* for the preservation of health." *Austin*, 126. Leonard W. Levy, *The Law of the Commonwealth and Chief Justice Shaw* (New York, 1957), 268.

131. *Thorpe v. Rutland and Burlington Railroad Company*, 27 Vt. 140 (1855). The statute read: "Each railroad corporation shall erect and maintain fences on the lines of their road, . . . and also construct and maintain cattle-guards at all farm and road crossings, suitable and sufficient to prevent cattle and animals from getting on to the railroad. Until such fences and cattle guards shall be duly made, the corporation and its agents shall be liable for all damages which shall be done by their agents or engines to cattle, horses, or other animals thereon, if occasioned by want of such fences and cattle-guards." *Vermont Compiled Statutes*, sec. 41 (1849). Redfield discusses *Brick Presbyterian Church* and *Coates* at 153.

132. *Thorpe v. Rutland*, 144, 147, 156.

133. Ibid., 149–50.

134. Ibid., 150, 155. Among the "thousand things" to be regulated on railroads: "the supervision of the track, tending switches, running upon the time of other trains, running a

road with a single track, using improper rails, not using proper precaution by way of safety beams in case of the breaking of axle-trees, the number of brakemen on a train with reference to the number of cars, employing intemperate or incompetent engineers and servants, running beyond a given rate of speed."

135. Redfield's police list looked like this: "The expense of sidewalks and curbstones in cities and towns has been imposed upon adjacent lots, chiefly for general comfort and convenience. *Paxson v. Sweet*, 1 Greenleaf 196; *City of Lowell v. Hadley*, 1 Metcalf 180. Unlicensed persons not allowed to remove house-dirt and offal from the streets. *Vandine's Case*, 6 Pick. 187. Prohibiting persons selling produce not raised upon their own farms, from occupying certain stands in the market. *Nightingale's Case*, 11 Pick. 168. See also *Buffalo v. Webster*, 10 Wendell 99; *Bush v. Seabury*, 8 Johns. 327. Prohibiting the driving or riding horses faster than a walk in certain streets. *Commonwealth v. Worcester*, 3 Pick. 462. Prohibiting bowling-alleys. *Tanner v. Trustees of the City of Albion*, 5 Hill 121, or the exhibition of stud horses or stallions in public places. *Nolan v. Mayor of Franklin*, 4 Yerger 163. . . . The destruction of private property in cities and towns, to prevent the spread of conflagrations, is an extreme application of the rule, compelling the subserviency of private rights to public security, in cases of imperious necessity. But even this has been fully sustained after the severest scrutiny. *Hale v. Lawrence*, 1 Zabriskie 714." *Thorpe v. Rutland*, 156. For discussions of *Vandine, Nightingale, Webster*, and *Bush* see the earlier discussion of market regulations. For *Tanner, Nolan*, and *Hale*, see chapters 2, and 5.

136. James Bradley Thayer, *Cases on Constitutional Law*, 2 vols. (Cambridge, Mass., 1895), 1:715.

137. Thomas M. Cooley, *A Treatise on the Constitutional Limitations* (Boston, 1868), 575–76.

138. Christopher G. Tiedeman, *A Treatise on the Limitations of Police Power in the United States* (St. Louis, 1886), 578.

139. Cooley, *Limitations*, 282–84; Tiedeman, *Limitations of Police Power*, 582.

140. *Boston Beer Company v. Massachusetts*, 97 U.S. 25 (1877); *Northwestern Fertilizing Company v. Hyde Park*, 97 U.S. 659 (1878). See also *Stone v. Mississippi*, 101 U.S. 814 (1880). For an excellent general discussion of the doctrine of inalienable police power, see Benjamin Fletcher Wright Jr., *The Contract Clause of the Constitution* (Cambridge, Mass., 1938), 195–213.

141. *The People v. Pullman's Palace Car Company*, 175 Ill. 125 (1898), 153.

142. *Brown v. Maryland*, 12 Wheat. 419 (U.S., 1827); Philip B. Kurland and Gerhard Caspar, eds., *Landmark Briefs and Arguments of the Supreme Court of the United States: Constitutional* (Washington, D.C., 1978), 2:428.

143. Massachusetts declared, "Whereas the observance of the Lord's Day is highly promotive of the welfare of a community . . . no person or persons whatsoever shall keep open his, her or their shop, ware-house or work-house, nor shall, upon land or water, do any manner of labour, business or work . . . on the Lord's Day." Stearns and Metcalf, *Laws of Massachusetts*, 1 (1792), 407, 2 (1815), 403. Also see *Laws of New York* (1813), 2:446.

144. McCord, *Statutes at Large of South Carolina, 1632–1838*, 7 (1807), 122; *Laws of New York* 2 (1813), 447, 429; Stearns and Metcalf, *Laws of Massachusetts*, 1 (1783), 85, 2 (1800), 45, 3 (1823), 32; Dorsey, *Law of Maryland*, 1 (1787), c. 26, 249; 1 (1803), c. 63, 483.

Chapter Four

1. Michael Mann, "The Autonomous Power of the State: Its Origins, Mechanisms and Results," in *States in History*, ed. John A. Hall (New York, 1986), 113, 117. For an excellent

and illuminative case study of the significance of the infrastructural power of the United States Postal Service, see Richard R. John, *Spreading the News: The American Postal System from Franklin to Morse* (Cambridge, Mass., 1995).

2. Pasquale Pasquino, "*Theatrum Politicum*: The Genealogy of Capital—Police and the State of Prosperity," in *The Foucault Effect: Studies in Governmentality*, ed. Graham Burchell, Colin Gordon, and Peter Miller (Chicago, 1991), 111.

3. George R. Taylor, *The Transportation Revolution, 1815–1860* (White Plains, N.Y., 1951); Carter Goodrich, *Government Promotion of American Canals and Railroads, 1800–1890* (New York, 1960); Harry N. Scheiber, *Ohio Canal Era: A Case Study of Government and the Economy, 1820–1861* (Athens, Ohio, 1968); Edward Chase Kirkland, *Men, Cities and Transportation, 1820–1900* (Cambridge, Mass., 1948); Paul Wallace Gates, *History of Public Land Law Development* (Washington, D.C., 1968); Nathan Miller, *Enterprise of a Free People* (Ithaca, N.Y., 1962). For a more complete bibliography and historiography, see Harry N. Scheiber, "The Transportation Revolution and American Law: Constitutionalism and Public Policy," in *Transportation and the Early Nation* (Indianapolis, Ind., 1982), 1–29.

4. Elizabeth Blackmar, *Manhattan for Rent, 1785–1850* (Ithaca, N.Y., 1989); Mary P. Ryan, *Women in Public: Between Banners and Ballots, 1825–1880* (Baltimore, 1990); David Scobey, "Anatomy of the Promenade: The Politics of Bourgeois Sociability in Nineteenth-century New York," *Social History* 17 (1992): 203–27; Christine Stansell, *City of Women: Sex and Class in New York, 1789–1860* (New York, 1982), especially ch. 10 "The Uses of the Streets."

5. For the most part, social and cultural historians have neglected this preliminary point. The fact that the "streets" were made "public" in one sense (i.e., that state and municipal control had been established over these spaces) often meant that in fact they were hardly "public" in another sense (i.e., open to all and tolerant of a fluid range of communication and activity). The streets were not simply an open arena for cultural ritual and contest. Long before a parade or demonstration or promenade began, the force and violence of law and the state had already stacked the deck in favor of certain kinds of behavior and access and proscribed alternatives. In the shadow of the substantial legal, disciplinary, and police institutions and traditions created in the nineteenth century, the symbolic gestures, winks, poses, and sartorial embellishments accompanying public events and displays seem more like window dressing for a more effective power and authority wielded earlier and elsewhere.

6. For an excellent example of this, see Roy Rosenzweig and Elizabeth Blackmar's wonderful discussion of the creation of New York's Central Park as a "violent act" from the perspective of poor "park dwellers" with prior-use claims. Roy Rosenzweig and Elizabeth Blackmar, "Private to Public Property," in *The Park and the People: A History of Central Park* (Ithaca, N.Y., 1992), ch. 3. Also see Hendrik Hartog, "Pigs and Positivism," *Wisconsin Law Review* (1985): 899–935.

7. In the early nineteenth century all roads, navigable rivers, and harbors were treated under the law of highways.

8. James Madison, *Federalist*, No. 14, in *The Federalist Papers*, ed. Clinton Rossiter (New York, 1961), 102–3.

9. Joseph Angell and Thomas Durfee, *A Treatise on the Law of Highways* (Boston, 1857), 34.

10. *Wharf Case*, 3 Bland Ch. 361 (Maryland, 1831), 370; Levi Lincoln, "Message of the Lieutenant-Governor of the Commonwealth of Massachusetts," January 26, 1809, quoted in Kirkland, *Men, Cities and Transportation*, 32.

11. Francis Lieber, *On Civil Liberty and Self-Government*, 3d ed. (Philadelphia, 1891), 87.

12. Angell and Durfee, *Highways*, 3.

13. Albert Gallatin, "Report on Roads and Canals," in *The Government and the Economy: 1783–1861*, ed. Carter Goodrich (New York, 1967), 5.

14. See, for example, *The Revised Statutes of the Commonwealth of Massachusetts* (Boston, 1836), title 11; *The Revised Statutes of the State of Michigan* (Detroit, 1838), title 6; *Revised Statutes of New York* (Albany, N.Y., 1835), title 16.

15. *Laws of New York* (1826), c. 183, 192.

16. *Public Laws of the State of New York* (Albany, N.Y., 1810), ch. 119, 37.

17. *Canal Laws, Regulations, Rates of Toll, and Names of the Principal Places, with Their Distances from Each Other on the New-York State Canals* (Albany, N.Y., 1846).

18. William Blackstone, *Commentaries on the Laws of England: A Facsimile of the First Edition of 1765–1769*, 4 vols. (Chicago, 1979), 4:167.

19. Horace G. Wood, *A Practical Treatise on the Law of Nuisances*, 2d ed. (Albany, N.Y., 1883), chs. 3, 7, and 14.

20. Thomas M. Cooley, *A Treatise on the Constitutional Limitations* (Boston, 1868), 588–94; John F. Dillon, *The Law of Municipal Corporations*, 2d ed., 2 vols. (New York, 1873), chs. 6, 12, and 18. Cooley's brief analysis of the police power of the states contained an unusually large discussion of highways, and Dillon's understanding of the powers of municipal corporations would not have been complete without his sections on streets and wharves. The work of Joseph Angell perhaps best expressed the role of roads and waterways in American law. He devoted full treatises to both subjects. Angell and Durfee, *Highways*; Joseph K. Angell, *A Treatise on the Common Law in Relation to Watercourses* (Boston, 1833). Also see Nathan Dane, *General Abridgment and Digest of American Law* (Boston, 1823), 3:242–80; James Kent, *Commentaries on American Law*, 4 vols. (New York, 1826), 2:338–39.

21. *Palmer v. Mulligan*, 3 Caine 307 (N.Y., 1805); *Callender v. Marsh*, 1 Pick. 417 (Mass., 1823); *Gibbons v. Ogden*, 9 Wheat. 1 (U.S., 1824); *Willson v. Black-Bird Creek Marsh Company*, 2 Pet. 245 (U.S., 1829); *New York v. Miln*, 11 Pet. 102 (U.S., 1837); *Charles River Bridge v. Warren Bridge*, 11 Pet. 420 (U.S., 1837); *Commonwealth v. Tewksbury*, 11 Metc. 55 (Mass., 1846); *Passenger Cases*, 7 How. 283 (U.S., 1849); *Commonwealth v. Alger*, 7 Cush. 53 (Mass., 1851); *Cooley v. Board of Wardens*, 12 How. 299 (U.S., 1851); *Genesee Chief v. Fitzhugh*, 12 How. 443 (U.S., 1851); *Wheeling Bridge Case*, 13 How. 518 (U.S., 1852); *Munn v. Illinois*, 94 U.S. 113 (1877); *Penasocola Telegraph Co. v. Western Union Telegraph Co.*, 96 U.S. 1 (1877).

22. Kent, *Commentaries*, 3:348.

23. Ibid., 349.

24. Wood, *Nuisances*, 251.

25. Angell and Durfee, *Highways*, 281.

26. Wood, *Nuisances*, 295.

27. Molly Selvin, "The Public Trust Doctrine in American Law and Economic Policy," *Wisconsin Law Review* (1980): 1403–42; Harry N. Scheiber, "The Road to Munn: Eminent Domain and the Concept of Public Purpose in the State Courts," *Perspectives in American History* 5 (1971): 327–402. Hale's discussion of *juris publici* was first brought to the attention of Americans by Francis Hargrave who published Hale's manuscript *A Treatise in Three Parts*, which included "*De Jure Maris et Brachiorum ejusdem*" and "*De Portibus Maris*," in *A Collection of Tracts Relative to the Law of England*, ed. Francis Hargrave (Dublin, 1787). Hale was so influential that his argument was published verbatim as an appendix to the New York case, *Ex Parte Jennings*, 6 Cow. 518 (N.Y., 1826). Although Hale's manuscripts dealt primarily with public rights in the sea, navigable waters, and ports, American jurists eagerly applied his constructions to highway law generally. See Angell and Durfee, *Highways*, 35–36. Also see "Navigable Rivers," *American Law Review* 2 (1868): 589–98.

28. Hargrave, *Tracts*, 84–87.

29. *O'Connor v. Pittsburgh*, 18 Pa. St. Rep. 187 (1851). For more on Justice Gibson's "commonwealth" orientation, see Stanley Kutler, "John Bannister Gibson: Judicial Restraint and the Positive State," *Journal of Public Law* 14 (1965), 181–97.

30. Cooley, *Constitutional Limitations*, 588; Wood, *Nuisances*, 296, 307.

31. Of course, the most direct way to expropriate private property in the nineteenth century was through the use of the state's eminent domain powers. For the best historical studies of eminent domain, see Harry N. Scheiber, "Property Law, Expropriation, and Resource Allocation by Government: The United States, 1789–1910," *Journal of Economic History* 33 (1973): 232–51; Scheiber, "The Road to *Munn*"; Harry N. Scheiber and Charles W. McCurdy, "Eminent Domain and Western Agriculture, 1849–1900," *Agricultural History* 49 (1975): 112–30; Tony A. Freyer, *Producers versus Capitalists: Constitutional Conflict in Antebellum America* (Charlottesville, Va., 1994), 137–66.

32. The best discussion of this doctrine is Carol Rose, "The Comedy of the Commons: Custom, Commerce, and Inherently Public Property," *University of Chicago Law Review* 53 (1986): 711–81.

33. According to Wood, "when the owner of land permits the free and uninterrupted use of a way over his premises by the public for such a length of time as to warrant the presumption that he intended to dedicate it to the public, this is regarded as sufficient to prove the existence of a highway, whether the owner of the soil is known or not." Wood, *Nuisances*, 254.

34. Rose, "Commons," 727. Also on dedication, see Angell and Durfee, *Highways*, secs. 131–35; "Dedication to Public Use," *American Decisions* 27 (1881): 559. This note was appended to the decision of the Vermont Supreme Court in *State v. Trask*, 27 Am. Dec. 554 (1834); *Smith v. State*, 3 Zabr. 712 (N.J., 1852); and *Harding v. Jasper*, 14 Cal. 642 (1860).

35. *State v. Wilkinson*, 2 Vt. 480 (1829).

36. Ibid., 485.

37. See *Commonwealth v. M'Donald*, 16 Serg. & R. 390 (Pa., 1827); *Rung v. Shoneberger*, 2 Watts 23 (Pa., 1833); *Smith v. State*.

38. In *Commonwealth v. Wright and Dame* (Mass., 1829), for example, defendants were fined a mere twenty dollars for the maintenance of a public nuisance. But their 100-foot wharf was also destroyed. See the reprint of this case in *American Jurist* 3 (1830): 185–201.

39. *People v. Cunningham*, 1 Den. 524, 43 Am. Dec. 709 (N.Y., 1845).

40. Ibid., 710.

41. Ibid.

42. Ibid., 711.

43. Ibid., 712–13.

44. Ibid., 714. This language is from Lord Ellenborough's opinion in *Rex v. Jones*, 3 Camp. 230 (Eng., 1812), an indictment against a timber merchant for obstructing part of a London street with his logs.

45. *People v. Cunningham*, 715.

46. This mode of delivering slops was initially sanctioned by the city council. Still, the court refused to "vest" a property right in an obstruction to a public way. This reflected the degree to which "public rights" in this period did not simply coincide with the paper enactments or recommendations of a city council.

47. *State v. Morris and Essex Railroad Company*, 3 Zabr. 360 (N.J., 1852); *Morton v. Moore*, 81 Mass. 573 (1860).

48. *Morris and Essex Railroad*, 371–72. On the police power and corporate status, see chapter 3.

49. *Morton*, 576.

50. See Morton J. Horwitz, *The Transformation of American Law, 1780–1860* (Cambridge, Mass., 1977), 47–54.

51. *Dygert v. Schenck*, 23 Wend. 446, 35 Am. Dec. 575 (N.Y., 1840).

52. Ibid., 576, 580.

53. *Dimmett v. Eskridge*, 6 Munf. 308 (Va., 1819), 308. Private abatement was another powerful instrument in the state's grab bag of regulatory authority. Throughout this period, courts allowed private individuals to pull down obstructions to public ways when they were "specially" affected or injured. For further examples of private abatement in public roads cases, see *Stetson v. Faxon*, 19 Pick. 147, 31 Am. Dec. 123 (Mass., 1837), and the exhaustive list of cases in the appended note. For an example of the limits of private abatement, see *Hopkins v. Crombie*, 4 N.H. 520 (1829). On private abatement in public morals and health regulation, see chapters 5 and 6. For an interesting discussion of the contending interests involved in the private abatement of milldams, see Gary Kulik, "Dams, Fish, and Farmers: Defense of Public Rights in Eighteenth-Century Rhode Island," in *The Countryside in the Age of Capitalist Transformation*, ed. Stephen Hahn and Jonathan Prude (Chapel Hill, N.C., 1985).

54. *People v. Carpenter*, 1 Mich. 273 (1849), 295.

55. *Commonwealth v. King*, 13 Metc. 115 (Mass., 1847), 118; *Dickey v. Maine Telegraph Co.*, 46 Me. 483 (1859).

56. *Commonwealth v. Wilkinson*, 16 Pick. 175 (Mass., 1834).

57. *Commonwealth v. King*; *Linsley v. Bushnell*, 15 Conn. 225 (1842); *Hyde v. County of Middlesex*, 68 Mass. 267 (1854); *Runyon v. Bordine*, 14 N.J. Law 472 (1834); *Harrow v. State*, 1 Greene 439 (Ia., 1848).

58. *Commonwealth v. Passmore*, 1 Serg. & R. 217 (Pa., 1814), 221–22.

59. *Davis v. Mayor of New York*, 14 N.Y. 506 (1856), 525. Denman's decision and rhetoric in *King v. Ward*, 4 Adolph. & Ellis 384 (Eng., 1836), was extremely influential. See the discussion of Angell and Durfee, *Highways*, 212.

60. On the American revival of criminal equity, see Edwin S. Mack, "The Revival of Criminal Equity," *Harvard Law Review* 16 (1903): 389–403; Charles Noble Gregory, "Government by Injunction," *Harvard Law Review* 11 (1898): 487–511; Cyrus D. Shabaz, "The Historical Development of the Power of Equity Courts to Enjoin Nuisances," *Marquette Law Review* 11 (1926): 32–38.

61. *Attorney General v. Richards*, 2 Anstr. 603 (Eng., 1795). It should be noted here that English courts refused to follow their American counterparts and allow the enjoining of public nuisances generally. See *Baines v. Baker*, 1 Ambl. 158, 27 E. Repr. 105 (Eng., 1752); *London v. Bolt*, 5 Ves. Jr. 129, 31 E. Repr. 507 (Eng., 1799); *Attorney General v. Cleaver*, 18 Ves. Jr. 211, 34 E. Repr. 297 (Eng., 1811); *Crowder v. Tinkler*, 19 Ves. Jr. 617, 34 E. Repr. 645 (Eng., 1816); *Attorney General v. Forbes*, 2 M. & C. 123 (Eng., 1836).

62. Hendrik Hartog's *Public Property and Private Power: The Corporation of the City of New York in American Law, 1730–1870* (Chapel Hill, N.C., 1983) is an unparalleled discussion of contemporaneous developments involving the public capacities of the municipal corporation of New York. By the mid-nineteenth century, New York's public powers had less to do with its corporate land holdings than its status as a governmental entity.

63. Joseph Story's *Commentaries on Equity Jurisprudence*, 3 vols. (Boston, 1836), challenged the prevailing wisdom and caution of James Kent. In *Attorney General v. Utica Insurance Co.*, 2 Johns. Ch. R. 371 (N.Y., 1817), Chancellor Kent denied equity's power to enjoin a *public* nuisance that only contravened general policy. Story, in contrast, argued that this jurisdiction had been the norm since the reign of Elizabeth. Joseph Story, *Commen-*

taries on *Equity Jurisprudence*, 376; *Attorney General v. Utica Insurance Co.* But compare Kent's opinion in *Utica* to *Corning v. Lowerre*, 6 Johns. Ch. 439 (N.Y., 1822).

64. *Commonwealth v. Rush*, 14 Pa. St. 186 (1850).

65. Ibid., 195–96.

66. *State v. Mayor of Mobile*, 5 Port. 279 (Ala., 1837); *Mayor of Columbus v. Jacques*, 30 Ga. 506 (1860).

67. *People v. Vanderbilt*, 28 N.Y. 396 (1863); *Attorney General v. Cohoes Co.*, 6 Paige 133 (N.Y., 1836); *Georgetown v. Alexandria Canal Co.*, 12 Pet. 91 (U.S., 1838). *Georgetown* represented the U.S. Supreme Court's acceptance of Story's view on the availability of the injunction in public nuisance and purpresture cases. North Carolina courts in particular were quick to use the injunctive remedy against milldams. See *Attorney General v. Hunter*, 16 N.C. 12 (1826); *Attorney General and Bell v. Blount*, 4 Hawks. 384 (N.C., 1826); *Attorney General v. Lea*, 38 N.C. 265 (1844).

68. Horwitz, *Transformation, 1780–1860*, 77; Paul M. Kurtz, "Nineteenth Century Anti-Entrepreneurial Nuisance Injunctions—Avoiding the Chancellor," *William and Mary Law Review* 17 (1976): 621–70.

69. *Attorney General v. Hunter*, 18.

70. *Attorney General and Bell v. Blount*, 527.

71. *Governor and Company of the British Cast Plate Manufacturers v. Meredith*, 4 T.R. 794 (1792); see the discussion in Angell and Durfee, *Highways*, 181–83. *Meredith* also figured prominently in the New York fire cases examined in chapter 2.

72. *Meredith*, 797.

73. *Callender v. Marsh*. See the discussions of Horwitz, *Transformation, 1780–1860*, 72–73; William E. Nelson, *Americanization of the Common Law: The Impact of Legal Change on Massachusetts Society, 1760–1830* (Cambridge, Mass., 1975), 132; Stanley K. Schultz, *Constructing Urban Culture: American Cities and City Planning, 1800–1920* (Philadelphia, 1989), 46–47.

74. *Callender*, 430.

75. Ibid., 430–31.

76. *Gardner v. Trustees of the Village of Newburgh*, 2 Johns. Ch. 162 (1816). In *later* additions of his *Commentaries*, James Kent also included a footnote hostile to the "consequential" damages doctrine articulated in *Callender*. He considered this a clear case of eminent domain. Joseph Story's less direct objection occurred in his dissent in the *Charles River Bridge Case*. Kent, *Commentaries*, 2:340, n. "c." *Charles River Bridge v. Warren Bridge* (1837), 638, 641. See also the contrary opinions of the Ohio courts, for example, *Goodloe v. Cincinnati*, 4 Ohio 500 (1831), and *Rhodes v. City of Cleveland*, 10 Ohio 159 (1840).

77. *Radcliff's Executors v. Mayor of Brooklyn*, 4 Comst. 195 (N.Y., 1850), 206–7.

78. *Charles River Bridge v. Warren Bridge* (1837), 553; *Barron v. Baltimore*, 7 Pet. 243 (U.S., 1833).

79. See Joseph William Singer, "The Legal Rights Debate in Analytical Jurisprudence from Bentham to Hohfeld," *Wisconsin Law Review* (1982): 975–1059.

80. Taylor, *Transportation Revolution*, 15.

81. Ibid., 56.

82. Scheiber, *Ohio Canal*, 9.

83. Angell and Durfee, *Highways*, 36.

84. Louis Houck, *A Treatise on the Law of Navigable Rivers* (Boston, 1868). As will be made clear momentarily, the common law rule identified here is a vast oversimplification of English experience. Nevertheless, it was constantly referred to as the "common law rule" by American courts and commentators.

85. Hale, "*De Juris Maris*." It should be pointed out here that there is some controversy over Hargrave's attribution of authorship to Hale. See Houck, *Navigable Rivers*, 17–19; "Navigable Rivers," 589.

86. Hale, "*De Juris Maris*," 8–9.

87. Almost every discussion of public rights in American rivers began with long excerpts from Hale and lavish praise. One commentator gushed, "With a mind beaming the efful-gence of noonday, he sat on the bench like a descended god!" See Wood, *Nuisances*, 525–28; Angell and Durfee, *Highways*, 35; Houck, *Navigable Rivers*, 16–25; Angell, *Common Law in Relation to Watercourses*, 201–2; *Ex Parte Jennings*, 6 Cow. 518 (N.Y., 1826), 536.

88. Houck, *Navigable Rivers*, 29.

89. Though the Supreme Court formally repudiated the common law definition of "navi-gability" in 1851, state courts began revising the standard as early as 1807. See *Genesee Chief v. Fitzhugh*; *Carson v. Blazer*, 2 Binney 475 (Pa., 1807). State reaction was diverse, however. North Carolina, South Carolina, Tennessee, and Alabama followed Pennsylvania in depart-ing from the common law rule. New York went through a long protracted debate on this subject, keeping the common law definition of navigability until 1865. Massachusetts regu-lated its navigable waters by statute, dividing public and private rights in waters at the low-water mark. Further west, one sees less and less of the common law definition. Article 4 of the Northwest Ordinance of 1787 declared the Mississippi, St. Lawrence, and all navigable waters leading into them to be common highways, forever free and public. Francis Newton Thorpe, *The Federal and State Constitutions*, 7 vols. (Washington, D.C., 1909), 2:961. A 1796 act of Congress respecting the surveying of the Northwest Territory declared all navigable rivers therein "public highways," not to be surveyed or sold. *United States Statutes at Large*, 1 (1796), 464. Needless to say, there were no tides in the rivers of the territory. An anony-mous author in the *American Law Review* (whom I assume to be Louis Houck) asserted that this law "by gradual legislation, has been extended over the domain of the Union." "Navigable Rivers," 594. States also enacted a deluge of legislation after the Revolution de-claring certain rivers public and regulating rights and duties therein. They were quicker than courts in carving out exceptions or making wholesale departures from the common law rule. See the detailed state-by-state discussion of Houck, *Navigable Waters*, 65–75.

90. See Wood, *Nuisances*, 529 and cases cited therein.

91. Despite their interpretive disagreements, that is the basic gist of the following discus-sions of antebellum water law: James Willard Hurst, *Law and the Conditions of Freedom in the Nineteenth-Century United States* (Madison, Wis., 1956), 3–32; Stanley I. Kutler, *Privi-lege and Creative Destruction: The Charles River Bridge Case* (New York, 1971); Horwitz, *Transformation, 1780–1860*, 41–47; Theodore Steinberg, *Nature Incorporated: Industrializa-tion and the Waters of New England* (Cambridge, 1991).

92. *Palmer v. Mulligan*.

93. These rules held that (1) any interference with the natural flow of water was unallow-able and (2) any injurious interference with a previous riparian owner's property was un-lawful. Morton Horwitz's argument goes something like this: this case signified a marked departure from the common law rule against obstructing or interfering with the flow of water, diluting the antidevelopmental doctrines of "natural use" and "priority." By not al-lowing damages or the abatement of the upstream dam in this case, the court sanctioned and subsidized upstream economic development. See Horwitz, *Transformation, 1780–1860*, 37–38.

94. *Palmer v. Mulligan*, 312. Chief Justice Kent's concurring opinion relied heavily on Hale in determining the public character of the Hudson. Ibid., 319.

95. Ibid., 313.

96. *Hecker v. New York Balance Dock Company*, 13 How. Pr. 549 (N.Y., 1857).

97. Ibid., 550.

98. Ibid., 551.

99. The court angrily challenged the defendant's claim that he had a permit from the dockmaster. "The object of the dock-master's office," the court argued, "is to secure, not sell or infringe, the equal rights of all; to prevent encroachments, and not to create or defend them." The dockmaster was not "intrusted with the sovereign power of granting monopolies." Ibid., 552–54.

100. *Veazie v. Dwinel*, 50 Me. 479 (1862). Justice Rice's opinion was deemed important enough to be republished in the *American Law Register* with an adulatory note by Isaac Redfield. Isaac Redfield, "Recent American Decisions," *American Law Register* 3 (1864): 715–28.

101. *Veazie v. Dwinel*, 484–86.

102. Ibid., 490.

103. Ibid., 487.

104. *People v. City of St. Louis*, 10 Ill. 351 (1848), 372.

105. *Commonwealth v. Church*, 1 Pa. St. 105 (1845), 110.

106. *Dugan v. Bridge Co.*, 27 Pa. St. 303 (1856), 305.

107. *French v. Camp*, 18 Me. 433 (1841), 434.

108. Ibid., 435.

109. *Gerrish v. Brown*, 51 Me. 256 (1863); *Penniman v. New York Balance Co.*, 13 How. Pr. 40 (N.Y., 1856); *Shaw v. Crawford*, 10 Johns. 236 (N.Y., 1813); *Stump v. McNairy*, 5 Humph. 363 (Tenn., 1844); *Gates v. Blincoe*, 2 Dana 158 (Ky., 1834); *Walker v. Shepardson*, 2 Wisc. 384 (1853); *Stoughton v. Baker*, 4 Mass. 522 (1808). New York was the site of some of the great exceptions before the Civil War. For two examples of the way New York courts limited the applicability of public nuisance doctrines see *People v. Platt*, 17 Johns. 195 (N.Y., 1819) (navigability); *Clark v. Mayor of Syracuse*, 13 Barb. 32 (N.Y., 1852) (against summary destruction).

110. An interesting example of this is the way the court in *Shaw v. Crawford* cited *Palmer v. Mulligan* along with Hale as establishing New York standards for *public* nuisances in the Battenkill River. *Shaw v. Crawford*, 237.

111. George Dargo, *Jefferson's Louisiana: Politics and the Clash of Legal Traditions* (Cambridge, Mass., 1975), especially 74–101. Dargo is nicely supplemented by Molly Selvin, *This Tender and Delicate Business: The Public Trust Doctrine in American Law and Economic Policy, 1789–1920* (New York, 1987), 78–91.

112. *Civil Code of 1808*, art. 6, p. 94; *Compiled Edition of the Civil Codes of Louisiana* (Baton Rouge, La., 1940), p. 257.

113. *Civil Code of 1808*, arts. 7 and 8, pp. 94–96; *Compiled Edition*, 257–58.

114. *Louisiana Civil Code of 1825*, art. 448; *Compiled Edition*, 259.

115. One of the conditions of Louisiana's entrance into the Union was that the Mississippi should be an open and common highway. Louis Houck captured the consensus when he asked rhetorically: "Can it, then, be said, . . . in view of the grandeur and magnificence of the river, the character stamped upon it by the laws of nature, the various treaties made in reference to it by the great maritime powers of the globe, the solemn compacts made by the sovereign States on its borders with each other and the United States,—that this vast stream, this great inland sea, the subject of so much jealous solicitude, is a mere private stream, belonging to the private individuals, who occupy and may own an acre on the verge of its banks, and subject only to the servitude of the public for the purposes of navigation?" Houck, *Navigable Waters*, 69–70, 76–77; *United States Statutes at Large*, 2 (1811), 642.

116. For excellent discussions and analyses, see Dargo, *Jefferson's Louisiana*, 74-101; and Selvin, *Tender and Delicate Business*, 84-85.

117. Selvin, *Tender and Delicate Business*, 81. In a remarkable indicator of the degree to which the common law has permeated our culture and language, *Webster's Third New International Dictionary* (Springfield, Mass., 1986) holds "alluvion" to belong to the property owner as a matter of *definition.*

118. *Hanson v. City Council of Lafayette*, 18 La. 295 (1841).

119. Ibid., 301, 303.

120. Ibid., 303. The events were probably not unrelated. The opinion hints that several adjoining property owners may have intentionally cut down parts of the levee to erect their buildings.

121. In this case, the most important law regulating the banks of the Mississippi was an 1816 act of the Louisiana legislature requiring proprietors adjacent to the river to leave sufficient space (up to sixty feet) for the making and repairing of levees, roads, and other public or common works. *Louisiana Laws, 1816*, 2 Martin's Digest 594; *Hanson*, 305. In addition, an earlier 1808 law imposed penalties "for constructing works which shall hinder or obstruct the free use of the shores of the Mississippi." *Louisiana Laws, 1808*, 1 Moreau's Digest 651; *Hanson v. City Council*, 305-6.

122. *Hanson v. City Council*, 307.

123. Ibid., 304. Not one of the owners in this case left more than thirty-five feet between buildings and water. Some built within inches. Garland found this a flagrant disregard of the rights of public use as well as a violation of the 1816 statute requiring sixty feet.

124. Ibid., 306; *Acts of 1833*, p. 146; *Acts of 1836*, p. 131.

125. *Hanson v. City Council*, 306-7.

126. Buildings on the banks of other navigable rivers in Louisiana fared no better. In *Natchitoches v. Coe* (1824) and *Herbert v. Benson* (1847), a warehouse on the bayou Teche and a house on the Red River were demolished for interrupting public use of the banks for mere "private emolument." The court in *Herbert* was straightforward: "It has been so often and so uniformly held by the former Supreme Court, that public places . . . cannot be appropriated to private use . . . that the question can no longer be considered an open one." *Trustees of Natchitoches v. Coe*, 3 Martin (N.S.) 140 (La., 1824); *Herbert v. Benson*, 2 La. Ann. 770 (1847), 771.

127. Quoted in Ronald E. Shaw, *Erie Water West: A History of the Erie Canal* (Lexington, Ky., 1966), 280.

128. Shaw, *Erie Water West*, 280-81; John J. McEneny, *Albany: Capital City on the Hudson* (Woodland Hills, Calif., 1981), 91; Codman Hislop, *Albany: Dutch, English, and American* (Albany, N.Y., 1936), 274-75.

129. *General Index of the Laws of the State of New York* (Albany, N.Y., 1859), 280-81.

130. *Laws of New York* (1823), c. 111, p. 128.

131. *Laws of New York* (1826), c. 185, p. 185, "An Act to Amend the Several Acts Relating to the City of Albany." The regulatory power discussed here is granted in section 15 of the act, "The Several Police Powers of the Common Council Specified."

132. *Hart v. Mayor of Albany*, 9 Wend. 571 (N.Y., 1832).

133. *Hart and Hoyt v. Mayor of Albany*, 3 Paige Ch. 213 (N.Y., 1832).

134. *Hart v. Mayor of Albany.*

135. Ibid., 584.

136. Ibid.

137. Ibid., 608.

138. Ibid., 590, 608. As Justice Sutherland put it, "[A]ny one may pull down or otherwise destroy a common nuisance, as a new gate or even a house created in a highway; for if one, whose estate is prejudiced by a private nuisance, may justify the entering into another's grounds, and pulling down and destroying it, it cannot but follow *a fortiori* that any one may lawfully destroy a common nuisance."

139. Ibid., 609.

140. Ibid., 591; *Laws of New York* (1826), c. 185., p. 184.

141. *Hart v. Mayor of Albany*, 600.

142. Ibid., 594.

143. Ibid., 582, 592, 596. The dock's owners contested throughout this litigation that their float was "beneficial to the public" and promoted one of the leading objects of the basin, "to facilitate transhipments of produce and merchandise."

144. *Lansing v. Smith*, 4 Wend. 9, 21 Am. Dec. 89 (N.Y., 1829).

145. Ibid., 94.

146. Ibid., 96.

147. Ibid., 97. This argument from public rights was quite congruent with the opinion reached by Chief Justice Taney in *Charles River Bridge* a year earlier.

148. *Vanderbilt v. Adams*, 7 Cow. 349 (N.Y., 1827).

149. *Laws of New York* (1819), c. 18, p. 24.

150. The wharf belonged to William Gibbons, but was being leased at this time by Thomas Gibbons of *Gibbons v. Ogden* fame.

151. *Vanderbilt v. Adams*, 350–51.

152. Ibid., 351–52.

153. *Commonwealth v. Tewksbury*; *Laws of Massachusetts* (Boston, 1845), c. 117.

154. *Commonwealth v. Tewksbury*, 57.

155. Ibid.

156. Ibid., 58. It is important to note, however, that the commonwealth's legislature did not feel so bound. In 1846, it passed a law granting Tewksbury $500 compensation for being debarred from the use of his land. *Laws of Massachusetts* (Boston, 1846), c. 206. *Commonwealth v. Tewksbury*, 59. Also see the excellent discussion of Leonard W. Levy, *The Law of the Commonwealth and Chief Justice Shaw* (Cambridge, Mass., 1957), 246–54.

157. *Commonwealth v. Alger.*

158. Ibid., 85.

159. *Commonwealth v. Wright and Dame* (Mass., 1829), reprinted in *American Jurist* 3 (1830): 185–201.

160. *Commonwealth v. Wright*, 193.

161. Ibid., 189.

162. Ibid., 188.

163. Ibid., 201.

164. *People v. Corporation of Albany*, 11 Wend. 539 (N.Y., 1834), 540.

165. *Commonwealth v. Rush.* The attorney general actually brought the suit in equity, requesting an injunction.

166. Ibid., 191–93.

167. *State v. Woodward*, 23 Vt. 92 (1850), 99.

168. Ibid., 99.

169. *Commonwealth v. Bowman and Duncan*, 3 Pa. St. 202 (1846), 206.

170. See also *Commonwealth v. Passmore* and *State v. Atkinson*, 24 Vt. 448 (1852). In *Passmore*, the defense counsel for a *public* auctioneer accused of keeping his goods in a Philadelphia street attempted to argue for a special privilege for his client stemming from

public "needfulness" and "expediency." Chief Justice Tilghman refused to balance or trade-off the public right to the full highway. In *Atkinson*, even a public schoolhouse was deemed a violation of a public common.

171. *Barker v. Commonwealth*, 19 Pa. St. 412 (1852).

172. Ibid., 412–13.

173. Ibid., 413. Also see *Gilbert v. Mickle*, 4 Sandf. Ch. 357 (N.Y., 1846); and *Adams v. Rivers*, 11 Barb. 390 (N.Y., 1851); Wood, *Nuisances*, 309.

Chapter Five

1. American Law Institute, *Model Penal Code. Tentative Draft No. 4* (Philadelphia, 1955), 207. For the great jurisprudential debate on law and morality catalyzed by the English Wolfenden Report on Homosexual Offenses and Prostitution, see Lord Devlin, *The Enforcement of Morals* (Oxford, 1959); H. L. A. Hart, *Law, Liberty, and Morality* (Stanford, Calif., 1963); Ronald Dworkin, "Lord Devlin and the Enforcement of Morals," *Yale Law Journal* 75 (1966): 986; Herbert L. Packer, *The Limits of the Criminal Sanction* (Stanford, Calif., 1968). Of course, the U.S. Supreme Court has recently made clear the limits of this tendency in *Bowers v. Hardwick*, 478 U.S. 186 (1986). The *Model Penal Code* itself retains ample provisions for sexual misconduct and offenses against public order and decency.

2. Emmerich de Vattel, *The Law of Nations*, ed. Edward D. Ingraham (Philadelphia, 1852), bk. 1, ch. 13, sec. 174.

3. Gerhard Oestreich, *Neo-Stoicism and the Early Modern State*, trans. D. McLintock (Cambridge, 1983), 157. Also see Colin Gordon, "Governmental Rationality: An Introduction," in *The Foucault Effect: Studies in Governmentality*, ed. Graham Burchell, Colin Gordon, and Peter Miller (Chicago, 1991), 1–51.

4. Christopher L. Tomlins, *Law, Labor, and Ideology in the Early American Republic* (New York, 1993); Amy Dru Stanley, "Beggars Can't Be Choosers: Compulsion and Contract in Postbellum America," *Journal of American History* 78 (1992): 1265–93; Elizabeth Blackmar, *Manhattan for Rent, 1785–1850* (Ithaca, N.Y., 1989); Allen Steinberg, *The Transformation of Criminal Justice: Philadelphia, 1800–1880* (Chapel Hill, N.C., 1989); John F. Kasson, *Rudeness and Civility: Manners in Nineteenth-Century Urban America* (New York, 1990). A good bit of this scholarship is creatively synthesized in David Montgomery's "Policing People for the Free Market," in his *Citizen Worker: The Experience of Workers in the United States with Democracy and the Free Market during the Nineteenth Century* (New York, 1993), 52–114. The debt of this scholarship to an earlier generation is obvious. See E. P. Thompson, *The Making of the English Working Class* (New York, 1964); E. P. Thompson, *Customs in Common: Studies in Traditional Popular Culture* (New York, 1991); Herbert G. Gutman, *Work, Culture, and Society in Industrializing America: Essays in Working-Class and Social History* (New York, 1976); and Daniel T. Rodgers, *The Work Ethic in Industrial America, 1850–1920* (Chicago, 1978).

A weakness in this interpretive tradition is a tendency to oversimplify causation and to adopt a rather monolithic conception of the role of law and the state in this process. For example, Marc Raeff, relying heavily on Oestreich and Albert Hirschmann, argues that German police ordinances regulating society and culture were quite consciously directed at stamping out traditional, premodern folkways ("eliminating outright, the 'superfluous' purposeless, unstructured, and fickle elements of society") and creating disciplined, rational, and productive attitudes toward work among the populace. While the linkages between police and capitalism are crucial, eighteenth- and nineteenth-century morals regulation was about more than patricians preparing plebs for profit making. Marc Raeff, *The*

Well-Ordered Police State: Social and Institutional Change through Law in the Germanies and Russia, 1600–1800 (New Haven, Conn., 1983), 85–92; Albert O. Hirschmann, The Passions and the Interests (Princeton, N.J., 1977). Hirschmann, of course, is well aware of the complexities and unintended consequences accompanying the important transition from the regulation of passion to the release of self-interest.

5. Beccaria argued in Elements of Public Economy (1769): "But neither the products of the earth, nor those of the work of the human hand, nor mutual commerce, nor public contributions can ever be obtained from men with perfection and constancy if they do not know the moral and physical laws of the things upon which they act, and if the increase of bodies is not proportionately accompanied by the change of social habits; if, among the multiplicity of individuals, works and products one does not at each step see shining the light of order, which renders all operations easy and sure. Thus, the sciences, education, good order, security and public tranquillity, objects all comprehended under the name of police, will constitute the fifth and last object of public economy." Quoted in Pasquale Pasquino, "Theatrum Politicum: The Genealogy of Capital—Police and the State of Prosperity," Ideology and Consciousness 4 (1978): 45. Beccaria's Essay on Crimes and Punishments (1764) greatly impressed, among others, John Adams, Thomas Jefferson, and Nathaniel Chipman, as well as American criminal law reformers Benjamin Rush, William Roscoe, and Edward Livingston. Beccaria's late nineteenth-century successor Cesare Lombroso also wrapped his criminal law concerns in the broader context of police and welfare experiments to secure social peace and security: universal suffrage; productive and distributive cooperation; state provision for sickness, premature death, old age, and accidents; mutual benefit societies; prevention of child labor; factory inspection; progressive taxation; and worker's compensation. See Charles Richmond Henderson, An Introduction to the Study of Dependent, Defective, and Delinquent Classes (Boston, 1893), 263–64.

6. Jacob D. Wheeler, Reports of Criminal Law Cases, 3 vols. (New York, 1854), 1:4–6. Echoing James Wilson on the social nature of man, Wheeler elaborated: "What is man out of the operations of these principles? As an individual he is solitary, and would be a most miserably wretched being. He was made for society, and to it he must fly for happiness—nay, he must fly to it for existence; he will do it and has done it in all ages. Experience has shown us, what common sense had instructed us before, that society without rules and laws to regulate it is no society at all." In addition to imbibing fully the rhetoric of the well-regulated society, Wheeler's analysis was also replete with 1850s assumptions about the roles of race and youth in crime and immorality, condemning the proportion of "boys and girls" (33 percent) and "colored people" (33 percent) brought before the New York Police Court in 1850. Wheeler, Reports, 11–12. For more on the close relation of penal laws and the well-regulated society, see Nathaniel Chipman, Principles of Government: A Treatise on Free Institutions (Burlington, Vt., 1833), 209–17.

7. Joel Prentiss Bishop, Commentaries on the Criminal Law, 4th ed., 2 vols. (1856; Boston, 1868), 1:545.

8. The Book of the General Laws and Liberties concerning the Inhabitants of Massachusetts (Cambridge, Mass., 1648). For the best discussions of colonial law and morality, see David H. Flaherty, "Law and the Enforcement of Morals in Early America," in Law in American History, ed. Donald Fleming and Bernard Bailyn (Boston, 1971), 203–53; William E. Nelson, Americanization of the Common Law: The Impact of Legal Change on Massachusetts Society, 1760–1830 (Cambridge, Mass., 1975), ch. 3.

9. Increase Mather, An Arrow against Profane and Promiscuous Dancing. Drawn out of a Quiver of the Scriptures (Boston, 1684); John Barnard, The Throne Established by Righteous-

ness (Boston, 1734), reprinted in *The Puritans*, ed. Perry Miller and Thomas H. Johnson, rev. ed., 2 vols. (New York, 1963), 1:272.

10. Quoted in Flaherty, "Law and Morals," 212.

11. Once again, the colonial urban surveys of Carl Bridenbaugh are invaluable and intimidatingly thorough. Bridenbaugh, *Cities in the Wilderness: The First Century of Urban Life in America, 1625–1742* (New York, 1938), 71–73, 226–30, 386–87; Bridenbaugh, *Cities in Revolt: Urban Life in America, 1743–1776* (New York, 1955), 119–22. Puritan and colonial morals cases are notorious and entertaining—I've restrained myself. For nice summations, see Lawrence M. Friedman, *A History of American Law*, 2d ed. (New York, 1985), 68–75; Kermit L. Hall, *The Magic Mirror: Law in American History* (New York, 1989), 30–35.

12. Roscoe Pound, *The Formative Era of American Law* (Boston, 1938). For an extreme and proudly ahistorical restatement of this theme, see Grant Gilmore, *The Ages of American Law* (New Haven, Conn., 1977).

13. William E. Nelson, "Emerging Notions of Modern Criminal Law in the Revolutionary Era: An Historical Perspective," *New York University Law Review* 42 (1967): 451; Nelson, *Americanization of the Common Law*; Flaherty, "Law and Morals," 245–53; Hall, *Magic Mirror*, 169.

14. Lawrence M. Friedman, *Crime and Punishment in American History* (New York, 1993), 125–40.

15. See the subsequent work of Steinberg, *The Transformation of Criminal Justice*; Friedman, *Crime and Punishment*.

16. This disparateness is mirrored in a massive literature including: Ronald G. Walters, *American Reformers, 1815–1860* (New York, 1978); Clifford S. Griffin, *Their Brothers' Keepers: Moral Stewardship in the United States, 1800–1865* (New Brunswick, N.J., 1960); Paul S. Boyer, *Urban Masses and Moral Order in America, 1820–1920* (Cambridge, Mass., 1978); Carroll Smith-Rosenberg, *Religion and the Rise of the American City: The New York City Mission Movement, 1812–1870* (Ithaca, N.Y., 1971); Lori D. Ginzberg, *Women and the Work of Benevolence: Morality, Politics and Class in the Nineteenth-Century United States* (New Haven, Conn., 1990).

17. Cotton Mather, *Bonifacius: An Essay upon the Good* (Boston, 1710); Paul E. Johnson, *A Shopkeeper's Millennium: Society and Revivals in Rochester, New York, 1815–1837* (New York, 1978); Timothy L. Smith, *Revivalism and Social Reform: American Protestantism on the Eve of the Civil War* (Baltimore, 1980); Donald G. Mathews, "The Second Great Awakening As an Organizing Process," *American Quarterly* 21 (1969): 23–43.

18. Lyman Beecher, "A Reformation of Morals Practicable and Indispensable," in Beecher, *Works*, 3 vols. (Boston, 1852), 2:75–113; Beecher, *The Autobiography of Lyman Beecher*, ed. Barbara M. Cross, 2 vols. (Cambridge, Mass., 1961) 1:185–93, 251–56; Boyer, *Urban Masses*, 12–13.

19. Swift also authored the first comprehensive analyses of American common law. Zephaniah Swift, *A System of the Laws of Connecticut* (Windham, Conn., 1795); Swift, *Digest of the Laws of Connecticut* (New Haven, Conn., 1822). For more on these connections see Beecher's sermons "The Government of God Desirable" and "The Bible a Code of Laws," in Beecher, *Works*, 2:5–32, 154–203.

20. Beecher's Society was not the first moral reform organization. In his sermons, he relied on ample English precedents dating back to the late seventeenth century. The resonances of Mather's *Bonifacius* in his "Reformation of Morals" are striking. Yale had established a student Moral Society as early as 1797, and New York, Philadelphia, and Pittsburgh had short-lived societies for the "Suppression of Vice" in the first decade of the nineteenth

century. Boyer, *Urban Masses*, 14. On English precedents, see Sidney Webb and Beatrice Webb, *The History of Liquor Licensing in England Principally from 1700 to 1830* (London, 1903), 137–51.

21. Charles I. Foster, *An Errand of Mercy: The Evangelical United Front, 1790–1837* (Chapel Hill, N.C., 1960), 275–79.

22. Walters, *American Reformers*, 31.

23. Patrick Colquhoun, *A Treatise on the Police of the Metropolis* (London, 1796). For an excellent discussion of these theorists and the constriction of police, see Tomlins, *Law, Labor, and Ideology*, 78–80.

24. Charles Christian, *A Brief Treatise on the Police of the City of New-York* (New York, 1812), 4.

25. Ibid., 30; James F. Richardson, *The New York Police: Colonial Times to 1901* (New York, 1970); Roger Lane, *Policing the City: Boston, 1822–1885* (Cambridge, Mass., 1967); Eric H. Monkkonen, *Police in Urban America, 1860–1920* (New York, 1981); Eric H. Monkkonen, "A Disorderly People? Urban Order in the Nineteenth and Twentieth Centuries," *Journal of American History* 68 (1981): 539; John C. Schneider, *Detroit and the Problem of Order, 1830–1880: A Geography of Crime, Riot, and Policing* (Lincoln, Neb., 1980); Steinberg, *The Transformation of Criminal Justice*; Paul A. Gilje, *The Road to Mobocracy: Popular Disorder in New York City, 1763–1834* (Chapel Hill, N.C., 1987), 267–82. *People v. Draper*, 25 Barb. 344 (N.Y., 1857); *People v. Draper*, 15 N.Y. 532 (1857); *Mayor of Baltimore v. State*, 15 Md. 376 (1860).

26. Daniel DeFoe, *Poor Man's Plea* (London, 1698). DeFoe was also one of the earliest commentators to point out the double standard behind bourgeois moral reform: "These are all cobweb laws, in which the small flies are catched, and the great ones break through. . . . 'Tis hard, gentlemen, to be punished for a crime by [men] as guilty as ourselves; this is really punishing men for being poor, which is no crime at all." Also see Gilje, *Mobocracy*; David J. Rothman, *The Discovery of the Asylum: Social Order and Disorder in the New Republic* (Boston, 1971); Kasson, *Rudeness and Civility*.

27. John Allen Krout, *The Origins of Prohibition* (New York, 1925); Griffin, *Their Brothers' Keepers*; Walters, *American Reformers*.

28. Joseph R. Gusfield, *Symbolic Crusade: Status Politics and the American Temperance Movement* (Urbana, Ill., 1963); Ian R. Tyrrell, *Sobering Up: From Temperance to Prohibition in Antebellum America, 1800–1860* (Westport, Conn., 1979); Robert L. Hampel, *Temperance and Prohibition in Massachusetts, 1813–1852* (Ann Arbor, Mich., 1982). The classic text for a later period is, of course, Richard Hofstadter, *Age of Reform* (New York, 1955).

29. Rodgers, *The Work Ethic*; Gutman, *Work, Culture and Society*.

30. Gilje, *Mobocracy*; Christine Stansell, *City of Women: Sex and Class in New York, 1789–1860* (New York, 1982), 65; Timothy J. Gilfoyle, *City of Eros: New York City, Prostitution, and the Commercialization of Sex, 1790–1920* (New York, 1992); Marilynn Wood Hill, *Their Sisters' Keepers: Prostitution in New York City, 1830–1870* (Berkeley, Calif., 1993); Ginzberg, *Women and Benevolence*.

31. Cover's essays are collected in *Narrative, Violence, and the Law: The Essays of Robert Cover*, ed. by Martha Minow, Michael Ryan, and Austin Sarat (Ann Arbor, Mich., 1992). See especially "Nomos and Narrative" and "Violence and the Word."

32. Beecher, *Autobiography*, 192; Boyer, *Urban Masses*, 18–19.

33. *Constitution or Form of Government for the Commonwealth of Massachusetts* (Boston, 1780), part I, art. 18.

34. As Bishop made perfectly clear, the common law continued to play an important role in criminal jurisprudence into the late nineteenth century despite the postrevolutionary

debate over federal common law crimes and the extraordinary commentary produced in Ohio (Ohio, Indiana, Florida, and Missouri all severely restricted use of the common law in criminal cases by midcentury). John Milton Goodenow's *Historical Sketches of the Principles and Maxims of American Jurisprudence* (Steubenville, Ohio, 1819) is a fascinating and innovative attack on common law crimes, but its historical significance may have been exaggerated by legal historians given Goodenow's caution upon its 1821 printing: "Sixty copies, only, of this work were printed [in 1819]; none were sold; and all the copies are within my knowledge." For influential discussions of common law crimes and Goodenow, see Morton J. Horwitz, *The Transformation of American Law, 1780–1860* (Cambridge, Mass., 1977), 9–30; G. Edward White, *The Marshall Court and Cultural Change, 1815–1835,* abr. ed. (New York, 1991), 139–47; Friedman, *A History of American Law,* 290.

35. Bishop, *Commentaries,* 1:545–50.

36. *Public Statute Laws of the State of Connecticut* (1830), c. 1, 268–76. The criminal codes of New York, Iowa, and Georgia tell similar stories. *The Revised Statutes of the State of New York,* 3 vols. (Albany, N.Y., 1860), 3: title 5, "Offenses against the Public Peace and Public Morals," 966–70 (adding restrictions on dueling and poisoning cattle); *Statutes of a General Nature of the State of Iowa* (Des Moines, Iowa, 1860), c. 172, "Offenses against Chastity, Morality, and Decency," 744–47 (adding "enticing virtuous females to bad houses," cruelty to animals, and disturbing worshiping congregations); *The Code of the State of Georgia* (Atlanta, 1867), tenth division, "Offenses against the Public Morality, Health, Police, Etc.," 875–85 (adding "marrying white and colored," "adultery with negroes," "retailing near church," and "illegal bathing").

37. Bishop, *Commentaries,* 15. On private prosecution, see Steinberg, *The Transformation of Criminal Justice.*

38. For example, Jacksonville, Illinois, site of several midcentury battles over local option, was chartered in 1849 with ample powers to regulate "disorders, indecencies, and obscenities." *Goddard v. Jacksonville,* 15 Ill. 588 (1854), 589. See also *President v. Holland,* 19 Ill. 271 (1857); *Block v. Jacksonville,* 36 Ill. 301 (1865); *Kettering v. Jacksonville,* 50 Ill. 39 (1869).

39. See, for example, Daniel Davis, *A Practical Treatise upon the Authority and Duty of Justices of the Peace* (Boston, 1824); Rudolphus Dickinson, *A Compilation of the Laws of Massachusetts Comprising the Titles of Assessors, Auctioneers, Clerks, Commissioners of Sewers, Etc.* (Boston, 1811).

40. See, for example, *Nott's Case,* 11 Me. 208 (1834), and *Portland v. Bangor,* 42 Me. 403 (1856).

41. For the most innovative examination of this hard-to-get-at phenomenon (and its limits), see Stansell, *City of Women.*

42. Thomas M. Cooley, *A Treatise on the Constitutional Limitations* (Boston, 1868), 596 (emphasis added). By 1886, Cooley's more radical scion, Christopher Tiedeman, strenuously objected to this linkage of government and morality, vice and crime: "The police power of the government cannot be brought into operation for the purpose of exacting obedience to the rules of morality, and banishing vice and sin from the world." Christopher G. Tiedeman, *A Treatise on the Limitations of Police Power in the United States* (St. Louis, 1886), 150.

43. *Mayo v. Wilson,* 1 N.H. 53 (1817), 57. On Sunday laws, see William Addison Blakely, *American State Papers Bearing on Sunday Legislation* (Washington, D.C., 1911). For an excellent discussion of the continuation of religious regulatory laws in Massachusetts (including prosecutions for blasphemy), see Leonard W. Levy, *The Law of the Commonwealth and Chief Justice Shaw* (New York, 1957), 29–58.

44. *Jones v. People,* 14 Ill. 196 (1852), 197.

45. *State v. Haines*, 30 Me. 65 (1849), 75. New York Justice Cowen argued similarly in *Tanner v. Albion*, "A useless establishment wasting the time of the owner, tending to fasten his own idle habits on his family, and to draw the men and boys of the neighborhood into a bad moral atmosphere—a place which, in despite of every care, will be attended by profligates, with evil communication, and at best with a waste of time and money, followed by the multiplication of paupers and rogues—has always been considered an obvious nuisance." *Tanner v. Trustees of Albion*, 5 Hill 121 (N.Y., 1843), 128. Also see *Hackney v. State*, 8 Ind. 494 (1856); and *State v. Hall*, 32 NJL 158 (1867), *contra*.

46. *State v. Roper*, 18 N.C. 208 (1835); *Nolin v. Mayor of Franklin*, 12 Tenn. 163 (1833); *State v. Toole*, 106 N.C. 736 (1890); *Jacko v. State*, 22 Ala. 73 (1853).

47. Friedman, *A History of American Law*, 314.

48. William Pitt, *Speech on the Excise Bill*, quoted in Jacob W. Landynski, *Search and Seizure and the Supreme Court* (Baltimore, 1966), 26.

49. *State v. Buckley*, 5 Del. 508 (1854), 508.

50. *Commonwealth v. Stewart*, 1 S&R 342 (Pa., 1815), 346. Yeates elaborated: "The entertaining of persons of both sexes, of evil name and fame, and of dishonest conversation, at unseasonable hours, and suffering them to remain tippling and misbehaving themselves, necessarily eventuates in riots and disorders, injurious to the peace and quiet of the neighbours." The *sic utere tuo* rationale was ubiquitous in disorderly house cases. New York's Justice Cowen invoked the spirit of the well-regulated society: "Men must act in good faith, and with due reference to the interests of others." *Brockway v. People*, 2 Hill 558 (N.Y., 1842), 564. The typical nineteenth-century complaint hinged on *sic utere tuo*, holding that disorderly houses existed "to the great damage and common nuisance of all the citizens." For a sampling of typical disorderly house complaints, see Davis, *The Authority and Duty of the Justices of the Peace*, 335–39.

51. Blackstone was unequivocal: "All disorderly inns or ale-houses, bawdy-houses, gaming-houses, . . . and the like, are public nuisances, and may upon indictment be suppressed and fined." William Blackstone, *Commentaries on the Laws of England: A Facsimile of the First Edition of 1756–1769*, 4 vols. (Chicago, 1979), 4:168. Also see William Hawkins, *A Treatise of the Pleas of the Crown* (London, 1716), 1:196–200.

52. Horace G. Wood, *A Practical Treatise on the Law of Nuisances* 2d. ed. (Albany, N.Y., 1883), 36. The classic statement on public nuisances per se is *Tanner v. Trustees v. Albion*. *Contra* in cases of bowling alleys, theaters, and landlords, see *People v. Baldwin*, 1 Wheeler Cr. Cas. 279 (NY, 1823); *Bloomhuff v. State*, 8 Blackf. 205 (Ind., 1846); *State v. Hall*; *State v. Lewis*, 5 Mo. App. 465 (1878). For a similar prioritization of disorderly houses, see Matthew Bacon, *A New Abridgment of the Law*, ed. John Bouvier (Philadelphia, 1852), 7:223–26.

53. *State v. Roper*; *Miller v. People*, 5 Barb. 203 (N.Y., 1849); *State v. Rose*, 32 Mo. 560 (1862).

54. *Alfred S. Pell's Case*, 3 City Hall Recorder 141 (N.Y., 1818). This particular case was occasioned when an irate husband assaulted the servant providing the obligatory light.

55. *Commonwealth v. Barker*, 19 Pa. St. 412 (1852).

56. *State v. Mathews*, 19 N.C. 424 (1837); *State v. Wright*, 51 N.C. 25 (1858). In the latter, Chief Justice Pearson threw out a disorderly house indictment against a father bringing up five drunkard sons who, "when in that situation," had a tendency to "wrangle, curse and swear most profanely, and make a loud noise; that the father, at times, would try to keep them in order; that this loud noise and profane swearing would continue until after midnight, in so loud a manner as to be heard at a distance." Pearson explicitly distinguished country and town life arguing, "if this disorder had been in a town, where all the good people of the State had a right to be, and to pass and repass, or on or near a public highway . . . it would have amounted to a common as distinguished from a private nui-

sance, so as to be indictable, yet it is clearly not so, having been committed in the country to the disturbance of only two families residing in the vicinity." *Wright*, 26 – 27. For a similar requirement of "publicity" for violation of the Sabbath, see *Hall v. State*, 4 Harr. 132 (Del., 1844), 140.

57. Gilfoyle, *City of Eros*.

58. *Commonwealth v. Stewart*, 1 S&R 342 (Pa., 1815), 345.

59. *State v. Williams*, 30 NJL 102 (1862), 104. Chief Justice Whelpley elaborated, "Any place of public resort, whether an inn, a dwelling house, a storehouse, or any other building or garden, is a public nuisance . . . when it becomes the habitual resort of thieves, drunkards, prostitutes, or other idle, vicious, and disorderly persons, who gather together there for the purposes of gratifying their own depraved appetites, or to make it a rendezvous where plans may be concocted for depredations upon society. . . . No private individual has a right, for his own amusement or gain, to carry on a public business clearly injurious to and destructive of the public quiet, health, or morals, and is indictable for so doing, because the injury is of a public character to the public, and not merely private, or to a single individual."

60. *Martha Boyd's Cases*, 3 City Hall Recorder 134 (N.Y., 1818); *People v. Carey*, 4 Parker Cr. Rep. 238 (N.Y., 1857).

61. *Amos Broad's Case*, 3 City Hall Recorder 7 (N.Y., 1818); ibid., 2 City Hall Recorder 25 (N.Y., 1817). For an extended discussion of Broad's tempestuous ministry, see Gilje, *Mobocracy*, 214 – 20.

62. An 1809 Washington, D.C., ordinance proscribed EO, ABC, LSD, faro, rolly-bolly, shuffle-board, equality tables, and other devices used with cards, balls, dice, coin, or money for the purposes of gaming for money. *United States v. Holly*, 3 Cranch, C.C. 656 (1829), Fed. Cas. #15,381.

63. Blackstone, *Commentaries*, 4:172; Christian, *Police of New York*, 20.

64. *State v. Layman*, 5 Harr. 510 (Del., 1854), 511; Nathan Dane provided the fullest statement of this threat: "Gaming, and immoralities in gaming-houses, inns, retailers' shops, play-houses, and idleness, are offenses always associated and in company. Men are so made and constituted, that idleness is tedious, and constantly wants relief. How to pass away, or in other words, to kill time, is ever an inquiry among idle men, or men who want the steady and regular employments of industry, and rational pursuits. With such, one mode of relief has ever been, to resort to gaming, to gaming-houses, to taverns, grog-shops, play-houses, billiard-tables, etc. These, in their turn have a direct and irresistible tendency to produce idleness, intemperance, and habits the most immoral and vicious. These are the places in which men often become intemperate, lazy, and immoral; and men, any way inclined to be of this description, are almost instinctively drawn to these places. Then, to regulate and keep in good order these places, is in effect, to correct, as well as to prevent, in many cases, intemperate and vicious habits. But idleness is sometimes sluggish and solitary, earns nothing, but consumes and corrupts the man who lives by himself, and makes him a vagabond, and worse than useless." Dane, *A General Abridgment and Digest of American Law*, 8 vols. (Boston, 1823), 7:41. Class tension and allegiance were at the heart of such antigambling sentiment, but jurists often dwelled more on the temptations to "the middling ranks of life" than on the criminality of the "horde of low gamblers." When the "genteel" Park Coffee-House in New York fell victim to a gambling prosecution, the reporter noted, "Although, on this occasion, the court could have wished that this offence could have been fastened on a defendant who had kept a house of worse description, . . . yet Courts and Juries have no choice. They are bound as conservators of the morals of the community, to endeavor to check the progress of this vice, whenever it may fall under their cognizance."

James Butler's Case, 1 City Hall Rec. 66 (N.Y., 1816), 67; Christian, *Police*, 20–21. One of the earliest English gaming statutes (33 Hen. VIII. c. 9) was distinctly class-based, prohibiting all but gentlemen the games of tennis, tables, cards, dice, bowls, and the like, except at Christmas. But by the late eighteenth century, William Blackstone was less concerned with common gamblers than "gaming in high life." Blackstone, *Commentaries*, 4:171. On the social and political history of gambling, see John M. Findlay, *People of Chance* (New York, 1986).

65. *United States v. Ismenard*, 1 Cranch, C.C. 150 (1803), Fed. Cas. #15,450; *State v. Doon and Dimond*, R.M. Charlt. 1 (Ga., 1811); *Alexander Cuscadden's Case*, 2 City Hall Rec. 53 (N.Y., 1817); *Commonwealth v. Hyde*, Thach. Crim. 19 (Mass., 1823); *United States v. Holly*, 3 Cranch, C.C. 656 (1829), Fed. Cas. #15,381; *Lockhart v. State*, 10 Tx. 275 (1853); *Rice v. State*, 10 Tx. 545 (1853); *Vanderworker v. State*, 13 Ark. 700 (1853); *Commonwealth v. Stahl*, 89 Mass. 304 (1863).

66. "An Act for the better Preventing of excessive and deceitful Gaming," *Statutes at Large of South Carolina, 1682–1838*, ed. David J. McCord, 10 vols. (Columbia, S.C., 1841), 2 (1712), 565; "An Additional Act for the more effectual Prevention of Gaming," ibid., 5 (1802), 432.

67. "For the rub" indicated play for rental of the table. *David and Anthony Lyner's Case*, 5 City Hall Rec. 136 (N.Y., 1820); *State v. Leighton*, 23 N.H. 167 (1851). Justice Gilchrist of New Hampshire elaborated on the dangers inherent even in playing dominos for food and drink: "A common gaming-house is indictable as a nuisance . . . 'because they are temptations to idleness and because they are apt to draw together great numbers of disorderly persons.' These mischiefs are quite as likely to result from the kind of gaming described in the instructions of the court, as from gaming for money whether in large sums or small. Each form of the vice might afford peculiar attractions for its appropriate class of idlers, and give occasion for its appropriate train of social disorders." *Lord v. State*, 16 N.H. 325 (1844), 330. For a more tolerant perspective, see *People v. Sergeant*, 8 Cow. 139 (N.Y., 1844).

68. In *Willis v. Warren* (1859), Police Justice Connolly without charge or warrant burst into a private card game, arresting all present and confiscating equipment and obscene pictures. New York Justice Brady defended this process and the ultimate destruction of such property: "It is the policy of the law to destroy gambling apparatus . . . which is considered by the law most mischievous in its consequences to society." *Willis v. Warren*, 1 Hilt. C.P. 590 (NY, 1859), 594. For an early and eloquent defense of notice and procedural due process, see *State v. Savannah*, T.U.P. Charl. 235 (Ga., 1809), 236: "[E]ven God himself, did not pass sentence upon Adam, before he was called upon to make his defence. Adam (says God), where art thou; has thou eaten of the tree, whereof I commanded thee that they should not eat? And the same question was put to Eve also." As further testament to such limitations, see *State v. Lafferty*, 5 Harr. 491 (Del., 1854), where the city watchman was fined $5 and costs for using unnecessary force in the arrest of a domino player.

69. *Commonwealth v. Tilton*, 49 Mass. 232 (1844), 234; *Charles Meyer's Case*, 1 City Hall Rec. 67 (N.Y., 1816); *John I. Moore's Case*, 6 City Hall Rec. 87 (N.Y., 1821).

70. One of the implications of the well-regulated society is that the divisions imperative to Jürgen Habermas's blueprint of the eighteenth-century public sphere, that is, the separation of public from private and the public sphere from both civil society and the state, are remarkably attenuated if not nonexistent in the antebellum United States. Jürgen Habermas, *The Structural Transformation of the Public Sphere: An Inquiry into a Category of Bourgeois Society*, trans. Thomas Burger (Cambridge, Mass., 1989).

71. *Jacob Hall's Case*, 1 Mod. 76 (Eng., 1683); also see *King v. Betterton and Others*, 5 Mod. 142 (Eng., 1696). The most revealing and entertaining commentary on *Hall's Case* came via

Justice Cowen in *Tanner v. Trustees of Albion*, 342: "Surely we have not come to an age when the morality of the law is relaxed beyond what it was in the reign of Charles II., the date of Hall's booth, erected, as he said, by license from the king. This was a very probable account. Charles was known to be the most careless in his moral conduct of any man in his kingdom, and to keep a court which was abandoned to all sorts of licentiousness. The Duke of Buckingham, his principal adviser, was said himself to have been a rope-dancer. It is not very likely that a king whose palace was distinguished for being the largest brothel in Europe, and is known to have dismissed Lord Clarendon on the advice of Buckingham and the Duchess of Cleveland, a prostitute, would hesitate to license a vicious establishment for which such courtiers might invoke his patronage. The rule of the common law becomes more evident, and the precedent referred to more imposing, when placed in contrast with the moral waste by which it was surrounded. I must be allowed to protest against the supposition that the same law will, in this age and country, and in such a village as Albion, hold practices to be innocent which were denounced as offenses against public morals and economy in the reign of Charles II."

72. Wood, *Nuisances*, 87; Bishop, *Commentaries*, 627; Dane, *Abridgment*, 7:47–48.

73. *Jacko v. State*; *Thurber v. Sharp*, 13 Barb. 627 (N.Y., 1852); *Knowles v. State*, 3 Day 103 (Conn., 1808); *Commonwealth v. Haines*, 4 Clark 17 (Pa., 1824). In *Commonwealth v. Gee*, 60 Mass. 174 (1850), the court drew the line at the indictment of a dancing school.

74. *People v. Baldwin*, 1 Wheeler Cr. Cas. 279 (N.Y., 1823), 285; *Berry v. People*, 1 N.Y. Crim. Rep. 43 (1878), 44. Also see *State v. Fox*, 12 Vt. 22 (1843); *Pike v. Commonwealth*, 63 Ky. 89 (1865). Matthew Bacon suggested that theaters became nuisances when "they pervert their original institution, by recommending vicious and loose characters under beautiful colours to the imitation of the people, and make a jest of things commendable, serious, and useful." Bacon, *Abridgment*, 7:224.

75. Building on an English theatrical licensing and censorship tradition dating from the sixteenth century, Massachusetts banned stage plays in 1750 because of their tendency to "discourage industry and frugality" and "increase immorality, impiety and a contempt of religion." By 1806, however, the commonwealth adopted a more discriminatory licensing policy salvaging those performances, as Hawkins put it, "recommending Virtue . . . and exposing Vice and Folly." Unvirtuous or immoral theatrics remained subject to nuisance proscriptions. By the 1830s and 1840s, the Astor Place Riot and the emergence of the "guilty third-tier" as a site of prostitution and scandal brought even stricter control. "An Act for Preventing Stage-Plays and Other Theatrical Entertainments," *Laws of Massachusetts Bay* (1750), c. 24; "An Act for Preventing Public Stage Plays, Interludes, and Other Theatrical Entertainments, in Certain Cases," *Laws of Massachusetts* (Boston, 1806), 117. Virginia Crocheron Gildersleeve, *Government Regulation of the Elizabethan Drama* (New York, 1908); L. W. Conolly, *The Censorship of English Drama, 1737–1824* (San Marino, Calif., 1976); Hawkins, *A Treatise of the Pleas of the Crown*; Richard Hofstadter and Michael Wallace, eds., *American Violence: A Documentary History* (New York, 1970), 453–57; Claudia D. Johnson, "That Guilty Third Tier: Prostitution in Nineteenth-Century American Theaters," in *Victorian America*, ed. Daniel Walker Howe (Philadelphia, 1976), 111–20; Abe Laufe, *The Wicked Stage: A History of Theater Censorship and Harassment in the U.S.* (New York, 1978). By the 1890s, even baseball games were suspect; see *Commonwealth v. Meyers*, 8 Pa. Co. Ct. R. 435 (1890). As testament to the dogged persistence of this strand of morals regulation, on the day these paragraphs were drafted the Dallas police cited the Dallas Theater Center for a nude scene in the play "Six Degrees of Separation." *New York Times*, November 4, 1993.

76. *Stephanes v. State*, 21 Tx. 206 (1858); *Dunnaway v. State*, 17 Tenn. 350 (1836); *Henry v.*

Commonwealth, 48 Ky. 361 (1849); *United States v. Prout*, 1 Cranch, C.C. 203 (1804), Fed. Cas. #16,093; *United States v. Coulter*, 1 Cranch, C.C. 203 (1804), Fed. Cas. #14,875; *United States v. Lindsay*, 1 Cranch, C.C. 245 (1805), Fed. Cas. #15,602. As *Stephanes* and *Dunnaway* made clear, appellate courts did not hesitate to override lower-court convictions based on inadequate evidence, for example, an allegation that "negroes got drunk there." See also *Frederick v. Commonwealth*, 43 Ky. 7 (1843). The infrequency of references to the race of defendants in northern disorderly house cases makes it difficult to assess its overall impact there.

77. *Smith v. Commonwealth*, 45 Ky. 21 (1845), 22 (emphasis added).

78. Ibid., 23. See also *Wilson v. Commonwealth*, 51 Ky. 2 (1851).

79. *State v. Boyce*, 32 N.C. 536 (1849), 537. This was one of those cases of almost absurd disparity between indictment and reality. The indictment charged that Boyce "did keep and maintain a certain common, ill governed, and disorderly house, and in said house, for his own lucre and gain, certain persons, both men and women, and white and black, of evil name and fame, and of dishonest and lewd conversation, to frequent and come together at unlawful times, as well in the night as the day, and on Sundays, and there to be and remain, drinking, tippling, and otherwise misbehaving themselves." Similarly extreme was the elaborate planning that went into the suppression of this Christmas celebration, which was provoked by an uneasiness with a similar gathering at Christmas, 1845. The fiddler at the party was sent there by one of the slave patrol.

80. In the end, Ruffin deferred to the need for seasonal merrymakings, but his racial assumptions were as significant a regulatory tool as the slave patrol's whip: "If slaves would do nothing, tending more to the corruption of their morals or to the annoyance of whites, than seeking the exhilaration of their simple music and romping dances, they might be set down as an innocent and happy class. We may let them make the most of their idle hours, and may well make allowances for the noisy outpourings of glad hearts, which providence bestows as a blessing on corporeal vigor united to a vacant mind." Ibid., 539–41.

81. Osgood Bradbury, *Female Depravity; or, The House of Death* (New York, 1857).

82. Christian, *Police*, 18–19.

83. Hill, *Their Sisters' Keepers*; Gilfoyle, *City of Eros*; Barbara Meil Hobson, *Uneasy Virtue: The Politics of Prostitution and the American Reform Tradition* (New York, 1987); Stansell, *City of Women*; Boyer, *Urban Masses*. On prostitution in the early twentieth century, see Ruth Rosen, *The Lost Sisterhood: Prostitution in America, 1900–1918* (Baltimore, 1982); and in the West, see Marion S. Goldman, *Gold Diggers and Silver Miners: Prostitution and Social Life on the Comstock Lode* (Ann Arbor, Mich., 1981); Anne M. Butler, *Daughters of Joy, Sisters of Misery: Prostitutes in the American West, 1865–90* (Urbana, Ill., 1985). The definitive study of prostitution in Britain is Judith R. Walkowitz, *Prostitution in Victorian Society: Women, Class, and the State* (Cambridge, 1980).

84. Daniel Rogers, ed., *The City-Hall Recorder* (New York, 1816–1820), 1:iii.

85. Daniel A. Cohen, *Pillars of Salt, Monuments of Grace* (New York, 1993).

86. *Mary Rothbone's Case*, 1 City Hall Rec. 26 (N.Y., 1816).

87. Ibid., 26–27. On private prosecution, see Steinberg, *The Transformation of Criminal Justice*.

88. *Mary Rothbone's Case*, 27.

89. Ibid. See for example, Nancy F. Cott, *The Bonds of Womanhood: 'Woman's Sphere' in New England, 1780–1835* (New Haven, Conn., 1977); Mary P. Ryan, *Cradle of the Middle Class: The Family in Oneida County, New York, 1790–1865* (New York, 1981); Kathryn Kish Sklar, *Catharine Beecher: A Study in American Domesticity* (New Haven, Conn., 1973). It should be noted that this moralism also cut in the other direction, especially regarding the

proper "place" for a married man. In *Mary Hagerty's Case*, 1 City Hall Rec. 108 (N.Y., 1816), the judge lectured a married man at length for being at a house of ill-fame at unseasonable hours rather than at home with his family.

90. True to form, Rothbone's defense focused exclusively on the reputation of the daughter as "of an infamous abandoned character." *Mary Rothbone's Case*, 27.

91. *Joanna Clark's Case*, 1 City Hall Rec. 136 (N.Y., 1816); *People v. Foot*, 1 Wheeler Cr. Cas. 70 (N.Y., 1822); *People v. Rowland*, 1 Wheeler Cr. Cas. 286 (N.Y., 1823); *People v. Clark*, 1 Wheeler Cr. Cas. 288 (N.Y., 1823); *State v. Nixon*, 18 Vt. 70 (1846); *State v. Bentz*, 11 Mo. 27 (1847); *Commonwealth v. Ashley*, 68 Mass. 356 (1854); *Maine v. Homer*, 40 Me. 438 (1855); *Maine v. Stevens*, 40 Me. 559 (1855); *Commonwealth v. Hart*, 76 Mass. 465 (1858); *Commonwealth v. Davis*, 77 Mass. 48 (1858); *Commonwealth v. Langley*, 80 Mass. 21 (1859); *McAlister v. Clark*, 33 Conn. 91 (1865); *Barnesciotta v. People*, 10 Hun. 137 (N.Y., 1877); *Commonwealth v. Ballou*, 124 Mass. 26 (1878); *United States v. Rollinson*, 2 Cranch, C.C. 13, Fed. Cas. #16,191 (1810); *United States v. Nailor*, 4 Cranch, C.C. 372, Fed. Cas. #15,853 (1833); *United States v. Jourdine*, 4 Cranch, C.C. 338, Fed. Cas. #15,499 (1833); *United States v. Stevens*, 4 Cranch, C.C. 341, Fed. Cas. #16,391 (1833); *United States v. McDowell*, 4 Cranch, C.C. 423, Fed. Cas. #15,671 (1834).

92. *Childress v. Mayor of Nashville*, 35 Tenn. 347 (1855), 352, 357.

93. *Neaf v. Palmer*, 45 S.W. 506 (1898).

94. Jacob D. Wheeler, *Reports of Criminal Law Cases* (New York, 1854), 1:290.

95. *Brockway v. People*, 2 Hill 558 (N.Y., 1842).

96. New York courts split on the criminal liability of landlords and the voidability of leases. On voidability, see *Updike v. Campbell*, 4 E.D. Smith 570 (N.Y., 1855) and the cases discussed therein. One reason for caution on the voidability issue was the potential for cohabiting tenants to use their "immoral" status to escape rent obligations. See *Trovinger v. M'Burney*, 5 Cow. 253 (N.Y., 1825). Justice Cowen's dissent in *Brockway v. People* employed the classic *sic utere tuo* argument against landlord's property interests: "It may be said—indeed, it is always said in cases of this kind—that men may sell or demise their property for what price or rent they please. No one will deny this, when taken with the proper qualification, viz.: that they shall not couple with such a transaction any criminal stipulations or understanding. Men must act in good faith, and with due reference to the interests of others. *Sic utere tuo ut alienum non laedas.*" *Brockway v. People*, 563. *People v. Erwin*, 4 Denio 129 (N.Y., 1847), explicitly overrode Nelson in *Brockway* and held the landlord indictable as a "keeper" of a bawdyhouse. Also see *Lowenstein v. People*, 54 Barb. 299 (N.Y., 1863). Nationally, most states followed the Massachusetts rule that landlords were indictable. *Commonwealth v. Harrington*, 20 Mass. 26 (1825); *Ross v. Commonwealth*, 41 Ky. 417 (1842); *Smith v. State*, 6 Gill 425 (Md., 1848); *Commonwealth v. Johnson*, 2 Am. L. J. 359 (Pa., 1849). Other states insisted on some proof that landlords had knowledge of the "immoral" usage made of their properties. *State v. Abrahams*, 4 Ia. 541 (1857); *State v. Lewis*, 5 Mo. App. 465 (1878).

97. *Hamilton v. Whitridge*, 11 Md. 128 (1857). Some classic cases in the legal evolution of progressive "injunction and abatement" are *State v. Crawford*, 28 Kan. 726 (1882); *Mugler v. Kansas*, 123 U.S. 623 (1887); *Cranford v. Tyrell*, 128 N.Y. 341 (1891); *State v. Canty*, 207 Mo. 439 (1907). On the extent and efficacy of this legislation, passed in thirty-eight states, see Charles S. Ascher and James M. Wolf, "'Red Light' Injunction and Abatement Acts," *Columbia Law Review* 20 (1920): 605–8; Robert McCurdy, "The Use of the Injunction to Destroy Commercialized Prostitution in Chicago," *Journal of Criminal Law* 19 (1929): 513–17.

98. Timothy J. Gilfoyle's *City of Eros* is the most recent example of a more widespread and problematic historical bias against law-on-the-books. Gilfoyle's thoroughly researched

monograph rightly exposes a gap between public rhetoric about law and morality and the proliferation of establishments for rhetoricians (among others) to indulge private vice. But after restricting research into "the enforcement question" to official district attorney indictment records and police court papers—rather than, for example, private nuisance suits or equity court records—Gilfoyle then posits a more general sexual revolution supported by official "toleration," "leniency," and a legal and governmental order "devoted primarily to protecting the interests of taxpayers and private property." Gilfoyle, 83. For more on enforcement and the separation of law and society, see chapter 2, n. 46.

99. *People v. Clark*, 1 Wheeler Cr. Cas. 288 (N.Y., 1823), 290.

100. Ernst Freund, *The Police Power: Public Policy and Constitutional Rights* (Chicago, 1904), 226. For Freund, all prostitutes were women, and the illicit sex to be regulated was heterosexual. He added, "For the purposes of the police power prostitution may be defined as the promiscuous admission of men to intercourse for gain and as a means of livelihood." Though indictments and judges sometimes referred to houses of ill fame as containing prostitutes "of both sexes," I have not come across an early nineteenth-century indictment of a male prostitute. Such cases might have been prosecuted under antisodomy statutes. *People v. Clark.*

101. See *Brooks v. State*, 10 Tenn. 482 (1831); *State v. Botkin*, 71 Ia. 87 (1887).

102. Bacon, *Abridgment*, 7:223. *People v. Brougham*, 1 Wheeler Cr. Cas. 40 (N.Y., 1822). Wheeler cited Bacon in his reporter suggesting, "A wife as well as a husband, may be indicted for keeping a disorderly house, because the charge does not respect the ownership, but the criminal management of the house." 1 Wheeler Cr. Cas. 291. *Commonwealth v. Lewis*, 42 Mass. 151 (1840). For an interesting example of the continued liability of husbands after the Married Women's Property Acts, see *Commonwealth v. Wood*, 97 Mass. 225 (1867). On coverture, see Michael Grossberg, *Governing the Hearth: Law and the Family in Nineteenth-Century America* (Chapel Hill, N.C., 1985), 18–24. Linda Kerber, *Women of the Republic: Intellect and Ideology in Revolutionary America* (Chapel Hill, N.C., 1980), 120–36.

103. *State v. Evans*, 27 N.C. 603 (1845).

104. Ibid., 605. Ultimately North Carolina's Justice Ruffin overturned the verdict on the grounds that unless the visits amounted to cohabitation, the simple admission of men to "the residence of an unchaste woman" was beyond the reach of statute and common law. The correction of morals in such cases, he suggested, was left to the realm of "spiritual supervision and penances." Ibid., 607.

105. *State v. McDowell*, Dud. 346 (S.C., 1838), 349–50.

106. Ibid., 350.

107. Though some jurisdictions did resist the "reputation rule," the very notion of a house of "ill fame" implied continued reliance on popular assessments of character and virtue in the law's morals campaign. The following cases upheld the "reputation rule": *Clements v. State*, 14 Mo. 112 (1851); *State v. M'Gregor*, 41 N.H. 407 (1860); *Commonwealth v. Gannett*, 83 Mass. 7 (1861); *Harwood v. People*, 16 Abb. Pr. 430 (N.Y., 1863). *Cadwell v. State*, 17 Conn. 467 (1846) and *State v. Main*, 31 Conn. 572 (1863) tried to preserve some role for "general reputation" evidence. Those opposed: *Rex v. Doaks*, Quincy 90 (Mass., 1763); *Commonwealth v. Harwood*, 70 Mass. 41 (1855); *State v. Hand*, 7 Ia. 411 (1858). In *People v. Mauch* (1862), Justice Ingraham presented the most enlightened opposition case: "There is no other offence in which general reputation is considered sufficient to convict a man of crime, and when we reflect how such reputation is made up, not from proof of facts, nor from the relation of actual occurrences, but rather from gossip, tale-bearing, prejudices, and other similar means, we may well hesitate at the propriety of permitting such evidence to be sufficient to blast a man's character, or to consign him to a prison." *People v. Mauch*,

24 How. Pr. 276 (N.Y., 1862), 277. Also see the note accompanying *Henson v. State*, 50 Am. Rep. 204 (1884).

108. "An Act for suppressing and punishing Rogues, Vagabonds, common Beggars, and other idle, disorderly and lewd persons," *The General Laws of Massachusetts, 1780–1822*, ed. Asaheal Stearns and Lemuel Shaw, 2 vols. (Boston, 1823), 1 (1787), c. 54, 322. See also "An Act for the Promotion of Industry, and for the Suppression of Vagrants and other Idle and Disorderly Persons," McCord, *Statutes at Large of South Carolina, 1682–1838*, 6 (1787), no. 1376, 554; "An Act relating to Vagrants in the City of Baltimore," in *The General Public Statutory Law and Public Local Law of the State of Maryland, 1692–1839*, ed. Clement Dorsey, 5 vols. (Baltimore, 1804), 3 (1804), c. 96, 1620.

109. Stearns and Shaw, *Laws of Massachusetts, 1780–1822*, 1:323. Baltimore's list went like this: "every person who has no visible means of maintenance from property or personal labour, and lives idle, without employment, and every person who wanders about and begs in the streets from door to door, and any person who wanders about and lodges in out-houses, market places, or in the open air, and cannot give a good account of the means by which he, she or they, procure a livelihood, and every woman who is generally reputed a common prostitute, and every juggler or fortune-teller, or common-gambler." Dorsey, *Law of Maryland*, 3:1621. South Carolina reserved a special place for suspicious horse traders and horse thieves. McCord, *Statutes at Large of South Carolina, 1682–1838*, 6 (1787), 554.

110. *Morgan v. Nolte*, 37 Ohio St. 23 (1881), 25–26.

111. On English precedents, see Blackstone, *Commentaries*, 4:256. Daniel Davis, solicitor general, reported on the Massachusetts statutory practice in *Laws of Massachusetts* (1787), c. 54: "Any justice of the peace (as well as the Court of Sessions) may send and commit unto the said house (of correction) to be kept and governed according to the rules and orders thereof, all rogues, vagabonds, and idle persons, going about in any town or place in the county, begging; or persons using any subtle craft, juggling, or unlawful games or plays, or feigning themselves to have knowledge in physiognomy, palmistry, or pretending that they can tell destinies or fortunes, or discover where lost or stolen goods may be found; common pipers, fiddlers, runaways, stubborn servants or children, common drunkards, common nightwalkers, pilferers, wanton and lascivious persons, in speech, conduct, or behavior; common railers or brawlers, such as neglect their callings and employments, mispend what they earn, and do not provide for themselves, or the support of their families." Davis, *The Authority and Duty of Justices of the Peace in Criminal Prosecutions*, 255–61.

112. South Carolina provided for a trial by freeholders, but allowed a convicted vagrant to be jailed, bound out for one year's service, whipped, or banished from the county. For the best discussion of vagrancy laws in the Reconstruction era, see Stanley, "Beggars Can't Be Choosers."

113. *Portland v. Bangor*, 42 Me. 403 (1856), 404, 410.

114. A further oddity in this pauperism prosecution (which the judge termed a "correctional rather than a penal proceeding") was the primary evidence of running a house of ill fame. If the house was as "notorious" as depicted, the Browns were certainly capable of supporting themselves. The defense, in fact, offered evidence that these "supposed paupers" were "in a condition to support themselves, and were not in distress and standing in need of immediate relief." Ibid., 404, 410. The rules for the Massachusetts house of correction included the following: "The master of such house of correction . . . shall have power and authority, and shall set all such rogues, vagabonds, beggars, and other lewd, idle and disorderly persons as aforesaid, that shall be duly sent or committed unto his custody, to work and labour (if they be able) for such time as they shall continue to remain in the said house; and to punish them by putting shackles or fetters upon them; and also from time to

time, in case they be stubborn, disorderly, idle or refractory, and do not perform their tasks, and in good condition, according as they shall be reasonably stinted, or to abridge them of their food, as the case shall require, until they be reduced to better order." *Laws of Massachusetts* (1787), c. 54.

115. *Nott's Case.* The wording of the Maine statute at issue was "Any two or more of the overseers in any town are hereby authorized, empowered, and directed to commit to [the workhouse] . . . all persons of able body to work and not having estate or means otherwise to maintain themselves, who refuse or neglect so to do; live a dissolute vagrant life, and exercise no ordinary calling or lawful business, sufficient to gain an honest livelihood." *Laws of Maine* (1821), c. 124, s. 6, 7.

116. *Nott's Case,* 211.

117. *Shafer v. Mumma,* 17 Md. 331 (1861), 336; *Commonwealth v. Doherty,* 137 Mass. 245 (1884); *Commonwealth v. Hart,* 137 Mass. 247 (1884). Also see Hill, *Their Sisters' Keepers,* ch. 4.

118. *Harwood v. People,* 16 Abb. Pr. 430 (N.Y., 1863), 431 (emphasis added).

119. In commenting on the discretion given English justices of the peace over the poor, Rudolf Gneist declared: "Even the presently applicable Vagrants Act contains many vague, police-like clauses such as 'suspicious persons' and 'known thieves,' etc., which in the hands of authorities other than English Justices of the peace would serve as an alarming exercise of arbitrary power." Rudolf Gneist, *Selfgovernment: Communalberfassung und Verwaltungsgerichte in England* (Berlin, 1871), sec. 46, 260–61.

120. See, for example, *James Butler's Case; Alfred S. Pell's Case.*

121. *Portland v. Bangor,* 65 Me. 120 (1876), 121.

122. Ibid. Justice Rice's complete statement was: "Pauperism works most important changes in the condition of the citizen. Through its influence, he is deprived of the elective franchise, and of the control of his own person. The pauper may be transported from town to town, and place to place against his will; he loses the control of his family; his children may be taken from him without his consent; he may himself be sent to the work-house, or made the subject of a five years contract, without being personally consulted. In short, the adjudged pauper is subordinated to the will of others, and reduced to a condition but little removed from that of chattel slavery, and until recently, by statute of 1847, c. 12, like the slave, was liable to be sold upon the block of the auctioneer, for service or support." *Portland v. Bangor,* 42 Me. 403 (1856), 411.

123. Eric Foner, *Reconstruction: America's Unfinished Revolution, 1863–1877* (New York, 1988), 228–80; Robert J. Kaczorowski, "To Begin the Nation Anew: Congress, Citizenship, and Civil Rights after the Civil War," *American Historical Review* 92 (1987): 45–68.

124. *People v. Turner,* 55 Ill. 280 (1870): *American Law Register* 10 (1871): 366.

125. *People v. Turner,* 368. *People v. Turner,* of course, was also a pivotal case in American family law, particularly in the area of child custody. Though I have not systematically included family law in this study (like labor law it is a huge subject already outlined by some of our best legal historians), before the Civil War and before *Turner,* it too resonated with the vision of a well-regulated society. After declaring marriage "an organic institution in every civilized and well regulated nation," a Kentucky judge declared in 1838: "Marriage, though, in one sense, a contract . . . is nevertheless, *sui generis,* and unlike ordinary or commercial contracts, is *publici juris,* because it establishes fundamental and most important domestic relations. And therefore, as every well organized society is essentially interested in the existence and harmony and decorum of all its social relations, marriage, the most elementary and useful of them all, is regulated and controlled by the sovereign power of the state. . . . Such a remedial and conservative power is inherent in every independent nation,

and cannot be surrendered or subjected to political restraint or foreign control consistently with the public welfare." *Maguire v. Maguire,* 7 Dana 181 (Kentucky, 1838), 184. Such rhetoric conflicts with Michael Grossberg's overarching story of a nineteenth-century shift from contract to status—from the "initial promotion of private rights to a later imposition of greater public controls." Michael Grossberg, "Guarding the Altar: Physiological Restrictions and the Rise of State Intervention in Matrimony," *American Journal of Legal History* 26 (1982): 198.

126. Isaac F. Redfield, "Note to *People v. Turner,*" *American Law Register* 10 (1871): 372–75. Also see the response of Wisconsin Supreme Court Chief Justice Ryan to Redfield's note in *Milwaukee Industrial School v. Supervisor of Milwaukee County,* 22 Am. Rep. 702 (1876). David Tanenhaus argues that Ryan co-opted Redfield's critique of reformers to create a new vision for the relationship of the child to the state, which paved the way for the creation of juvenile courts at the turn of the century. Tanenhaus, "Creating the Child and State" (unpublished manuscript).

127. Christopher G. Tiedeman, *The Unwritten Constitution* (New York, 1890); Tiedeman, *Limitations of Police Power in the United States,* 11, 135, 556. Tiedeman also eloquently opposed antimiscegenation laws.

128. Indeed, on the limits of *People v. Turner,* see *Ex Parte Ferrier* 103 Ill. 367 (1882). There the simple inclusion of a "judicial hearing" before commitment quickly revived the practice of removing "wayward" children to industrial schools.

129. Freund suggested, "A conviction can be based only on the proof of specific [criminal] acts and notoriety cannot create a presumption of guilt. . . . [T]he sound doctrine is undoubtedly that vagrancy and criminal idleness do not constitute in the eye of the law a social status to be dealt with by police control, but criminal acts to be punished by the criminal courts." Freund, *Police Power,* 95–100.

130. In the vast literature on this topic, I have found most useful Krout, *Origins of Prohibition*; Jack S. Blocker Jr., *American Temperance Movements* (Boston, 1989); Tyrrell, *Sobering Up*; Hampel, *Temperance and Prohibition in Massachusetts, 1813–1852*; C. C. Pearson and J. Edwin Hendricks, *Liquor and Anti-Liquor in Virginia, 1619–1919* (Durham, N.C., 1967); W. J. Rorabaugh, *The Alcoholic Republic: An American Tradition* (New York, 1979); Gusfield, *Symbolic Crusade*; Ernest H. Cherrington, *The Evolution of Prohibition in the United States of America* (Westerville, Ohio, 1920); August F. Fehlandt, *A Century of Drink Reform in the United States* (Cincinnati, 1904).

131. Thomas S. Grimké, *Address on the Patriot Character of the Temperance Reformation* (Charleston, S.C., 1833), 3; Benjamin Rush, *An Inquiry into the Effects of Ardent Spirits upon the Human Body and Mind* (1814), reprinted in Yandell Henderson, *A New Deal in Liquor: A Plea for Dilution* (New York, 1934), 197.

132. Act of 5 & 6 Edw. VI, c. 25 (1552). As the Webbs summed up the deep roots of liquor control, "It is easy to find, in such scanty records of the fourteenth and fifteenth centuries as are yet printed, curiously exact precedents, in one town or manor or another, at one period or another, for almost every modern expedient of dealing with the liquor traffic." Webb and Webb, *Liquor Licensing in England.* Also see C. M. Iles, "Early Stages of English Public House Regulation," *Economic Journal* 13 (1903): 251–62; Frederick A. Johnson and Ruth R. Kessler, "The Liquor License System—Its Origin and Constitutional Development," *New York University Law Quarterly Review* 15 (1937–38): 210–51, 380–424; Krout, *Origins of Prohibition*; Clark Warburton, "Prohibition," in *Encyclopaedia of the Social Sciences* (New York, 1933), 12:499–510. Also see the brief discussion of licensed houses in chapter 3.

133. See Peter Clark, *The English Alehouse: A Social History, 1200–1830* (London, 1983).

134. This argument conflicts with Hendrik Hartog's contention that by the 1780s and

1790s (at least in Middlesex County) the license had become "private property" and "a guarantee of a livelihood." Hendrik Hartog, "The Public Law of a County Court: Judicial Government in Eighteenth Century Massachusetts," *American Journal of Legal History* 20 (1976): 291.

135. Bishop, *Commentaries on Criminal Law*, 613–15. On licensed houses as disorderly houses, see *United States v. Elder*, 4 Cranch, C.C. 507 (1835), Fed. Cas. #15,039; *United States v. Bede*, Fed. Cas. #14,558 (1837); *United States v. Benner*, 5 Cranch, C.C. 347 (1837), Fed. Cas. #14,569; *State v. Bertheol*, 6 Blackf. 474 (Ind., 1843); *State v. Mullikin*, 8 Blackf. 260 (Ind., 1846); *State v. Burchinal*, 4 Harr. 572 (Del., 1847); *Cable v. State*, 8 Blackf. 531 (Ind., 1847); *State v. Buckley*, 5 Harr. 508 (Del., 1854); *State v. Paul*, 5 R.I. 185 (1858); *Commonwealth v. Howe*, 79 Mass. 26 (1859); *Garrison v. State*, 14 Ind. 287 (1860); *Commonwealth v. Davenport*, 84 Mass. 299 (1861); *Meyer v. State*, 12 Vroom 6 (N.J., 1879). Also see the discussion of Wood, *Nuisances*, 60.

136. Although I have surveyed statute and case law from a variety of states, the Massachusetts legal record is simply unequaled in completeness and clarity. The opinions of the Shaw court provide an unparalleled discussion of the legal context of temperance and prohibition. And Massachusetts was no anomaly. Massachusetts's temperance and prohibition experiments were copied directly by other states, and the perspective of the Massachusetts Supreme Judicial Court on liquor regulation became the "law of the land" in the *License Cases*.

137. "An Act for the Due Regulation of Licensed Houses," in Stearns and Shaw, *Laws of Massachusetts, 1780–1822*, 1 (1787), c. 68, 297–304. The liquor oath read as follows: "I, A.B. do swear, that I will bear true faith and allegiance to the Commonwealth of Massachusetts, and that I will, to the utmost of my power, defend the Constitution and Government thereof, against traitorous conspiracies, and all hostile and violent attempts whatsoever."

Selectmen certification took the form: "We, the subscribers, selectmen of the town, . . . do hereby recommend the said, A.B., as a person of sober life and conversation, suitably qualified and provided for the exercise of such an employment and firmly attached to the Constitution and laws of this Commonwealth."

Similar community tests of "good rule and order" attended annual license renewal. Licenses could not be renewed without the following review: "We, the subscribers, selectmen of the town, . . . do hereby certify, that we have maturely considered the returned list of such persons as were licensed in the year past, and, to the best of our knowledge, the following persons named therein have maintained good rule and order in their respective houses or shops, and have conformed to the laws and regulations respecting licensed persons, and are firmly attached to the Constitution and laws of this Commonwealth." Also see "An Act for Licensing and Regulating Ordinary-Keepers," *Law of Maryland* 1 (1780), c. 24, 158–60.

138. The indictment in most of these cases took the form: "Presentment for selling rum, gin, brandy and other strong liquors by retail, and in less quantities than twenty eight gallons. . . . All of which is contrary to the form of the Statute." *Plymouth Court Records, 1686–1859*, ed. David Thomas Konig, 16 vols. (Wilmington, Del., 1978–81). *Commonwealth v. Edward Ells & Samuel Little* Case 96 (April 1816); *Commonwealth v. Ephraim Stetson* Case 97 (April 1816); *Commonwealth v. Rizpah Brewer* Case 84 (August 1816); *Commonwealth v. Ephraim Stetson* Case 219 (August 1817); *Commonwealth v. Ephraim Stetson* Case 157 (August 1818); *Commonwealth v. Samuel Oakman Ruggles* Case 141 (August 1820); *Commonwealth v. Nehemiah Leonard* Case 109 (August 1821); *Commonwealth v. Samuel Oakman Ruggles* Case 79 (November 1821); *Commonwealth v. Charles Lane, Jr.* Case 85 (August 1822); *Commonwealth v. Spencer Churchill* Case 85 (April 1823); *Commonwealth v. Stephen*

Bradford Case 86 (April 1823); *Commonwealth v. Thomas Long* Case 93 (April 1824); *Commonwealth v. Lewis Keith* Case 55 (August 1824); *Commonwealth v. John Foster, Jr.* Case 56 (August 1824); *Commonwealth v. Elkanah Finney* Case 57 (August 1824); *Commonwealth v. Barker Ramsdell, Reuben Estis and William Estis* Case 89 (April 1825); *Commonwealth v. William & John Salmond* Case 70 (August 1825); *Commonwealth v. Ezra Sturtevant* Case 73 (August 1825); *Commonwealth v. Joshua Gates* Case 67 (November 1825); *Commonwealth v. Dexter Vinal* Case 99 (November 1826); *Commonwealth v. Leonard Hammond* Case 102 (November 1826); *Commonwealth v. James Ames* Case 64 (August 1840); *Commonwealth v. Darius Eldridge* Case 39 (December 1842); *Commonwealth v. Darius Eldridge* Case 40 (December 1842); *Commonwealth v. Isaac B. Leonard* Case 41 (December 1842); *Commonwealth v. Leonard Ayres* Case 46 (August 1843); *Commonwealth v. Seth Perry* Case 47 (August 1843); *Commonwealth v. Seth Perry* Case 48 (August 1843); *Commonwealth v. Abiel Gibbs* Case 47 (December 1843); *Commonwealth v. Abiel Gibbs* Case 48 (December 1843); *Commonwealth v. Darius Eldridge* Case 49 (December 1843); *Commonwealth v. Thomas Holmes* Case 50 (December 1843); *Commonwealth v. Gilbert O. Clark* Case 37 (April 1844); *Commonwealth v. Darius Eldridge* Case 29 (December 1844); *Commonwealth v. Darius Eldridge* Case 30 (December 1844); *Commonwealth v. George P. Fowler* Case 24 (August 1845); *Commonwealth v. John Harlow* Case 34 (December 1847); *Commonwealth v. Martin Hendrick* Case 33 (December 1848); *Commonwealth v. Abiel Gibbs* Case 34 (December 1848); *Commonwealth v. John McGowan* Case 48 (December 1850); *Commonwealth v. Abiel Gibbs* Case 49 (December 1850); *Commonwealth v. Patrick Harvey* Case 50 (December 1850); *Commonwealth v. Henry Smith* Case 51 (December 1850); *Commonwealth v. Moses Cleaveland* Case 52 (December 1850); *Commonwealth v. Henry W. B. Cordell* Case 55 (December 1850); *Commonwealth v. Henry W. B. Cordell* Case 56 (December 1850).

139. See G. Thomann, *Colonial Liquor Laws* (New York, 1887); Henry H. Faxon, *Laws Relating to the Sale of Intoxicating Liquors* (Boston, 1884); Bishop, *Commentaries*, 619–39; "An Act for vesting in the Town Council of Camden the exclusive power of granting Licences for retailing spiritous and other liquors," McCord, *Statutes at Large of South Carolina, 1682–1838*, 5 (1792), 211. Even the United States Congress legislated early on the subject of liquor and Indians in "An Act to Regulate Trade and Intercourse with the Indian Tribes, and to Preserve Peace on the Frontiers" (U.S., 1802). On Sunday laws and liquor, see "An Act providing for the due Observation of the Lord's Day," Stearns and Shaw, *The General Laws of Massachusetts, 1780–1822*, 1 (1791), c. 58, 407. "An Act to prohibit the sale of spirituous liquors, or other articles, at or near places assigned for divine worship," McCord, *Statutes at Large of South Carolina, 1682–1838*, 5 (1809), 599; and Blakely, *American State Papers Bearing on Sunday Legislation* (1911). For a detailed account of the prosecution of common drunkards, see Hampel, *Temperance and Prohibition*, 33, 152.

140. "An Act for the Due Regulation of Licensed Houses," *Laws of Massachusetts* (March 24, 1832), c. 166. Wendell D. Howie, "Three Hundred Years of the Liquor Problem in Massachusetts," *Massachusetts Law Quarterly* 18 (1933): 75–284; Hampel, *Temperance and Prohibition*; Blocker, *American Temperance Movements*, 25–26. As Blocker notes, Rhode Island, New Hampshire, Connecticut, and Illinois simultaneously explored local option on liquor licensing at this time.

141. Quoted in Howie, "The Liquor Problem in Massachusetts," 130. Lincoln went on, "An inordinate appetite for the use of spirituous liquors, too often gratified by their free and unlicensed sale, has given occasion for immediate and greatest apprehension. If experience has shown, that, by moral influences alone, the former can be corrected, it becomes the more imperative that by wise enactments, and their rigid enforcement, the latter should be effectually restrained."

142. Leonard Levy deserves credit for first bringing this extraordinary series of cases to the attention of legal historians. Levy's interpretation, however, is a bit presentist and overly constitutional, portraying Shaw as the innovator of a positivist and plenary conception of legislative power. See Levy, *The Law of the Commonwealth and Chief Justice Shaw*, 232–37, 259–65. The series—*Commonwealth v. Blackington, Commonwealth v. Kimball, Commonwealth v. Kimball* (II), *Commonwealth v. Thurlow*—is located on consecutive pages in 24 *Pickerings Reports* 352–81 (Mass., 1837).

143. *Commonwealth v. Blackington*, 24 Pick. 352 (Mass., 1837). The statute at issue in *Blackington* was a slightly revised version of the 1832 licensing law (which in turn was only a slight revision of 1787). "Of the Regulation of Licensed Houses," *Massachusetts Revised Statutes* (Boston, 1836), c. 47.

144. Rantoul also argued that the license system as a whole involved a grant of "exclusive privileges" in violation of the Declaration of Rights: "Article 6. No man, nor corporation, or association of men, have any other title to obtain advantages, or particular and exclusive privileges, distinct from those of the community, than what arises from the consideration of services rendered to the public."

Attorney General Austin countered again with article 18: "A frequent recurrence to the fundamental principles of the constitution, and a constant adherence to those of piety, justice, moderation, temperance, industry, and frugality, are absolutely necessary to preserve the advantages of liberty, and to maintain a free government. The people ought, consequently, to have a particular attention to all those principles, in the choice of their officers and representatives: and they have a right to require of their lawgivers and magistrates an exact and constant observance of them, in the formation and execution of the laws necessary for the good administration of the commonwealth."

145. *Commonwealth v. Blackington*, 355.

146. Ibid., 356 (emphasis added).

147. As Shaw put it, "It must never be forgotton, that [the constitution] was not intended to contain a detailed system of practical rules, for the regulation of the government or people in after times; but that it was rather intended, after an organization of the government, and distributing the executive, legislative, and judicial powers, amongst its several departments, to declare a few broad, general, fundamental principles for their guidance and general direction." Ibid.

148. Ibid., 357 (emphasis added).

149. Ibid., 358.

150. *Commonwealth v. Kimball*, 24 Pick. 359 (Mass., 1837). *Gibbons v. Ogden*, 9 Wheat. 1 (U.S., 1824); *Brown v. Maryland*, 12 Wheat. 419 (U.S., 1827). Also see *Commonwealth v. Kimball* (II), 24 Pick. 366 (Mass., 1837).

151. *Commonwealth v. Kimball*, 360–61.

152. Ibid., 361–63.

153. *License Cases*, 5 Howard 504 (U.S., 1847). Also at issue were the licensing and taxation statutes of New Hampshire and Rhode Island. See *Pierce v. State*, 13 N.H. 536 (1843); *State v. Fletcher*, 1 R.I. 193 (1846). The particulars of these three cases and three state statutes get as complicated and idiosyncratic as the six arguments of counsel and nine judicial opinions. The following discussion attempts a rough synthesis on the constitutionality of liquor licensing as a form of state police power.

154. Taney argued: "What are the police powers of the state? They are nothing more or less than the powers of government inherent in every sovereignty to the extent of its dominion, and whether a state passes a quarantine law, or a law to punish offenses, or to establish courts of justice, or requiring certain instruments to be recorded, or to regulate

commerce within its own limits, in every case it exercises the same power: that is to say, this power of sovereignty, the power to govern men and things within the limits of its own dominions. It is by virtue of this power that it legislates." *License Cases*, 583. Here Taney clearly moved well beyond Lemuel Shaw's distinction between common law police measures and the power to regulate interstate commerce. Taney's attempt to highlight general, open-ended powers of "state sovereignty," including a *concurrent* power to regulate commerce, was part of his long-standing attack on Joseph Story's position of *exclusive* federal powers over interstate commerce. The emergence of this artificially heightened divide on state police power versus federal commerce power in formal constitutional discourse (as opposed to state and local adjudication) had everything to do with the incipient crisis over slavery. Historiographically, the commerce-clause issue has become so bound up with ex post facto positions on capitalism, the Civil War, and the New Deal that it has yet to receive a fair hearing. For some useful but problematic efforts, see W. G. Hastings, "The Development of Law As Illustrated by the Decisions Relating to the Police Power of the State," *Proceedings of the American Philosophical Society* 39 (1900): 359–554; Felix Frankfurter, *The Commerce Clause under Marshall, Taney, and Waite* (Chapel Hill, N.C., 1937); William Winslow Crosskey, *Politics and the Constitution in the History of the United States*, 3 vols. (Chicago, 1953).

155. *License Cases*, 589.

156. Ibid., 631–32.

157. Beginning in the 1830s, numerous indictments were issued against individuals for violating the state's licensing laws. Forty-three such cases were appealed to Massachusetts's highest court; it upheld convictions more than 70 percent of the time. For examples of these early decisions, see *Commonwealth v. Estabrook*, 10 Pick. 293 (1831); *Commonwealth v. Markoe*, 17 Pick. 465 (1835); *Commonwealth v. Jordan*, 18 Pick. 228 (1836); *Commonwealth v. Kimball*, 21 Pick. 373 (1836); *Commonwealth v. Odlin*, 23 Pick. 275 (1839); *Harris v. The Commonwealth*, 23 Pick. 280 (Mass., 1839); *Commonwealth v. Thurlow*, 24 Pick. 374 (1840); *Commonwealth v. Churchill*, 1 Met. 118 (1840).

158. Webster argued *Thurlow v. Massachusetts* before the Supreme Court. See *License Cases*, 511–14, 538–39.

159. For the definitive discussion on the issue of liquor licenses and contract, see *Calder v. Kurby*, 5 Gray 597 (Mass., 1856), 597–98, in which the Massachusetts court held that "A license to retail spirituous liquors . . . is not a contract. . . . This statute, like those authorizing the licensing of theatrical exhibitions and shows, sales of fireworks, sales by auctions, and other similar enactments, was a mere police regulation, intended to regulate trade, prevent injurious practices, and promote the good order and welfare of the community, and liable to be modified and repealed whenever by the judgment of the legislature it failed to accomplish these objects." Also see *Metropolitan Board of Excise v. Barrie*, 34 N.Y. 657 (1866).

160. Also see *Heisembrittle v. City of Charleston*, 2 McMul. Law 233 (S.C., 1842); *Pierce v. State*; *Austin v. State*, 10 Mo. 591 (1847); *State v. Burchinal*; *Cable v. State*; *Bode v. State*, 7 Gill 326 (Md., 1848).

161. J. D. B. De Bow's Compendium of the 1850 Census, cited in *Herman v. State*, 8 Ind. 545 (1855), 561.

162. Cooley, *Constitutional Limitations*, 583–84. Remarkably, given his reputation as an opponent of police power, Cooley had little trouble upholding the constitutionality of state prohibition, suggesting that, "Perhaps there is no instance in which the power of the legislature to make such regulations as may destroy the value of property, without compensation to the owner, appears in a more striking light than in the case of these statutes." On Cooley as laissez-faire constitutionalist, see Clyde E. Jacobs, *Law Writers and the Courts:*

The Influence of Thomas M. Cooley, Christopher G. Tiedeman, and John F. Dillon upon American Constitutional Law (Los Angeles, 1954); Benjamin R. Twiss, *Lawyers and the Constitution: How Laissez-Faire Came to the Supreme Court* (New York, 1962). Alan Jones contributes the requisite revision in "Thomas M. Cooley and 'Laissez-Faire Constitutionalism': A Reconsideration," *Journal of American History* 53 (1967): 751–71.

163. John Stuart Mill, *On Liberty* (1859; Harvard Classics reprint, New York, 1909), 284–85. For the temperance critique of Mill, see Robert C. Pitman, *Alcohol and the State: A Discussion of the Problem of Law as Applied to the Liquor Traffic* (New York, 1877), 117–29.

164. I owe this point to many conversations with Hendrik Hartog.

165. Blocker, *Temperance Movements*, 53–54.

166. John Miller, "The License Law," in *The Lights of Temperance*, ed. James Young (Louisville, Ky., 1851), 212; J. T. Crane, "The License System," *American Temperance Magazine* 1 (1851): 221–23. Crane was particularly incensed by the legal benefits bestowed on the licensed liquor merchant: "The whole thing struts boldly forth, invested with the majesty of the law. The vender is now doing a lawful business, and he can hold up his head in the community. He feels that he occupies a dignified position. The State has laid its hands upon his head, and solemnly set him apart to deal out alcohol to its thirsty citizens."

167. H. L. Dawes, "The Maine Liquor Law a Part of the Criminal Code," in *The Maine Liquor Law: Its Origin, History, and Results*, ed. Henry S. Clubb (New York, 1856), 230.

168. "An Act for the Suppression of Drinking Houses and Tippling Shops," *Laws of Maine* (1851), c. 211.

169. The Maine law required that all seized liquors be forfeited and destroyed unless the owner could show "by positive proof, that said liquors are of foreign production, that they have been imported under the laws of the United States, and in accordance therewith— that they are contained in the original packages in which they were imported, and in quantities not less than the laws of the United States prescribe." This qualification was in direct accordance with John Marshall's dictum in *Brown v. Maryland* that foreign products in their original packages were subject solely to the commercial, import, and taxing regulations of Congress not state legislatures. *Brown v. Maryland.*

170. Ernst Freund produces a very useful chart for gauging the extent, duration, and state constitutional reception of prohibition:

CONSTITUTIONAL

Connecticut, 1853–72. Constitutionality upheld in *State v. Wheeler*, 25 Conn. 290 (1856).

Delaware, 1855–57. Upheld in *State v. Allmond*, 2 Houst. 612 (1856).

Illinois, 1851–53. Upheld in *Jones v. People*, 14 Ill. 196 (1852).

Iowa, 1851–84 (partial). Upheld in *Santo v. State*, 2 Iowa 165 (1855).

Maine, 1846–51, 1851–. Upheld in *State v. Gurney*, 37 Me. 156 (1853).

Massachusetts, 1838–40, 1852–75. Upheld in *Commonwealth v. Kendall*, 12 Cush. 414 (1853).

Michigan, 1855–58. Upheld in *People v. Gallagher*, 4 Mich. 244 (1856).

Nebraska, 1855–58.

New Hampshire, 1855–1903.

Rhode Island, 1852–63. Upheld in *State v. Paul*, 5 R.I. 185 (1858).

Vermont, 1850–1903. Upheld in *Lincoln v. Smith*, 27 Vt. 328 (1855).

UNCONSTITUTIONAL

Indiana, 1855–58. Declared unconstitutional in *Beebe v. State*, 6 Ind. 501 (1855).

New York, 1855. Declared unconstitutional in some particulars in *Wynehamer v. People*, 13 N.Y. 378 (1856).

See Freund, *Police Power*, 202–3. Some of these statutes are conveniently listed in Clubb, *The Maine Liquor Law*, 299–415.

171. Clubb, *The Maine Liquor Law*, 31.

172. *State v. Gurney*. The court did, however, strike down section 6 of the Maine law which used recognizances, bonds, and threats of double fines to discourage appeals, thus hindering the defendant's right to a trial by jury.

173. See again Ernst Freund's constitutionality survey, n. 170.

174. *Lincoln v. Smith*, 337.

175. *State v. Wheeler*, 298.

176. *People v. Gallagher*, 257.

177. *State v. Allmond*, 632–33.

178. *Lincoln v. Smith*, 336.

179. *State v. Wheeler*, 637–38.

180. *Fisher v. McGirr*, 1 Gray 1 (Mass., 1854); "An Act concerning the Manufacture and Sale of Spirituous or Intoxicating Liquors," *Laws of Massachusetts* (1852), c. 322.

181. Clubb, *The Maine Liquor Law*, 155.

182. On appeal to Shaw's court, this case was accompanied by *Commonwealth v. Albro* (a conviction for keeping intoxicating liquors that involved a fine of $20, $20.91 in costs, and the destruction of the liquors) and *Herrick v. Smith* (Herrick was suing for habeas corpus after being imprisoned for thirty days when he did not pay the liquor fines). Certainly the stakes and costs of prohibition were high.

183. This process began with *Commonwealth v. Kendall*.

184. As Shaw put it, "We have no doubt that it is competent for the legislature to declare the possession of certain articles of property, whether absolutely, or when held in particular places, and under particular circumstances, to be unlawful, because they would be injurious, dangerous or noxious; and by due process of law, by proceedings in rem, to provide both for the abatement of the nuisance and the punishment of the offender, by the seizure and confiscation of the property, by the removal, sale, or destruction of the noxious articles." He noted the examples of infectious materials and gunpowder. *Fisher v. McGirr*, 27.

185. Ibid., 29.

186. Ibid., 36–37.

187. "An Act concerning the Manufacture and Sale of Spirituous and Intoxicating Liquors," *Laws of Massachusetts* (1855), c. 215.

188. *Fisher v. McGirr*, 32.

189. Edward S. Corwin, "The Doctrine of Due Process before the Civil War," *Harvard Law Review* 24 (1911): 366–85, 460–79; Rodney L. Mott, *Due Process of Law* (Indianapolis, 1926).

190. Levy, *Law of the Commonwealth*, 283.

191. *Fisher v. McGirr*, 40.

192. Once again, as in *Commonwealth v. Alger*, Shaw made absolutely clear the distinction between the police power and a "taking" of private property in violation of article 12 of the state Declaration of Rights, arguing that that clause had "no bearing on this subject." The Massachusetts "takings clause" was "related to another class of subjects and rights." Shaw concurred with an even stronger argument made by Attorney General Rufus Choate: "The suggestion . . . that this may be regarded as a taking of private property for public uses without compensation, is purely fanciful. . . . It might as well be said that the life of a murderer is taken for public uses. . . . There is no distinction, as to the power of the legislature in this respect between this case, and the cases of counterfeiters' tools, implements of gaming, lottery tickets, obscene or incendiary pamphlets, bowie knives and pistols, or goods on

board a ship in a state of rapid decay, all of which are subjects of property, and entitled to protection as such, when not held for purposes declared unlawful. The law destroys all these for the public benefit, but on the principle that they are not fit to be used for sale at all, and that they are kept in violation of law, and are, under such conditions an evil, and to be destroyed accordingly. When prohibited by law, they are no longer protected as property by the constitution." *Fisher v. McGirr*, 17, 41. Though twentieth-century constitutionalism has obscured the line between the police power and eminent domain, nineteenth-century jurists were all too clear about their jurisprudential separateness.

193. *People v. Gallagher*, 259–60.

194. *State v. Prescott*, 27 Vt. 194 (1855), 200. *Prescott* was a companion case to *Lincoln v. Smith*.

195. It is worth reminding readers just how infrequently judicial review was exercised before the Civil War. From 1790 to 1860, the United States Supreme Court invalidated acts of Congress in only two cases, *Marbury v. Madison* and *Dred Scott*. Clear and unequivocal invalidations of general state statutes were also relatively rare. In the 1840s and 1850s, liquor laws, along with married women's property acts and public works legislation, seemed to attract particularly determined review. See William E. Nelson, "Changing Conceptions of Judicial Review: The Evolution of Constitutional Theory in the States, 1790–1860," *University of Pennsylvania Law Review* 120 (1972): 1166–85.

196. *Beebe v. State*; *Herman v. State*. The Indiana prohibition statute at issue was admittedly one of the more stringent restrictions, specifically outlawing the *drinking* of alcoholic beverages (except for medicinal purposes).

197. *Beebe v. State*, 506–8.

198. Ibid., 506–7.

199. Ibid., 508.

200. *Herman v. State*, 563.

201. Ibid. (emphasis added).

202. *Beebe v. State*, 506–8.

203. *Wynehamer v. People*. Also see *People v. Toynbee*, 10 Barb. 168 (1855).

204. *Wynehamer v. People*, 385.

205. Ibid., 387.

206. Ibid., 392–93.

207. It is important to point out that even Justice Comstock in *Wynehamer* hesitated to root constitutional limitations in such higher law vagaries as "fundamental principles" or "common reason and natural rights." He defended his own notion of limitations as rooted in specific constitutional provisions. Ibid., 389–90.

208. *Boston Beer Company v. Massachusetts*, 97 U.S. 25 (1877), 33. For a hint of early ambiguity (and a flirtation with *Wynehamer*, especially in dissent), see *Bartemeyer v. Iowa*, 18 Wall. 129 (U.S., 1873).

209. See Daniel T. Rodgers, *Contested Truths: Keywords in American Politics since Independence* (New York, 1987), 147–75.

210. *Boston Beer Company v. Massachusetts*, 32. The court defined "inalienability" this way: "[The police power] does extend to the protection of the lives, health, and property of the citizens, and to the preservation of good order and the public morals. The legislature cannot, by any contract, divest itself of the power to provide for these objects. They belong emphatically to that class of objects which demand the application of the maxim, *salus populi suprema lex*: and they are to be attained and provided for by such appropriate means as the legislative discretion may devise. That discretion can no more be bargained away than the power itself." Ibid., 33.

211. *Wynehamer v. People*, 451.

212. Ibid.; *Boston Beer Company v. Massachusetts*. Two other key cases on "inalienability" involved lotteries: *Boyd v. Alabama*, 94 U.S. 645 (1877); *Stone v. Mississippi*, 101 U.S. 814 (1880). Despite this obvious significance in the constitutionalism of the time, the leading surveys of American legal and constitutional history fail to discuss the role of state prohibition experiments at all. Alfred H. Kelly, Winfred A. Harbison, and Herman Belz, *The American Constitution: Its Origins and Development*, 6th ed. (New York, 1983); Hall, *Magic Mirror*.

Chapter Six

1. Eli F. Heckscher, *Mercantilism* (London, 1934), especially 2:158–61; Michael Ignatieff and Istvan Hont, *Wealth and Virtue: The Shaping of Political Economy in the Scottish Enlightenment* (Cambridge, 1983); Steven L. Kaplan, *Bread, Politics and Political Economy in the Reign of Louis XV* (The Hague, 1976); Pasquale Pasquino, "*Theatrum Politicum*. The Genealogy of Capital—Police and the State of Prosperity," *Ideology and Consciousness* 4 (1978): 45; Albion Small, *The Cameralists: The Pioneers of German Social Polity* (Chicago, 1909); Marc Raeff, *The Well-Ordered Police State: Social and Institutional Change through Law in the Germanies and Russia, 1600–1800* (New Haven, Conn., 1983). See generally Christopher L. Tomlins, *Law, Labor, and Ideology in the Early American Republic* (New York, 1993), 35–59.

2. Erna Lesky, ed., *A System of Complete Medical Police: Selections from Johann Peter Frank* (Baltimore, 1976). See generally George Rosen, "Cameralism and the Concept of Medical Police," *Bulletin of the History of Medicine* 27 (1953): 21–42; George Rosen, *A History of Public Health* (New York, 1958).

3. Petty quoted in Charles Webster, *The Great Instauration: Science, Medicine and Reform, 1626–1660* (London, 1975), 421.

4. Michel Foucault, "The Subject and Power," in *Michel Foucault: Beyond Structuralism and Hermeneutics*, ed. Hubert L. Dreyfus and Paul Rabinow (Chicago, 1982), 208–26; Michel Foucault, "The Politics of Health in the Eighteenth Century," in *Power/Knowledge: Selected Interviews and Other Writings, 1972–1977* (New York, 1980), 166–82; Jacques Donzelot, *The Policing of Families* (New York, 1979).

5. Lesky, *Selections from Johann Peter Frank*, 12.

6. By 1849 German pathologist Rudolph Virchow could conclude, "Medicine is a social science . . . whose greatest task is to build up society on a physiological foundation. . . . Politics is nothing but medicine on a large scale." Quoted in Rosen, *Public Health*, 13.

7. John Bell, *Report on the Importance and Economy of Sanitary Measures to Cities* (New York, 1860), 32.

8. *Report of the Select Committee Appointed to Investigate the Health Department of the City of New York* (Albany, N.Y., 1859), 23.

9. Nathan Dane, *A General Abridgment and Digest of American Law* (Boston, 1823), 7:69; William Blackstone, *Commentaries on the Laws of England: A Facsimile of the First Edition of 1765–1769*, 4 vols. (Chicago, 1979), 3:122.

10. *Gibbons v. Ogden*, 9 Wheat. 1 (U.S., 1824), 203, 205.

11. *Report of the Board of Health of the City of Chicago for 1867, 1868, and 1869; And a Sanitary History of Chicago from 1833 to 1870* (Chicago, 1871), 10–11.

12. George Wilson, *Handbook of Hygiene and Sanitary Science*, 7th ed. (1877; Philadelphia, 1892), 1.

13. Rosen, *Public Health*, 464–70; George Rosen, "Political Order and Human Health in Jeffersonian Thought," in *From Medical Police to Social Medicine* (New York, 1974), 246–58.

14. Rosen, *Public Health*, 248; Also see Gert H. Brieger, "Sanitary Reform in New York City: Stephen Smith and the Passage of the Metropolitan Health Bill," in *Sickness and Health in America: Readings in the History of Medicine and Public Health*, ed. Judith Walzer Leavitt and Ronald L. Numbers, rev. ed. (Madison, Wis., 1985), 399–413. Louisiana actually formed the first state board of health in 1855, but Rosen described it as ineffective.

15. Stuart Galishoff, *Newark: The Nation's Unhealthiest City, 1832–1895* (New Brunswick, N.J., 1988); Judith Walzer Leavitt, *The Healthiest City: Milwaukee and the Politics of Health Reform* (Princeton, N.J., 1982); Charles Rosenberg, *The Cholera Years: The United States in 1832, 1849, 1866* (Chicago, 1962); Barbara Gutmann Rosenkrantz, *Public Health and the State: Changing Views in Massachusetts, 1842–1936* (Cambridge, Mass., 1972). One reason for this interpretation in traditional public health histories is an underappreciation of the role of courts as agents of public policy. For exceptions old and new, see John Duffy, *A History of Public Health in New York City, 1625–1866* (New York, 1968); Margaret Humphreys, *Yellow Fever and the South* (New Brunswick, N.J., 1992); James C. Mohr, *Doctors and the Law: Medical Jurisprudence in Nineteenth-Century America* (New York, 1993). One of the more interesting counters to the liberal tradition is Susan Wade Peabody, *Historical Study of Legislation regarding Public Health in the States of New York and Massachusetts* (Chicago, 1909). From a legal-institutional perspective on nineteenth-century health regulation, Peabody offered up this early twentieth-century assessment: "The sanctions of the early laws were vigorous, their enforcement often drastic; modern methods lean more toward education and persuasion; yet the time may come when it will be made a crime to aid in disseminating any form of disease germ." Peabody, 2.

16. As the Massachusetts Sanitary Commission argued in 1850, "If a municipal or state authority neglects to make and execute those sanitary laws and regulations on which the health and life of the people depend they violate a known duty, and are justly chargeable with guilt and its consequences; and they will certainly be punished either by means of less capacity for labor, of increased expenditures, of diminished wealth, of more abject poverty and atrocious crime, or of more extended sickness and a greater number of deaths; or in some other form. These are the physical and social consequences of a neglect of sanitary duty." Massachusetts Sanitary Commission, *Report of a General Plan for the Promotion of Public and Personal Health* (Boston, 1850), 277.

17. Mohr's critique of Rosen is pointed: "In the United States people like Thomas Cooper, whose political philosophy could hardly be characterized as cameral, not only went along with but actually took the lead in pushing a medico-legal agenda. Indeed, in almost direct rebuttal of Rosen's explicit arguments about Jeffersonianism, it was Jefferson himself who asked Dunlinson, a professional trained in the German tradition, to come to the University of Virginia to build medical jurisprudence." Mohr, *Doctors and the Law*, 279.

18. Quoted in Mohr, *Doctors and the Law*, 8.

19. Charles Caldwell, *Thoughts on Hygiene* (New Orleans, 1836), 65–66.

20. Henry I. Bowditch, *Public Hygiene in America: Being the Centennial Discourse Delivered before the International Medical Congress, Philadelphia, September, 1876* (Boston, 1877), 1; John S. Billings, "Jurisprudence of Hygiene," in *A Treatise on Hygiene and Public Health*, ed. Albert H. Buck (New York, 1879), 1:34–63; Thomas J. Turner, *Some Remarks upon National and International Sanitary Jurisprudence* (Boston, 1882).

21. Billings, "Jurisprudence of Hygiene," 9, 36–37. Billings vision was not uncontested. Theodore Woolsey argued in his *Political Science*: "Sanitary regulations tend to preserve health and life, but only in an indirect way, and so they are not a necessary part of state action. It is not evident that a swamp ought to be drained by the state, or under its direction by the district for the purpose of diminishing malaria because the right to life requires it,

any more than physicians and medicine ought to be supplied by the state because the right to life requires it. The right to life is of another sort; and it does not say to the state 'thou shalt keep this or that man from sickness such as the soil or climate may bring upon him,' any more than the rights of property say 'thou shalt keep this or that man from poverty occasioned by his neighbor's superior skill.'" Theodore D. Woolsey, *Political Science or The State Theoretically and Practically Considered* (New York, 1877), 1:219–20.

22. As enumerated by Shaw, such reasonable regulations included: "[L]aws to prohibit the use of warehouses for the storage of gunpowder near habitations or highways; to restrain the height to which wooden buildings may be erected in populous neighborhoods, and require them to be covered with slate or other incombustible material; to prohibit buildings from being used for hospitals for contagious diseases, or for the carrying on of noxious or offensive trades; to prohibit the raising of a dam, and causing stagnant water to spread over meadows, near inhabited villages, thereby raising noxious exhalations, injurious to health and dangerous to life." *Commonwealth v. Alger*, 7 Cushing 53 (Mass., 1851), 85–86; Billings, "Jurisprudence of Hygiene," 37–38.

23. Massachusetts Sanitary Commission, *Report of a General Plan for the Promotion of Public and Personal Health*, 285.

24. Ibid., 286–88. *Shaw v. Cummiskey*, 7 Pick. 76 (Mass., 1828); *Baker v. Boston*, 12 Pick. 184 (Mass., 1831).

25. *Baker v. Boston*, 193.

26. Ibid., 194.

27. Ibid., 191, 194.

28. Leroy Parker and Robert H. Worthington, *The Law of Public Health and Safety, and the Powers and Duties of Boards of Health* (Albany, N.Y., 1892), xxxviii. The epigram for this treatise is *Salus populi est suprema lex.*

29. *Laws and Ordinances Relative to the Preservation of the Public Health in the City of New York*, ed. George W. Morton (New York, 1860). Also see generally Parker and Worthington, *The Law of Public Health and Safety, and the Powers and Duties of Boards of Health.*

30. *Manual of the Board of Health of the Health Department of the City of New York* (New York, 1872), 38–114.

31. A reasonably good survey of state-by-state legislation can be found in H. G. Pickering, "Digest of American Sanitary Law," in Bowditch, *Public Hygiene in America*, 299–440.

32. Joel Prentiss Bishop, *Commentaries on the Criminal Law*, 4th ed., 2 vols. (1865; Boston, 1868), 1:542–44.

33. Bowditch, *Public Hygiene in America*, 45–46. The argument from lack of state and especially federal legislative initiatives was made all the time by nineteenth-century reformers and has passed (without critical reflection) into current historiography. The indictment of early American health policy via state budget analysis is also something of a red herring—though Henry W. Broude used it to undermine the whole commonwealth notion of a role for "the state" in the antebellum economy. See Broude, "The Role of the State in American Economic Development, 1820–1890," in *United States Economic History: Selected Readings*, ed. Harry N. Scheiber (New York, 1964), 114–35.

34. The best overviews of these institutional/legislative initiatives are John Duffy, *The Sanitarians: A History of American Public Health* (Urbana, Ill., 1990), and Peabody, *Legislation regarding Public Health.*

35. "A Supplement to the act, entitled, 'An act for establishing an health office, for otherwise securing the city and port of Philadelphia from the introduction of pestilential and contagious diseases, and for regulating the importation of German and other passengers,'"

The Statutes at Large of Pennsylvania from 1682 to 1809 (Harrisburg, Pa., 1911) (1794), c. 1789; "An Act for establishing an health office, for securing the city and port of Philadelphia from the introduction of pestilential and contagious diseases," ibid. (1799), c. 2094. Powers of appointment fluctuated from the mayor, aldermen, and justices of the peace to 1806, the governor to 1818, municipal election to 1854, and judicial selection to 1885. The charters of Pittsburgh (1851–52), Harrisburg (1872), and Williamsport (1872), included provisions for the establishment of municipal boards of health. But there was no state board of health in Pennsylvania until 1885. Peabody, *Legislation regarding Public Health*, 114–22; J. H. Powell, *Bring Out Your Dead: The Great Plague of Yellow Fever in Philadelphia in 1793* (Philadelphia, 1949), 174–75.

36. "Act to empower the town of Boston to choose a Board of Health, and for removing and preventing nuisances," *Laws of Massachusetts* (1799), c. 10; "An act to empower the town of Boston to choose a Board of Health, and to prescribe their power and duty," *Laws of Massachusetts* (1816), c. 44. Boards of health were created in Salem (1799), Marblehead (1801), and Plymouth (1809). In 1822 these public health powers were transferred to the city council. See generally Peabody, *Legislation regarding Public Health*, 51–57.

37. *Laws of New York* (1796), c. 38; *Laws of New York* (1805), c. 31. For a very close analysis of these developments, see Duffy, *Public Health in New York City, 1625–1866*, 101–75. Also see Peabody, *Legislation regarding Public Health*, 3–14.

38. *Metropolitan Board of Health v. Heister*, 37 N.Y. 661 (1868). Also see *Van Wormer v. Mayor of Albany*, 15 Wend. 262 (N.Y., 1836); *Reed v. People*, 1 Park. Cr. R. 481 (N.Y., 1854); *People ex. rel. Cox v. The Court of Special Sessions*, 7 Hun. 214 (N.Y., 1876) ; *Health Department v. Knoll*, 70 N.Y. 530 (1877); *Polinsky v. People*, 73 N.Y. 65 (1878); *Boehm & Loeber v. Mayor of Baltimore*, 61 Md. 259 (1883); *Hengehold v. City of Covington*, 57 S.W. 495 (Ky., 1900). See generally "Powers Which May Be Delegated to Boards of Health," *American State Reports* 80 (Ind., February 1900): 212.

39. State health organizations established by 1880 included: Louisiana (1855), Massachusetts (1869), California (1870), Minnesota (1872), Virginia (1872), Michigan (1873), Maryland (1874), Alabama (1875), Wisconsin (1876), Illinois (1877), Mississippi (1877), New Jersey (1877), North Carolina (1877), Tennessee (1877), Connecticut (1878), Kentucky, (1878), Rhode Island (1878), South Carolina (1878), Delaware (1879), Iowa (1880), New York (1880). James A. Tobey, *The National Government and Public Health* (Baltimore, 1926), 12. The Louisiana Board was a direct outgrowth of the yellow fever epidemic that struck New Orleans in 1853. See John Duffy, *Sword of Pestilence: The New Orleans Yellow Fever Epidemic of 1853* (Baton Rouge, La., 1966).

40. See especially John H. Griscom, *The Sanitary Condition of the Laboring Population of New York* (New York, 1845); *Minutes of the Proceedings of the Quarantine Convention* (Philadelphia, 1857); Duffy, *The Sanitarians*, 93–109. The United States sanitary movement was directly influenced by the work of Edwin Chadwick in England and Louis René Villermé and the Paris "Conseil de Salubrité" in France. See especially Edwin Chadwick, *On the Sanitary Condition of the Laboring Population of Great Britain* (London, 1842).

41. Billings, "Jurisprudence of Hygiene," 55. For a remarkably complete survey of state board of health legislation to 1876, see Pickering, "Digest of American Sanitary Law."

42. Massachusetts Sanitary Commission, *Report of a General Plan for the Promotion of Public and Personal Health*, 109–11. The Massachusetts State Board of Health was empowered "to take cognizance of the interests of life and health among the citizens . . . [to] make sanitary investigations and inquiries in respect to the people, the causes of disease, and especially of epidemics and the sources of mortality and the effects of localities, employments, conditions, and circumstances on the public health . . .; [to] gather such informa-

tion in respect to those matters as they may deem proper, for diffusion . . .; [to] advise the government in regard to the location of public institutions. . . . [To] examine into and report . . . the effect of the use of intoxicating liquor, as a beverage, on the industry, prosperity, happiness, health and lives of citizens." The board was also required to "make [a] report to the legislature of their doings, investigations and discoveries . . . with suggestions as to legislative action." *Laws of Massachusetts* (1869), c. 420; Peabody, *Legislation regarding Public Health*, 58. In 1871 the board gained further power to investigate and order the removal of offensive trades and buildings. *Laws of Massachusetts* (1871), c. 167. In 1879 it became the State Board of Health, Lunacy, and Charity. *Laws of Massachusetts* (1879), c. 291.

43. Samuel P. Hays, "The New Organizational Society," in *American Political History as Social Analysis* (Knoxville, Tenn., 1980), 244–63.

44. A good example of this tendency is the amount of attention paid to the creation of New York's Metropolitan Board of Health in 1866 and a relatively uncritical acceptance of indictments of Tammany Hall health policy like that of Andrew D. White: "The condition of things in the city of New York had become unbearable; the sway of Tammany Hall had gradually brought out elements of opposition such as before that time had not existed. . . . The city system was bad throughout; but at the very center of this evil stood what was dignified by the name of the 'Health Department.' At the head of this was a certain Boole, who, having gained the title of 'city inspector,' had the virtual appointment of a whole army of so-called 'health inspectors,' 'health officers,' and the like, charged with the duty of protecting the public from the inroads of disease; and never was there a greater outrage against a city than the existence of this body of men absolutely unfit both as regarded character and education for the duties they pretended to discharge. . . . Whole districts in the most crowded wards were in the worst possible sanitary condition. There was probably at that time nothing to approach it in any city in Christendom save, possibly, Naples. Great blocks of tenement houses were owned by men who kept low drinking-bars in them, each of whom, having secured from Boole the position of 'health officer,' steadily resisted all sanitary improvements or even inspection. Many of these tenement houses were known as 'fever nests.'" Andrew D. White, *Autobiography of Andrew Dickson White*, vol. 1 (New York, 1905), 107–8. Similar charges of a "corrupt" public health apparatus leveled at Louisiana's Reconstruction legislature now appear to be unfounded. See the discussion of the *Slaughterhouse Cases* later in this chapter.

45. Charles Caldwell summed up the sanitarian take on intoxicating liquors, "Temperance in all things [is] important to the preservation of sound health in all places." Caldwell, *Thoughts on Hygiene*, 73–77. Also see Massachusetts Sanitary Commission, *Report of a General Plan for the Promotion of Public and Personal Health*, 183; Citizens' Association of New York, *Report upon the Sanitary Condition of the City* (New York, 1866), 196–221.

46. *Baker v. Boston*, 193.

47. *Brick Presbyterian Church v. Mayor of New York*, 5 Cow. 538 (N.Y., 1826); *Coates v. Mayor of New York* (also *Slack* and *Stuyvesant*), 7 Cowen 585 (New York, 1827), 605. See the discussion in chapter 3.

48. S. Oakley Vanderpoel, "General Principles Affecting the Organization and Practice of Quarantine," *American Public Health Reports* 1 (1873): 402–29. Also see Heber Smith, "Sailors As Propagators of Disease," *American Public Health Reports* 1 (1873): 447–53.

49. *Morgan's Steamship Co. v. Louisiana Board of Health*, 118 U.S. 455 (1886), 463.

50. Peabody, *Legislation regarding Public Health*, 40–41.

51. "An Act in Addition to an Act entitled 'An Act providing in case of sickness,'" *Laws of Massachusetts* 2 (1717–18), c. 14; Peabody, *Legislation regarding Public Health*, 43.

52. "An Act to empower the Inhabitants of the Town of Salem to choose a Board of

Health, and for removing and preventing Nuisances in said Town," *Laws of Massachusetts* (1799), c. 14; "An Act to empower the Town of Boston to choose a Board of Health, and for removing and preventing Nuisances," *Laws of Massachusetts* (1799), c. 10 (emphasis added).

53. *Laws Relative to Quarantine and to the Public Health of the City of New-York* (New York, 1858).

54. Following Boston's lead, this particular station and hospital were first established after the bout with yellow fever in 1799. By 1845 the thirty acres that comprised the Quarantine Grounds were fairly well developed, including three multiple-story hospitals accommodating 450 to 850 patients (one nine-month period logged 7,000 patients), officer and physician housing, houses for steward, farmer, bargemen, and others, a workhouse, office, boathouse, carpenter's shop, icehouse and coalhouse, wagon house, and barn. *Report of a Special Committee of the House of Assembly of the State of New-York on the Present Quarantine Laws* (Albany, N.Y., 1846), 59–60. The Staten Island location was a source of constant friction in the 1850s culminating in a full-scale riot by the citizens of nearby Castleton worried about threats to their own health as well as economic discrimination. The Castleton Board of Health labeled the station and hospital a public "nuisance," and urged the citizens to "abate it." For an excellent discussion, see Duffy, *Public Health in New York, 1625–1866*, 330–53.

55. Vessels subject to quarantine between April 1 and November 1 included (1) all vessels from any place where "pestilential, contagious, or infectious disease" existed at time of departure; (2) all vessels on which any case of disease occurred during the voyage; (3) all vessels from Asia, Africa, the Mediterranean, the West Indies, Bahama, Bermuda, Western Islands, or from any place in America in the ordinary passage from which they pass south of Cape Henlopen. *Laws Relative to Quarantine*, sec. 2, pp. 8–9.

56. For the destruction of cargo, the health officer was required to obtain the ascent of the mayor or commissioners of health. The mayor and commissioners also served as the general Board of Appeal through which to contest health officer directives.

57. Obstructing or violating quarantine was a misdemeanor punishable by $100–$500 fine and/or 3–6 months in the penitentiary.

58. *Laws Relative to Quarantine*, sec. 14, p. 16.

59. "Rules and Regulations to be Observed by Masters of Vessels under Quarantine. Quarantine Ground. Staten Island, 1858," in *Laws Relative to Quarantine*, 62–65.

60. According to Staten Island rules: "No boat shall be permitted to come on shore without an officer in it, and only between sun rising and sun setting, unless in cases of distress or sickness; and all boats must be alongside or on board by sun-down. The bell of the Health Office boat-house will be rung ten minutes before sun-down, to give notice to all boats to go off to their respective vessels.

"On Sundays, all boats must put off to their vessels by ten o'clock in the morning, when the bell will be rung to give such notice; and the boats must not come on shore again before six o'clock in the evening.

"Provisions and other necessaries, intended to be sent on board of a vessel at Quarantine, must be embarked from the Health Office wharf only." "Rules and Regulations of Quarantine. Staten Island," 62–63.

61. *Mitchell v. City of Rockland*, 41 Me. 363 (1856); *Beers v. Board of Health*, 35 La. Ann. 1132 (1883).

62. *Laws Relative to Quarantine*, 58.

63. "An Act Relating to Alien Passengers," *Laws of Massachusetts* (1837), c. 238. The act denied landing to any "lunatic, idiot, maimed, aged, or infirm person" or "pauper or in-

competent" unless the master of the vessel gave $1,000 bond to the city guaranteeing that such person would not become a public charge within ten years of landing. See *Norris v. Boston*, 4 Metc. 282 (1842); *Passenger Cases*, 7 How. 283 (U.S., 1849).

64. Massachusetts Sanitary Commission, *Report of a General Plan for the Promotion of Public and Personal Health*, 79. According to this report, "two persons who scuttled her, and some others who happened to be passing in a sail-boat, took the disease and died."

65. Pierre Bourdieu, *Outline of a Theory of Practice*, trans. Richard Nice (New York, 1977), 193.

66. *Mayor of New York v. Miln*, 11 Pet. 102 (U.S., 1837).

67. Joseph Jones, *Acts of the Legislature of Louisiana Establishing and Regulating Quarantine* (New Orleans, 1880), 38.

68. Africa, Austria, British America, Belgium, Canada, China, Denmark, England, Finland, France, Germany, Greece, Holland, Ireland, Italy, Louisiana, Mexico, Norway and Sweden, Poland, Portugal, Russia, Scotland, At Sea, South America, Spain, Switzerland, United States, Wales, West Indies.

69. Jones, *Louisiana Quarantine*, 92–97.

70. Michel Foucault, *Discipline and Punish* (New York, 1979), 140.

71. Ditto Augustin Averill, Robert Kermit, Charles Marshall, William Whitlock, William Nelson, William DeForest, George DeForrest, J. M. Woodward, Andrew Patrullo, James Tapscott, James McMurray, and William Roy. *Report of a Special Committee of the House of Assembly of the State of New York on the Present Quarantine Laws*, 241–305, quotations at 276, 288, 254–59.

72. For the most judicious assessment of merchant reaction to quarantine in the South, see Margaret Humphreys, *Yellow Fever and the South* (New Brunswick, N.J., 1992). Also see Duffy, *Public Health in New York, 1625–1866*, 350–51.

73. *Dubois v. City Council of Augusta*, Dud. 30 (Ga., 1831), 30–31.

74. *Harrison v. Mayor of Baltimore*, 1 Gill 264 (Md., 1843), 276.

75. *City of St. Louis v. McCoy*, 18 Mo. 238 (1853), 242; *Metcalf v. City of St. Louis*, 11 Mo. 102 (1847); *City of St. Louis v. Boffinger*, 19 Mo. 13 (1853).

76. See also *Board of Health v. Loyd*, 1 Phila. 20 (Pa., 1850); *Rudolphe v. City of New Orleans*, 11 La. Ann. 242 (1856). In *Mitchell v. Rockland*, a case inspired by a health officer's negligent burning of a quarantined ship, one does get a sense of some legal limits on local discretion. But here the court's close reading of health officer powers is used to *insulate* the city from liability. See *Mitchell v. City of Rockland*, 41 Me. 363 (1856); *Mitchell v. City of Rockland* (II), 52 Me. 118 (1860).

77. "An Act Relative to Quarantine," *United States Statutes at Large*, 1 (1799), c. 12, 619; *United States Statutes at Large*, 1 (1796), 31, 474.

78. Quoted in Joseph Jones, *Outline of the History, Theory and Practice of Quarantine* (New Orleans, 1883), 12.

79. *License Cases*, 5 How. 504 (U.S., 1847), 580–81. John Marshall explicitly referred to the 1796 and 1799 quarantine statutes in upholding state health and quarantine powers in *Gibbons v. Ogden*, 205–6.

80. *License Cases*, 632.

81. Ibid.

82. *New York v. Miln*, 11 Pet. 102 (U.S., 1837), 139.

83. Ibid., 110, 128–29.

84. *Passenger Cases*, 408, 423. The issue of powers over passengers, freight, and immigration was constitutionally volatile from an early date. In *Miln*, Justices Story and Baldwin did battle over the Marshall legacy on commerce and national versus state power. In the

late nineteenth century, that battle continued in *Henderson v. Mayor of New York*, 92 U.S. 259 (1875); *Chy Lung v. Freeman*, 92 U.S. 275 (1875); *Railroad Company v. Husen*, 92 U.S. 465 (1877).

85. *Peete v. Morgan*, 86 U.S. 581 (1873), 582. Like the *Passenger Cases, Peete* ultimately denied states the power to levy a direct tonnage tax on cargo despite this defense of general health regulatory authority.

86. On state pilotage regulations, see *Cooley v. Board of Wardens*, 12 How. 299 (U.S., 1851).

87. Quoted in Duffy, *Public Health in New York, 1625–1866*, 353; Blewett Harrison Lee, "Limitations Imposed by the Federal Constitution on the Right of the States to Enact Quarantine Laws," *Harvard Law Review* 2 (1889): 269.

88. For the unparalleled general discussion of cholera in 1832, see Rosenberg, *The Cholera Years*.

89. *Albany Argus*, June 16 and 18, 1832.

90. George Rogers Howell and Jonathan Tenney, *History of the County of Albany, New York, from 1609 to 1886* (New York, 1886), 214.

91. *Van Wormer v. Mayor of Albany*, 264. "An Act for the Preservation of Public Health," *Laws of New York* (1832), c. 333. Also see *People v. Corporation of Albany*, 11 Wend. 539 (N.Y., 1834).

92. See, for example, *Laws of New York* (1823), c. 333; *Laws of Louisiana* (1835), c. 162. Peabody, *Legislation regarding Public Health*, 75.

93. *Annual Report of the Board of Health of the State of Louisiana for the Year 1877* (New Orleans, 1878), 24–25.

94. *Commissioners of Salisbury v. Powe*, 51 N.C. 134 (1858).

95. *Aull v. City of Lexington*, 18 Mo. 401 (1853), 402.

96. *Ferguson v. City of Selma*, 43 Ala. 398 (1869), 399, 401.

97. *People v. Roff*, 3 Park. Crim. R. 216 (N.Y., 1856), 233.

98. *Pinkham v. Dorothy*, 55 Me. 135 (1868); *Lynde v. City of Rockland*, 66 Me. 309 (1876). Also see *Boom v. City of Utica*, 2 Barb. 104 (N.Y., 1848).

99. *Pinkham v. Dorothy*, 138. Chief Justice Appleton admitted that municipal officers were duly authorized to (1) remove persons with disease; (2) provide hospitals for reception; and (3) impress houses and stores for the safekeeping of infected articles. Appleton's only quibble here was that the legislature did not provide for impressing "the means of removal."

100. For two excellent later discussions of these issues, see *Raymond v. Fish*, 51 Conn. 80 (1883); *Spring v. Inhabitants of Hyde Park*, 137 Mass. 554 (1884).

101. *Willson v. Black Bird Creek Marsh Company*, 2 Pet. 245 (U.S., 1829).

102. I owe this way of stating the problem to Nayan Shah whose dissertation "San Francisco's 'Chinatown': Race and the Cultural Politics of Public Health, 1854–1952" (Ph.D. diss., University of Chicago, 1995), nicely illustrates the benefits of a cultural history approach in exploring the role of race and gender in constructions of public health and public power.

103. The directive read: "It is ordered that no Indian shall come to towne into the street after sufficient notice upon penalty of 5 s. or be whipped until they be free of the small poxe; but that they may come where they have corne on the back side and call; and if any English or Indian servant shall go to their wigwams they shall suffer the same punishment." Quoted in Elizabeth C. Tandy, "Local Quarantine and Inoculation for Smallpox in the American Colonies, 1620–1775," *American Journal of Public Health* 13 (1923): 204.

104. *First Biennial Report of the State Board of Health of California* (Sacramento, 1871), 9, 44–48; Austin Lewis, "Municipal Boards of Health and Quarantine Regulations," *American Law Review* 34 (1900): 722–25. *Jew Ho v. Williamson*, 103 Fed. 10 (1900).

105. *Meeker v. Van Rensselaer*, 15 Wend. 397 (N.Y., 1836), 398. *Albany Argus*, June 18, 1832.

106. Joel Munsell, ed., *The Annals of Albany* (Albany, N.Y., 1858), 9:248. The tenements abated in *Ferguson v. City of Selma* were described as "two old and almost worthless houses, filthy and crowded with filthy tenants." *Ferguson*, 401. In *Frank v. City of Atlanta*, 72 Ga. 428 (1884), the court felt compelled to add, "Some complaint was heard about her tenants, who were negroes." Also see Dr. Henry I. Bowditch's overlapping health, crime, and morals concerns in his verdict on the so-called Crystal Palace tenements in Boston. Bowditch argued that such buildings should not be allowed and, if built, should be summarily removed: "Any large tenement house, occupied by the lowest classes, who are accustomed to filth, and are regardless of making filth on the common territory, is in itself bad for the health and morality of the community. The long, dark, common corridors, in which vice can lurk wholly hidden at night, are of themselves provocative of the worst crimes." Bowditch, *Public Hygiene in America*, 80–89.

107. *Annual Report of the Board of Health of the State of Louisiana for the Year 1877*, 65, 67.

108. *Report of a General Plan for the Promotion of the Public and Personal Health*, 200–201. In recommendation 20, this report urged that "local Boards of Health endeavor to prevent or mitigate the sanitary evils arising from over-crowded lodging-houses or cellar-dwellings." Ibid., 164. Caldwell, *Thoughts on Hygiene*, 86.

109. Albert H. Buck, ed., *A Treatise on Hygiene and Public Health*, 2 vols. (New York, 1879), 1:41–43; *American Public Health Association Reports* 3 (1877): 50.

110. Again, this conceptualization of the problem of public health and state power owes much to an ongoing conversation with Nayan Shah.

111. For the best example of this kind of investigation for a later period, see George Chauncey, *Gay New York: Gender, Urban Culture, and the Making of the Gay Male World, 1890–1940* (New York, 1994), especially ch. 5 "Urban Culture and the Policing of the 'City of Bachelors.'"

112. In taking this more comprehensive approach to nuisance law and offensive trades, I will be glossing over several technical, doctrinal distinctions and stories. I will be combining results from equity and common law courts, public and private nuisance cases, and statutory and common law processes. My objective is to get an *overall* picture of the extent to which private businesses and manufactories were subject to publicly enforced penalties and sanctions when their actions harmfully affected others in the community. Lawyers will accuse me of mixing oil and water. I would argue that only by giving oil and water a vigorous shake are we at least temporarily able to gain a new perspective. Nineteenth-century citation patterns and the larger arguments of cases and treatises suggest that judges and commentators borrowed freely from a whole range of nuisance cases to make their points. Their minds were more supple and their rules more flexible than modern treatises suggest.

113. *Society for Establishing Useful Manufactures v. Morris Banking Co.*, 1 New Jersey Equity (NJE) 157 (1830), 192. Also see *Attorney General v. New-Jersey Railroad and Transportation Co.*, 3 NJE 136 (1834), on a railroad bridge; *Shreve v. Voorhees*, 3 NJE 25 (1834), on diverting a stream; *Browning v. Camden and Woodbury Railroad*, 4 NJE 47 (1837), on a railroad; *Shields v. Arndt*, 4 NJE 234 (1842), on diverting a watercourse; *Morris Canal and Banking v. Fagan*, 18 NJE 215 (1867), on obstruction of canal; *Higbee & Riggs v. Camden and Amboy Railroad*, 19 NJE 276 (1868), on a depot; *Delaware & Raritan Canal Co. v. Wright*, 21 New Jersey Law (NJL) 469 (1848), on obstruction of a watercourse; *Delaware & Raritan Canal Co. v. Lee*, 22 NJL 243 (1849), on obstruction of a watercourse; *State v. Morris and Essex Railroad*, 23 NJL 360 (1852), on a depot; *State v. Morris and Essex Railroad*, 25 NJL 437 (1856), on a depot; *Morris Canal and Banking v. Ryerson*, 27 NJL 457 (1858), on obstructing a watercourse; *State v. Babcock and Babcock*, 30 NJL 29 (1862), on obstructing a river. For a

variety of reasons, procedural, factual, and doctrinal, the court did not grant damages or an injunction in the following cases: *Quackenbush v. Van Riper*, 3 NJE 350 (1835), on a mill; *Vanwinkle v. Curtis*, 3 NJE 422 (1836), on diverting a stream; *Perkins v. Collins*, 3 NJE 483 (1835), on obstructing a street; *Hulme v. Shreve*, 4 NJE 116 (1837), on a mill gate; *Society for Useful Manufactures v. Holsman*, 5 NJE 126 (1845), on diverting water; *Morris Canal and Banking v. Society for Useful Manufactures*, 5 NJE 203 (1845), on diverting water; *Warne v. Morris Canal and Banking*, 5 NJE 410 (1846), on diverting water; *Gilbert v. Morris Canal and Banking*, 8 NJE (1850), on obstructing a creek; *Attorney General v. Hudson River Railroad*, 9 NJE 526 (1853), on a railroad bridge; *Newark Plank Road v. Elmer*, 9 NJE 754 (1855), on a railroad bridge; *Hinchman v. Paterson Horse Railroad*, 17 NJE 75 (1864), on a railroad; *Hogencamp v. Paterson Horse Railroad*, 17 NJE 83 (1864); *Beavers v. Trimmer and Cole*, 25 NJL 97 (1855), on a dam; *State v. Passaic Turnpike*, 27 NJL 217 (1858), on a turnpike gate. As in the famous case of *Charles River Bridge*, there were several nuisance actions in New Jersey to restrain competing corporations from infringing on previously granted chartered rights. *Bordentown and S. Amboy Turnpike Road v. Camden and Amboy Railroad*, 17 NJL 314 (1839); *Delaware and Raritan Canal and Camden and Amboy Railroad v. Atlantic Railroad*, 15 NJE 321 (1863); *Charles River Bridge v. Warren Bridge*, 23 Mass. 376 (1828); *Charles River Bridge v. Warren Bridge*, 24 Mass. 345 (1829). For a further discussion of the obstruction of public ways, see chapter 4.

114. *Kennedy v. Board of Health*, 2 Pa. St. 366 (1845), on stagnant water; *Brick Presbyterian Church v. Mayor of New York*, 5 Cow. 538 (N.Y., 1826), on a cemetery; *Coates v. Mayor of New York*, 7 Cow. 585 (N.Y., 1827), on a cemetery; *Commonwealth v. Patch*, 97 Mass. 221 (1867), on a swine; *Ashbrook v. Commonwealth*, 1 Bush 139 (Ky., 1867), on cattle and swine; *Milne v. Davidson*, 5 Martin, N.S. 409, 16 Am. Dec. 189 (La., 1827), on a hospital; *Green v. Mayor and Aldermen of Savannah*, 6 Ga. 1 (1849), on rice.

115. *Coates v. Mayor of New York* (decided with *Stuyvesant v. Mayor of New York* and *Slack v. Mayor of New York*), 604. For a discussion of *Coates* in the context of early American corporation and contract law, see chapter 3.

116. *Rhodes v. Dunbar*, 57 Pa. St. 274 (1868), 275. Also see William P. Prentice, *Police Powers Arising under the Law of Overruling Necessity* (New York, 1894), 167–181; Thomas W. Waterman, *Waterman's Eden on the Law and Practice of Injunctions*, 3d ed., 2 vols. (New York, 1852), 2:259–68; Francis Wharton, *A Treatise on the Criminal Law of the United States* (Philadelphia, 1846), 503–21. English common law held that some of these businesses, for example, a glasshouse, a candle factory, a tannery, a tobacco mill, a swinesty, a limekiln, and a smelting house for lead, were of such a hurtful character as to be nuisances per se. The deleterious effects of such trades were taken for granted and did not have to be independently proved in a court of law. Horace G. Wood, *A Practical Treatise on the Law of Nuisances*, 2d ed. (Albany, N.Y., 1883), 656.

117. Martin V. Melosi, ed., *Pollution and Reform in American Cities, 1870–1930* (Austin, Tex., 1980); Terence McLaughlin, *Dirt: A Social History As Seen through the Uses and Abuses of Dirt* (New York, 1971).

118. *Norcross v. Thoms*, 51 Me. 503, 81 Am. Dec. 588 (1863), 589.

119. *Ross v. Butler*, 19 NJE 294, 97 Am. Dec. 654 (1868), 659. Also see *Fuselier v. Spalding*, 2 La. Ann. 773 (1847); *Dennis v. Eckhardt*, 3 Grant's Cases 390 (Pa., 1862), 390; *Hutchins v. Smith*, 63 Barb. 251 (N.Y., 1872); *Campbell v. Seamen*, 63 N.Y. 568 (1876). *Campbell v. Seamen* was typical in its reliance on English common law, citing ten English brick-burning decisions since 1736 to support its award of injunction and damages. These cases also relied on American court decisions against cemeteries, livery stables, and steam-powered manufac-

tories, which will be discussed later. There were limits to courts' willingness to restrain noxious traditional trades, especially in parts of cities already devoted to industrial, polluting enterprises. In *Huckenstine's Appeal*, 70 Pa. St. 102, 10 Am. Rep. 669 (1872), the Pennsylvania Supreme Court refused to enjoin a brickkiln in Allegheny County: "The properties of the plaintiff and defendant lie adjoining each other on the hillside overlooking the city, whose every-day cloud of smoke from thousands of chimneys and stacks, hangs like a pall over it, obscuring it from sight. This single word [smoke] describes the characteristics of this city, its kind of fuel, its business, the habits of its people and the industries which give it prosperity and wealth."

120. *Holsman v. Boiling Spring Bleaching Co.*, 14 NJE 335 (1862).

121. *Whitney v. Bartholomew*, 21 Conn. 213 (1851).

122. Ibid., 217–19.

123. *General Statutes of Massachusetts* (1860), c. 88, 458–60. *Call v. Allen*, 83 Mass. 137 (1861).

124. *Davidson v. Isham*, 9 NJE 186 (1852). Also see *Fish v. Dodge*, 4 Denio 311 (N.Y., 1847); *Thebaut and Glazier v. Canova*, 11 Fla. 143 (1866); *McKeon v. See*, 51 N.Y. 300 (1873); *Ditman and Berger v. Repp*, 50 Md. 516 (1878). In *Davidson*, Williamson denied the injunction in equity as the same case was pending at law.

125. *Wesson v. Washburn Iron Co.*, 13 Allen 95 (Mass., 1866); *Ottawa Gas-Light and Coke Co. v. Thompson*, 39 Ill. 598 (1864); *Pottstown Gas Co. v. Murphy*, 39 Pa. St. 257 (1861); *Cleveland v. Citizens Gas Light Co.*, 20 NJE 201 (1869); *Milhau v. Sharp*, 27 N.Y. 611 (1863); *City of Salem v. Eastern Railroad Co.*, 98 Mass. 431 (1868); *King v. Morris and Essex Railroad Co.*, 18 NJE 397 (1867); *Attorney General v. Morris and Essex Railroad Co.*, 19 NJE 386 (1869). See also *Hay v. Cohoes Co.*, 2 N.Y. 159 (1849), on blasting; *Holsman v. Boiling Spring Bleaching Co.*, 14 NJE 335 (1862); *Adams v. Michael*, 38 Md. 123 (1873), on a felt-roofing factory.

126. *Call v. Allen*. Even here, however, the court held out the possibility that, if the plaintiff could prove actual nuisancelike damage (rather than merely relying on these mills' lack of a license), it might intervene.

127. They did so in *Holsman v. Boiling Spring Bleaching Co.* and *Cleveland v. Citizens Gas Light Co.* In *Cleveland*, Chancellor Zabriskie enjoined the gas company from using the lime process in purifying its gas. The New Jersey Court of Equity refused injunctions in *Tichenor v. Wilson*, 8 NJE 197 (1849); *Durant v. Williamson*, 7 NJE 547 (1849); *Butler v. Rogers*, 9 NJE 487 (1853); *Rogers v. Danforth*, 9 NJE 289 (1853); *Wolcott v. Melick*, 11 NJE 204 (1856); *Duncan v. Hayes and Greenwood*, 22 NJE 25 (1871).

128. *Cleveland v. Citizens Gas Light Co.*, 209.

129. *Gilbert v. Showerman*, 23 Mich. 448 (1871), 456. Also see the torn opinions of the Pennsylvania Supreme Court in *Rhodes v. Dunbar*.

130. *Budd v. New York*, 143 U.S. 517 (1892).

131. *Rhodes v. Dunbar*.

132. Ibid., 277–78.

133. *Coker v. Birge*, 9 Ga. 425, 54 Am. Dec. 347 (1851).

134. Ibid., 348. For similar rulings on livery stables, see *Burditt v. Swenson*, 17 Tx. 489 (1856); *Dargan v. Waddill*, 9 Ire. Law 244 (N.C., 1848); *Morris v. Brower, Thompson and Fish*, Anthony's Nisi Prius 368 (N.Y., 1851), in which $500 damages were awarded by jury; *Aldrich v. Howard*, 8 R.I. 246 (1865); *Shiras v. Olinger*, 50 Ia. 571 (1879).

135. Livery stables were not held to be nuisances per se — in and of themselves. As was the case with most private nuisance law, courts determined the existence of an injury or potential injury on the basis of specific, local circumstances. Thus some courts, while upholding

the general decisions in *Coker, Burditt, Dargan, Morris,* and *Aldrich,* refused an injunction or damages given a different set of facts. See, for example, *Harrison v. Brooks,* 20 Ga. 537 (1856); *Kirkman v. Handy,* 11 Humph. 406 (Tenn., 1850).

136. *Report of the Council of Hygiene and Public Health of the Citizen's Association of New York upon the Sanitary Condition of the City* (New York, 1865), xciv, cxxviii, 86–87, 175, 294. In one case, the council reported on a Forty-sixth Street slaughterhouse "built on the rear of the lot, the drainage is over the surface of the yard over the sidewalk into the street gutter, where the blood is mixed with water; it then runs two-thirds of the entire block before it finds its way into the inlet of the sewer. The children of the neighborhood play in this mixture." Ibid., 294.

137. *Catlin v. Valentine,* 9 Paige 575 (N.Y., 1842); *Taylor v. People,* 6 Parker's Crim. 347 (N.Y., 1867); *Brady v. Weeks,* 3 Barb. 157 (N.Y., 1848). In issuing an injunction against a slaughterhouse on Twelfth Street in New York City, the court argued in *Brady,* "When the slaughterhouse was erected [ten to fourteen years earlier], it was remote from the thickly settled parts of the city; but it seems that the city has now grown up to it. . . . When the slaughter house was erected, it incommoded no one; but now it interferes with the enjoyment of life and property, and tends to deprive the plaintiffs of the use and benefit of their dwellings. . . . As the city extends, such nuisances should be removed to the vacant ground beyond the immediate neighborhood of the residences of the citizens. This, public policy, as well as health and comfort of the population of the city, demand." *Brady,* 159. The idea of "coming to the nuisance" bears a resemblance to the process of turning private property into public roads discussed in chapter 4. The destruction of established private rights and older expectations was a constant part of the expansion and movement of early nineteenth-century populations. See Stanley I. Kutler, *Privilege and Creative Destruction: The Charles River Bridge Case* (New York, 1971).

138. *Commonwealth v. Upton,* 6 Gray 473 (Mass., 1856), 475–76 (emphasis added). Also see *State v. Wilson,* 43 N.H. 415 (1862); *Taylor v. People,* 6 Parker's Crim. 347 (N.Y., 1867); *Allen v. State,* 34 Tx. 230 (1871); *Minke v. Hopeman,* 87 Ill. 450 (1877); *Pruner v. Pendleton,* 75 Va. 516 (1881). The injunction also remained a key regulatory tool. See *Bishop v. Banks,* 33 Conn. 118 (1865).

139. *Milwaukee v. Gross,* 21 Wis. 241 (1866); *Ex Parte Shrader,* 33 Cal. 279 (1867). As will be seen momentarily, some of these municipal regulatory schemes would become controversial. The *Slaughterhouse Cases,* 83 U.S. 36 (1872), were a product of one of the more famous attempts to establish a public abattoir system like that in Paris. See also *Wreford v. People,* 14 Mich. 41 (1865); *Chicago v. Rumpff,* 45 Ill. 90 (1867).

140. Alexander W. Winter, *Winter's Handy Book of Reference for Packers, Butchers, Abattoirs, Meat Markets and Stockmen* (Chicago, 1894), 43–44. Winter also described how to arrange catch basins to avoid the loss of grease in washing floors (recipe 36) and how to prepare blood and offal for fertilizer (recipes 32 and 33).

141. *Peck v. Elder,* 3 Sandf. 126 (N.Y., 1849).

142. *Howard v. Lee,* 3 Sandf. 281 (N.Y., 1849), 283. See also *Blunt and Murray v. Hay,* 4 Sandf. Ch. 362 (N.Y., 1846); *Burk v. State,* 27 Ind. 430 (1867); *Francis v. Schoellkopf,* 53 N.Y. 152 (1873). In *Francis v. Schoellkopf,* the New York Court of Appeals reacted hostilely to the defense's contention that a private individual could not bring suit against a public nuisance without proving a "special" injury: "The idea that if by a wrongful act a serious injury is inflicted upon a single individual a recovery may be had therefore against the wrong-doer, and that if by the same act numbers are so injured no recovery can be had by anyone, is absurd" (154). See the discussion of this topic in Wood, *Nuisances,* 737–54, and the extensive list of cases cited there. My own research tends to back up Wood's conclusion: "Injury to

one's private property or to his health or comfort is special." Wood, 754. Also see the excellent discussion of the special damage requirement in *Wesson v. Washburn Iron Co.*

143. *Commonwealth v. Rumford Chemical Works*, 16 Gray 231 (Mass., 1860), 234.

144. *Kennedy v. Phelps*, 10 La. Ann. 227 (1855).

145. Duffy, *Public Health in New York City, 1625–1866*; John Duffy, *A History of Public Health in New York City, 1866–1966* (New York, 1974).

146. *Laws of New Jersey* (1865), c. 493, 917.

147. *Babcock v. The New Jersey Stock Yard Co.*, 20 NJE 296 (1869).

148. Ibid., 298–99.

149. *Manhattan Manufacturing and Fertilizing Co. v. New Jersey Stock Yard and Market Co.*, 23 NJE 161 (1872). In this case, the fertilizing company brought suit to prevent the stockyard from giving its offal to another party.

150. *Meigs v. Lister*, 23 NJE 199 (1872). This first establishment was the subject of an earlier public nuisance indictment.

151. Ibid., 200–201.

152. Ibid., 205–6.

153. *Manhattan Fertilizing Co.*

154. Ibid., 251–52.

155. See chapter 2.

156. *Laws of New Jersey* (1871), c. 424, 1107.

157. *Manhattan Fertilizing Co.*, 255.

158. See Alpheus T. Mason and Gerald Garvey, eds., *American Constitutional History: Essays by Edward S. Corwin* (New York, 1964); Benjamin R. Twiss, *Lawyers and the Constitution: How Laissez-Faire Came to the Supreme Court* (New York, 1962); Charles Grove Haines, *The Revival of Natural Law Concepts* (Cambridge, Mass., 1930); Benjamin Fletcher Wright Jr., *American Interpretations of Natural Law: A Study in the History of Political Theory* (Cambridge, Mass., 1931).

159. The persistence of the doctrine *salus populi* in public health history is extraordinary. George Rosen concludes the preface of his classic survey of public health history with "*Salus publica suprema lex.*" Susan Wade Peabody concludes her dissertation on legislation and public health similarly: "Without private health the individual is useless, without protection of the public health government is a failure. *Salus populi suprema lex.*" Rosen, *History of Public Health*, 19; Peabody, *Legislation regarding Public Health*, 113.

160. *Coe v. Schultz*, 47 Barb. 64 (N.Y., 1866); *Stewart v. Schultz*, 33 How. Prac. 3 (N.Y., 1867); *Cooper v. Schultz*, 33 How. Prac. 5 (1866); *Weil v. Schultz* (decided with *Eckel v. Schultz*), 33 How. Prac. 7 (N.Y., 1866); *Gies v. Schultz* (decided with *Westheimer v. Schultz, Eisner v. Schultz, Schwartzchild v. Schultz,* and *Donahue v. Schultz*), 33 How. Prac. 11 (N.Y., 1866); *Schuster v. Metropolitan Board of Health*, 49 Barb. 450 (N.Y., 1867); *Metropolitan Board of Health v. Heister*, 37 N.Y. 661 (1868). As one might have guessed, Schultz was the commissioner of the Metropolitan Board of Health.

161. *Coe v. Schultz*, 65.

162. Ibid., 67.

163. *Metropolitan Board of Health v. Heister.*

164. Ibid., 670. See also *Stewart v. Schultz*, 33 How. Prac. 3 (N.Y., 1866); *Gies v. Schultz*; *Weil v. Schultz*, 33 How. Prac. 7 (N.Y., 1866).

165. *Laws of New York* (1857), c. 569. *People v. Draper*, 25 Barb. 344 (N.Y., 1857); *People v. Draper*, 15 N.Y. 532 (1857).

166. *Village of Jamaica v. Long Island Railroad Co.*, 37 How. Prac. 379 (N.Y., 1869).

167. See also the dissent of Justice Miller in *Metropolitan Board of Health v. Heister*, 674.

168. The Metropolitan Board of Health itself fell victim to municipal/state political wrangling in 1870. See Duffy, *Public Health in New York City, 1866–1966,* 1–90. In New Jersey, the summary authority granted boards of health was particularly suspect. See *Attorney General v. Steward & Taylor,* 20 NJE 415 (1869); *Weil v. Ricord,* 24 NJE 169 (1873); *State, Marshall, Prosecutors v. Cadwalader,* 36 NJL 283 (1873); *Hutton v. City of Camden,* 39 NJL 122 (1876). In Massachusetts, see *Belcher v. Farrar,* 8 Allen 325 (Mass., 1864); *City of Taunton v. Taylor,* 116 Mass. 254 (1874).

169. Frank J. Goodnow, a founder of American administrative law, pursued those linkages in "Summary Abatement of Nuisances by Boards of Health," *Columbia Law Review* 2 (1902): 203–22. Also see Christopher G. Tiedeman, *A Treatise on the Limitations of the Police Power in the United States* (St. Louis, 1886), 422–33; Ernst Freund, *Administrative Powers over Persons and Property: A Comparative Survey* (Chicago, 1928).

170. For the best overview of these developments, see Duffy, *The Sanitarians,* 102–74.

171. *Northwestern Fertilizing Company v. Hyde Park,* 97 U.S. 659 (1878); *Northwestern Fertilizing Company v. Hyde Park,* 70 Ill. 634 (1873). See also *Boyd v. Alabama,* 94 U.S. 645 (1877); *Boston Beer Company v. Massachusetts,* 97 U.S. 25 (1878); and the discussion of corporate charters and the contract clause in chapter 3.

172. The best indicator of this governmental tendency toward higher legal powers and forms is Willard Hurst's chronology of milk regulation in Wisconsin. James Willard Hurst, *Law and Social Process in United States History* (Ann Arbor, Mich., 1960), 93–102. *Statutes of Wisconsin Territory* (1839), p. 350; *Wisconsin Revised Statutes* (1849), c. 140; *Wisconsin Laws* (1883), c. 308; *Wisconsin Laws* (1887), c. 157; *Wisconsin Laws* (1889), chs. 425, 452; *Wisconsin Laws* (1939), c. 492.

173. *Slaughterhouse Cases,* 83 U.S. 36 (1872). The Louisiana decision is *State v. Fagan,* 22 La. Ann. 545 (1870). Loren P. Beth, "The Slaughter-House Cases—Revisited," *Louisiana Law Review* 23 (1963): 487–505.

174. *Slaughterhouse,* 109, 111.

175. Herbert Hovenkamp, *Enterprise and American Law, 1836–1937* (Cambridge, 1991), 116–24. Hovenkamp's innovative discussion of *Slaughterhouse* nicely rebuts interpretations based on "corruption" and charges of "monopoly." The Crescent City facilities were not monopolistic; they were open to all butchers who could either do their own work there or have it done for them at legislatively set rates. Hovenkamp also admits to the prominent role of public health in the cases. But his overarching economic interpretation unduly marginalizes legal discourse and practice. His contention, for example, that prior to *Slaughterhouse* slaughtering "had always been a common right undertaken in competitive markets" neglects the long public regulatory tradition discussed here. Ibid., 121, 116.

176. *State v. Fagan,* 553.

177. Ibid., 555–57.

178. *Slaughterhouse Cases,* 21 L. Ed. 394 (1872), 399. The lawyer's edition of the U.S. Supreme Court reports contains this more complete record of the arguments of counsel.

179. Ibid., 398.

180. Robert J. Kaczorowski, "To Begin the Nation Anew: Congress, Citizenship, and Civil Rights after the Civil War," *American Historical Review* 92 (1987): 45–68.

181. Citing Adam Smith, Justice Field opined that "equality of right, with exemption from all disparaging and partial enactments, in the lawful pursuits of life, throughout the whole country, is the distinguishing privilege of citizens of the United States. . . . That only is a free government, in the American sense of the term, under which the inalienable right of every citizen to pursue his happiness is unrestrained, except by just, equal, and impartial laws." *Slaughterhouse,* 83 U.S. 36, 109–111. Justice Bradley argued similarly that "a law

which prohibits a large class of citizens from adopting a lawful employment, or from following a lawful employment previously adopted, does deprive them of liberty as well as property, without due process of law. Their right of choice is a portion of their liberty; their occupation is their property." Ibid., 122. For telling insights into the limits of Bradley's commitment to economic freedom, see his majority opinion in the very next case in the Supreme Court Reporter, *Bradwell v. Illinois*, 83 U.S. 130 (1873). There he denied Myra Bradwell's right to practice law with a spirited defense of the "natural law" of domesticity and patriarchy.

182. *Slaughterhouse Cases*, 83 U.S. 36 (1872), 62.

183. *Slaughterhouse Cases*, 21 L. Ed. 394 (1872), 400.

184. *Slaughterhouse Cases*, 83 U.S. 36 (1872), 77.

Conclusion

1. Albert Shaw, "The American State and the American Man," *Contemporary Review* 51 (1887): 696; James Bryce, *The American Commonwealth*, 3 vols. (London, 1888), 3:266–88. In the third edition, Bryce removed the legislative and regulatory charts that clashed so sharply with the ideology of laissez-faire. For an excellent discussion of Shaw and Bryce and the American regulatory/administrative state after 1865, see William R. Brock, *Investigation and Responsibility: Public Responsibility in the United States, 1865–1900* (Cambridge, 1984).

2. Theodore J. Lowi, "American Business, Public Policy, Case-Studies, and Political Theory," *World Politics* 16 (1964), 677.

3. See George M. Fredrickson, *The Inner Civil War: Northern Intellectuals and the Crisis of the Union* (New York, 1965); Morton Keller, *Affairs of State: Public Life in Late Nineteenth Century America* (Cambridge, Mass., 1977), ch. 1; James M. McPherson, *Battle Cry of Freedom: The Civil War Era* (New York, 1988); Harold M. Hyman, *A More Perfect Union: The Impact of the Civil War and Reconstruction on the Constitution* (New York, 1973). Also see Eric Foner, *Reconstruction: America's Unfinished Revolution, 1863–1877* (New York, 1988); Robert J. Kaczorowski, "To Begin the Nation Anew: Congress, Citizenship, and Civil Rights after the Civil War," *American Historical Review* 92 (1987): 45–68; William E. Nelson, *The Fourteenth Amendment: From Political Principle to Judicial Doctrine* (Cambridge, Mass., 1988).

4. Max Weber, *Economy and Society*, ed. Guenther Roth and Claus Wittich, 2 vols. (Berkeley, 1978), 1:56.

5. Samuel P. Hays, "The New Organizational Society," in *American Political History as Social Analysis* (Knoxville, Tenn., 1980), 244–63.

6. For an excellent example, see Hendrik Hartog's marvelous discussion of Dillon's Rule wherein municipal governments were legally allowed "only such powers as were granted to it in specific and unambiguous statutory language." Hendrik Hartog, *Public Property and Private Power: The Corporation of the City of New York in American Law, 1730–1870* (Chapel Hill, N.C., 1983), 222–23.

7. Stephen Skowronek, *Building a New American State: The Expansion of National Administrative Capacities, 1877–1920* (Cambridge, Mass., 1982); William E. Nelson, *The Roots of American Bureaucracy, 1830–1900* (Cambridge, Mass., 1982). Also see Robert Wiebe, *The Search for Order, 1877–1920* (New York, 1967). On the limits of such developments, see Barry Karl, *The Uneasy State: The United States from 1915 to 1945* (Chicago, 1983); Morton Keller, "(Jerry-) Building a New American State," *Reviews in American History* 11 (1983): 248–51.

8. Alexis de Tocqueville, *Democracy in America*, ed. Phillips Bradley, 2 vols. (New York, 1945), 61–101; James Bryce, *The American Commonwealth*.

9. Classic statements on the nature of Union after the start of the Civil War include Sydney G. Fisher, *The Trial of the Constitution* (Philadelphia, 1862); J. A. Jameson, *The Constitutional Convention* (New York, 1866); Elisha Mulford, *The Nation* (New York, 1870); John C. Hurd, *The Union State* (New York, 1890).

10. Woodrow Wilson, *The State* (Boston, 1889); W. W. Willoughby, *An Examination of the Nature of the State* (New York, 1896). Also see John W. Burgess, *Political Science and Comparative Constitutional Law* (Boston, 1890). The best historical discussions of these works can be found in Charles Edward Merriam, *A History of American Political Theories* (New York, 1915), and Daniel T. Rodgers, *Contested Truths: Keywords in American Politics since Independence* (New York, 1987), 144–75.

11. Theodore D. Woolsey, *Political Science* (New York, 1877).

12. J. K. Bluntschli quoted in Christopher G. Tiedeman, *A Treatise on the Limitations of Police Power in the United States* (St. Louis, 1886), 3–4.

13. *United States v. DeWitt*, 9 Wall. 41 (U.S., 1869). *DeWitt* held that the federal government did not have the power to prohibit the manufacture and sale of dangerous, flammable materials like naphtha, illuminating oils, and petroleum. Police powers were the province of state governments; the national government remained a government of specifically delegated powers, for example, commerce and taxation.

14. Henry Adams, "The Anglo-Saxon Courts of Law," in *Essays in Anglo-Saxon Law* (Boston, 1876), 4.

15. Otto von Gierke, *The German Law of Fellowship*, volume 1, *The Legal and Moral History of the German Fellowship*, trans. Antony Black, in *Community in Historical Perspective* (Cambridge, 1990), 112.

16. *Dred Scott v. Sandford*, 19 How. 393 (U.S., 1857).

17. See, for example, William Hosmer, *The Higher Law, in Its Relations to Civil Government: With Particular Reference to Slavery, and the Fugitive Slave Law* (New York, 1852).

18. Charles M. Cook, *The American Codification Movement: A Study of Antebellum Legal Reform* (Westport, Conn., 1981); Maxwell Bloomfield, *American Lawyers in a Changing Society, 1776–1876* (Cambridge, Mass., 1976), ch. 3; Luther Hamilton, ed., *Memoirs, Speeches, and Writings of Robert Rantoul, Jr.* (Boston, 1954).

19. Theodore Sedgwick, *A Treatise on the Rules Which Govern the Interpretation and Application of Statutory and Constitutional Law* (New York, 1857). See also E. Fitch Smith, *Commentaries on Statute and Constitutional Law* (Albany, N.Y., 1848); and Platt Potter, *Dwarris on Statutes* (Albany, N.Y., 1871).

20. Michael Kammen, *A Machine That Would Go of Itself: The Constitution in American Culture* (New York, 1986).

21. Thomas M. Cooley, *A Treatise on the Constitutional Limitations* (Boston, 1868); Tiedeman, *Limitations on Police Power*.

22. *Munn v. Illinois*, 94 U.S. 113 (1877); *Mugler v. Kansas*, 123 U.S. 623 (1887); *Powell v. Pennsylvania*, 127 U.S. 678 (1888); *Budd v. New York*, 143 U.S. 517 (1892); *Lawton v. Steele*, 152 U.S. 133 (1894).

This book uses standard sources and conventional research techniques in American legal and constitutional history. But since one of its objectives is the integration of legal and political history, this selected bibliography is designed to familiarize students of government and public power with the key sources and literatures on nineteenth-century American public law. It is divided into four categories: cases, statutes, primary treatises, and secondary works. For a more complete listing of the sources used in this book, consult the notes for each chapter.

Cases

Adams v. Mayor of Somerville, 39 Tenn. 363 (1859).
Adams v. Michael, 38 Md. 123 (1873).
Adams v. Rivers, 11 Barb. 390 (N.Y., 1851).
Administrators of Byrne v. Administrators of Stewart, 3 Des. Eq. 466 (S.C., 1812).
Aldrich v. Howard, 8 R.I. 246 (1865).
Alexander Cuscadden's Case, 2 City Hall Rec. 53 (N.Y., 1817).
Alexander v. Town Council of Greenville, 54 Miss. 659 (1877).
Alfred S. Pell's Case, 3 City Hall Recorder 141 (N.Y., 1818).
Allen v. State, 34 Tx. 230 (1871).
American Land Co. v. Zeiss, 219 U.S. 47 (1911).
American Print Works v. Lawrence, 3 Zabr. 590, 57 Am. Dec. 420 (N.J., 1851).
Amos Broad's Case, 3 City Hall Rec. 7 (N.Y., 1818).
Anderson v. City of Savannah, 69 Ga. 472 (1882).
Anonymous, 12 Mod. 342 (1700).
Ash v. People, 11 Mich. 347 (1863).
Ashbrook v. Commonwealth, 1 Bush 139 (Ky., 1867).
Attorney General v. Cleaver, 18 Ves. Jr. 211, 34 E. Repr. 297 (Eng., 1811).
Attorney General v. Cohoes Co., 6 Paige 133 (N.Y., 1836).
Attorney General v. Forbes, 2 M. & C. 123 (Eng., 1836).
Attorney General v. Hunter, 16 N.C. 12 (1826).
Attorney General v. Lea, 38 N.C. 265 (1844).
Attorney General v. Morris and Essex Railroad Co., 19 NJE 386 (1869).
Attorney General v. New-Jersey Railroad and Transportation Co., 3 NJE 136 (1834).
Attorney General v. Richards, 2 Anstr. 603 (Eng., 1795).
Attorney General v. Steward and Taylor, 20 NJE 415 (1869).
Attorney General v. Utica Insurance Co., 2 Johns. Ch. R. 371 (N.Y., 1817).
Attorney General and Bell v. Blount, 4 Hawks. 384 (N.C., 1826).
Aull v. City of Lexington, 18 Mo. 401 (1853).
Babcock v. The New Jersey Stock Yard Co., 20 NJE 296 (1869).
Badkins v. Robinson, 53 Ga. 613 (1875).
Baines v. Baker, 1 Ambl. 158, 27 E. Repr. 105 (Eng., 1752).

Baker v. Boston, 12 Pick. 184 (Mass., 1831).

Bank of Augusta v. Earle, 13 Pet. 519 (U.S., 1839).

Barker v. Commonwealth, 19 Pa. St. 412 (1852).

Barnesciotta v. People, 10 Hun. 137 (N.Y., 1877).

Barron v. Baltimore, 7 Pet. 243 (U.S., 1833).

Bartemeyer v. Iowa, 18 Wall. 129 (U.S., 1873).

Baumgartner v. Hasty, 100 Ind. 575 (1884).

Beebe v. State, 6 Ind. 501 (1855).

Beers v. Board of Health, 35 La. Ann. 1132 (1883).

Belcher v. Farrar, 8 Allen 325 (Mass., 1864).

Berks County v. Bertolet, 13 Pa. St. 522 (1850).

Berry v. People, 1 N.Y. Crim Rep. 43 (1878).

Bethune v. Hughes, 28 Ga. 560, 73 Am. Dec. 789 (1859).

Bishop v. Banks, 33 Conn. 118 (1865).

Block v. Hirsch, 256 U.S. 135 (1921).

Block v. Jacksonville, 36 Ill. 301 (1865).

Bloomhuff v. State, 8 Blackf. 205 (Ind., 1846).

Blunt and Murray v. Hay, 4 Sandf. Ch. 362 (N.Y., 1846).

Board of Health v. Loyd, 1 Phila. 20 (Pa., 1850).

Bode v. State, 7 Gill 326 (Md., 1848).

Boehm and Loeber v. Mayor of Baltimore, 61 Md. 259 (1883).

Boom v. City of Utica, 2 Barb. 104 (N.Y., 1848).

Booth v. State, 4 Conn. 65 (1821).

Boston Beer Company v. Massachusetts, 97 U.S. 25 (1877).

Bowditch v. Boston, 101 U.S. 16 (1879).

Bowers v. Hardwick, 478 U.S. 186 (1986).

Bradley v. People, 56 Barb. 72 (N.Y., 1866).

Bradwell v. Illinois, 83 U.S. 130 (1873).

Brady v. Northwestern Insurance Co., 11 Mich. 425 (1863).

Brady v. Weeks, 3 Barb. 157 (N.Y., 1848).

Brick Presbyterian Church v. Mayor of New York, 5 Cow. 538 (N.Y., 1826).

Briscoe v. Bank of Kentucky, 11 Pet. 257 (U.S., 1837).

Brockway v. People, 2 Hill 558 (N.Y., 1842).

Brooks v. State, 10 Tenn. 482 (1831).

Brown v. Maryland, 12 Wheat. 419 (U.S., 1827).

Browning v. Camden and Woodbury Railroad, 4 NJE 47 (1837).

Budd v. New York, 143 U.S. 517 (1892).

Burditt v. Swenson, 17 Tx. 489 (1856).

Burk v. State, 27 Ind. 430 (1867).

Bush v. Seabury, 8 Johns. R. 418 (N.Y., 1811).

Butchers' Union Slaughter-House and Livestock Landing Co. v. Crescent City Live-Stock Landing and Slaughter-House Co., 111 U.S. 746 (1883).

Butler v. Rogers, 9 NJE 487 (1853).

Cable v. State, 8 Blackf. 531 (Ind., 1847).

Cadwell v. State, 17 Conn. 467 (1846).

Calder v. Bull, 3 Dallas 386 (U.S., 1798).

Calder v. Kirby, 5 Gray 597 (Mass., 1856).

Caldwell v. City of Alton, 33 Ill. 416, 85 Am. Dec. 282 (1864).

Call v. Allen, 83 Mass. 137 (1861).

Callender v. Marsh, 1 Pick. 417 (Mass., 1823).

Campbell v. Seamen, 63 N.Y. 568 (1876).

Canepa v. City of Birmingham, 92 Ala. 358 (1890).

Carson v. Blazer, 2 Binney 475 (Pa., 1810).

Case of the King's Prerogative in Salt-peter, 12 Coke 13 (Eng., 1607).

Catlin v. Valentine, 9 Paige 575 (N.Y., 1842).

Charles River Bridge v. Warren Bridge, 23 Mass. 376 (1828).

Charles River Bridge v. Warren Bridge, 24 Mass. 345 (1829).

Charles River Bridge v. Warren Bridge, 11 Pet. 420 (U.S., 1837).

Cheatham v. Shearon, 1 Swan. 213, 55 Am. Dec. 734 (Tenn., 1851).

Cherokee Nation v. Georgia, 5 Pet. 1 (U.S., 1831).

Chicago v. Rumpff, 45 Ill. 90 (1867).

Charles Myer's Case, 1 City Hall Rec. 67 (N.Y., 1816).

Childress v. Mayor of Nashville, 35 Tenn. 347 (1855).

Chy Lung v. Freeman, 92 U.S. 275 (1875).

Cincinnati v. Buckingham, 10 Oh. 257 (1840).

Cincinnati R.R. Co. v. Commonwealth, 80 Ky. 137 (1882).

City and County of Sacramento v. Crocker, 16 Cal. 119 (1860).

City Council of Charleston v. Goldsmith, 2 Spear's Law 428 (S.C., 1844).

City Council of Montgomery v. Louisville & N.R. Co., 84 Ala. 127 (1887).

City of Bowling Green v. Carson, 73 Ky. 64 (1873).

City of Brooklyn v. Cleves, Hill & Denio 231 (N.Y., suppl., 1843).

City of Charleston v. Reed, 27 W. Va. 681 (1886).

City of Cincinnati v. Buckingham, 10 Oh. 257 (1840).

City of Des Moines v. Gilchrist, 67 Ia. 210 (1885).

City of London v. Wood, 12 Mod. 669 (Eng., 1702).

City of New Orleans v. Heirs of Guillotte, 12 La. Ann. 818 (1857).

City of New Orleans v. Stafford, 27 La. Ann. 417, 21 Am. Rep. 563 (1875).

City of Olympia v. Mann, 1 Wash. St. 389 (1890).

City of Raleigh v. Sorrell, 1 Jones Law 49 (N.C., 1853).

City of Richmond v. Dudley, 129 Ind. 112 (1891).

City of Salem v. Eastern Railroad Co., 98 Mass. 431 (1868).

City of St. Louis v. Boffinger, 19 Mo. 13 (1853).

City of St. Louis v. Jackson, 25 Mo. 37 (1857).

City of St. Louis v. McCoy, 18 Mo. 238 (1853).

City of St. Louis v. Weber, 44 Mo. 547 (1869).

City of St. Paul v. Colter, 12 Minn. 41 (1866).

City of St. Paul v. Laidler, 2 Minn. 159, 72 Am. Dec. 89 (1858).

City of Taunton v. Taylor, 116 Mass. 254 (1874).

Clark v. City of South Bend, 85 Ind. 276 (1882).

Clark v. Mayor of Syracuse, 13 Barb. 32 (N.Y., 1852).

Clements v. State, 14 Mo. 112 (1851).

Cleveland v. Citizens Gas Light Co., 20 NJE 201 (1869).

Coates v. Mayor of New York, 7 Cow. 585 (N.Y., 1827).

Coe v. Schultz, 47 Barb. 64 (N.Y., 1866).

Coffin v. Nantucket, 5 Cush. 269 (Mass., 1850).

Coker v. Birge, 9 Ga. 425, 54 Am. Dec. 347 (1851).

Commissioners of Salisbury v. Powe, 51 N.C. 134 (1858).

Commonwealth v. Alger, 7 Cush. 53 (Mass., 1851).

Commonwealth v. Ashley, 68 Mass. 356 (1854).

Commonwealth v. Ballou, 124 Mass. 26 (1878).

Commonwealth v. Blackington, 24 Pick. 352 (Mass., 1837).

Commonwealth v. Bowman and Duncan, 3 Pa. St. 202 (1846).

Commonwealth v. Church, 1 Pa. St. 105 (1845).

Commonwealth v. Churchill, 1 Met. 118 (Mass., 1840).

Commonwealth v. Davenport, 84 Mass. 299 (1861).

Commonwealth v. Davis, 77 Mass. 48 (1858).

Commonwealth v. Doherty, 137 Mass. 245 (1884).

Commonwealth v. Estabrook, 10 Pick. 293 (Mass., 1831).

Commonwealth v. Gannet, 83 Mass. 7 (1861).

Commonwealth v. Gee, 60 Mass. 174 (1850).

Commonwealth v. Haines, 4 Clark 17 (Pa., 1824).

Commonwealth v. Harrington, 20 Mass. 26 (1825).

Commonwealth v. Hart, 76 Mass. 465 (1858).

Commonwealth v. Hart, 137 Mass. 247 (1884).

Commonwealth v. Harwood, 70 Mass. 41 (1855).

Commonwealth v. Howe, 79 Mass. 26 (1859).

Commonwealth v. Hyde, Thach. Crim. 19 (Mass. 1823).

Commonwealth v. Johnson, 2 Am. L. J. 359 (Pa., 1849).

Commonwealth v. Jordan, 18 Pick. 228 (Mass., 1836).

Commonwealth v. Kimball, 21 Pick. 373 (Mass., 1836).

Commonwealth v. Kimball, 24 Pick. 359 (Mass., 1837).

Commonwealth v. Kimball, 24 Pick. 366 (Mass., 1837).

Commonwealth v. King, 13 Metc. 115 (Mass., 1847).

Commonwealth v. Langley, 80 Mass. 21 (1859).

Commonwealth v. Lewis, 42 Mass. 151 (1840).

Commonwealth v. Markoe, 17 Pick. 465 (Mass., 1835).

Commonwealth v. M'Donald, 16 Serg. & R. 390 (Pa., 1827).

Commonwealth v. Meyers, 8 Pa. Co. Ct. R. 435 (1890).

Commonwealth v. Nightingale, Thach. Crim. Cas. 251 (Mass., 1830).

Commonwealth v. Odlin, 23 Pick. 275 (Mass., 1839).

Commonwealth v. Parks, 155 Mass. 531 (1892).

Commonwealth v. Passmore, 1 Serg. & R. 217 (Pa., 1814).

Commonwealth v. Patch, 97 Mass. 221 (1867).

Commonwealth v. Rice, 9 Metc. 253 (Mass., 1845).

Commonwealth v. Ruggles, 10 Mass. 391 (1813).

Commonwealth v. Rumford Chemical Works, 16 Gray 231 (Mass., 1860).

Commonwealth v. Rush, 14 Pa. St. 186 (1850).

Commonwealth v. Stahl, 89 Mass. 304 (1863).

Commonwealth v. Stewart, 1 S&R 342 (Pa., 1815).

Commonwealth v. Tewksbury, 11 Metc. 55 (Mass., 1846).

Commonwealth v. Thurlow, 24 Pick. 374 (1837).

Commonwealth v. Tilton, 49 Mass. 232 (1844).

Commonwealth v. Upton, 6 Gray 473 (1856).

Commonwealth v. Wilkinson, 16 Pick. 175 (Mass., 1834).

Commonwealth v. Wood, 97 Mass. 225 (1867).

Commonwealth v. Wright and Dame, in *American Jurist* (Mass., 1829), 3 (1830): 185.

Conwell v. Emrie, 2 Ind. 35 (1850).

Cooley v. Board of Wardens, 12 How. 299 (U.S., 1851).

Cooper v. Schultz, 33 How. Prac. 5 (N.Y., 1867).

Corning v. Lowerre, 6 Johns. Ch. 439 (N.Y., 1822).

Corporation of Brick Presbyterian Church v. Mayor of New York, 5 Cow. 538 (N.Y., 1826).

Corporation of Knoxville v. Bird, 80 Tenn. 121 (1883).

Cougot v. City of New Orleans, 16 La. Ann. 21 (1861).

Cousins v. State, 50 Ala. 113 (1874).

Cranford v. Tyrrel, 128 N.Y. 341 (1891).

Crowder v. Tinkler, 19 Ves. Jr. 617, 34 E. Repr. 645 (Eng., 1816).

Daggett v. State, 4 Conn. 60 (1821).

Dargan v. Waddill, 9 Ire. Law 244 (N.C., 1848).

Dartmouth College v. Woodward, 4 Wheat. 518 (U.S., 1819).

Davenport v. Kelly, 7 Ia. 102 (1858).

Davenport v. Richmond City, 81 Va. 636 (1886).

David and Anthony Lyner's Case, 5 City Hall Rec. 136 (N.Y., 1820).

Davidson v. Isham, 9 NJE 186 (1852).

Davis v. Mayor of New York, 14 N.Y. 506 (1856).

Dennis v. Eckhardt, 3 Grant's Cases 390 (Pa., 1862).

Dickey v. Maine Telegraph Co., 46 Me. 483 (1859).

Dimmett v. Eskridge, 6 Munf. 308 (Va., 1819).

Ditman and Berger v. Repp, 50 Md. 516 (1878).

Douglass v. Commonwealth, 2 Rawle 262 (Pa., 1830).

Dred Scott v. Sandford, 19 How. 393 (U.S., 1857).

Dubois v. City Council of Augusta, Dud. 30 (Ga., 1831).

Dugan v. Bridge Co., 27 Pa. St. 303 (1856).

Dumesnil v. Dupont, 18 B. Monroe 800, 68 Am. Dec. 750 (Ky., 1858).

Duncan v. Hayes and Greenwood, 22 NJE 25 (1871).

Dunnaway v. State, 17 Tenn. 350 (1836).

Durant v. Williamson, 7 NJE 547 (1849).

Dygert v. Schenck, 23 Wend. 446 (N.Y., 1840).

Ex Parte Ferrier, 103 Ill. 367 (1882).

Ex Parte Jennings, 6 Cow. 518 (N.Y., 1826).

Ex Parte Shrader, 33 Cal. 279 (1867).

Ferguson v. City of Selma, 43 Ala. 398 (1869).

First Municipality v. Cutting, 4 La. Ann. 335 (1849).

Fish v. Dodge, 4 Denio 311 (N.Y., 1847).

Fisher v. McGirr, 67 Gray 1 (Mass., 1854).

Fletcher v. Peck, 6 Cranch 87 (U.S., 1810).

Foote v. Fire Department of the City of New-York, 5 Hill 99 (N.Y., 1843).

Ford v. Thralkill, 84 Ga. 169 (1889).

Francis v. Schoellkopf, 53 N.Y. 152 (1873).

Frank v. City of Atlanta, 72 Ga. 428 (1884).

Frederick v. Commonwealth, 43 Ky. 7 (1843).

French v. Baker, 36 Tenn. 193 (1856).

French v. Camp, 18 Me. 433 (1841).

Fuselier v. Spalding, 2 La. Ann. 773 (1847).

Gardner v. Trustees of the Village of Newburgh, 2 Johns. Ch. 162 (1816).

Garrison v. State, 14 Ind. 287 (1860).

Gates v. Blincoe, 2 Dana 158 (Ky., 1834).

Genesee Chief v. Fitzhugh, 12 How. 443 (U.S., 1851).

Georgetown v. Alexandria Canal Co., 12 Pet. 91 (U.S., 1838).

Gerrish v. Brown, 51 Me. 256 (1863).

Gibbons v. Ogden, 9 Wheat. 1 (U.S., 1824).

Gies v. Schultz, 33 How. Prac. 11 (N.Y., 1867).

Gilbert v. Mickle, 4 Sandf. Ch. 357 (N.Y., 1846).

Gilbert v. Showerman, 23 Mich. 448 (1871).

Goddard v. Jacksonville, 15 Ill. 588 (1854).

Goodloe v. City of Cincinnati, 4 Oh. 500 (1831).

Governor and Company of the British Cast Plate Manufacturers v. Meredith, 4 T.R. 794 (Eng., 1792).

Green v. Mayor and Aldermen of Savannah, 6 Ga. 1 (1849).

Hackney v. State, 8 Ind. 494 (1856).

Hale v. Lawrence, 21 N.J. 714, 47 Am. Dec. 190 (N.J., 1848).

Hall v. State, 4 Harr. 132 (Del., 1844).

Hamilton v. Whitridge, 11 Md. 128 (1857).

Hanson v. City Council of Lafayette, 18 La. 295 (1841).

Harding v. Jasper, 14 Cal. 642 (1860).

Harris v. The Commonwealth, 23 Pick. 280 (Mass., 1839).

Harrison v. Brooks, 20 Ga. 537 (1856).

Harrison v. Mayor of Baltimore, 1 Gill 264 (Md., 1843).

Harrow v. State, 1 Greene 439 (Ia., 1848).

Hart v. Mayor of Albany, 9 Wend. 571 (N.Y., 1832).

Hart and Hoyt v. Mayor of Albany, 3 Paige Ch. 213 (N.Y., 1832).

Harwood v. People, 16 Abb. Pr. 430 (N.Y., 1863).

Hatch v. Pendergast, 15 Md. 251 (1859).

Hay v. Cohoes Co., 2 N.Y. 159 (1849).

Health Department v. Knoll, 70 N.Y. 530 (1877).

Hecker v. New York Balance Dock Company, 13 How. Pr. 549 (N.Y., 1857).

Heeg v. Licht, 80 N.Y. 579 (1880).

Heisembrittle v. City of Charleston, 2 McMul. Law 233 (S.C., 1842).

Henderson v. Mayor of New York, 92 U.S. 259 (1875).

Hengehold v. City of Covington, 57 S.W. 495 (Ky., 1900).

Henry v. Commonwealth, 48 Ky. 361 (1849).

Henson v. State, 62 Md. 231 (1884), 50 Am. Rep. 204.

Herbert v. Benson, 2 La. Ann. 770 (1847).

Herman v. State, 8 Ind. 545 (1855).

Holsman v. Boiling Spring Bleaching Co., 14 NJE 335 (1862).

Hopkins v. Crombie, 4 N.H. 520 (1829).

Howard v. Lee, 3 Sandf. 281 (N.Y., 1849).

Hubbard v. Town of Medford, 20 Or. 315 (1891).

Huckenstine's Appeal, 70 Pa. St. 102, 10 Am. Rep. 669 (1872).

Hulme v. Shreve, 4 NJE 116 (1837).

Hutchins v. Smith, 63 Barb. 251 (N.Y., 1872).

Hutton v. City of Camden, 39 NJL 122 (1876).

Hyde v. County of Middlesex, 68 Mass. 267 (1854).

Inter-City Coach Lines v. Harrison, 172 Ga. 390 (1930).

Iowa and Dubuque v. Leiber, 11 Ia. 407 (1861).

Jacko v. State, 22 Ala. 73 (1853).

Jacob Hall's Case, 1 Mod. 76 (Eng., 1683).

Jacobson v. Massachusetts, 197 U.S. 11 (1905).

James Butler's Case, 1 City Hall Rec. 66 (N.Y., 1816).

Jew Ho v. Williamson, 103 Fed. 10 (1900).

Joanna Clark's Case, 1 City Hall Rec. 136 (N.Y., 1816).

John I. Moore's Case, 6 City Hall Rec. 87 (N.Y., 1821).

Jones v. People, 14 Ill. 196 (1852).

Keller v. Corpus Christi, 1 Tx. 614 (1879).

Kennedy v. Board of Health, 2 Pa. St. 366 (1845).

Kennedy v. Phelps, 10 La. Ann. 227 (1855).

Keokuk v. Scroggs, 39 Ia. 447 (1874).

Ketchum v. City of Buffalo and Austin, 14 N.Y. 356 (1856).

Kettering v. Jacksonville, 50 Ill. 39 (1869).

King v. Betterton and Others, 5 Mod. 142 (Eng., 1696).

King v. Davenport, 98 Ill. 305 (1881).

King v. Morris and Essex Railroad Co., 18 NJE 397 (1867).

King v. Ward, 4 Adolph. & Ellis 384 (Eng., 1836).

Kirkman v. Handy, 11 Humph. 406 (Tenn., 1850).

Kneedler v. Norristown, 100 Pa. St. 368 (1882).

Knowles v. State, 3 Day 103 (Conn., 1808).

Lansing v. Smith, 4 Wend. 9 (N.Y., 1829).

Lawton v. Steele, 152 U.S. 133 (1894).

License Cases, 5 How. 504 (U.S., 1847).

Lincoln v. Smith, 27 Vt. 328 (1855).

Linsley v. Bushnell, 15 Conn. 225 (1842).

Lochner v. New York, 198 U.S. 45 (1905).

Lockhart v. State, 10 Tx. 275 (1853).

London v. Bolt, 5 Ves. Jr. 129, 31 E. Repr. 507 (Eng., 1799).

Lord v. State, 16 N.H. 325 (1844).

Lowenstein v. People, 54 Barb. 299 (N.Y., 1863).

Lynde v. City of Rockland, 66 Me. 309 (1876).

Maguire v. Maguire, 7 Dana 181 (Ky., 1838).

Maine v. Homer, 40 Me. 438 (1855).

Maine v. Stevens, 40 Me. 559 (1855).

Maleverer v. Spinke, 1 Dyer 32 (Eng., 1538).

Manhattan Manufacturing and Fertilizing Co. v. New Jersey Stock Yard and Market Co., 23 NJE 161 (1872).

Manhattan Manufacturing and Fertilizing Co. v. Van Keuren, 23 NJE 251 (1872).

Marbury v. Madison, 1 Cranch 137 (U.S., 1803).

Martha Boyd's Cases, 3 City Hall Rec. 134 (N.Y., 1818).

Mary Hagerty's Case, 1 City Hall Rec. 108 (N.Y., 1816).

Mary Rothbone's Case, 1 City Hall Rec. 26 (1816).

Mayo v. Wilson, 1 N.H. 53 (1817).

Mayor and Council of Atlanta v. White and Kreis, 33 Ga. 229 (1862).

Mayor and Council of Monroe v. Hoffman, 29 La. Ann. 651, 29 Am. Rep. 345 (1877).

Mayor of Baltimore v. State, 15 Md. 376 (1860).

Mayor of Columbus v. Jacques, 30 Ga. 506 (1860).

Mayor of Hudson v. Thorne, 7 Paige ch. 261 (N.Y., 1838).

Mayor of Mobile v. Yuille, 3 Ala. 137, 36 Am. Dec. 441 (1841).

Mayor of New York v. Lord (I), 17 Wend. 285 (N.Y., 1837).

Mayor of New York v. Lord (II), 18 Wend. 126 (N.Y., 1837).

Mayor of Rochester v. Rood, Hill & Denio 146 (N.Y., suppl., 1843).

McAlister v. Clark, 33 Conn. 91 (1865).

McAndrews v. Collerd, 42 N.J. 189 (1880).

McCloskey v. Kreling, 76 Cal. 511 (1888).

McCulloch v. Maryland, 4 Wheat. 316 (U.S., 1819).

McDonald v. City of Red Wing, 13 Minn. 38 (1868).

McKeon v. See, 51 N.Y. 300 (1873).

Meeker v. Van Rensselaer, 15 Wend. 397 (N.Y., 1836).

Meigs v. Lister, 23 NJE 199 (1872).

Metcalf v. City of St. Louis, 11 Mo. 102 (1847).

Metropolitan Board of Excise v. Barrie, 34 N.Y. 657 (1866).

Metropolitan Board of Health v. Heister, 37 N.Y. 661 (1868).

Meyer v. State, 12 Vroom. 6 (N.J., 1879).

Milhau v. Sharp, 27 N.Y. 611 (1863).

Miller v. People, 5 Barb. 203 (N.Y., 1849).

Mills v. Hall and Richards, 9 Wend. 315 (N.Y., 1832).

Milne v. Davidson, 5 Martin, N.S. 409, 16 Am. Dec. 189 (La., 1827).

Milwaukee Industrial School v. Supervisor of Milwaukee County, 22 Am. Rep. 702 (1876).

Milwaukee v. Gross, 21 Wis. 241 (1866).

Minke v. Hopeman, 87 Ill. 450 (1877).

Missouri v. Whittaker, 33 Mo. 457 (1863).

Mitchell v. City of Rockland, 41 Me. 363 (1856).

Mitchell v. City of Rockland, 52 Me. 118 (1860).

Morano v. Mayor, 2 La. 217 (1831).

Morgan v. Nolte, 37 Ohio St. 23 (1881).

Morgan's Steamship Co. v. Louisiana Board of Health, 118 U.S. 455 (1886).

Morris v. Brower, Thompson and Fish, Anthony's Nisi Prius 368 (N.Y., 1851).

Morton v. Moore, 81 Mass. 573 (1860).

Mouse's Case, 12 Coke 63 (Eng., 1609).

Mugler v. Kansas, 123 U.S. 623 (1887).

Munn v. Illinois, 94 U.S. 113 (1877).

Myers v. Malcolm, 6 Hill 292, 41 Am. Dec. 744 (N.Y., 1844).

Nagle v. City Council of Augusta, 5 Ga. 546 (1848).

Neaf v. Palmer, 45 S.W. 506 (1898).

New York v. Miln, 11 Pet. 102 (U.S., 1837).

Nightingale's Case, 11 Pick. 168 (Mass., 1831).

Norcross v. Thoms, 51 Me. 503, 81 Am. Dec. 588 (1863).

Norris v. Boston, 4 Metc. 282 (Mass., 1842).

Northwestern Fertilizing Company v. Hyde Park, 70 Ill. 634 (1873).

Northwestern Fertilizing Company v. Hyde Park, 97 U.S. 659 (1878).

Nott's Case, 11 Me. 208 (1834).

O'Connor v. Pittsburgh, 18 Pa. St. Rep. 187 (1851).

Ogden v. Saunders, 12 Wheat. 213 (U.S., 1827).

Ottawa Gas-Light and Coke Co. v. Thompson, 39 Ill. 598 (1864).

Palmer v. Mulligan, 3 Caine 307 (N.Y., 1805).

Parsons v. Pettingell, 11 Allen 507 (Mass., 1866).

Passenger Cases, 7 How. 283 (U.S., 1849).

Peck v. City of Austin, 22 Tx. 261 (1858).

Peck v. Elder, 3 Sandf. 126 (N.Y., 1849).

Peete v. Morgan, 86 U.S. 581 (1873).

Pensacola Telegraph Co. v. Western Union Telegraph Co., 96 U.S. 1 (1877).

Penniman v. New York Balance Co., 13 How. Pr. 40 (N.Y., 1856).

Pennsylvania v. Wheeling Bridge Co., 13 How. 518 (U.S., 1851).

Pennsylvania Coal Co. v. Mahon, 260 U.S. 393 (1922).

People v. Baldwin, 1 Wheeler Cr. Cas. 279 (N.Y., 1823).

People v. John Brougham and Bridget His Wife, 1 Wheeler Cr. Cas. 40 (N.Y., 1822).

People v. Budd, 117 N.Y. 1 (1889).

People v. Carey, 4 Parker Cr. Rep. 238 (N.Y., 1857).

People v. Carpenter, 1 Mich. 273 (1849).

People v. City of St. Louis, 10 Ill. 351 (1848).

People v. Clark, 1 Wheeler Cr. Cas. 288 (N.Y., 1823).

People v. Corporation of Albany, 11 Wend. 539 (N.Y., 1834).

People v. Cunningham, 1 Den. 524 (N.Y., 1845).

People v. Draper, 25 Barb. 344 (N.Y., 1857).

People v. Draper, 15 N.Y. 532 (1857).

People v. Erwin, 4 Denio 129 (N.Y., 1847).

People ex rel. Cox v. The Court of Special Sessions, 7 Hun. 214 (N.Y., 1876).

People v. Foot, 1 Wheeler Cr. Cas. 70 (N.Y., 1822).

People v. Gallagher, 4 Mich. 244 (1856).

People v. Mauch, 24 How. Pr. 276 (N.Y., 1862).

People v. Naglee, 1 Calif. 232 (1850).

People v. Platt, 17 Johns. 195 (N.Y., 1819).

People v. Roff, 3 Park. Cr. R. 216 (N.Y., 1856).

People v. Rowland, 1 Wheeler Cr. Cas. 286 (N.Y., 1823).

People v. Sands, 1 Johns. 78 (N.Y., 1806).

People v. Sergeant, 8 Cow. 139 (N.Y., 1844).

People v. Toynbee, 10 Barb. 168 (1855).

People v. Turner, 55 Ill. 280 (1870), *American Law Register* 10 (1871): 366.

People v. Vanderbilt, 28 N.Y. 396 (1863).

Perdue v. Ellis, 18 Ga. 586 (1855).

Pierce v. Bartrum, 1 Cowp. 269 (Eng., 1775).

Pierce v. State, 13 N.H. 536 (1843).

Pike v. Commonwealth, 63 Ky. 89 (1865).

Pinkham v. Dorothy, 55 Me. 135 (1868).

Polinsky v. People, 73 N.Y. 65 (1878).

Portland v. Bangor, 42 Me. 403 (1856).

Portland v. Bangor, 65 Me. 120 (1876).

Pottstown Gas Co. v. Murphy, 39 Pa. St. 257 (1861).

Powell v. Pennsylvania, 127 U.S. 678 (1888).

President v. Holland, 19 Ill. 271 (1857).

Prigg v. Pennsylvania, 16 Pet. 539 (U.S., 1842).

Pruner v. Pendleton, 75 Va. 516 (1881).

Pye v. Peterson, 45 Tx. 312 (1876).

Quackenbush v. Van Riper, 3 NJE 350 (1835).

Radcliff's Executors v. Mayor of Brooklyn, 4 Comst. 195 (N.Y., 1850).

Railroad Company v. Husen, 95 U.S. 465 (1877).

Raymond v. Fish, 51 Conn. 80 (1883).

Reed v. People, 1 Park. Cr. R. 481 (N.Y., 1854).

Respublica v. Duquet, 2 Yeates 493 (Pa., 1799).

Respublica v. Sparhawk, 1 Dallas 357 (Pa., 1788).

Rex v. Doaks, Quincy 90 (Mass., 1763).

Rex v. Ivens, 7 Car. & P. 213 (Eng., 1835).

Rex v. Jones, 3 Camp. 230 (Eng., 1812).

Rex v. Marsden, 3 Burr. 1812 (Eng., 1765).

Rex v. Taylor, 2 Str. 1167 (Eng., 1742).

Rhodes v. City of Cleveland, 10 Oh. 159 (1840).

Rhodes v. Dunbar, 57 Pa. St. 274 (1868).

Rice v. State, 10 Tx. 545 (1853).

Roe v. Wade, 410 U.S. 113 (1973).

Rogers v. Danforth, 9 NJE 289 (1853).

Ross v. Butler, 19 NJE 294, 97 Am. Dec. 654 (1868).

Ross v. Commonwealth, 41 Ky. 417 (1842).

Rudolphe v. City of New Orleans, 11 La. Ann. 242 (1856).

Ruggles v. Inhabitants of Nantucket, 11 Cush. 433 (Mass., 1853).

Rung v. Shoneberger, 2 Watts 23 (Pa., 1833).

Runyon v. Bordine, 14 N.J. Law 472 (1834).

Rutgers v. Waddington (1784), in *Select Cases of the Mayor's Court of New York City, 1674–1784*, ed. Richard B. Morris (Washington, D.C., 1935).

Russell v. Mayor of New York, 2 Denio 461 (N.Y., 1845).

Santa Clara v. Southern Pacific Railroad, 118 U.S. 394 (1886).

Schuster v. Metropolitan Board of Health, 49 Barb. 450 (N.Y., 1867).

Shafer v. Mumma, 17 Md. 331 (1861).

Shaw v. Crawford, 10 Johns. 236 (N.Y., 1813).

Shaw v. Cummiskey, 7 Pick. 76 (Mass., 1828).

Shelton v. Mayor of Mobile, 30 Ala. 540 (1857).

Shields v. Arndt, 4 NJE 234 (1842).

Shiras v. Olinger, 50 Ia. 571 (1879).

Slack v. Mayor of New York [no citation listed].

Slaughterhouse Cases, 21 L. Ed. 394 (1872).

Slaughterhouse Cases, 83 U.S. 36 (1872).

Smith v. Commonwealth, 45 Ky. 21 (1845).

Smith v. State, 6 Gill 425 (Md., 1848).

Smith v. State, 3 Zabr. 712 (N.J., 1852).

Smith v. Turner, 48 U.S. 283 (1849).

Sparf v. United States, 15 S. Ct. 273 (1895).

Spaulding v. City of Lowell, 23 Pick. 71 (Mass., 1839).

Spring v. Inhabitants of Hyde Park, 137 Mass. 554 (1884).

State v. Abrahams, 4 Ia. 541 (1857).

State v. Allmond, 2 Houston 612 (Del., 1856).

State v. Atkinson, 24 Vt. 448 (1852).

State v. Bentz, 11 Mo. 27 (1847).

State v. Bertheol, 6 Blackf. 474 (Ind., 1843).

State v. Botkin, 71 Ia. 87 (1887).

State v. Boyce, 32 N.C. 536 (1849).

State v. Buckley, 5 Harr. 508 (Del., 1854).

State v. Burchinal, 4 Harr. 572 (Del., 1847).

State v. Canty, 207 Mo. 439 (1907).

State v. Crawford, 28 Kan. 726 (1882).

State v. Doon and Dimond, R.M. Charlt. 1 (Ga., 1811).

State v. Evans, 27 N.C. 603 (1845).

State v. Fagan, 22 La. Ann. 545 (1870).

State v. Fletcher, 1 R.I. 193 (1846).

State v. Fox, 12 Vt. 22 (1843).

State v. Gurney, 37 Me. 156 (1853).

State v. Haines, 30 Me. 65 (1849).

State v. Hall, 3 Vroom. 158 (N.J., 1867).

State v. Hand, 7 Ia. 411 (1858).

State v. Johnson, 114 N.C. 846 (1894).

State v. Lafferty, 5 Harr. 491 (Del., 1854).

State v. Layman, 5 Harr. 510 (Del., 1854).

State v. Leighton, 23 N.H. 167 (1851).

State v. Lewis, 5 Mo. App. 465 (1878).

State v. Main, 31 Conn. 572 (1863).

State, Marshall, Prosecutors v. Cadwalader, 36 NJL 283 (1873).

State v. Mathews, 19 N.C. 424 (1837).

State v. Mayor of Mobile, 5 Port. 279 (Ala., 1837).

State v. McDowell, Dud. 346 (S.C., 1838).

State v. M'Gregor, 41 N.H. 407 (1860).

State v. Morris and Essex Railroad Company, 3 Zabr. 360 (N.J., 1852).

State v. Mullikin, 8 Blackf. 260 (Ind., 1846).

State v. Nixon, 18 Vt. 70 (1846).

State v. Paul, 5 R.I. 185 (1858).

State v. Prescott, 27 Vt. 194 (1855).

State v. Rose, 32 Mo. 560 (1862).

State v. Savannah, T.U.P. Charl. 235 (Ga., 1809).

State v. Toole, 106 N.C. 736 (1890).

State v. Trask, 27 Am. Dec. 554 (1834).

State v. Wheeler, 25 Conn. 290 (1856).

State v. Wilkinson, 2 Vt. 480 (1829).

State v. Williams, 1 Vroom. 102 (N.J., 1862).

State v. Wilson, 43 N.H. 415 (1862).

State v. Woodward, 23 Vt. 92 (1850).

State v. Wright, 51 N.C. 25 (1858).

State of Pennsylvania v. Wheeling Bridge Co., 13 How. 518 (U.S., 1852).

Stephanes v. State, 21 Tx. 206 (1858).

Stetson v. Faxon, 19 Pick. 147 (Mass., 1837).

Stewart v. Schultz, 33 How. Prac. 3 (N.Y., 1867).

Stone v. Mayor of New York, 25 Wend. 157 (N.Y., 1840).

Stone v. Mississippi, 101 U.S. 814 (1880).

Stoughton v. Baker, 4 Mass. 522 (1808).

Stump v. McNairy, 5 Humph. 363 (Tenn., 1844).

Sturges v. Crowninshield, 4 Wheat. 122 (U.S., 1819).

Stuyvesant v. Mayor of New York, 7 Cow. 588 (N.Y., 1827).

Surocco v. Geary, 3 Cal. 69 (1853).

Swift v. Tyson, 16 Pet. 1 (U.S., 1842).

Talbot v. Janson, 3 Dallas 133 (U.S., 1795).

Tanner v. Trustees of Albion, 5 Hill 121 (N.Y., 1843).

Taylor v. Inhabitants of Plymouth, 49 Mass. 462 (1844).

Taylor v. People, 6 Parker's Crim. 347 (N.Y., 1867).

Thebaut and Glazier v. Canova, 11 Fla. 143 (1866).

Thomas v. Town of Vernon, 9 Oh. 290 (1839).

Thorpe v. Rutland and Burlington Railroad Company, 27 Vt. 140 (1855).

Thurber v. Sharp, 13 Barb. 627 (N.Y., 1852).

Tichenor v. Wilson, 8 NJE 197 (1849).

Tinkham v. Tapscott, 17 N.Y. 141 (1858).

Town Council of Winnsboro v. Smart, 11 Rich. 551 (S.C. Law, 1858).

Trovinger v. M'Burney, 5 Cow. 253 (N.Y., 1825).

Trustees of Natchitoches v. Coe, 3 Martin (N.S.). 140 (La., 1824).

Trustees of Rochester v. Pettinger, 17 Wend. 265 (N.Y., 1837).

Turner v. Maryland, 107 U.S. 38 (1882).

Tuttle v. State, 4 Conn. 68 (1821).

United States v. Bede, Fed. Cas. #14,558 (1837).

United States v. Benner, 5 Cranch, C.C. 347 (1837), Fed. Cas. #14,569.

United States v. Coolidge, 25 Fed. Cases 619 (1813).

United States v. Coulter, 1 Cranch, C.C. 203 (1804), Fed. Cas. #14,875.

United States v. Dewitt, 9 Wall. 41 (U.S., 1869).

United States v. Elder, 4 Cranch, C.C. 507 (1835), Fed. Cas. #15,039.

United States v. Holly, 3 Cranch, C.C. 656 (1829), Fed. Cas. #15,381.

United States v. Ismenard, 1 Cranch, C.C. 150 (1803), Fed. Cas. #15,450.

United States v. Jourdine, 4 Cranch, C.C. 338 (1833), Fed. Cas. #15,499.

United States v. Lindsay, 1 Cranch, C.C. 245 (1805), Fed. Cas. #15,602.

United States v. McDowell, 4 Cranch, C.C. 423 (1834), Fed. Cas. #15,671.

United States v. Nailor, 4 Cranch, C.C. 372 (1833), Fed. Cas. #15,853.

United States v. Prout, 1 Cranch, C.C. 203 (1804), Fed. Cas. #16,093.

United States v. Rollinson, 2 Cranch, C.C. 13 (1810), Fed. Cas. #16,191.

United States v. Stevens, 4 Cranch, C.C. 341 (1833), Fed. Cas. #16,391.

Updike v. Campbell, 4 E.D. Smith 570 (N.Y., 1855).

Vanderworker v. State, 13 Ark. 700 (1853).

Van Wormer v. Mayor of Albany, 15 Wend. 262 (N.Y., 1836).

Vanderbilt v. Adams, 7 Cow. 349 (N.Y., 1827).

Vandine's Case, 23 Mass. 187 (1828).

Veazie v. Dwinel, 50 Me. 479 (1862).

Village of Buffalo v. Webster, 10 Wend. 99 (N.Y., 1833).

Village of Jamaica v. Long Island Railroad Co., 37 How. Prac. 379 (N.Y., 1869).

Wadleigh v. Gilman, 12 Me. 403 (1835).

Walker v. Shepardson, 2 Wisc. 384 (1853).

Wartman v. City of Philadelphia, 33 Pa. St. 202 (1859).

Weil v. Ricord, 24 NJE 169 (1873).

Weil v. Schultz, 33 How. Prac. 7 (N.Y., 1867).

Wesson v. Washburn Iron Co., 13 Allen 95 (Mass., 1866).

West River Bridge v. Dix, 6 How. 507 (U.S., 1848).

Wharf Case, 3 Bland Ch. 361 (Maryland, 1831).

White v. City Council of Charleston, 2 Hill 571 (S.C., 1835).

Whitney v. Bartholomew, 21 Conn. 213 (1851).
Whitten v. Mayor and Council of Covington, 43 Ga. 421 (1871).
Wier's Appeal, 74 Pa. St. 230 (1873).
Willis v. Warren, 1 Hilt. C.P. 590 (N.Y., 1859).
Willson v. Black Bird Creek Marsh Company, 2 Pet. 245 (U.S., 1829).
Williams v. The City Council of Augusta, 4 Ga. 509 (1848).
Woelpper v. City of Philadelphia, 38 Pa. St. 203 (1861).
Wolcott v. Melick, 11 NJE 204 (1856).
Wreford v. People, 14 Mich. 41 (1865).
Wight v. Curtis, 29 Fed. Cases 1170 (1845).
Wynehamer v. People, 13 N.Y. 378 (1856).

Statutes and Reports

American Law Institute, *Model Penal Code. Tentative Draft No. 4*. Philadelphia, 1955.
(Boston). *By-Laws and Orders of the Town of Boston*. Boston, 1818.
————. *Reports of Criminal Cases, Tried in the Municipal Court of the City of Boston*. Edited by Horatio Woodman. Boston, 1845.
————. *Faneuil Hall Leases*. Boston, 1856.
(Charleston). *Digest of the Ordinances of the City Council of Charleston, 1783–1818*. Edited by John Geddes. Charleston, S.C., 1818.
(Chicago). *Laws and Ordinances Governing the City of Chicago, 1837*. Edited by Joseph E. Gary. Chicago, 1866.
————. *Report of the Board of Health of the City of Chicago for 1867, 1868, and 1869; And a Sanitary History of Chicago from 1833 to 1870*. Chicago, 1871.
(Connecticut). *Laws of Connecticut, 1673*. Edited by George Brinley. Hartford, Conn., 1865.
Dickinson, Rudolphus. *A Compilation of the Laws of Massachusetts Comprising the Titles of Assessors, Auctioneers, Clerks, Commissioners of Sewers, Etc.* Boston, 1811.
(Georgia). *The Code of the State of Georgia*. Atlanta, 1867.
(Illinois). *Laws of the Illinois Territory, 1809–1818*. Edited by Francis Philbrick. Springfield, Ill., 1950.
————. *Pope's Digest of the Laws of the Illinois Territory, to 1815*. Edited by Francis Philbrick. Springfield, Ill., 1950.
(Indiana). *Laws of the Indiana Territory, 1801–1809*. Edited by Francis Philbrick. Springfield, Ill., 1930.
Jones, Joseph. *Acts of the Legislature of Louisiana Establishing and Regulating Quarantine*. New Orleans, 1880.
————. *Outline of the History, Theory and Practice of Quarantine*. New Orleans, 1883.
(Louisiana). *Acts of the Legislature, 1804–1827*. Edited by L. Moreau Lislet. 2 vols. New Orleans, 1828.
————. *Annual Report of the Board of Health of the State of Louisana for the Year 1877*. New Orleans, 1878.
————. *Compiled Edition of the Civil Codes of Louisiana*. Baton Rouge, La., 1940.
(Maryland). *The General Public Statutory Law and Public Local Law of the State of Maryland, 1692–1839*. Edited by Clement Dorsey. 3 vols. Baltimore, 1840.
(Massachusetts). *The Book of the General Laws and Liberties Concerning the Inhabitants of Massachusetts*. Cambridge, Mass., 1648.
————. *General Laws of Massachusetts, 1780–1835*. Edited by Asaheal Stearns and Theron Metcalf. 4 vols. Boston, 1823–36.

————. *The Revised Statutes of the Commonwealth of Massachusetts.* Boston, 1836.

————. *Acts and Resolves of the Province of Massachusetts Bay, 1692–1780.* 21 vols. Boston, 1869.

————. *Colonial Laws of Massachusetts, 1660–1686.* 2 vols. Boston, 1889.

Massachusetts Sanitary Commission. *Report of a General Plan for the Promotion of Public and Personal Health.* Boston, 1850.

(Michigan). *Territorial Laws of Michigan.* 4 vols. Lansing, Mich., 1871.

————. *The Revised Statutes of the State of Michigan.* Detroit, 1838.

————. *Compiled Laws of Michigan, to 1857.* Edited by Thomas M. Cooley. 2 vols. Lansing, Mich., 1857.

Minutes of the Proceedings of the Quarantine Convention. Philadelphia, 1857.

(New Hampshire). *Laws of New Hampshire, 1679–1835.* Edited by Albert Stillman Batchellor. 10 vols. Manchester, N.H., 1904.

(New Jersey). *A Digest of the Laws of New Jersey, 1709–1861.* Edited by John T. Nixon. 3d ed. Trenton, N.J., 1861.

————. *General Statutes of New Jersey, 1709–1895.* 3 vols. Jersey City, N.J., 1896.

————. *Index of Colonial and State Laws of New Jersey, 1663–1903.* Edited by John Hood. Camden, N.J., 1905.

————. *Compiled Statutes of New Jersey.* 5 vols. Newark, N.J., 1911.

(New Orleans). *Ordinances Ordained and Established by the Mayor and City Council of the City of New-Orleans.* New Orleans, 1817.

(New York City). *Laws and Ordinances Ordained and Established by the Mayor, Aldermen, and Commonalty of the City of New-York.* New York, 1799.

————. *The City-Hall Recorder.* Edited by Daniel Rogers. New York, 1816–20.

————. *Laws Relative to Quarantine and to the Public Health of the City of New-York.* New York, 1858.

————. *Report of the Select Committee Appointed to Investigate the Health Department of the City of New York.* Albany, N.Y., 1859.

————. *Laws and Ordinances Relative to the Preservation of the Public Health in the City of New York.* Edited by George W. Morton. New York, 1860.

————. Citizens' Association of New York. *Report upon the Sanitary Condition of the City.* New York, 1866.

————. *Manual of the Board of Health of the Health Department of the City of New York.* New York, 1872.

(New York State). *Laws of New York, 1781–1801.* 2 vols. Albany, N.Y., 1802.

————. *Public Laws of the State of New York.* Albany, N.Y., 1810.

————. *Laws of the State of New York.* 2 vols. Albany, N.Y., 1813.

————. *Canal Laws, Regulations, Rates of Toll, and Names of the Principal Places, with Their Distances from Each Other on the New-York State Canals.* Albany, N.Y., 1846.

————. *Report of a Special Committee of the House of Assembly of the State of New-York on the Present Quarantine Law.* Albany, N.Y., 1846.

————. *Laws of New Netherland, 1638–1674.* Edited by E. B. O'Callaghan. Albany, N.Y., 1868.

————. *Colonial Laws of New York, 1664–1775.* 5 vols. Albany, N.Y., 1894.

————. *General Index to the Laws of the State of New York, 1777–1901.* Edited by Archie E. Baxter. 3 vols. Albany, N.Y., 1902.

(Ohio). *Statutes of Ohio and of the Northwestern Territory Adopted or Enacted from 1788 to 1833.* Edited by Salmon P. Chase. Cincinnati, 1833.

(Pennsylvania). *Duke of Yorke's Book of Laws, 1676–1700*. Edited by John Blair Linn. Harrisburg, Pa., 1879.

———. *Stewart Purdon's Digest: A Digest of the Statute Law of the State of Pennsylvania from the Year 1700 to 1903*. 13th ed. 5 vols. Philadelphia, 1905.

———. *The Statutes at Large of Pennsylvania from 1682 to 1809*. 18 vols. Harrisburg, Pa., 1911.

(Philadelphia). *Ordinances of the Corporation of the City of Philadelphia*. Edited by John C. Lowber. Philadelphia, 1812.

(Rhode Island). *Public Laws of the State of Rhode Island*. Providence, 1798.

———. *Public Laws of the State of Rhode Island*. Providence, 1822.

———. *Public Laws of the State of Rhode Island*. Providence, 1844.

(South Carolina). *Statutes at Large of South Carolina, 1682–1841*. Edited by Thomas Cooper. 10 vols. Charleston, S.C., 1836.

———. *The Statutes at Large of South Carolina, 1682–1838*. Edited by David J. McCord. 10 vols. Columbia, S.C., 1841.

Swift, Zephaniah. *Digest of the Laws of Connecticut*. New Haven, Conn., 1822.

Thomann, G. *Colonial Liquor Laws*. New York, 1887.

(Vermont). *The Laws of Vermont of a Public and Permanent Nature, to 1824*. Edited by William Slade. Windsor, Vt., 1825.

(Virginia). *Virginia Statutes at Large, 1619–1792*. Edited by William W. Hening. 13 vols. New York, 1823.

Wheeler, Jacob D. *Reports of Criminal Law Cases*. 3 vols. New York, 1854.

Treatises, Articles, and Lectures

Angell, Joseph K. *A Treatise on the Common Law in Relation to Watercourses*. 2d ed. Boston, 1833.

Angell, Joseph K., and Thomas Durfee. *A Treatise on the Law of Highways*. Boston, 1857.

Bacon, Matthew. *A New Abridgment of the Law*. Edited by John Bouvier. 10 vols. Philadelphia, 1852.

Baldwin, Henry. *A General View of the Origin and Nature of the Constitution and Government of the United States*. Philadelphia, 1837.

Bateman, Joseph. *A Practical Treatise on the Law of Auctions*. Boston, 1883.

Bell, John. *Report on the Importance and Economy of Sanitary Measures to Cities*. New York, 1860.

Bishop, Joel Prentiss. *Commentaries on the Criminal Law*. 4th ed. 2 vols. 1865; Boston, 1868.

———. *Commentaries on the Written Laws and Their Interpretation*. Boston, 1882.

Blackstone, William. *Commentaries on the Laws of England: A Facsimile of the First Edition of 1765–1769*. 4 vols. Chicago, 1979.

Blakely, William Addison. *American State Papers Bearing on Sunday Legislation*. Washington, D.C., 1911.

Bouvier, John. *Institutes of American Law*. Philadelphia, 1854.

Bowditch, Henry I. *Public Hygiene in America: Being the Centennial Discourse Delivered before the International Medical Congress, Philadelphia, September, 1876*. Boston, 1877.

Brackenridge, Hugh Henry. *Law Miscellanies*. Philadelphia, 1814.

Broom, Herbert. *A Selection of Legal Maxims, Classified and Illustrated*. London, 1845.

Buck, Albert H., ed. *A Treatise on Hygiene and Public Health*. 2 vols. New York, 1879.

Caldwell, Charles. *Thoughts on Hygiene*. New Orleans, 1836.

Chadwick, Edwin. *On the Sanitary Condition of the Laboring Population of Great Britain.* London, 1842.

Chipman, Nathaniel. *Principles of Government: A Treatise on Free Institutions.* Burlington, Vt., 1833.

Chitty, Joseph. *A Treatise on the Law of the Prerogatives of the Crown.* London, 1820.

Christian, Charles. *A Brief Treatise on the Police of the City of New-York.* New York, 1812.

Clubb, Henry S. *The Maine Liquor Law: Its Origin, History, and Results.* New York, 1856.

Colquhon, Patrick. *A Treatise on the Police of the Metropolis.* London, 1796.

Cooley, Thomas M. *A Treatise on the Constitutional Limitations.* Boston, 1868.

———. *A Treatise on the Law of Taxation.* Chicago, 1876.

Cooper, James Fenimore. *The American Democrat: Or Hints on the Social and Civil Relations of the United States of America.* Cooperstown, N.Y., 1838.

Cooper, Thomas. *Two Essays: 1. On the Foundation of Civil Government; 2. On the Constitution of the United States.* Columbia, S.C., 1826.

Crane, J. T. "The License System." *American Temperance Magazine* 1 (1851): 212–37.

Dana, David D. *The Fireman: The Fire Departments of the United States.* Boston, 1858.

Dane, Nathan. *A General Abridgment and Digest of American Law.* 8 vols. Boston, 1823.

Davis, Daniel. *A Practical Treatise upon the Authority and Duty of Justices of the Peace.* Boston, 1824.

"Destruction of Private Property to Prevent the Spread of Fires." *Law Journal* 9 (1874): 484.

DeVoe, Thomas F. *The Market Book: A History of the Public Markets of the City of New York.* 1862. Reprint, New York, 1970.

Dillon, John F. *The Law of Municipal Corporations.* 2d ed. 2 vols. New York, 1873.

———. *The Laws and Jurisprudence of England and America.* Boston, 1894.

Dodge, Allen W. *A Prize Essay on Fairs.* Boston, 1858.

Du Ponceau, Peter S. *A Dissertation on the Nature and Extent of the Jurisdiction of the Courts of the United States.* Philadelphia, 1824.

Eden, Robert Henley. *A Treatise on the Law of Injunctions.* New York, 1839.

Endlich, G. A. *A Commentary on the Interpretation of Statutes.* Jersey City, N.J., 1888.

Faxon, Henry H. *Laws Relating to the Sale of Intoxicating Liquors.* Boston, 1884.

Fisher, Sydney G. *The Trial of the Constitution.* Philadelphia, 1862.

Freund, Ernst. *The Police Power: Public Policy and Constitutional Rights.* Chicago, 1904.

Goodenow, John Milton. *Historical Sketches of the Principles and Maxims of American Jurisprudence.* Steubenville, Ohio, 1819.

Goodrich, Charles B. *The Science of Government.* Boston, 1853.

Griscom, John H. *The Sanitary Condition of the Laboring Population of New York.* New York, 1845.

Grotius, Hugo. *De Jure Belli Ac Pacis Libri Tres.* Translated by Francis W. Kelsey. New York, 1964.

Hale, Sir Matthew. "*De Juris Maris et Brachiorum ejusdem.*" In *A Collection of Tracts Relative to the Law of England,* edited by Francis Hargrave. Dublin, 1787.

———. "*De Portibus Maris.*" In *A Collection of Tracts Relative to the Law of England,* edited by Francis Hargave. Dublin, 1787.

———. *The Prerogatives of the King.* Edited by D. E. C. Yale. London, 1976.

Hargrave, Francis. *A Collection of Tracts Relative to the Law of England.* Dublin, 1787.

Hawkins, William. *A Treatise of the Pleas of the Crown.* London, 1716. Reprint, New York, 1973.

Henderson, Charles Richmond. *An Introduction to the Study of Dependent, Defective, and Delinquent Classes.* Boston, 1893.

Hickey, W. *The Constitution of the United States of America*. Philadelphia, 1854.

Hilliard, Francis. *The Elements of Law: Being a Comprehensive Summary of American Civil Jurisprudence*. Boston, 1835.

Hoffman, David. *A Course of Legal Study: Respectfully Addressed to the Students of Law in the United States*. Baltimore, 1817.

Holmes, John. *The Statesman, or Principles of Legislation and Law*. Augusta, Me., 1840.

Holmes, Oliver Wendell, Jr. *The Common Law*. 1881. Edited by Mark DeWolfe Howe. Boston, 1963.

Hosmer, William. *The Higher Law, in Its Relations to Civil Government: With Particular Reference to Slavery, and the Fugitive Slave Law*. New York, 1852.

Houck, Louis. *A Treatise on the Law of Navigable Rivers*. Boston, 1868.

Jameson, J. A. *The Constitutional Convention*. New York, 1866.

Kent, James. *Commentaries on American Law*. 4 vols. New York, 1826.

———. *Commentaries on American Law*. 12th ed. Edited by Oliver Wendell Holmes Jr. 4 vols. Boston, 1873.

———. "An Introductory Lecture to a Course of Law Lectures." In *American Political Writing during the Founding Era, 1760–1805*, edited by Charles S. Hyneman and Donald S. Lutz, 2:936–49. Indianapolis, Ind., 1983.

Lieber, Francis. *Manual of Political Ethics Designed Chiefly for the Use of Colleges and Students at Law*. 2 vols. Boston, 1838–39.

———. *Legal and Political Hermeneutics*. Boston. 1839.

———. "Inaugural Address of Francis Lieber." *Addresses of the Newly-Appointed Professors of Columbia College, February 1858*. New York, 1858.

———. *On Civil Liberty and Self-Government*. 1853. 3d ed., Philadelphia, 1891.

Mansfield, Edward D. *The Political Grammar of the United States*. New York, 1834.

M'Kinney, Mordecai. *The United States Constitutional Manual*. Harrisburg, Pa., 1845.

"Navigable Rivers." *American Law Review* 2 (1868): 589–98.

Parker, Leroy, and Robert H. Worthington. *The Law of Public Health and Safety, and the Powers and Duties of Boards of Health*. Albany, N.Y., 1892.

Pitman, Robert C. *Alcohol and the State: A Discussion of the Problem of Law as Applied to the Liquor Traffic*. New York, 1877.

Potter, Platt. *Dwarris on Statutes*. Albany, N.Y., 1871.

Prentice, William P. *Police Powers Arising under the Law of Overruling Necessity*. New York, 1894.

Redfield, Isaac. "Note to *People v. Turner*." *American Law Register* 10 (1871): 372–75.

Rutherford, Thomas. *Institutes of Natural Law*. 2 vols. Philadelphia, 1799.

Sedgwick, Theodore. *A Treatise on the Rules Which Govern the Interpretation and Application of Statutory and Constitutional Law*. New York, 1857.

Smith, E. Fitch. *Commentaries on Statute and Constitutional Law*. Albany, N.Y., 1848.

Story, Joseph. *Commentaries on the Constitution of the United States*. 3 vols. Boston, 1832.

———. *Commentaries on Equity Jurisprudence as Administered in England and America*. Boston, 1836.

Sullivan, James. *The History of Land Titles in Massachusetts*. Boston, 1801.

Sullivan, William. *The Political Class Book: Intended to Instruct the Higher Classes in Schools in the Origin, Nature, and Use of Political Power*. Boston, 1831.

Swift, Zephaniah. *A System of the Laws of the State of Connecticut*. 2 vols. Windham, Conn., 1795.

Taylor, John. *Construction Construed and Constitutions Vindicated*. Richmond, Va., 1820.

Thayer, James Bradley. *Cases on Constitutional Law*. 2 vols. Cambridge, Mass., 1895.

Thorpe, Francis Newton. *The Federal and State Constitutions.* 7 vols. Washington, D.C., 1909.

Tiedeman, Christopher G. *A Treatise on the Limitations of Police Power in the United States.* St. Louis, 1886.

Turner, Thomas J. *Some Remarks upon National and International Sanitary Jurisprudence.* Boston, 1882.

Vattel, Emmerich de. *The Law of Nations.* 1759. Edited by Edward D. Ingraham. Philadelphia, 1852.

Waterman, Thomas W. *Waterman's Eden on the Law and Practice of Injunctions.* 3d ed. 2 vols. New York, 1852.

Webster, Daniel. *The Papers of Daniel Webster: Legal Papers.* Volume 1, *The New Hampshire Practice.* Edited by Alfred S. Konefsky and Andrew J. King. Hanover, N.H., 1982.

Wharton, Francis. *A Treatise on the Criminal Law of the United States.* Philadelphia, 1846.

Wilson, James. *The Works of James Wilson.* Edited by Robert Green McCloskey. 2 vols. Cambridge, Mass., 1967.

Wood, Horace G. *A Practical Treatise on the Law of Nuisances.* 1875. 2d ed., Albany, N.Y., 1883.

Woolsey, Theodore D. *Political Science or the State Theoretically and Practically Considered.* New York, 1877.

Secondary Sources

Ackerman, Bruce A. *We the People: Foundations.* Cambridge, Mass., 1991.

Adair, Douglass. *Fame and the Founding Fathers.* Williamsburg, Va., 1974.

Agnew, Jean-Cristophe. *Worlds Apart: The Market and Theater in Anglo-American Thought, 1550–1750.* Cambridge, 1987.

Appleby, Joyce Oldham. *Economic Thought and Ideology in Seventeenth-Century England.* Princeton, N.J., 1978.

———. *Capitalism and a New Social Order: The Republican Vision of the 1790's.* New York, 1984.

———. *Liberalism and Republicanism in the Historical Imagination.* Cambridge, 1992.

Arendt, Hannah. *The Human Condition.* Chicago, 1958.

Atiyah, P. S. *The Rise and Fall of Freedom of Contract.* Oxford, 1979.

Ayers, Edward L. *Vengeance and Justice: Crime and Punishment in the Nineteenth-Century American South.* New York, 1984.

Bailyn, Bernard. *The Ideological Origins of the American Revolution.* Cambridge, Mass., 1967.

———. *The New England Merchants in the Seventeenth Century.* Cambridge, Mass., 1979.

Baker, Paula. "The Domestication of Politics: Women and American Political Society, 1780–1920." In *Women, the State, and Welfare*, edited by Linda Gordon, 55–91. Madison, Wis., 1990.

Beard, Charles A. *The Supreme Court and the Constitution.* New York, 1912.

———. *An Economic Interpretation of the Constitution of the United States.* New York, 1913.

Benedict, Michael Les. "Laissez-Faire and Liberty: A Re-evaluation of the Meaning and Origins of Laissez-Faire Constitutionalism." *Law and History Review* 3 (1985): 293–331.

Berle, Adolf A., and Gardiner C. Means. *The Modern Corporation and Private Property.* Rev. ed. New York, 1968.

Bernstein, Iver. *The New York City Draft Riots: Their Significance for American Society and Politics in the Age of the Civil War.* New York, 1990.

Blackmar, Elizabeth. *Manhattan for Rent, 1785–1850.* Ithaca, N.Y., 1989.

Blocker, Jack S., Jr. *American Temperance Movements.* Boston, 1989.

Bloomfield, Maxwell. *American Lawyers in a Changing Society, 1776–1876.* Cambridge, 1976.

Bone, Robert G. "Normative Theory and Legal Doctrine in American Nuisance Law: 1850 to 1920." *Southern California Law Review* 59 (1986): 1101–1226.

Boorstin, Daniel J. *The Mysterious Science of the Law.* Cambridge, Mass., 1941.

———. *The Genius of American Politics.* Chicago, 1953.

———. *The Americans: The National Experience.* New York, 1965.

———. "The Perils of Indwelling Law." In *The Rule of Law,* edited by Robert Paul Wolff, 79–97. New York, 1971.

Boudin, Louis B. *Government by Judiciary.* 2 vols., New York, 1932.

Boyer, Paul S. *Urban Masses and Moral Order in America, 1820–1920.* Cambridge, Mass., 1978.

Brenner, Joel Franklin. "Nuisance Law and the Industrial Revolution." *Journal of Legal Studies* 3 (1974): 403–33.

Bridenbaugh, Carl. *Cities in the Wilderness: The First Century of Urban Life in America, 1625–1742.* New York, 1938.

———. *Cities in Revolt: Urban Life in America, 1743–1776.* New York, 1955.

Bright, Charles C. "The State in the United States During the Nineteenth Century." In *Statemaking and Social Movements,* edited by Charles C. Bright and Susan Harding, 121–58. Ann Arbor, Mich., 1984.

Brock, William R. *Investigation and Responsibility: Public Responsibility in the United States, 1865–1900.* New York, 1984.

Bruchey, Stuart. *The Wealth of the Nation: An Economic History of the United States.* New York, 1988.

Bryce, James. *The American Commonwealth.* 2d ed. 2 vols. New York, 1891.

———. *Studies in History and Jurisprudence.* New York, 1901.

Bourdieu, Pierre. *Outline of a Theory of Practice.* Translated by Richard Nice. New York, 1977.

———. "The Force of Law: Toward a Sociology of the Juridical Field." *Hastings Law Journal* 38 (1987): 805–13.

Cherrington, Ernest H. *The Evolution of Prohibition in the United States of America.* Westerville, Ohio, 1920.

Clark, Victor S. *History of Manufactures in the United States.* 1929. 2 vols. New York, 1949.

Cohen, Daniel A. *Pillars of Salt, Monuments of Grace.* New York, 1993.

Cohen, Felix S. *The Legal Conscience: Selected Papers of Felix S. Cohen.* New Haven, Conn., 1960.

Cohen, Morris R. *Law and the Social Order: Essays in Legal Philosophy.* New York, 1933.

Cohen, Morris R., and Felix S. Cohen. *Readings in Jurisprudence and Legal Philosophy.* Boston, 1951.

Commons, John R. *Legal Foundations of Capitalism.* New York, 1924.

Cook, Charles M. *The American Codification Movement: A Study of Antebellum Legal Reform.* Westport, Conn., 1981.

Corwin, Edward S. "The 'Higher Law' Background of American Constitutional Law." *Harvard Law Review* 42 (1929): 149–85, 365–409.

———. *The Twilight of the Supreme Court.* New Haven, Conn., 1934.

———. "The Doctrine of Due Process of Law before the Civil War." *Harvard Law Review* 24 (1911): 366–85, 460–79.

———. "The Basic Doctrine of American Constitutional Law." *Michigan Law Review* 12 (1914): 247–76, 538–72.

———. *Liberty against Government: The Rise, Flowering and Decline of a Famous Juridical Concept.* Baton Rouge, La., 1948.

Cover, Robert M. *Justice Accused: Antislavery and the Judicial Process.* New Haven, Conn., 1975.

———. *Narrative, Violence, and the Law: The Essays of Robert Cover.* Edited by Martha Minow, Michael Ryan, and Austin Sarat. Ann Arbor, Mich., 1992.

Crosskey, William W. *Politics and the Constitution in the History of the United States.* 2 vols. Chicago, 1953.

Curtis, George B. "The Checkered Career of *Parens Patriae*: The State as Parent or Tyrant?" *DePaul Law Review* 25 (1976): 895–915.

Dargo, George. *Jefferson's Louisiana: Politics and the Clash of Legal Traditions.* Cambridge, Mass., 1975.

Davis, Joseph S. *Essays in the Earlier History of American Corporations.* 2 vols. Cambridge, Mass., 1917.

Diggins, John P. *The Lost Soul of American Politics: Virtue, Self-Interest, and the Foundations of Liberalism.* New York, 1984.

Dodd, E. Merrick, Jr. *American Business Corporations until 1860.* Cambridge, Mass., 1954.

Duffy, John. *A History of Public Health in New York City, 1625–1866.* New York, 1968.

———. *A History of Public Health in New York City, 1866–1966.* New York, 1974.

———. *The Sanitarians: A History of American Public Health.* Urbana, Ill., 1990.

Dunlavy, Colleen A. *Politics and Industrialization: Early Railroads in the United States and Prussia.* Princeton, N.J., 1994.

Dunn, John. *Locke.* Oxford, 1984.

Dworkin, Ronald. *Taking Rights Seriously.* Cambridge, Mass., 1978.

Einhorn, Robin L. *Property Rules: Poltical Economy in Chicago, 1833–1872.* Chicago, 1991.

Ely, Richard T. *Property and Contract in Their Relations to the Distribution of Wealth.* 2 vols. New York, 1914.

Engelstein, Laura. "Combinded Underdevelopment: Discipline and the Law in Imperial and Soviet Russia." *American Historical Review* 98 (April 1993): 338–53.

Evans, George Heberton, Jr. *Business Incorporations in the United States, 1800–1943.* New York, 1948.

Farnam, Henry W. *Chapters in the History of Social Legislation in the United States to 1860.* Washington, D.C., 1938.

Farnham, Wallace D. "'The Weakened Spring of Government': A Study in Nineteenth Century American History." *American Historical Review* 68 (1963): 662–80.

Ferguson, Robert A. *Law and Letters in American Culture.* Cambridge, Mass., 1984.

Fine, Sidney. *Laissez Faire and the General-Welfare State: A Study of Conflict in American Thought, 1865–1901.* Ann Arbor, Mich., 1956.

Fisher, David Hackett. *Albion's Seed: Four British Folkways in America.* New York, 1989.

Fisher, William W. "The Law of the Land: An Intellectual History of American Property Doctrine, 1776–1880." Ph.D. dissertation, Harvard University, 1991.

———. "Making Sense of Madison: Nedelsky on Private Property." *Law and Social Inquiry* 18 (1993): 547–72.

Flaherty, David H. "Law and the Enforcement of Morals in Early America." In *Law in American History*, edited by Donald Fleming and Bernard Bailyn, 203–53. Boston, 1971.

Foner, Eric. *Reconstruction: America's Unfinished Revolution, 1863–1877.* New York, 1988.

Foucault, Michel. *Discipline and Punish.* New York, 1979.

———. "The Politics of Health in the Eighteenth Century." In *Power/Knowledge: Selected Interviews and Other Writing, 1972–1977,* edited by Colin Gordon, 166–82. New York, 1980.

———. "*Omnes et Singulatim*: Towards a Criticism of 'Political Reason.'" *The Tanner Lectures on Human Values II,* edited by Sterling M. McMurrin, 225–54. Stanford, Calif., 1979.

———. "Governmentality." In *The Foucault Effect: Studies in Governmentality,* edited by Graham Burchell, Colin Gordon, and Peter Miller, 87–104. Chicago, 1991.

Fredrickson, George M. *The Inner Civil War: Northern Intellectuals and the Crisis of the Union.* New York, 1965.

Freidel, Frank. *Francis Lieber: Nineteenth-Century Liberal.* Baton Rouge, La., 1947.

Freund, Ernst. *Standards of American Legislation.* Chicago, 1917. 2d ed., Chicago, 1965.

———. *Administrative Powers over Persons and Property: A Comparative Survey.* Chicago, 1928.

———. *Legislative Regulation: A Study of the Ways and Means of Written Law.* New York, 1932.

Freyer, Tony. "Reassessing the Impact of Eminent Domain in Early American Economic Development." *Wisconsin Law Review* (1981): 1263–86.

———. *Producers versus Capitalists: Constitutional Conflict in Antebellum America.* Charlottesville, Va., 1994.

Friedman, Lawrence M. "Heart against Head: Perry Miller and the Legal Mind." *Yale Law Journal* 77 (1968): 1244–59.

———. "Some Problems and Possibilities of American Legal History." In *The State of American History,* edited by Herbert J. Bass, 2–21. Chicago, 1970.

———. *A History of American Law.* 2d ed. New York, 1985.

———. *Crime and Punishment in American History.* New York, 1993.

Gates, Paul Wallace. *History of Public Land Law Development.* Washington, D.C., 1968.

Gierke, Otto von. *The German Law of Fellowship.* Volume 1, *The Legal and Moral History of the German Fellowship.* Translated by Antony Black in *Community in Historical Perspective.* Cambridge, Mass., 1990.

Gilfoyle, Timothy J. *City of Eros: New York City, Prostitution, and the Commercialization of Sex, 1790–1920.* New York, 1992.

Gilje, Paul A. *The Road to Mobocracy: Popular Disorder in New York City, 1763–1834.* Chapel Hill, N.C., 1987.

Gilmore, Grant. *The Ages of American Law.* New Haven, Conn., 1977.

Goebel, Julius. "Constitutional History and Constitutional Law." *Columbia Law Review* 38 (1938): 555–77.

———. *The Oliver Wendell Holmes Devise History of the Supreme Court of the United States.* Volume 1, *Antecedents and Beginnings to 1801.* New York, 1971.

Goodrich, Carter. *Government Promotion of American Canals and Railroads, 1800–1890.* New York, 1960.

Gordon, Linda, ed. *Women, the State, and Welfare.* Madison, Wis., 1990.

Gordon, Robert W. "Introduction: J. Willard Hurst and the Common Law Tradition in American Legal Historiography." *Law and Society Review* 10 (1976): 9–56.

———. "Critical Legal Histories." *Stanford Law Review* 36 (1984): 57–125.

Gough, John W. *The Fundamental Law in English Constitutional History.* Oxford, 1961.

Grey, Thomas C. "Origins of the Unwritten Constitution: Fundamental Law in American Revolutionary Thought." *Stanford Law Review* 30 (1978): 843–93.

Griffin, Clifford S. *Their Brothers' Keepers: Moral Stewardship in the United States, 1800–1865.* New Brunswick, N.J., 1960.

Grossberg, Michael. "Guarding the Altar: Physiological Restrictions and the Rise of State Intervention in Matrimony." *American Journal of Legal History* 26 (1982): 197–226.

———. *Governing the Hearth: Law and the Family in Nineteenth-Century America.* Chapel Hill, N.C., 1985.

Gusfield, Joseph R. *Symbolic Crusade: Status Politics and the American Temperance Movement.* Urbana, Ill., 1963.

Habermas, Jürgen. *The Structural Transformation of the Public Sphere: An Inquiry into a Category of Bourgeois Society.* Translated by Thomas Burger. Cambridge, Mass., 1989.

Hahn, Steven, and Jonathan Prude, eds. *The Countryside in the Age of Capitalist Transformation: Essays in the Social History of Rural America.* Chapel Hill, N.C., 1985.

Haines, Charles Grove. *The Revival of Natural Law Concepts.* Cambridge, Mass., 1930.

Hale, Robert L. "Coercion and Distribution in a Supposedly Non-Coercive State." *Political Science Quaterly* 38 (1923): 470–94.

———. "Force and the State: A Comparison of 'Political' and 'Economic' Compulsion." *Columbia Law Review* 35 (1935): 149–201.

Hall, Kermit L. *The Magic Mirror: Law in American History.* New York, 1989.

Handlin, Oscar, and Mary Flug Handlin. *Commonwealth: A Study of the Role of Government in the American Economy: Massachusetts, 1774–1861.* New York, 1947.

———. "Origins of the American Business Corporation." In *Enterprise and Secular Change,* edited by Frederic C. Lane and Jelle C. Riemersma, 102–24. Homewood, Ill., 1953.

———. *The Dimensions of Liberty.* New York, 1966.

Hartog, Hendrik. "The Public Law of a County Court: Judicial Government in Eighteenth Century Massachusetts." *American Journal of Legal History* 20 (1976): 282–326.

———. "Distancing Oneself from the Eighteenth Century: A Commentary on Changing Pictures of American Legal History." In *Law in the American Revolution and the Revolution in the Law,* edited by Hendrik Hartog, 229–57. New York, 1981.

———. *Public Property and Private Power: The Corporation of the City of New York in American Law, 1730–1870.* Chapel Hill, N.C., 1983.

———. "Pigs and Positivism." *Wisconsin Law Review* (1985): 899–935.

———. "The Constitution of Aspiration and 'The Rights That Belong to Us All.'" *Journal of American History* 74 (1987): 1013–34.

Hartz, Louis. "The Individualist Philosophy of John Harlan, 1833–1911." Honors thesis, Harvard University, 1940.

———. *Economic Policy and Democratic Thought: Pennsylvania, 1776–1860.* Cambridge, Mass., 1948.

———. *The Liberal Tradition in America: An Interpretation of American Political Thought since the Revolution.* New York, 1955.

Haskins, George Lee. *Law and Authority in Early Massachusetts.* New York, 1960.

Hastings, W. G. "The Development of Law as Illustrated by the Decisions Relating to the Police Power of the State." *Proceedings of the American Philosophical Society* 39 (1900): 359–554.

Hay, Douglas, et al. eds. *Albion's Fatal Tree: Crime and Society in Eighteenth-Century England.* New York, 1975.

Hays, Samuel P. *American Political History as Social Analysis.* Knoxville, Tenn., 1980.

Heath, Milton. *Constructive Liberalism: The Role of the State in Economic Development in Georgia to 1860.* Cambridge, Mass., 1954.

Heckscher, Eli F. *Mercantilism.* London, 1934.

Higham, John, and Paul K. Conkin, eds. *New Directions in American Intellectual History.* Baltimore, 1979.

Hill, Marilynn Wood. *Their Sisters' Keepers: Prostitution in New York City, 1830–1870.* Berkeley, Calif., 1993.

Hirschmann, Albert O. *The Passions and the Interests.* Princeton, N.J., 1977.

Hofstadter, Richard. *The American Political Tradition.* New York, 1948.

Hollinger, David A. *In the American Province: Studies in the History and Historiography of Ideas.* Bloomington, Ind., 1985.

Horwitz, Morton J. *The Transformation of American Law, 1780–1860.* Cambridge, Mass., 1977.

———. "The History of the Public/Private Distinction." *Pennsylvania Law Review* 130 (1982): 1423–28.

———. "Progressive Legal Historiography." *Oregon Law Review* 63 (1984): 679–87.

———. *The Transformation of American Law, 1870–1960: The Crisis of Legal Orthodoxy.* New York, 1992.

Hovenkamp, Herbert. *Enterprise and American Law, 1836–1937.* Cambridge, Mass., 1991.

Huntington, Samuel P. *Political Order in Changing Societies.* New Haven, Conn., 1968.

Hurst, James Willard. *The Growth of American Law: The Law Makers.* Boston, 1950.

———. *Law and the Conditions of Freedom in the Nineteenth-Century United States.* Madison, Wis., 1956.

———. *Law and Social Process in United States History.* Ann Arbor, Mich., 1960.

———. *Law and Economic Growth: The Legal History of the Lumber Industry in Wisconsin, 1836–1915.* Cambridge, Mass., 1964.

———. *The Legitimacy of the Business Corporation in the Law of the United States, 1780–1970.* Charlottesville, Va., 1970.

———. *Dealing with Statutes.* New York, 1982.

Hyman, Harold M. *A More Perfect Union: The Impact of the Civil War and Reconstruction on the Constitution.* New York, 1973.

Hyman, Harold M., and William M. Wiecek. *Equal Justice under Law: Constitutional Development, 1835–1875.* New York, 1982.

Ignatieff, Michael, and Istvan Hont, eds. *Wealth and Virtue: The Shaping of Political Economy in the Scottish Enlightenment.* Cambridge, 1983.

Jacobs, Clyde E. *Law Writers and the Courts: The Influence of Thomas M. Cooley, Christopher G. Tiedeman, and John F. Dillon upon American Constitutional Law.* Los Angeles, 1954.

John, Richard R. *Spreading the News: The American Postal System from Franklin to Morse.* Cambridge, Mass., 1995.

Jones, Alan. "Thomas M. Cooley and 'Laissez-Faire Constitutionalism': A Reconsideration." *Journal of American History* 53 (1967): 751–71.

Kaczorowski, Robert J. "To Begin the Nation Anew: Congress, Citizenship, and Civil Rights after the Civil War." *American Historical Review* 92 (1987): 45–68.

Kairys, David, ed. *The Politics of Law: A Progressive Critique.* New York, 1982.

Kammen, Michael. *A Machine That Would Go of Itself: The Constitution in American Culture.* New York, 1986.

Karsten, Peter. "Explaining the Fight over the Attractive Nuisance Doctrine: A Kinder, Gentler Instrumentalism in the 'Age of Formalism.'" *Law and History Review* 10 (1992): 45–92.

Kasson, John F. *Rudeness and Civility: Manners in Nineteenth-Century Urban America.* New York, 1990.

Katz, Stanley N. "The American Constitution: A Revolutionary Interpretation." In *Beyond Confederation: Origins of the Constitution and American National Identity*, edited by Richard Beeman, Stephen Botein, and Edward C. Carter II, 23–37. Chapel Hill, N.C., 1987.

Keller, Morton. *Affairs of State: Public Life in Late Nineteenth Century America.* Cambridge, Mass., 1977.

———. "The Pluralist State: American Economic Regulation in Comparative Perspective, 1900–1930." In *Regulation in Perspective*, edited by Thomas K. McCraw, 56–94. Cambridge, Mass., 1981.

———. "(Jerry-) Building a New American State." *Reviews in American History* 11 (1983): 248–51.

———. "Powers and Rights: Two Centuries of American Constitutionalism." *Journal of American History* 74 (1987): 675–94.

Kelley, Donald R. *The Human Measure: Social Thought in the Western Legal Tradition.* Cambridge, 1990.

Kelly, Alfred H., Winfred A. Harbison, and Herman Belz. *The American Constitution: Its Origins and Development.* 6th ed. New York, 1983.

Kennedy, Duncan. "Form and Substance in Private Law Adjudication." *Harvard Law Review* 89 (1976): 1685–1778.

———. "The Structure of Blackstone's Commentaries." *Buffalo Law Review* 28 (1979): 209–382.

———. "The Role of Law in Economic Thought: Essays on the Fetishism of Commodities." *American University Law Review* 34 (1985): 939–1001.

———. "The Stakes of Law, or Hale and Foucault!" *Legal Studies Forum* 15 (1991): 327–65.

Kloppenberg, James T. *Uncertain Victory: Social Democracy and Progressivism in European and American Thought, 1870–1920.* New York, 1986.

———. "The Virtues of Liberalism: Christianity, Republicanism, and Ethics in Early American Political Discourse." *Journal of American History* 74 (1987): 9–33.

———. "The Theory and Practice of American Legal History." *Harvard Law Review* 106 (1993): 1332–51.

Krout, John Allen. *The Origins of Prohibition.* New York, 1925.

Kulikoff, Alan. "The Transition to Capitalism in Rural America." *William and Mary Quarterly* 46 (1989): 120–44.

Kutler, Stanley I. *Privilege and Creative Destruction: The Charles River Bridge Case.* New York, 1971.

Lane, Roger. *Policing the City: Boston, 1822–1885.* Cambridge, Mass., 1981.

Lerner, Max. "The Supreme Court and American Capitalism." *Yale Law Journal* 42 (1933), 668.

Leuchtenberg, William E. "The Pertinence of Political History: Reflections on the Significance of the State in America." *Journal of American History* 73 (1986): 585–99.

Levy, Leonard W. *The Law of the Commonwealth and Chief Justice Shaw.* New York, 1957.

———. ed. *American Constitutional Law: Historical Essays.* New York, 1966.

Lively, Robert A. "The American System: A Review Article." *Business History Review* 29 (1955): 81–96.

Llewellyn, Karl N. *The Bramble Bush: On Our Law and Its Study.* 1930. Reprint, New York, 1960.

———. *The Common Law Tradition: Deciding Appeals.* Boston, 1960.

———. *Jurisprudence: Realism in Theory and Practice.* Chicago, 1962.

Lowi, Theodore J. "American Business, Public Policy, Case-Studies, and Political Theory." *World Politics* 16 (1964): 677–715.

Macpherson, C. B. *The Political Theory of Possessive Individualism*. Oxford, 1962.

Mann, Michael. "The Autonomous Power of the State: Its Origins, Mechanisms and Results." In *States in History*, edited by John A. Hall, 109–36. New York, 1986.

Mason, Alpheus T., and Gerald Garvey, eds. *American Constitutional History: Essays by Edward S. Corwin*. New York, 1964.

McCloskey, Robert G. *The American Supreme Court*. Chicago, 1960.

———, ed. *Essays in Constitutional Law*. New York, 1957.

McCormick, Richard L. *The Party Period and Public Policy: American Politics from the Age of Jackson to the Progressive Era*. New York, 1986.

McCraw, Thomas K. "Regulation in America: A Review Article." *Business History Review* 49 (1975): 159–83.

———. *Prophets of Regulation*. Cambridge, Mass., 1984.

———, ed. *Regulation in Perspective: Historical Essays*. Cambridge, Mass., 1981.

McCurdy, Charles. "Justice Field and the Jurisprudence of Government-Business Relations: Some Parameters of Laissez-Faire Constitutionalism." *Journal of American History* 61 (1975): 970–1005.

McDonald, Forrest. *Novus Ordo Seclorum: The Intellectual Origins of the Constitution*. Lawrence, Kans., 1985.

McDonald, Terrence J. "The Burdens of Urban History: The Theory of the State in Recent American Social History." *Studies in American Political Development* 3 (1989): 3–29.

McEvoy, Arthur F. *The Fisherman's Problem: Ecology and Law in the California Fisheries, 1850–1980*. New York, 1986.

McIlwain, Charles H. *The High Court of Parliament and Its Supremacy*. New Haven, Conn., 1910.

———. *Constitutionalism and the Changing World*. Cambridge, 1939.

———. *Constitutionalism: Ancient and Modern*. Ithaca, N.Y., 1947.

McLaren, John P. S. "Nuisance Law and the Industrial Revolution—Some Lessons from Social History." *Oxford Journal of Legal Studies* 3 (1983): 155–221.

McLaughlin, Andrew C., and Albert Bushnell Hart, eds. *Cyclopaedia of American Government*. 3 vols. New York, 1914.

Melosi, Martin V., ed. *Pollution and Reform in American Cities, 1870–1930*. Austin, Tex., 1980.

———. *Garbage in the Cities: Refuse, Reform, and the Environment, 1880–1980*. College Station, Tex., 1981.

Merriam, Charles Edward. *A History of American Political Theories*. New York, 1915.

Meyers, Marvin. *The Jacksonian Persuasion: Politics and Belief*. Stanford, Calif., 1957.

Miller, Perry. *The Life of the Mind in America: From the Revolution to the Civil War*. New York, 1965.

———, ed. *The Legal Mind in America*. Ithaca, N.Y., 1962.

Mohr, James C. *Doctors and the Law: Medical Jurisprudence in Nineteenth-Century America*. New York, 1993.

Monkkonen, Eric H. "A Disorderly People? Urban Order in the Nineteenth and Twentieth Centuries." *Journal of American History* 68 (1981): 539–59.

———. *Police in Urban America, 1860–1920*. New York, 1981.

Montgomery, David. *Citizen Worker: The Experience of Workers in the United States with Democracy and the Free Market during the Nineteenth Century*. New York, 1993.

Morgan, Edmund S. *American Slavery, American Freedom: The Ordeal of Colonial Virginia*. New York, 1975.

Morris, Richard B. *Government and Labor in Early America*. New York, 1946.

Mott, Rodney L. *Due Process of Law*. Indianapolis, Ind., 1926.

Murphy, Earl F. *Water Purity: A Study of Legal Control of Natural Resources.* Madison, Wis., 1961.

Murphy, Paul L. "Time to Reclaim: The Current Challenge of American Constitutional History." *American Historical Review* 69 (1963): 64–79.

Nash, Gerald D. *State Government and Economic Development: A History of Administrative Policies in California, 1849–1933.* Berkeley, Calif., 1964.

Nedelsky, Jennifer. *Private Property and the Limits of American Constitutionalism: The Madisonian Framework and Its Legacy.* Chicago, 1990.

Nelson, William E. "Emerging Notions of Modern Criminal Law in the Revolutionary Era: An Historical Perspective." *New York University Law Review* 42 (1967): 450–82.

———. "Changing Conceptions of Judicial Review: The Evolution of Constitutional Theory in the States, 1790–1860." *University of Pennsylvania Law Review* 120 (1972): 1166–85.

———. "The Impact of the Antislavery Movement upon Styles of Judicial Reasoning in Nineteenth Century America." *Harvard Law Review* 87 (1974): 513–66.

———. *Americanization of the Common Law: The Impact of Legal Change on Massachusetts Society, 1760–1830.* Cambridge, Mass., 1975.

———. *The Roots of American Bureaucracy, 1830–1900.* Cambridge, Mass., 1982.

———. *The Fourteenth Amendment: From Political Principle to Judicial Doctrine.* Cambridge, Mass., 1988.

Newmyer, R. Kent. *Supreme Court Justice Joseph Story: Statesman of the Old Republic.* Chapel Hill, N.C., 1985.

———. "Harvard Law School, New England Legal Culture, and the Antebellum Origins of American Jurisprudence." *Journal of American History* 74 (1987): 814–35.

Oestreich, Gerhard. *Neo-Stoicism and the Early Modern State.* Translated by D. McLintock. Cambridge, 1983.

Orren, Karen. *Belated Feudalism: Labor, the Law, and Liberal Development in the United States.* New York, 1991.

Orren, Karen, and Stephen Skowronek, eds. *Studies in American Political Development.* New Haven, Conn., 1987–.

Paul, Arnold. *Conservative Crisis and the Rule of Law: Attitudes of Bar and Bench, 1887–1895.* Ithaca, N.Y., 1960.

Peabody, Susan Wade. *Historical Study of Legislation regarding Public Health in the States of New York and Massachusetts.* Chicago, 1909.

Pocock, J. G. A. *The Ancient Constitution and the Feudal Law.* Cambridge, 1957.

———. *Politics, Language and Time: Essays on Political Thought and History.* New York, 1973.

———. *The Machiavellian Moment: Florentine Political Thought and the Atlantic Republican Tradition.* Princeton, N.J., 1975.

———. *Virtue, Commerce, and History: Essays on Political Thought and History, Chiefly in the Eighteenth Century.* Cambridge, Mass., 1985.

Poggi, Gianfranco. *The Development of the Modern State: A Sociological Introduction.* Stanford, Calif., 1978.

Polanyi, Karl. *The Great Transformation.* New York, 1944.

Pound, Roscoe. "Liberty of Contract." *Yale Law Journal* 18 (1909): 454–87.

———. "The Scope and Purpose of Sociological Jurisprudence." *Harvard Law Review* 24 (1911): 591–619; 25 (1912): 140–68, 489–516.

———. *The Spirit of the Common Law.* Boston, 1921.

———. *The Formative Era of American Law.* Boston, 1938.

Raeff, Marc. *The Well-Ordered Police State: Social and Institutional Change through Law in the Germanies and Russia, 1600–1800.* New Haven, Conn., 1983.

Read, Conyers, ed. *The Constitution Reconsidered.* New York, 1938.

Reid, John Phillip. *Constitutional History of the American Revolution: The Authority of Rights.* Madison, Wis., 1986.

Reznick, Scott M. "Empiricism and the Principle of Conditions in the Evolution of the Police Power: A Model for Definitional Scrutiny." *Washington University Law Quarterly* (1978): 1–92.

Rodgers, Daniel T. *Contested Truths: Keywords in American Politics since Independence.* New York, 1987.

———. "Republicanism: The Career of a Concept." *Journal of American History* 79 (1992): 11–38.

Rose, Carol M. "The Comedy of the Commons: Custom, Commerce, and Inherently Public Property." *University of Chicago Law Review* 53 (1986): 711–81.

———. *Property and Persuasion: Essays on the History, Theory, and Rhetoric of Ownership.* Boulder, Colo., 1994.

Rosen, Christine Meisner. *The Limits of Power: Great Fires and the Process of City Growth in America.* Cambridge, 1986.

Rosen, George. "Cameralism and the Concept of Medical Police." *Bulletin of the History of Medicine* 27 (1953): 21–42.

———. *A History of Public Health.* New York, 1958.

Rosenberg, Charles E. *The Cholera Years: The United States in 1832, 1849, and 1866.* Chicago, 1962.

Rosenkrantz, Barbara Gutmann. *Public Health and the State: Changing Views in Massachusetts, 1842–1936.* Cambridge, Mass., 1972.

Ross, Dorothy. *The Origins of American Social Science.* New York, 1991.

Rothman, David J. "The State as Parent: Social Policy in the Progressive Era." In *Doing Good: The Limits of Benevolence,* edited by Willard Gaylin, 67–98. New York, 1978.

———. *The Discovery of the Asylum: Social Order and Disorder in the New Republic.* Boston, 1971.

Ryan, Mary P. *Women in Public: Between Banners and Ballots, 1825–1880.* Baltimore, 1990.

Sandel, Michael J. *Liberalism and the Limits of Justice.* New York, 1982.

Scheiber, Harry N. *Ohio Canal Era: A Case Study of Government and the Economy, 1820–1861.* Athens, Ohio, 1968.

———. "The Road to Munn: Eminent Domain and the Concept of Public Purpose in the State Courts." *Perspectives in American History* 5 (1971): 327–402.

———. "Government and the Economy: Studies of the 'Commonwealth' Policy in Nineteenth-Century America." *Journal of Interdisciplinary History* 3 (1972): 135–51.

———. "Property Law, Expropriation, and Resource Allocation by Government: The United States, 1789–1910." *Journal of Economic History* 33 (1973): 232–51.

———. "American Constitutional History and the New Legal History." *Journal of American History* 68 (1981): 337–50.

———. "Public Rights and the Rule of Law in American Legal History." *California Law Review* 72 (1984): 217–51.

———. "Instrumentalism and Property Rights: A Reconsideration of American 'Styles of Judicial Reasoning' in the Nineteenth Century." *Wisconsin Law Review* (1985): 1–18.

Schneider, John C. *Detroit and the Problem of Order, 1830–1880: A Geography of Crime, Riot, and Policing.* Lincoln, Neb., 1980.

Schultz, Stanley K. *Constructing Urban Culture: American Cities and City Planning, 1800–1920.* Philadelphia, 1989.

Seligman, Edwin R. A., and Alvin Johnson, eds. *Encyclopaedia of the Social Sciences*. 15 vols. New York, 1930.

Sellers, Charles G. *The Market Revolution: Jacksonian America, 1815–1846*. New York, 1991.

Selvin, Molly. *This Tender and Delicate Business: The Public Trust Doctrine in American Law and Economic Policy, 1789–1920*. New York, 1987.

Shah, Nayan. "San Francisco's 'Chinatown': Race and the Cultural Politics of Public Health, 1854–1952." Ph.D. dissertation, University of Chicago, 1995.

Shalhope, Robert E. "Toward a Republican Synthesis: The Emergence of an Understanding of Republicanism in American Historiography." *William and Mary Quarterly* 29 (1972): 49–80.

———. "Republicanism in Early American Historiography." *William and Mary Quarterly* 39 (1982): 334–56.

Shaw, Albert. "The American State and the American Man." *Contemporary Review* 51 (1887): 695–711.

Singer, Joseph William. "The Legal Rights Debate in Analytical Jurisprudence from Bentham to Hohfeld." *Wisconsin Law Review* (1982): 975–1059.

Skinner, Quentin. *Meaning and Context: Quentin Skinner and His Critics*. Edited by James Tully. Princeton, N.J., 1988.

Skocpol, Theda. "Bringing the State Back In: Strategies of Analysis in Current Research." In *Bringing the State Back In*, edited by Peter R. Evans, Dietrich Rueschemeyer, and Theda Skocpol, 3–37. Cambridge, 1985.

———. *Protecting Soldiers and Mothers: The Political Origins of Social Policy in the United States*. Cambridge, Mass., 1992.

Skowronek, Stephen. *Building a New American State: The Expansion of National Administrative Capacities, 1877–1920*. Cambridge, 1982.

Small, Albion W. *The Cameralists: The Pioneers of German Social Polity*. Chicago, 1909.

Soifer, Aviam. "The Paradox of Paternalism and Laissez-Faire Constitutionalism: United States Supreme Court, 1888–1921." *Law and History Review* 5 (1987): 249–79.

Stanley, Amy Dru. "Beggars Can't Be Choosers: Compulsion and Contract in Postbellum America." *Journal of American History* 78 (1992): 1265–93.

Stansell, Christine. *City of Women: Sex and Class in New York, 1789–1860*. New York, 1982.

Steinberg, Allen. *The Transformation of Criminal Justice: Philadelphia, 1800–1880*. Chapel Hill, N.C., 1989.

Steinberg, Theodore. *Nature Incorporated: Industrialization and the Waters of New England*. Cambridge, 1991.

Steinfeld, Robert J. *The Invention of Free Labor: The Employment Relation in English and American Law and Culture, 1350–1870*. Chapel Hill, N.C., 1992.

———. "*The Philadelphia Cordwainers' Case* of 1806: The Struggle over Alternative Legal Constructions of a Free Market in Labor." In *Labor Law in America: Historical and Critical Essays*, edited by Christopher L. Tomlins and Andrew J. King, 20–43. Baltimore, 1992.

Stoner, James R., Jr. *Common Law and Liberal Theory: Coke, Hobbes, and the Origins of American Constitutionalism*. Lawrence, Kans., 1992.

Sunstein, Cass R. *The Partial Constitution*. Cambridge, Mass., 1993.

"Symposium: The Republican Civic Tradition." *Yale Law Journal* 97 (1988): 1493–1723.

Taylor, George Rogers. *The Transportation Revolution, 1815–1860*. White Plains, N.Y., 1951.

Teaford, Jon C. *The Municipal Revolution in America: Origins of Modern Urban Government, 1650–1825*. Chicago, 1975.

Teichgraeber, Richard, III. "*Free Trade*" *and Moral Philosophy: Rethinking the Sources of Adam Smith's Wealth of Nations*. Durham, N.C., 1986.

Thompson, E. P. *The Making of the English Working Class*. New York, 1964.

———. *Whigs and Hunters: The Origin of the Black Act*. New York, 1975.

———. *Customs in Common: Studies in Traditional Popular Culture*. New York, 1991.

Tomlins, Christopher L. *Law, Labor, and Ideology in the Early American Republic*. New York, 1993.

Tomlins, Christopher L., and Andrew J. King, eds. *Labor Law in America: Historical and Critical Essays*. Baltimore, 1992.

Tully, James. *A Discourse on Property: John Locke and His Adversaries*. Cambridge, 1980.

Twiss, Benjamin R. *Lawyers and the Constitution: How Laissez-Faire Came to the Supreme Court*. New York, 1962.

Unger, Roberto Mangabeira. *Knowledge and Politics*. New York, 1975.

———. *Law in Modern Society: Toward a Criticism of Social Theory*. New York, 1976.

———. *Social Theory: Its Situation and Its Task. A Critical Introduction to Politics, a Work in Constructive Social Theory*. Cambridge, 1987.

Wade, Richard C. *The Urban Frontier: Pioneer Life in Early Pittsburgh, Cincinnati, Lexington, Louisville, and St. Louis*. Chicago, 1959.

Warren, Charles. *A History of the American Bar*. Boston, 1911.

———. *The Supreme Court in United States History*. 2 vols. Boston, 1926.

Watson, Harry L. *Liberty and Power: The Politics of Jacksonian America*. New York, 1990.

Webb, Sidney, and Beatrice Webb. *The History of Liquor Licensing in England Principally from 1700 to 1830*. London, 1903.

———. *The Development of English Local Government, 1689–1835*. London, 1963.

Weber, Max. *Economy and Society*. Edited by Guenther Roth and Claus Wittich. 2 vols. Berkeley, 1978.

White, G. Edward. *The Marshall Court and Cultural Change, 1815–1835*. Abr. ed. New York, 1991.

Wiebe, Robert H. *The Search for Order, 1877–1920*. New York, 1967.

———. *The Opening of American Society: From the Adoption of the Constitution to the Eve of Disunion*. New York, 1984.

Wilentz, Sean. "Society, Politics, and the Market Revolution, 1815–1848." In *The New American History*, edited by Eric Foner, 51–71. Philadelphia, 1990.

Williams, Joan C. "Critical Legal Studies: The Death of Transcendence and the Rise of the New Langdells." *New York University Law Review* 62 (1987): 429–96.

Winch, Donald. *Adam Smith's Politics: An Essay in Historiographical Revision*. Cambridge, 1978.

Wolin, Sheldon S. *Politics and Vision: Continuity and Innovation in Western Political Thought*. Boston, 1960.

Wood, Gordon S. *The Creation of the American Republic, 1776–1787*. Chapel Hill, N.C., 1969.

———. *The Radicalism of the American Revolution: How a Revolution Transformed a Monarchical Society into a Democratic One Unlike Any That Had Ever Existed*. New York, 1992.

Woodard, Calvin. "Reality and Social Reform: The Transition from Laissez-Faire to the Welfare State." *Yale Law Journal* 72 (1962): 286–328.

Wright, Benjamin Fletcher, Jr. *American Interpretations of Natural Law: A Study in the History of Political Thought*. Cambridge, Mass., 1931.

———. *The Contract Clause of the Constitution*. Cambridge, Mass., 1938.

Business. *See* Corporations; Economy; Manufactories; Offensive trades

Butchers, 97–101, 288 (n. 31); Melting Association, 223. *See also* Slaughterhouses

Bylaws, 11, 99–100, 244, 254 (n. 34). *See also* Self-government

Caldwell, Charles, 195; *Thoughts on Hygiene*, 215–16

California, 79; licensing, 91, 94; health regulation of Chinese in, 215

Callender v. Marsh, 129–30, 147, 197

Cameralism, 14, 87, 150, 191

Campbell, John A.: argument in *Slaughterhouse*, 231–33

Canals, 116, 118, 120

Capitalism: and liberalism, ix, 6, 112–13; and legal instrumentalism, 22–23, 61–62, 85–86; and morals regulations, 153–54. *See also* Economy; Market revolution

Carriers and carting, 93–94

Castleton, N.Y., 214

Catlin v. Valentine, 222

Cemeteries: regulation of, 50, 70, 108–9, 217–18, 296 (n. 130). *See also* Public health

Centralization, x, 170, 183, 188, 203, 237; and prohibition, 177–79; of public health authority, 228–30; of state power, 240–43

Chadwick, Edwin, 332 (n. 40)

Character, 165–70; as evidence, 318 (n. 107)

Charles River Bridge v. Warren Bridge, 106–7, 130

Charleston, S.C.: fires, 55–56; safety regulations, 58–59, 67–68; public markets, 98, 101; Temperance Society, 172; police powers of, 273 (n. 37)

Charleston v. Goldsmith, 101

Charters. *See* Corporations

Cheatham v. Shearon, 64–65

Chemical works, 223–24

Chicago, Ill.: regulatory powers, 3–6; reform school, 171; public health, 193; offensive trades, 223, 229

Children, 171

Chinese, 215

Chipman, Nathaniel: *Principles of Government*, 27, 261 (n. 26); on man and social nature, 27–32; on social rights, 32–34; on common law, 38–39; on governance, 42; on *sic utere tuo*, 44–45; on *salus populi*, 46

Cholera, 193, 212–13, 215. *See also* Public health

Christian, Charles: *Treatise on Police*, 153; on gambling, 160; on prostitution, 163

Christianity, 150, 155; and public safety, 52. *See also* Religion

Church, C.J. (Conn.), 219

Churches, 108–9, 159

Cicero, 26, 263 (n. 43)

Cincinnati, Oh.: fires, 55; offensive trades, 222–23

Cincinnati v. Buckingham, 101

Cities. *See* Municipal corporations

Citizens Association of New York, 222

Citizenship: and participation, x, 248; and self-government, 10–11, 244; and common law, 38; and public safety, 52, 54; and service, 57, 212; and corporations, 108; national, 231–33, 242. *See also* Self-government

Civil law tradition, 136–39

Civil liberty. *See* Liberty: regulated

Civil rights, 237, 245, 248

Civil society, ix–x, 236

Civil War: impact on well-regulated society, 17, 170, 240–44, 246

Class: conflict, 17, 117, 153, 162, 286 (n. 16); and economy, 87; legislation, 102; "dangerous," 150, 154, 216; and health regulations, 215–16, 337 (n. 106); and morals regulations, 313–14 (n. 64). *See also* Poor; Vagrancy

Coates v. Mayor of New York, 108–9, 204, 217

Cockfighting, 160

Codification, 174, 178, 246

Coe v. Schultz, 228

Coke, Edward, 40, 157–58

Coker v. Birge, 21

Colman, Benjamin, 96

Colonies: fire regulations, 56–58; morals regulations, 151; liquor regulations, 172; health regulations, 201, 205, 215; governance of, 238–39; legal history of, 251 (n. 15)

Colquhoun, Patrick, 153
Comfort. *See* Public comfort
Commerce. *See* Economy
Commerce clause. *See* Constitution, U.S.
Commissioners of Salisbury v. Powe, 213
Common, 41, 167–68, 237
Common good. *See* Public good
Common law, 25; and American government, 11–12, 266 (n. 93), 267 (n. 95);
   and experience (history), 18, 29, 36–37,
   38–41, 265–66 (n. 82); and the well-
   regulated society, 35–50, 70–71, 237,
   239–40; tributes to, 38; and consent,
   38–39; and change, 40–41; and public
   good, 41–42; and *sic utere tuo*, 44–45;
   and *salus populi*, 45–47; and police, 52;
   and nuisance, 60–71; and legislation,
   63; destruction of property in, 68–69;
   necessity, 71–79; navigability, 132–33;
   and civil law, 139; and morality, 155; and
   constitution, 175; and public health,
   201; superseded by constitutional law,
   240–41, 245–48; crime, 310–11 (n. 34).
   See also Nuisance law
Commons, 115–21
Commons, John: on state, 252 (n. 22)
Common sense, 36, 41–42, 265–66 (n. 82).
   See also Scottish Enlightenment
Commonwealth, 41, 46, 74–79, 122, 143
Commonwealth studies, 2, 284 (n. 6), 286
   (n. 17)
Commonwealth v. Alger, 19–25, 48, 67, 70,
   81, 110, 143–45, 147, 196, 227, 257 (nn. 1, 2,
   3, 6), 258 (n. 7), 260 (n. 21)
Commonwealth v. Blackington, 174–76
Commonwealth v. Bowman and Duncan,
   147
Commonwealth v. Kimball, 176
Commonwealth v. Passmore, 126
Commonwealth v. Rice, 101
Commonwealth v. Rush, 128
Commonwealth v. Tewksbury, 144–45
Commonwealth v. Wright and Dame, 145
Communications, 41, 115–21, 131; and
   police, 14, 86. *See also* Public ways
Community, 29–31, 41; to society, 6; and
   individualism, 49; and necessity, 72; and
   state, 242
Community rights. *See* Rights, public

Compensation. See *Damnum absque
   injuria*; Eminent domain
Compulsory service: regarding fires, 56–57,
   73
Comstock, George F., 186–87, 245
Confiscation. *See* Forfeiture; Summary
   destruction
Congress, U.S.: quarantine acts, 210
Connecticut: Supreme Court, 33, 219;
   Missionary Society, 152; Society for the
   Suppression of Vice, 152; criminal code,
   155; prohibition, 179–81
Consent, 37, 43; and common law, 38–39
Constitution, U.S.: and local authority,
   10; Tenth Amendment, 13 (*see also*
   Federalism); Fifth Amendment, 16, 20,
   59, 75, 130 (*see also* Eminent domain);
   preamble, 41, 52, 268 (n. 118); contract
   clause, 47–48, 107–9; habeas corpus, 52;
   and *Brown v. Maryland*, 53; commerce
   clause, 54, 87, 176–77, 205, 207, 210–11,
   324–25 (n. 154); Fourteenth Amendment, 104, 107, 170, 230–33, 242, 244,
   246; Thirteenth Amendment, 104, 242,
   244, 246; privileges and immunities,
   108, 232; and laissez-faire, 110, 230, 245,
   281–82 (n. 147); Bill of Rights, 171; Fifteenth Amendment, 244. *See also* Due
   process; Supreme Court, U.S.
Constitutional law: and constitutional
   limitations, 7, 12, 22, 28–29, 81, 170–71,
   185–88, 228, 236, 246, 328 (n. 207); and
   liberalism, 7, 21–23; and common law,
   11–12, 41, 237; and history, 22, 28; critique
   of, 36–38, 266 (n. 89); interpretation,
   47–48; and necessity, 74–79; and corporations, 106–8; and public morality, 157,
   168–69; invention (ascendancy) of, 170,
   174, 231–33, 240–41, 245–48; and well-
   regulated society, 175–76; and public
   health, 193–94; influence of *Slaughterhouse Cases* on, 230–33. *See also* Due
   process; Judicial review; Liberal legalism
Contract: and liberalism, 6; status to, 6;
   and police power regulation, 17, 47–48,
   54, 105–11, 142; and legal transformation,
   23; absolute rights of, 28; and prostitution, 165; and liquor licensing, 177, 325
   (n. 159); and public health, 204

DuBois v. Augusta, 209

Dueling, 152

Due process, 22, 104, 107, 226, 228–29; and morals regulation, 167–71; procedural, 181–83, 212, 245, 314 (n. 68); substantive, 184–88, 232, 244–45, 246; Justices Field and Bradley on, 342–43 (n. 181). *See also* Constitution, U.S.; Procedure

Du Ponceau, Peter, 25, 261 (n. 27); on common law, 38, 40, 266 (n. 93)

Du Pont, 63

Duties: and moral philosophy, 27; relation to rights in the well-regulated society, 32–36, 244, 253 (n. 30), 264–65 (nn. 66, 68); and nuisance law, 62

Dygert v. Schenk, 125–26

Easement, 121, 138–39

Economy: market, ix, 7, 95–96, 98, 102–4, 291 (n. 65) (*see also* Great transformation; Market revolution); and police power regulation, 14–16, 53–54, 83–113, 236; and legal instrumentalism, 22–23, 285 (n. 8); invisible hand of, 35, 42; and public safety, 51–52, 59, 62–63, 65, 67; and nuisance law, 61–62, 275 (n. 51), 276 (n. 61); definitions of, 86–87; moral, 87; and corporations, 105–8, 295–96 (nn. 119, 120, 121); and transportation and communications, 115–21, 131; and public order, 149–50; and liquor, 178; and public health, 194, 204–12. *See also* Offensive trades; Public economy

Edmunds, Sen. (N.Y.), 140–41

Education, 49, 150

Edwards, Sen. (N.Y.), 77

Emancipation, 231, 241, 244

Emerson, George B., 30, 34; on golden rule, 69 (n. 138)

Eminent domain (takings), 49, 106, 130; police power distinguished from, 16, 20, 69, 109, 197, 206–7, 257 (n. 5), 278 (n. 94), 282 (n. 153), 327 (n. 192); destruction of property and, 59, 68–69, 75–79, 137–39, 140–42, 180, 226–27; and highways, 123–24; and public property, 146–47. *See also Damnum absque injuria*; Summary destruction

Enforcement: of law, 2, 60, 153, 249 (n. 1),

273–74 (n. 46); of fire regulations, 58, 282 (n. 150); of morals regulations, 165–66, 173, 317–18 (n. 98); of health regulations, 208–9, 213, 330 (n. 15); of economic regulations, 291–92 (nn. 72, 74, 76)

England: and law of necessity, 74; market regulations, 87, 95–96; equity and purpresture in, 127–28; rule of navigability, 132; private rights in, 157; morals regulation, 161, 315 (nn. 71, 74, 75); vagrancy law, 167; poor law, 168; liquor licensing, 172, 321 (n. 132)

Engrossing. *See* Forestalling, engrossing, and regrating

Enlightenment: and natural law, 29. *See also* Scottish Enlightenment

Environment: and public health, 192–94; and pollution, 218–21, 274 (n. 50). *See also* Offensive trades

Epidemic, 52–53, 55, 193, 201, 212–14, 215. *See also* Public health

Equity, 127–28, 156, 165–66, 220

Erie Canal, 116, 130, 139–42

Ethnicity: conflicts over, 16–17, 154, 170; and health regulations, 208, 215–16. *See also* Immigrants

Ewing, C.J. (Ky.), 162

Experience: in common law thinking, 29, 36–37, 39–41, 265–66 (n. 82); and regulation, 43

Exports/Imports, 53–54, 88–90

Factories. *See* Manufactories

Family, 87, 150, 152; and prostitution, 163; and children, 171; and police power, 320–21 (n. 125)

Federalism, 13, 54, 81, 176–77, 210–11; post–Civil War challenges to, 231–33, 242–43

Federalists, 25, 43

Federal police power, 243, 246

Ferguson v. City of Selma, 213

Ferries, 118–20

Fertilizer companies, 222–27

Field, Stephen J.: dissent in *Slaughterhouse*, 230, 232, 342 (n. 181)

Field codes, 178, 246

Fifteenth Amendment. *See* Constitution, U.S.

Fifth Amendment. *See* Constitution, U.S.; Eminent domain

Fines: and fire regulations, 56–60, 67–68, 273 (n. 39); and nuisance law, 61, 300 (n. 38); and morals regulations, 155; and quarantine regulations, 206

Fire: and regulation, 51–82, 282 (n. 150); examples, 55; and disorder, 55–56; London, 58; and gunpowder, 62–66; and wooden buildings, 66–71; and necessity, 71–79; and official destruction of property, 73–78, 280 (n. 124). *See also* Public safety

Fire limits, 57–58, 66–71

Fireworks, 57

Fish, 88–89

Fisher v. McGirr, 181–83, 187, 245

Food, 62, 87, 94. *See also* Markets, public; Slaughterhouses

Foreign policy, 53

Forestalling, engrossing, and regrating, 87, 94–102, 290 (n. 57), 291–92 (n. 72). *See also* Public economy

Forfeiture: and fire regulations, 58–59, 65; and market regulations, 97; and morals regulations, 155; and liquor regulations, 179–83. *See also* Summary destruction

Formalism, legal, 40, 247–48

Fornication, 155

Foucault, Michel: on police, 14, 191–92; on liberal state, 252 (n. 19); on governmentality, 252 (n. 20)

Founders, 38, 192

Fourteenth Amendment. *See* Constitution, U.S.; Due process

Frank, Johann Peter, 191–92

Franklin, Benjamin: and fire department, 58; and public markets, 98

Fraud, 87–90, 287 (n. 30); and markets, 96–102. *See also* Public economy

Freedom. *See* Liberty

French v. Baker, 91

French v. Camp, 135

Freund, Ernst: on police power, 13, 80, 254 (n. 34); on nuisance law, 44, 61; on corporations, 106, 294–95 (n. 116)

Friedman, Lawrence M., 151–52, 156; on legal thought, 260 (n. 23)

Fundamental law. *See* Natural law

Gallatin, Albert, 118, 210

Gambling/gaming, 153, 155–56, 159–60, 313–14 (nn. 62, 64, 67, 68). *See also* Public morality

Gardner v. Newburgh, 129

Garland, J. (La.), 138

Gemeinschaft to *Gesellschaft*, 6

Gender: conflicts, 16–17, 117, 154; and disorderly house prosecutions, 159, 162–70, 316–17 (n. 89), 318 (nn. 100, 102); and health regulations, 208; and due process, 343 (n. 181). *See also* Patriarchy; Sexuality; Women

General incorporation laws, 105–8, 178, 246, 294 (n. 111)

General will, 42

Georgia, 128; market regulations, 102–3; Supreme Court, 209; offensive trades, 221

Gibbons v. Ogden, 176, 193, 210, 211, 214, 232

Gibson, John Bannister, 122, 135, 147

Gierke, Otto von: on state and individuality, 243–44; on fellowship, 252 (n. 21)

Gilfoyle, Timothy J., 159; on enforcement, 274 (n. 46), 317–18 (n. 98)

Gneist, Rudolf von, 242, 320 (n. 119)

Golden rule, 34, 46, 62, 269 (n. 138)

Goodenow, John Milton, 310–11 (n. 34)

Goodnow, Frank J., 342 (n. 169)

Goodrich, Carter, 116

Goodrich, Charles B.: *Science of Government*, 11; on regulation, 11, 43, 47, 269 (n. 131); on rights, 33; on *sic utere tuo*, 44; on public good, 46; on public economy, 86

Governance, ix; practice of, 8–10, 13, 48–49, 237–39, 252 (n. 20); local, 10–11; and well-regulated society, 11, 13–14, 26–27, 32–35, 42–50, 51, 235–40; science of, 11, 14; powers of, 46–50; and public safety, 51–53, 56, 59; and nuisance law, 60–62; and economy, 83–88; and infrastructure, 115–21; and morality, 149–57; and paternalism, 184–85; and public health, 191–204; and vital statistics, 207–8; transformation of, 228–30, 233, 240–48; American regimes of, 238–39. *See also* State

Government. *See* Governance

talism, 22–23, 259 (n. 16), 284 (n. 7), 285 (n. 8); on nuisance law and legal transformation, 61–62, 275 (n. 51), 276 (n. 70); on corporations, 295 (n. 120); on *Palmer v. Mulligan*, 303 (n. 93)

Hospitals, 62, 68, 206, 217, 334 (n. 54); seizure of buildings for, 214; Marine Hospital Service, 229. *See also* Public health

Hotels, 159, 214

Households, 86–87

Housing, 215–16. *See also* Buildings; Disorderly houses

Hovenkamp, Herbert, 230, 285 (n. 8); on classical political economy and corporations, 106, 295 (n. 119); on *Slaughterhouse*, 342 (n. 175)

Hubbard, J. (N.Y.), 188

Hudson River, 132–34, 139–42; and offensive trades, 224–26

Hume, David, 29

Hunt, C.J. (N.Y.), 228–29

Hurst, James Willard: and Wisconsin Pike Creek Claimants Union, 10–11; and legal instrumentalism, 22–23, 284 (n. 7), 294 (n. 109); *Law and Conditions of Freedom*, 85, 105, 257 (n. 58), 285 (n. 7); on enforcement, 273 (n. 46); on corporate regulation, 295–96 (nn. 116, 121)

Hygiene. *See* Public health

Idleness, 313 (n. 64), 314 (n. 67). *See also* Vagrancy

Illinois, 102; Supreme Court, 111, 135, 170–71

Immigrants, 206, 215–16, 218; and passenger laws, 207–8, 210–11, 334–35 (n. 63)

Imports/Exports: regulation of, 53–54, 88–90

Impressment, 214

Imprisonment: and fire regulations, 58; and morals regulations, 155; and quarantine regulations, 206. *See also* Prisons

Improvement: and law, 40–41, 43, 46

Indiana, 79, 161; prohibition, 184–86

Indians, 53, 271 (n. 11); and liquor, 161, 323 (n. 139); and health, 215, 336 (n. 103)

Indictment: and nuisance law, 61, 217

Individualism, ix-x, 6–7, 35; possessive, 11,

32, 236, 263 (n. 41); versus the state, 21–23, 184–88, 238; and natural law, 28–29; versus social nature of man, 29–32; and common law, 38, 41–42; limitations on, 44–45, 70–71; and public good, 46, 49, 74–79; and public safety, 52, 56, 80–81; and public economy, 84–88; and public health, 194–95; late nineteenth-century expansion of, 240–41, 243–45; Roscoe Pound on, 268 (n. 115). *See also* Liberalism; Rights

Industry. *See* Economy; Manufactories; Offensive trades

Informers, 173

Infrastructure, 115–21, 131, 133. *See also* Public ways

Ingersoll, Jared, 67

Injunction: and nuisance law, 61, 302 (n. 67); and gunpowder regulation, 65; and highways, 127–28, 140–42, 276 (n. 75); and morals regulation, 156, 165–66; and offensive trades, 217, 220–22, 224–26

Inns and taverns: regulation of, 61–62, 87, 92, 155, 158, 160; and liquor licensing, 172–77. *See also* Disorderly houses; Liquor

Inspection: fire, 57–58; of products, 88–90, 288 (n. 32); of inns and taverns, 92, 173; public health, 205–8, 212–13

Instrumental rationality, ix, 248. *See also* Legal instrumentalism

Insurance: fire, 73

Insurrection, 53. *See also* Riots

Intellectual history. *See* History: intellectual

Intoxicants. *See* Liquor

Invasion, 52–53

Iredell, James: on public safety, 53, 271 (n. 9)

Irish, 215

Jacksonianism, 43, 194, 230

Jay, John, 51

Jefferson, Thomas, 137; Willard Hurst on, 295–96 (n. 121); and medical police, 330 (n. 17)

Jeffersonianism, ix, 43

Jersey City, N.J., 224–27

Jewell, Wilson, 203
Jewett, J. (N.Y.), 124–25
Johnson, J. (Mich.), 180
Jones, James, 203
Judicial review, 22, 182–83, 185–88, 246, 328
   (n. 195); and natural law, 28–29
Judiciary: power and role of, 1, 21–22, 60;
   and legislatures, 246
Jurisprudence: and governance, 32, 42, 51.
   See also Legal thought
Jury, 138, 141, 226
Justi, Johann: on *Polizeiwissenschaft*, 14, 255
   (n. 46)
Justices of the peace. *See* Officers, public

Keller, Morton: on polity, 252 (n. 20); on
   brevity of American history, 270 (n. 158)
Kelley, Donald R.: on instrumentalism in
   Western law, 259 (n. 16)
Kennedy, Duncan: on the liberal rule of
   law, 22, 258 (n. 12)
Kent, James, 30, 197, 232, 261 (n. 25); on
   public good trumping private interest, 9,
   75, 125; *Commentaries on American Law*,
   25, 35, 50; on law as moral philosophy,
   26–27; on Vattel, 29; on property and
   regulation, 49–50, 75; on nuisance law,
   61, 158; on highways, 121; in *Gardner v.
   Newburgh*, 129; on common law, 267
   (n. 95); on criminal equity, 301 (n. 63)
Kentucky: Supreme Court, 162
Kenyon, C.J. (Eng.), 129
Kerber, Linda: on liberalism, 251 (n. 18)
King's Prerogative in Salt-peter, 74–76
Kloppenberg, James T.: on liberalism, 250
   (n. 14); on pragmatic hermeneutics, 260
   (n. 22)
Kuhn, Thomas: and hermeneutic method,
   24
Kulikoff, Alan, 283–84 (n. 5)
Kurtz, Paul M.: on nuisance law, 275
   (n. 51), 276 (n. 70)

Labor: and police, 14, 150, 236, 307 (n. 4);
   and economy, 85–86; and morality,
   153–54; law, 253 (n. 24). *See also* Public
   economy
Lafayette, La., 137–39
Laissez-faire, ix, 3, 11, 49, 84–88, 102, 107,

116, 156, 250 (n. 8), 251 (nn. 18, 19), 291
   (n. 65); constitutionalism, 110, 230, 245,
   281–82 (n. 147); and regulation, 236–37
Landlords: and prostitution, 165, 317
   (n. 96)
Land-use: and nuisance law, 60–62; regulation, 67, 277 (n. 83)
Lane, C.J. (Oh.), 101–2
Lansing v. Smith, 142, 197
Law: and political economy, 2, 23, 83–88;
   enforcement of, 2, 60, 153, 249 (n. 1),
   273–74 (n. 46); constitutive power of,
   8–9, 23, 236, 285 (n. 7) (*see also* Legal-
   political construction of reality); and
   society (culture), 21–23, 60, 117, 247, 249
   (n. 1), 273–74 (n. 46), 298 (n. 5); and
   ideas, 24–26, 51, 260 (nn. 23, 24); and
   moral philosophy, 26–27; tributes to, 35;
   history and, 36–37, 39–41, 267 (n. 103);
   public versus private, 49–50 (*see also*
   Public-private distinction); higher,
   244–45; and morality, 307 (n. 1). *See
   also* Common law; Constitutional law;
   Criminal law; Natural law
Law, American: economic transformation
   of, 6–7, 23, 61–62, 151–52, 217, 275 (n. 51),
   285 (n. 8), 288 (n. 32) (*see also* Great
   transformation; Market revolution);
   "formative era" of, 7, 23, 151; and self-
   government, 10–11, 36, 163 (*see also* Citizenship); and governance, 11–12; liberal
   interpretations of, 12, 21–22 (*see also*
   Legal instrumentalism; Liberal legalism); and police power, 13–17, 70–71;
   and moral philosophy, 26–27; and the
   well-regulated society, 35–50; reason
   versus experience in, 36–37; and public
   economy, 83–88; and moral reform, 163;
   and public health, 214–15; constitutionalization of, 240–41, 245–48
Law, common. *See* Common law
Law, constitutional. *See* Constitutional law
Law, criminal. *See* Criminal law
Law, natural. *See* Natural law
Law, nuisance. *See* Nuisance law
Law, rule of, 22, 246–48; as a public ideal,
   12; E. P. Thompson on, 258 (n. 12)
Law of nations, 28–32. *See also* Natural law
Law of nature. *See* Natural law

London: Great Fire of 1666, 58, 73–74, 280 (n. 117)

Lotteries, 155–56

Loudon, Samuel, 28

Louisiana: Supreme Court, 71, 224; market regulations, 103–4; Civil Code, 136–37; water law, 136–39; board of health, 202, 208; and *Slaughterhouse Cases*, 230–33

Love: and the well-regulated society, 34, 45–46, 269 (n. 138)

Lowell, Mass., 220

Lowi, Theodore J., 239

Lumpkin, J. (Ga.), 102–3

Luxury, 87, 94

McCloskey, Robert G.: on naysaying judiciary, 22

McCormick, Richard L., 286 (n. 17)

McCraw, Thomas K., 83, 294 (n. 107)

McDonald, Forrest: on Blackstone, 264 (n. 62)

McDonald, Terrence J., 251 (n. 16)

McDowall, John R., 163

McEvoy, Arthur F.: on enforcement, 273 (n. 46)

McLean, John, 177; on public safety regulation (*License Cases*), 66

Madison, James, 117–18

Magic, 155, 156, 161

Maine: Supreme Court, 68–70, 134–35, 156, 170, 214, 218; highway regulation, 126; poor law, 168–70; Temperance Union, 178; prohibition, 178–79

Maleverer v. Spinke, 74–75

Man, theory of: and social nature, 26–35, 47–48, 150, 196, 308 (n. 6)

Manhattan Manufacturing and Fertilizing Company v. Van Keuren, 225–28

Mann, Michael, 116

Manners, 149–57; and police, 14. *See also* Public morality

Mansfield, Edward D., 25, 100, 261 (n. 25)

Manufactories: regulation of, 57, 62, 71; gunpowder, 62–63; liquor, 171; as nuisances, 218–21. *See also* Offensive trades

Marbury v. Madison, 185, 244

Market, free. *See* Economy: market

Market revolution, 85, 95–96, 98, 105, 283–84 (n. 5), 288 (n. 32), 291 (n. 65);

and legal instrumentalism, 22–23. *See also* Economy: market; Great transformation

Markets, public (urban marketplace), 70, 95–105, 290–91 (nn. 63, 65). *See also* Public economy

Marr, J. (La.), 71

Marriage, 320–21 (n. 125)

Married women's property acts, 178, 246

Marshall, John, 37, 247; in *Brown v. Maryland*, 54, 111, 257 (n. 1), 326 (n. 169); on corporations, 106–9, 294 (n. 114); in *Barron v. Baltimore*, 130; on commerce clause and police power, 176; on public health, 193, 210, 214; cited in *Slaughterhouse*, 232

Marx, Karl, ix, 87; on history, 18

Maryland: regulation of merchants, 53–54; product laws, 88–90; licensing, 91–94; Supreme Court, 169, 209

Massachusetts, 38; Supreme Judicial Court of, 19–21, 100; fire regulations, 58, 79; product laws, 88–89; inns and taverns, 92; provisions, 94; highway regulations, 126; harbor regulations, 136, 144–45; *Laws and Liberties*, 151; morals regulations, 151; Declaration of Rights, 154, 174, 182; vagrancy laws, 167–68; liquor regulation, 172–78, 181–83, 188; boards of health, 196, 201–3, 332–33 (n. 42); Sanitary Survey and Commission, 196–97, 215; quarantine, 205–6; offensive trades, 220, 223–24

Mather, Cotton, 151, 152

Mather, Increase, 151

May, Henry F., 26

Mayor of Monroe v. Hoffman, 71

Mayors. *See* Officers, public

Mayor v. Lord, 76–77

Meat. *See* Butchers; Slaughterhouses

Medical police, 191–204, 329 (n. 6), 330 (n. 16). *See also* Police; Public health

Meeker v. Van Rensselaer, 215

Melosi, Martin V.: on nuisance, 274 (n. 50)

Mercantilism, 14, 49, 84–88, 191

Merchants: regulation of, 53–54; licensing, 90–95; opposition to quarantine, 209. *See also* Public economy

Passaic River: and offensive trades, 219, 225
Passenger Cases, 211
Passenger laws, 207–8, 210–11, 334–35
   (n. 63)
Patriarchy, 157, 162–64, 236, 248. *See also*
   Gender
Paupers. *See* Poor
Peddlers, 87, 94–102
Peete v. Morgan, 211
Pell's Case, 158
Penn, William: and fire regulations, 58; and
   market regulations, 97
Pennsylvania: fire legislation, 56, 58;
   Supreme Court, 65, 74, 99, 122, 128;
   licensing, 91; corporations, 106; health
   regulations, 201, 332 (n. 35); offensive
   trades, 218, 221
Pennsylvania Coal v. Mahon, 81–82, 282
   (nn. 152, 153)
Penobscot River, 134–35
People v. Brougham, 166
People v. Cunningham, 124–25, 134, 140, 147
People v. Gallagher, 180, 183
People v. Sands, 63–65
People v. Turner, 170–71, 320 (n. 125)
Perfectionism, 45–46, 72, 269 (n. 137)
Perkins, J. (Ind.), 184–85
Peters, J. (Ala.), 213
Petty, William, 191
Philadelphia, Pa.: fires, 54–56, 58; building
   regulations, 67–68, 80; public markets,
   97–99; boards of health, 201–3, 332
   (n. 35); offensive trades, 221; police
   powers granted, 277 (n. 86)
Philosophy, legal. *See* Legal thought
Philosophy, moral. *See* Moral philosophy
Philosophy, political. *See* Political thought
Pierce v. Bartrum, 100
Pilot laws, 112
Pitt, William, 157
Pittsburgh, Pa.: fires, 55; streets, 147–48;
   offensive trades, 220
Planning, 67
Plymouth, Mass.: County Court, 173
Pocock, J. G. A., 10, 26; on Matthew Hale,
   40
Polanyi, Karl, 283 (n. 4). *See also* Great
   transformation
Police (*Polizei*), ix, 13–15, 255–56 (nn. 46,

48); ordinances, 11, 52; English, French,
   German, and Scottish influences, 14;
   and public safety, 52–53; medical, 53,
   191–204; and economy, 86–88; and infrastructure, 115–21; and morality, 149–51,
   153–56, 307 (n. 4); and crime, 153, 308
   (n. 5); challenged, 184–88
Police, municipal: and fires, 55–56; and
   crime, 153, 163; reform, 246
Police power: regulations (examples of,
   lists), 3–6, 15–17, 21, 50, 87–89, 91, 93–94,
   155, 198–200, 203, 232, 256 (nn. 54, 55),
   297 (n. 135), 331 (n. 22); explained, 13–15,
   47–50, 235–37, 239–40, 255 (n. 44);
   distinguished from eminent domain,
   16, 20, 69, 257 (n. 5), 278 (n. 94), 282
   (n. 153), 327 (n. 192); significance of
   Commonwealth v. Alger, 19–21; and
   legal thought, 25–26; and nuisance law,
   44–45, 60–62; James Kent on, 49–50;
   Oliver Wendell Holmes on, 50; and
   Brown v. Maryland, 53–54; and public
   safety, 56–60, 65–71; and destruction
   of property, 68–69; and private right,
   69–71, 157–59; and necessity, 72–79; and
   economy, 86–88, 96–97, 104–5, 111–13;
   and corporations, 105–11; inalienable,
   111, 188, 229, 232, 243, 246, 328 (n. 210);
   and transportation and communications, 115–27, 136, 137–45, 147; and
   morality, 149–57, 176–77; and race, class,
   and gender, 161–70, 215–16; and health,
   191–204; constitutionalization of, 243,
   245–48; federal, 243, 246. *See also* Well-
   regulated society
Political development, American: histories
   of, 2; and liberalism, 7; and morality,
   154; and public health, 192–97; role of
   well-regulated society in, 235–40; and
   liberal state, 240–48
Political science, 2; and moral philosophy,
   33; and the state, 242
Political thought (theory), 8–10, 26; of the
   well-regulated society, 25–26; on social
   nature of man, 26–27; and moral philosophy, 27
Polizei. See Police
Pollution, 218–21, 274 (n. 50). *See also*
   Offensive trades

Poor, 14; regulatory proceeds to, 97, 291 (n. 71); and morals regulation, 153–54, 167–70, 172, 310 (n. 26), 320 (n. 122); and immigration, 206–8, 210–11; and health regulation, 215–16. *See also* Class; Vagrancy

Poor law, 155, 168–70

Popular sovereignty. *See* Self-government

Population: and police, 14; and public safety, 52–54; and health, 191–93, 207–8

Porter, J. (N.Y.), 77

Portland, Me., 168–70

Ports. *See* Harbors

Posse comitatus, 212

Poughkeepsie, N.Y.: public markets, 99–100

Pound, Roscoe: on individualism and common law, 38, 41, 268 (n. 115)

Powell v. Pennsylvania, 246–47

Pratt, J. (Mich.), 183

Prerogative. *See* Sovereign prerogative

Prices, 90, 92, 96–97, 292 (n. 81). *See also* Public economy

Prisons, 153, 163; and houses of correction (workhouses), 319–20 (nn. 114, 115)

Privacy, 149, 156, 157. *See also* Rights

Private property. *See* Property, private

Private prosecution. *See* Prosecution, private

Pro bono publico, 74

Procedure: summary, 168–70, 173, 181–83, 314 (n. 68). *See also* Due process

Product laws, 88–90

Profanity, 152, 155, 158–59

Professions: licensing of, 90–95

Progressivism, 8, 67, 166, 171, 194, 236; and historiography, 28

Prohibition (state), 172, 177–89, 246, 326 (nn. 166, 169); and state power, 243. *See also* Public morality

Property, private: and liberalism, 6; and police power regulation, 13, 17, 19–21, 24, 47, 49–50, 236; as a social, conventional right, 20, 33; and legal transformation, 23, 151–52; and natural law, 28–32, 185–88; James Kent on, 49–50; and public safety limitations, 51–56, 59, 65–66, 67–71, 80–81; destruction of, 57–59, 65, 68–69, 72–79, 121–31, 137–39, 140–42, 145,

180, 206–7, 212–15, 217, 226–27 (*see also* Abatement; Summary destruction); and nuisance law, 60–62; and necessity, 72; and economy, 85; and public rights, 136–45; and liquor regulation, 174–78, 180–88; and public health, 194, 204, 212–14; and offensive trades, 217–28; and *Slaughterhouse*, 231–33. *See also* Nuisance law; *Sic utere tuo*

Property, public, 41, 115–48. *See also* Public ways; Public works

Prosecution, private, 155; and fire regulations, 58; and morals regulation, 164

Prostitution, 153, 155–56, 159; and bawdy house regulation, 163–70; treatment of women versus men, 316–17 (n. 89), 318 (nn. 100, 102); and landlord liability, 317 (n. 96). *See also* Disorderly houses

Providence, R.I.: fire regulations, 58; offensive trades, 224

Public comfort: and civil liberty, 11; and police power, 13–16; and public safety, 52, 71

Public economy, 1, 83–113, 286 (n. 13); and police power, 13–16, 83–84, 86–88, 111–13; and product laws, 88–90; and licensing, 90–95; and markets, 95–105, 291–92 (nn. 65, 72, 74, 76); and corporations, 105–11; and offensive trades, 217–33

Public good (welfare), x, 2, 9–10, 35, 45–47; in American political ideology, 6; and regulated liberty, 11, 44–45; and police power, 13–16, 20; and private right, 23, 46–47, 49, 69–71, 74–79, 133–36, 185–88; and legal thought, 25–26, 36, 41–42; and natural law, 28–32; and social nature of man, 29–32; and common law, 36, 41–42; and well-regulated governance, 42–50; and public safety, 51–53, 55–56, 59, 65–66, 69–71, 80–81; and nuisance law, 62; and necessity, 71–72, 74–79; and economy, 86–88, 96–97, 100–101, 104–5; and public property, 115–21; and morality, 149–57, 169, 175–76; and race, class, gender, 161–70, 215–16; and health, 191–204; and vital statistics, 207–8. *See also* Republicanism; *Salus populi*

Public health, 2, 191–233; and civil liberty,

public safety, 51–54; economic, 53–54, 83–88, 96–97, 104–5; fire, 56–60, 65–67; and summary destruction, 59, 68–69; and nuisance law, 60–62; of corporations, 105–11; transportation and communications, 115–21, 127, 136; and morality, 149–57, 180–88; and public health, 191–204; constitutionalization of, 233, 245–47. *See also* Police power; Well-regulated society

Religion: and police, 14; and regulation, 47, 311 (n. 43); and morality, 150–56. *See also* Public morality

Representation, 267 (n. 101), 269 (n. 140)

Republicanism, 2, 9–10, 37, 41, 46, 49, 235, 264 (n. 61); and liberalism, 6; and law, 12

Reputation, 165–70; as evidence, 318 (n. 107)

Respublica v. Duquet, 67–68, 71

Respublica v. Sparhawk, 74–75

Rhode Island: fire regulations, 58; offensive trades, 221

Rhodes v. Dunbar, 218

Rice, J. (Me.), 134–35, 170

Richardson, C.J. (N.H.), 156

Rights: and public good, 9, 13, 41, 46–47, 49, 157–58, 235–37, 239–40, 268–69 (n. 130); social and relative nature of, 17, 27–36, 38, 236–37; liberal conception of, 21–23, 32–33, 265 (n. 73); vested, 22, 54, 99, 108–9, 121–31, 141; and *sic utere tuo*, 44–45, 117; and public safety, 53–55, 69–71, 80–81; summary destruction and, 59; and nuisance law, 60–62; and necessity, 72–79; economic, 86–88, 95–96, 99–105; of corporations, 106–11; and public property, 121–48; and morals regulation, 167–70, 180–88; late nineteenth-century redefinition of, 170–71, 182–83, 185–88, 228, 230–33, 240–41, 243–45; and public health, 196–97, 214. *See also* Individualism; Liberalism; Property, private

Rights, public, 20, 24, 34, 41, 45–47; and nuisance law, 60–62; and public safety, 65–66, 80–82; and necessity, 74–79; James Kent on, 75; and highways, 115–31; and rivers, 131–36; and harbors, 136–45; and public squares, 145–47. *See also* Public good

Riots, 153, 155, 159; health, 334 (n. 54)

Riparian rights, 132–36, 137–39

Rivers, 115–21, 131–36, 303 (n. 89); banks, 136–39; and pollution, 219, 224–25, 230–31 (*see also* Offensive trades). *See also* Public ways

Roads, 3, 115–31; as public property, 121–23; encroachments on, 123–27, and *damnum absque injuria*, 127, 128–31; and injunctions, 127–28. *See also* Public ways

Roe v. Wade, 187

Root, Jesse, 33–34

Rose, Carol, 123

Rosen, George, 194

Rosenberg, Charles E.: on health law enforcement, 273 (n. 46)

Rothbone's Case, 163–65

Rousseau, Jean Jacques, 27, 35–36

Ruffin, Thomas, 162, 213

Rule of law. *See* Law, rule of

Rush, Benjamin, 17, 194–95

Russell v. Mayor of New York, 77

Rutgers v. Waddington, 28–29

Rutherford, Thomas, 29; on necessity, 72

Ryan, Mary P., 117

Sabbath. *See* Sunday laws

Safety. *See* Public safety

Sailors, 159

St. Louis, Mo.: fires, 55; markets, 103; quarantine, 209–10

Salem, Mass., 205

Sales, 88, 90. *See also* Licensing

Salesmen, 87, 94–102

Saloons. *See* Inns and taverns

Salus populi, 34, 70, 81; explained, 9–10, 42–50, 235–40; and natural law, 29; and public safety, 52–53, 55, 59, 65, 108; and necessity, 71–72, 74–79; and economy, 88, 104, 109, 112; and public property, 115, 121, 128–29, 147; and public morality, 156, 157–58, 177; challenged (demise of), 184–88, 232, 240–48; and public health, 192, 195–97, 213, 341 (n. 159); and offensive trades, 228. *See also* Public good; Well-regulated society

San Francisco, Ca.: fires, 55; Chinatown, 215; offensive trades, 222

Sanger, William, 163

Sanitation. *See* Public health

Santa Clara v. Southern Pacific Railroad, 106–8

Savage, C.J. (N.Y.), 100, 108, 213, 215

Savannah, Ga., 55

Scheiber, Harry N., 116, 122, 257 (n. 3); on eminent domain, 278 (n. 94); on public rights, 284 (n. 6)

Scobey, David, 117

Scottish Enlightenment: and moral philosophy, 6, 14, 36, 265–66 (n. 82)

Search and seizure: and liquor regulations, 179–83; and offensive trades, 226

Security. *See* Public safety

Sedgwick, Theodore, 246

Self-defense, 72

Self-government, x; local, 10–11, 237, 240, 244, 254 (nn. 31, 32, 34); and regulation, 43; challenges to, 187–88

Selma, Ala., 213

Selvin, Molly, 122

Separate spheres, 164

Servants, 215. *See also* Labor

Service, compulsory: regarding fires, 56–57, 73

Sexuality, 154, 155–56, 162, 163; transformation in, 166. *See also* Public morality

Shafer v. Mumma, 169

Shah, Nayan, 336 (n. 102)

Shattuck, Lemuel, 203

Shaw, Albert, 237

Shaw, Lemuel: on constitution and common law, 12; defense of well-regulated society in *Commonwealth v. Alger,* 19–25, 48, 69, 82, 143–45, 227, 247, 257 (n. 4), 258 (n. 7), 259–60 (nn. 20, 21); on gunpowder regulations, 65; on market regulations, 100–101; on public rights, 126, 220; on public morality, 160; defense of well-regulated society in *Commonwealth v. Blackington,* 174–76; and liquor regulation, 174–77, 181–84; and procedural due process (*Fisher v. McGirr*), 181–84, 187, 245; and public health, 196–97; on police power, 327 (n. 192), 331 (n. 22)

Shaw v. Cummiskey, 196

Shepley, C.J. (Me.), 156

Sheriff: and fires, 57. *See also* Officers, public

Sherman, Sen. (N.Y.), 77

Shippen, C.J. (Pa.), 67–68

Shows, 155–56, 159–61, 315 (nn. 74, 75). *See also* Theaters

Sic utere tuo, 34, 70–71, 81, 126, 128, 135, 144; in *Commonwealth v. Alger,* 20; explained, 42–50; and public safety, 53, 59, 63–66, 109; and nuisance law, 60–62; and public morality, 157–58, 312 (n. 50); attacked, 185, 244; and public health, 195–97; and offensive trades, 217–28. *See also* Nuisance law

Sinclair, Upton, 223

Skepticism, 29

Slaughterhouse Cases: and police power, 14–15, 230–33

Slaughterhouses: regulation of, 50, 61–62, 65–66, 222–33, 340 (nn. 136, 137). *See also* Offensive trades

Slavery, 16–17, 53, 98, 161–62, 170–71, 188, 210, 231–32, 236, 241, 248, 271 (n. 11), 316 (nn. 79, 80)

Smith, Adam: on police, 14, 255 (n. 46); criticized, 30, 35, 46; on public safety, 52; *Wealth of Nations,* 84–87; revisionism, 263 (n. 53)

Smith, Stephen, 203

Smith v. Commonwealth, 161–62

Smoke, 62, 217–20

Soap, 23

Social Darwinism, 245

Social history. *See* History: social

Socialism, ix-x

Society: law and, 21–23; theory of man in, 26–35, 47–48

Sociological jurisprudence, 2

Sodomy, 155

South Carolina: fire and watch, 56, 58–59; product laws, 88; licensing, 92, 94; rivers, 131; gambling regulations, 160; Supreme Court, 167

Sovereign prerogative: and necessity, 72; and markets, 95; and highways, 122, 142

Sovereignty: and police power, 13, 21–22, 70, 177, 188, 192; and the modern state, 241–43; and individuality, 243–45; and legislation, 246. *See also* State

Spencer, Herbert: *Man Versus the State,* 21

Spencer, J. (N.Y.), 133–34

Stables, 61–62, 221–22

Stafford, Ward, 154

State, ix-x; welfare, ix, 3, 236, 248; historiography of, 2; negative, 3, 7, 35, 43, 47; theory, 3, 8–9, 238–39, 252–53 (nn. 19, 20, 21, 22); as a constitutive force, 8–9, 236; creation of modern American liberal, 17–18, 170–71, 183, 187–88, 228, 233, 237, 240–48; and the individual, 21–23, 35, 243–45; and public safety, 52–53; and nuisance law, 62; and public economy, 83–87; and corporations, 107–11; and infrastructure, 115–21, 127, 131, 133, 136, 146–47; and morality, 149–52, 154–55, 163; and race, class, and gender, 161–70, 215–16; and public health, 191–204; and vital statistics, 207–8; Max Weber on, 241. *See also* Governance

Statelessness: myth of, 3, 56, 236–37

State police power. *See* Police power

State v. Allmond, 180

State v. Evans, 166–67

State v. Gurney, 179

State v. Morris and Essex Railroad, 125

State v. Wheeler, 179–80

State v. Wilkinson, 123

State v. Woodward, 146–47

Statistics, 207–8

Statutes. *See* Legislation

Statutory construction, 109, 141, 142, 246, 267 (n. 95)

Steam engines, 62, 218, 220

Steinberg, Allen, 250 (n. 7)

Stoicism. *See* Neo-Stoicism

Stoner, James R., Jr., 40

Stone v. Mayor of New York, 77

Storrs, J. (Ct.), 179–81

Story, Joseph: on corporations, 107, 109; on equity, 128, 301 (n. 63); constitutionalism of, 247

Street commissioners, 68. *See also* Officers, public

Streets. *See* Roads

Sturges v. Crowninshield, 48

Stuyvesant, Peter, 56–57

Stuyvesant v. Mayor of New York, 70

Substantive due process. *See* Due process

Sullivan, James: on common law, 38–39, 41, 267 (n. 95)

Sullivan, William, 25, 261 (n. 25); *Political Class Book*, 27, 30; on government, 43; on *sic utere tuo*, 44; on people's welfare, 46; on contract clause, 47–48

Summary destruction, 57–59, 65, 68–69, 123–24, 137–39, 140–42, 145, 177, 180, 183, 278 (n. 92), 314 (n. 68), 327–28 (nn. 184, 192); and necessity, 72–79; and public health, 206–7, 212–15; and offensive trades, 217, 226–27. *See also* Abatement

Summary justice. *See* Procedure, summary

Sumner, William Graham, 254

Sunday laws, 21, 112, 152, 155–56, 173, 297 (n. 143); and liquor, 323 (n. 139). *See also* Religion

Supreme Court, U.S., 37, 53, 90; and liberal constitutionalism, 22; and contract clause, 48; and *Brown v. Maryland*, 53–54; and necessity, 79; on inalienable police power, 111, 229; and *License Cases*, 176–77, 179; and prohibition, 187–88; on public health, 193, 205; on quarantine, 210–11; and *Slaughterhouse Cases*, 231–33; on federal police power, 243. *See also* Constitutional law

Surety and recognizance, 92, 94, 173

Sutherland, J. (N.Y.), 140–41, 228

Swift, Zephaniah, 25, 27, 152, 242, 261 (n. 26); on social nature of man, 30, 32; on common law, 40–41; on property and regulation, 47; on representation, 267 (n. 101), 269 (n. 140)

Tacitus, 160

Takaki, Ronald: *Iron Cages*, 16

Takings. *See* Eminent domain

Taliaferro, J. (La.), 104, 231

Tanenhaus, David S., 321 (n. 126)

Taney, Roger: in *Brown v. Maryland*, 53–54, 66, 111; on corporations, 106–9, 130; in *License Cases*, 177, 179; on health and quarantine, 210; on police power and sovereignty, 324–25 (n. 154)

Taverns. *See* Inns and taverns

Taxation, 49; and licensing, 53–54, 90–95; and Civil War, 242

Taylor, George Rogers, 116

Taylor, John, 261 (n. 26); on property and regulation, 47; on experience, 265 (n. 82)

Teaford, Jon, 291 (n. 65)

Temperance, 152–54, 171–89, 237. *See also* Liquor

Tennessee: Supreme Court, 64–65, 165; licensing, 91

Tenth Amendment. *See* Constitution, U.S.

Texas: offensive trades, 221

Thacher, Peter O., 100, 145

Thayer, James Bradley, 110, 257 (n. 1)

Theaters, 62, 155, 159–61, 315 (nn. 74, 75). *See also* Public morality

Theft, 72

Thirteenth Amendment. *See* Constitution, U.S.

Thompson, E. P., 87; on rule of law, 258 (n. 12); on law and society, 260–61 (n. 24)

Thomson, James, 19

Thompson, R. H., 206

Thornton, J. (Ill.), 171

Thorpe v. Rutland and Burlington Railroad Company, 109–10

Tiedeman, Christopher G.: on police power, 80–81, 110, 171, 281–82 (n. 147); constitutionalism of, 245, 246; on morals regulation, 311 (n. 42)

Tocqueville, Alexis de: *Democracy in America*, 2, 7; on federalism, 242; on associations, 252 (n. 21)

Tomlins, Christopher L.: on law as a modality of rule, 12, 254 (n. 41)

Torts: and nuisance law, 61

Trade. *See* Economy; Offensive trades

Trades, offensive. *See* Offensive trades

Transportation, 86, 115–21, 131; and nuisance law, 62; revolution, 116. *See also* Carriers and carting; Public ways

Treatises (legal), 25–26, 150, 246

Trial, right to, 168, 182–83

Trippe, J. (Ga.), 103

Turner v. Maryland, 90

Ultra vires, 106, 111

Union, 242

United States Constitution. *See* Constitution, U.S.

United States Sanitary Commission, 229

United States Supreme Court. *See* Supreme Court, U.S.

United States v. Dewitt, 81, 243, 344 (n. 13)

Urban policy. *See* Municipal corporations

Usury, 87

Utility, 141, 147

Vaccination, 206, 215

Vagrancy, 153, 155, 167–71, 319–20 (nn. 108, 109, 111, 112, 114, 115, 119, 122). *See also* Idleness; Poor

Vanderbilt v. Adams, 21, 70, 143–44, 147, 197

Van Keuren, Benjamin (street commissioner), 226–27

Van Wormer v. Mayor of Albany, 212–13

Vattel, Emmerich de, 36, 263 (nn. 46, 47); *Law of Nations*, 29–30; on rights, 33, 264–65 (n. 68); on governance, 42; on perfectionism, 45; on economy, 86; on order and morality, 149; on police, 255–56 (n. 48)

Veazie v. Dwinel, 134–35

Vermont: railroad regulation, 109–10; Supreme Court, 123, 146–47; prohibition, 179–81, 183–84

Vice. *See* Public morality

Village of Buffalo v. Webster, 70, 99–100, 103

Village of Jamaica v. Long Island Railroad Company, 229

Virginia, 126

Wadleigh v. Gilman, 68–71, 78, 81

Walton, J. (Me.), 170

Walworth, Ch. (N.Y.), 76–77, 140, 142, 222

Wardlaw, J. (S.C.), 101

Warner, J. (Ga.), 221

Warren, Charles, 53

Watch, 52, 56, 58

Webb, Sidney and Beatrice: on nuisance law, 62

Weber, Max, 87; on the state, 241

Webster, Daniel, 177, 247; on self-government, 254 (n. 31)

Weights and measures, 87, 90, 96-97, 101–2. *See also* Product laws

Welfare. *See* Public good

Welfare state, ix, 3, 236, 248

Well-regulated society: defined, x, 1–2, 9–13, 174–77, 235–40; and liberalism, 6; European influence on, 7; and law, 11–12, 35–38; and police, 13–15; demise of, 17,

184–88, 240–48; and social nature of man, 26–32, 308 (n. 6); and social rights, 32–35; and history, 36–37, 39–41; and common law, 38–50; and public safety, 51–54, 59, 65–66, 69–71, 80–81; and summary destruction, 59; and nuisance law, 60–62; and necessity, 71–79; and public economy, 83–88, 100–101, 104–5, 109, 111–13; and corporations, 108–11; and transportation and communications, 115–21, 136, 139, 142, 147; and morality, 149–57, 169–70, 174–77; and race, class, and gender, 161–70, 215–16; and prohibition, 180–88; and public health, 191–204; and offensive trades, 219, 222, 227, 228; and *Slaughterhouse Cases*, 231–33. *See also* Police power; *Salus populi*

Weston, C.J. (Me.), 68–71

Wharfs, 19–21, 49, 89, 130, 143

Wheeler, Jacob, 150, 165, 308 (n. 6)

Whigs, 43

White, Andrew D., 333 (n. 44)

Whitney v. Bartholomew, 219

Wilde, J. (Mass.), 100, 197

Williamson, Ch. (N.J.), 220

Willoughby, W. W.: *Nature of the State*, 242

Willson v. Black Bird Creek Marsh Company, 214

Will theory of law, 37. *See also* Legal positivism

Wilson, George, 193

Wilson, James, 242, 261 (n. 25); on freedom and police, 11; law lectures, 19, 25; on

man and social nature, 27–32, 263–264 (n. 54, 64), 269 (n. 138); on social rights, 32–35; on reason versus experience, 36–37, 265 (n. 82); critique of legal positivism, 37; on common law, 38–40, 267 (n. 103); on regulated governance, 43, 70; and *salus populi*, 45–47; on U.S. Constitution, 268 (n. 118)

Wilson, Woodrow, 28; *The State*, 242

Winthrop, John, 205

Wisconsin: Pike Creek Claimants Union of, 10–11

Wolin, Sheldon, 27, 262 (nn. 29, 37)

Women: and suffrage, 153; and prostitution, 163–70; and married women's property acts, 178, 246. *See also* Gender

Wood, Gordon S.: on liberalism, 251 (n. 18)

Wood, Horace G.: *Law of Nuisances*, 44–45, 60–62; on highways, 120–22; on disorderly houses, 158

Wooden buildings, 55, 58–59; regulation of, 66–71. *See also* Public safety

Woodworth, J. (N.Y.), 21, 143–44

Woolsey, Theodore D., 242; versus sanitary police, 330–31 (n. 21)

Work ethic, 150, 153–54

Worthington, Robert, 197

Wright, Benjamin Fletcher, 28

Wynehamer v. People, 186–88, 245

Yeates, J. (Pa.), 158

Zabriskie, Ch. (N.J.), 224–25

Zoning, 67, 277 (n. 83)